SOCIAL WORK PRACTICE AND SOCIAL WELFARE POLICY IN THE UNITED STATES

Social Work Practice and Social Welfare Policy in the United States

A History

Philip R. Popple

UNIVERSITY OF TEXAS AT ARLINGTON

OXFORD
UNIVERSITY PRESS

OXFORD
UNIVERSITY PRESS

Oxford University Press is a department of the University of Oxford. It furthers
the University's objective of excellence in research, scholarship, and education
by publishing worldwide. Oxford is a registered trade mark of Oxford University
Press in the UK and certain other countries.

Published in the United States of America by Oxford University Press
198 Madison Avenue, New York, NY 10016, United States of America.

Library of Congress Cataloging-in-Publication Data
Names: Popple, Philip R., author.
Title: Social work practice and social welfare policy in
the United States : a history / Philip R. Popple.
Description: New York, NY : Oxford University Press, [2018] |
Includes bibliographical references and index.
Identifiers: LCCN 2017027261 (print) | LCCN 2017038949 (ebook) |
ISBN 9780190607333 (updf) | ISBN 9780190607340 (epub) |
ISBN 9780190607326 (alk. paper)
Subjects: LCSH: Social service—United States—History. |
Public welfare—United States—History.
Classification: LCC HV91 (ebook) | LCC HV91 .P6785 2018 (print) |
DDC 361.973—dc23
LC record available at https://lccn.loc.gov/2017027261

9 8 7 6 5 4 3 2 1
Printed by Webcom, Inc., Canada

CONTENTS

SOCIAL WORK PRACTICE AND SOCIAL WELFARE POLICY IN THE UNITED STATES

INTRODUCTION

The senior pastor at my church ascended into the pulpit, looked over the waiting congregation and, after allowing a few moments of silence for tension to build, boomed out: *Give people fish, feed them for a day; teach them to fish, feed them for a lifetime.* My pastor was introducing a sermon on the subject of social welfare. "Give people fish" is a metaphor for that part of our social welfare system historically referred to as charity, now more formally called social provision. It involves providing needy people with cash and a variety of in-kind benefits that will meet their immediate survival needs. "Teach them to fish" refers to helping people solve problems preventing them from being economically independent (i.e., needing charity), but it also refers to the related problems of taking adequate care of their children, living as good citizens, maintaining stable relationships, not abusing addictive substances, and numerous other problems preventing people from being fully contributing citizens in our society. The provision of charity to relieve the suffering of people with obvious needs dates back to the beginning of civilization. The provision of services to attempt to help people solve the problems that lead to their dependency has a much shorter history. My pastor's little bromide, advocating providing services to help people solve problems rather than simply providing them stuff to meet immediate needs, has been the theme of Sunday sermons and Thursday Rotary Club talks, probably thousands of times, because it just seems to make so much sense. However, behind its seeming clarity and simplicity lies a problem so difficult and complex that after more than 100 years of concentrated effort we have made little progress toward its solution. Social work is the profession that has been given the major responsibility for developing and applying social service techniques that will solve these problems, metaphorically, teaching people to fish.

This book is a survey of the history of the social welfare system in the United States. It is written by a social worker and is aimed primarily at the needs of social work students. So although of necessity a great deal of content is provided regarding the development of our system of social provision, the heart of the book regards our efforts to develop, implement, and administer social services that seek to help people solve the problems that contribute to their dependency, that is, teaching them to fish. Particular attention will be paid to the social work profession's search for the elusive techniques that enable practitioners to more effectively help people solve problems and develop strengths.

THE RATIONALE FOR THIS BOOK

This book was written based on a belief, a fact, and a problem. The belief is that it is critical for social workers to have a fairly sophisticated understanding of the history of the social welfare institution and of the social work profession. The self-image of social work is that of being an empirical, science-based profession. Although this goal is a good one, the truth of the matter is that social work can, at best, be science based to only a limited degree. Social work and the social welfare institution in which it functions are primarily based on values, cultural traditions, and belief systems and any number of myths based on these. These myths have proven to be surprisingly resistant to disconfirmation from data and scientific inquiry. For example, even though it has been empirically demonstrated a number of times that the non-poor benefit from transfer payments to a far greater degree than the poor, the American public continues to hold firmly to the belief that the poor are the only ones "getting something for nothing" and by doing so are sucking the life blood out of the economy.[1] It is only through historical study that social workers can come to understand the cultural context of their profession, including the myths, and appreciate why they are members of what has been referred to as "the unloved profession."[2]

The fact upon which this book is based is that, fortunately for people who share the belief that social workers should have a sophisticated understanding of the history of the social welfare institution and of the social work profession, a fair amount of time and effort is devoted to developing historical literacy among social work students. The standards of the accrediting body for social work education, the Council on Social Work Education (CSWE), have always required that social work programs include historical content in their curriculums. The most recent version of the Educational Policy and Accreditation Standards (EPAS), following current educational fashion, eliminates all curriculum requirements, substituting in their stead a set of competencies. Competency 5, Engage in Policy Practice, includes the expectation that "social workers understand the history and current structures of social policy [and] the historical . . . influences that affect social policy."[3] A doctoral student, Ms. (now Dr.) Alicia Patterson and I conducted a survey of all accredited social work programs in the United States to assess the place of historical content in their curriculums. Major findings were that faculty members assess their program curriculums as containing a medium amount of historical content.[4] Deans and directors assessed historical content as making a large contribution to students' mastery of core competencies. Thirty-two percent of the programs included a historical survey of social work and social welfare in at least one required course. Another survey, this one done by Michael Reisch, yielded similar results.[5]

1. See for, example, Thomas H. Walz and Gary Askerooth, *The Upside Down Welfare State* (Minneapolis, MN: Elwood Printing, 1973); Mimi Abramovitz, "Everyone Is on Welfare: 'The Role of Redistribution in Social Policy' Revisited," *Social Work* 28 (December 1983): 440–445; Mimi Abramovitz, "Everyone Is Still on Welfare: The Role of Redistribution in Public Policy," *Social Work* 46 (October 2001): 297–308.

2. Willard C. Richan and Allan R. Mendelsohn, *Social Work: The Unloved Profession* (New York: New Viewpoints, 1973).

3. Council on Social Work Education, *Educational Policy and Accreditation Standards* (Alexandria, VA: CSWE, 2015), 8.

4. Faculty members were asked to rate the amount of historical content in their school's curriculum on a Likert scale ranging from a seven, which denoted substantial content, to a one, which denoted minimal content. The average rating was 4.7.

5. Michael Reisch, "The End of Social Welfare History: Implications for Social Work Education," Paper presented at the Council on Social Work Education—Annual Program Meeting, October 25, 2014.

The problem upon which this book is based is that although most social workers and social work educators share my belief in the importance of history, and because of this they accord history an adequate space in the social work curriculum, there has been little historical scholarship aimed at the needs of social workers written in the past twenty years.[6] While I will not use the loaded words "fault" or "blame" I will say that the reasons for this dearth of new material can be shared by both the historical and the social work professions. As for the historical profession, the topic of social welfare was at its margins until the late twentieth century. Although for historians interested in social welfare it was not a good thing to be marginalized by their own profession, for the allied profession of social work this had a salutary effect. In order to find colleagues with similar interests, sometimes even to find employment related to their field, a number of talented historians became involved with the social work profession.[7] Fortunately for historians, but unfortunately for social workers, this has now changed. Social welfare history is now at the very center of the historical profession and historians no longer find it necessary to reach out to their applied social work colleagues. Fisher, a historian on the faculty of a school of social work, has observed that "From the 1970s onward, the field of social welfare history as written by historians had a history of its own . . . undermining the need for cooperation with the social work profession."[8]

On the other side of the relationship, academic social work has increasingly deemphasized history as an area of research and scholarship. Fisher and Dybicz have studied the interest in historical scholarship by social workers and found that the number of historical dissertations declined from over 40 percent in the 1940s to currently "an almost negligible amount." They conclude that the reason for this has been the development of a "social scientific culture" of social work research that has come to dominate the profession.[9] Recently minted social work Ph.D. assistant professors seeking promotion and tenure are acutely aware that their research had better be in an area that is defined as "fundable" and at a high level, and this generally means empirical social science research rather than qualitative approaches such as most historiography. The result of this mutual disengagement of the historical and social work professions has been that the flow of new material specifically aimed at the needs and interests of social workers has virtually ceased.

Some might argue that the fact that no new historical surveys of social work and social welfare have been written in the past twenty years does not constitute a problem. They might argue that given the sweep of history, twenty years is the blink of an eye. This might be a good

---

6. The books currently in print, and used by most social work programs, are all in the sixth or seventh editions: June Axinn and Mark Stern, *Social Welfare: A History of the American Response to Need,* 7th ed. (Boston: Allyn & Bacon, 2008), first edition, written by Axinn with Herman Levin, in 1975; Phyllis Day and Jerome Schiele, *A New History of Social Welfare,* 7th ed. (Boston: Allyn & Bacon, 2013), first edition, 1989; Bruce Jansson, *The Reluctant Welfare State; American Social Welfare Policies: Past, Present, and Future,* 6th ed. (Belmont, CA: Brooks/Cole, 2008), first edition, 1988; Walter Trattner, *From Poor Law to Welfare State: A History of Social Welfare in America,* 6th ed. (New York: Free Press, 1999), first edition, 1974.

7. Robert Fisher, " 'Speaking for the Contribution of History': Context and Origins of the Social Welfare History Group," *Social Service Review* 73, no. 92 (June 1999): 191–217.

8. Robert Fisher, "Speaking for the Contribution of History," 204.

9. Robert Fisher and Phillip Dybicz, "The Place of Historical Research in Social Work," *Journal of Sociology and Social Welfare* 26 (September 1999): 105–124.

argument except for the fact that, after ignoring social welfare history for most of the twenti-eth century, historians have now found the area to be of intense interest. In the late 1970s the "new social history" emerged and, as noted by Fisher, "took the historical profession by storm, transforming the discipline . . . " The result has been an explosion of research and publication on topics related to social welfare history. This scholarship has developed a bewildering vari-ety of perspectives from which to approach the topic. Katz has referred to these as segmented visions, which he sees as "limiting rather than incorrect."[10] Among the approaches taken are the policy centered approach represented by Theda Skocpl in *Protecting Soldiers and Mothers*; the gender approach taken by Linda Gordon in *Pitied But Not Entitled: Single Mothers and History*; the racial lens illustrated by Michael Brown's *Race, Money, and the American Welfare State*; and interestingly, a whole gaggle of books on the relation of business and social welfare such as Isabela Mares's *The Politics of Social Risk: Business and Welfare State Development*, and by Harvard Business School's David Moss, *When All Else Fails: Government as the Ultimate Risk Manager*.[11] Katz argues that "No historian has written about social welfare comprehensively."[12] One seg-ment conspicuously absent in this new flurry of research by historians has been the vision and needs of the social work profession.

Although recent scholarship by social welfare historians is not aimed at the needs of social work, it contains much that can benefit the profession. One of the major criticisms that practi-tioners of the new social history level at traditional social welfare history as written by and for social workers is that the older work tends to be written from the top down.[13] That is, it is writ-ten from the perspective of the elites who were developing and implementing policies and pays little attention to the perspectives and lives of the intended beneficiaries of the programs or of the people charged with implementing them.[14] A great deal of work that incorporates the lived experiences of clients has been produced in recent years, including studies by Eric Schnieder, Beverly Stadum, Michael Katz, Lynn Hollen Lees, Billy G. Smith, David Wagner, and Mark Peel, among others.[15] The lives and perspectives of the social workers and other professionals charged

10. Michael Katz, "Segmented Visions: Recent Historical Writing on American Welfare," *Journal of Urban History* 24 (1998): 245.

11. Theda Skocpol, *Protecting Soldiers and Mothers: The Political Origins of Social Policy in the United States* (Cambridge, MA: Harvard University Press, 1992); Linda Gordon, *Pitied but Not Entitled: Single Mothers and the History of Welfare* (New York: The Free Press, 1994); Michael K. Brown, *Race, Money, and the American Welfare State* (Ithaca, NY: Cornell University Press, 1999); Isabela Meres, *The Politics of Social Risk: Business and Welfare State Development* (New York: Cambridge University Press, 2003); David A. Moss, *When All Else Fails: Government as the Ultimate Risk Manager* (Cambridge, MA: Harvard University Press, 2002).

12. Katz, "Segmented Visions," 245.

13. Raymond Mohl, "Review: Mainstream Social Welfare History and Its Problems," *Reviews in American History* 7 (1979): 469–476.

14. Mohl, for example, in an otherwise positive review of James Leiby's *A History of Social Welfare and Social Work in the United States*, criticizes it as being "history viewed only from the top, from the legal, administrative, and institutional perspectives." Raymond Mohl, "Review: Mainstream Social Welfare History and Its Problems," 473.

15. Eric Schneider, *In the Web of Class: Delinquents and Reformers in Boston, 1810-1930* (New York: New York University Press, 1992); Beverly Stadum, *Poor Women and Their Families: Hard Working Charity Cases, 1900–1930* (Albany: State University of New York, 1992); Michael B. Katz, "The History of an Impudent Poor Woman in New York City from 1918 to 1923," in *The Uses of Charity: The Poor on Relief in the Mid-Nineteenth Century Metropolis*, ed. Peter Mandler (Philadelphia: University of Pennsylvania Press, 1990); Lynn Hollen Lees, *The Solidarities of Strangers: The English Poor*

with implementing the policies developed by elites have not received as much attention. As Katz has noted, historians "neglect the paid agents and early social workers interposed between reformers or agency officials and clients . . . The daily background, careers, and work experience of these proto– and early social workers remains dimly lit territory."[16] Only a small amount of work has emerged discussing the perspective of the front line social workers, notably Karen Tice's *Tales of Wayward Girls and Immoral Women: Case Records and the Professionalization of Social Work.*[17]

The purpose of this book is to survey social welfare history, addressing the needs and reviving the vision segment of the social work profession. I cover most of the areas discussed in the old institutional and administrative histories of social welfare—the Elizabethan Poor Laws, the Flexner report, the Social Security Act, the War on Poverty, and all that—but I add to these the recent historical scholarship that looks at how these interacted with the lives of the poor and how benefits and services were often negotiated arrangements that included the poor as active participants in the course of their own lives. I also include as much as has been produced about the lives, work, and perspectives of the practitioners who were charged with actually implementing the plans of the elites and negotiating with the intended beneficiaries of these plans. I include a modest amount of original research that I have conducted as a response to the still extremely sparse amount of work published in this area. This research included visits to archives at Columbia University (Society for Improving the Condition of the Poor records and annual reports, and New York Charity Organization Society records, case records, annual reports); University of Massachusetts—Boston Archives (Boston Children's Aid Society papers and annual reports, Boston Society for Prevention of Cruelty to Children records); Philadelphia City Archives (Philadelphia Almshouse records); University of Wisconsin—Green Bay Cofrin Library Archives (Green Bay Department of Public Welfare records and case files); and University of Minnesota Social Welfare History Archives (Minneapolis Family and Children's Services records; Family Service Society of America records). Records in these archives provided a refreshing look at the actual day-to-day practice of social workers (and proto–social workers) with clients as a counterbalance to the often wishful thinking describing practice found in the works of academics and agency administrators.

Laws and the People, 1700–1948 (New York: Cambridge University Press, 1998); Billy G. Smith, ed., *Down and Out in Early America* (University Park, PA: Pennsylvania State University Press, 2004); David Wagner, *Ordinary People: In and Out of Poverty in the Gilded Age* (Boulder, CO: Paradigm Publishers, 2008); Mark Peel, *Miss Cutler and the Case of the Resurrected Horse* (Chicago: University of Chicago Press, 2012).

16. Katz, "Segmented Visions," 249–250. Clarke Chambers made basically this same point six years earlier, saying " . . . but what is missing in most of these accounts is some description and assessment of those who actually did the work. The daily routine of family caseworkers, group workers, probation officers, visiting teachers, workers engaged in child protection, and county welfare workers has rarely been examined . . . Scholars have worked the macro- and to a lesser degree the microlevels of welfare without attending to the mezzo, or middle, level of the narrative." Clarke A. Chambers, " 'Uphill All the Way': Reflections on the Course and Study of Welfare History," *Social Service Review* 6, no 4 (December 1992): 495.

17. Karen W. Tice, *Tales of Wayward Girls and Immoral Women: Case Records and the Professionalization of Social Work* (Urbana, IL: University of Illinois Press, 1998).

SOCIAL WELFARE AND SOCIAL WORK
AS DEFINED IN THIS BOOK

Social welfare and social work are vague, imprecise terms, used by many people in many different ways. The policy analyst Joseph Heffernan once observed that "while politics and economics are fuzzy at their boundaries, social welfare is fuzzy at its core."[18] So, it is probably a good idea to define these terms as used in this book before proceeding further.

Social Welfare

Most social welfare historians employ the economist's definition of social welfare as being economic transactions outside the market system, particularly those aimed at bringing the poor up to some marginal level of material well-being. Katz uses this definition in a recent book discussing the welfare state as including all "programs designed to assure economic security to all citizens by guaranteeing the fundamental necessities of life . . . "[19] But, at least from the point of view of a social worker, social welfare includes much more than this. It includes programs to protect the vulnerable from harm regardless of their economic situation; programs such as child and adult protective services. It includes services to help people suffering various maladjustments; examples being mental health and relationship counseling. It includes programs to facilitate human growth and development through recreation, socialization, and life transitions; services provided by agencies such as the YMCA, YWCA, JCCA, community centers, and the Boy and Girl Scouts. For the purposes of this book then, from the social workers perspective, the economic definition is not, by itself, adequate.

In order to capture the meaning of social welfare in all of its dimensions I employ a two-pronged definition. One part of this definition is a description of what social welfare looks like, the other part describes the social function of social work and social welfare.[20] The descriptive part of the definition views social welfare as the provision of goods and services aimed at bringing people up to some minimal level of social and personal functioning. The philosopher Nicholas Rescher notes that "This characterization—with its explicit reference to the basic—makes transparently clear one critical negative feature of welfare in its relationship to human well-being in general, namely, that welfare is a matter of 'well-being' not in its global totality but in its 'basic requisites,' its indispensable foundations."[21] By this definition social welfare is broader than physical and material

---

18. Joseph Heffernan, *Introduction to Social Welfare Policy: Power, Scarcity and Common Human Needs* (Itasca, IL: F. E. Peacock, 1979), 8.

19. Michael Katz, *The Price of Citizenship: Redefining the American Welfare State* (New York: Metropolitan Books, 2001), 9.

20. A more detailed description of this definition can be found in chapter 2, "Social Welfare: Basic Concepts," in Philip Popple and Leslie Leighninger, *Social Work, Social Welfare, and American Society*, 7th ed. (Boston: Allyn & Bacon, 2008), 27–58.

21. Nicolas Rescher, *Welfare: The Social Issue in Philosophical Perspective* (Pittsburgh: The University of Pittsburgh Press, 1972), 4–5.

welfare. It includes people's relations with one another and their personal and close-range inter-actions (family contacts, occupational interactions, friendships, and other human relationships), which are key aspects of well-being. Therefore, this means of defining social welfare includes serv-ices such as recreation and socialization, personal and relationship counseling, and protective services. "Yet," Rescher cautions, "it is important to recognize that despite its diversified and mul-tifaceted character, the issue of a [person's] welfare has a certain minimality about it. Welfare—in all its dimensions—deals only with the basic essentials."[22]

The second part of my definition of social welfare describes its social function: what the motiva-tion of society is for providing these services that have no obvious payback. The social worker and historian Ralph Pumphrey argued that all social welfare activities are driven by two more or less compatible motives. On the one hand there is the desire of people to make the lives of others better. "This aspect of philanthropy may be designated as compassion: the effort to alleviate present suffer-ing, deprivation, or other undesirable conditions to which a segment of the population, but not the benefactor, is exposed." On the other side are aspects of social welfare policies and programs that are designed for the benefit of their promoters and of the community at large. Pumphrey called this motivation protection and stated, "It may result either from fear of change or from fear of what may happen if existing conditions are not changed."[23] So we grant people financial assistance because we feel bad about their poverty and want to help reduce it, but also out of fear of what they may do if help is not provided, things like crime, begging, or ultimately engaging in political rebellion, all consequences we wish to avoid. And we provide mental health services because we want to help people suffering psychological pain, but we also fear people who we see as unstable, and we wish to reduce anti-social behavior. And we provide protective services for maltreated children because we feel these children deserve better, but also because poorly cared for children wander the streets, disrupt classrooms, and are a generally disruptive presence in the community.

Pumphrey's conceptualization of the functions of social welfare is particularly useful because it highlights one of the least recognized attributes of social welfare—that is, its essentially con-servative nature. Almost everyone recognizes the stingy nature of social welfare in the United States—that we want to take care of problems at the least possible cost—but generally picture the motivations of the programs themselves as basically liberal, always pushing for expansion and more spending. But however liberal the motivations and intentions of advocates for social welfare may be, the social function is conservative: maintaining a smoothly operating society with the least possible threat to the status quo.

Social Work

Another problem for the social welfare historian is defining exactly what a social worker is. Traditional histories tend to accept the argument aggressively advanced by the professional

---

22. Rescher, *Welfare*, 8.

23. Ralph Pumphrey, "Compassion and Protection: Dual Motivations in Social Welfare," *Social Service Review* 23 (1959): 21–29.

elite that the only legitimate social workers are those with training from a professional school, generally at the graduate level (the MSW degree) and, added recently, having a social work license. These social workers tend to cluster disproportionately in private sector agencies and in the practice areas of mental health and medical health. A recent labor market analysis found that 87 percent of licensed social workers were graduate trained, 50 percent were employed in mental or medical health, and that 67 percent worked in either private sector organizations or were in private practice.[24] The problem is that this group has never constituted more than 25 percent of people holding jobs that are defined by the Bureau of Labor Statistics as social work jobs.

The majority of social work jobs are held by two other groups. The first are professional social workers trained at the baccalaureate level (BSWs). This group did not officially exist until 1974, when the major social work professional organizations finally gave in to what most observers had recognized for years, that there were never going to be enough graduate trained social workers to fill all positions, and granted formal recognition to the BSW degree. After a slow start, undergraduate social work programs have rapidly developed until BSW programs now outnumber MSW programs. There are currently over 600 BSW programs either accredited or in candidacy for accreditation, compared to fewer than 300 MSW programs. However, because graduate programs are generally much larger than undergraduate programs, MSW programs graduate about 16,000 social workers per year while BSW programs graduate about 15,000. Traditional histories of social work and social welfare have tended to criticize the direction the profession has gone, Katz, for example, saying: "Social work never managed to limit entry as successfully as other occupations. Nor has it successfully established its claim to professional standing. One reason is that it chose the wrong alternative. As social workers rejected urban mediation and abandoned social reform, they became second class therapists, inferior in standing, if not in competence, to psychologists and psychiatrists. No other group . . . picked up the task that social work abandoned early in the twentieth century. None claimed a 'generalized mandate' to integrate individuals, institutions, and groups; to help individuals negotiate their way through the thickening maze of social services and bureaucracies; or to stimulate 'social legislation.' "[25] This criticism specifically addresses MSW programs and accepts the elite conception of the profession as being composed of only graduate trained social workers, a conception that has been uncritically accepted by historians. The problem that Katz identifies is precisely the problem that the social work profession addressed when it recognized and developed BSW programs. These programs are specifically prohibited by accreditation standards from training therapists (second rate or otherwise) and are required to train workers with a generalist focus that addresses exactly those areas about which Katz expresses concern. The 2015 accreditation standards give the following description of BSW level social work practice: "To promote human and social well-being, generalist practitioners

24. National Association of Social Workers, *Assuring the Sufficiency of a Frontline Workforce: A National Study of Licensed Social Workers—Preliminary Report,* (Washington, D.C.: National Association of Social Workers, 2005), 10–12.

25. Michael Katz, *In the Shadow of the Poorhouse: A Social History of Welfare in America, Tenth Anniversary Edition, Revised and Updated* (New York: Basic Books, 1996), 172.

use a range of prevention and intervention methods in their practice with individuals, families, groups, organizations, and communities . . . Generalist practitioners engage diversity in their practice and advocate for human rights and social and economic justice. They recognize, support, and build on the strengths and resiliency of all human beings. The baccalaureate program in social work prepares students for generalist practice."[26]

The final group of social workers is those who have no professional training or certification at all. Until after 1974, when BSW programs began to turn out trained generalist practitioners, this group constituted by far the largest number of people holding social work jobs. A 1970 analysis of social work manpower found " . . . that workers who have not earned a professional degree in social work [staff] more than 80 percent of the direct service positions in public and voluntary agencies . . . It is not uncommon that workers with and without the MSW degree are assigned to the same kinds of tasks."[27] In one critical area of public social work practice, child protective services, a 1988 study found that 72 percent of professional staff did not have a social work degree.[28] Another study of child welfare staff in Georgia found that as recently as 2003 less than 20 percent of professional staff had formal social work training and, more startling yet, 10 percent listed a high school diploma or GED as their highest level of education.[29] Since the inception of BSW programs, the percentage of social work jobs held by people with at least a basic social work credential has steadily increased, but it remains far from 100 percent. How far short is difficult to tell as there is no specifically applicable data. However, we do know that in the year 2000, the *Current Population Survey* reported that of 840,000 people identifying themselves as holding social work jobs, 240,000 held less than a bachelor's degree, and only 300,000 held social work licenses.[30] So extrapolating from this data we can infer that we still have a situation where fewer than 50 percent of social work jobs are held by fully qualified professional social workers.

If we accept the rather circuitous definition of a social worker as someone who holds a social work job, as opposed to the definition of elites of a social worker as someone with a professional social work credential (preferably a graduate degree and a license), we are looking at a considerably larger and more diverse group of people. Because social services continue to be provided largely by people who are social workers by self-identification or by job identification, rather than by professional credentials, it is important that the story of these people be included in the history of social work and social welfare. This is another story I include in this book, to the extent this is possible, given the sparse record available regarding this group.

26. Council on Social Work Education. *Educational Policy and Accreditation Standards* (2015): 7–8.

27. Frank M. Loewenberg, "Toward a Systems Analysis of Social Welfare Manpower Utilization Patterns," *Child Welfare* 49 (May 1970): 252–253.

28. Alice Leiberman, H. Hornby, and M. Russell. "Analyzing the Educational Backgrounds and Work Experiences of Child Welfare Personnel: A National Study," *Social Work* 33 (1988): 485–489.

29. A. J. Ellert, C. D. Ellert, and J. K. Rugutt, *A Study of Persoanal and Organizational Factors Contributing to Employee Retention and Turnover in Child Welfare in Georgia* (Athens, GA: University of Georgia Press, 2003).

30. National Association of Social Workers, *Assuring the Sufficiency of a Frontline Workforce: National Study of Licensed Social Workers Preliminary Report* (Washington, DC: NASW, 2005), 16, n. 1.

THE PLAN OF THIS BOOK

In this book I attempt to tell the story of social work and social welfare in the United States in an accurate, thorough, but reasonably brief manner. I tell this story on four levels. First I describe the general social history of each era—economics, technology, population shifts, prevailing social philosophy, and emerging social problems. Second, I discuss the development of societal responses to these emerging problems, responses that eventually came to be referred to as our social welfare system. Third, I describe the emergence of various technologies to staff the social welfare institution, technologies that in the twentieth century became recognized as the profession of social work. And fourth, I look at attempts by the profession of social work to develop practice techniques to enable its practitioners to effectively and efficiently implement social welfare policies and aid individuals in the solution to their problems. In chapters covering the early years of the history of social welfare, all four levels are dealt with in single chapters. Chapters dealing with the late nineteenth century onward divide each era into two chapters, one describing general social history and social welfare developments, and one describing the social work profession and the development of practice theory and technique.

It is important to note that although this book is intended to be a survey of the history of social work and social welfare in the United States, I make no claim that it is a comprehensive history. Such a history would be a multi-volume project and would greatly exceed the rather limited purpose of this book. That purpose is to provide a fairly brief but high-quality survey of those aspects of social welfare history that a social worker needs to comprehend in order to understand his or her role in the social welfare institution. Thus, many topics are either left out or given short shrift; for example, international social welfare and the self-help movement are barely touched. Also, some currently very vibrant areas of academic inquiry, such as welfare state theory, while potentially very useful for understanding the developments described in this book, are very briefly, if at all, dealt with because they are so rich and complex that to do more would expand the book far beyond its targeted scope.

CHAPTER 1

OLD WORLD AND COLONIAL BACKGROUND

In 1781 a physician in Newport, Rhode Island closed John Treby's eyes and declared him dead, thus ending a six year stint in Newport as an officially recognized pauper and public charge. Treby had begun his adult life with a promising start, but a combination of bad luck, bad family relations, and bad health had eventually brought things to a bad end. Trained as a goldsmith who designed and made jewelry, decorative art objects, and high-end carriage fittings, and also educated to a high degree of literacy, Treby began his adult life with a bright future. He completed his apprenticeship and began practice as a goldsmith in Newport in 1761 when he was in his early twenties. After doing business in Newport for a year or two, Treby relocated to Providence, exactly why is not known, but probably because he thought business opportunities would be better in this larger and richer town. Goldsmithing was, after all, a trade that was completely dependent on a population of wealthy people with discretionary income to spend on luxuries. While in Providence, Treby married the daughter of a prominent businessman and they had several children. In the mid-1760s the Trebys moved once again to Newport, where John Treby became a merchant, running a business that may or may not have been related to his training as a goldsmith. At this time his luck began to turn sour. In June of 1769 one of his largest accounts declared bankruptcy while owing Treby a large sum of money, apparently causing his business to fail. Treby and his family moved back to Providence and he once again took up the trade of goldsmithing. After his return to Providence things for Treby went from bad to worse. His goldsmithing business did not prosper, his relations with his wife, children, and in-laws became estranged, and he suffered a health crisis. His situation was so grim that in 1775 he was summoned before the Providence town council and examined to ascertain if he was likely to become "chargeable to the town," the term used to describe a person who needed to be supported by pubic aid. The determination of the council was that he was likely to become a public charge and, further, that his place of legal settlement was Newport, where he had been born, operated a business, and paid taxes. Trelby was "warned out" of town, transported by the Providence town sergeant to Newport, where he was delivered to John Pitt, one of Newport's overseers of the poor. His wife and children were not warned out and remained in Providence, presumably living with her father, Ebenezer Richardson. It is not clear how Overseer Pitt and the town council in Newport supported John Treby during the six years between his relocation to Newport and his death. It is known that he was destitute and in failing health. Most likely he was boarded in a private home at public expense, provided with medical care such as it was in the eighteenth century, and perhaps given a small amount of cash to cover personal expenses. When he died the town undoubtedly paid for a pauper's burial.[1]

When John Treby found himself in trouble and at the mercy of the Newport town fathers for help, he was judged and assisted under a system that was both ancient and rapidly evolving. The system for dealing with the dependent poor in colonial Rhode Island was based on values that can be traced back to the Egyptians, added to by the Jews, and expanded by the Christians. The town fathers in Providence and Newport realized, just like the early Greeks and Romans had, that although the poor had little influence or power, they were still a political faction and cost the taxpayers money, so a politician could gain or lose support by either paying more or less attention to their needs. The legal basis of the treatment that Treby received was one imported from England, where a complex set of laws regarding treatment of the poor and dependent had been formulated over the course of 200 years when it became increasingly clear that they were a threat to social stability and that some rational, clearly structured, governmental response was called for. Finally, the response to Treby's dependency was guided by the unique situation in America, an evolving society that prized work and feared leisure even more than the English forefathers, strongly preferred private action to that of government, and firmly believed that the poor were a local responsibility; a person's neighbors in that person's place of legal residence were the ones, and the only ones, responsible for providing anything more than emergency assistance.

SOCIAL WELFARE IN THE ANCIENT WORLD

Social welfare is generally considered to be a product of liberal political ideology—kindly people wanting to make life better for the poor and oppressed. It is not. As we shall see throughout the history discussed in this book, social welfare programs generally arise out of a need to promote social order in a disorderly society, to quell social unrest, or simply as one tool a politician can use to curry favor with various segments of the population. We see all of these elements in the beginning of formal social welfare benefit programs in the early Greco-Roman world. In ancient Athens, with unemployment on the rise, a form of work relief was instituted in the fifth century BCE In 400 BCE the Council of Athens, in response to a rise in street begging, began providing a type of public welfare. The amount given was very small, one obol a day, approximately one sixth of the wage of a common laborer. By 325 BCE this amount had been increased to two obols per day. At this time a means test was instituted to insure in a systematic way that only the very poorest citizens would be eligible to receive this meager benefit. Elsewhere in Greece, but not in Athens, there were programs for the regular distribution of grain to the poor at public expense. Once the

---

1. Ruth Wallis Herndon, *Unwelcome Americans—Living on the Margin in Early New England* (Philadelphia, PA: University of Pennsylvania Press, 2001), 109–111.

practice of providing public aid was established, it quickly became part of the political process. The Greek historian Plutarch reports how the leader Pericles, lacking the wealth of his competitor Cimons, "turned to the distribution of public monies" and thereby in a short time "brought the people over" to become his supporters.[2]

When Rome became the dominant force in the western world it too made provisions for public welfare to help support the poor. In 123 BCE Rome began a program of distributing grain at about one-half the market price to its citizens. There were apparently no eligibility criteria for receiving the bargain grain, but the intent was for only the poor to take advantage of the program. This program was so costly that at times it came close to bankrupting the state. By the time Caesar became dictator in 46 BCE the grain dole had changed from a subsidized purchase program to being free. The number of people receiving the free dole was nearly 320,000 and the cost approached 20 percent of Rome's budget. In addition to the grain dole, which can be viewed as a precursor to today's general assistance programs, Rome developed programs foreshadowing modern unemployment compensation, old age and disability benefits, and public works employment. In the first century CE a policy providing support to poor families with children was established in an effort to increase the population. In the second century an administrative office was established to oversee distribution of benefits from the treasury, thus establishing a forerunner of the modern welfare bureaucracy. The cost of welfare programs in Rome eventually became the second largest public budget item, exceeded only by the military budget.[3]

Although the proliferation of public programs in Greece and Rome provides an interesting tidbit of social welfare history, and it does illustrate how social welfare programs have always contributed to social stability and political processes, there is no direct link between these programs and what later developed in England and was eventually imported to the New World. This is not the case in relation to the development of social values guiding charity and welfare. Greece was a pagan society as was Rome, and by the time of the fall of Rome pagan religions had been replaced by Christianity. One of the major reasons for the triumph of Christianity was its value base of love, charity, and mutual social support. These values constitute a direct line from fifth century Rome to the modern day United States and continue to form the basis for our social welfare beliefs and practices.

The pagan religion of the Romans worshipped a number of gods such as Jupiter, the ruler of the gods; Mars, the god of war; Neptune, the god of the sea; as well as many others. Notably missing from this pantheon was a god of charity, or a god of neighborly love. There was, of course, Venus, who is generally referred to as the love goddess, but she was more a goddess of romantic love and beauty rather than brotherly love. There was no god telling the people and their rulers to be kind to one another, to help each other, and particularly to take care of the old, sick, orphaned children, and the helpless. Quite the opposite, in Greco-Roman society the poor, particularly the very poor referred to as the *ptochoi*, were loathed and despised. Plato, in his book *The Republic*, in which he described what he believed to be the ideal state, said beggars would be banished because they were likely to be thieves, pickpockets, temple robbers, or other types of criminals. The Latin

2. Merritt Ierley, *With Charity for All—Welfare and Society, Ancient Times to the Present* (New York: Praeger, 1984), 3.
3. Ierley, *With Charity for All*, 14–20.

poet Plautus voiced a contemporary sounding sentiment when he said, "You do a beggar bad service by giving him food and drink."[4]

Rome for centuries occupied and ruled Jewish communities and oppressed and occasionally attempted to eliminate this faith. The Jews were monotheistic and their religion, unlike that of the pagan Romans, paid a good deal of attention to follower's duties to their more unfortunate brethren. Following the Egyptians before them, the Jewish scriptures contain a number of injunctions against doing harm to the poor and weak, such as Exodus 22:21–27:

> You shall not wrong or oppress a resident alien, for you were aliens in the land of Egypt. You shall not abuse any widow or orphan. If you do abuse them, when they cry out to me, I will surely heed their cry; my wrath will burn, and I will kill you with the sword ... If you lend money to my people, to the poor among you, you shall not deal with them as a creditor; you shall not exact interest from them. If you take your neighbor's cloak in pawn, you shall restore it before the sun goes down; for it may be your neighbor's only clothing to use as cover; in what else shall that person sleep? And if your neighbor cries out to me, I will listen, for I am compassionate."

The Jewish scriptures go beyond injunctions against doing harm to include assertions that individuals also have a positive obligation to perform acts of helping and doing good for others such as Deuteronomy 15:11:

> There will always be poor people in the land. Therefore I command you to be openhanded toward your brothers and toward the poor and needy in your land.

Based on this belief in a positive obligation to do good, the Jews developed a number of social welfare practices. Among these were hospitable reception of strangers, education of orphans, redemption of lawbreakers, endowment of marriages, visitation of the ill and infirm, burial of the dead, consolation of the bereaved, care of widows, slaves, divorcees, and the aged.[5] Provision for the poor was mainly through various agricultural practices such as those specified in Leviticus 19:9–18:

> When you reap the harvest of your land, you shall not reap to the very edges of your field, or gather the gleanings of your harvest. You shall not strip your vineyard bare, or gather the fallen grapes of your vineyard; you shall leave them for the poor and alien.

In addition to the these practices, Jews were expected to give alms for the poor. Almsgiving was connected to one of the supreme Jewish virtues, "deeds of lovingkindness."

> Almsgiving and deeds of lovingkindness are equal to all the commandments of the Law. Almsgiving is exercised toward the living, deeds of lovingkindness toward the living and the dead; almsgiving

---

4. Birger A. Pearson, *Ancient Roots of Western Philanthropy: Pagan, Jewish, and Christian* (Indianapolis, IN: Indiana University Center on Philanthropy, 1997), 7.

5. Robert Morris, *Rethinking Social Welfare: Why Care for the Stranger* (New York: Longman, 1986), 66.

to the poor, deeds of lovingkindness to the poor and to the rich; almsgiving is done with a man's money, deeds of lovingkindness either with his money or personally.[6]

The historian of religion Birger Pearson concludes, "Indeed, the special concern of the God of Israel for the poor runs like a thread through the entirety of the Hebrew Bible."[7]

When Christianity emerged in the first century CE and the New Testament was written over the next hundred and fifty years, Jewish ideas of love and charity were adopted and expanded. This is hardly surprising when we remember that the early Christians were themselves Jews. In the New Testament an emphasis on love and compassion was added to the moral teachings and concept of justice found in the Old Testament. The theological virtues were set forth as faith, hope, and charity, the greatest of these being charity. The basis of the Christian approach to social welfare is generally considered to be in Jesus' depiction of the welcome to the righteous as blessed inheritors of the Kingdom:

> "For I was hungry and you gave me food, I was thirsty and you gave me drink, I was a stranger and you welcomed me, I was naked and you clothed me, I was sick and you visited me, I was in prison and you came to me." Then the righteous will answer him, "Lord, when did we see thee hungry and feed thee, or thirsty and give thee drink? And when did we see thee a stranger and welcome thee, or naked and clothe thee? And when did we see thee sick or in prison and visit thee?" And the King will answer them, "Truly, I say to you, as you did it to one of the least of these my brethren, you did it to me." [Matthew 25:35–40]

The early Christian church, and the generations that followed, took seriously the command of Jesus to carry out the expression of love that occurs so frequently in the New Testament. Since its earliest days, the church has engaged in at least twelve areas of social ministry: the care of widows, orphans, the sick, the poor, the disabled, prisoners, captives, slaves, and victims of calamity; burial of the poor; provision of employment services; and meals for the needy.

Largely due to the Christian's ideas of love and mutual support they gradually gained ascendency in the Roman Empire until eventually they came to dominate it when the Emperor Constantine converted to Christianity in 312 CE. In 313 CE Constantine issued the Edict of Toleration that marks the beginning of the development of a Christian empire. At this time the church's already highly developed social welfare system was augmented by contributions from the state. Eventually the entire administration of the state program of food distribution was given over to the churches and their leaders, who then became functionaries of the state.

The Christian Roman Empire lasted only about 150 years, falling in the late fifth century when it was overrun by Ottoman Turks led by Mehmed II in the east and by Germanic Huns led by Odoacer in the west. A few years later Odoacer was himself defeated by Theodoric, King of the Ostrogoths, who took for himself the title of Governor of the Romans. Although Rome had been conquered, many of its customs continued, prominently including provisions for the poor. The

---

6. George F. Moore, *Judaism in the First Centuries of the Christian Era: The Age of the Tannaim* (Cambridge, MA: Harvard University Press, 1927), 171.

7. Pearson, *Ancient Roots of Western Philanthropy*, 12.

historian Procopius recorded that Theodoric "ordered that the needy gathering about the Church of St. Peter the Apostle should forever be supplied by the treasury with 3,000 measures of free grain a year."[8]

THE ENGLISH HERITAGE

Following the fall of Rome the western world entered a period of history known as the Middle Ages. The common belief is that in this period of history the pace of science, scholarship, and the arts slowed to a crawl, with little significant progress being recorded on any front. This belief is not entirely true. The medieval period in Western Europe really encompassed three distinct periods. The first of these, beginning about 400 CE, when the process of Roman decline was nearly complete, and extending until about 1000 CE was the early Middle Ages. It was this period alone that was distinguished by most of those attributes commonly referred to as "medieval," referring to primitivism, violence, abysmal ignorance, and superstition. The early Middle Ages petered out with the emergence of a new period, the high Middle Ages, which lasted from around 1000 until about 1300, followed by the late Middle Ages, which lasted until the mid-fifteenth century. In the high and late Middle Ages Europe slowly began to emerge from the backwardness of earlier times with a decline of otherworldliness and an emerging determination to live in this world and to mold the environment to humanity's own advantage. The causes of this change in attitude were many, but notable among them were the contact with the Saracenic and Byzantine civilizations, the increase in economic activity and security, and the influence of monastic education. In addition, the revival of trade in the eleventh and twelfth centuries and the corresponding growth of cities led to an increase in prosperity and sophistication that greatly stimulated the forward thrust of society.

Following the death of Charlemagne in 814 strong government in Western Europe collapsed. In response, a system of social organization emerged that could establish order without a strong central government. This came to be known as the feudal or manorial system. This was a system of governance similar to the bureaucratic hierarchal system of a large organization. At the top of the social and economic structure was the king who owned all of the land. He would keep a certain amount of the land for his own use, but would lease out the majority of his holding to a number of high-ranking members of the aristocracy, known as barons. The land holdings these people leased were known as manors, and the baron or prince was known as the Lord of the Manor. In return for these grants of land, the lords had to pledge an oath of loyalty to the king, agree to pay rent to the king's treasury, to serve on the royal council, and to provide knights for military service when needed by the king. The baron would, in turn, keep as much of the land he was leasing for his own use as he wished, and lease the remainder out to knights. The knight was given the land in return for agreeing to provide military service when needed, paying rent to the Lord of the Manor, and protecting the manor from attack. Finally, the knight would keep as much of his land holding as he wished for his own use, and would divide the remainder among a number of people at the bottom of society, known variously as villeins, serfs, or peasants.

---

8. Ierley, *With Charity for All*, 20.

The peasant was basically a tenant farmer who was given the land in return for giving a portion of the crops and animals produced on the holding to the knight as rent. He and his family were also required to provide other domestic services for the knight as demanded. Peasants had few rights. For example, they were not permitted to travel or marry without permission. Although the lot of the medieval peasant was generally very hard, there were some positive aspects. One is that the peasant had no obligation to provide military service. But more germane to our discussion here is that fact that the medieval manor in many ways constituted a mini welfare state. Many of the fears and anxieties that plagued the poor in later centuries meant nothing to the serf. He was in very little danger of loss of employment or of starving in old age. It was a principle of feudal law that the peasant could not be deprived of his land. If the land was sold, the serf went with it and retained the rights to work the land as before. When he became too old or feeble to work, it was the duty of the lord to care for him for the remainder of his days. Peasants were poor but secure. The small proportion of the population who were not serfs generally lived in the few cities and towns, and they made their living as merchants or craftspeople of various sorts. Security was provided for these people through the development of merchant's or craft guilds, which, among other functions, served as mutual protection societies that provided insurance against disability, old age, and widowhood. The few common people who did not come under the feudal or the guild system, or who did but found themselves in need due to traveling or serious illness, were provided some protection by the Catholic Church. The church ran hospitals that cared for the sick, the lame, and distressed travelers. Finally, people who fell between the cracks were under the charge of the bishop of their diocese who had the responsibility for feeding and protecting the poor within his district.[9]

In the late Middle Ages beginning in the fourteenth century, the social and economic organization of England was changing. Initially, the changes stemmed from purely negative events. The historian J.C.L.S. de Sismonde summarized the century very simply when he said that it was "a bad time for humanity."[10] Tuchman has said that the disorders of the fourteenth century "cannot be traced to any one cause; they were the hoof prints of more than the four horsemen of St. John's version, which had now become seven—plague, war, taxes, brigandage, bad government, insurrection, and schism in the church."[11] The events most relevant for our discussion of the emergence of governmental provisions for social welfare were a couple of calamities that befell the land in rapid succession—crop failures that resulted in a famine that lasted from 1315 to 1321, and the bubonic plague that swept across Europe from 1348 to 1349 and killed almost one-third of England's population. By this time, the feudal system had begun to break down, and the tenant farming and guild systems were rapidly being replaced by a system of wage labor. The plague created a labor crisis in that so many workers died that an extreme labor shortage was created. This resulted in a situation in which workers could come and go as they pleased, travel where they wanted, and demand much higher wages than in the past. The owners of the farms and businesses that employed the workers saw this as an intolerable situation.

9. Walter Trattner, *From Poor Law to Welfare State: A History of Social Welfare in America*, 6th ed. (New York: Free Press, 1999), 4–5.

10. Quoted in Barbara Tuchman, *A Distant Mirror: The Calamitous 14th Century* (New York: Alfred A. Knopf, 1978), xiv.

11. Tuchman, *A Distant Mirror*, xiii.

The travails of the fourteenth century resulted in what de Schweinitz argues was the first step in the development of a social security system in England and by extension in the United States. This was the passage of the Statute of Laborers in 1349. This act sought to solve the labor problem by setting a maximum wage, compelling unattached workers to accept employment from whoever wanted to hire them, restricting the travel rights of workers, and making it illegal for able-bodied men to beg. de Schweinitz observes that the Statute of Laborers illustrates that "The King and his lords saw begging, movement and vagrancy, and the shortage of labor as essentially the same problem, to be dealt with in one law."[12] It may seem a stretch to consider this act, which was completely repressive and clearly in the interests of the owners of the means of production and not of those who worked in them, as a piece of social welfare legislation. de Schweinitz, however, argues that because it was the foundation for later, more progressive, true social security legislation it should be considered the beginning of both the British and American social welfare systems. The Statute of Laborers was a systematic attempt by government to deal with begging and the consequences that go with it, and was thus the first law to try to do something about the poor created by the decline of feudalism and the emerging market economy and wage system. An important aspect of the act is that it constituted, for the first time, a formal recognition of the existence of a free labor force with problems of safety and security.

Following the fourteenth century, the pace of change in England quickened and many of the changes were part of what we generally think of as progress. As the feudal system declined, trade routes opened, new industries (particularly woolen textiles) developed, the New World began to open up, and in general the potential for greater prosperity was everywhere. This emerging economic system, concerned with international trade, particularly with exports exceeding imports and the resulting accumulation of gold and other precious metals, was known as mercantilism. Along with the progress, however, these developments brought serious problems. The major problems had to do with the supply of labor and the growing insecurity of life. When the majority of people had been serfs, they were poor, but at least they had a form of security. No matter how hard times were, the serfs at least had the land and whatever sort of shelter they had erected on it. With the coming of industrialization and the beginning of a capitalist economy, and the growth of urban areas, most people no longer had any right either to the land that they lived on or to their dwellings. The feudal system had, for the common person, been replaced by the wage system. Under this system the majority of people were one payday away from destitution. This led to a continuation of the perception of a threat to the social order that had begun with the labor shortage following the bubonic plague. However, the threat rapidly came to be perceived not as a shortage of laborers but rather as an excess of unemployed and unattached people who wandered the countryside begging and stealing. The situation was made worse during the Protestant Reformation, when in 1536 Henry VIII expelled the Catholic Church from England. This act basically kicked most of the social welfare provisions out of England along with the church, because it was the church that had been given the primary responsibility for caring for the old, the sick, travelers, and the poor in general.

12. Karl de Schweinitz, *England's Road to Social Security* (New York: A. S. Barnes, 1943), 6.

The Statute of Laborers, with a few minor revisions, remained the basis for the official English response to poverty until well into the sixteenth century. At this time something happened that directed much greater attention to the problem of poverty. Several explanations of what this "something" was have been offered by historians. The first explanation, referred to by Slack as the "high pressure" interpretation, asserts that the poor laws were stimulated by economic circumstances and by population pressure.[13] This is the explanation subscribed to by Trattner, who argues that social and economic changes occurring in the sixteenth century were causing problems that were more powerful than the Statute of Laborers was able to handle. The rapid transformation of English society and economy from feudalism toward a wage system based on capitalism and democracy—a change described by Trattner as "one of the most profound upheavals civilization has known"—continued, and the accompanying problems of dependency, manifested by begging, crime, and vagabondage, became ever more pronounced and worrying.[14] The second interpretation looks at changes in public attitudes; a new conception, inspired by humanism, Protestantism, and Puritanism, was developing within the population of what government could and should do for the poor. The third explanation has to do with the process of state formation. According to this explanation, England in the sixteenth century was experiencing an expansion in both the scope and capabilities of the organs of governance, and part of this process, according to Healey, was that "the establishment of the poor law in early modern times represents a major step toward the modern idea that one of the state's crucial aims should be to provide a minimum standard of living for its citizens.[15] Probably as a result of a combination of these reasons, beginning in 1531 England enacted a series of poor laws, culminating in a piece of summary legislation passed in 1601, 43 Elizabeth, An Act for the Relief of the Poor. This act, with minor revisions, remained the basis of the social welfare systems both in England and the United States for well over two hundred years.

The first of this series of sixteenth century welfare laws in England was 22 Henry VIII, An Act Concerning Punishment of Beggars and Vagabonds, enacted in 1531. The motivation for passing this act is stated in the act's preamble as, "In all places throughout this realm of England, vagabonds and beggars have of long time increased, and daily do increase in great and excessive numbers, by the occasion of idleness, mother and root of all vices, whereby hath insurged and sprung, and daily insurgeth and springeth, continual thefts, murders, and other heinous offences and great enormities, to the displeasure of God, the unquietation and damage of the king's people, and to the marvelous disturbance of the commonweal of this realm."[16] This act took the provisions of the Statute of Laborers regarding begging and made them more severe. Whereas under the Statute of Laborers the penalty for an able-bodied person begging was confinement in the stocks, under the new law such offenders were to be tied naked to the end of a cart, and be whipped while being dragged throughout the town "tyll his Body be bloody by reason of suche whypping." The offender was then to be returned to his place of legal residence and there "put himself to labor like as a true man oweth to do," and not to leave this place for a period of three years. The law also made it illegal

13. Paul Slack, *The English Poor Law, 1531–1782* (Cambridge, UK: Cambridge University Press, 1990), 3.

14. Trattner, *From Poor Law to Welfare State*, 8.

15. Jonathan Healey, "The Development of Poor Relief in Lancashire, c. 1598–1680," *The Historical Journal*, 53 (September 2010), 552.

16. Quoted in de Schweinitz, *England's Road to Social Security*, 20.

to give aid to able-bodied beggars and set fines as the penalty for those who did so. Finally, this law did have one slightly progressive feature—it recognized that there were people, mainly the old and disabled, who were unable to live by working, and it set up a procedure for licensing these people to beg and assigning territories in which they could do so legally.

In 1536, 22 Henry VIII was revised. The revision kept the repressive provisions regarding punishment for sturdy vagabonds and beggars, in fact making them more severe by specifying capital punishment for the third offence of begging without license. But significantly, the act paid more attention to those who were considered to be legitimate poor. This law, for the first time, established that the legitimate poor should not have to beg, that society had an obligation to tend to their needs. This act required local magistrates to obtain resources, through voluntary contributions collected in churches, to care for the lame, the sick, and the aged (these were the groups considered to be "legitimate" poor). The parish was the unit assigned responsibility for administration of poor relief. In addition to providing aid to the legitimate poor, the parish was made responsible for providing work for returned vagabonds and finding apprenticeships for needy children.

The poor law was subjected to minor revisions in 1547, 1550, 1552,1555, and 1563. The next revision of any significance came in 1572 with a revision that can be seen, with some imagination, as the origin of social work. This act, titled 14 Elizabeth, An Act for the Punishment of Vagabonds and for Relief of the Poor and Impotent, repealed all previous statutes and replaced them with a new piece of summary legislation. Most of the provisions of the previous statutes were retained with some revision: in addition to being whipped, vagabonds were now to be burned through the ear, unless taken into service; beggars were still to be licensed; returned vagabonds were to be set to work; poor children were to be bound to service. There were some new features. Justices of the Peace (the primary governmental administrative official in the parish) were to register the names of all "aged, decayed, and impotent poor" in their parish, decide how much they require to live, and assess "all the inhabitants" to contribute weekly to their relief.[17] What had under previous statute been a voluntary contribution was now a mandatory tax, referred to as the poor rate, and a citizen who did not make their contribution faced "pain of committal to gaol" (jail). Finally, and most significant for our purposes here, the law created a new public official, the Overseer of the Poor, who was appointed by the local justice of the peace and to whom most of the administration of the poor law was delegated.

In 1576 this act was amended to recognize that a person could be able-bodied but unable to find work. The act extended the duties of the overseer of the poor to require that this official provide work relief to the able-bodied poor. The overseer was required to amass "a competent store and stock of wool, hemp, flax, iron or other stuff" to be distributed to the poor to use in their own homes to produce products such as yarn or cloth that could then be sold by the parish to partially compensate for the cost of caring for the poor. For those poor who were judged to be able-bodied, yet refused to work either inside or outside of their own homes, each parish was directed to build a house of correction to which they could be sent. In these facilities, later called workhouses, the poor would be forced to labor, with whips and chains if necessary.

---

17. Paul Slack, *The English Poor Law, 1531–1782*), 52.

In 1597/98 Parliament chose to assemble in one law all of the measures experimented with over the previous seventy-five years. This legislation was in turn reenacted in 1601 into the most famous of the poor laws, as mentioned earlier, 43 Elizabeth, An Act for the Relief of the Poor, commonly known as the Elizabethan or the English poor law. This act contained little that was new, but it is significant because it remained, with only minor modifications, the basis for the English and American social welfare systems for over 200 years and elucidated basic values and principles that still provide the foundation for our social welfare policies and practices. The first of these is the principle that one of the foremost reasons for, and goals of, social welfare programs is the regulation of labor. The market economy and free labor system that evolved in England during the late Middle Ages contains an inherent contradiction; that is, due to the fundamental instability of the system, some provisions must be made to support workers who at any particular time cannot be used by the system and hence have no source of support, but this must be done so in a way that ensures that they remain ready and able to rejoin the workforce when needed. This was accomplished by the poor laws, and continues to be accomplished today, by the principle labeled by the Royal Poor Law Commission of 1834 as "less eligibility." This principle means that the highest standard of living provided to a person on public relief must be lower than the lowest standard of living provided to an employed person. In other words, the poorest working person must be better off than the most comfortable person on relief. In addition to this doctrine, which was intended to ensure that the unemployed were motivated to work, the poor laws also contained a number of provisions requiring people to work whether they were motivated to do so or not. An unemployed person was required to accept any work that was offered; the children of the poor were to be bound out as apprentices, a practice that set them immediately to work, as well as preparing them for useful future careers as adults; finally, if people could not find any other work, the poor laws specified that they be provided with the raw material necessary to work within their own homes.

The poor laws also established the central concern of social welfare legislation, continuing until the present day, as the maintenance of social order. It is for this reason that de Schweinitz identifies the Statute of Laborers, an act totally concerned with controlling the behavior of workers and with no concern for assisting them in any way, as the first piece of social welfare legislation. With the breakdown of feudalism and the rise of a wage economy, England was faced with a mobile labor force who wandered about seeking work. People did not like strangers on the roads and in their towns, fearing that these people might be thieves and or prone to violence. Michael Dalton, in his 1618 handbook for rural Justices the Peace titled *The Country Justice*, devotes nine pages to describing poor law provisions for controlling rogues and vagabonds. Included in the list of people described as rogue and vagabond are people using any subtle craft or game (presumably gamblers), fortune tellers, jugglers, those using "any other like crafty science," patent gatherers, collectors for prisons or hospitals (presumably people begging by using the scam of collecting for a charity), fencers, minstrels, and tinkers. About the only legitimate reason that a person could be traveling was if he was a punished vagabond under order to return to his place of residence, a soldier or sailor returning home, or a "poor diseased person traveling to the baths for remedy of their grief." These people were required to carry with them letters of testament from a Justice of the Peace or, in the case of soldiers or sailors, from a commanding officer.[18] As the poor law

18. Michael Dalton, *The Country Justice* (London: Society of Stationers, 1643), 87, 108–116.

evolved from its origin in the 1349 Stature of Laborers roots to its summary and restatement in the Elizabethan Poor law of 1601, it gradually evolved to recognize that to reduce the number of wandering strangers it was not sufficient to merely punish the unemployed, regardless how savagely, but also was necessary to meet their needs. As the English social policy scholar Richard Tawney observed, officials found that "the whip had no terror for the man who must either tramp or starve."[19]

The poor laws also established the principle that the care of the poor, or the setting to work of the idle, was a local responsibility. People who found themselves destitute in a town or parish where they did not have legal residence were to be sent home. *Home* was defined as the parish in which a person was born, or if this was not known, the person was to be sent "to the Parish where such person last dwelt by the space of one year."[20] The person ordered to return to his home parish was expected to travel at least ten miles per day. Having traveled at least this distance, and entering a new parish, upon presentation of a letter from a Justice of the Peace in the sending parish, officials were required to provide one meal and one night's lodging before sending the traveler on his way.

The poor laws also established the principle of family responsibility. People were, to the extent they could afford to do so, responsible for caring for family members to an extent of two generations. Thus a person could be required to support his children, grandchildren, parents, and grandparents. This principle has eroded over the years to the extent that people are now only legally liable for the support of their children. However, the social norm of family responsibility remains.

The poor laws were the first step in the development of the professions of social work and social administration through the creation of the position of overseer of the poor. The clergy had traditionally assumed caring for the poor and dependent as one of their key roles. With the creation of the office of overseer of the poor this became, for the first time, the responsibility of a public official. The overseer was generally responsible for conducting the census of the poor, assessing their level of need, assessing and collecting the poor rate sufficient to cover this need, and keeping careful records of all collections and disbursements. For each parish, depending on its size, two to four overseers were appointed each year by the Justices of the Peace for the county in which the parish was located. The overseers were assigned to work with parish churchwardens to deal with the poor in the parish by arranging apprenticeships for poor children and deciding whether poor adults were able to work or not. For those able to work, the overseers had the responsibility of setting them to work; for those unable to work, they were to decide their level of need and provide funds sufficient to meet this need. This work was funded by means of the overseers estimating the amount of money needed each year and then collecting taxes from every inhabitant of the parish in amounts sufficient to fund the program. If the parish was too poor to fully fund its own program, then the overseer could tax the residents of neighboring, wealthier parishes. Although this system of funding sounds as though it was loose and flexible, the overseer was held tightly accountable for administration of the funds he raised. At the end of the year the overseers and church wardens were required to provide a "true and perfect accounting" of the poor funds; at the end of their

19. Richard Tawney, *Religion and the Rise of Capitalism* (New York: Harcourt, Brace: 1937).

20. Michael Dalton, *The Country Justice*, 108.

terms transferring all money remaining in the accounts to the new overseers. Failure to do either of these things would result in being jailed, without bail, until such time as the accounts were settled.

Overseers of the poor were given some guidance in two books published in the early 1600s. which, with a little imagination, can be considered the first social work and social administration textbooks. One was Michael Dalton's *The Country Justice*, a summary of the law mainly aimed at Justices of the Peace, but containing sections of relevance to the overseer of the poor position. The increasing recognition of the complexity and importance of the overseer's role is illustrated by the section on the poor in Dalton's book having grown from six and a half pages in the first edition published in 1618 to thirteen pages in the 1643 edition to twenty-seven pages in the 1697 edition. The second book was a handbook specifically aimed at the tasks and responsibilities of the overseer's position. This book was published in 1601 by Cambridge University and was titled *An Ease for Overseers of the Poor*. These books constitute the first attempt to provide guidelines for assessing the poor and for deciding on appropriate help based on this assessment.

The *Country Justice* and *An Ease for Overseers of the Poor* provided overseers with a system for classifying the poor and directions as to the proper treatment of people falling into each category. The first category was the willful and incorrigible poor, also referred to as the thriftless poor, later in history called the unworthy poor. This group comprised four subcategories: " the riotous person that consumes all with play, drinking, etc; the dissolute person, as the strumpet, pilferer, etc; all such as willfully spoil their work; and the vagabond that will abide in no service or place." The proper response by the overseer and the Justice of the Peace to the willful and incorrigible poor was clear: "For all these . . . the house of correction, or common jail is fitted; And yet such persons being able in body, are to be compelled to labor, for the rule of the Apostle is, that such as would not work should not eat."[21]

The second category was the willing and tractable poor; later known as the worthy poor. This group was divided into two subgroups, the first being the poor by impotence, which in turn comprised four types of persons: "the aged and decrepit, that are past labor; the infant, fatherless and motherless, and not able to work; the person naturally disabled, either in wit, or member, as an idiot, lunatic, blind, lame, etc; the person visited with grievous disease or sickness, though casually, yet thereby for the time being impotent." The second subgroup was the poor by casualty. This group comprised three types of persons: "the persons casually disabled, or maimed in his body, as the soldier or laborer maimed in their lawful calling; the householder decayed by casualty or fire, water, robbery, etc; the poor man overcharged with children."[22] By the nineteenth century, the man who was poor because of too many children would be classified as unworthy because he was guilty of violating the moral principle of abstinence; however, in the seventeenth century children were deemed to result from divine providence rather than human action, thus having more children than one could afford could be seen as being poor by casualty.

What to do with the worthy poor was a somewhat more complicated decision than that regarding the unworthy poor. The first principle was that, if at all possible, the poor should be set to work. To do this the overseer was given the authority to purchase out of the poor tax, a stock of supplies

21. Michael Dalton, *The Country Justice*, 87.
22. Michael Dalton, *The Country Justice*, 87.

to enable the poor to work in their homes. This was most often a stock of wool and flax that could be spun into thread and then woven (probably by a different person) into fabric. Using this stock as a means of employment the overseer was told that he must hold the poor to work, keep account of their work, and arrange to sell the products of their work. Although work was presented as the primary goal for the poor, the overseers were cautioned to not go overboard and treat the poor with harshness. *An Ease for Overseers of the Poor* advises that overseers "must tend the poor and lay no more upon them than they are able to bear, as we entreat God to lay no more upon us then he will make us able to bear, and those whom God doth punish with poverty, let no man seek to oppress with cruelty, as the taskmasters did the Israelites in Egypt."[23]

The children of the dependent poor were to be apprenticed at an early age, generally specified as seven years. They were to be apprenticed so young because ". . . the poor are by nature much inclined to ease and idleness and therefore they are to be put forth very timely for as a twig will bend when it is green, so children are fittest to be bound when they are young, otherwise by reason of their idle and base educations, they will . . . sooner be disposed to vagrancy then activity, to idleness than to work."[24] The apprenticeship was most often to last for males until age twenty-four and for females until age twenty-one.

Finally, the poor law, as explained by Dalton and in the *Ease for Overseers of the Poor*, recognized that some people were unable to work, even in subsidized labor, and had a right to "relief with money." The term relief is used, it is explained, because "it is an ease or lightening of the burden . . . that the poor endure many burdens, and that a little thing will ease where there is want or oppression." The overseer is advised not to be harsh, but to be sure that a person is actually unable to work. It is explained that a person who loses an eye still has one good eye and is therefore not impotent; likewise, the person who loses a leg still has a good leg and therefore is still able to work. "So long as there is any natural or necessary means left to live, none must depend upon the help of the law." After the overseer determined that a person was truly impotent, his next job was to ascertain whether or not there were relatives available to whom the support of the poor person was chargeable under the provisions of the poor law. The *Ease for Overseers of the Poor* bemoans the fact that "miserable is this age, that [people] must be compelled by penalty of law, to do that it should extend by instinct of nature."[25] Finally, the overseer is instructed to relieve with money those assessed to be truly unable to do any work and for whom no relatives can be found to provide support. No guidance was given to the overseer as to the size of the benefit to be given to these people.

SOCIAL WELFARE IN THE COLONIES

It has long been a myth of American history that poverty was rare in colonial America; that it was, to use a phrase written by indentured servant and diarist William Moraley, "the best poor

---

23. Anonymous, *An Ease for Overseers of the Poor* (Cambridge, England: John Legat, Printer, 1601), 20.

24. Anonymous, *An Ease for Overseers of the Poor*, 27.

25. Anonymous, *An Ease for Overseers of the Poor*, 23.

man's country in the world."[26] This myth has been passed along by prominent historians, including Pulitzer Prize winner Gordon Wood, who asserted that "Poverty and economic deprivation were not present in colonial America," and economic historians John McCusker and Russell Menard, who conclude that "the colonies experienced little if any of the abject poverty found in contemporary Europe."[27] The belief has been that two factors present in early America created a situation where anyone could prosper. These factors were an unlimited supply of unsettled land, making it possible for anyone to establish a farm, and a shortage of labor, enabling workers to negotiate for favorable wages. These analyses recognize that slaves and Native Americans could well be impoverished, but that there was little reason for European immigrants to find themselves in this situation.

There were, of course, no central data bases as we have today to track and measure poverty during the colonial era. However, the data that we do have, as well as simple logic, point to the conclusion that assertions of a nearly poverty-free colonial American society are nonsense and that poverty during this era was a huge problem just as it was before and after. Jackson Turner Main, in his study *The Social Structure of Revolutionary America*, concluded that, even discounting slaves, as much as one-third of the population in the northern colonies lived in poverty in the years preceding the American Revolution.[28] This is not surprising when you consider that the majority of immigrants arrived in this country not only penniless, but actually in debt. During the seventeenth and eighteenth centuries about two-thirds of all white immigrants arrived as indentured servants, this being the only way they could finance the voyage to the new world. The myth is that these people served their terms of indenture and then, taking advantage of the limitless land available, became prosperous farmers or, taking advantage of the labor shortage, negotiated jobs at good salaries and perhaps saved enough to become business owners themselves. The reality, according to quantitative studies by Abbott Smith and others, was somewhat different. Abbott Smith found that of every ten indentured servants only one ended up as a self-sufficient farmer and one achieved the position of artisan or craftsman. "The other eight died before they obtained their freedom or became propertyless day laborers, vagrants, or denizens of the local almshouse after completing their indentures."[29]

The reasons that the early American dream did not work out for so many people are many. First, the notion that the large amount of available land and the shortage of labor would translate into opportunity for all is flawed. There may have been ample real estate, but in order to take advantage of this a person still needed capital to purchase or rent the land and to buy the many things necessary to establish a functioning farm. People arriving in poverty (perhaps as much as 90 percent of immigrants) and people completing a term of indentured servitude were lucky to have a good pair of boots, much less enough money to set up a farm. Then there is the fact that it takes knowledge and skill to be a farmer, something that most of the immigrants, being simple

26. Susan E. Klepp and Billy G. Smith, eds., *The Infortunate—The Voyage and Adventures of William Moraley, an Indentured Servant* (State College, PA: Pennsylvania State University Press, 1992), 88–89. (Originally published: Newcastle, 1743.)

27. Cited in Billy G. Smith, *Down and Out in Early America* (University Park, PA: Pennsylvania State University Press, 2004), xii.

28. Jackson Turner Main, *The Social Structure of Revolutionary America* (Princeton, NJ: Princeton University Press, 1965).

29. Gary B. Nash, "Poverty and Politics in Early American History," in Billy G. Smith, *Down and Out in Early America*, 7–8.

laborers, did not have. Second, although there was a shortage of labor in the colonies, this shortage was seasonal. During the spring, summer, and early fall, healthy laborers could generally find ample work. However, during the winter months, agriculture, businesses supporting agriculture, and the maritime industry shut down. Common laborers employed in these industries did not earn enough to see themselves and their families through these lean months, so even the young, able-bodied, and healthy were likely to face four or five months of deprivation each year. Add to these reasons for poverty environmental factors such as recurrent wars and economic downturns, and personal crises such as sickness, death, and the difficulty of most to accumulate enough assets to move beyond a hand-to-mouth life style, and the existence of significant amounts of poverty in colonial America becomes easy to envision.

There is evidence that as the process of colonization continued and the population increased, the problem of poverty increased also. Gary Nash studied poverty in colonial America and found that during the eighteenth century

- The rate of indigence, as measured by the poor tax rate and the number of people receiving assistance, steadily rose.
- Widows, orphans, the sick, aged, and disabled among the poor were joined increasingly by able-bodied men.
- Private aid and church charity were insufficient to assist all the "deserving" poor in the major cities during cyclical economic downturns in the 1720s and 1730s, and these sources were even more stressed by the 1750s and 1760s in trying to cope with the large number of immigrants and the growing number of unemployed.
- The numbers of "strolling poor" (those called vagabonds and rogues in England) were steadily increasing in both eastern seaboard and frontier towns.
- All major cities responded to increased relief costs by building poorhouses by the end of the century.
- Poverty was becoming increasingly feminized because the social and economic structure afforded few opportunities for single, abandoned, or widowed women.
- The number of children placed in apprenticeships, sometimes without their parents' consent, increased as the number of parents unable to support their children rose.
- Lifelong landlessness expanded markedly.[30]

As each colony was faced with the problem of caring for the old, the blind, the disabled, the widowed, and the orphaned, as well as for the seasonally unemployed, each in turn passed legislation closely modeled on the English Poor Law of 1601. Plymouth Colony was the first, adopting the law in 1642, followed by Virginia in 1646, Rhode Island in 1647, Connecticut in 1673, and Massachusetts in 1692. Eventually, all the colonies adopted a poor law. True to the English law on which they were closely modeled, the colonial poor laws stressed public responsibility for the dependent and legally enforceable family responsibility, and they identified the smallest unit of

---

30. Nash, "Poverty and Politics in Early American History," 3–4.

government (the township or the county) as being responsible for caring for its own poor and dependent.

Although the colonies leaned heavily on the English experience in shaping their approach to the problem of poverty and dependence, a unique American approach began to emerge very early. In England, most poor relief was furnished under the public poor law, supplemented by a small amount of aid from the church. In America the poor law was also the major instrument of aid, but a dual system emerged that provided a substantial amount of assistance from private social welfare organizations that were frequently affiliated with churches. Responsibility for social welfare was divided between the public and private sectors, and although the majority of relief has always been public, Americans have had a strong preference for private provision of benefits and services. Concurrently with the passage of the poor laws in the different colonies, private organizations emerged such as the Scots Charitable Society in Boston in 1657, the Friends Almshouse in Philadelphia in 1713, the Boston Episcopal Society in 1724, and the Society House of Carpenters in New York in 1767.

The poor law was implemented and administered in the colonies in a manner very similar to England's but with a couple of subtle differences. The first difference is that in the New World, the emphasis on work was even greater than in England. This emphasis on work stemmed from two sources—economic and cultural. The economic reasons are fairly clear and straightforward. In the colonies there was a shortage of both labor (during periods of good weather) and wealth. In order to survive and to develop a store of excess wealth, it was of paramount importance that everyone who could work did so. The cultural factors are related to what later came to be called the Protestant ethic or simply the work ethic. This is the strong belief that work is innately good and that hard work indicates a person of quality—hard work may even be essential for earning salvation. The flip side of this belief system is that idleness, laziness, and sloth are sinful (sloth being, after all, one of the seven deadly sins). This belief in work and fear of idleness was reflected in the colonial poor laws. As in England, the laws called for children of the poor to be bound out as apprentices and the able-bodied poor to be set to work, and they also contained provisions for the development of home industry, mainly related to linen spinning, to enable people to work off their assistance payments.

The second difference is that colonial poor laws demonstrated much less concern with what the English called vagabonds and rogues, referred to in the colonies by the much more gentle appellation "the strolling poor." In England there was extreme concern with controlling the movement of people, probably a throwback to the feudal system, where people were legally bound to one place. The colonists, it can be surmised, probably after traveling thousands of miles seeking opportunity, would have thought of attempts to restrict movement as absurd and intolerable. The fact that colonists were relatively free to travel did not mean, however, that they were free to receive assistance wherever they happened to be when hardship struck. The colonial poor laws were clear in that people were entitled to assistance only where they had established legal settlement.

Under the colonial poor laws, either the county court or the town council, assisted in more populous regions by one or more overseers of the poor, had the responsibility of making decisions regarding persons' eligibility for assistance, along with the type and amount of assistance they could receive. The first and most critical decision was whether or not the person had legal settlement in the town or county. In colonial America the term "transient" did not refer to a person who was on the move. Rather, it referred to a person living in a town who did not have legal settlement. Legal settlement could be achieved in one of five ways: having been born in the town; by completing an apprenticeship in the town; by purchasing land within the town's jurisdiction; in the case of a woman, by marrying a man who had legal settlement in the town; or by living in a town for one year without being warned out. This final way of establishing settlement rarely worked because towns and counties kept tabs on people without legal settlement and issued yearly citations that kept transients "under warning," meaning that they were blocked from gaining legal settlement.[31] If it was decided that persons applying for assistance did not have legal settlement, arrangements would be made to send them back to the place where they did have settlement. If for some reason (e.g., a pregnant woman nearing her delivery date) a person could not be relocated, the process of applying for reimbursement from the place that did have legal responsibility was begun. Once legal settlement was determined, the town council/county court, in consultation with the overseers of the poor, decided what type of support to grant the person.

In addition to the English options of assisting the poor through outdoor financial relief, binding out of children, tax abatement, and in a few large cities commitment to a poorhouse, the colonists developed a unique approach. This approach, which in fact became the colonists preferred approach to helping the poor and dependent, involved placing needy people in private homes at public expense. While policies and procedures for boarding the dependent poor varied from place to place, the situation is Somerset County Maryland described by Geoffrey Guest was probably fairly typical. The process began when a person needing assistance would petition the county court at its regular session for relief. The court clerk would read the petition and then the petitioner was interrogated by the sitting Justices of the Peace. The court would then deliberate and render a decision. If the decision was favorable, the court would inquire if any of the householders in attendance would take the petitioner into their home for an agreed on sum. It was rare that anyone present volunteered, so the court would usually delegate the case to one or two of the Justices and the overseer of the poor to seek out (often to strong-arm) a householder into assuming responsibility for the person needing care.[32]

Because of the difficulty in finding people willing to agree to care for a dependent person in their home, a selection of four administrative procedures were developed. The first was the payment of fairly generous compensation to householders for caring for a poor person. In Somerset County the payment for in-home care of the poor was more than three times the amount the court granted a poor person as support to stay in his or her own home. In addition, when householders petitioned the court for an increase in the amount of support, the request was virtually always approved; however, when the poor receiving outdoor relief petitioned for an increase, it was very rarely granted. The second procedure was to not make a permanent placement for the poor person, but to place them "round the town." That is, people would take turns caring for the poor person for two weeks or a month, and then pass the person on to the next householder.[33] The third method was referred to as "venduing." In this procedure, rather than offering the people

31. Ruth Wallis Herndon, *Unwelcome Americans—Living on the Margins in Early New England*, 5.

32. Geoffrey Guest, "The Boarding of the Dependent Poor in Colonial America," *Social Service Review* 63 (March 1989), 92–112.

33. Trattner, *From Poor Law to Welfare State*, 19.

attending the court session a set amount for caring for a person, the court would solicit bids for the payment a householder would require to perform the requested service. The court would then employ the person willing to provide the care for the least amount of money, a sum undoubtedly much more than the amount originally offered. This basically amounted to a reverse auction. The fourth method was known as contracting. This procedure involved the county contracting with one or two individuals to provide care for a set amount of money for a period of one year for all persons needing such care. Basically this amounted to the setting up of small, private poorhouses. If no person could be found willing to care for all the poor, then the county or township would contract to have the poor cared for one individual at a time.[34]

When the colonies adopted the poor law, they also adopted the position of overseer of the poor as the public official responsible for its administration. Each year at an annual meeting, the town or county would elect between one and five overseers of the poor. The role was similar to that of the English position it was modeled on, but there were some differences. First, in England the position appears to have been a desired one. The overseer was an important component of a social process in England of state formation; the establishment of central governmental authority. It was a position appropriate for people aspiring to be recognized as members of a new and growing middle class, sometimes referred to as the "middling sorts." By contrast, in the colonies the position of overseer of the poor does not appear to have been a highly prized one. The role carried a high degree of responsibility, was only part time, and paid only enough to be a modest supplement to the office holder's income. In addition, unlike some other government appointments, the position of overseer did not involve any fees that could be exploited for personal gain. In spite of the meager benefits derived from this position, the overseer of the poor in colonial America had a great amount of power. Perhaps the greatest power of the overseer was to determine who was needy, a status referred to at the time as "likely to become chargeable" to the town budget. Once an overseer made this determination, the pauper lost most of his or her legal rights and the person's relationship to the overseer ceased to be one of legal equality and became much more similar to that of father and child. Once an overseer determined that a person was likely to become chargeable to the town or county, he then was responsible for determining whether the person had legal settlement in the town. If he determined that the person did not, he would then "warn out" the person; in some cases the sheriff would actually force the person to leave and return to his or her home but in other cases allowed the person to remain while being on formal notice that he or she was ineligible for any services or benefits in the town or county. If a person had legal settlement and was determined to be needy, the overseer had the responsibility of deciding what type of relief should be granted—whether the poor person should be supported in his or her own home, in a publically run workhouse or poorhouse, or in another citizen's private home. In the case of poor children who were old enough to work, the overseer would arrange for them to be bound out as apprentices, regardless of their parent's wishes.[35]

34. Gabriel J. Loiacono, *Poverty and Citizenship in Rhode Island, 1780–1870*, Ph.D. Dissertation, Brandeis University, August, 2008, 54–55.

35. Loiacono, *Poverty and Citizenship in Rhode Island, 1780–1870*, 52–56.

CONCLUSION

By the time the United States was established it had a stable and workable system of provision for the dependent poor in place and operating. This system was based on ancient Judeo-Christian values that the colonists took very seriously. Its legal basis was the system that had been developed in England over a period of more than a century of trial and error. A few features had been developed that were unique to the situation in the colonies.

Social welfare in pre-revolutionary America was a response to problems in a society characterized by low population, ample land, and a situation in which many people were poor but few who were so destitute that they needed ongoing assistance. Most towns and counties had only a handful of people in this situation. Social and economic life in the colonies was fairly stable, and change occurred in a gradual and orderly fashion. Also, and very important, social relations were, for the most part, personal and face-to-face. The person needing help was likely to be a neighbor and probably the factors leading to his or her problems were very familiar.

The system of relief programs established in the colonies provided a flexible response to the problem of dependency and did so while maintaining social order. The poor during this era were considered an organic part of society. Poverty was accepted as just being part of humanity's lot. The belief was that there was nothing surprising or urgent about the fact that some people were poor, and certainly no one harbored any expectations about eliminating, or even reducing, poverty. People believed that the most that could be done was to ease the suffering of the poor while maintaining an orderly, hierarchal society.

It would probably be an overstatement to say that the response to the poor in pre–Revolutionary War America was warm and generous. However, it can be said that it was not overly harsh and punitive. People expected that there would be poverty, accepted their religious and civic duty to aid the poor, had a pretty good understanding of why specific individuals were poor, harbored no expectation of changing or fixing the poor, and generally accepted that poverty was just part of the human condition. This was all about to change very rapidly.

CHAPTER 2

SOCIAL WELFARE IN THE NEW NATION, 1776–1865

In 1818 Lydia Bates, born in Scituate Rhode Island in 1800, applied for and was granted public assistance by the overseer of the poor of that town.[1] Although this was almost two hundred years ago, Ms. Bates fit many of the negative stereotypes of a 21st century welfare recipient. She was part of a multi-generational welfare family, there being evidence that she was supported by the town for at least part of her childhood. She was poorly educated; as she signed her name with an x, she apparently was illiterate. She appears to have had a fondness for spending time in taverns in the company of, perhaps disreputable, friends. Finally, she appears to have been a little free and indiscriminate in her relationships with men, as would come out later in a state Supreme Court case regarding the paternity of her child. As was the practice in Rhode Island at the time, the overseer of the poor auctioned off Lydia's care to the property holder who would take on the task of caring for her at the lowest expense to the town. Between being declared eligible for aid from the town until nine years later when she disappeared from town records, Lydia was cared for in the homes of at least six citizens of Scituate.

In 1819, while living in the home of William and Lydia Phillips, Lydia Bates became pregnant. Our forebears were at least as concerned as we are about deadbeat dads, and so when an unmarried woman, particularly one who either was or was likely to become a charge to the town (a category that included almost all unwed mothers), came to the attention of town officials they exerted great effort to establish paternity and to hold the putative father responsible for the financial support of the child. Lacking any kind of physical tests such as blood typing or DNA, establishment of paternity was almost totally based on information provided by the mother. Officials expected midwives to question mothers as to paternity while they were in labor based on the seemingly sensible belief that a woman in the throes of childbirth was unlikely to be other than truthful about the father's

---

1. The case of Lydia Bates is based on research by Gabriel Loiacono and reported in his article "Economy and Isolation in Rhode Island Poorhouses, 1820–1850," *Rhode Island History* 65, no. 2 (Summer 2007): 30–47, and in his dissertation, *Poverty and Citizenship in Rhode Island, 1780–1870*, Brandeis University, Department of History, August 2008, 135–141; and in personal communications, May 25–May 29, 2011.

identity. If the midwife did not establish the father's identity, or if officials wanted to answer this question prior to the child's birth, they would sometimes resort to questioning the mother at an official council meeting. At the meeting, on the record, they would ask questions such as "Who is the father of the child you are now pregnant with?" "At what time was it when [he] had the carnal knowledge of your body?" "Hath any other person except [him] had carnal knowledge of your body?" When a woman revealed a name, and if the person could not disprove her assertion, he was legally judged to be the child's father.[2] Once the identity of the father was established, he would be arrested and brought before a Justice of the Peace who would issue an order for support of the child. The father would then be jailed and would not be released until he either paid the support or posted a bond that guaranteed that payment would be made.

Officials of the town of Scituate set out to determine the father of Lydia Bates' child. This proved to be an easy task as Lydia, before, during, and after the birth of her daughter, Rhoda Martha, consistently identified the father as Thomas T. Hill, a resident of Providence and native of the neighboring town of Foster. Hill was a traveling salesman who peddled earthenware jars and other sundries from a cart he would drive from town to town. It was established that Lydia and Hill were acquainted, she having gone from the home of the Phillips to meet him at the road and, having spent some time with him, retuned with an earthenware jug. The jug may have been a gift, may have been payment for services rendered, or could have been a purchase, although this seems unlikely, as Ms. Bates probably had little, if any, cash. On order of the Justices of the Peace, the Scituate town sergeant located Hill and brought him before town officials, who ordered that he pay $23.46 immediately and then 50 cents a week for as long as Rhoda Martha was supported by the town.[3] It is interesting that no obligation was established from Hill to the child, only to the town. If Ms. Bates had found some means of support and thus was no longer a charge to the town, Hill would have had no obligation to continue supporting the child.

Thomas T. Hill was not at all happy about being identified as Rhoda's father and, in fact, vigorously denied that he was. He hired a lawyer to represent him in the matter, who filed an appeal with the Rhode Island Supreme Judicial Court. In preparation for the case, Hill's lawyer interviewed a number of acquaintances and neighbors of Ms. Bates. The purpose of these interviews was to establish that Lydia Bates was a women of questionable morals, who had relations with numerous men, and that any one of them could be the father. Hill and his lawyer were successful in impugning Bates' character and the court ruled that he was not Rhoda's father and was therefore not responsible for her support. The people of Scituate were not so willing to accept Hill's story, however, and continued to refer to Rhoda in official documents (and probably unofficial conversations) as "the child Lydia Bates had by T. T. Hill."

---

2. Ruth Wallis Herndon, *Unwelcome Americans; Living on the Margin in Early New England* (Philadelphia: University of Pennsylvania Press, 2001), 28–29.

3. Translating sums of money from 1819 to the present day is a tricky business for a number of reasons and, consequently, there are a number of ways to do this. Using the Consumer Price Index (CPI), the lump sum Hill was ordered to pay works out to $415 2010 dollars, and the weekly support amount works out to $8.84. However, if you use the unskilled wage method that looks at the amount of time Hill would have had to work to earn these sums, the answer is that he would have had to work as long as it takes a 2010 unskilled worker to earn $5,020 for the lump sum payment, and $112 for the weekly support payment. The bottom line is that the support Hill was ordered to pay was not insignificant, which at least partially explains his wish to escape responsibility for Rhoda's support.

What became of Lydia and Rhoda is not clear. Town records indicate that they were both supported by Scituate until 1827 when support was discontinued. By 1828 the Scituate overseers had assumed responsibility for Rhoda with the intention of placing her in an apprenticeship. This would not have been an unusual occurrence, as binding out the children of the poor, with or without parental consent, was the most common plan for their long-term support, and age nine would have been considered an appropriate age to do this. Whether a placement was ever secured for Rhoda is not known. Bates does not show up in the Scituate records in any fashion after 1827. It seems likely that she married, either legally or common law, and this enabled her to cease to be dependent on the town for support.

The case of Lydia Bates serves as a useful example of social welfare practices in the early years of the nineteenth century. There are several significant aspects to the way in which she was treated. The first is the relative willingness of the town to accept responsibility for the support of Lydia, and later of her daughter. The town leaders may not have been happy about supporting her (public assistance was, after all, the largest item in the town budget and must have been a constant source of concern) but there was absolutely no question that doing so was their duty. While tongues may have wagged behind closed doors, there seems to have been no official or public condemnation of her or her behavior. There seems to have been little concern about why Lydia was poor and needed support. The overseer of the poor and Justices of the Peace appear to have simply accepted that a young woman from a poor family, with no husband and no resources, would not be able to be self-supporting. They did not search for character flaws or psychopathology as explanations for her situation. They also seem to have given no thought to the possibility that Lydia could be somehow "fixed" or reformed and thereby made self-supporting. Finally, and perhaps most significantly, Lydia was cared for in the context of the community; there was no attempt to exclude or isolate her; there is no evidence of her having been stigmatized. She lived with town residents, participated in their lives and in the life of the community, and appears to have had a rich and full social life. She was, in other words, a full citizen of the town even though she was totally dependent upon it for her support.

It was only a matter of a few short years before the experience of paupers who followed Lydia Bates was completely different. As a result of rapid social, economic, and philosophical changes in the nation, the approach to poverty and dependency were radically altered. As the nineteenth century progressed, the nation became focused, almost obsessed, with studying and classifying people experiencing poverty and a number of related problems such as mental illness, crime, dependent children, and disability, among others. People's problems ceased to be viewed as simply fated conditions; they were seen instead as having causes that could be understood and, once understood, could be prevented or fixed. People like Lydia were no longer considered unfortunate victims of non-preventable conditions (i.e., being a single young woman from a pauper family with no resources who could not reasonably be expected to support herself) but as people with flaws that were responsible for their situations, flaws that could be fixed. These flaws were most commonly moral characteristics such as insufficient attention to virtues like abstinence, diligence, and thrift.

AMERICA 1776–1850: SOCIAL, DEMOGRAPHIC, AND ECONOMIC DEVELOPMENT

Poverty and related social problems were not given much attention in the years immediately following the American Revolution, even though they were widespread and very costly, because the population was fairly small, homogeneous, and stable. People needing assistance were likely neighbors, perhaps even family and friends, and people felt a moral, religiously based duty to help. Also, the problem was fairly stable. Except for years plagued by easily understandable problems such as crop failures, severe weather, outbreaks of disease, and the like, the number of people needing assistance was pretty constant from one year to the next. Leiby refers to American society at this time as the "rural democracy," a society of communities characterized by a stable population, a well-established culture, and a clear hierarchal class structure.[4] As the nineteenth century dawned and progressed, this situation changed quickly and dramatically. The change was caused by three related factors—industrialization, urbanization, and population growth increasingly composed of immigrants, all of which combined to move concern for poverty and related social welfare problems from the margins to the very center of American thought.

Following ratification by eleven states, the last being New York in July 1788, the Constitution replaced the Articles of Confederation as the framework for the government of the United States. The Constitution contains the provision that the federal government will "promote the general welfare" of the country, but the word "welfare" at this time was synonymous with "well-being" or perhaps "prosperity"; it in no way referred to helping the poor and dependent, as the word is currently used. The Constitution is completely silent regarding all matters that we now classify as social welfare. Because the Constitution, reflecting the earlier Articles of Confederation, delegates to the separate states all duties and rights not specifically assigned to the federal government, the result has been that the United States has as many social welfare systems as it has states and territories. This can be contrasted with more centrally governed countries such as England, where Parliament passes social welfare legislation and it applies uniformly to all political jurisdictions across the country.

In the years following the ratification of the Constitution there were many rapid changes forcing the new nation to deal with poverty and dependency. These changes accompanied the rapid geographic expansion of the country. In 1776 the country was bounded by the Atlantic coast on the east, the border with Spanish Florida on the south, the Mississippi River on the west, and the border with British North America (Canada) on the north. As a result of the 1803 Louisiana Purchase, the Florida Purchase in 1821, the 1845 Texas Annexation, the extinguishing of British claims to the Oregon Territory in 1846, the Mexican Cession of 1848, and the Gadsden Purchase of 1853, the United States achieved the dream of manifest destiny by controlling the entire area now constituting the lower 48 states. Because the country was so huge, and the various regions so diverse (ranging from areas in the west where the number of native Americans exceeded European Americans, to densely populated urban centers such as New York City and Philadelphia), there was

---

4. James Leiby, *A History of Social Work and Social Welfare in the United States* (New York: Columbia University Press, 1978), 36.

no uniform approach to problems of poverty and dependency. The South was rural and agricultural with much of the labor provided by slaves who were cared for, sometimes well but frequently not so well, by their owners. There were a number of free blacks who were largely excluded from any form of public or private organized assistance and who, as a consequence, developed various means of self-help. In the South there were also poor whites, abandoned and orphaned children, elderly people, and other groups who found themselves in need. These folks were treated with the warmer and more accepting approach that characterized charity in the colonial era; with relatively little need, the more prosperous segments of the population were not threatened by dependent people and dealt with them in the manner of *noblesse oblige*. The heavily populated urban areas along the Atlantic seaboard and the northeast were the harbingers of things to come, with dependency being increasingly perceived as a threat to social order and to town budgets, thus causing civic leaders to scramble to develop responses that would efficiently and effectively manage these problems. Eventually the whole country would resemble the heavily populated and urbanized east and would share the same problems and responses to poverty and dependency.

One of the major factors that disrupted the relatively stable and orderly economic structure of colonial America was changes in the labor market. The work force at the beginning of this era comprised four basic groups—agricultural workers, a small group of mostly urban professionals (doctors, lawyers, preachers, and the like), artisans and mechanics, and a group of workers who performed the many tasks requiring little skill but a strong back and a willing spirit. Many of this latter group earned at least part of their livelihood through what is known as the putting-out system. Under this system local merchants furnished ("put out") raw materials to rural households and paid a piece rate for the labor that converted the raw materials into manufactured products. The artisans/mechanic group was the backbone of the American economy. This group included carpenters, cabinet makers, silversmiths, cobblers, and the dozens of other skilled crafts needed to run an economy. People entered these trades by way of an apprenticeship, which was a legal arrangement whereby a master craftsman took on the responsibility of teaching a young person (generally a child at the beginning of the arrangement) the "art and mystery" of his craft. The apprenticeship period was generally for six or more years. In addition to providing training in the craft, the master was obligated to arrange for a certain number of months of formal schooling and at the end of the apprenticeship to provide specific benefits to help the young person get a start in life. A fairly typical example is that of Betsey Allen, bound out by the Philadelphia Board of Alms House Managers in 1799, with the arrangement being described as "a female orphan child admitted for the purpose of being bound aged ten years five months twenty five days . . . bound to Doctor George Bensel of German Town to learn the art and mystery of Housewifery—to serve him seven years, six months & five days, to have eight quarters half days of schooling one half of which schooling to be given after she is fourteen years of age & when she is free, two suits of clothes one of which to be new & forty Dollars in cash."[5] Girls were almost always bound out as domestic servants (housewifery); boys were apprenticed to a wide variety of trades ranging from the lowly (agriculture or shoe making) to the prestigious (goldsmith or apothecary). Once a young man completed an apprenticeship, generally in his late teens, he would become a

5. Philadelphia Guardians of the Poor, *Alms House Managers Minutes, 1788–1828*, December 9, 1799, Philadelphia City Archives.

journeyman. A journeyman was a fully qualified, beginning level, craftsman. A journeyman generally lacked the capital to set up his own shop, plus could probably benefit from additional experience, so in the early years of his career he would work as an employee for a master craftsman, often the same person he had apprenticed under. If things worked well for the journeyman, he would save his money and hone his skills, eventually qualifying as a master craftsman and opening his own shop, thereby earning an income that would enable him to support a family and take on apprentices or his own.

The increasing industrialization during this era had a great impact on the American workforce. First there was an emergence of a fifth group of workers, those with relatively low skills who worked for hourly wages in emerging industries. As the nineteenth century progressed there was a steady and increasing redeployment of more of the labor force from agricultural to industrial employment. In 1820, 80 percent of the free labor force worked in agriculture. By 1850, 45 percent of the labor force were non-farm workers. Another consequence of the industrial revolution for American workers was the development of technology that made production much more efficient. This technology began with the development of water power and the invention of means of using it for mass production in factory settings. Soon there were developments in steam power that had the advantage of freeing manufacturers from the necessity of locating near rapidly flowing rivers. These technologies were first applied to the textile industry, initially powering machines that spun cotton and other fibers into thread and then machines that wove the thread into finished cloth. Steam power was quickly applied to transportation, high-speed printing presses, and machines that carried out numerous industrial tasks such as stamping out metal parts, turning wooden dowels, and so forth. These technologies made more goods available at cheaper prices and as such were largely beneficial to American workers.

A trend that had an even greater effect on American workers than the technical innovations of the era were innovations in management and the division of labor according to the jobs' most basic parts and assigning only one part to a worker, which then required very little skill to perform. Adam Smith, author of the famous *Wealth of Nations* described the process thus:

> To take an example . . . the trade of the pin-maker; a workman . . . could scarce, perhaps, with his utmost industry, make one pin in a day, and certainly could not make twenty. But in the way in which this business is now carried on . . . it is divided into a number of branches, of which the greater part are likewise peculiar trades. One man draws out the wire, another straights it, a third cuts it, a fourth points it, a fifth grinds it at the top for receiving the head; to make the head requires two or three distinct operations; to put it on, is a peculiar business, to whiten the pins is another, it is even a trade by itself to put them into the paper; and the important business of making a pin is, in this manner, divided into about eighteen distinct operations . . . I have seen a small manufactory of this kind where ten men only were employed, and where . . . they could, when they exerted themselves, make among them . . . upwards of forty-eight thousand pins in a day. But if they had all wrought separately and independently . . . they certainly could not each of them have made twenty.[6]

6. Adam Smith, *An Inquiry into the Wealth of Nations* (London: W. Strahan, 1776).

Accompanying this new means of dividing labor was the development, by Eli Whitney in 1798, of interchangeable parts. Whitney developed this as a means of mass producing muskets for the US Army. Just like Smith's pin makers, with this new system Whitney did not need to hire journeyman or master gunsmiths to produce his product, but only to train men in the much simpler operations of grinding the sight, fitting the trigger, or carving the stock.

The factory system that developed from the new manufacturing technologies and processes had the effect of undercutting both the household and artisanal manufacturing systems that had been the backbone of the American economy. At the beginning of this era, goods were produced both by hand and by manufacturing centers and were produced in homes as well as in factories. As the nineteenth century progressed, a reorganization of economic life fueled by the new manufacturing and management technologies led to a deterioration of the position of home workers and independent journeymen. Nearly all of them became wage laborers employed by others rather than independent workers owning their raw materials, tools, place of work, and selling their products directly. Their skills also lost much of their value as the new production technologies subdivided work into smaller and smaller tasks that required little skill and time to learn. The result was a poorer and less secure workforce totally at the mercy of a relatively unstable market economy. With nine recessions between 1800 and 1860, each lasting from one to three years, and four depressions during the same period, lasting one to six years, the economy had become very unstable with workers at constant risk.

The era between the signing of the Constitution and the outbreak of the Civil War was also one of great population growth. The population in 1790 was slightly less than four million. Each year from 1790 to 1860 the population grew at a rate of around three percent, so by the end of the era the total population was 31.4 million. Although most of this population growth was due to natural increase resulting from a high birth rate of native born families, immigration was beginning to have an effect. About six million people immigrated to the United States during this era, the greatest number coming after 1845, mostly impoverished Germans and Irish. The Irish tended to remain in large cities, along the eastern seaboard, while the Germans dispersed into rural areas with many becoming successful farmers. Although one would think that people from Western Europe would be perceived as being similar to the native population, this was not always the case. The native population was overwhelmingly Protestant, and many of the immigrants were Catholic. The immigrants exhibited customs and habits, for example congregating in neighborhood bars and taverns even on Sundays, that often alarmed the Protestant majority who were dedicated to maintaining order in what they were beginning to perceive as a disorderly society.[7]

Industrialization and population growth were accompanied by the beginning of a change in where Americans lived. The United States remained a rural society until considerably after the end of this era, but urbanization was already well under way. In 1790 only 3 percent of Americans lived in cities with populations greater than 10,000; by 1860 this had increased to 16.4 percent.[8] In 1790 there were only five cities with populations greater than 10,000, and the largest, New York City,

---

7. Walter Trattner, *From Poor Law to Welfare State—A History of Social Welfare in America,* 6th ed. (New York: The Free Press, 1999), 55.

8. Jane Riblett Wilke, "The United States by Race and Urban-Rural Residence 1790–1860: Reference Tables," *Demography,* 13, (Feb., 1976): 139–148.

had a population of only 33,131 (if Philadelphia and its suburbs, called the Northern Liberties, were considered to be one urban area, it would have been the largest with a population of just over 40,000). By the mid-1800s there were 93 cities over 10,000 and the largest, still New York City, had grown to 813,669.

AMERICA 1776–1850: SOCIAL PROBLEMS

It is a truism that any great social advance has a flip side of one or more serious problems. Such was the case in the United States during its early years. The almost unimaginable increases in geographic size, population, wealth, and technology were accompanied by a darker side. Historian Steven Mintz observes, "A nightmare haunted early-nineteenth-century America—the specter of social breakdown."[9] The new nation was experiencing unprecedented levels of crime, vice, violence, poverty, and numerous other problems. European observers of the American scene such as Alexis de Tocqueville and William Chambers saw the new country in a generally favorable light, but were concerned about emerging problems. de Tocqueville looked "upon the size of certain American cities, and especially on the nature of their populations, as a real danger." Chambers expressed concern that the political fabric of the United States may not last, that it might "contain within itself the germs of dissolution."[10]

For an issue to be considered a social problem two things are required. First, of course, is empirical evidence that a problem exists—number of people in poverty, number of crimes, rate of births to single women, and the like. Second, and equally important, is that the issue must be perceived as a problem. For example, domestic violence has been around forever as an empirical phenomenon, but it was not defined as a social problem until the 1980s when, largely due to the women's movement, the public began to define it as something that should be dealt with.[11] Social problems play a very large role in the history of the 1788—1865 era because the actual incidence of problems greatly increased, and probably more important, people began to acutely perceive the problems and to be fearful of what they meant for day-to-day life and for the future of the republic.

Perhaps the most worrisome problem for the average American was the increase in crime. A British observer of the American experiment in democracy, one not particularly favorable to its prospects for success, Thomas Brothers, asserted in 1840 that with the founding of the United States "a new era came; and what were the consequences? Lynching, firing, stabbing, shooting and rioting are daily taking place." Brothers buttressed his conclusions about the violent nature of American society by reproducing 238 pages of newspaper reporting that read for all the world like present-day cable TV reality crime shows. The articles focus heavily on family murders, murders

9. Steven Mintz, *Moralists and Modernizers—America's Pre-Civil War Reformers* (Baltimore, MD: The Johns Hopkins University Press, 1995), 3.

10. Alexis de Tocqueville, *Democracy in America,* Vol. 1 (New York: Random House, Vintage Books, 1945), 300; William Chambers, *Things as They Are in America* (London and Edinburgh: William and Robert Chambers, 1854), 351–352.

11. Malcome Spector and John Kutsuse, *Constructing Social Problems,* 2nd ed. (New York: Aldine de Gruyter, 1987); Pierre L. van den Berghe, "How Problematic Are Social Problems?" *Social Problem Theory Division Newsletter, The Society for the Study of Social Problems* 4 (Summer 1975): 17.

and assaults on law enforcement officers, lynchings, and other examples of mob violence. Notable attention was paid to the Charleston Massachusetts Ursuline Convent riots, where a large mob, reacting to rumors that a young Protestant woman was being held in the convent against her will, rioted for three days and burned down the convent and destroyed its grounds and orchards.[12] The news articles furnished by Brothers are, of course, anecdotal data and illustrate more the level of popular concern with crime than they do the actual level. There is, however, some empirical data to support Brothers' contentions. The Boston Police Court, one of the first institutions to regularly report crime statistics, recorded prosecutions for violent crimes of 1,430.5 per 100,000 population in 1824, a number nearly four times the level today, and imprisonments of 16.8 per 100,000, a level three times that reported by the end of the nineteenth century.[13]

Americans were also becoming concerned that they were living in a nation of hard drinkers. In the larger cities such as New York and Boston people staggered down the streets, begging for money, brawling with one another, and accosting pedestrians. Journalists reported seeing street children taking bottles from gutters and drinking the dregs. By 1830, consumption of alcohol in the United States had reached an all-time high of 9.1 gallons of pure alcohol per year for every American over the age of thirteen, about three times present-day levels. By 1835 there were nearly three thousand bars in New York City, which works out to one for every fifty persons age fifteen or older. Accompanying the problem of alcohol abuse were related vice issues, notably gambling and prostitution. An expose published in 1830 by anti-prostitution crusader John R. McDowall alleged that there were over 10,000 prostitutes plying their trade in New York City.[14]

Perhaps the most significant problem to emerge in the years between the American Revolution and 1850 is that of poverty. Many of the problems I have described reached their peak during these years and then rapidly declined. Alcohol consumption fell from its high of 9.1 gallons per person per year to less than two gallons by 1845; violent crime decreased until by the end of the nineteenth century it was at levels about one-third of its peak; mob violence and lynching, while never completely disappearing, decreased as the century moved on. This was not the case with poverty. It came to be perceived as a major problem during the early years of the nineteenth century, and this perception continues to the present day. It is impossible to be highly specific and quantitative about poverty in the early years of the country for a couple of reasons. The first is that there was no definition of poverty; a definition would not be developed in the United States until the mid-twentieth century. However, even though there was no official, social scientific definition of poverty, it is fairly easy to figure out what the working definition was from the records of the era. Poverty was a far more serious condition during this era than it is presently. In modern times we consider a person poor if they lack the resources to be full participating members of the community; if they are "maimed in body and spirit, existing at levels beneath those necessary for human

---

12. Thomas Brothers, *The United States of North America as They Are; Not as They Are Generally Described: Being A Cure for Radicalism* (London: Orme, Brown, Green & Longman, Paternoster-Row, 1840).

13. Roger Lane, "Crime and Criminal Statistics in Nineteenth-Century Massachusetts," *Journal of Social History* 2 (Winter, 1968): 158–163.

14. Paul Boyer, *Urban Masses and Moral Order in America, 1820–1920* (Cambridge, MA: Harvard University Press, 1978), 18.

decency."[15] Thus today a person can have food, clothing, and some form of shelter and still be considered to be living in poverty. In the early years of this nation poverty did not mean simply to be poor. The majority of the population was poor in the sense that they had little or no cash, perhaps only a suit or two of clothes, and during good weather may not have even had any permanent shelter. To be in poverty was to be what was called a pauper, a person not just lacking the means to a decent life but actually facing a threat to survival. The intake entries in the Daily Occurrence Docket of the Philadelphia Almshouse frequently note the condition of persons admitted with terms such as "wretchedly naked and badly diseased."[16]

Related to the fact that there was no definition of poverty during the nineteenth century is that no one was keeping count in any systematic way, so it is hard to say just how large the problem was and to what degree it was increasing. The Constitution requires that a census be taken every ten years, but the original purpose was only to count the population for the purposes of political representation. It was not until 1930 that questions were added about unemployment and income. The United States did not even have an official poverty line until 1965; much less keep data on the number of people in poverty. So statistics on the actual poverty rate during the early years of the nation are largely a matter of conjecture and rough estimation. The evidence exists that poverty was, in Rockman's words, "the most pressing issue facing the United States."[17] His research demonstrates that in the early years of the Republic poor relief was the largest single item in the budget of most townships.[18] Concentrating on the development of poverty programs in the south, Elna Green argues that "poor relief was one of the most important functions of local governments in early American history."[19] Studying poverty in Pennsylvania, the contemporary observer Charles Burroughs found that between 1800 and 1820, expenditures for relief increased by 370 percent and the number of recipients increased from one of every 333 residents to one of every 100.[20]

The increase in poverty, both empirically and perceptually, was mainly due to the reorganization of work and labor relations that characterized this period. Prior to the nineteenth century, the overwhelming majority of Americans worked for themselves as farmers, craftsman, or merchants. As the new century progressed, more and more people became wage earners in the employ of someone else. The percentage identified on the New York City tax roles as wage laborers increased from 6 percent to 27 percent between 1750 and 1850. New York City censuses and city directories report that for most trades the ratio was ten or eleven employees for every proprietor by 1850.

15. Maghnad Desai, "Drawing the Line: On Defining the Poverty Threshold," in *Excluding the Poor*, ed. Peter Golding (London: Child Poverty Action Group, 1986); Michael Harrington, *The Other America: Poverty in the United States* (Baltimore, MD: Penguin Books, 1963), 9.

16. Daily Occurrence Docket of the Philadelphia Almshouse, Saturday 21 November 1789, Record Group 35.75, Philadelphia City Archives, Philadelphia, PA.

17. Seth Rockman, *Welfare Reform in the Early Republic—A Brief History with Documents* (Boston and New York: Bedford/St. Martin's, 2003), 1.

18. Rockman, *Welfare Reform in the Early Republic*, 2–3.

19. Elna C. Green, *This Business of Relief—Confronting Poverty in a Southern City, 1740–1940* (Athens, GA: University of Georgia Press, 2003), 9.

20. Charles Burroughs, "A Discourse Delivered in the Chapel of the New Almshouse, in Portsmouth, N.H. Dec. 15, 1834, on the Occasion of Its First Being Opened for Religious Services," reprinted in David J. Rothman, advisory editor, *The Jacksonians on the Poor: Collected Pamphlets* (New York: Arno Press & The New York Times, 1971), 49–50.

A person who lived in a rural area as a farmer or an independent craftsman who owned land, had some form of shelter and a garden on it, and was able to hunt, fish, and gather could withstand periods of economic hardship. Likewise, a master craftsman in an urban area who owned his home, his shop, and his tools, and perhaps had a garden in his yard and a few animals could also weather a crisis, at least for a short while. However, a laborer whose total wealth consisted of a few personal items and a weekly paycheck was instantly in peril if he lost his job. Katz identifies two factors that added to the precarious position of working people during this era. One is that apprenticeships were shortened and the labor market had become glutted, resulting in lower wages for skilled trades. Even with lower wages and increasing instability in employment, workers had no cushion against unemployment. There was no such thing as unemployment compensation or disability payments, and few workers earned enough to be able to save for a rainy day.[21]

As the country became more and more a nation of employees, the availability of work became a major issue. As Katz has observed, the availability of work for every able-bodied person who really wants a job is one of the enduring myths of American history. In the nineteenth century work was no more universally available than it is today. Unskilled and semiskilled workers overstocked the labor market. There was also the problem of the seasonality of work. Most of the unskilled labor that was available—unloading ships, digging canals, and building railways—took place outdoors during periods of good weather. In northern regions these opportunities for employment ended with the onset of winter, meaning that most unskilled workers faced four or more months of unemployment each year.[22]

Although poverty in rural areas was not as great a problem as in urban areas, it too was on the increase. One of the factors accounting for this increase was shared with urban areas—mechanization. Just as new machines were replacing workers in urban factories, innovations such as threshing machines were replacing low-skill laborers on farms. Also, the increasing population, especially in long settled areas in the east, was leading to the land becoming less productive and farmers no longer having enough land to subdivide among their children. Rural poverty also resulted from periodic crop failures due to weather conditions or insect infestations. Farm work was, even more than urban work, seasonal. Following the fall harvest farm employment ended until the time for spring planting.

It is clear that the increasing concern with poverty in the eighteenth century was not merely a figment of the popular imagination—poverty was indeed increasing and doing so at a rapid rate. There were, however, a number of factors other than the statistical increase in the number of poor that served to fan the flames of public concern and to put poor relief squarely in the sites of public policy reformers. The first of these factors is that due to the increase in population, diversity, and urbanization, the poor came to more and more be considered to be "the other." In previous times, when most people lived in small towns with homogeneous populations and personal relationships, the people who needed help (such as Lydia Bates) were friends and neighbors or were at least familiar. In this type of setting people understood why someone needed relief, and they tended to be sympathetic to the plight of the less fortunate, because the cause of their poor fortune

---

21. Michael B. Katz, *In the Shadow of the Poorhouse: A Social History of Welfare in America*, 10th anniversary edition (New York: Basic Books, 1996), 4.

22. Katz, *In the Shadow of the Poorhouse*, 3–6.

was generally obvious. As the nineteenth century progressed it became less likely that you would personally know the poor and perceive them to be less fortunate versions of yourself. It was easy to see that Mrs. Armstrong needed help because her husband had been a drunk and was run over by a horse while on a bender, leaving her with nothing but four kids and a load of debt. The poor dear had done her best but life dealt her a bad hand and she really does need and deserve help. As the population became larger and more diverse it also was easy to see that Mrs. O'Conner was asking for help because she is Irish and those people drink too much, fight with each other, have more kids than they can afford, and are lazy to boot. If she would just learn to act like a good American she wouldn't need to ask for help all of the time.

DISCOVERY OF THE SOCIAL ENVIRONMENT

Prior to the American Revolution, thinking in America, as well as in Western Europe, included several ideas that shaped responses to social problems. Life in general was viewed as largely a matter of fate; you were born to be poor or to be rich and there was really not much to be done about it. Explanations of most phenomena, social as well as physical, were supernatural, generally religious; the sun rose in the east and some people were poor and others rich because this was all part of God's plan. Personal and social problems were largely a result of the sinful nature of humans; people committed crimes because of their selfish nature and were poor because they are lazy by nature and therefore will not work if there is any way they can avoid it.

During the seventeenth and eighteenth centuries, developments in religion, philosophy, and politics, collectively referred to as the Enlightenment, resulted in changes in the way many people in the west viewed the natural and social world. Enlightenment thinkers were heavily influenced by the Newtonian conception of a harmonious, law-governed universe, a rational system ruled by the mathematical laws of cause and effect. The assumption was that people, as a part of this rational universe, could understand it through their own reason; it was no longer necessary to view the universe as a mystery only partially explained by divine revelation. It was thought that religious doctrines could be tested by reason and should be accepted only if found to be in accord with a great rational design of the universe as comprehended by the human mind. God was viewed as the great watchmaker, having set the universe in motion according to natural law and afterward being largely uninvolved.

According to the philosophy of the Enlightenment, human nature was not predetermined by God, but was the natural result of the environment that molded it. People possessed no innate ideas; a person's mind was the product of her or his experiences, both good and bad. The doctrine of the depravity of humanity was viewed as a religious fiction invented by priests to gain control over the gullible. If human nature contained large elements of evil, this was simply the result of natural causes, mainly irrational environmental conditions and authoritarian training. People had the power to improve their own nature by improving the environment through science and education so it would accord with reason and natural law. Enlightenment thinkers conceived of human nature in optimistic terms.

Although Enlightenment thinking had a great influence in America, informing both the American Revolution and the form and content of the Constitution, most Americans were

Christians who took their bible seriously and literally. These people did not accept the notion that God was uninvolved in human affairs and that everything could be eventually understood as a result of natural law. However, even the thinking of fundamentalist Christians changed to accommodate a more optimistic view of human nature and to give more recognition to the power of people's social environment. What brought about these changes in thinking was the rise of two religious movements called the First and the Second Great Awakening. The First Great Awakening originated in England and spread to the colonies, where it exerted influence from the 1730s to the 1770s and can be described as a revitalization of religious piety. It was a new age of faith that arose to counter the currents of the Enlightenment, to reaffirm the view that being truly religious meant trusting the heart rather than the head, prizing feeling more than thinking, and relying on biblical revelation rather than human reason. The Second Great Awakening, lasting from about 1830 to 1850, was a religious movement that provided a framework for Christians to respond to the rapid social and technological changes that were occurring all around them. The Second Great Awakening proposed the belief, new to mainstream Protestantism, that anyone who sought salvation could attain it, not just those whom God had predestined to be saved. In both spiritual and secular realms, individuals were accountable for their own actions. Through Christian activism, individuals could strive toward moral perfectibility. Social evils, and the sinful consequences of economic and social changes, could be cleansed only if good Christians helped others find the path of righteousness. Although fundamentalist Christians arrived by taking a different route than more liberal Enlightenment thinkers, they eventually arrived at the same destination—that people were not inherently bad, that they were largely shaped by their social and physical environment, and that it was the moral duty of their fellow citizens to shape that environment for the betterment of humanity.

Prior to the 1800s Americans had displayed a strong preference for voluntary efforts to cope with crime, poverty, and other forms of social deviance. With the influence of the Enlightenment and the Second Great Awakening, Americans began to suspect that these efforts were inadequate and reformers turned to public authorities to establish a host of new institutions to deal with social problems. All these public institutions reflected a new attitude toward conditions that until then had been regarded as inevitable and irreversible. This new thought was that individual deviant behavior was a result of a chaotic and improperly structured social environment that tended to confuse individuals and derail proper moral development and behavior. It became a popular theory that by isolating people afflicted by various social problems in institutions dedicated to eradicating the causes of these problems, the problems could be corrected. In the properly ordered environment of the new institutions, discipline and moral character would be instilled in paupers, criminals, and other deviants who lacked the self-control to resist the society's corruption, vices, and temptations.

CRIME AND PUNISHMENT

The first problem to be addressed with the new Enlightenment inspired approach, and the related faith in the institution as a means of reform, was crime. The philosophic foundation of the new approach to crime was provided by the Italian criminologist Cesar Beccaria who, in his 1764 book *Essays on Crimes and Punishments*, argued that much crime was a direct result of the criminal justice system itself—it was too harsh and was unjust in that the severity of penalties far exceeded the crimes they were attached to. Beccaria argued for changes in the way criminal justice was administered—crimes should be defined clearly and systematically and the law should be codified so the suspect could better defend himself against unjust or untrue accusations. Punishments should be set to fit the crime in an explicit and fair way so the offender could understand his risk and the judge could not be arbitrary in passing sentence. The result of overly severe punishment, Beccaria argued, was that "The severity of punishment of itself emboldens men to commit the very wrongs it is supposed to prevent. . . [lawbreakers] are driven to commit additional crimes to avoid the punishment for a single one. The countries and times most notorious for severity of penalties have always been those in which the bloodiest and most inhumane of deeds were committed."[23]

Prior to this time the notion that a criminal's sentence could serve the purpose of rehabilitating him would have been considered laughable. Sentences for crimes were for the purpose of social vengeance or retaliation, and the only positive effect anticipated was that if the punishment was severe enough it would perhaps serve as an example for others and deter them from risking the same fate. Jails and prisons at this time were not places where convicted criminals spent long periods of time as payment for their misdeeds. Rather, they were places of detention while the accused awaited trial, and after sentence was passed they detained the now convicted criminal until the sentence could be carried out. Sentences generally consisted of fines, or, for those who could not afford to pay a fine, flogging, mutilation, or placement in the stocks for public humiliation. Capital punishment was the prescribed punishment for a remarkable number of offenses. Beccaria argued that these brutal punishments should be replaced with a policy of imprisoning the guilty for varying periods of time, related in a rational way to the seriousness of their offense. While locked up the convict should be put about various constructive tasks for the purpose both of contributing to her or his own self-support while locked up, and to develop good habits of labor and industry and some useful skills.

Beccaria's reforms found fertile ground in the new United States. The prison reformer Samuel Gridley Howe wrote that "Thousands of convicts are made so in consequence of a faulty organization of society . . . "[24] In the properly ordered environment of new institutions, discipline and moral character would be instilled in criminals and other deviants who lacked the self-control to resist the society's corrupting vices and temptations. Programs for lengthy incarceration with the goal of reforming the miscreant were implemented at the Walnut Street Prison in Philadelphia in 1790, at state prisons in New York and New Jersey in 1797, Virginia in 1800, and in most other states within a few years. This initial reform was quickly perceived as not successful as the inmates tended to develop their own social organization within the walls, with their own leaders and norms of behavior, and quickly gained virtual control of the prison. Rather than reforming the convicts, putting them in close association with one another for long periods of time appeared to be having

---

23. Quoted in David J. Rothman, *The Discovery of the Asylum* (Boston and Toronto: Little Brown and Company, 1971), 59–60.

24. Cited in David Goldfield, Carl Abbott, Virginia Anderson, Jo Ann E. Argersinger, Peter H. Argersinger, William L Barney, Robert M. Weir, *The American Journey: A History of the United States* (Upper Saddle River, NJ: Pearson, 2009), 319.

exactly the opposite effect. In response to this problem the new approach to penology was revised under one of two similar models. One approach was known as the "silent system" and was piloted at Auburn Prison in New York between 1816 and 1821. Under this system the prisoners were kept in separate cells with no chance for communication between them. They worked and ate together but were required to do so in complete silence. When they were moved from one daily activity to the next they were made to line up single file, place one hand on the shoulder of the prisoner in front of them, and look at the ground as they were lead to their destination, a procedure that became known as "lockstep." The other system was known as the "separate system" and was developed in Pennsylvania at Eastern State Penitentiary in 1829 and refined at Cherry Hill Prison in 1831. Under this system the isolation of the prisoners was absolute. They slept, ate, and worked in individual cells, each opening on to a small exercise yard where the prisoner would also be alone. Under both of these systems the prisoners were given nothing except a bible to provide distraction. The theory was that spending time in a completely controlled environment, free from the pressures and evil influences of a disorderly society, with a bible to read and time to reflect, that some sort of transformation would miraculously occur that would turn the former anti-social actor into a useful and law abiding citizen.

Although the idea of the penitentiary as a correctional approach enjoyed a great deal of support, it was criticized as being inhumane and counterproductive almost from the beginning. The famous French observers of American society, Alexis de Tocqueville and Gustave Auguste de Beaumont commented in an 1831 book: "The silence within these vast walls . . . is that of death . . . We felt as if we traversed catacombs; there were a thousand living beings, and yet it was desert solitude." As prisons proliferated and their size grew, officials found maintaining order, especially the total silence, to be increasingly difficult. Prisoners found ways of talking to each other, cursed, and sang obscene songs even on the Sabbath as a way of defying the guards. Arson, assaults on guards, and prison escapes became common. In an attempt to maintain order, prison officials resorted to increasingly barbaric punishments such as those at Eastern State Penitentiary described by Thomas Brothers in an 1833 letter to the British Parliament: long periods in a dark cell with no bed or blanket, being fed only a small ration of bread and water; denial of food for as long as six days; "ducking," which was a procedure resembling water boarding; and various means of restraint meant to cause excruciating pain such as the tranquillizing chair, the strait jacket, and the iron gag. In less than twenty five years it became clear that prisons were not living up to the promises and expectations of their founders. As Mintz concludes ". . . the penitentiary aimed to achieve a series of contradictory and ultimately irreconcilable goals: to punish and reform; to deter and rehabilitate; to segregate and resocialize. By mid-century, the institution's custodial role had superseded its rehabilitative aims."[25]

WAYWARD AND DEPENDENT CHILDREN

The institution as a response to social problems also proved very appealing to those concerned with children who were dependent because they had been arrested for a crime, or because they

25. Mintz, *Moralists and Modernizers,* 88.

either did not have parents to care for them or they had parents who were thought to be inadequate. The problem with juvenile lawbreakers was that they were subject to exactly the same laws and penalties as adult offenders. This led to two possible outcomes when a child was put on trial, each viewed as equally undesirable. The child could be convicted as an adult and sent to an adult prison where they were likely to mix with hardened adult criminals and as a result were "liable to acquire bad habits and principles, and lay the foundation for a career of worthlessness and improvidence," according to a committee in Philadelphia studying the problem of juvenile crime.[26] The other was that the jury, faced with the only option of a conviction and severe adult penalty, would often find the child not guilty even in the face of evidence of guilt, and let him or her escape any consequences for the bad behavior.

The solution for this group of children was the house of refuge, a residential facility in which an orderly environment and lifestyle could be imposed on the residents with the goal of instilling lifelong habits of work, orderliness, and moral behavior. The founders of the houses of refuge insisted that they were not prisons, but rather were asylums for "friendless and unfortunate children." Be that as it may, the houses of refuge looked for all the world like prisons with their strict routines and severe methods of enforcing discipline. The children lived by the bell: at the New York house of refuge, a typical example, they woke up to a bell at 5:00 a.m. After they washed and made their beds, another bell summoned them to the yard where they were examined for cleanliness and proper dress; the bell then summoned them to morning prayers and school; the bell then directed them to gather for breakfast; the bell continued throughout the day calling the children for work, for lunch, for dinner, and then for more school. This continued until 8:00 p.m., when they had a short time for personal chores and relaxation until the bell finally ended its duties for the day by indicating time for bed at 9:00 p.m. Discipline and order were enforced by a combination of positive and negative means. Good behavior was rewarded by extra privileges such as passes to go outside of the institution and appointments to positions of authority such as monitor of the younger children. Undesirable behavior was punished harshly by whippings, solitary confinement, deprivation of meals, leg irons, and handcuffs.[27]

The first house of refuge was opened in New York in 1825, followed by Boston and Philadelphia, who opened their own three years later. Although houses of refuge were private institutions they received a significant amount of operating funds through public sources. Because states and municipalities were devoting a great deal of money to opening multipurpose children's homes, the establishment of houses of refuge slowed after the establishment of only a few. However, the movement soon regained popularity to the point that by the 1840s houses were opened in Rochester, Cincinnati, and New Orleans. In the 1850s they were opened in Providence, Baltimore, Pittsburgh, Chicago, and St. Louis. The movement had spread to a point that in 1857 a convention of refuge superintendents was held in New York.[28] At this meeting it was reported that seventeen

---

26. Mintz, *Moralists and Modernizers*, 90.

27. Alexander W. Pisciotta, "Treatment on Trial: The Rhetoric and Reality of the New York House of Refuge, 1857–1935," *The American Journal of Legal History*, 29 (April 1985), 151–181.

28. Managers and Superintendents of Houses of Refuge and Schools of Reform, *Proceedings of the First Convention* (New York, 1857).

houses of refuge were in operation, with a combined population of over 20,000 residents, residential plant value totaling nearly $2 million, and total budgets in excess of $330,000.[29]

It is ironic that about the same time the superintendents of houses of refuge were holding their first meeting to celebrate their accomplishments and to share and hone their techniques, the movement was reaching its zenith and beginning its decline. Increasing population, especially low-income immigrant population, was causing a massive increase in the number of both juvenile delinquents and neglected children. The houses of refuge, being private organizations, did not have the resources to deal with the emerging demand. As a result states began to establish totally state-funded reform schools to deal with the problem. The reform schools on the surface shared the reform rhetoric of the houses of refuge, but most people accepted that they were in fact little more than junior jails. The reality of large numbers of inmates from the immigrant lower classes led to a deterioration of the spirit of reform, while at the same time the faith that a correctly structured environment could improve character and inculcate good habits in this group of children waned.

In addition to the problem of what to do with juvenile offenders, there was also concern over the increasing number of young people who had somehow become separated or alienated from their families and were attempting to live on their own. The reasons for these children's lack of parental care and supervision were many: medical and public health knowledge was poor, leading to many deaths of parents from diseases, particularly contagious diseases contracted in overpopulated and poorly ventilated housing and working conditions; little attention was paid to industrial safety resulting in frequent death or incapacitation of parents due to industrial accidents; extreme poverty sometimes led to mothers abandoning their infant children, or to older children simply leaving homes where parents were unable to feed or clothe them. These were children who in modern terminology would be classified as abandoned, neglected, or as children in need of supervision (CHINS). They had not been charged with breaking any laws but were without homes and were probably considered to be unruly and therefore not ready to be bound out as apprentices. Even in the case of a child deemed suitable for an apprenticeship, the likelihood of one being available became lower as the apprenticeship system declined.

Prior to the development of orphanages, dependent children were dealt with like any other pauper. County or town overseers of the poor would first determine if the child was chargeable to the town (i.e., had legal residence). Any child who was determined to be the responsibility of another town was transported to that location and that town's overseers took over the process. The first choice of the overseers after residency was established was generally to see if the child could be bound out as an apprentice. This could be done with children as young as three years, although in these cases the master was generally given a cash stipend to compensate for the time it would take the child to grow into economic usefulness. If the child could not be placed in an apprenticeship, he or she was then placed in the care of a local property owner. As many towns contracted with one or two people for care of all their poor, this meant that the child was placed in what was for all practical purposes a poorhouse. A report submitted to the Senate and Assembly of New York in 1823 found 2,604 children living in poorhouses in that state.

---

29. Adjusting these figures to 2010 dollars using the Consumer Price Index, residential plant value would be $51,500,000, and total budgets in excess of $7,730,000.

As the population, and particularly the urban population, grew, the number of unsupervised children increased to immense levels. In New York City alone, with a population of around a half million people, the police estimated that there were ten thousand children living on the streets. Charity workers estimated that the number was as high as thirty thousand.[30] The traditional method of caring for dependent children came under increasing attack. First, critics charged that the existing method neglected the moral and educational development of the children. Referring to these children, a 1819 report of the New York Society for the Prevention of Pauperism expressed worry that "Thousands of children are growing up . . . destitute of . . . superintendence over their minds and morals . . . a class more dangerous to the community can hardly be imagined."[31] Second, people who visited poorhouses came away shocked at the conditions under which children were living. These children, they charged, were growing up in the company of elderly, alcoholic, sick (often contagious), insane, and feeble minded people. Finally, changes in the labor market, mainly the growth of industrialization and mechanization, led to a sharply reduced demand for child labor, including a reduction in the number of available apprenticeships and an increase in the age at which apprenticeships began.[32]

Similar to the response to other social problems, the response to criticisms of the existing means of assisting dependent children was to build specialized institutions to house them and shape their characters. It was believed that only in an institution could the regimen necessary for character reform and moral development be established. A few children's homes, generally called orphanages at the time, had been opened prior to the nineteenth century. A home for girls was founded by the Ursuline Sisters in New Orleans in 1729; the Bethesda House for Boys was opened near Savannah, Georgia, in 1740; and the Charleston Orphans Home was established in 1790 in Charleston, South Carolina. These early children's homes were for the most part anomalies, established in response to specific events such as plagues and Indian wars. After the beginning of the nineteenth century, however, children's homes became a significant movement with 150 private orphanages established between 1820 and 1860: 11 in the 1820s, 36 in the 1830s, 39 in the 1840s, and 64 in the 1850s. In 1790 the total population of all orphanages in the United States was only 200 children. By 1850 this number had expanded to nearly 8,000.[33]

Children's homes continued to expand until well past 1865, in fact not reaching their peak until well into the twentieth century. However, like other forms of institutional care, they were subjected to criticism from their early years. The most common criticism of children's homes was that they were large, impersonal, rigid, authoritarian, and generally antifamily. One of the leading critics, the Reverend Charles Loring Brace, felt that "The impersonal custodial care of an institution . . . not only stunted children, it destroyed them . . . The regimentation did little to build self-reliance, to prepare the child for practical living. . . Institutional life, like charity handouts, perpetuated pauperism, and both were dismal failures when it came to helping people to learn to

---

30. Annette Riley Fry, "The Children's Migration," *American Heritage 26* (January 1974), 4–10, 79–81.

31. *Second Annual Report of the Managers of the Society for the Prevention of Pauperism in the City of New York* (New York: E. Conrad, 1820), 16.

32. Susan Whitelaw Downs and Michael Sherraden, "The Orphan Asylum in the Nineteenth Century," *Social Service Review* 57, (June 1983), 272–290.

33. Susan Whitelaw Downs and Michael Sherraden, "The Orphan Asylum in the Nineteenth Century," 273.

stand on their own."[34] Bryce went on to found the New York Children's Aid Society, which pioneered an early form of foster care, a practice that would eventually eclipse children's homes as the preferred method to provide care for dependent children.

THE MENTALLY ILL

Prior to the nineteenth century mental illness was viewed as a social and economic problem rather than a medical one. This was a holdover from pre-Enlightenment thinking that viewed mental illness as a fated condition that nothing much could be done about. Mental illness disrupted family relationships and separated the afflicted person from any means of self-support. Because of this attitude, the mentally ill were dealt with by the existing poor law system. A mentally ill person would be brought before a county or township's overseers of the poor, who would decide on a course of action. The plan implemented was similar to that for other categories of the poor, generally provision of financial assistance to help the person's family care for him or her, placement with a host family who would be compensated by the town or county, or, in more populous areas, consignment to a poorhouse. Because the mentally ill can be difficult to control and there were no drugs or behavioral interventions to help, the means of care often left much to be desired. Reports from the era are rife with stories of mentally disturbed people being kept in chains or other restraints and often being locked in sheds, basements, or back yards. The early reformer Dorothea Dix, while teaching Sunday school at the East Cambridge Jail in Massachusetts, reported on mentally ill people who were confined in the jail in unheated cells during harsh northeastern winters based on the belief that they did not feel the cold.[35]

Toward the end of the eighteenth century physicians, who, would now be called psychiatrists but at the time were known as alienists, began to argue that insanity was curable, and in fact was more curable than purely physical ailments. It was not a result of God's inevitable will. Dr. Benjamin Rush, a prominent political as well as scientific leader in the United States, began to experiment with physical treatments for insanity, including such things as bleeding, blistering, and mechanical devices such as the tranquilizer chair that spun the patient around at a high speed. In France, Dr. Phillipe Pinel developed a new theory of treating mental illness that argued that treatment should not be physical but rather moral or psychological. He argued that the mentally ill should be treated with gentleness and respect and subjected to an environment and experience that would lead them back to health. Dr. Pinel laid out the fundamentals of his new approach, which came to be known as moral treatment, in his *Traitise de la Folie*, which was published in France in 1801 and translated into English and published in the United States in 1806. Dr. Pinel's approach quickly gained strong support in the United States, including that of Dr. Rush.

At the heart of moral treatment was the belief that mental illness was a result of the disorderly character of modern society that could overwhelm the coping capabilities of many people and cause them to become mentally unhinged. It was believed that America had a significantly

34. Annette Riley Fry, "The Children's Migration," 6.
35. James Leiby, *A History of Social Work and Social Welfare*, 67.

higher rate of mental illness than did Europe, and moral treatment theory explained this as being a result of the exceptionally open and fluid quality of American society. America may have been a land of freedom and opportunity, but it was also a land without boundaries, structure, and limits, and many people's psyches were unable to cope with this. The solution recommended by advocates of moral treatment was to create a different kind of environment, one that would correct the deficiencies of the community, create an orderly and non-stressful living situation, and this would, over time, result in a cure. It was believed that the only place that this controlled environment could be created was within the walls of an institution, or asylum as it was then known. The asylum would create and administer a disciplined routine that would control impulsive behavior without resorting to cruelty, excessive restraint, or unnecessary punishment. The institution would restore order and stability in the patient's life and compensate for the irregularities of society.[36]

Moral treatment was based on three basic principles. The first was that the insane had to be removed from the community as soon as possible, preferably as soon as the first symptoms appeared. Allowing the person to remain in the disorderly environment that was causing the condition could quickly result in severity of the illness becoming too great to treat, so immediate placement in a mental hospital was imperative. The second principle was that the institution was, like the patient, to be as separate from the community as possible. Most mental hospitals were, as a result, built in rural areas far from population centers. This had the additional salutary benefit of decreasing the cost of hospital construction because land was cheaper far from urban centers. The third and most important principle of moral treatment was the daily program prescribed for the mentally ill. The patient had to be governed but not irritated or excited; order had to be imposed but in a humane manner; discipline had to be enforced without harshness; and finally, regularity had to be imposed on chaotic lives, but done so in a way that did not cause agitated reactions. The hospital would counteract the stressful environment of the community. As one physicians explained, "the hours for rising, dressing and washing . . . for meals, labor, occupation, amusement, walking, riding, etc., should be regulated by the most *perfect precision*. . . . The utmost *neatness* must be observed in the dormitories; the meals must be *orderly* and comfortably served. . . . The physician and assistants must make their visits at *certain* hours."[37] The patients were also expected to work while in the hospital, not so much to offset the cost of their care (although this was certainly considered a benefit) but because steady employment at some useful task would contribute to the development of proper habits and bring regularity and predictability to patients' lives.

Just as the criminal justice system began to revolve around the prison, the institution became the center of the mental health system. Based on the curative power of the asylum utilizing moral treatment, along with a number of exposes revealing the inhumane conditions that the mentally ill were often subjected to in the homes, poorhouses, and jails that were their usual abodes, the number of hospitals grew steadily. Prior to 1810 there were a few private mental

---

36. David Rothman, *The Discovery of the Asylum*, 132–133.

37. Quoted in Rothman, *The Discovery of the Asylum*, 144.

hospitals in eastern seaboard states and only Virginia had a public mental hospital. These institutions combined treated fewer than 500 patients a year. Quakers in Pennsylvania opened an asylum applying moral treatment at Frankford in 1817; Massachusetts General Hospital opened the McLean Asylum in 1821; in Connecticut, Hartford Retreat was opened in 1824. These were private institutions that served mostly paying patients, although they were reimbursed with public funds for the treatment of a limited number of paupers. Industrial states like New York and Massachusetts built institutions in the 1830s as well as the agricultural states of Vermont, Ohio, Tennessee, and Georgia. By 1860, 28 of 33 states had public mental hospitals. Although not every mentally ill person was cared for in a mental hospital, the institutionalization of the insane became the preferred procedure of American society. As Rothman notes "A cult of asylum swept the country."[38]

The accelerating pace of mental hospital construction can be partially attributed to what would later turn out to be wildly inflated claims of the success of moral treatment. Dr. Eli Todd published a report in 1827 in which he claimed a recovery rate exceeding 91 percent at his facility, the Hartford Retreat. In 1834 Samuel Woodward, superintendent of the Massachusetts hospital at Worcester, calculated an 82.25 percent recovery rate at his facility. In 1840 Dr. Luther Bell at Mc Lean Hospital in Boston asserted that all recent cases had been cured. One hundred percent cure rates were also claimed by John Galt at the Virginia State Hospital in 1842 and Dr. William Awl of the Ohio Asylum in 1843. Before the Civil War these claims were simply accepted as true because the people asserting them were experts and no one saw any reason to doubt them; there was an almost complete lack of dissent. It was not until 1887 that the validity and reliability of these incredible claims were attacked and the uncritical support of moral treatment began to erode.[39]

The new social concern with mental illness and the optimistic promises of advocates of moral treatment led to one of the earliest and most remarkable examples of grass roots organizing in the United States. Dorothea Dix was a teacher who had retired early due to health issues and was living on the proceeds of a small inheritance. While teaching Sunday school as a volunteer in the East Cambridge Massachusetts jail in 1841, she was appalled by the treatment of inmates who were there for no reason other than their mental illness. She went to court to protest the conditions that these people were living under and was successful in getting an order to improve their level of care, specifically to provide them with heat in their cells. Based on this experience Dix read widely of the literature on insanity, such as it was at the time, and was strongly influenced by the work on moral treatment, especially its advocates' claims of success. She spent two years visiting the mentally ill in Massachusetts in jails, poorhouses, private homes, and a few in asylums, and compiled a case-by-case report chronicling the wretched conditions under which they lived. In 1843 she presented her report to the Massachusetts legislature with the result that funds were appropriated to expand and improve the state hospital at Worchester.

38. David Rothman, *The Discovery of the Asylum*, 130.

39. Pliny Earle, *The Curability of Insanity* (Philadelphia: J. B. Lippincott, 1887), 27–29.

Dix continued her activities organizing on behalf of the mentally ill until 1848. She moved her campaign beyond Massachusetts, preparing reports and presenting "memorials" to the legislatures in twelve additional states, six in the north and six in the south. The results of her efforts were the construction or expansion of 32 mental hospitals. Dix presented the same arguments everywhere she visited, buttressing her argument with specific local cases at each setting. Her argument was based on assertions of moral treatment: that insanity was curable; and that the cure was only possible in institutional settings that were properly structured and, most important, provided high-quality, humane, care. Dix argued that high-quality moral treatment was already being provided, with good results, to the well-to-do in expensive private hospitals. The poor were the ones being neglected and mistreated, so there should be special state institutions constructed with substantial state funding because the cost of their care was beyond the resources of private charity and local governments.

Because even at the state level there was a shortage of money to pay for the care of the insane poor, Dix, in her final supreme effort, turned to the US Congress for help. In 1848 she was successful in getting a bill introduced that would have appropriated ten million acres of federal government land to state governments to be used to generate funds for the building, expansion, and operation of state mental hospitals. This was the same method that the federal government would use later in the century to support other activities, notably the construction of railroads and the establishment or expansion of state agricultural universities. It took six years for the bill to finally come up for a vote, with the result that in 1854 both houses of congress passed the measure and sent it to President Pierce. Tragically for Dix, her supporters, and the indigent mentally ill, the President vetoed the bill. His decision to do this was one that was to have ramifications for the social welfare system in the United States for years to come. Pierce objected to the "Ten Million Acre Bill" on two related constitutional grounds. The first was that he did not believe that the Constitution provided the federal government with the power to determine the activities of state governments, citing the Tenth Amendment, which reserves all powers not granted to the Congress to the states. His second objection was that he did not believe the Constitution granted any authority to the federal government to provide assistance to the poor. In his veto message he explained, "If Congress has the power to make provision for the indigent insane . . . it has the same power to provide for the indigent who are not insane; and thus to transfer to the Federal Government the charge of all the poor in all the States . . . I . . . acknowledge the duty incumbent on us all . . . to provide for those who . . . are subject to want and to disease of body or mind, but I cannot find any authority in the Constitution for making the Federal Government the great almoner of public charity throughout the United States."[40]

By the time of the Civil War the care and treatment of the mentally ill had been radically transformed in the United States through the efforts of physicians such as Benjamin Rush and Phillippe Pinel, progressive superintendents at newly emerging mental hospitals, and crusaders such a Dorothea Dix. Through these people's efforts the idea had been firmly planted that insanity was an illness and required medical treatment. Although claims of treatment success turned out

---

40. President Franklin Pierce's veto the bill resulting from Miss Dix's efforts, *Congressional Globe*, 33rd Congress, 1st sess. May 3, 1854, 1061–1063.

to be greatly exaggerated, the fact that people began to see mental illness as curable was itself a major step forward. Along with the expansion of institutions came a body of law that specified procedures for declaring a person *non compos mentis*, for committing a person to an institution, and the rights of the person committed. Most important, standards for the treatment of the mentally ill were formulated with a clear focus on humane and positive care. Although these institutions, bogged down by too many patients and too little money, by new psychiatric theories that stressed the physical basis of insanity and its curability, would themselves eventually become objects of scorn and targets for reform, during the pre-Civil War era they stand out as shining examples of the hope and optimism of enlightened and scientific thinking.

CONCLUSION

In 1820, the same year that Lydia Bates' daughter Rhoda was born in Scituate Rhode Island, another child, William Fales, was born in nearby Portsmouth.[41] Unlike Rhoda, who seemed to be blessed with good health, Fales was sick from childhood on. At the age of six he was diagnosed as having inflammatory rheumatism, an inflammation of the joints that causes severe pain and greatly restricts mobility. By the time he was sixteen he could not stand, and by twenty could not sit upright in a chair. His mother cared for him at home until he was twenty-five, at which time, with her financial resources depleted, and probably her own health on the decline, she could no longer care for him. Mrs. Fales appealed to the Portsmouth overseers of the poor for assistance, and in response they placed William in the newly constructed Portsmouth poorhouse.

William Fales was unusual among paupers in that he was gregarious and extremely literate. He was also a devout Christian. While in the poorhouse he carried on a correspondence with a number of prominent Philadelphia Christians, as well as with "Sheppard" Tom Hazard, a Rhode Island activist for better treatment of the poor. Fales eventually published a book based on his correspondence. Because of his outgoing nature, his Christian friends, and his writings, Fales became a bit of a celebrity, popularly referred to as "the Portsmouth cripple."

Although Fales was an unusual poorhouse resident, probably having more friends and outside contact than was usual, his writing clearly and movingly demonstrates that his experience as a pauper in a poorhouse was very different, and much worse, than the experience Lydia Bates had only a generation earlier as a pauper who was allowed to remain in the community. Whereas Lydia had a full and robust social life, Fales's experience was of isolation and loneliness. In a journal entry written in 1849, for example, he wrote, "I often think if I had a friend near at hand to whom I might unburden my troubled mind, it would alleviate my sorrows. But, alas! I have no such a one here (except it is the lord)."

---

41. The case of William Fales, like that of Lydia Bates, is based on research done by Gabriel Loiacono and reported in his article "Economy and Isolation in Rhode Island Poorhouses, 1820–1850," *Rhode Island History* 65 (Summer 2007): 30–47, and in his dissertation, *Poverty and Citizenship in Rhode Island, 1780–1870*, Brandeis University, Department of History, August 2008, 135–141; and in personal communications, May 25–May 29, 2011.

William Fales could have been cared for in a manner similar to the way Lydia Bates was treated only a generation earlier. Perhaps a small cash grant to his mother would have been sufficient to enable her to continue to care for him at home. Or perhaps, like Lydia, he could have been cared for in the home of a local resident. But neither option was considered because long-term poverty, like crime, child dependency, and mental illness, had been defined as an individual and social pathology that threatened community order and could only be managed in an institutional setting. The era of the poorhouse had arrived.

CHAPTER 3

AMERICA CONFRONTS POVERTY, 1776–1860

T he week of June 29, 1800 was a typical one at the Philadelphia Almshouse.[1] Fifteen people were admitted over the course of the week which, given a total admission of 800 for the year, was right at the average. Most of the fifteen were people who were sick or injured and had no one in their lives to care for them. The admission note for Mary McNeal stated " . . . this poor creature had the Misfortune of breaking one of her thighs, last Wednesday, by falling down a pair of Stairs; her Husband John McNeal is a poor laboring man and not being able to support himself and her in the situation she is In . . ." Jane Crawford was admitted because she " . . . is much afflicted with the rheumatism, which renders her incapable of working for a livelihood, for which reason she is sent here. . . " James Cody was admitted with ". . . a very bad sore leg also the Rheumatism. . . " Cody was one of many people the almshouse staff referred to as a "repeat customer," noting in his case "he's been here twice before this with the same complaint, and was discharged, so late as the 15th last April at his own request, finding himself he thought cured." A couple of the admissions were due to some kind of mental illness, such as Amelia Corsign who was "subject to fits at periodi-cal times, and [is] a little deranged," and Ernest Beathgen, who was noted to be "somewhat flighty." An elderly woman, Elizabeth Conven, was admitted, but the docket entrance did not identify age as the reason for her admission but rather that she "seems a good deal deranged." Finally, four children were admitted along with their ill parents.

Six people were discharged during the week of June 29. Two children, Thomas and William Stanfield, were returned to the care of their mother after she promised to "take care and provide for them as a Parent ought to do." They had resided in the Almshouse for slightly more than nine months. Sophia Fister had been admitted with a sore leg that had gotten better and, in addition, upon release she was reported to be "decently clothed." One man, Thomas Parmer, who was

---

1. Billy G. Smith and Cynthia Shelton, "The Daily Occurrence Docket of the Philadelphia Almshouse: Selected Entries, 1800–1804," *Pennsylvania History*, 52 (July 1985): 182–204.

admitted the previous June on "account of derangement in Mind," was released to his wife "who got permission of Mr. Ashley [and the] Visiting Committee to take him away." Two people were discharged, presumably involuntarily, on account of being troublesome. One, Mary Ashman, was discharged with the note that "the institution is rid of a troublesome body." The other, Oliver Lynch, "has been a very troublesome to and fro customer, too lazy to work out doors, or in doors, although he can eat two men's allowance and was punished with two days confinement for his idleness, but all to no purpose." In addition to the formal discharges, four people eloped (ran away): Thomas Scott, who was admitted following a fall from a third story window, had been given liberty to visit friends and did not return. Aaron Larkin had been admitted with venereal disease "and for being made sound again has taken this ungrateful method of acknowledging Thanks to his benefactors." Mathew Richards, in spite of being seventy years old, scaled the almshouse wall and ran away. The docket reported that he "is much addicted to liquor . . . has been here often, and always took this method of getting out."

In addition to admissions, discharges, and the like, routine business was conducted during the week to keep the almshouse running. Four women, Lydia McCulloch, Mary Dixon, Sarah Ferry, and Mary Hudson were paid to wet nurse children who were either there by themselves or else had mothers who were too ill to care for them. The inmates who were able to work spun twelve pounds of flaxen yarn, thirteen pounds of tow yarn, and two pounds of woolen yarn. They also wove thirty six pounds of flaxen yarn into 53 yards of linen. Four pairs of women's shoes and four pairs of men's shoes were made, as well as "Mending and Cobbling as usual." Inmates who were able to work but were not skilled as spinners, weavers, or cordwainers (shoe makers and repairers), spent the week picking oakum. Oakum was a material made by picking jute or hemp fibers from old ropes, which was mixed with tar and used for caulking small spaces in wooden ships, thereby rendering them watertight.

The Philadelphia Almshouse was not the typical approach to poverty and related social problems at the beginning of the 1776–1850 era. Established as the Friends Almshouse in 1713, in 1800 it was one of only a handful of institutions to care for the poor, most located in the few large urban areas such as New York City, Boston, and Baltimore. The more common approach to poverty was, as illustrated by the case of Lydia Bates in the last chapter, for public officials to arrange for the elderly, disabled, single mothers, and orphaned children to receive care in a private household at taxpayer's expense. Overseers of the Poor had little interest in studying why some people became impoverished, exploring ways to reform the poor, or classifying the poor beyond ascertaining whether or not a person had legal residence in the county or township. Poverty, they figured, was simply the lot of some people and there was little that could be done about it except to find ways to care for the poor at the lowest possible cost. By the end of the era all of this had changed. Poorhouses had become the public response of choice to the problem of poverty in the more heavily settled areas of the United States. In addition, the seeds of the social work profession were planted by the establishment of private urban charities—agencies dedicated to helping people who generally were in need of short-term assistance (hence were not appropriate for almshouse care), with the goal of studying, classifying, and reforming them to ensure their future self-sufficiency. Both institutions and urban charities viewed poverty as a condition not to be accepted, but to be studied, classified, and fixed.

AMERICA'S WAR ON POVERTY BEGINS

Concern about poverty as a serious social problem grew slowly in the years immediately following the American Revolution. However, this concern was not great, being roughly analogous to concern about any other growing item in town budgets. Attitudes toward the poor and methods of dealing with them changed little from the colonial practices. It took a major financial panic, lasting from 1819 to 1823, to focus attention on poverty as a problem threatening American life and prosperity. During this period of economic depression a record number of banks failed, factories were shut down, home mortgages were foreclosed upon, and unemployment was estimated to be as high as a half a million workers. The scope and impact of the depression was frightening. At a time when it was still possible to be sent to prison for unpaid debt, the numbers so incarcerated in Philadelphia reached 1,808 and in Boston 3,500. The depression was over by 1823, but it left a lasting impression on the American psyche, particularly on attitudes toward poverty and the poor.

At the same time that the depression of 1819–1823 was sharpening concern about poverty, the beginning of large and visible urban slums was providing people with graphic depictions of poverty and the lives of the poor. Perhaps the most famous slum was the neighborhood in New York City known as Five Points, named after an intersection in the middle of the area. Located just a few minutes' walk from Broadway, Five Points became infamous for its crime, filth, and depravity. It was, in the words of Anbinder, "ground zero for wretchedness." The streets of Five Points were lined with saloons and brothels, full of dirt and disease, and home to the city's most destitute and degraded citizens. A single block in Five Points housed seventeen houses of prostitution, with names such as the infamous Palace of the Passions. One tenement house, known as the Old Brewery, housed over a thousand people, averaged a murder a night, and was described in New York's *Police Gazette* as "the wickedest house on the wickedest street that ever existed in New York, yes, and in all the country and possibly all the world."[2] Although not as infamous as Five Points, similar large and visible slum neighborhoods developed during the 1820s in Boston, Philadelphia, Baltimore, and other urban areas. These slum neighborhoods became the beats of reporters for urban daily newspapers, assuring that the most lurid and sensational depictions of poor people and their lives became part of popular culture.

The increasing size and cost of the poverty population in the United States, highlighted by the depression of 1819–1823 and exacerbated and illustrated by sensational journalistic accounts of life of the poor in slums such as Five Points, led to increasing categorization of the poor into groups of worthy and unworthy. These distinctions had been around since the English poor laws and were actually written into these laws. However, in the colonies and in the early years of the republic, relatively little attention was paid to them. This changed in the 1820s when popular public attitudes began to depict the poor as immoral, licentious, irresponsible, and largely at fault for their own condition. In 1834 Burroughs reviewed the leading scholars and concluded that by far the greatest cause of poverty was intemperance. He concluded that "from three fourths to nine tenths of all paupers in our country can trace their destitution" to alcohol abuse. Lesser, but still

---

2. Tyler Anbinder, *Five Points: The 19th Century New York City Neighborhood That Invented Tap Dance, Stole Elections, and Became the World's Most Notorious Slum* (New York: Plume, 2002).

significant, causes of poverty identified by Burroughs were lack of diligence and thrift by the poor, all kinds of gaming, dissipation, and extravagance in living. There were a few dissenting voices, notably Mathew Carey, who argued forcefully that poverty had little to do with individual characteristics and much to do with the organization of the economy. Carey argued that the solution to poverty was for an economic and social organization that enabled everyone wanting work to be able to find work, and that wages be high enough so "the poor . . . may at all times support themselves comfortably without eleemosynary aid [charity]." Carey supported his argument with an analysis of economic data through which he concluded that the annual living expenses of a family of four totaled $166.21 per year, but that a typical laborers family income was only $136.00 per year, even with the wife working part time, leaving a deficit of $30.21 per year. He criticized the leading free market economists of the time saying that they "are not ashamed to stigmatize [poor laborers] as worthless and improvident, because they do not, forsooth, save enough out of their miserable wages, to support themselves and families in times of scarcity. . ."[3] It appears that Charles Burroughs had either not read or he chose to ignore Carey when he identified savings banks as one of the solutions to poverty. Burroughs waxed eloquently about the intelligent men of business who were "not only becoming faithful guardians of the earnings of the laborer, but the rewarders of industry and economy." He believed that workers, "By availing themselves of the benefit of these banks the laboring classes soon learn the value of money; and also are led to become more frugal and diligent."[4] Burroughs appeared to be unconcerned that the laborer, as calculated by Carey, did not earn enough to live on, much less have an excess to save for a rainy day. Although it would seem that a major economic depression like the Panic of 1819 would lend credence and support to Carey's arguments and criticism of those like Burroughs, it did not. The individualistic explanation of poverty, which has come to be referred to as "blaming the victim," became the explanation of choice for the increase in the cost of poverty.

Beginning in the 1820s the old poor law system of relief, which gave people a little assistance to allow them to remain in their own homes or with family or else boarded them out with local homeowners, was largely replaced. It was replaced with three new methods of relief that were roughly in response to the type of poverty being addressed. Cases that were considered to be unworthy poor, usually able bodied men who were not working, often transient, sometimes supporting themselves through begging, were to be sent to the workhouse. Cases that were generally considered worthy poor, what we would now call residual, persistent, or permanent poverty, were to be dealt with by placement in a publically supported poorhouse. These were cases where people were old, sick, mentally ill, handicapped, or single mothers without family support; cases where the prospect was that they would need long-term assistance. The poorhouse was seen as the proper response to this type of poverty because it was less costly than other approaches, could monitor and perhaps improve the behavior of the pauper, and, a very important aspect, it was a prospect so bleak that no one would use its services unless they truly had no other option. In other words,

3. Mathew Carey, *Appeal to the Wealthy of the Land, Ladies as Well as Gentlemen, on the Situation, and Prospects of Those Whose Sole Dependence for Subsistence Is on the Labor of Their Hands* (Philadelphia: stereotyped by L. Johnson, 1823), 3–34.

4. Charles Burroughs, "A Discourse Delivered in the Chapel of the New Almshouse in Portsmouth, N.H. Dec. 15, 1834 on the Occasion of Its First Being Opened for Religious Services," reprinted in David J. Rothman, ed., *The Jacksonians and the Poor* (New York: Arno Press and New York Times, 1971), 81.

it was an early response to the perceived problem of welfare cheating. Finally, there were a number of people needing assistance that we would now call marginal or transitional poor who were not appropriate candidates for the poorhouse. These people were poor in response to some life situation—short-term unemployment, curable illness, family breakdown, or life transitions such as being newly arrived immigrants—who needed short-term assistance or who needed assistance in amounts less than full support. For this group, a group often suspected of being unworthy, a new form of assistance began to emerge. This was assistance through urban charities, agencies that would provide small amounts of short-term support. But assistance was provided only after careful investigation of the situation of the person requesting aid, and it required that the recipient accept personal services from the agency to assure that they were truly needy, were spending the money in ways acceptable to the agency, and were working with the agency on self-improvement projects aimed at assuring that they would become better citizens both in terms of self-support and moral behavior.

Although the terms almshouse (or poorhouse) and workhouse are sometimes used interchangeably, and in some instances the two institutions were combined into one facility, they were not the same thing. The workhouse was a punitive institution and was often attached to a jail. The purpose of the workhouse was to deal with the able bodied who were perceived as being unwilling to work, preferring to rely on begging or petty crime. It was aimed at putting to some useful employment the idle, disorderly, and vagrant. The poorhouse, on the other hand, was viewed primarily as a shelter for the helpless and disabled, and only secondarily for the provision of work to the unemployed. Employment in the poorhouse was not provided for punitive reasons, but rather as a means of reform of people who did not have sufficient work habits or skills and as a way of defraying some of the costs of operating the institution.

THE RISE OF THE POORHOUSE

As population rapidly increased, accompanied by great increases in poverty and poor relief budgets, civic leaders began to look for better ways of managing the problem of the dependent poor. Pauperism in most areas was dealt with at this time through a combination of methods. People who were incapable of caring for themselves, referred to as the permanent poor, were generally placed in private homes at public expense, as had been the practice during the preceding colonial era. People, who were temporarily poor because of illness, injury, or just bad luck, were generally aided in their own homes through the provision of a small amount of cash, or in-kind benefits such as food, coal, and clothing, a practice referred to as "outdoor relief." The colonial practice of placing poor people in private homes worked fairly well in small rural areas where only a handful of people needed care each year, but in larger, more populous areas the system tended to break down. As a result, a few of the larger towns and counties constructed poorhouses in the 18th and early 19th centuries to provide what was known as "indoor relief." It was not until the 1820s, however, when the new faith in institutions, combined with several influential reports, resulted in a shift to a predominantly institutional system of poor relief. The reports, which did not so much cause the change in approach as focus on factors already in the wind, were the 1821 *Report of the Committee on the Pauper Laws of this Commonwealth* written, by Josiah Quincy for the Massachusetts legislature; the 1824 *Report on the Relief and Settlement of the Poor,* written by New York Secretary of State J. V. N. Yates; and the *Report by The Committee Appointed by the Board of Guardians of the Poor of the City and Districts of Philadelphia,* written in 1827. Charitable leaders in the United States were in frequent contact with their peers in England who, in 1834, released the *Report of the Royal Poor Law Commission for Inquiring in the Administration and Practical Operation of the Poor Laws.* This report embraced ideas and recommendations even more drastic than those of the reports in the United States.

These reports were all heavily influenced by changes in economic thinking that had been most clearly and forcefully stated in Adam Smith's famous 1776 book *An Inquiry into the Nature and Causes of the Wealth of Nations.* Smith sought to establish principles of economics that would demonstrate predictability and regularity just as Isaac Newton had done for physics. Smith's main principle was that of the invisible hand, by which he meant that when individuals each sought their own self-interest, free of any external interference, the result would be maximum social good. He asserted that even though every individual "intends only his own security, only his own gain . . . he is led by an invisible hand to promote an end which was no part of his intention. By pursuing his own interest he frequently promotes that of society more effectually than when he really intends to promote it."[5] Smith's theory of economics—at the time known as liberal economics and sometimes referred to as laissez-faire, free market, or classical economics—revolved around the central principle that nothing, especially government, should interfere with individual economic choices. This approach was a radical departure from the prevailing approach, known as mercantilism, which was based on the idea that the economy should be centrally planned by a benevolent government.

The primary impact of liberal economic theory on poor relief was the idea that the public provision of assistance as a right of citizenship, as was the case under the poor laws, was bad economic policy for several reasons. The first was that providing people with assistance not tied to work would drive up the cost of labor, as employers would have to compete with the public dole for the services of workers. Even more important was the impact of public relief on the morals of recipients. One poorhouse report succinctly stated the issue as, "That of all modes of providing for the Poor, the most wasteful, the most expensive, and the most injurious to their morals, and destructive of their industrious habits, is that of supply in their own families. . . The manner in which public charity is too often administered affords encouragement to idleness, intemperance, and improvidence. The idle will beg, in preference to working: relief is extended to them without suitable discrimination. They are not left to feel the just consequences of their own idleness. The industrious poor are discouraged, by observing the bounty bestowed upon the idle, which they can only obtain by the sweat of their brow. . . [irresponsible behavior by the poor is encouraged because] they have a resource in the charity of individuals, and if not, they can obtain relief by application to the overseers of the poor."[6] The conclusion drawn by all of the reports was that the provision of outdoor relief to the poor resulted not in the reduction of poverty, but in its increase

5. Adam Smith, *An Inquiry into the Nature and Causes of the Wealth of Nations* (London: W. Strahan and T. Cadell, 1776).

6. Report from the Beverly Poor House," quoted in *Report of the Committee Appointed by the Board of Guardians of the Poor of the City and Districts of Philadelphia, to Visit the Cities of Baltimore, New York, Providence, and Salem* (Philadelphia: Samuel Parker, 1827), 24–25.

through rewarding idleness and sloth. The poor relief system itself became viewed as a cause of poverty. The conclusion, as stated in the Philadelphia report was that "no money in any case to be given." Any system that did so ". . . is essentially founded in error, and its parts are consequently defective." Quincy similarly concluded that "supplies, if given in money, are mischievous and often misapplied; when given for necessaries, as expended by the men, in ale, and by the women, for tea and sugar . . . and promoted habits of indolence and dissipation; and that the great object of . . . policy ought to be to eradicate this mode of . . . support."[7]

The Philadelphia pamphleteer Mathew Carey was one of the few people to argue against the assertion that the poor's "sufferings and distresses chiefly, if not wholly, arise from their idleness, and their dissipation, and their extravagance," and "That taxes for the support of the poor, and aid afforded them by charitable individuals, or benevolent societies, are pernicious, as, by encouraging the poor to depend on them, they foster their idleness and improvidence, and thus produce, or at least increase, the poverty and distress they are intended to relieve."[8] Carey viewed these as evil and destructive beliefs that served the main purpose of hardening the hearts of the rich against the poor and doing nothing more than prolonging and intensifying the suffering of the needy. Carey's arguments, which now sound very modern, fell on deaf ears. The liberal economists with their belief in the moral culpability of the poor for their own situations and of the role of charity in exacerbating the problem it was meant to solve, totally won the day.

The acceptance of critiques of the poor relief system from the perspective of liberal economics in the United States led to the consideration of two questions succinctly stated in the Yates report. The first question was, "Ought the whole system to be abolished, and the support of the poor left altogether to the voluntary contribution of the charitable and humane." Yates noted that many "men of great literary acquirements" had made convincing arguments that the poor relief system not only failed to reduce poverty, but in fact increased it through providing perverse incentives for people to accept public aid rather than exert the effort required to provide for their own support. All of the American reports on the poor relief system agreed that the arguments for total elimination of the public system were valid and made sense, yet in the words of the Yates report, "the total want of a pauper system, would be inconsistent with a humane, liberal, and enlightened policy."[9]

This acceptance of the failure of the prevailing system, combined with the belief that the total abolition of the system would be inconsistent with American values, led Yates to the second question, which he stated as "If the system ought not to be abolished, is it susceptible of improvement, and in what mode can it be best effected." He felt that there were a couple of additional problems with the poor relief system that required reform. One was that disproportionate shares of poor relief budgets were expended to determine questions of settlement, that is, which town or county was responsible for assisting an individual in need. Yates estimated that at least one-ninth of poor relief budgets were expended on "appeals and law suits concerning the settlement, maintenance, and removal of paupers . . . in the payment of fees of justices, overseers, lawyers and constables . . . " Another aspect of the problem of settlement was that when a person was determined not to have settlement in the location where he or she applied for aid, the process of transferring them to

---

7. *Report of the Committee Appointed by the Board of Guardians of the Poor of the City and Districts of Philadelphia,* 25.

8. Mathew Carey, "*Appeal to the Wealthy of the Land,*" Essay I, 7.

9. J. V. N. Yates, *Report of the Secretary of State in 1824 on the Relief and Settlement of the Poor* (New York, 1824), 950.

their place of legal residence was often inhumane. This was a result not of purposeful infliction of punishment, but of young, elderly, disabled, sick, or late-stage pregnant individuals having to undergo a long trip "frequently at inclement seasons of the year, regardless of the claims of age, sex, or condition." Yates concluded, "The removal of so many human beings, like felons, for no other fault than poverty, seems inconsistent with the spirit of a system professing to be founded on principles of pure benevolence and humanity." Another defect in the poor relief system in the early nineteenth century is that, although historians have often referred to the "warmer Colonial approach of placing the poor in individual's homes," the practice was frequently subject to abuses. Yates identifies this problem as, "The poor, when farmed out, or sold, are frequently treated with barbarity and neglect by their keepers." The final problem identified with the existing system of relief was that it neglected the needs, particularly the didactic and moral education, of the children of the poor. Yates asserted that they "grow up in filth, idleness, ignorance and disease, and many become early candidates for the prison or the grave."[10]

These reports all concluded, without equivocation, that public support of the poor was essential, but that outdoor relief should be ended, and that a poorhouse system should be adopted. The Philadelphia report stated, "The first and most grievous error of our unwieldy system is the abuse of the administration of relief, other than in the Alms House." The Quincy report concluded "that it is the duty of society by general arrangements, to attempt to diminish the increase of pauperism, as well as to make provision for that which is inevitable;—that diminution of the evil, is best, and most surely to be effected by making Alms Houses . . . and denying for the most part all supply from public provision, except on condition of admission into the public institution . . . " The Yates Report concluded "that the adoption of the poorhouse plan, in every county, is recommended by the proposed bill; and it may safely be affirmed, that wherever that plan has been fairly tried, the expense of supporting paupers has decreased 33, and in many instances 50 percent." These reports received widespread and nearly instant acceptance and support resulting in rapid spread of almshouses as the main public response to poverty. By way of example, in Massachusetts sixty towns built poorhouses between 1820 and 1840; by 1860 the state had a total of 219 almshouses. By 1860 Pennsylvania had 31 county almshouses in addition to an unknown but presumably large number of local institutions, and Maryland had an almshouse in every county except for one, and this county was allowed to use a facility in Baltimore. In New York only thirty out of a sample of 130 towns had poorhouses when the Yates report was written in 1824. By 1835, such institutions had been established in all but four of the state's fifty-five counties. In Rhode Island, thirteen of thirty-one towns built poorhouses between 1820 and 1850.[11]

There were a number of poorhouses that had been established prior to the Yates and Quincy reports, but these were a different type of institution than that developed afterward. The earlier poorhouses were really an extension of the practice of placing the poor in individual homes. When the number of poor needing assistance exceeded the capacity of individual home placement, towns often contracted with one or two individuals to care for all of the poor. In larger towns, such as New York and Philadelphia, even the capacity of this approach was exceeded, so larger

10. J. V. N. Yates, *Report of the Secretary of State*, 951–952.

11. David J. Rothman, *The Discovery of the Asylum* (Boston and Toronto: Little, Brown and Company, 1971).

facilities, the early poorhouses, were constructed.[12] Although these institutions shared the size and basic organization of the later poorhouses, they did not share the goals of protecting the community from being taken advantage of by unworthy poor, of regimenting and controlling the lives of their residents, or of facilitating moral character reform of the poor. These organizations were much looser than their later namesakes, often permitting alcohol, tobacco, and contact between the sexes, and residents were fairly free to leave the poorhouse to visit family and friends in the surrounding community. An example of the rather loose reins with which early poorhouse residents were supervised, as well as that our colonial forebears really did have a sense of humor, is that of Sarah Lackey, who was a resident of the Philadelphia Almshouse in September 1800. Sarah was pregnant and was released from the almshouse to go before the Justice of the Peace to swear as to the paternity of the child. She agreed that she would return again on time, and sober, neither of which did she do" When questioned by the Justice of the Peace it was revealed that she had become pregnant while a resident of the almshouse, and the father of the child was the brother of the almshouse baker and that he "came back & forward to assist his Brother Samuel in the Bake house, but if he had heated one Oven only, it would have been better for him."[13]

Although the new generation of poorhouses all shared the same basic philosophy and approach to poverty, there was great variability in their facilities. Some, like the Philadelphia Almshouse, the Newport Asylum, the Dexter Asylum in Providence Rhode Island, and Bellevue in New York, were modern, purpose built, architect designed, and appear to have initially been sources of public pride. The Dexter Asylum was financed and built according to the will of a wealthy local philanthropist, and contemporary reports describe it as being a high-quality building. The Newport Asylum design specified the "best cedar shingles" and "Thomaston or Dexter Lime of first quality." Both the Philadelphia Almshouse and the Bellevue Asylum had hospitals attached that were among the best in the country. Bourque notes that much more effort and expense tended to be devoted to the exterior of these buildings, including expensive fashionable design features such as cupolas, than was expended on the interiors, which tended to be cramped and plain. Other facilities, however, particularly those that were located in existing, repurposed buildings that were sometimes remodeled, sometimes not, tended to be far less adequate. "Sheppard" Tom Hazard, in his tour of Rhode Island poorhouses, described the facility in Coventry: "The house in which they were huddled was old and dilapidated—and the furniture was absolutely unfit for the use of the most degraded of savages." In addition, Hazard found the diet provided to the residents to be entirely inadequate, meals often consisting of only watery soup made with unripe potatoes, and provided in quantities too small to satisfy their hunger.[14]

The old expression about there being "many a slip twixt the cup and the lip" is well illustrated in the case of the poorhouse. The gap between the optimistic and high minded plans of the originators and the reality of the poorhouse was great indeed. According to the original intentions

12. Gerald N. Grob, *Mental Institutions in America; Social Policy to 1875* (New York: The Free Press, 1973), 13–16.

13. Billy G. Smith and Cynthia Shelton, "The Daily Occurrence Docket of the Philadelphia Almshouse," 185–186.

14. Gabriel Loiacono, "Economy and Isolation in Rhode Island Poorhouses, 1820–1850," *Rhode Island History*, 65 (Summer 2007): 30–37; Ruth Wallis Herndon, *Unwelcome Americans: Living on the Margin in Early New England* (Philadelphia: University of Pennsylvania Press, 2004); Monique Bourque, "The Peculiar Characteristic of Christian Communities—The County Almshouses of the Delaware Valley, 1790–1860," *Perspectives in Vernacular Architecture*, 6 (1997): 60–73.

of poorhouse advocates, the new Jacksonian era institution was to bear little resemblance to the facilities of the previous century. The new poorhouse, like prisons, houses of refuge, and mental asylums, was to be based upon order, discipline, and exacting routine. The behavior of the residents was to be strictly monitored (for their own good, of course) with alcohol, tobacco, and contact between the sexes strictly prohibited. Healthful work, preferably in agriculture, was to be provided to inculcate good habits of labor and industry. Because so many poorhouse residents were elderly, handicapped, or critically ill, the expectations for reform were never as great as that of prison, youth, or mental health institutional advocates, but some expectation of reform remained. Burroughs stated that "The infirm and helpless poor, incapable of work, are here furnished with a most comfortable asylum." However, "the able bodied paupers, before they can eat, are compelled to labor; and thus . . . brought into good habits."[15]

Poorhouse designers and administrators devoted a great deal of time and thought to developing programs that would meet these goals. A comfortable facility was to be provided for the old, sick, and disabled where they could spend their days in peace and tranquility. Ideally, specialized wings or buildings were to be provided for infants, orphans, and those needing medical attention. Work was to be provided, actually insisted upon, for the able bodied poor who were not criminals but who lacked means of support. The program for these people was to be carefully administered. The key was to provide a disciplined environment that would impose a rigid routine to bring new habits of industry to the idle and prevent them from becoming dependent on charity, as was feared would happen if they were given outdoor relief. They were to wear uniforms, be closely supervised at all times, sleep in congregate cells, and follow a strict schedule ruled by a series of bells to indicate times to move on to the next daily activity. Under the principle that was known as "less eligibility," the life of the able bodied poorhouse resident was to be inferior to that of the poorest self-supporting person in the community. Those residents who followed the poorhouse rules were rewarded with privileges such as occasional passes to visit family and friends in the community. Those who violated the rules were punished with curtailed food rations or placement in solitary confinement. More severe punishments, such as whippings, were also occasionally administered to particularly recalcitrant residents.

The performance of poorhouses in meeting the goals of providing good quality care for the aged, ill, and children, and providing a structured program of character reform for the able bodied unemployed was recognized to be a failure almost from the beginning. The reasons for this failure were many. Staff and management of the facilities lacked any type of specialized training to help them carry out their mission of reform, and probably more important, there was virtually no body of knowledge to base such training upon even if it did exist. The programs were based on a fundamentally flawed theory of dependency, one that continues to exist even to the present day, that the almost exclusive cause of poverty and dependency is individual moral failure. The fact that if there was no job available for a man, regardless of how strong a person's motivation or how sterling his character, he was going to be unemployed, never seemed to enter the minds of the poorhouse advocates. Finally, the poorhouses were almost immediately swamped with many more residents

15. Charles Burroughs, "A Discourse Delivered in the Chapel of the New Almshouse in Portsmouth, N.H.," 87.

than they were designed for, resulting in a program that could only struggle to keep up with basic survival needs of residents, much less provide any kind of positive care or reform activities.

A number of investigations of poorhouses beginning with a legislative committee in Massachusetts in 1833 confirmed the failure of the idea. All of the studies found that the facilities were badly overcrowded and that even newly constructed facilities quickly became run down. Systems of classification of residents had either broken down or had never been implemented in the first place, resulting in residents being all lumped together, so children were living with people who were insane, had contagious diseases, or were simply of questionable character. A state committee in New York in 1857 came to a typical conclusion that "As receptacles for adult paupers, the committee do not hesitate to record their deliberate opinion that the great mass of the poor houses. . . are most disgraceful memorials of the public charity. Common domestic animals are usually more humanely provided for than the paupers in some of these institutions."[16]

A small window into the decline of poorhouses is found in the daily occurrence dockets of the Philadelphia Almshouse, the official record of activities in that facility. From these documents it can be theorized that the institution was simply overwhelmed by the demands for its services. In 1800 the total number of admissions for the year was 800. As many residents remained for only a part of the year, the average daily census was much lower. By 1850 the number of admissions had swelled to over 4000. On July 5, 1858, a typical but by no means a record day, the number of residents was 2216, with weekly admission figures sometimes being as high as 90. The effect of these escalating numbers can be seen in the knowledge of individual cases evidenced by the staff. In the early years the docket contains brief descriptions of each resident who is admitted, discharged, died, or eloped. The descriptions are, by modern standards, sometimes judgmental and negative, but they at least demonstrate some individualization of the residents and knowledge and concern about their lives. Here are some examples:[17]

SATURDAY, NOVEMBER 21, 1789

> Admitted Hugh O'Harra—a very worthless young fellow. He was admitted here 30th Dec. last in a very wretched condition, with disease & rags. Wintered here, got cured & clothed, and went off in the spring, day 11th March & immediately sold most of his clothing and soon drank the whole they produced & hath ever since lived about in that way & sometimes in the Work House. He is now as wretchedly naked & badly diseased as before & returned as a pauper from the city tho he belongs to the NL [Philadelphia suburbs called the Northern Liberties].

16. David Rothman, *The Discovery of the Asylum*, 195–198.

17. Cases and statistics are from Philadelphia City Archives, Record Group 35, Philadelphia Guardians of the Poor; specifically 35.75, Daily Occurrence Docket, 1787–1888, 58 volumes.

WEDNESDAY, NOVEMBER 18, 1789

Died James Williams—a lame sailor who hath been in this house upwards of 20 years—was honest, manly & well behaved—and most of the time in trust as a useful man in many ways—among them yarn and linen boiling in the garden & over the oakum pickers in turn.

TUESDAY, MAY 11, 1790

Admitted Mary Smith—A common Hussey with the venereal disease. Sent in as a pauper from a common bawdy house.

Admitted Rachel Ward—Of the same character & disease as the above. She was of our Polishing Room gang all last winter & ran away. The disorder now affects her eyes so that she is almost blind.

MONDAY, SEPTEMBER 4, 1800

Admitted Joseph Webb—An old house carpenter who hath legal residence. Is poor and destitute and has been here several times before this, in the same predicament. He is agèd but healthy, and perhaps rather too fond of the liquor, which probably may be the cause of being troublesome to his friends.

SUNDAY, SEPTEMBER 17, 1809

Admitted Lucy W. Pherson LR [legal resident]. 55 years old, born in Ireland. Served her time in this city. Her husband is a brick layer and lives in Southwark. It is said he is subject to intemperance, and where so, beats her and abuses her in a cruel manner; has lost the use of her right arm, and is sick, so sent in per order of Andrew Powele & John Rutter [Overseers of the Poor]

Admitted Mary McCoy LR. About 21 years old, born in Springfield New Jersey—came from there to this city 17 months ago—had lived in various places, her husband John McCoy has deserted her 5 weeks ago. With her were two children—Daniel—2 years and Mary, 8 months.

In the years after 1800 a gradual change can be seen in the Philadelphia Almshouse records. The entries become briefer and demonstrate less knowledge of individual residents and their condition and situation. By 1849 the Daily Occurrence Docket contains only lists of names of those admitted, discharged, deaths, elopements, and births. By 1858 even the names are omitted with only bare bones summary statistics reported. It is ironic that as the almshouse evolved from the older style facility that made no claim regarding character reform and behavior control and management, to the new model that was entirely about these things, just the opposite of the designers' intentions appears to have happened. It is often said that the opposite of love is not hate but indifference. The earlier Philadelphia Almshouse probably could not be said to love the residents, but the docket provides clear evidence that the staff at least had the time and inclination to get to know each resident individually and to understand, if not always empathize, with each situation. In the later almshouse, regardless of ideology that preached character reform and rehabilitation, staff did not even have time to enter an individualized note about each resident.

Following the heyday of the poorhouse, a short period from the mid-1820s until the late 1840s, construction of new facilities slowed to a crawl. The glowing reports of poorhouse advocates such as Charles Burroughs ceased, and the reports that did appear were almost all critical of the approach. The poorhouse as a public response to poverty remained, however, until well into the twentieth century. David Wagner argues that poorhouses are in fact still with us in the form of low-quality, Medicaid funded nursing homes.[18] Their continued existence long after most people agreed that they were a failure and an embarrassment to a humane society can be linked to two factors. The first is that although poorhouse advocates had failed to provide a good solution as to how to manage poverty, they had been very successful in inculcating in American society the fear of poor people and the belief that helping the poor in the community (outdoor relief) would only exacerbate the problem. In the words of a popular song from the 1990s, they convinced the rest of society that it was cruel to be kind. The other reason that poorhouses continued to exist for so long is that there were very few good ideas going around about what else to do. There was, however, one idea that was beginning in the voluntary sector that was eventually to grow and form the basis not only for the profession of social work, but also for a new approach to public assistance to the poor. This idea was urban charities.

THE DEVELOPMENT OF URBAN CHARITIES

At the same time that enlightenment thinkers with their belief in liberal economics and the power of the institution were addressing social problems, these problems were also drawing intense attention from religious leaders. To these leaders the social and economic changes that accompanied the American market revolution were disorienting and even frightening. They saw signs of moral wickedness and disorder all around them and felt that the moral decline evident in large cities, particularly the evils of drink, were causing workers to forsake God and their families. Alarmed by what they believed was a breakdown of moral authority, they sought new ways to impose moral discipline on Americans.

The result of the concerns of religious leaders, notably Presbyterian minister Lyman Beecher, and backed by the financial and organizational strength of eastern business leaders, was a network of voluntary, church-affiliated reform organizations that has come to be known as the benevolent empire. This network included the American Board of Commissioners for Foreign Missions founded in 1810, the American Bible Society (1816), the American Sunday School Union (1824),

---

18. David Wagner, *The Poorhouse—America's Forgotten Institution* (Lanham, MD: Rowman & Littlefield, 2005).

the American Tract Society (1825), and the American Home Missionary Society (1826). These organizations developed modern and sophisticated means of operation that maintained a constant pressure for reform. They were led by national and local boards of directors who supervised the work of salaried managers, who in turn recruited and trained legions of volunteers to combat sin that was viewed as racking the nation. An innovation of these groups was that many of the volunteers were women. The rationale for this was, as noted by the Baltimore Bible Society in 1822, "men might be regarded as intruders, but what door would be rudely closed against female loveliness; what heart so hard, as to be insensible to the soft and imploring tones of her voice?"[19] When steam presses halved the cost of printing, they were the first organizations to recognize and exploit the power of print media. These groups pioneered techniques that continue to inform the best practices of the voluntary social welfare sector up to the present day.

The basic idea of all the organizations that formed the benevolent empire was that the distribution of God's word would have a "restraining effect on vicious habits" and that this would "strengthen the fabric of civil society." Initially this was to be accomplished by distribution of copies of the bible. The Bible, however, had a number of disadvantages. It was large, which meant that only a few could be carried at one time, it was costly to print and ship, but mostly it was long and difficult to read and to understand. Beginning in the 1820s interest began in writing and distributing tracts, which were short, pithily written, Bible based moral lessons that could be printed, carried, and distributed in the thousands by a single person. In 1825 representatives of various groups who were distributing these met and formed the American Tract Society. These tracts were meant to be informal, personal, and easily read. They contained wording such as "My dear friend, Will you permit one, with the best of intentions, to converse with you on a very important subject? As a friend, I feel interested in your welfare." The tract writer would then go on to deliver a message aimed at a specific category of reader: children, young people, parents, the ill, the poor, alcohol abusers, and numerous others. The tract would generally implore the reader to abandon any "vice and impropriety," and would hold out the hope of eternal salvation as the reward for following the advice contained in the tract.[20]

The expectations of the tract societies were high and exceedingly naïve. For example, the Reverend Justin Edwards, a tract society leader from Massachusetts, relayed the following case example at an American Tract Society meeting to illustrate the "ease and effect" of accomplishing reform through the distribution of tracts. The story goes that a volunteer visited in the home of a drunkard. Upon arriving he found the home in a shambles. The place was filthy, the wife and children were dressed in rags, no food was in evidence, and the kids were loud and disrespectful. He put his discomfort aside and had a short visit with the wife and left her with a tract he felt was appropriate for an alcohol abuser. An undisclosed period of time later he made a return visit to the drunkard's home and found the place completely transformed. The fighting, disorder, and grim indications of poverty had disappeared. Now, he reported, "neatness and comfort characterized the dwelling, and peace smiled on every countenance." The wife joyously explained the change,

---

19. Paul Boyer, *Urban Masses and Moral Order in America, 1820–1920* (Cambridge, MA: Harvard University Press, 1978), 24.

20. Paul Boyer, *Urban Masses and Moral Order*, 17–29.

"O, the Tract—the Tract has got us all these nice things! My husband never drank after you gave him the Tract."[21]

Staff and volunteers of tract societies and other organizations making up the benevolent empire were naïve not because they were stupid, but because there was almost no knowledge available about the problems they were addressing. No one had any idea about the roots and dynamics of alcohol abuse, prostitution, violence and crime, family disorganization, or poverty in general. It was only natural that these people looked to the main source of guidance in their lives, their religion and the Bible, and concluded that the source of all these problems was that some people's lives were not guided by this document. However, as they visited the homes of the poor, visited hospitals and jails, and were confronted with the stark realities of urban poverty, their naivety quickly faded and they became the first experts on social problems. They did not abandon their belief in the importance of tracts and moral guidance for the poor, but came to realize that more was needed. They quickly began to supplement their moral guidance with the provision of material assistance, helping the poor with rent, food, coal in the winter, clothing, as well as concrete advice on problems such as how and where to find a job or a better and more affordable apartment.

THE SOCIETY FOR THE PREVENTION
OF PAUPERISM

The poorhouses that were emerging in the early nineteenth century were recognized as not being the solution to all types of poverty. The poorhouse was viewed as a public response, and it was targeted at what were classified as the impotent poor—those too young, old, sick, handicapped, or deranged for there to be any expectation of self-support. This left a large number of people in need who did not fit this category. Mostly living in urban areas, this other group of the poor comprised the temporarily ill or injured, the occasionally unemployed, families whose number of children exceeded their earning capacity, recent immigrants who were without resources or connections, and those who no matter how hard or long they worked were not able to earn enough to sustain life. These people excited the compassion of nineteenth century urbanites, but even more they excited their fear. These paupers were not appropriate subjects for poorhouse care, but neither were they willing to starve or freeze to death. They would resort to any means necessary to survive—begging on the street, coming into prosperous neighborhoods and going door-to-door to request leftover food (referred to as cold victuals at the time), and engaging in illegal activities such as prostitution, gambling, or outright theft. Most feared was the person who would game the system by going to numerous charities or individuals to obtain assistance far in excess of their need, if such need ever really existed.

In response to this type of poverty, a series of agencies emerged during the second and third decade of the nineteenth century that were very much in sync with the poorhouse movement and with the moral vision and organizational expertise of the benevolent empire. The first, and generally

---

21. Justin Edwards, "Usefulness of Tracts," *Tracts of the American Tract Society*, general series (n.d., New York), III, no. 104: 5, 19, quoted in Paul Boyer, *Urban Masses and Moral Order*, 25.

recognized as the leader among these agencies, was the New York Society for the Prevention of Pauperism. This agency was established in 1817 and within a few years was emulated by similar organizations in every large city in the country, notably the Pennsylvania Society for the Promotion of Public Economy (1817), the Baltimore Society for the Prevention of Pauperism (1820), the Boston Society for the Moral and Religious Instruction of the Poor (1820), and a latecomer, the Boston Society for the Prevention of Pauperism (1835).

The New York Society for the Prevention of Pauperism (SPP) was formed by a small group of New York City activists, under the moral and intellectual leadership of John Griscom, a Columbia University chemistry professor and prominent civic leader.[22] The purpose of the agency as stated by Griscom and co-founder John Pintard was "To see if we cannot check in some degree the growth of the present system of relieving the poor." Significant, but hardly surprising for a scientist such as Griscom, was that its founders viewed the SPP only secondarily as a direct service and relief organization, but primarily as an instrument of social investigation. Toward this end, Article Two of the Society's constitution identified its main purpose as "To investigate the circumstances and habits of the poor," only after this was done would the agency ". . . devise means for improving their situation, both in a physical and moral point of view . . ."

One of the first things the SPP board did was to appoint Griscom to chair a committee to study the problem of poverty and poor relief in New York City. The Griscom Committee worked fast and completed their report on March 8, 1818. The report's main argument was that any workable poor relief system had to be able to discriminate between unavoidable indigence (later referred to as the "worthy poor") and artificial indigence (the "unworthy poor"). The committee estimated that 90 percent of the poor fell into the artificial category. The committee argued that poverty was due to ten factors:

"1st. Ignorance, arising either from inherent dullness or from want of opportunities for improvement [that] is particularly great among the foreign born that annually accumulate in this city; 2nd. Idleness. A tendency to this evil may be more or less inherent; 3rd. Intemperance in drinking . . . This evil, in relation to poverty and vice, may be emphatically styled, the *Cause of Causes* . . . we cannot but regard it as the crying and increasing sin of the nation, and as loudly demanding the solemn deliberations of our legislative assemblies; 4th. Want of economy. [This] prevails to a great extent, in an inattention to those small, but frequent savings when labor is plentiful, which may go to meet the privations of unfavorable seasons; 5th. Imprudent and hasty marriages; 6th. Lotteries, [that] divert the labourer from his employment, to weaken the tone of his morals, to consume his earnings, and consequently to increase his poverty; 7th. Pawnbrokers. The establishment of these offices is considered as very unfavorable to the independence and welfare of the middling and inferior classes . . . not to mention the facilities which they afford to the commission of theft; 8th. Houses of Ill Fame. Among the causes of poverty, those houses, where all the base-born passions are engendered—where the vilest profligacy receives a forced culture, must hold an eminent rank; 9th. The numerous charitable institutions of the city. [Relief giving agencies, especially public] with whatever zeal they may be conducted, never can effect the removal of poverty, nor lessen its general amount; but that indigence

22. This discussion is based on Raymond A. Mohl, "Humanitarianism in the Preindustrial City: The New York Society for the Prevention of Pauperism, 1817–1823," *The Journal of American History*, 57 (Dec. 1970): 576–599.

and helplessness will multiply nearly in the ratio of those measures which are ostensibly taken to prevent them . . . to prevent the misapplication and abuse of public charity, demands the utmost vigilance, and wisest precaution, and the most elaborate system of inspection and oversight; Lastly, War . . . But as this evil lies out of the immediate reach of local regulation, and as we are now happily blest with a peace which we hope will be durable, it is deemed unnecessary further to notice it."[23]

The clear conclusion of this report was that poverty was entirely due to defects in the poor themselves. There was recognition of some environmental factors (lotteries, pawnbrokers, prostitution) but these were viewed as significant because they contributed to the faults of the poor. Particularly significant not only because it shaped the SPP's approach to poverty, but also because it has continued to ring through the years right up to the present day, is the strong condemnation of anti-poverty programs based on the belief that they mainly allow the poor to "get away" with being lazy and behaving badly by shielding them from the natural consequences of such behavior.

The methodology of the SPP was greatly influenced by the tract societies. The city was divided into small districts and a volunteer was appointed to provide guidance, counsel, advice, and moral exhortation to the poor in each. In addition to providing direct services to the poor in their districts, each visitor was viewed as a social investigator with the responsibility of collecting data about the poor in their district including name and age of family head, occupation and character, church membership, family size, race and ethnicity, handicaps, number unable to care for themselves, and whether the family possessed a bible. Based partially on the data they collected, but probably more on the member's basic moral beliefs, the society embarked on wide-ranging campaigns for reform. They proposed and lobbied for municipal regulations and state laws calling for marriage reform, theater and gambling taxes, tavern and liquor licenses, restriction of billiard tables and the sale of playing cards, revision of the poor law and penal code, standards for prison construction and criminal court procedure, and immigration reform.

Their zealous pursuit of moral reform legislation led to the SPPs, in New York and elsewhere, to come to a rather quick end. As long as these moral reformers were down in the slums providing one-on-one counseling to the poor, few people had any objections to their activities. However, when they began trying to reform liquor and gambling laws, they ran afoul of powerful political forces who did not appreciate their efforts. In New York very few of the Society's reform proposals resulted in any legislative or public policy changes. As a result of this failure the Society began to look for a narrower and potentially more effective focus. After some study, Griscom and the board concluded that delinquent and abandoned children formed the "core of pauperism" and decided to focus on the needs of this group. At the beginning of 1825 the Society dismantled its programs and in their stead founded the New York House of Refuge, a residential program for dependent, neglected, and delinquent youth. This facility was deemed to be an instant success. Likewise, the Baltimore Society for the Prevention of Pauperism, founded in 1820, came to an end after only two years. This group's legislative and organizational efforts resulted in two public rallies protesting its activities and the publication of a widely distributed pamphlet titled "A Warning to the Citizens of Baltimore." The pamphlet began "Citizens Awake! Under the cover of religion and

---

23. New York Society for the Prevention of Pauperism, *Report of a Committee on the Subject of Pauperism* (New York: Samuel Wood & Sons, 1818), 5–10.

benevolence, but with little of either at heart, men now conspire to erect in our city an inquisitorial power; [the Society for the Prevention of Pauperism] proposes not only to assume the attributes of the legislature, it proposes not only to interfere with the customs, and habits, and manners of the community, but to interrupt the common legalized current of trade. [The society is] in fact the foundation of a fanatic and gloomy despotism [which will lead to the prohibition of] every rational and elegant amusement in Baltimore."[24] The society launched a public relations campaign to try to counteract the bad publicity it was receiving, but these efforts were unsuccessful and it closed operations before the end of 1822.

Although they met with little success, the SPPs can be viewed as the first step in the development of the profession of social work and the development of social work methods to help the poor and dependent. The SPP founders were aware of the work in Germany of Benjamin Thompson Rumford, in Scotland of Thomas Chalmers, and, perhaps the greatest influence, Patrick Colquhoun of the London Society for the Betterment of the Poor. All these men advocated an approach of dividing the city into small areas, appointing one visitor for each area, individualizing the poor, and using a personal relationship to help the poor help themselves. The SPP applied this approach to the communities in which they were operating. Unfortunately, their theory of poverty was so flawed and their understanding of human behavior in the social environment so lacking, that they did not even begin to develop an effective methodology of helping. However, their recognition of the importance of personal relationships, collection of data, and careful organization of services into manageable geographic areas represented a giant step toward the eventual development of effective helping methods and programs.

Association for Improving the Condition of the Poor

When the SPPs faded from the charity scene, a source for leadership and innovation disappeared. Relief-giving agencies continued to be established—there were thirty to forty operating in New York City by 1840—but they were limited in scope, uncoordinated, and lacking in any particular vision. This problem became apparent when the financial panic of 1837 hit, causing great hardship to the working classes of the city. Believing what was needed was a single city-wide agency for the general amelioration of poverty that would provide coordination between charitable groups, "a few friends of the poor became deeply impressed with the importance on ascertaining their [existing agencies] failure, and of devising, if practicable, a better system of dispensing relief."[25] In the winter of 1842–43, a select committee was appointed and Robert Hartley, a prominent temperance society leader, was hired as the committee's agent, and the problem was referred to the committee for careful examination.

The committee's report, authored by Hartley, concluded that there were three fundamental problems with the system of charity in New York City, and by extension elsewhere. The first

24. Quoted in Blanche D. Coll, "The Baltimore Society for the Prevention of Pauperism, 1820–1822," *American Historical Review* (October 1955): 84.

25. New York Association for Improving the Condition of the Poor, *First Annual Report* (New York: John F. Trow, 1845), 15.

problem was that there was a lack of discrimination in giving, mainly a result of there being no arrangement for learning the character and condition of applicants. The second problem was that existing charities operated independently of each other: they were ignorant of each other's operations, and artful mendicants so turned this ignorance to their own advantage, as often to obtain assistance from many of the societies at the same time without detection ... while the better class of the needy ... obtained less aid [than they needed]." Finally, existing charities made no provision for personal contact with recipients of aid, depriving them of "sympathy and counsel as would tend to encourage industrious and virtuous habits and foster among them a spirit of self-dependence." Following the completion of the report, the committee sent Hartley on a tour of other major cities to ascertain how they organized their charitable systems.

Based on what he learned on his tour of other cities, but probably more his knowledge of the experience of the SPP and the tract and temperance societies with which Hartley had previously worked, a plan for organization of charity in New York City was developed and implemented. The city was divided into sixteen districts corresponding to its political wards. These sixteen districts were in turn divided into 278 sections. Each of these districts was controlled by an advisory committee of at least five members, and each advisory committee appointed at least one visitor for its section. The visitors were all men, all volunteers, and their job was to visit the poor in their homes in order to elicit information on their condition, their worthiness, and to distribute relief if they felt it was warranted. By 1852 the number of sections had increased to 337. If size is any measure, the Association for Improving the Condition of the Poor (AICP) was an instant and huge success. In its first year of operation the agency had 244 volunteer visitors, and this number increased to 357 by 1853. The average annual number of cases receiving assistance between 1846 and 1854 was 5830. During one six-month period in 1848 the agency recorded more than 27,000 visits made by its volunteers.[26]

The basic charge given to visitors was that they were to "carefully investigate all cases referred to them before granting relief, ascertain their [the applicants] condition, their habits of life, and means of subsistence; and extend to all such kind services, counsel, and assistance, as a discriminating and judicious regard for their present and permanent welfare requires." In their investigations of applicants and their decisions regarding the granting of relief, the visitors were to be guided by the fundamental rules of the association:

- To give what is least susceptible of abuse.
- To give necessary articles in small quantities, in proportion to immediate need.
- To give assistance, both in quantity and quality, inferior, except in case of sickness or old age, to what might be procured by labor.
- To give assistance at the right moment; and not to prolong it beyond the duration of the necessity which calls for it; but to extend, restrict, and modify it with that necessity.[27]

26. Lilian Brandt, *Growth and Development of AICP and COS (A Preliminary and Exploratory Review)*, Report to the Committee on the Institute of Welfare Research, Community Service Society of New York, 1942; New York Association for Improving the Condition of the Poor, *Fifth Annual Report* (New York: Leavitt, Trow & Co., 1848), 14.

27. New York Society for Improving the Condition of the Poor, *First Annual Report* (New York: Society for Improving the Condition of the Poor, 1844), 21.

To help the visitors carry out their charge and follow the fundamental principles, a short pamphlet, *Visitor's Manual,* was prepared by Hartley, which could be considered as the first social work practice text to be released since the *Ease for Overseers of the Poor* in seventeenth-century England. The pamphlet begins by cautioning the visitor to use careful and discriminating judgment when distributing relief to prevent abuse by applicants. It then goes on to present the agencies' typology of the poor, which consists of three categories. The first is those who are poor due to unavoidable misfortune such as age, illness, or disability; the second is "those who have brought themselves to want and suffering by their improvidence and vices"; the third is people who are simply too lazy to work, preferring to live as vagrants and support themselves by begging. The manual explains that these groups should be treated differently: "And as this cannot be applied without a knowledge of their character and circumstances, your first duty is, *to withhold all relief from unknown persons.* Let this rule be imperative and unalterable."[28]

Modern concepts of helping such as communication skills, interviewing techniques, relationship building, and so forth, were not even on the radar screen in the age of the AICP. In the hierarchical, patriarchal society of the time, it was assumed that the poor would recognize that the visitors were their social, economic, and moral betters, and so would naturally listen to and respond to advice given. The heart of the association's helping technique, which in modern terminology would be referred to as "use of self," is summarized in Article iii of the *Visitor's Manual*:

> . . . visit [applicants in your district] in their homes; personally examine every case; ascertain their character and condition; and carefully inquire into the causes which have brought them into a state of destitution. You will become an important instrument of good to your suffering fellow-creatures, when you aid them to obtain this good from resources within themselves. To effect this, show them the true origin of their suffering, when these sufferings are the result of imprudence, extravagance, idleness, intemperance, or other moral causes which are within their own control; and endeavor, by all appropriate means, to awaken their self-respect, to direct their exertions, and to strengthen their capacities for self-support. In your intercourse with them, avoid all appearance of harshness, and every manifestation of an obtrusive and a censorious spirit. . . The most effectual encouragement for such persons is not *alms chiefly*, or any other form of charity as a substitute for alms, but that sympathizing counsel which re-kindles hope, and that expression of respect for character which such individuals never fail to appreciate.[29]

Showing the tract society heritage of the AICP, visitors were given tracts to distribute to recipients. These tracts were less overtly religious than those distributed by the tract societies, being aimed at specific character needs of the poor. Two of the most popular were *The Economist* and *The Way to Wealth. The Economist* explained to the poor that they were actually better off than they thought, and needed mostly to carefully manage their money by, for example, buying Indian meal (corn meal) instead of potatoes because it was cheaper and, supposedly, more nutritious. The *Way to*

28. New York Society for Improving the Condition of the Poor, *First Annual Report,* Appendix A, "Visitor's Manual," 2.
29. New York Society for Improving the Condition of the Poor, "Visitor's Manual," 4.

Wealth was mostly a reprint of Benjamin Franklin's popular collection of sayings related to wealth from *Poor Richard's Almanac,* with several exerts from Proverbs and Ecclesiastes appended to supply what was regarded as a lack of religious sentiment in the original. Nuggets of wisdom thought useful for impoverished New Yorkers included "There are no gains without pains"; "He that hath a trade hath an estate"; and "At the working man's house hunger looks in, but dares not enter."

Although the *Manual for Visitors* pays lip service to the power of personal relationships, and the expectation that visitors will, through these relationships, effect character reform and improvement among their cases, it is clear that the main expectation of visitors was to make proper decisions about who was, and who wasn't, to receive assistance, being sure that only the "worthy" were helped, and were helped for the shortest time at the least cost possible. This decision process was to be implemented through the use of a series of "tickets" and forms for collecting data about aid recipients. The association printed and distributed three types of ticket books (Figure 3.1).

The first were books of tickets given to members of the AICP (anyone who donated was considered a member). These were referral tickets and the idea was that when a person approached a member for a handout, the member would give them a completed ticket to give to the district visitor, requesting that the visitor make an assessment of the person and a decision about whether to give assistance. Publicity campaigns implored New Yorkers to not give aid to strangers who approached them on the street, but rather to direct beggars to members of the AICP who could in turn direct them to the proper district visitor. The visitor also had a book of tickets. These were to be given to applicants when and if a decision was made to help them. The ticket indicated how much help was to be given and what type of help. The third type of ticket was designed specifically to deal with the problem of beggars coming to the door of prosperous homes and requesting to be given leftover food (cold victuals). The association asked homeowners to sign an agreement to only give left-over food to people with a ticket from the district visitor attesting that they were worthy of such help (Figure 3.2).

In addition to their tickets, the visitors were required to complete forms that listed the names, descriptive data, and information on the type and amount of aid given to every person who applied for help in their district. These forms were turned in to the central office, where they were compiled on a master sheet that listed every person who received aid in the city. Visitors were directed to check the master sheet before giving anyone a ticket to receive aid to prevent dishonest applicants from moving from district to district to get more aid than they deserved.

Based on their system of organization and helping technique, charity in New York City, and in the many other cities that adopted the AICP model, was supposed to work like this: a person in need of assistance (or not) would approach a citizen at his home, business, church, or on the street and ask for a hand-out. Based on AICP publicity, that citizen would not turn a deaf ear to the request, but rather than giving any help he would say something like, "Mr. Davis at such and such an address is a member of the AICP. Go see him and he'll give you a ticket to see a visitor." The person would do this and would fairly quickly be seen by a visitor who would gather information about his situation. The visitor would also check AICP records to see if the person had previously received aid. If the visitor decided that the applicant was a drunk, a criminal, could work but was too lazy, or had been previously helped by the agency but had not taken its advice about changes

AICP Visitor's Tickets

Ticket of Reference for the Use of Members.

Mr.   Visitor,

  No.   St.

is requested to visit

at No.

                                                       Member

N. Y. Association for the
Improvement of the Condition of the Poor.

Visitor's Order.

  Mr.

No.   *St.*

Please let

have the value of

in

184

                                                              Vis.

N. Y. Association for the
Improvement of the Condition of the Poor.

COLD VICTUALS.

To the

          No.   Street,

M .... *Residence,*

No. .... *Street,*

Will give Cold Victuals on the Orders of your Visitors.

FIGURE 3.1. AICP Visitor's Tickets

he or she needed to make, aid would be refused. In this case the person had two choices—they could go to work and support themselves, or they could receive public relief in the form of admission to the poorhouse. If the visitor found the applicant worthy, he would decide how much relief the person needed and was entitled to and give him or her tickets to receive this aid, almost always

AICP Visitor's Monthly Report

New-York Association for the Improvement of the Condition of the Poor.

VISITOR'S MONTHLY REPORT, OF SECTION No.   DISTRICT No.   Dated

☞ *A mark with a pen thus ɪ, in the columns, will point out the class to which the person named belongs.* ☜

Nos. of Persons.	Names of Persons Visited.	Residence of Persons.	Foreigners.	Natives.	Colored Persons.	Males.	Females.	Kind of occupation.	Time in City.	No. in Family.	No. of Visits.	Character: Temperate.	Intemperate.	Provident.	Improvident.	Virtuous.	Vicious.	Industrious.	Idle.	Unavoidable causes: Sickness.	Infirmity.	Misfortune.	Old Age.	Education: Can'd & write	Cannot do.	Child'n to S.	do. Public.	Kind of Relief: Food.	Fuel.	Clothing.	Shelter.	Money.	Medicine.	Physician.	Amount Expended. Dols	cts.	Remarks.

Total,

Remarks.

Signed,

Visitor.

FIGURE 3.2. AICP Visitor's Monthly Report

in kind (coal, rent voucher, food) and rarely money. It was always to be made clear that aid was to be given on a temporary basis. An example of the work of a visitor who had received a referral ticket is given in a letter from a visitor to Robert Hartley, the general secretary:

> I go *direct* to the room of the applicant and find everything clean and neat, with a pleasant woman perhaps at a sewing machine to work, with three or four small children around her. Stating my business her eyes brighten with the prospect of some help. I find that she pays about eight dollars per month rent, and by working early and late she can earn about four dollars per week, which is sixteen dollars per month, leaving her after paying her rent, eight dollars to support herself and her children, only two dollars per week. I give her assistance about one dollar per week up to about April, and exert myself to get her some *better* work. When I tell her in April that I am obliged to discontinue the relief she looks very sorrowful, but thanks me kindly, and hopes God will reward me for what I have done for her and her little children during the winter.[30]

The visitor does not indicate if he was successful in finding her better work, or what else changed that led to his decision that aid was no longer needed.

A significant area of activity by the AICP was in efforts it referred to as incidental labors. These were activities that would now be referred to as macro social work: efforts to remediate aspects of the social environment that negatively impact the lives of the poor. The first incidental labor the agency addressed was housing reform. In 1846 it appointed a committee to study housing of the city's poor. Another housing committee was appointed in 1853 that conducted a study and produced a report that served for many years as the model for housing and public health reformers in nineteenth century America. In 1855, based on the housing studies, the agency opened its Workingmen's House, a model tenement in lower Manhattan. Another study begun in 1845 produced a plan to develop health facilities in New York City, and in 1851 the association opened the Demelt Dispensary, followed by the Northern Dispensary, opened in 1869. In 1849 a nursing committee was organized by the AICP that visited and reported on conditions in the children's institutions on Randall's Island. The tract *The Economist,* first published in 1847 with thousands of copies distributed, described the basics of nutrition and home economics, other areas in which the agency pioneered. Robert Hartley, the general agent, led a campaign against tainted milk that resulted in an official state investigation in 1858 followed by pure milk legislation. In 1852 the agency opened the first public bath, and in 1862 founded the Society for the Ruptured and Crippled, which opened a facility devoted to helping injured workers.[31]

In its main approach to poverty, registering cases, providing individual services, closely monitoring recipients, the AICP did little that was new or innovative. All of these had been tried, admittedly with less success, by earlier agencies, notably the Societies for the Prevention of Pauperism. Likewise, its evaluation of poverty as being the result of individual moral failure was previously stated in the many reports on the problem of poverty, notably those by the Quincy and Yates committees. By the time of the AICP's founding this explanation was typical and well accepted.

---

30. Dorothy Becker, "The Visitor to the New York City Poor, 1843–1920," *The Social Service Review*, 35 (Dec. 1961): 392.

31. Peter Romanofsky, *Social Service Organizations*, Vol. 2 (Westport, CT: Greenwood Press, 1978), 623–628.

Where it was innovative was in its incidental labors that for the first time established the connection between poverty and environmental conditions. Although the AICP never wavered from its insistence that poverty was basically a moral problem, the concern with the relationship between poverty and the environment set a precedent for future social workers.

CONCLUSION

Continental Army veteran John Baker moved to Thetford, Vermont in August of 1781 and, using his bonus from having served four years in the army, purchased a farm of fifty acres. The next year he married Elizabeth Rich and by 1792 they had six children. Sometime during this decade John Baker became mentally ill, to the extent that in 1792 the Selectmen of the town declared him legally insane and took over his affairs, including responsibility for caring for his wife and children. The town placed the children in apprenticeships that apparently worked out satisfactorily for the children as evidenced by the fact that one of the girls included the name of her master's family in the name of her own first born child. John and Elizabeth were cared for by the town for twenty years, sometimes they were boarded with a town family and sometimes rent was paid for them to have their own dwelling. Although according to the Vermont Poor Law the town could have charged John and Elizabeth's expenses to their several living relatives or, after the children had grown charged the expenses to them, there is no evidence that this was ever done. Town records show that in addition to a place to live, the town paid for food, clothing, sundries, and fairly extensive medical expenses. The last expenses paid for Elizabeth were for her burial in 1812. Following Elizabeth's death the town supported John until he wandered off in 1817, never to be seen again. Even though he was a pauper, totally supported by the town, the selectman placed a notice in three issues of a statewide newspaper announcing that John had wandered away and asking "Whoever will give notice to the subscriber where such Baker can be found will exercise an act of humanity, and shall be handsomely rewarded."[32]

Contrast the treatment of the Baker's needs with that of Mrs. Snow, who approached an AICP visitor in 1846. The visitor investigated Mrs. Snow and found that she had "intemperate habits" (i.e., she drank) and was therefore not a good candidate for assistance, which he refused her. Mrs. Snow was a widow, who had lived on the edge for a number of years and was desperate for help. She went over the visitor's head and made a complaint and renewed request for assistance to the general office. Arriving at the office she was met by Robert Hartley, the general secretary himself. He asked her if she had been aided previously by the Association, and she replied that she had not. Secretary Hartley looked up Mrs. Snow in the Association's Register of Cases and found that she had been helped on several occasions over the previous years. He then asked again if she had been previously helped, to which she replied, "And sure, no one knows better than myself that I never had anything from your Society." Showing Mrs. Snow the record, Hartley said, "But, good woman, two years since, you lived in Houston Street, and were helped one month by the visitor; next you

32. Mary L. Eysenbach, "Caring for the Poor: Thetford and the Baker Family, 1792–1817," *Vermont History* 72 (Winter/Spring 2004): 55–62.

moved to Ludlow Street, where you were helped until your character was found out; then you went to Forsyth Street, and being sick, a physician was sent to you, and you were aided until you recovered; now you live in Mott Street, and because of your intemperance, the Visitor believes it is to be his duty to refuse you relief." At this point, realizing that she was no match for the power of a modern bureaucracy, and wishing to preserve some of her pride, Mrs. Snow got directly in Mr. Hartley's face and spit out, "Och, if your honor has nothing better to do than to follow honest women about the streets, I'll have nothing to do with your Society."[33]

The years between the end of the American Revolution and the middle of the nineteenth century are of momentous importance for social welfare in this country. It was in these years that attitudes, values, and approaches were formed that continue to shape our responses to social welfare up to the present day. At the beginning of this era we considered poverty and related social problems as things that were fated, inevitable, and that just had to be accepted. By the end of the era we considered these as things that needed to be aggressively managed and that, if this was done correctly, they could be fixed. At the beginning of the era we viewed people afflicted with problems as unfortunates who probably did not deserve their afflictions and did deserve our sympathy and charity. By the end of the era we considered victims of social problems as being at fault for their own conditions, and that this fault was largely due to moral shortcomings. At the beginning of the era the poor were cared for in the community as neighbors and, perhaps, sometimes friends. By the end of the era the poor were isolated in poorhouses, other institutions, and in urban ghettos. At the beginning of the era assistance may not have been generous, and may not have been gladly given, but such assistance was considered a social obligation of those better off and simply viewed as a social cost. By the end of the era assistance was itself considered to be a major contributor to social problems, mainly poverty, and withholding assistance was seen as the most productive response.

As Mintz has observed, it is easy to ridicule these early reformers. From the perspective of a twenty-first century social worker, it is also easy to become angry and judgmental when reading the smug, self-serving, and social class–serving statements of the poorhouse advocates and the AICP members. It is true that initially these moral reformers were extraordinarily naïve; they were largely blind to the intrusive nature of their reforms and had little sensitivity to the obstacles faced by their working class neighbors. But it has to be said that over time they learned. They learned about problems of public health, housing, the legal system, and many other environmental conditions that were more important in determining the situation of the poor than individual moral deficiencies. They also learned that helping people with serious problems was not something that could be entirely trusted to volunteers who had little more to offer than time and a helpful nature. Social problems, and means and methods of helping the victims of these problems, were topics needing serious study, needing the application of scientific methods, and needing paid professionals to apply the results. This, however, did not fully dawn on people until the second half of the century.

33. New York Association for Improving the Condition of the Poor, *Fourth Annual Report* (New York: Leavitt, Trow & Company, 1847), 17.

CHAPTER 4

MODERN AMERICA— MODERN PROBLEMS: 1860–1900

The author's great grandmother Marie Movius was a homemaker and mother living in Lidgerwood North Dakota during the latter half of the nineteenth century. She was married to the Reverend E. F. Movius, pastor of the Evangelical Lutheran Church, small farmer, and small businessman. Lidgerwood was a farm service center with a population of 800, with four bars on Main Street. This worked out to a bar to citizen ratio of 1 to 200; 1 to 100 male citizens; and 1 to 65 male citizens over the age of twenty-one. Lidgerwood, North Dakota today still has a population of 800, still has four bars on main street, but with the greater likelihood of women going to bars and the change in the age structure of the town to a greater proportion over twenty-one, the bar to adult male ratio has deteriorated somewhat.

It would seem that Lidgerwood in the late nineteenth century, being hundreds of miles from any significant urban area, would have been immune to the problems of an emerging urban industrial society. This was not the case. Family lore passed down over the last one hundred fifty years documents that urban social problems frequently visited Lidgerwood in the form of the "tramp problem." Once or twice a month Great Grandmother Movius would be in her house cooking, cleaning, reading, or whatever, and her peace would be disrupted by a knock on the back door. Looking out the door she would see a small group of ragged and disheveled strangers. These would turn out to be what had recently come to be called "tramps"; unemployed men, mostly from large cities in the East, who were heading west by hopping trains and riding from town to town. Railroad tracks connecting the East Coast to the west passed on the outskirts of Lidgerwood, and it was not uncommon to see strangers who had jumped off the train wandering into town seeking something to eat. Mrs. Movius, anticipating the arrival of tramps, kept several outside jobs undone so she could ask the men to mow or rake the lawn, weed the garden, or some similar task while she prepared them a meal. The work was generally only a token, but she believed that doing something in payment for the food received added to the dignity of the men. After the men had completed their tasks, Mrs. Movius would provide soap and towels so they could wash up, would serve them a meal on the back porch, and would give the men a box of additional food to tide them over for a few days. Looking at the behavior of Great Grandmother Movius from the perspective of the twenty-first century it appears that she was an unusually kind and generous individual, but this is not the case. In his "Report on Tramps" read at the Fourth Annual Conference of Charities and Corrections in 1877, Edward E. Hale identified the typical generosity of Americans as one of the factors contributing to the continuation of the tramp problem. He observed that in American culture to refuse to give food to a wayfarer had been "for centuries regarded a sign of utter meanness—almost unheard of . . . in the popular estimation, the meanest man has almost a right to food without work."[1]

The "tramp problem" hit mid-nineteenth century America with the suddenness of a spring thunderstorm. There had always been poor people who wandered the countryside—sometimes referred to as the strolling poor—but they were few in number and were not seen as any particular threat to social order. Shortly after the end of the Civil War, however, the problem grew at an exponential rate and assumed a new and threatening character. It is not possible to come up with any accurate report on the number of tramps, statistics on such matters were not compiled at the time, but some rough estimates are available. Police during the latter half of the nineteenth century would allow homeless men to sleep in the station, often on the floor, during periods of bad weather. They kept records of the number of men they boarded, so these numbers give some idea of the size of the tramp problem. Eric Monkkonen, using police lodging data, found that that in 1880 631,637 and in 1890 615,131 persons stayed in police stations. These figures were for the nation as a whole and counted individuals who spent at least one night in a police station. Based on these police lodging figures, census data, and other sources he estimates somewhere between 10 and 20 percent of the US population in the late nineteenth century came from families with at least one member who had tramped in search of work.[2]

The "tramp problem" was a direct consequence of a number of rapid social and economic changes that characterized America during the last half of the nineteenth century, changes that continued America's transformation from the relatively stable rural democracy described by Leiby into a volatile and insecure urban industrial society.[3] These changes included an increasingly rich, but unstable, laissez-faire economy that was prone to recessions and depressions that would leave millions of men out of work at the same time. The work that many of these men did had also deteriorated from well-paying skilled craft jobs, to jobs in industrial production that required little skill and provided little security. Even these low level jobs were becoming highly competitive as the population grew at an unprecedented rate, both as a result of natural increase and ever increasing immigration. Finally, when people found themselves out of work they had few resources to draw upon. The American belief in rugged individualism, combined with newly popular social

1. Edward E. Hale, "Report on Tramps," in *Proceedings of the Fourth Annual Conference of Charities and Correction* (1877), cited in Michael B. Katz, *Poverty and Policy in American History* (New York: Academic Press, 1983), 159.

2. Eric H. Monkkonen, "Introduction," in Eric Monkkonen (ed.), *Walking to Work: Tramps in America, 1790—1935* (Lincoln, NE: University of Nebraska Press, 1984), 9; Eric Monkkonen, *Police in Urban America, 1860–1920* (New York, NY: Cambridge University Press, 1981), 93–97.

3. James Leiby, *A History of Social Work and Social Welfare in the United States* (New York: Columbia University Press, 1978).

philosophies such as the Gospel of Wealth and Social Darwinism, created an environment in which very little social welfare help was to be found.

This period of American history can be subdivided into two parts. The first part was during the years between 1850 and 1877 that were dominated by events leading up to the Civil War, the war itself, and a time referred to as the Reconstruction when attempts were made to repair the devastation the war had wrought on the South and to help African Americans transition from slavery to life as a free people. The second part was during the years 1877 to 1900, an era referred to as the Gilded Age, a name taken from the title of a novel co-written by Mark Twain that satirized the material excesses of the day.[4] This was an age of massive wealth, massive poverty, and the birth of inequality as a problem that still takes center stage in American social and economic life. It was the era in which modern America was born.

THE CIVIL WAR AND RECONSTRUCTION

The American Civil War, lasting from 1861 to 1865, was of massive consequence for the young United States. Over the years of the war, over 2.5 million men served in the armed forces, more than 1.5 million on the Union side and over one million on the Confederate side. The death rate was 23 percent for northern forces and 24 percent for southern, totaling more than 618,000 young men killed. The main issue of the Civil War was, of course, slavery, and at the end four million African Americans were emancipated from slavery into a society that had little commitment to offering them equal citizenship. One thing that the war definitely decided was that the federal government was supreme over the states and had broad constitutional authority to act on matters affecting the general welfare. The southern principle of almost complete state sovereignty ended with the war, thus sending the United States on its way to becoming a true nation-state with an effective central government. Although the states retained many powers and the Constitution placed limits on what the national government could do, the war ended all question about where ultimate authority rested.

The Federal Government Enters the Social Welfare Arena

The Civil War and its aftermath had two major long-term effects on social welfare policy in the United States. The first was a result of the war's establishment of the primacy of the federal government over the states. In his 1844 veto of legislation to provide financial aid to states for the building and operation of mental hospitals, President Pierce reaffirmed the principle that the federal government was not authorized by the constitution to engage in social welfare activities.[5]

---

4. Mark Twain and Charles Dudley Walker, *The Gilded Age: A Tale of Today* (New York: American Publishing Company, 1873).

5. Walter I. Trattner, "The Federal Government and Needy Citizens in Nineteenth Century America," *Political Science Quarterly* 103 (Summer, 1988): 347–356.

Several developments from the Civil War began a process of repudiation of this doctrine. The first development was the establishment of the Sanitary Commission, a body that was appointed by Secretary of War Cameron. The term "sanitary" referred to what we would currently call public health. Military leaders and many civilians were familiar with the horrors of the Crimean War, where many more deaths among soldiers were due to contagious diseases than to battlefield wounds. Based on this concern, a large number of voluntary organizations emerged at the beginning of the Civil War dedicated to improving the health and welfare of the troops. These organizations raised a tremendous amount of money and had many people wanting to volunteer their time and skills, but lacking coordination their potential was being wasted. The Sanitary Commission, a federal level coordinating and planning body, housed in the Department of War, was established to deal with this issue. This commission was composed of military officers, medical men, and "civilians distinguished for their philanthropic experience and acquaintance with sanitary matters." The duties of the Commission were, first, to investigate "the best means of methodizing and reducing to practical service the already active but undirected benevolence of the people toward the army," and, second, to study and suggest ways of preventing sickness and unnecessary suffering among soldiers. The Commission raised money, coordinated collection and distribution of medical and hygiene supplies, promoted the practice of battlefield nursing, and pioneered the construction of inexpensive and roomy pavilion hospitals that eventually proved to be among the major lifesaving advances of the war. Allen Nevins wrote of the Sanitary Commission: "Nothing quite like it, in its combination of specialized skill, sturdy common sense, and consecrated devotion to a great aim, had previously been known in American annals; and its success was to show that a new era of national organization was opening."[6]

In addition to the coordinating activities of the Sanitary Commission, the federal government became involved in direct social provision in the form of cash and housing benefits to northern military veterans. This began in 1861 when legislation was passed granting pensions and disability benefits to union veterans and their dependents. A military draft was not instituted until 1863, and lacking this, in the words of a policy historian, "our Government had to resort to the policy of persuasion."[7] The policy of a pension and protection from financial consequences of disability was a strong marketing tool for recruitment. The pension system was made more generous in 1862, when dependents of those who died for causes traceable to their Union military service became eligible to receive pensions equal to the rate for veterans with total disability; in 1879 when, under the Arrears Act soldiers with newly discovered Civil War related disabilities could receive a lump sum payment of all benefits back to the date of their military service; and in 1890 when the Dependent Pension Act expanded pension eligibility to veterans who were disabled even if the disability was not related to their military service. In 1906 old age became defined as a disability making virtually every Union Civil War veteran eligible for a pension. By 1895 nearly three-quarters of a million veterans were receiving federal pensions; by 1915 over 93 percent of Union veterans were enrolled in the program. Skocpol asserts that "Ultimately, the system became a kind

6. Robert H. Bremner, *The Public Good: Philanthropy & Welfare in the Civil War Era* (New York: Alfred A. Knopf, 1980), 37–40.

7. Theda Skocpol, "America's First Social Security System: The Expansion of Benefits for Civil War Veterans," *Political Science Quarterly* 108 (Spring 1993): 85–116.

of precocious social security system for those U.S. citizens of a certain generation and region who were deemed morally worthy of enjoying generous and honorable public aid."[8]

THE CREATION OF A SEMI-PERMANENT UNDERCLASS

Although slavery was ended in the United States by the passage of the Thirteenth Amendment in 1865 and its imposition on the South by the Union's military victory that shortly followed, the southern states were unrepentant and quickly moved to assure that blacks remained in their subservient status. In late 1865, the newly elected southern state legislatures revised their slave codes into what were called black codes. These laws allowed local officials to arrest black people who could not document employment or residence, or who were deemed to be "disorderly," and sentence them to forced labor on farms or road crews. Black people were also restricted by the codes from many occupations, barred from jury duty, and forbidden from owning guns.

In an attempt to deal with the problems of the mass of newly freed black citizens, Congress established the first federal agency charged with directly delivering social welfare services. This was the Bureau of Refugees, Freedmen, and Abandoned Lands, established in March of 1865. This agency, popularly known as the Freedmen's Bureau, was located in the US War Department and was authorized to administer a program of temporary relief for the remainder of the war and for one year after. In 1866, one year after the conclusion of the war, Congress voted to reauthorize the Bureau, but President Johnson vetoed the extension, referencing Pierce's veto of aid to states for mental hospitals and saying, "A system for the support of indigent persons in the United States was never contemplated by the authors of the Constitution."[9] Unlike the Pierce veto, Congress voted to override Johnson's veto, extending the life of the Freedmen's Bureau for six years and establishing the principle that it was constitutional for the federal government to directly or indirectly support the provision of social welfare benefits and services.

In some areas the Freedmen's Bureau did not live up to expectations. Freed blacks and their white supporters hoped that the Bureau would serve the function of redistributing abandoned and otherwise unoccupied lands to former slaves, enabling them to become independent farmers (the famous "forty acres and a mule" story).[10] In this area the Bureau achieved little success, facing massive political pressure to return lands to former owners. In other areas, however, the Bureau accomplished a great deal. Over the seven years of its existence, the Bureau, working closely with the army, distributed twenty-one million rations, established forty hospitals, and spent over $2 million providing medical care to 450,000 sick people of both races. The Bureau's greatest success was in education. Its agents established a variety of schools that included day schools, Sunday

---

8. Theda Skocpol, *Protecting Soldiers and Mothers—The Political Origins of Social Policy in the United States* (Cambridge, MA: The Belnap Press of Harvard University Press, 1992), pp. 103–118.

9. John Abel and LaWanda Cox, "Andrew Johnson and His Ghost Writers: An Analysis of the Freedman's Bureau and Civil Rights Veto Messages," *The Mississippi Valley Historical Review* 48 (December, 1961) 460–479.

10. Walter Fleming, "Forty Acres and a Mule," *The North American Review*.

schools, industrial schools, and colleges and universities. By 1870, more than 250,000 blacks were in 4,300 schools aided by the Bureau and various philanthropic and religious groups. By the final year of its existence the Bureau had deemphasized the welfare and education parts of its mission and increased its efforts to get freedmen back to work. In the words of W. E. B. Du Bois the agency had become "a vast labor bureau," the agents of which directed their energies to negotiating and enforcing contracts between planters and former slaves. The contracts negotiated set up what became known as the tenant farm system whereby blacks, in exchange for their labor, could live on the land and receive a share ranging from one-tenth to one-third of the crop harvested.[11] The Freedmen's Bureau ended operations in 1872 when its congressional extension expired.

From 1867 to 1876 was a period known as Congressional Reconstruction in which the Republican-dominated Congress attempted to reform southern society so as to guarantee an equal place for black citizens. The Fourteenth Amendment guaranteed all citizens equality before the law. Two key sections prohibited states from violating the civil rights of their citizens, thus outlawing the black codes, and gave the states the choice of enfranchising black people or losing representation in Congress. The Fifteenth Amendment, passed in 1869, guaranteed the right of every American man to vote regardless of race. As a result of these laws and their vigorous support by three groups—southern yeoman farmers known by opponents as scalawags, northern transplants to the south known as carpetbaggers, and southern blacks whose voting rights were temporarily being protected—progress was made in the position of blacks in the South and further improvement seemed possible.

The most visible area of improvement was that of elected representation. The number of black congressmen in the US House of Representatives increased from two in 1869 to seven in 1873, and more than 600 African Americans were elected to southern state legislatures between 1867 and 1877. In addition, the provision of state services to lower income citizens, both black and white, greatly expanded during the period of Congressional Reconstruction. Under Republican leadership states built hospitals, schools, and children's homes. Stepping further into social policy than most northern states at the time, Republican governments in the South expanded women's property rights, enacted legislation against child abuse, and required child support from fathers of mixed race children. In South Carolina, the state government provided medical care for the poor, and the Alabama state government provided free legal aid for needy defendants.

This period of hope and optimism that a more just and equal society could emerge out of the ashes of the Civil War was short lived. By 1877, fueled by a combination of white hostility toward blacks in the South and by weariness and apathy of northerners, reconstruction ended. Whites in the South, acting as individuals, ad hoc groups, or formally organized groups such as the Knights of the Golden Circle and the Ku Klux Klan, employed violence and intimidation to prevent blacks from voting, thus crippling the Republican Party in the South. The economic Panic of 1873 caused extended suffering, particularly among working class Americans, and focused attention away from

11. Although sharecropping has been taken to characterize the life of black farmers in the entire South following Reconstruction, it actually applied to only about half (54 percent). By 1900, an impressive 27 percent of black farmers in the South had managed to amass savings or sufficient credit to buy their own land. See Stanley Legergott, *The Americans—An Economic Record* (New York: W. W. Norton & Company, 1984), 254–255.

reconstruction in the South. And, truth be known, northerners had mostly been abolitionists, but they were hardly advocates of civil rights and of an equal place for blacks in American society. For the most part northerners believed in the genetic inferiority of blacks and doubted if they had the capacity for full citizenship. As evidence of this consider the fact that black northerners could vote in only eight of twenty-two states, and between 1865 and 1869 white northerners rejected suffrage referendums in eight of eleven elections. The national level legal system also moved rapidly to relegate blacks to the status of second class citizens. In the Slaughterhouse case in 1873, and *United States v. Cruikshank* in 1876, the Supreme Court decreed that most citizenship rights remained under the states and outside of federal control, and that the federal government had jurisdiction only over rights violations by the states, not by individuals. Over the remainder of the nineteenth century, the Supreme Court would uphold the legality of racial segregation and black disfranchisement, in effect declaring that the Fourteenth and Fifteenth Amendments did not apply to African Americans. The Civil War had ended slavery and killed secession forever, but states' rights and white dominance over blacks enjoyed a remarkable recovery.

THE END OF NATIVE AMERICAN SOVEREIGNTY

In terms of shamefulness, the re-subjugation of blacks in the south following reconstruction can only be matched, perhaps exceeded, by white America's treatment of American Indians during the latter nineteenth century. In a progression of aggressive steps the white majority stole Indian land, militarily defeated those that resisted, violated virtually every treaty that had been agreed upon, and, finally, attempted systematically to destroy Indian religion and culture.

Prior to the middle of the nineteenth century the US government used the western half of the country as "one big reservation." This territory was also referred to as the "great American desert," reflecting the belief of most people that the land was of little value. This half of the continent was designated as Indian Country. Eastern Indian tribes were relocated to this territory with the idea that the West would be a permanent frontier and would be Indian owned as one huge reservation. This relocation involved about 90 percent of the Indians living east of the Mississippi, more than one hundred thousand people. Of these, about forty thousand died during the process of being relocated.[12] In 1834 Congress passed the Indian Intercourse Act that allowed white people access to Indian Territory only with a license.

This plan lasted for only a short period, falling prey to a number of factors. The first was the acquisition by the United States of the western territories of Texas, California, and Oregon. Some in the east wanted to immigrate to these new territories, and others wanted to open the territories up to eastern business for the purpose of trade, resulting in the opening up of trails across Indian Territory to provide access to these new territories and markets. The trails were typically guarded by a series of forts staffed by the US Army with the mission of protecting the transients from Indian resistance to the territorial violation posed by the settlers crossing their lands and

12. Robert W. Venables, *American Indian History—Five Centuries of Conflict and Coexistence, Volume II, Confrontation, Adaption & Assimilation 1783–Present* (Santa Fe, NM: Clear Light Publishers, 2004), 80–82.

disrupting their hunting grounds. Shortly following the acquisition of California, gold was discovered there and, a quarter century later, in the Black Hills of South Dakota, causing what had been a trickle of whites crossing the territories into a flood. In the case of the gold prospectors, the encroachers had come to stay and to take possession of the land, not merely to cross it. Once whites began to cross and in some cases to settle in the West, they quickly discovered and communicated to those still in the east that this territory was not for the most part a great American desert but was, in fact, arable and valuable farm and ranch land. This knowledge unleashed another group of people wanting to settle on Indian land. The final factor opening the west up to massive white encroachment was the development and the expansion of railroads, which made the territory much more easily and safely accessible, and made the importation of supplies and the exportation of goods to sell practical and profitable. Venables describes the well-known ceremony whereby the railroad tracks being constructed from the east are joined with those from the west with a golden spike, making the first transcontinental railroad a reality, as "The auspicious ceremony was also a spike through the Plains Indian's way of life."[13] Bowing to the pressure of people wanting to cross over or to settle upon Indian Territory, in the 1850s the federal government abandoned the Indian Country policy and substituted for it a policy of removing tribes to specific and separated reservations. Not coincidentally, the reservations developed for the various tribes were for the most part made up of the most barren and least desirable land available. Summarizing the prevailing Indian belief that the last chapter of their independence was being written, the Apache leader Cochise said in 1866: "When I was young I walked all over this country, east and west, and saw no other people than the Apaches. After many summers I walked again and found another race of people had come to take it. How is it? Why is it that the Apaches wait to die—that they carry their lives on their finger nails? They roam over the hills and plains and want the heavens to fall on them."[14]

The years from the 1850s to the 1880s was a period of sporadic conflict between the tribes and the US government, as more and more whites moved onto former Indian Territory and tribes were relocated to smaller and bleaker reservations. Most of the smaller tribes capitulated to the government's demands because they had little choice to do otherwise. The larger tribes often chose to fight. Occasionally they even won, as when the Sioux and allied tribes resisted the opening of the Bozeman trail, a war that ended with the Treaty of Fort Laramie. Under the terms of this treaty the United States abandoned the Bozeman trail and the forts constructed to protect it, as well as other trails and military posts on Sioux territory. The tribe was granted permanent ownership of the western half of South Dakota and the right to inhabit and hunt in the Powder River country in Wyoming and Montana; this whole area was to be closed to white people. It turned out that "permanent" meant four years, until 1872, when the Northern Pacific Railroad began to build a route into Sioux territory and the government sent an army to protect the surveying parties hired by the railroad. After four more years of war, which included the defeat of Custer's Seventh Calvary at the Battle of Little Bighorn, the Indians were crushed by the industrial might and seemingly

13. Robert W. Venables, *American Indian History*, 207.

14. Dee Brown, *Bury My Heart at Wounded Knee: An Indian History of the American West* (New York: Henry Holt, 2007); Frederick E. Hoxie, A Final Promise: The Campaign to Assimilate the Indians, 1880–1920 (Lincoln, NE: University of Nebraska Press, 1984).

endless supply of soldiers of the US Army. The remaining Sioux, under the leadership of Sitting Bull, retreated to Canada during the winter of 1876–1877, and others who remained in the territory surrendered. By 1876 the Navajos, the Comanche, and the Apaches had all been defeated, their leaders imprisoned, and the tribes relegated to small reservations on land so bad that no one was interested in stealing it from them.[15]

As soon as the tribes were conquered and relegated to dismal reservations, the government's attention turned to Indian welfare. A number of programs were implemented, ostensibly for the benefit of native peoples but with the real objective of destroying their culture and eradicating tribal society. These programs, spoke of "civilizing" or "Americanizing" the Indians. Under the banner of charity, the government—aided by private, generally Protestant, philanthropic groups—used education, land policy, proselytization, and finally the near total destruction of the buffalo in an attempt to eliminate Indian values, traditions, and life style. In the area of education, 227 boarding schools were established to which 14,300 Indian children, often seized by Army troops, were sent far from their homes.[16] At these schools, where they were generally confined until after adolescence, the children were forced to speak English and dress in the style of white society, were given Christian religious education and required to attend church services, and were expected to profess white American values. Land policy was used to attempt to change Indian values of communal ownership and rejection of private property by, under the Dawes Act, distributing Indian land to individuals along with farm implements. The hope was that this would inculcate in the Indians the value of personal success that lay at the heart of capitalism. In the words of one Bureau of Indian Affairs official, this would teach the Indians to be more "mercenary and ambitious to obtain riches." White religious activists sought to destroy Indian religion because they viewed it as "pagan" and because it helped Indians resist assimilation. Under the influence of Protestant missionary groups the Bureau of Indian Affairs developed a criminal code in 1884 that prohibited tribal religious practices. The code remained in effect until 1933. The code was first used to ban the Sun Dance, a significant part of Plains Indian religion. To enforce the ban the government withheld rations and disrupted religious ceremonies that transmitted traditional values. In 1890, to suppress the Ghost Dance religion, the army resorted to brute force, using artillery to bombard a ceremony at Wounded Knee, South Dakota, killing at least 200 Sioux men, women, and children.[17]

The government's war on American Indian culture was not successful in destroying it, but did do massive, probably irreparable, damage to the Indian peoples and their way of life. The result has been a group that has suffered, and continues to suffer, from a far greater than average rate of nearly every social problem. The rates of poverty, unemployment, family violence, alcoholism, suicide, to name a few, are all much higher among Indians than the population as a whole.

15. David Goldfield, Carl Abbott, Virginia DeJohn Anderson, JoAnn E. Argersinger, Peter H. Argersinger, William L. Barney, and Robert M. Weir, *The American Journey—A History of the United States*, Vol. 2 (Upper Saddle River, NJ: Prentice Hall, 1998), 634–636.

16. Joe R. Feagin, *Racial and Ethnic Relations*, 2nd ed. (Englewood Cliffs, NJ: Prentice-Hall, 1984), 194–195.

17. Thorsten Veblen, *The Theory of the Leisure Class* (New York: MacMillan, 1899).

THE SOCIAL-ECONOMIC ENVIRONMENT, 1850–1900: THE BIRTH OF MODERN AMERICA

The era of American history in which Great Grandmother Movius confronted the tramp problem was one of cataclysmic changes in nearly all areas of American life. Old paradigms were fading out and being replaced by new ones in almost every aspect of existence; modern America was emerging. It would probably not be an exaggeration to say that if you were to get in a time machine and return to 1850 you would be a stranger in a strange land—very little would seem recognizable or comfortable. However, if you were to return to 1900 you would not feel nearly so out of place. You would recognize and be familiar with most aspects of life: there was not email, but there was the telegraph; cell phones did not exist, but land lines did and you could call across the nation or even overseas; air travel was not available, but fairly rapid trains connected most areas of the country and the replacement of sails by steam power had reduced travel time from London to New York from fourteen to eight days; if you were sick you could not expect the miracle cures of today, but medicine was firmly based on science and, for the first time in history, people went to the hospital with the expectation that they would get better rather than die. The modern era had arrived and it was a mixed blessing.

Industrial and Economic Transformation

Between 1870 and 1900 the United States transformed itself from an agricultural nation into the world's foremost industrial power, producing more than one-third of the world's manufactured goods. During these years trends that had begun earlier in the century became even more pronounced, with the result that the position of the average working and lower class American became even more precarious. The most important of these trends for the well-being of American workers were the concentration of economic power in the form of the corporation; the deterioration of jobs as corporations adopted mass production technologies that broke formerly skilled jobs down into simple tasks that could be performed by unskilled labor earning subpoverty-level wages; the neglect of working conditions by corporate employers, leading to unsafe working conditions and numerous industrial accidents, often resulting in worker disability or death; and, finally, the expansion of the labor pool to include large numbers of low-power, easily exploitable employees, including children, women, and recent immigrants.

In 1860, 140,000 factories were turning out products valued at $1.9 billion. By 1900 207,000 factories and shops were producing goods valued at $11.4 billion. The number of companies had grown at a pace far slower than the growth of production, illustrating the trend toward much larger employers. At the end of the Civil War a factory with forty or fifty workers was considered a fair sized business. By 1900 many industries employed thousands of workers in a single plant. During these forty years numerous mergers and takeovers occurred in which some companies disappeared and a few became huge corporations. By the turn of the century, only 1 percent of all manufacturing plants were turning out nearly two-thirds of the nation's manufactured goods. The largest manufacturers by the turn of the century were, in order of size, iron and steel, meat packing, foundry and machine shop products, lumber and timber products, and flour and gristmill products.

The new large corporations provided American workers with many jobs, but they also firmly controlled pay and working conditions and were constantly seeking ways to organize work to make each job more productive and more efficient. The deskilling process that had begun earlier in the century accelerated in response to new technologies, new workers, and workplace reorganization. A US Department of Labor report issued shortly after the end of the nineteenth century concluded that industrial labor had been reduced to minute, low-skilled operations, making skilled artisans obsolete. However, on the other end of the labor spectrum, the advance of workplace technology had the effect of upgrading unskilled workers into semi-skilled workers: the ditch digger was replaced by the steam shovel operator; the railroad track layer by the mechanical crane operator; the hod carrier by the elevator and hoist operator. The zenith of this work reorganization process occurred in the persona of Frederick Taylor, an industrial engineer and one of the country's first management consultants. Taylor became famous and rich by contracting with companies to show them how to scientifically analyze every task in the production process, break all the tasks down into their simplest components, and develop and train workers to perform each task in the "one best way." Using Taylor's methods employers were able to make workers just one more tool in the production process, one that could be paid the smallest possible amount, and one that could be easily replaced if he or she became inefficient or troublesome. Taylor's approach to management did indeed yield higher productivity and higher profits for corporations but, as Legergott notes, "it likewise generated a burning sense of outrage among those who felt that man was not to be confounded with material nature, and that to make a profit from human labor was essentially immoral."[18]

An example of the deskilling process and its effect on American workers can be found by looking at the plight of carpenters. Prior to the 1870s, carpenters had been highly skilled and well paid artisans who were required to have years of training to ply their trade. This level of training and skill was necessary because carpenters were required to be able to hand carve moldings, furniture parts, and decorative house features such as gargoyles; to be able to turn banisters on a lathe; to be able to design and construct staircases; to construct doors and window casings; and hundreds of other labor-intensive, high-skill tasks. This situation began to change in the 1870s when factories began to turn out machine-made millwork that could be manufactured and sold for a fraction of the cost of a carpenter fabricating it by hand. They also began to mass produce building products such as staircases, doors, columns, windows, and decorative features, also at a much reduced cost. As these ready-made items streamed out of factories the skill needed to build houses and other wood using products was greatly reduced. A carpenter no longer needed any more skill than that required to measure for fit and then to nail the part in place. With a long apprenticeship no longer needed the trade of carpenter was opened to lower skilled workers, with a corresponding loss of status and income. Traditionally trained carpenters referred to these new entrants to their profession as the "saw and hatchet brigade" or as "botches." This resulted in a chronic oversupply of carpenters, causing many to go on the road in search of work. It is likely that some of the visitors

---

18. Stanley Lebergott, *The Americans—An Economic Record* (New York: W.W. Norton & Company, 1984), 148, 382.

to Great Grandmother Movius's back stoop were carpenters who were forced by mass production to tramp in search of work.[19]

While manufacturers were making record profits for their shareholders by streamlining production methods and employing less skilled workers, they were not showing any inclination to plow money into making working conditions more pleasant or safer. In one year, 1881, in one industry, the railroads, on the job accidents disabled or killed 30,000 workers. In the meatpacking plants of Chicago, workers who had grown careless from fatigue and long hours, using sharp knives, under pressure to work rapidly, often sliced fingers off their numb hands. Upton Sinclair in *The Jungle*, his famous novel about the killing floors of meatpacking plants in Chicago, wrote: "It was to be counted as a wonder that there were not more men slaughtered than cattle." The typical schedule for a factory worker was ten hours a day, six days per week in the 1880s. Steel workers labored 12 hours per day and, because the plants operated 24/7, once every two weeks when the workers changed shifts, one group was required to take a "long turn" and stay on the job for 24 hours. To make matters worse, workers who bore these conditions were paid subsurvival-level wages. For example, workers for U.S. Steel were paid less than $12.50 per week, almost 17 percent below the $15.00 per week that the federal government estimated that an urban family needed to subsist.

Corporations were able to get away with such poor working conditions and pay partially because competition for jobs was intense due to an expansion of the size of the labor pool. Many industries were beginning to employ children and women to perform rote, low-skilled, often highly dangerous, tasks. Children were frequently employed in the garment industry as bobbin boys and girls, bastings pullers, and similar tasks. Girls under 16 made up over half of the workforce in the silk mills of Scranton and Wilkes-Barre, Pennsylvania. In the coal mining industry, breaker boys stood on ladders day-after-day to remove waste matter from the coal, breathing in harmful coal dust with no protective gear whatsoever. Reformers in the 1890s told shocking tales of the effect of factory labor on children's lives, citing cases like the seven-year-old girl whose legs were paralyzed and deformed after toiling "day after day with little legs crossed, pulling out bastings from garments." John Spargo in *The Bitter Cry of Children* (1906) reported that in 1900 there were 1,752,187 children under sixteen working full time—later estimates concluded that this figure was probably unrealistically low. Women accompanied children into the workforce in increasing numbers after 1870. The low wages of unskilled male factory workers often made two incomes a necessity for family survival. Between 1870 and 1920, the number of women and children in the labor force more than doubled. However, most working women were single women who had to work to support themselves; in 1900 85 percent of working women were single and under the age of 25. Corporations liked employing women and children because they could pay them even less than they paid their unskilled male workers. In one St. Louis factory in 1896 women were paid $4.00 per week for work that the company paid men $16.00.

19. Jules Tygiel, "Tramping Artisans: Carpenters in Industrial America, 1880–1890," in Eric Monkkonen (ed.), *Walking to Work: Tramps in Industrial America, 1790–1935* (Lincoln, NE: University of Nebraska Press, 1981), 87–117.

POPULATION AND IMMIGRATION

Between 1850 and 1900 the population of the United States grew at a staggering pace. In 1850 the total population was only a little over 23 million people. By 1900 the population had grown to nearly 76 million. In percentage terms, the population between 1850 and 1870 grew by 66 percent, between 1850 and 1880 it grew by 116 percent, and between 1850 and 1900 the growth rate was 228 percent.

The majority of the population increase during this era was a result of natural growth; people in the nineteenth century married young and had large families. However, a significant factor in the population growth was a marked increase in immigration. A major reason that corporations were able to find easily exploitable workers who would accept sub-poverty wages was this flood of immigrants entering the United States during the late nineteenth century. From 1840 to 1870, approximately 2.5 million immigrants arrived in the country each decade, but in the last three decades of the century the number was nearly 5 million. Between 1870 and 1910 the total number of immigrants to arrive in the United States was almost twenty million. These people arrived in the country as a result of both the pull of perceived opportunity in the new land and the push of various factors in their countries of origin. Italians first came in large numbers to escape an 1887 cholera epidemic in southern Italy; tens of thousands of Jews sought refuge from the pogroms (anti-Jewish massacres) that swept Russia and Poland after 1880. Chinese and Japanese immigrants also came to the United States in large numbers during this era. Most Chinese immigrants came from Canton in South China, a region of great poverty. They worked building railroads and in mines throughout the West and as farm laborers in California. Many eventually settled in cities such as San Francisco, Seattle, and Vancouver, where they established residential and retail enclaves referred to as Chinatowns. The Chinese population peaked in the United States at about 125,000 in 1882, sharply declining after the Chinese Exclusion Act of 1883. Japanese began immigrating to the U.S. in the late 1880s, driven by severe overpopulation and land shortage in their country of origin. Most settled on farms on the west coast, taking the place of Chinese who had moved to the cities. By 1900, there were approximately 50,000 Japanese immigrants to the United States, nearly all on the West Coast. The total immigration during the late nineteenth century was so great that by the century's end about 15 percent of the US population was foreign-born.

Most, about two-thirds, of the huge wave of immigrants were young men, most between the ages of 15 and 40. They were, in nearly all cases, property-less and with few skills and came in search of work where they could make enough money to be able to save and later send for their families. They tended to crowd into northern seaboard cities, settling in areas where others of their nationality or region had settled.

The new population of immigrants posed a challenge for social order and social welfare in the United States for a number of reasons. First, and most obvious, was that the new immigrants, generally lacking skills and often lacking knowledge of the English language and American customs, were easily exploited. When they were working they were generally paid subpoverty-level wages, and when the economy took a downturn, as it frequently did in this age of no macro-economic regulation or intervention by the government, they were the first to be laid off, leaving them with no means of support. Second, immigrants crowded into large cities, adding to already existing problems of housing, public health and sanitation, crime, and the total panoply of emerging urban problems. Finally, in addition to adding to the objective social problems referred to already, they added to subjective social problems. Not only had the number of immigrants increased in the late nineteenth century, they were coming from different places. Immigrants in the earlier part of the century had mainly come from Northern Europe. Most came from England, and the more exotic came from Ireland and Germany. In the later years of the century many more came from southern and Eastern Europe—those arriving on the East Coast often came from Italy, Austria-Hungary, Poland, and Russia. Many did not speak English, they were Catholics and Jews rather than Protestants, and they often had strange customs, habits, and beliefs. This led to the common perception that American values and the American way of life was under assault. Social welfare programs were developed with the dual mission of providing support for the needy and also with socializing them away from their odd foreign habits and making them more American, a process referred to as "Americanization." Early schools of social work often had one or more courses in this subject.

URBANIZATION ACCELERATES

Historian Richard Hofstadter has said that "The United States was born in the country and moved to the city."[20] Much of that movement occurred during the nineteenth century when the United States was the most rapidly urbanizing nation in the world. Between 1850 and 1900 the proportion of the nation's population living in cities with populations over 100,000—swelled by immigrants from Europe and Asia and by internal migrants from rural areas—increased from less than 5 percent to nearly 20 percent of the population. The nation's population tripled between 1860 and 1920, but the urban population increased nine-fold. Of the 1,700 cities listed in the 1900 census, fewer than 2 percent even existed in 1800.

The rapid growth of cities during the latter half of the nineteenth century was made possible by a number of factors. The first was the development of power technologies that freed manufacturers to locate their plants away from the rivers that had been the source of power for most manufacturing. The development of the steam engine, which motivated manufacturers to locate near coal deposits rather than rivers, followed by the development of the electric grid which made power sources irrelevant for plant location and substituted factors such as proximity to raw materials and transportation networks, allowed manufacturing to spread out to hundreds of locations. The second factor was the development of rapid and cheap transportation networks that enabled the importation of food over long distances from agricultural regions to cities where it was possible to grow only a fraction of the amount of food necessary to support the population. Internal city transportation networks, mainly streetcars, allowed workers access to employers who were not within walking distance to their homes. Finally, the development of infrastructure such as sanitary water and sewage systems and fire protection systems, which prevented the massive death rates that resulted from disease epidemics and citywide fires, made living in cities safer and more pleasant.

20. Richard Hofstadter, *The Age of Reform: From Bryan to F.D.R.*(New York: Alfred A. Knopf, 1955), 23.

Once these technical blocks to urban growth, power, transport, and infrastructure had perhaps not been solved but at least brought under control, the reason for urban growth was simple—the labor market. Manufacturers located in cities because that was where the employees were. Employees located in cities because that was where the jobs were. As Lebergott notes, "Given a nickel for trolley fare in 1900, a Chicago worker could reach any one of almost 48,000 different employers ... Furthermore, the city offered immigrants many employers, some of whom spoke his own language, and competed for workers' skills much as workers competed for jobs. By contrast, in downstate Illinois the same nickel, plus a walk, gave a worker access to at most a dozen employers during the course of a day."[21]

The massive increase in urban population exacerbated the problems of social order and social control in the nation. Although there were many opportunities for employment in the city, there was also great risk of unemployment. As workers rarely owned their own homes, did not have unemployment compensation or any other kind of insurance, and rarely made enough to save for a rainy day, any period of unemployment lasting more than a few days could spell disaster for a family. The city also posed unexpected risks for families, mainly the breakdown of traditional control of children by parents. When families had lived on isolated farms the authority of parents was nearly unquestioned. In cities not only was the supervision that families were able to exercise over their children decreased, but children were also exposed to multiple role models because of their exposure to so many more people in their multiple dwelling units. With children persistently exposed to so many different family styles in their immediate neighborhood and their public school, the traditional authority of family declined.

NEW DEVELOPMENTS IN SOCIAL PHILOSOPHY

As with any era of massive social change, the latter half of the nineteenth century unsettled the minds of Americans. There were, of course, the easily observed social problems we have already discussed, but more troubling to the average citizen were the changes in the basic arrangements of the society. In a short time we had gone from a rural democracy where people may not have actually been equal but were at least kind of equal. The vast majority of the population was middle class, lived in the same neighborhoods or communities, went to the same churches, and generally believed themselves to be similar to their fellow countrymen; as the nineteenth century progressed this situation changed. There were suddenly masses of very poor people and a very visible group of people who appeared to be obscenely wealthy. Was this all right? Was this American? Was this Christian? As to the very poor, what was the obligation of other citizens, particularly those who obviously had much more than they needed to help? Questions of this type plagued Americans. In response, several new philosophies began to have influence and guide American's responses to their less fortunate brethren. Primary among these were Social Darwinism, the Gospel of Wealth, and the Social Gospel.

21. Stanley Lebergott, *The Americans*, 359.

SOCIAL DARWINISM

A major justification for increasing inequality, and argument against social reform to redress the problem, was expounded in the philosophy of social Darwinism. This philosophy was based on the evolutionary theories of Charles Darwin and the writings of English social philosopher Herbert Spencer. In several influential books, Spencer applied Darwinian principles of natural selection to society, combining biology and sociology in a theory of "social selection" that explained human progress. Like animals, society evolved slowly, by adapting to the environment. The "survival of the fittest"—an expression that Spencer, not Darwin, invented—preserved the strong and weeded out the weak. This expression appeared to legitimize existing social hierarchies as the outcome of natural selection. Social Darwinism had a number of influential followers in the United States, notably William Graham Sumner, a prominent professor at Yale University who was also a popular and forceful writer who wrote in 1883 that, "The millionaires are a product of natural selection, acting on the whole body of men to pick out those who can meet the requirement of certain work to be done. . . They get high wages and live in luxury, but the bargain is a good one for society."[22] Sumner argued that government action on behalf of the poor or weak interfered with evolution and sapped the strength from the species. Reform tampered with the laws of nature and was ultimately harmful to society as a whole.

THE GOSPEL OF WEALTH

Although the philosophy of social Darwinism viewed social welfare efforts, particularly those of the government and those aimed at the very poor, as unnecessary and perhaps even dangerous to the social structure (for these efforts permitted the "unfit" to survive and, worse, to reproduce) the wealthy were not completely blind to social problems and to their responsibility to give back to the society that had so richly benefitted them. Notable among these people, who could perhaps be called philanthropic social Darwinists, was the Pittsburgh steel magnate Andrew Carnegie. In two essays printed in the *North American Review*, Carnegie developed a philosophy that was later named in the British press as the Gospel of Wealth. Carnegie argued that millionaires had not created their wealth by themselves but, rather, had been supported by the communities in which the wealth was created. Because of this fact the wealthy individual had a moral obligation to return a substantial portion of his wealth to the community within which it had been created. The wealthy businessman who spent all of his money on himself was guilty of two sins: first keeping for himself that which did not belong to him, and second of depriving the larger community of his managerial talents. The same talents that had led the millionaire to accumulate his wealth were the talents needed to wisely distribute that wealth for the greater good. Indiscriminate giving wrecked lives and communities. It took a wise man to give money wisely. Interestingly, because Carnegie was

---

22. Quoted in Richard Hofstadter, *Social Darwinism in American Thought* (Boston: MA, 1955), 58.

no fan of government action, he felt that if the rich failed to give away their fortunes during their lifetimes, that the government should do so after their deaths. He supported a nearly 100 percent estate tax because he believed it provided an incentive for the rich to dispose of their fortunes while still alive.

There would seem to be an inherent contradiction between social Darwinism and the Gospel of Wealth. Social Darwinism argues that welfare for the poor is harmful because it reinforces negative characteristics of the poor, such as rewarding them for not working and allowing the unfit to survive and reproduce. The Gospel of Wealth argues that charity is good and is in fact a moral obligation of the wealthy. The two philosophies are actually not contradictory and are in fact in accord with one another for two reasons. First, the Gospel of Wealth provides a strong justification for a laissez-faire (hands off) position of government toward business. By permitting businessmen to seek as much profit as possible the government is in fact furthering the welfare of the larger society because by making huge sums of money the businessman will have more to give away to the larger community. In this vein it is significant to note that Carnegie's interest in philanthropy did not make him a more generous employer. On the contrary, he became, if anything, more ruthless in the pursuit of profits once he had determined that those profits would be distributed during his lifetime. The second way that the Gospel of Wealth was entirely consistent with social Darwinism was in the kind of charities identified as worthwhile. Carnegie had little if any interest in helping the very poor, that group that social Darwinists identified as unfit. He thought that to the extent these people should be helped that help should come from the government, probably in the form of incarceration in poor houses so that the very poor could not reproduce and otherwise drag down the rest of the community. Carnegie's favored targets for philanthropy were things he felt would help people lift themselves up and improve their productivity. Along this line his various foundations endowed schools, colleges, and built libraries in dozens of American towns.

CHALLENGES TO CONSERVATIVE SOCIAL THINKING

As the end of the nineteenth century drew near, a number of new currents in social thought were emerging that challenged the harsh, deterministic, philosophy of Social Darwinism and its charitable wing the Gospel of Wealth. A basis for these challenges was a best-selling book, *Progress and Poverty*, written by Henry George and published in 1879. George's book offered a critical appraisal of American society and questioned the assumptions of Social Darwinism. George wrote that "The present century has been marked by a prodigious increase in wealth-producing power . . . it was natural to expect, and it was expected, that . . . real poverty [would become] a thing of the past." This, however, had not happened. Instead, "the wealthy class is becoming more wealthy; but the poorer class is becoming more dependent." George proposed a solution to this situation, a highly progressive tax plan that would redistribute income from the rich to the poor. This "single tax" plan generated a good deal of popular support, with "Single-tax" clubs springing up across the country, but it was never taken seriously by policy makers. His analysis of the problem of the unequal distribution of wealth did, however, raise questions a new generation of citizens set out to answer.[23]

During this period economics was gaining influence as an independent profession and academic specialty. Richard T. Ely at the University of Wisconsin and other young economists set out to challenge traditional economic thought. Ely and his colleagues attacked classical economics, charging it with being dogmatic, questioning its faith in laissez-faire, and criticizing its reliance on self-interest as a guide for human conduct. In 1885 Ely and his associates founded the American Economic Association, which linked economics to social problems and urged government intervention in economic affairs. One of the associations founding members, social critic Thorstein Veblen, argued that traditional economic theory was really a mask for human greed. In his 1899 book *The Theory of the Leisure Class* Veblen presented an analysis of the "predatory wealth" and "conspicuous consumption" of the business class.[24]

Perhaps the most important force countering the influence of Social Darwinism was a movement among mostly Protestant clergy that came to be called the Social Gospel movement. A leader of the movement was Walter Rauschenbusch, a young Baptist minister who had read widely from the writings of George, Ely, and other social reformers. When he took his first pulpit at a church in Hell's Kitchen, a blighted area of New York City, he soon recognized the tremendous damage to people's lives caused by living in a slum environment. Rauschenbusch later became a professor at the Rochester Theological Seminary, a position from which he influenced hundreds of pastors to recognize and commit to change the environmental causes of poverty and related social problems. Another social gospel leader was Washington Gladden, pastor at First Congregational Church in Columbus, Ohio. In 1895 Gladden published an article titled "Tainted Money" in which he attacked practitioners of the Gospel of Wealth, calling them "robber barons," "Roman plunders," "pirates of industry," and "spoilers of the state." Gladden asked whether a charity or a university could take offerings of money made in reprehensible ways without condoning the methods and accepting the standards of the donor. He asked "Is this clean money? Can any man, or any institution, knowing its origin, touch it without being defiled?"[25] Gladden published widely, linking Christianity to the social and economic environment. He spent his career working for "social salvation." Emphasizing a fellowship of love, he denounced competition, urged an "industrial partnership" between employers and employees, and called for greater effort to help the poor.

Following the lead of pastors like Rauschenbusch and Gladden, by the end of the nineteenth century churches began establishing urban missions in the slums of large American cities. Living among the poor and homeless, the urban missionaries lost any faith they may have had in traditional religious doctrines that poverty was evidence of sinfulness and that religion should focus exclusively on individual salvation and preparation for life in the next world, not this one. As an alternative, the Social Gospel focused on improving living conditions in the present world, as well as preparation for the next. Urban churches became centers for social betterment as well as religious activity.

23. Henry George, *Progress and Poverty: An Inquiry into the Cause of Industrial Depression and of Increase of Want with Increase of Wealth: The Remedy* (New York: D. Appleton and Company, 1879).

24. Veblen, *The Theory of the Leisure Class.*

25. Quoted in Robert H. Bremner, *American Philanthropy,* 2nd ed. (Chicago, IL: University of Chicago Press, 1988), 107.

CONCLUSION

Although the winds of a more humane and generous social philosophy were blowing across the land in the late nineteenth century, the overall effect of increasingly visible social problems, combined with the spread of Social Darwinian thinking, resulted in an increasing emphasis on attributing the causes of social problems to the individuals affected. This is a tendency still characterizing American society and is often referred to as "blaming the victim."[26] This tendency can be illustrated by the reaction to the tramp problem that visited Great Grandmother Movius in Lidgerwood, North Dakota. From the perspective afforded by looking back from the twenty-first century, it is clear that the tramp problem was almost entirely a result of social and economic factors leading to disruptions in the lives of hundreds of thousands of workers. However, few contemporary observers recognized these factors; most attributed the problem to deficiencies in the moral character of the traveling men themselves. Even though statistics clearly demonstrated that the population of tramps was constantly shifting, most being on the road for only a short time as they sought work, the popular belief was that the population was stable, composed of a number of long-term tramps who chose the life in preference to the stability of home, family, and a job. Tramps were labeled as lazy, immoral, and shiftless. Professor Francis Wayland of Yale wrote a report in which he characterized the tramp as "a lazy, shiftless, incorrigible, cowardly, utterly depraved savage . . . Practically, he has come to consider himself at war with society and all social institutions . . . He has only one aim—to be supported in idleness."[27]

There is another factor that contributed to the huge number of wandering unemployed. This is that there was an almost total lack of a social welfare system to help regulate the labor market and cushion a brief period of unemployment to prevent it from becoming a disaster. Public aid, as we have seen, was limited in most cases to the poorhouse. Private charities were small, uncoordinated, short-term, and provided a level of aid generally far below what was needed to maintain a family at a level of even marginal comfort.

There were a number of people who recognized the problems illustrated by the great number of tramps, even though they poorly understood the causes. These people were experimenting with a number of new social institutions to deal with these. Institutions were emerging in which the shape of a modern social welfare system was faintly visible. Prominent among these was the Charity Organization Society, the Society for the Prevention of Cruelty to Children (placing out agencies that have come to be known as the orphan train movement) and settlement houses. We turn to these in the next chapter.

---

26. William Ryan. *Blaming the Victim* (New York: Pantheon Books, 1971).

27. Francis Wayland, "Paper on Tramps," 11, quoted in Michael B. Katz, *Poverty and Policy in American History* (New York: Academic Press, 1983), 159–161.

CHAPTER 5

SCIENTIFIC CHARITY, 1850–1900

The 1888 annual meeting of the National Conference of Charities and Corrections was held in Buffalo New York during the week of July 6. The participants enjoyed taking strolls under the balmy 78 degree Buffalo July weather with the result that Conference organizers experienced a bit of difficulty attracting participants off the streets and into the sessions which, according to a New York Times report, were "remarkably meaty" but were delivered in a somewhat less than stimulating manner. Of the keynote address, presented by Dr. Charles S. Hoyt, Secretary of the New York State Board of Charities, the Times report observed that "the doctor read it in so low a voice that very few people heard him."[1] This was not the case with one paper, read before the Out Door Poor Relief session by the Reverend Oscar C. McCulloch. McCulloch was a trained preacher, a graduate of the Chicago Theological Seminary, and senior pastor at the Plymouth Congregational Church in Indianapolis. McCulloch had presented many a sermon and knew how to project his voice and to be sure to keep his audience engaged. McCulloch also had an understanding of the importance of a catchy title to attract an audience, and the title he chose was inspired: "The Tribe of Ishmael: A Study in Social Degradation."

The Reverend McCulloch was what would be identified at a later point in history as a public intellectual. In addition to being a full-time minister he was a self-styled social scientist, a student of medicine and the life sciences, and a leading figure in the emerging world of social work. He was, among other appointments, the founder and President of the Indianapolis Charity Organization Society (COS) and Chair of the Indiana State Board of Charities. In his intellectual pursuits he was especially interested in the work of Charles Darwin and the extension of Darwin's theories to the social sphere by Herbert Spencer, and by Sir Frances Galton in his 1865 *Macmillan's Magazine* article "Hereditary Talent and Character." McCulloch's former pulpit was at a church in Sheboygan Wisconsin where his attempts to reconcile Darwin's theories with the bible created a schism leading to his resignation and acceptance of a call from the more progressive Plymouth Church in Indianapolis.

McCulloch stumbled upon the family that was to become the basis of his study in 1877 when he was requested to make a pastoral visit to a family of "extreme destitution." He visited the family

---

1. *New York Times*, July 6, 1888, 1.

in their home that turned out to be only a room not more than ten feet by ten feet. In this room, without even a fire, a half-made bed was the only furnishing. There was no other furniture, no cooking utensils, and seven people—an elderly blind woman, a man and his wife, their child, and his sister and her two children. McCulloch saw to the family's immediate needs and was a short time later called back by the family to perform a marriage for another Ishmael household. He found this branch of the family, eleven persons, living in one small room furnished by only two beds. He performed the marriage, waiving his usual fee, and when he later inquired about how the couple was doing he was told "Oh, Elisha don't live with her anymore." When asked why, he was told "Her other husband came back and she went to him. That made Elisha mad, and he left her."[2]

At the same time that McCulloch became aware of the Ishmael family, he was reading Richard Dugdale's book *The Jukes: A Study in Crime, Disease, and Heredity.* Dugdale, another self-styled social scientist and member of the Prison Association of New York, had been asked by the Association to carry out an inspection of county jails. Intrigued by the high incidence of kinship among inmates, Dugdale used his own funds to extend the study with the results published in his book. In reality, Dugdale's study was mainly a plea for public health reform, attributing the high kinship rate among criminals to intemperance, unsanitary environments, venereal disease, and other environmental conditions negatively affecting child development. It was, however, widely misinterpreted by people, including McCulloch, as proof of "hereditary criminality," that criminal tendencies are to be found in the genes.

Inspired by his misinterpretation of Dugdale's findings about inherited criminality and pauperism, and armed with the family study methodology Dugdale had developed for his work, McCulloch decided to look into the Ishmael family. His first stop was the office of the Township Trustee, a position that in an earlier era would have been called the overseer of the poor, and later would be called the director of public welfare. In the Trustee's records McCulloch discovered that the Ishmael's "had a pauper history of several generations, and so intermarried with others as to form a pauper ganglion of several hundreds." Over the next several years he added the records of the COS. He found that the "tribe" had grown from the first generation studied comprised of 30 families and 62 individuals, to the sixth generation with 57 families and 1750 individuals. His research showed the family to have had a continuous pauper record:

> They have been in the almshouse, the House of Refuge, the Women's Reformatory, the penitentiaries, and have received continuous aid from the township. They are intermarried with other members of the group, as you may see by the marriage lines, and with over two hundred other families. In this family history are murders, a large number of illegitimacies and of prostitutes. They are generally diseased. The children die young. They live by petty stealing, begging, ashgathering. In summer they "gypsy," or travel in wagons east or west. We hear of them in Illinois about Decatur and in Ohio about Columbus. In the fall they return. They have been known to live in hollow trees on the river bottoms or in empty houses. Strangely enough they are not intemperate to excess.[3]

2. Oscar C. McCulloch, "The Tribe of Ishmael: A Study in Social Degradation," Proceedings: Fifteenth National Conference of Charities and Corrections (Boston: George H. Ellis, 1888), 157.

3. Oscar C. McCulloch, "The Tribe of Ishmael," 155.

McCulloch illustrated the interrelationships between the members of the tribe by means of a chart with 1,720 names, which measured 3 × 12 feet, much too large to be bound with the Conference Proceedings. The COS of Indianapolis was happy to provide, upon request and for the fee of 50 cents, a version of the chart measuring a mere 29 × 66 inches.

For an explanation of his findings of intergenerational transmission of pauperism, McCulloch turned to the work of biologist Ray Lankaster, who had studied

"... a minute organism which is found attached to the body of the hermit crab. It has a kidney-bean-shaped body, with a bunch of root-like processes through which it sucks the living tissue of the crab. It is known as the Sacculina. It is a crustacean which has left the free, independent life common to its family, and is living as a parasite, or pauper. The young have the Nauplius form belonging to all crustacea: it is a free swimmer. But very soon after birth a change comes over it. It attaches itself to the crab, loses the characteristics of the higher class, and becomes degraded in form and function. An irresistible hereditary tendency seizes upon it, and it succumbs. A hereditary tendency I say, because some remote ancestor left its independent, self-helpful life, and began a parasitic, or pauper, life. Not using its organs for self-help, they have one by one disappeared,—legs and other members, —until there is left a shapeless mass, with only the stomach and organs of reproduction left. This tendency to parasitism was transmitted to its descendants, until there is set up an irresistible hereditary tendency; and the Sacculina stands in nature as a type of degradation through parasitism, or pauperism. . . So we have the same in the [human] pauper. Self-help disappears. All the organs and powers that belong to the free life disappear, and there are left only the tendency to parasitism and the debasement of the reproductive tendency.[4]

Although McCulloch's approach to the problem of pauperism was new, his recommendations based on his findings were hardly new or innovative. He used his findings mainly to rail against public relief and what he called "private and indiscriminate benevolence." He argued that charitable people when giving to paupers are giving them society's consent to exist. Charity, McCulloch believed, sent the pauper out with the benediction "be fruitful and multiply." He cautioned: "Such charity has made this element, has brought children to the birth, and insured them a life of misery, cold, hunger, sickness. So-called charity joins public relief in producing still-born children, raising prostitutes, and educating criminals." These views were very similar to those expressed in the English Poor Laws of the sixteenth century, and those of the Societies for the Prevention of Pauperism, and the Associations for Improving the Condition of the Poor earlier in the nineteenth century. These earlier beliefs, however, were based on moral reasoning and religious belief, and were subscribed to mainly because they seemed to make sense. McCulloch's contribution was that he added the awesome weight of science.

The meeting at which McCullough presented his paper, the National Conference of Charities and Corrections, was the first large, interdisciplinary organization devoted to sharing information and promoting research about practical responses to social problems. The organization met once

4. Oscar C. McCulloch, "The Tribe of Ishmael," 154.

a year at a conference with hundreds of attendees, representing dozens of organizations, spread across most of the country. This organization began in 1872 when the secretary of the Illinois Board of State Commissioners of Public Charities, Frederick Wines, and the president of the Wisconsin State Board of Charities and Reform, Andrew E. Elmore, spent a few days together visiting welfare institutions in Wisconsin and discussing thoughts about their field. At the end of their trip they decided it had been of great value and that they should write to other charity officials and invite them to a meeting to discuss common concerns. The result of their letters was a two day meeting held in Chicago in May of 1872. This meeting was considered so successful that another was held in Milwaukee on April 15, 1873. These conferences were deemed to be extremely useful and attracted the attention of the American Social Science Association (ASSA), an interdisciplinary group devoted to the furthering of social science in the U.S. that had been founded in Boston in 1865. Consequently, the ASSA invited the charity leaders to join them and to meet along with their section on social economy. This was done and, beginning in 1875, the newly named Conference of Charities began to hold annual sessions at the ASSA meeting. In 1879 the Conference of Charities withdrew from the ASSA, forming an independent organization that held its own annual meeting. After several name changes the organization became the National Conference of Charities and Corrections in 1884.

As illustrated by McCulloch's paper, the National Conference of Charities and Corrections was interested in applying the methods of science, which had been so dramatically demonstrated by the massive technological breakthroughs of the late nineteenth century, to the increasing social problems of the urban-industrial society. As Leiby has noted, "the conference carried forward old ideals of humanitarian reform and social justice, of social progress, but increasingly they aspired to be scientific. By this they meant secular, rational, and empirical as opposed to sectarian, sentimental, and dogmatic."[5] The association had begun as an information sharing mechanism for public boards of charities and of prisons. However, the conference quickly changed and became dominated by several large networks of private organizations that were emerging and gaining prominence. These organizations were child welfare agencies, which at the time were entirely private; charity organization societies, which were descendants of the societies for improving the conditions of the poor that had emerged earlier in the century; and a totally new approach to urban problems, the settlement house.

THE EMERGENCE OF SERVICES
FOR DEPENDENT CHILDREN

Children have always been a popular object of charity, defined as worthy because they are viewed as being in no way at fault for their own poverty and dependency. In children people have always seen the

---

5. James Leiby, *A History of Social Welfare and Social Work in the United States* (New York: Columbia University Press, 1978), 91.

possibility of constructive philanthropy, a good return on the investment of charitable resources and efforts. This belief became especially pronounced in America in the last half of the nineteenth century when social problems seemed to be exploding and science seemed to be offering the possibility for constructive responses. In 1894, in what was probably the first modern social work textbook, Amos Warner put it this way: "The work for dependent children is the most hopeful branch of charitable endeavor in that it affords more possibilities of constructive work than any other line... In work for the aged, the sick, the defective, even for the unemployed, one is conscious that for the individuals dealt with there is no possibility of any high measure of success. There is little else possible than to make the best of unfortunate circumstance... With children, on the other hand, especially for the quite young and tolerably healthy, there is a possibility of more positive results. The young life contains within itself the principles of growth, and may be enabled to expand into something actively useful."[6]

Prior to the mid-nineteenth century the response to dependent children had been to place them in poorhouses, orphanages, houses of refuge, or, the most popular solution, to place them as apprentices. Around mid-century it began to be clear that these responses were no longer adequate to manage the whole problem of child dependency. The classic response, the poorhouse, had lost popularity in the wake of a series of reports from visiting committees who uncovered shocking conditions for all residents, but especially for children. One of many possible examples is the report of the visiting committee of the New York State Charities Aid Association that described the plight of children in the Westchester County poorhouse in 1873 as follows:

> The children, about sixty in number, are in the care of an old pauper woman, whose daughter and whose daughter's child, both born in the poorhouse, make her one of three generations of paupers. The daughter assists in the care of the children. She has a contagious disease of the eyes, which is, apparently, communicated to them. The children are neither properly clothed nor fed; but saddest of all is to see the stolid look gradually stealing over the faces of these little ones, as all the joy of their lives is starved out of them.[7]

The people of New York State felt so strongly about the problem of children in poorhouses that in 1875 an Act to Provide for the Better Care of Pauper and Destitute Children was passed. This act made it illegal for a child over three and under sixteen to be committed to a poorhouse "unless such child be an unteachable idiot, an epileptic or paralytic, or... otherwise defective, diseased, or deformed, so as to render it unfit for family care."[8]

As poorhouses lost favor as resources for dependent children, but the faith in institutional solutions for social problems remained, the number of orphanages, or children's homes, increased. In 1800 there were 3 specialized children's homes, by 1851 there were 77, and by 1860 there were 124.[9] Although the children's homes were a great improvement over county poorhouses, they had

---

6. Amos G. Warner, *American Charities: A Study in Philanthropy and Economics* (New York: Thomas Y. Crowell & Company, 1894), 203–204.

7. Robert H. Bremner, ed., *Children and Youth in America: A Documentary History, Vol. 2: 1886–1932* (Cambridge, MA: Harvard University Press, 1971), 250–251.

8. Laws of the State of New York, "An Act to Provide Better Care of Pauper and Destitute Children," April 24, 1875.

9. Homer Folks, *The Care of Destitute, Neglected and Delinquent Children* (New York: Macmillan, 1911), 52–55.

many shortcomings. They were large, impersonal, rigid, authoritarian, and generally antifamily. Many argued that they were not appropriate places to rear children. In addition to these criticisms, other problems emerged that began to erode the acceptance these institutions had once enjoyed. One problem was that in spite of the great growth in the number of institutions, the number of dependent children was growing at a much faster pace. The overflow either ended up in the dreaded county poorhouse or, in the case of older children, became "street Arabs" living on their own by whatever means necessary. Another problem stemmed from the fact that children's homes were designed to take care of children for a relatively short time, "during which education and reeducation for orderly living were provided. Having satisfactorily completed this period of rehabilitation, the male child was placed out as an apprentice in a particular trade or occupation; the female child was indentured as a domestic servant."[10] But the spread of compulsory public education and the decline of the apprenticeship system greatly lengthened the period of time dependent children needed care. This further increased the pressure on already overcrowded institutions, because as children stayed longer, fewer children could be cared for. By mid-century people were recognizing that a new approach was needed, people such as the Reverend Charles Loring Brace, founder of the New York Children's Aid Society.

The New York Children's Aid Society and the Idea of Foster Family Care

Children for whom there was no space in an orphanage and no apprenticeship available, often, through choice or circumstance, ended up living on the street. By the mid-1800s the numbers were becoming so large in cities such as New York as to cause alarm among the public. In 1849 the semi-annual report of Captain Matsell, Chief of Police, gave statistical verification of this concern. Matsell reported that the number of children living on the streets of New York City was nearly 10,000. Of these, he asserted that 2,955 were engaged in thieving in order to support themselves, and two-thirds of this number was girls between the ages of 8 and 16. Among boys common crimes identified by Matsell, in addition to thieving, were pocket picking, impersonating baggage porters and then stealing the baggage, and stealing iron and cotton from the wharves. Girls, in addition to thieving, tended to engage in that "old debasement in the pure and sunny years of childhood," that is, prostitution.[11]

The report of Captain Matsell was read by three Protestant clergymen who were friends and shared a concern with the poor of New York, the Reverends William C. Russell, Benjamin Howland, and Charles Loring Brace. Brace had recently returned from a trip to Europe where he had observed the way that vagrant youth contributed to violence and revolutionary activity, an observation that further emphasized the danger contained in Matsell's statistics. In 1853 Russell, Howland, and Brace, along with other concerned citizens, began to meet and to work to assist

---

10. June Axinn and Herman Levin, *Social Welfare: A History of the American Response to Need* (New York: Dodd, Mead & Co., 1975), 48.

11. *First Annual Report of the Children's Aid Society*, Feb. 1854, 4–5.

groups of vagrant boys. They referred to their work as The Mission, and offered Brace the leadership of the new organization. In February of 1853 the organization became chartered as the Children's Aid Society (CAS) of New York.

The first steps of the CAS were to provide local services for the street children of New York. Following the example of the Reverend A. D. F. Randolph of the Carmine Street Presbyterian Church who had begun to meet with groups of vagrant boys in 1848 hoping that religious inspiration would reshape their broken lives, Brace and his colleagues began to hold boy's meetings and soon began similar ones for girls. The goal of these meetings "was to influence them through the *sympathy of an audience . . . Plain, practical addresses were to be delivered, and the effect of music and simple worship tried upon them.*"[12] These meetings were shortly followed by the opening of a News Boys Lodging House and vocational training classes to train young people in marketable industrial skills such as shoe making.

Although the local services of the CAS were useful and to all indications well received both by the street children and the community, there was nothing particularly innovative about them. The real innovation of the CAS was the pioneering, development, and expansion of a new process for dealing with dependent children called out placement. Brace recognized that the nation in the middle 1850s was characterized by a mismatch between jobs and workers. Large urban areas such as New York City had an excess of unskilled labor, while rural areas had an excess of work, mainly agricultural, needing to be done and a shortage of people to do it. From this recognition grew Brace's idea of taking homeless children from the streets of New York—where they had few options other than begging, crime, and vice and were therefore, as pointed out in Chief Matsell's report, a serious social problem—and transporting them to rural areas to live and work with farm families. There they would be assets since even fairly small children could be useful on a farm doing simple chores such as gathering eggs, weeding gardens, and so forth. Older children, particularly boys, could take on the tasks of full-fledged farm hands and girls could assume housekeeping tasks. In 1853 Brace and his associates settled on a plan for relocating children from the city to rural areas and advertised the plan among the city's homeless children, finding the response overwhelming. Brace recalled:

> "Most touching of all was the crowd of wandering little ones who immediately found their way to the office. Ragged young girls who had nowhere to lay their heads; children driven from drunkards' homes; orphans who slept where they could find a box or a stairway; boys cast out by step-mothers or step-fathers; newsboys, whose incessant answer to our question, 'Where do you live?' rung in our ears, '*Don't live nowhere!*' little bootblacks, young peddlers . . . who seem to drift into the city every winter, and live a vagabond life; pickpockets and petty thieves trying to get honest work; child beggars and flower-sellers growing up to enter courses of crime—all this motley throng of infantile misery and childish guilt passed through our doors, telling their simple stories of suffering and loneliness, and temptation, until our hearts became sick . . . "[13]

12. *First Annual Report of the Children's Aid Society,* Feb. 1854, 6.

13. Charles Loring Brace, *The Dangerous Classes of New York and Twenty Years' Work Among Them,* 3rd ed. (New York: Wynkoop & Hallenbeck, 1880), 88–89.

The methodology of the CAS was to reach out to homeless children through flyers, group meetings, and individual contact. Children who expressed an interest in leaving the city for life on a farm were gathered together in one of several temporary shelters run by the agency. When a large enough group was gathered, they traveled up the Erie Canal by boat and then were placed on a train bound, in the early years, for upstate New York, and in later years when this area became saturated the trains traveled farther and farther away with many ending in the mid-west and some traveling as far as Texas. Agents of the society preceded the train into each town to organize a local placement committee of prominent citizens and to advertise the location and date that the children would be available for placement. When the day arrived, local families would inspect the children, and families who were deemed suitable by both the society's agent and the local committee could select one or more of them. *Suitable* generally meant that the family was Protestant, self-supporting, and had no members with criminal records or who were known to drink excessively or be overly prone to violence. The prospective guardians promised to take good care of the children and to provide them with a Christian home and a basic education.

The CAS was able to make a significant dent in the number of children living on the streets of New York. By 1873, the CAS was placing more than 3000 children per year. Its peak year was 1875, when a total of 4,026 children were placed. The picture of the orphan trains portrayed in recent years by popular history is that they were carrying mostly small children who were orphans looking for new families. This picture is incorrect in two ways. First, while many of the orphan train riders were actually orphans, the majority were not. Most were either half-orphans (having one living parent) or had two living parents. Second, most of the riders were not small children, but were boys between the ages of twelve and seventeen. In most cases they were not looking for new families at all, but were looking for jobs.

Although an innovative organization for its time, the CAS had serious problems both in terms of its philosophy and its technique, and shortly after it began its work, criticisms began to surface. In terms of philosophy, Brace and his organization were anti-urban, anti-immigrant, and anti-Catholic. The sum of these characteristics made the CAS anti-family, at least anti-family of origin (they were very much pro mythical wholesome midwestern farm foster family). Even when a young person had a living parent, the CAS was happy to sever ties with this parent in order to get the child out of the city and on to a farm. Brace viewed farm life as ideal for child development. In the Society's annual report, he stated that "for an outcast or homeless or orphan child, not tainted with bad habits, the best possible place of shelter and education, better than any prison or public institution, was the farmer's home."[14]

The CAS worked from the assumption that the parents of dependent or neglected children were morally inadequate and viewed its role as rescuing these children both from the parents and the city. Catholics accused the CAS of snatching Catholic children off the streets of New York and sending them out of the city to be reared in Protestant homes. Although there is no evidence that the CAS sought out Catholic children as a matter of policy, it is clear that when a Catholic child came under the agency's care, the child was placed in a Protestant home, which staff considered a victory for the child.

14. Verlene McOllough, "The Orphan Train Comes to Clarion," *Palimpsest* (Fall 1988), 145.

The most serious criticism of the CAS regarded the techniques it employed to make and then to follow up placements. Critics charged that the placement process was overly casual and characterized by a lack of study of prospective homes. In 1894, Hasting Hart, Secretary of the Minnesota State Board of Charities, made a careful study of the children placed in that state. He found that 58 percent of the placements made by the CAS had turned out badly. Hart concluded that the primary reasons for the high failure rate were that the children had been hastily placed and that there had not been sufficient supervision of the placements to afford them reasonable protection.[15] This high failure rate was supported by data from other out-placement agencies that did do careful follow-up on their placements. For example, children under the care of the Pennsylvania Children's Aid Society for more than a year often were placed in four or more homes.[16]

Although the CAS program had many flaws, the basic idea of placing dependent children in a family setting caught on and had a tremendous impact of the development of child welfare practice in the United States. Toward the end of the nineteenth century, members of the newly emerging social work profession—notably, John Finley of the New York State Charities Aid Association, Charles Birtwell of the Boston Children's Aid Society, and Homer Folks of the Children's Aid Society of Pennsylvania—began to develop systematic and sound administrative procedures for child placement. The system they developed was called boarding out, and had several differences from the placing out system. First, the advocates of boarding out argued that children should be placed close to home and ties with their families of origin should not be broken. In fact, the main objective of boarding out placements was the eventual reunification of the family. Second, the boarding out system provided payment to the homes so the children would not have to work for their keep. Charles Loring Brace, the originator of the placing out (orphan train) system vigorously opposed the idea of payment for child care, arguing that this vulgarized the home placement movement, turning a Christian ideal into a crass business arrangement. Finally, the developers of boarding out established thorough investigative procedures to be followed prior to a child being placed in a home. These agencies believed that because they were paying for the placement, they had a right to demand that the family meet and adhere to high standards.[17]

By the turn of the century, although the orphan trains would run for another twenty-nine years and orphanages would continue to have wide support, boarding out was becoming the response of choice for the problem of dependent children. This approach came to be referred to as foster care and is still a mainstay (although an increasingly embattled one) of our 21st century child protective services system.

15. Frank J. Bruno, *Trends in Social Work as Reflected in the Proceedings of the National Conference of Social Work, 1874–1946* (New York: Columbia University Press, 1946), 59–60.

16. Pricilla Clement, "Families and Foster Care: Philadelphia in the Late Nineteenth-Century," *Social Service Review* (53, 1979), 406–420.

17. Leroy Ashby, *Endangered Children: Dependency, Neglect, and Abuse in American History* (New York: Twayne, 1997), 72–75.

The New York Society for the Prevention of Cruelty to Children and the Idea of Child Protective Services

Psycho-historian Lloyd DeMause has noted that "A child's life prior to modern times was uniformly bleak. Virtually every childrearing tract from antiquity to the modern century recommended the beating of children."[18] Even though cruelty by parents and caretakers was common and fairly open, few cases of child abuse and neglect were acted upon by the courts prior to the late nineteenth century. Protecting children from maltreatment was particularly difficult due to the strength of the presumption that parents should be free to choose forms and severity of punishment.

In the nineteenth century the idea that children had no rights and that parents were free to treat their children in any way they desired began to slowly change. Social attitudes began to evolve that included a conception of children as beings with unique needs and the right to have these needs fulfilled to a reasonable extent. Sociologist Viviana Zelizer documents in her book *Pricing the Priceless Child* how during the nineteenth century the concept of the "useful" child who made a valuable contribution to the family economy gradually evolved into the "useless" child of the twentieth century: the child who is economically useless, in fact very costly, to the family but is considered to be emotionally priceless. The reasons for this transformation were many, including the decline in useful tasks that could be performed by children in a maturing industrial economy, the decline of the birth and death rates, and the rise of the compassionate family.[19] Courts slowly began to recognize this changing conception of childhood and parental rights and to affirm the right of the government to intervene in cases of child maltreatment. For example, the Pennsylvania state court denied a writ of habeas corpus to the father of Mary Ann Crouse who had petitioned to have custody returned to him from the House of Refuge of Philadelphia, saying in part: "That parents are ordinarily entrusted with [child rearing responsibility], is because it can seldom be put in better hands; but where they are incompetent or corrupt, what is there to prevent the public from withdrawing their faculties, held, as they obviously are, at its sufferance? The right of parental control is a natural, but not an inalienable one."[20] The changing view of children, combined with the enlightened view of jurists that parental rights result from the carrying out of parents' duties to their children, created an atmosphere in which laws and programs to protect children were possible.

This expansion of the conception of children's rights and the mitigation of parental rights was part of an overall humanitarian trend in the nineteenth century that included a moral revulsion against physical suffering. Historian James Turner has shown that this moral revulsion was one of the central ideas in the animal protection movement that began shortly following the end of the Civil War.[21] Henry Bergh, a wealthy New Yorker, had traveled the world as a young man, and had

18. Lloyd DeMause, "Our Forebears Made Childhood a Nightmare," *Psychology Today* (April 1975): 85–88.

19. Viviana Zelizer, *Pricing the Priceless Child: The Changing Social Value of Children* (Princeton, NJ: Princeton University Press, 1994).

20. Ex Parte *Crouse*, 4 Wharton (Pa.) 9 (1838). Reprinted in Robert H. Bremner, ed., *Children and Youth in America: A Documentary History*, Vol. 1 (Cambridge, MA: Harvard University Press, 1971), 691–693.

21. James Turner, *Reckoning with the Beast: Animals, Pain, and Humanity in the Victorian Mind* (Baltimore, MD: Johns Hopkins University Press, 2000).

been deeply offended by cruelty to animals he witnessed at bullfights in Spain and by the treatment of horses by peasants in Russia. After observing the work of England's Royal Society for the Prevention of Cruelty to Animals he returned to New York and began a similar society in 1865. It is interesting that Bergh was not an animal lover in the commonly used sense of the term. He once admitted, "I was never especially interested in animals—though I always had a natural feeling of tenderness for creatures that suffer. What struck me most forcibly was that mankind derived immense benefits from these creatures, and gave them in return not the least protection."[22]

It was to Bergh and the SPCA that a charity worker named Etta Wheeler turned with her concern about the treatment of Mary Ellen Wilson, an eight-year old girl that neighborhood residents reported was being horribly abused and neglected by her stepparents. Bergh, acting through the attorney for the SPCA, Elbridge Gerry, agreed to help and, amid much publicity, was successful in removing the child, prosecuting and jailing the stepmother, and placing the child in Sheltering Arms, a local institution for dependent children (Mary Ellen was later placed in the care of Wheeler's mother and, upon the mother's death, with her sister, where she remained until grown). Media coverage of the Wilson case caused a flood of public opinion demanding protection of children from such cruelty and in the passage in New York in 1875 of "an Act of the incorporation of societies for the prevention of cruelty to children." Like animal protection agents, employees of these new societies were empowered to "prefer a complaint before any court or magistrate having jurisdiction of the violation of any law relating to or affecting children."[23] They carried badges and were considered to be law enforcement officers.

By 1879 the work of the New York Society had spread to seven other cities, and within six years there were societies in 30 more, and Gerry reported on their activities:

> In New York City alone 604 complaints were received, 569 convictions secured, and 1,161 children were rescued. In Pennsylvania, 900 complaints were received and 2,212 children were rescued. In Massachusetts, 712 complaints were received and 1,350 children rescued. In Wisconsin, 399 complaints were received, 681 cases examined, and 81 convictions secured.[24]

In 1886 the American Humane Association, a national organization comprised of Societies for the Prevention of Cruelty to Animals, amended its charter to officially include children in its agenda. By 1900, the membership of the American Humane Association included 150 anti-cruelty or humane societies throughout the United States. Most dealt with both child and animal protection, but about 20 restricted their activities to the protection of children only.

22. Eric A. Shelman and Stephen Lazoritz, *The Mary Ellen Wilson Child Abuse Case and the Beginning of Children's Rights in 19th Century America* (Jefferson, NC: McFarland & Company, 2005), 30.

23. G. C. Williams, Introduction to Part II/Protection of Children Against Abuse and Neglect: Historical Background," in G. J. Williams and J. Money (Eds.), *Traumatic Abuse and Neglect of Children at Home* (Baltimore, MD: Johns Hopkins University Press, 1980), 47–52.

24. Elbridge T. Gerry. "The Relation of Societies for the Prevention of Cruelty to Children to Child Saving Work," in *Proceedings of the National Conference of Charities and Corrections"* (Madison, WI: Midland Publishing Company, 1882), 637–654.

The societies for the prevention of cruelty to children viewed themselves as law enforcement agencies rather than as charitable organizations. In this regard it is interesting, perhaps predictable, that the SPCCs were nearly entirely staffed by men, as compared to other social welfare agencies that became more and more female dominated over time.[25] Like law enforcement agencies (which they were, for all practical purposes), the societies investigated cases of abuse, neglect, and exploitation. If a complaint was substantiated, criminal charges were initiated against the perpetrators and custody papers filed. An annual report of the American Humane Association stated that the societies were never intended to reform children or families. Rather, they were

> A hand affixed to the arm of the law by which the body politic reaches out and enforces the law. The arm of the law seizes the child when it is in an atmosphere of impurity, or in the care of those who are not fit to be entrusted with it, wrenches the child out of these surroundings, brings it to the court, and submits it to the decision of the court.[26]

Once they gained custody of the child, agents would place the child in a home or institution and close the case. Only in cases of lost or kidnapped children did the society ever consider reuniting children with their parents.

The Societies for the Prevention of Cruelty to Children considered themselves to be preventive agencies, intervening and removing children before too much damage had been done by their inadequate parents. They looked askance at agencies such as the CAS that waited to intervene in a family until after the damage had been done. SPCC advocates would tell the parable of the children in the river to illustrate this point:

> [There was] a river down which children who had been thrown in further up, no one knew by whom, were being swept down to destruction, except for the few that people were able to save as they passed along. At last a practical man got a gun and went up the river to see what could be done to stop the supply.[27]

In keeping with this preventive, law enforcement focus, SPCC agents were very aggressive about case finding and sometimes skirted very close to the edge of the law in investigations and prosecutions.

Gordon has studied the work of the Massachusetts Society for the Prevention of Cruelty to Children (MSPCC), an early child protection agency, and this study provides an illustration of the work of child protection agencies in general. The MSPCC was established in 1878 and within three years had handled 2,017 cases involving 3,660 children. Gordon identifies the zeal of the agents as the primary reason for the early large caseloads of the agency. Rather than waiting for referrals, the agents went out into the streets looking for abuses to correct. They looked for children begging,

25. Mike Reid, "At Last a Practical Man Got a Gun," The Masculinity of Children's Aid, 1893–1912," *Ontario History* (Autumn 2011), 150–168.

26. Robert H. Bremner, ed., *Children and Youth in America: A Documentary History*, Vol. 2 (Cambridge, MA: Harvard University Press, 1971), 214.

27. Mike Reid, "At Last a Practical Man Got a Gun," 150.

children playing when they should have been in school, children improperly dressed or excessively dirty, and children working as street performers or peddlers. They also wrote letters to newspapers advertising their work and asking the public for referrals. As a result the number of cases coming from non-staff, known to the agency as complainants, soon outnumbered the cases discovered by staff. In addition to abuse, neglect, and abandonment by caretakers, the MSPCC directed attention to several phenomena that were, or at least were considered to be by the MSPCC, social problems. One was a system of child labor known as the *padrone* system, where children of poor Italian families were recruited for labor in the United States in return for payment to their parents who remained in Italy. After arrival in the United States the *padrone* would provide care for the child while keeping his earnings, creating a situation where gross exploitation of the child was likely. Another group that attracted the attention of the MSPCC was child theater and circus performers. The MSPCC believed that the theater threatened all of the values of middle-class, Protestant America, namely immorality, irreverence, immodesty, intemperance, and children's "precocity." A final target of the Massachusetts, as well as the New York, society was that of "baby farming." Under this practice women would contract and be paid for the care of abandoned infants, and after being paid would kill the infant. In Boston in 1890, in one particularly gruesome case, the bodies of thirty infants were found within three quarters of a mile of a commercial nursery.[28]

Gordon notes that "Social worker's bias in their view of clients has been a consistent problem in child-protection work. In the nineteenth century, it was at its worst, because the social distance between clients and workers was greatest." Most of the society's agents were white, Anglo-Saxon, protestant men, were probably teetotalers, and were among Boston's politically active supporters of prohibition. The clients were nearly always poor, and were Italian or Irish immigrants. The clients were drinkers of beer if Irish, and wine if Italian, lived in cramped apartments that the agents considered to be filthy and disreputable, ate diets involving olive oil and garlic, which the agents considered unappetizing, unhealthy, and probably over stimulating if not actually aphrodisiac. Two themes dominated the agents analyses of child maltreatment: drunkenness and the cultural inferiority of the immigrants. The agents were convinced of the cultural superiority of Americans as demonstrated by what was believed to be their more humane treatment of children. An agent reported in one case that the "mother will never bring up her children according to American standards." In another case the "Worker pointed out [to the mother] that there were standards here she would be expected to meet and that we were interested in helping her in this."[29]

Both the Children's Aid Societies and the Societies for the Prevention of Cruelty to Children built their work on a rock solid belief in the rightness of what they were doing, and supreme confidence that they were doing it correctly. When first faced with criticism about the techniques and results of outplacement, Brace responded by writing *The Dangerous Classes of New York*, a 648 page defense of his organizations methods and results. Nowhere in the book does he indicate any awareness of actual problems with the organization or any need for study or reform of its methods. This was not the case with the next organization to emerge during the nineteenth century, the Charity Organization Society (COS). While based on a bedrock of beliefs every bit as sturdy as

28. Linda Gordon, *Heroes of Their Own Lives: The Politics and History of Family Violence, Boston 1880–1960* (New York: Viking, 1988), 32–46.

29. Linda Gordon, *Heroes of Their Own Lives*, 46–47.

those of the Children's Aid Societies and the Societies for the Prevention of Cruelty to Children, the COS became aware very quickly about the lack of good information to inform its work, the complexity of the work it was doing and, consequently, the need for well-trained staff and research to inform their work. These concerns were to provide the starting point for the development of the profession of social work.

Poverty and Relief: The Charity Organization Society and Scientific Philanthropy

In the 1870s many people feared that the United States was coming apart. The country was gripped by a severe depression that lasted from 1873 to 1878, a depression that saw the economy decline by an estimated 32 percent, bank holding drop by 40 percent, the index of railroad stock prices decline by nearly 60 percent, and retail prices, already down in 1873 from their wartime peak, fall another 20 percent. While the effects of the economic downturn on the propertied classes were severe, the real problem was with the poor. The Bureau of Labor Statistics was still in the future, so figures on unemployment were inexact, but estimates were possible. The New York Society for Improving the Condition of the Poor estimated that the unemployment rate in the winter of 1873–74 was 25 percent and in the following winter had risen further to 33 percent. The Society's assistance rolls reflected this condition by soaring from approximately 5,000 families receiving aid in 1873 to 24,000 in 1874, and leveling off at about 20,000 per year for the remainder of the decade.[30]

Although the depression of 1873–78 was certainly not the first severe depression in U.S. history, it did have one new feature. This is that the problem was cast, at least partially, as a result of the relationship of labor to management with the result that radical proposals for social and economic restructuring were frequent. In Chicago a demonstration of twenty thousand persons demanded that the city provide public works jobs for the unemployed; in New York City a mass meeting of unemployed persons got out of control and resulted in a battle with the police in what became known as the Tompkins Square Riot. A report on the incident by the New York Society for Improving the Condition of the Poor concluded that the incident was the product of "well-known Communists, Internationalists, and Free-thinkers, with a sprinkling of sympathizing natives." Resulting from the "mischievous intentions" of these groups were cries for "a complete overthrow of the social and political system" and to "hang the thieves and robbers in Wall and Broad Streets."[31]

Much of the suffering of the poor and the sometimes violent response of the unemployed was blamed on the system, or more pointedly lack of a system, of relief. The number of charities had grown steadily during the century, but there was little in the way of systematic procedures or coordination among them. Critics asserted that at least half of the money raised for the victims of the depression was wasted on imposters and con artists, and the amount that actually reached the needy was more likely to degrade than to elevate them, or to even encourage their demands for

30. Samuel Rezneck, "Distress, Relief, and Discontent in the United States During the Depression of 1873–78," *Journal of Political Economy*, 58 (Dec. 1950), 495–498.

31. New York Society for Improving the Condition of the Poor, *Thirty First Annual Report* (1874), 33.

better wages and working conditions. The New York Society for Improving the Condition of the Poor criticized the "outgush of morbid sympathy," in the form of free lunches and free dormitories, as offering an invitation to tramps and encouragement to workers to stay out on strike against the reduction of wages and as contributing to the demoralization of the poor.[32] An editorial in the *Journal of Social Sciences* estimated that there were twenty thousand imposter paupers living on charity in New York City alone; that soup kitchens were driving low cost diners in the city out of business; that petty crime and begging by a hoard of tramps supported by unwise charities had increased; and, worst of all, "charity assisted labor in the combat to keep up wages."[33] The problem of disorganization and inefficiency in the charitable world was summed up by sociologist Charles Henderson as "There are too many societies, especially too many bad ones . . . They overlap, duplicate and interfere with each other. . . The business man is vexed and perplexed to know which society is worthy of his gifts and which deserves his curses."[34]

In response to the suffering caused by the depression and by the failure of existing charities to effectively relieve it, efforts were made to improve the system. As has always been common in America, reformers first looked to Europe for ideas. Two that were found were the London and Elberfeld plans. The central feature of both of these approaches was dividing a city into districts, employing visitors to investigate cases in each district, and setting up a central case registration bureau to minimize duplication and fraud. In 1873 versions of these plans were implemented in Germantown and Indianapolis and in 1876 the Co-operative Society of Volunteer Visitors among the Poor was founded in Boston shortly followed by the establishment of a Case Registration Bureau. The movement did not really gain traction, however, until 1877 when S. Humphries Gurteen, Assistant Rector of St. Paul's Episcopal Church, supported by parishioner and wealthy young businessman T. Guilford Smith, became concerned with the plight of the poor in Buffalo, New York.

Gurteen and Smith had become alarmed over the suffering of the poor resulting from the depression and from the bitter winter of 1876, and were even more concerned with the violence that had accompanied labor strikes during that year. The two decided to take steps to find solutions to the problem. As part of their plan Gurteen spent the summer of 1877 in London observing the work of the Royal Society for Organizing Relief and Repressing Mendicancy. Gurteen returned to Buffalo late in the summer of 1877 and he and Smith began to implement their plans by establishing the Buffalo Charity Organization Society based on the London model. Resulting mainly from the desperate need that civic leaders had for a solution to the problem of relief during the depression, but in no small measure to Gurteen's power as a speaker and skill as a proselytizer, the Buffalo plan spread quickly and soon became known as the Charity Organization Society (COS) movement. These societies, based on the Buffalo model, had been established in seven additional cities within two years, and the movement had grown to 92 societies by 1892, and to 150 in 1904. These new organizations were usually called Charity Organization Societies, but occasionally had names such as the Central Relief Association, Bureau of Associated Charities, United Charities,

32. New York Society for Improving the Condition of the Poor, Thirty First Annual Report (1874), 52.

33. Editor, *Journal of Social Sciences*, No. 6 (1874), 74.

34. Charles R. Henderson, "The Place and Functions of Voluntary Associations," *American Journal of Sociology*, 1 (Nov. 1895): 334.

or sometimes the Provident Association. Books, articles, and lectures by Josephine Shaw Lowell, founder and "guiding spirit" of the New York Charity Organization Society, notably *Public Relief and Private Charity* (1884), provided the theoretical and philosophical basis for the movement; works by S. Humphries Gurteen, notably *Phases of Charity* (1878) and *Handbook of Charity Organization* (1882), provided practical organizational guidance as specific as sample forms, by-laws, and job descriptions.

One of the basic principles behind the COS movement was opposition to outdoor public assistance. Outdoor public assistance was viewed by the propertied class that supported and participated in COS work as the first step down the road to socialism and, at very least, government siding with labor in their struggle against capital because, it was thought, the availability of public relief would drive up the wages demanded by people to go to work. Public relief, where available, was often distributed by urban political machines as a form of patronage, and such relief was viewed as encouraging sloth and fraud, and also exacerbating social divisions by breeding a sense of entitlement among the poor and resentment among taxpayers. COS supporters believed that public outdoor relief would quickly lead to the belief that assistance was a right and they firmly believed, on moral grounds, that not only was it not a right, but was an injustice to taxpayers. New York COS leader Josephine Shaw Lowell put it this way:

> Every dollar raised by taxation comes out of the pocket of some individual, usually a poor individual, and makes him so much the poorer, and therefore the question is between the man who earned the dollar by hard work, and needs it to buy himself and his family a day's food, and the man who, however worthy and suffering, did not earn it, but wants it to be given to him to buy himself and his family a day's food. If the man who earned it wishes to divide it with the other man, it is usually a desirable thing that he should do so, and at any rate it is more or less his own business, but that the law, by the hand of a public officer, should take it from him and hand it over to the other man, seems to be an act of gross tyranny and injustice . . .

Lowell believed that very few people would work if they could be supported by someone else. Her opinion of public relief was "The less that is given, the better for everyone, the giver and the receiver."[35] The COS movement was viewed as a demonstration that the private sector could deal with the problem of poverty and unemployment in urban America and that involvement of the government was not necessary. The COS, along with other social forces, was successful in reducing the amount of public outdoor relief available. Beginning in the 1870s, cities across America abolished public outdoor relief. By 1900 such relief had been eliminated in New York, Baltimore, St. Louis, Washington, D.C., San Francisco, Kansas City, New Orleans, Louisville, Denver, Atlanta, Memphis, Charleston, S.C., Pittsburgh, and others.[36]

The most basic operational principle of the COS movement was that stated in its name—the coordination and rationalization of the provision of poor relief. The original idea of the COS

35. Josephine Shaw Lowell, "The Economic and Moral Effects of Public Outdoor Relief," *Proceedings of the National Conference of Charities and Corrections,* 1890 (Boston, 1890), 81–82.

36. Walter Trattner, *From Poor Law to Welfare State: A History of Social Welfare in the United States,* 6th ed. (New York: Free Press, 1999), 90.

was that it would not give any direct relief to poor people, but would instead serve as a central record keeping and referral center. COS offices frequently had signs out front reading "No relief given here," and one of the mottos of the movement was "Not alms, but a friend." Mrs. Lowell is reported to have answered the question of how much of a donor's gift would go to direct relief of poor people by saying "Not one cent."[37] The plan was that every agency in a city would turn over their application process to the COS. When a person applied for assistance the agency or individual being petitioned would refer the person to the COS. At the COS the applicant would be interviewed, a record set up, and the person's claims would be investigated by a salaried District Agent. After compiling all available information on the applicant the case would be referred to the volunteer District Committee and this group would make decisions regarding whether the person was "worthy" of relief, if so what kind and how much, and which agency was most appropriate to provide the assistance. The District Committee would then refer the person to the selected agency and would follow the case keeping careful records of all help the applicant was given. Finally, the District Committee would assign the case to a volunteer friendly visitor who would work with the family with the goal of finding solutions to problems that were preventing them from being self-supporting. It was thought that by administering charity in this way that fraud and duplication would be eliminated, charity would be put on a business like footing, and long term dependency would be prevented. COS advocates believed that there was plenty of money already available to adequately assist all of the needy; all that was needed was to ably and efficiently administer it.

Central to the COS idea of efficient administration of charity was the principle of repression of pauperism. A pauper, as the COS used the term, was a person who had been given relief unwisely, with no requirements for work or expectation of reform, and was thereby rendered forever unwilling to work and to be self-supporting. He or she was the Sacculina described by Oscar McCulloch in the paper summarized at the opening of this chapter. Reverend Gurteen railed against ". . . the fatal effects of indiscriminate charity upon the *individual*; how it unmans him, by destroying all self-respect and independence and ambition; how it encourages idleness and unthriftiness and improvidence." Even more serious than the effect of pauperism on individuals was the threat it posed to society: "Socially considered, the treatment of pauperism is a matter which bears directly upon our own homes, and our own safety in life and property." Gurteen drew an analogy between pauperism and Frankenstein's monster and even went so far as to attribute the decline and fall of the Roman Empire to indiscriminant charity and the accompanying growth of pauperism. Gurteen estimated that if agencies could be prevented from giving aid to unworthy or dishonest applicants, thereby contributing to their pauperization, that the cost of charity could be reduced by as much as fifty percent.[38]

The Charity Organizations took the idea of personal service, pioneered by the Associations for Improving the Condition of the Poor, and raised it to a whole new level, making it a central part of the COS approach. Josephine Shaw Lowell stressed that all true charity should "tend to raise the character and elevate the moral nature, and so improve the condition of those toward whom it is exercised." She stated the great rule of charity as "that the best help of all is to help people to

37. Robert H. Bremner, "Scientific Philanthropy," 1873–93," *Social Service Review* 30 (1956): 168–173.

38. S. Humphreys Gurteen, *A Handbook of Charity Organization* (Buffalo, New York: Published by the Author, 1882), 44.

help themselves."[39] Gurteen argued that "the chief need of the poor to-day, is not alms-giving, but the *moral support of true friendship*—the possession of a real friend, whose education, experience and influence, whose general knowledge of life, or special knowledge of domestic economy are placed at the service of those who have neither the intelligence, the tact nor the opportunity to extract the maximum of good from their slender resources." To provide this personal service the Charity Organizations recruited a corps of friendly visitors. Basic guidelines for the provision of friendly visiting were that the visitors were not to provide any material assistance, only guidance and support; they were under no circumstances to proselytize, and they were only to work with a few cases so they would have adequate time and energy for each one (Gurteen felt that one case per visitor would be ideal). Gurteen recommended the following process to guide the work of the friendly visitor:

- The visitor should first determine if the dwelling and neighborhood in which the recipient lives is "free from any immoral taint." If it is not the visitor should "urge removal to some more desirable dwelling . . . since no reform can be expected as long as parents and children are exposed to the contaminating influences of immoral surroundings."
- The visitor should determine if relatives are doing all that they can to assist in support of the family. This task is an extension of the concern with pauperization in that, just as individuals can come to rely on charity, indiscriminate and over generous relief by unwise charitable agencies can cause relatives to neglect their responsibilities.
- If the family is found to be entitled to relief, the visitor should make sure such relief is adequate and given promptly.
- The visitor should ascertain if the dwelling is up to code and not endangering the health of the residents and, if it is not, refer the matter to the District Committee "in order that a complaint may be made to the proper authorities and redress may be had."
- At the stage of the work where a family has become self-supporting, the visitor should endeavor to inculcate provident ideas and foster provident habits. Gurteen instructed visitors that "It must ever be borne in mind that the poor are seldom provident for themselves; they know little, if anything, of the laws of health or of domestic economy . . . In all these matters, and in others which we need not enumerate, the Visitor should place time, experience and education at the service of the poor. . . ."
- Finally, the visitor should be knowledgeable about other organizations in the city that could be helpful to a particular family and make referrals as appropriate. In this regard Gurteen particularly recommended child care centers (which he called Creches) and penny saving banks.

It is remarkable to note the smugness with which early COS participants approached their work. They cloaked their work in the shroud of Christian caring and sympathy, but it was pretty obvious that protection of the wealthy and control of the poor was their main agenda. They sought to cultivate relations of friendship between the rich and the poor, but there was no question of the

---

39. Michael Katz, *In the Shadow of the Poorhouse: A Social History of Welfare in America*, Tenth Anniversary Edition (New York: Basic Books, 1996), 74.

superiority of the rich. "We could not," Mrs. Lowell stated, "be charitable to our equals."[40] The worthy poor were viewed as not vicious or mean, but as wayward children incapable of discerning their own best interests. Their well-being would be improved if the rich and prosperous assumed the responsibilities of moral guardianship. The visitor was supposed to be sure families followed the advice they were offered, that they used any relief they were granted wisely, that they lived upstanding moral lives, that their children attended school, and that they recognized the value of work and the shame of receiving charity. In his study of the Chicago COS Kusmer concluded that "Many of the programs . . . can only be described as an attempt to impose bourgeois values on the poor."[41] Katz summarizes the role of the friendly visitor as ". . . to be at once a sympathetic friend, an official, a teacher, and a spy."[42]

Many people at the time recognized that the COS philosophy and methods were disingenuous, coercive, and condescending, and criticized the organization as such. In what is probably the most famous quote about the COS at the time, poet John Boyle O'Reilly wrote: "That Organized Charity, scrimped and iced, In the name of a cautious, statistical Christ." The Reverend James O. S. Huntington criticized the movement for its tendency to judge the worthiness of individuals by business standards, and for holding the poor accountable to standards of truthfulness and labor that were not applied to the well-to-do. Jane Addams spoke of the difficulties that volunteer friendly visitors encountered when they attempted to apply COS standards and methods to the lives of the poor they were assigned to help. She observed that the visitor was obliged by the Society to confine her work with families to what Addams called the industrial virtues, insisting that they must work and be self-supporting. The sensitive visitor, observed Addams, soon realizes "that she has no right to say these things; that she herself has never been self-supporting; that, whatever her virtues may be, they are not the industrial virtues; that her untrained hands are no more fitted to cope with actual conditions than are those of her broken-down family."[43]

Historian Michael Katz has studied the COS in the nineteenth century and concluded that it was a failure in every aspect of its work. He documents that although part of the original COS creed was to never give material relief, almost all agencies soon did so; that the COS intended to make public outdoor relief unnecessary, but that private relief never was successful in even equaling the amount of public aid, much less replacing it; that by never embracing the problems of workers the organizations became increasingly irrelevant to issues of labor; and finally that, as illustrated by the fact that more contributions to COS agencies were used for administrative purposes than for aid to the poor, the agencies were inherently inefficient.[44] Katz is correct in judging the COS movement to have been a failure if it is judged, as he does, on its original goals. However, what Katz fails to acknowledge is that based on other criteria the movement was a great success. This criteria is that the COS movement was the first approach to social welfare problems that demonstrated a willingness to learn, and to be open to change based on what was learned. COS

40. Josephine Shaw Lowell, *Public Relief and Private Charity* (New York, 1884), 89.

41. Kenneth L. Kusmer, "The Functions of Organized Charity in the Progressive Era: Chicago as a Case Study," *The Journal of American History* 60 (1973), 657–678.

42. Michael Katz, *In the Shadow of the Poorhouse*, 79.

43. Jane Addams, "The Subtle Problems of Charity," *The Atlantic Monthly* (February 1899), 164.

44. Michael Katz, *In the Shadow of the Poorhouse*, 83–87.

leaders were enthusiastic participants and often leaders in the National Conference of Charities and Corrections that we have previously described as an organization devoted to the scientific study of social problems and societal responses to these problems. In the context of the NCCC the COS leaders studied the problem of poverty and the methods they employed to deal with it. They studied the issues and quickly learned a great deal, and based on this new information began to modify their approach, something no previous social welfare organization had done. As Bremner has noted, "The important thing was that charity workers came into daily contact with the problem [poverty] and were constantly seeking answers to it."[45]

Just what did the COS learn? First the movement learned to question, if not entirely dismiss, the belief that goes back to the earliest English poor laws that the poor can be divided into the worthy and the unworthy. The Reverend Gurteen argued in his COS handbooks that most applicants for relief were imposters and frauds. He advised, "Refrain from giving a single cent until the individual case of each applicant has been thoroughly examined. The money which will be saved to the community by this means . . . will pay the additional expense involved, and leave a handsome surplus to the city."[46] A mere five years later COS and National Conference leader Alexander Johnson argued that there was no such thing as the "unworthy poor" and that charity workers, rather than classifying people into groups of worthy and unworthy should devote themselves to the scientific analysis of poverty.[47] In her 1897 guide for friendly visitors, Mary Richmond argued that the terms "worthy" and "unworthy" mean very little, and that their actual function is to "save us from thinking." She further argued that rather than being concerned with hard and fast classifications of cases that friendly visitors should devote themselves to the principle that "our relief should always have a future to it, should be given as part of a carefully devised plan for making the recipient permanently better off."[48]

As a corollary to rejecting the classification of the poor into groups of worthy and unworthy, the COSs steadily deemphasized the detective and repressive aspects of their work. In his handbooks, sermons, and public addresses, Gurteen hammered home the point that the first object of charity organization was "the repressing of pauperism." Early leaders in the organizations regarded the apprehension of imposters as the principle function of the investigations conducted by COS agents. They considered the files and family history data collected by each society as mainly means of exposing fraud and eliminating duplication. By the 1880s the societies began to downplay these functions and to emphasize the constructive purposes of investigation (which gradually became known as social case histories and later as assessments). They began to view detection of fraud and repression of pauperism as incidental to the positive benefits of scientific philanthropy, and defined investigations as the necessary prerequisite to the intelligent treatment of distress. Boston COS leader and social work education pioneer Zilpha Drew Smith asserted, "The possibility of imposture is not so much to be guarded against as the constant danger of mistakes . . . Two-thirds of the errors in charity work arise from misinformation or lack of information."[49]

45. Robert H. Bremner, "Scientific Philanthropy," 1873–93, 172.

46. S. Humphries Gurteen, *Handbook of Charity Organization*, 30.

47. Alexander Johnson, *Methods and Machinery of Organized Charity* (Chicago, 1887).

48. Mary E. Richmond, *Friendly Visiting Among The Poor: A Handbook for Charity Workers* (New York: Macmillan, 1899), 154.

49. Zilpha D. Smith, "Report of the Committee on Organization of Charities," *Proceedings of the National Conference of Charities and Correction, 1888* (Boston: George H. Ellis, 1888), 126–127.

At their beginning the Charity Organization Societies had an extreme individualistic explanation of the causes of poverty based on a pessimistic view of human nature. Josephine Shaw Lowell expressed her belief that "the usual cause of poverty is to be found in some deficiency—moral, mental, or physical—in the person who suffers." She assumed that people would not work if they could find any way not to, and that when pressure to work was relaxed workers inevitably tended to become idlers.[50] This belief began to change following an agreement among Charity Organizations, made at the 1888 National Conference of Charities and Corrections, to develop a schedule of causes of poverty to be used by all the societies with the data aggregated annually. The data they collected indicated that less than one-quarter of all COS cases were poor due to reasons of "personal misconduct" such as drinking, immorality, or laziness. They found that the explanation of poverty far more frequently lay in what they termed "causes indicating misfortune." These were mostly things that we would now identify as environmental causes, things such as a mother whose husband had been imprisoned, children who were orphaned or abandoned, unemployment due to economic conditions, underemployment or employment at a salary too low to live on, work caused disability, and similar factors largely out of the control of the person.[51] Based on this data, along with other emerging research such as Robert Hunter's classic study *Poverty*, COS leaders began to modify the organizations pessimistic individualistic explanation of poverty and substitute an analysis that recognized the importance of environmental factors. In 1895 Boston COS leader Robert Treat Paine speculated that much, if not most, causes of poverty and related problems were social rather than individual and if this were true, "how vain to waste our energies on single cases of relief when society should aim at removing the prolific sources of all woe." A year later, Josephine Shaw Lowell added her opinion: "It seems often as if [the] charities are the insults which the rich add to the injuries . . . they heap upon the poor."[52]

One more major lesson that was learned by the COS movement was that while the idea of personal service as an adjunct to material aid was extremely valuable, this was not something that could be effectively done by an all-volunteer staff. There were two reasons that the practice of relying on volunteers proved insufficient to the task. The first is the problem, familiar to any present day volunteer coordinator, of the fact that the number of volunteers, and the number of hours they were able to devote to the job, was never near adequate. Boston, which with 870 friendly visitors in 1884 was recognized for having the most successful volunteer recruitment program of any COS in the nation, served 160,000 families during its first ten years of operation, but was able to assign a friendly visitor to fewer than twenty five percent of these cases. Compounding this problem was that as opportunities for volunteer social reform activities for women increased during the late nineteenth century, the number signing on as COS friendly visitors declined. The annual reports of the New York COS indicate that the agency had 130 friendly visitors active in 1884, 109 in 1887, 71 in 1888, and by 1892 the number had declined to 58.

50. Kenneth L. Kusmer, "The Functions of Organized Charity in the Progressive Era," 670.

51. Amos G. Warner, *American Charities: A Study in Philanthropy and Economics* (New York: Thomas Y. Crowell & Company, 1894), 31–36.

52. Walter I. Trattner, *From Poor Law to Welfare State: A History of Social Welfare in America*, 6th ed. (New York: The Free Press, 1999), 101–102.

The second reason that volunteers were found to not be up to the task of providing effective social treatment is that as district agents and volunteers began the task of helping families it soon became apparent that the job required much more than a friendly manner and a willing spirit. As Leighninger has noted in her history of social work education, "it soon became clear that . . . on-the-job, rule-of-thumb training could not give people the broad principles and theory necessary for a consistent and effective practice of charitable work."[53] By the late years of the century, COS agencies, prominently in New York and Boston but also in Baltimore, Chicago, and St. Louis, had taken steps to initiate formal training programs to prepare people for the work of charity organization district agents. Beginning in 1890 Zilpha Drew Smith at the Boston COS began the practice of hiring an agent in training "in order that she may be trained in the details of the society's work and be ready to take a position as agent if required." In 1898 she expanded this into a formal study class for agents in training and volunteers, as well as staff of other charity agencies. By 1905 Ms. Smith's efforts had been expanded into the Simmons College School for Social Workers, one of the earliest uses of the term "social worker" to refer to a formal occupation.[54] In 1894 Anna Dawes presented a paper in which she called for training not so much of friendly visitors or district agents, but for agency executives. She lamented that "it is today impossible to get a suitable superintendent of charities . . . because no one knows anything about how to carry on the work . . . What is needed, it seems to me, is some course of study where an intelligent young person can. . . . be taught what is now the alphabet of charitable science—some knowledge of its underlying ideas, its tried and trusted methods."[55] In 1898, under the leadership of Charity Organization Society President Robert W. de Forest, a six-week summer course called the New York School of Philanthropy was initiated. This course quickly grew to a full academic year, affiliated with Columbia University and eventually became the Columbia University School of Social Work. Concurrent with the development of training programs for charity workers was the developing sentiment that the work constituted a career, a potential profession even, and as such provided the seeds for what was to grow into the profession of social work.

The state of the Charity Organization Society movement as the 19th century drew to a close can be illustrated by three groups of significant participants in the movement. The first group was comprised of hard line COS ideologues such as S. Humphries Gurteen. This group had become involved in COS work based on rigid conservative beliefs that poverty was almost entirely the result of moral defects among the poor, and that the main purpose of the COS was to organize charity in such a way that the poor were prevented from taking advantage of the well-to-do in society. As COS experience and research began to collect strong data that largely refuted these beliefs, and the approach of the organization began to change to reflect this new knowledge of the dynamics of poverty, people like Gurteen, rather than abandon their cherished ideals, quietly withdrew from participation

53. Leslie Leighninger, *Creating a New Profession: The Beginnings of Social Work Education in the United States* (Alexandria, VA: Council on Social Work Education, 2000), 1.

54. Zilpha D. Smith, Associated Charities of Boston, U.S., "The Training of District Agents, 1890—1899," Simmons College Archives, MS9, B1, F5; Zilpha D. Smith, Associated Charities of Boston, U.S.A., "Study Class. 1898—1900," Simmons College Archives, MS9, B1, F6; Simmons College, Boston, October 12, 1905, "Course of Twenty Lectures on Philanthropic Problems and Practice," Simmons College Archives, MS9, B1, F18.

55. Anna Dawes, "The Need for Training Schools for a New Profession," in A. G. Warner, ed., *Sociology in Institutions of Learning* (Baltimore, MD: Johns Hopkins Press, 1894), 14–20.

in the organization. The case of Gurteen himself is interesting. At about the time he was at the peak of his COS prominence, his clerical career began to unravel. Shortly after Easter in 1880 Gurteen was dismissed from his position as Assistant Rector of St. Paul's Church in Buffalo. He went from Buffalo to Toledo Ohio to take a position as Rector of Trinity Church. This job lasted only a little over a year, once again ending in his dismissal. In both cases his dismissal appears to have been over his insistence on adopting an Anglo-Catholic, "high church" form of worship that was contrary to the less formal Protestant style preferred by American congregations. Following this second dismissal, Gurteen tried to reenter the COS movement, this time as a paid employee by becoming General Secretary of the newly formed Chicago COS, a position he assumed in 1883. This job also did not work out, with Gurteen resigning after one year. There appear to be two reasons for Gurteen leaving this job. The first is that his views were somewhat out of sync with emerging mainstream COS attitudes and this probably put him in conflict with the current and sophisticated Chicago board. The second reason is that during this year he married the wealthy heiress Edith Carpenter, putting Gurteen, for the first time in his life, in a position where he did not need to work. Following his marriage Gurteen made several claims regarding his professional activities, none of which can be verified by records and for many reasons are subject to doubt. He claimed to have worked as an administrator and professor at Griswold College in Iowa, and further claimed that the college awarded him two honorary doctorates, a D.D. and a LL.D. Gurteen claimed to have received these degrees in the 1890s, but by this time Griswold College had closed. Also in the 1890s he published a couple of books, one on the tales of Arthur and the other on the songs of Caedmon, and on the title pages of both he lists himself as having an MA degree from Cambridge University. It is likely that he had a BA from that university, but no record exists of his having attended graduate school. The truth appears to be that following his leaving the Chicago COS job, and marrying into money, Gurteen adopted a life of leisure, living in a house in Gramercy Park New York and spending summers hosting afternoon wine and cheese receptions at his (actually his wife's) summer house near Jamestown Rhode Island.[56] In his time as a COS leader Gurteen railed against three types of people who he saw as major threats to society. These were posers, frauds, and paupers (defined by Gurteen as people who refuse to work once they learn that they could get someone to support them). It is a delicious irony that, in the end, Gurteen turned out to be all three.

The second group of Charity Organization leaders are those, illustrated by the journey of Josephine Shaw Lowell, who read and pondered the emerging research and data on the causes of poverty and suffering and, rather than throwing up their hands and withdrawing from the movement, integrated it into their thinking and broadened out their reform efforts beyond the boundaries of the COS movement. Historian Joan Waugh has documented Lowell's commitment to the application of social science to philanthropy and her resulting ". . . growing ability to recognize the complexity of the conditions of poverty that were being observed and studied."[57] Based on her emerging understanding of the dynamics of poverty Lowell, while still leading the New York COS, devoted an increasing proportion of her time to supporting the labor movement, playing an active role in settling labor conflicts, defending worker's right to strike, and advocating for

56. Verl S. Lewis, "Stephen Humphries Gurteen and the American Origins of Charity Organization," *Social Service Review* 1966, 40 (2), 190–201.

57. Joan Waugh, "Give This Man Work," *Social Science History* 25, no. 2 (Summer 2001): 220.

industrial conciliation on fair terms. In 1891 she helped found the Consumers' League of the City of New York, an advocacy group formed to protest the oppressive working conditions of women who were employed as department store clerks. Observing the life in New York slums, Lowell asked, "Where is fresh air to be found? Where is there any refuge from crowds and filth and vileness? There is scarcely an open place to be found in the crowded parts of the city; the children can only play in the gutters. . . The dead monotony of a life of poverty and labor must have some break, something to change the horror of incessant squalid misery. The mere physical exhaustion consequent on bad air, bad food, insufficient clothing calls for a stimulant."[58] This recognition of the complexity and environmental dimension of poverty led Lowell, as noted by Katz, "through scientific charity to the left wing of respectable reform."[59] In stark contrast to Gurteen and his supporters who were involved with the COS movement precisely because it was a means of repressing of the poor and defending the wealthy, Lowell reflected, "If the charity organization societies of the country are going to take the position of defenders of the rich against the poor which I do think is the danger. . . then I shall be very sorry that I ever had anything to do with the work."[60]

The final group of people to evolve within the COS movement were staff of the agencies. When the charity organizations had begun in the 1870s staff were low level, very poorly paid, and were expected to be handmaidens to the volunteer boards and friendly visitors. As the century progressed and the complexity of the task became more clear to organization leaders, staff began to advocate for improvement of their status and eventually became so bold as to argue that what they were doing was a profession on par with any other profession and deserving of equivalent status and reward. These were people such as Mary Richmond, who began work for the Baltimore COS as assistant treasurer and, when her intelligence and competence were quickly recognized, was promoted to general secretary (a position that would now be called executive director) of the agency. She went from Baltimore to Philadelphia where she directed its prominent COS, and then became director of the Charity Organization Department of the Russell Sage Foundation, one of the first privately funded research/think tanks. From these platforms she worked to develop social casework into a science, advocate for professional education, and lobby for improved status of the profession. In a similar pattern, Zilpha Drew Smith rose to become Associate Director of the Boston Charity Organization Society and worked to develop social work theory, methods, and data, and to transmit these to new workers through increasingly formalized training programs, eventually helping found the Simmons College School for Social Workers. Entering on a slightly different path was Edward T. Devine, a Johns Hopkins educated economist who was hired by Josephine Shaw Lowell in 1896 to direct the New York COS. Devine and Lowell worked together to explain the structural and environmental aspects of charity practice. As Waugh has noted, "Because of the forces they themselves set in motion with their support of a 'science' of charity, professionals were replacing devoted, unpaid volunteers (leaders and workers). With the change, which took place with great rapidity after the 1893 depression and into the first decades of the twentieth century, a professional ideal of objectivity replaced the passionate advocacy of the amateurs."[61]

58. Joan Waugh, "Give This Man Work," 231.
59. Michael Katz, *In the Shadow of the Poorhouse,*" 70.
60. Joan Waugh, "Give This Man Work," 231.
61. Joan Waugh, "Give This Man Work," 240.

THE SOCIAL SETTLEMENTS: APPROACHING
SOCIAL ISSUES FROM ANOTHER DIRECTION

A movement that was to prove of great import for the development of social welfare and social work developed during the final years of the nineteenth century and represented a fresh, new, perspective on social, particularly urban, issues in the United States. This is what was called the settlement house movement. Like many ideas in American social welfare the settlement movement was a transplant from England. An Anglican clergyman, Canon Samuel Barnett, shared a concern with his COS associates that a huge gap had developed between the social classes and that this gap posed a threat to the future of English society. Barnett believed that working men in the lower strata of society were cut off from culture and civilization and that college men from the upper crust of society were cut off from the actual work of the world and were restless for something useful to do. The idea Barnett hit upon to address this problem was to have college men move into St. Jude's "the worst parish in London" and get to know their neighbors and do what they could to help them improve their lives. To this end he built what was essentially a fraternity house in a London slum and moved a group of Oxford University graduates into the building which he soon christened Toynbee Hall, in memory of Arnold Toynbee, an Oxford University political economist who died at the age of thirty after authoring a book in which he coined the term "industrial revolution." Toynbee Hall was strongly Protestant in nature in that Barnett hoped that it would lead to a spiritual reawakening of both the laborer and the university man. Barnett believed "that the things which make men alike are finer and better than the things that keep them apart, and that these basic likenesses . . . easily transcend the less essential difference of race, language, creed, and tradition."[62]

Several young Americans touring Europe visited Toynbee Hall and came away impressed and convinced that Barnett's idea should be tried in the United States. The first was Stanton Coit who was traveling Europe following the receipt of a Ph.D. from the University of Berlin. Coit spent three months at Toynbee hall and returned to New York to found the Neighborhood Guild in 1888, renamed University Settlement in 1891. Shortly after Coit's visit, Jane Addams and her college classmate, Ellen Gates Starr, visited Toynbee Hall in 1887. They returned to Chicago and in 1889 founded Hull House, easily the most famous settlement house in history. The settlement idea caught on and grew rapidly in the U.S. In 1891 there were six settlements in the country, in 1897 there were seventy-four, and by the turn of the century there were over one hundred.

Unlike other proto-social workers in the nineteenth century, those in both the child protection and COS movements, who would enter a community from the outside, do their work, and then leave as soon as they were done, the settlement workers actually lived in the communities they sought to serve. Many settlement workers were college students who would live and work at a settlement house in return for receiving their room and board. Many were young professionals who pursued other careers during the business week lived in a settlement and provided services such as teaching classes or leading groups in evenings and weekends. This resulted in what would

---

62. Jane Addams, *Twenty Years at Hull House* (New York: Macmillan Publishing Company, 1938), 112.

turn out to be one of the most significant contributions of the settlement movement to the development of social welfare in the United States—the large number of young men and women who lived in settlements for a brief period and then continued their lives in their chosen professions with a heightened perception and expanded knowledge of social problems of urban America. Hull House it has been said probably had a greater influence on those who lived there than it did on those it sought to help. Davis and McCree observe: "Those who were influenced over the years by the atmosphere of intellectual freedom and by the amazing group of people at the settlement reads like a twentieth century Who's Who, and in itself is enough to insure the importance of Hull House in any account of recent history."

Whereas the people in the COS movement were becoming concerned with developing methods and techniques for helping the poor, the settlement workers only wanted to become neighbors. Their methodology, if it can even be called that, consisted of moving into a community, always low income and usually immigrant, and just getting to know the residents and waiting for them to say what it was that they needed. The settlement workers "tried, sometimes with limited success, to be more than missionaries from the outside, to become part of the community they sought to change."[63] While the COS viewed the individual or family as the client, the settlements focused on the community. Where the COS would work case-by-case to obtain child care for clients, a settlement would open a kindergarten for the entire neighborhood. Where the COS would work to get an individual help in qualifying for citizenship, the settlement would develop an Americanization class. Typical programs offered by settlements were adult education, child care, clubs for children and adults, citizenship classes, discussion groups often focusing on literature or politics, playgrounds and gyms for community residents, art classes and galleries, musical groups, as well as many other activities based on community needs and desires.

The settlements stressed the social and economic causes of poverty rather than the individual causes. Whereas the philosophy of the charity organizations led to private charity and spiritual uplift, the philosophy of the settlements led to social and economic change. The settlements stressed the neighborhood ideal and rejected the idea of enlightened self-interest, emphasizing instead the interdependence of social groups in an organically structured society. It would probably not be an over statement to say that the currently popular strengths based approach to social work has its origins in the settlement movement. Other social agencies in the nineteenth century assumed that society was functional and that if a person had problems fitting in it was undoubtedly due to some kind of personal defect that should be corrected. The settlements, on the other hand, assumed that in many cases it was the individual who was capable of adequate functioning and personal problems were often the result of some defect in the social and economic system. One settlement advocate suggested that the settlement was "a great modern protest against the heresy that wealth makes character, that education can establish an aristocracy; that one can rise to a social pinnacle without obligation to those who have contributed to that rise."[64]

During the early years of the settlement house movement there was often open hostility between the settlements and the charity organization societies. For their part the settlement

---

63. Allen F. Davis *Spearheads for Reform: The Social Settlements and the Progressive Movement, 1890–1914* (New York: Oxford University Press, 1967), 6.

64. Allen F. Davis, *Spearheads for Reform*, 18.

residents accused the COS people of being guided by ". . . an unconscious division of the world into the philanthropists and those to be helped. It is an assumption of two classes, and against this class assumption our democratic training revolts as soon as we begin to act upon it."[65] For their part the charity organizations were critical, almost contemptuous, of the settlements lack of interest in expert technique as can be illustrated by the following joke popular with COS staff: A settlement worker is walking down a city street and comes upon a drunk lying in the gutter. The worker stares down at the man and says "I can't do anything to help you, my friend, but I'll be glad to sit in the gutter beside you." This strain between the two movements lasted only a brief period as the leaders quickly recognized that they were concerned with the same issues and were approaching them from two equally legitimate perspectives. The National Conference of Charities and Corrections soon became common ground where settlement and COS leaders shared ideas and research. Julie Lathrop of Hull House was the first settlement worker invited to address the conference, this happening in 1894. In 1896 the Conference planned a whole section for settlement house issues. Shortly after the turn of the century a permanent department of the Conference was established called Neighborhood Improvement, which, of course, was the settlement house area of interest and expertise. The spirit of cooperation between the two movements became cemented as more and more COS workers and leaders became, sometimes for short periods and sometimes for extended stays, residents and volunteer workers in various settlement houses.[66]

SOCIAL SERVICES FOR BLACK AMERICANS DURING THE LATE NINETEENTH CENTURY

The history of social welfare we have been discussing in this chapter is largely a white history. Emerging social service agencies served a very diverse population, but it was diverse in terms of ethnicity, religion, and nationality, not race. A large proportion of the clientele served by Charity Organizations, children's homes, and orphan trains were first or second generation immigrants, Italians, Irish, Germans, and increasingly Eastern Europeans who were often Jewish, but they served few blacks. The neglect of this part of the population can be illustrated by Amos Warner's 1894 book American Charities that was the source authority on social welfare at the time. This book does not even have a single entry in the index for "negroes" or "colored," the terms that would have been used at the time to refer to the black population. Frank Dekker Watson's 1921 history of the charity organization movement includes only one reference to the black population, this being: "one is not surprised to learn that the problem of family rehabilitation among negroes . . . has remained largely untouched. During the period under review [1877–1921] the feeling seemed to have been fairly general that it was wiser to concentrate on the problem of poverty among the whites, leaving that among the colored for the future."[67]

65. Jane Addams, "The Subtle Problems of Charity," The Atlantic Monthly (February 1899), 163.

66. Allen F. Davis, Spearheads for Reform, 21–22.

67. Amos Warner, American Charities; Frank Dekker Watson, The Charity Organization Movement in the United States (New York: Macmillan, 1922), 357–358.

The vast majority of settlement houses focused their services on one neighborhood which, in the pattern of the time, was generally an ethnically homogeneous one. A few settlements, notably Lillian Wald's Henry Street Settlement, founded in 1893, and Mary Kingsbury Simkovitch's Greenwich House founded in 1902, both in New York, were open to the black population living in lower Manhattan. Other settlements opened segregated branches to serve African Americans. However, the mainstream settlement movement was, like the majority of social services at the time, primarily white.

Because blacks were largely excluded from services of existing social service organizations, they developed services on their own. Many of these services were provided by a black variation on the settlement house movement. The mainstream settlement movement, as discussed in this chapter, traces its roots to England and Toynbee Hall. The black settlement movement had different roots and, in fact, appears to have predated the white movement by a number of years. The black settlement house movement originated in institutional churches (sometimes white, but usually black) that after the Civil War began to establish missions in the rural south and, as black immigration to northern cities increased, in the new black neighborhoods of these cities.

Probably the first of what Luker calls proto-settlement houses was the New York Colored Mission.[68] This mission, supported by the Quakers, purchased a building in the Tenderloin district and began a school for black children. Within a short time the mission added a number of social service programs of a type that would become common among the later emerging white settlements. Among these were a nursery, a medical clinic, home visitors, an employment bureau, a temporary housing program, and a soup kitchen. Later added were programs to distribute low cost or free coal and food, a boy's club, Friday night socials, and classes in homemaking.

As the nineteenth century progressed, and the mainstream settlement movement became established, some of the missions transitioned into settlement houses. By the turn of the century Philadelphia had three settlements in black neighborhoods. These were Neighborhood House, the Eighth Ward Settlement House, and the Philadelphia College Settlement. The most important among these, the College Settlement, eventually owned a full city block that included Starr Garden, a gym, a playground, and a library. Classes in homemaking and carpentry were offered; a sick benefit society and a savings bank were established, as well as cooperative buying programs, subsidized lunches and milk for school children, university extension courses, and a medical clinic with a visiting nurse.

The black settlement house movement arose from needs and provided services very similar to the mainstream settlement houses. However, stemming from their origins as missions, they emphasized the religious aspect of their work a bit more than white settlements. Worship often was a part of the program at many settlements, but it was a secondary activity. At the settlements with their roots in institutional churches and missions, worship was the central feature of the community's life together.

---

68. Ralph E. Luker, *The Social Gospel in Black and White: American Racial Reform, 1885–1912* (Chapel Hill: University of North Carolina Press, 1991), 166.

CONCLUSION

The last half of the nineteenth century can be viewed as the nursery of the modern American social welfare system. It was during these years that age old beliefs, attitudes, and approaches toward social problems began to be seriously questioned and studied, and the faint outline of the current social welfare system can be seen. From the child protection movement emerged the principle, still controversial, that it is acceptable, perhaps mandatory, for external bodies to intervene in the relation between parents and children when it becomes obvious that parents are failing in their role. From the New York CAS to succeeding organizations such as the Boston CAS and the CAS of Pennsylvania, the idea of caring for dependent children in family settings, now called foster care emerged. Finally, and for our purposes probably the most important, the signature principle of social work, viewing problems as a result of interaction between individuals and their environment, began to emerge. The charity organization movement was the pioneer in developing knowledge and methods for dealing with the individual side of this equation and the settlements were the pioneers in studying and remediating the environmental factors. But, each organization realized by the end of the century that the perspective of the other was valuable and essential if there were to be any hope of solving, and increasingly the focus became preventing, individual and social problems that many still feared would lead to a cataclysmic social breakdown. As the new century arrived a new profession of social work was emerging that was to take center stage in "battling for social betterment."[69]

---

69. James E. McCulloch, editor, *Battling for Social Betterment: Proceedings of the Southern Sociological Congress*, Memphis, Tennessee, May 6–10, 1914.

CHAPTER 6

PROGRESS IN SOCIAL WELFARE, 1895–1929

Roger Nash Baldwin was born on January 21, 1884 into the comfort and affluence of an old-stock New England family. Both his father and mother were Mayflower descendants. Although how much family wealth was handed down to him is not known, it is a safe bet that he was at least fairly wealthy. This wealth was not, however, reflected in his life-style as his friends identified him as a tightwad who, when a young man, lived in a room in a settlement house or with the family of friends, owned only one suit of clothing for each required social function, and always rode public transportation rather than taking a taxi or owning a private car. In 1901 Baldwin entered Harvard University and left four years later with a BA and an MA in philosophy and anthropology. Upon finishing at Harvard Baldwin was encouraged by later Chief Justice of the Supreme Court Louis Brandeis to pursue a career in philanthropic work and consequently accepted a position in St. Louis as Director of Self-Cultural Hall, a settlement house in an Irish-Polish-Jewish ghetto. He also was hired to start a sociology program at Washington University even though he had never taken a sociology course at Harvard. In 1907, influenced by the pioneering work of Judge Ben Lindsey in Denver, Baldwin accepted the position of Chief Probation Officer for the St. Louis Juvenile Court. He soon became recognized as a national leader in the field of juvenile justice and in 1914 published *Juvenile Courts and Probation* with coauthor Bernard Flexner, the first text in juvenile justice and one that remained the standard in the field for many years. While on the faculty of Washington University, a segregated institution, Baldwin negotiated with the Chancellor to set up a "Special Course for Colored People," the first program at the University to graduate African American students. When World War I began in Europe and the drumbeat began for the United States to enter the war, Baldwin, who was becoming increasingly influenced by socialist thinkers, notably Emma Goldman the "Red Queen of Anarchy," became a dedicated pacifist and spent an increasing amount of time opposing the war. In 1915 he joined the American Union Against Militarism and in 1917 became the director if its newly formed Civil Liberties Bureau. In 1918 he refused to report for the draft and, as a result, served nine months of a one year prison sentence. In 1920 he became director of the newly formed American Civil Liberties Union, an outgrowth of the earlier Civil Liberties Bureau, a position he retained, becoming America's leading champion of free speech, until his retirement in 1950. Baldwin began his career as a social worker, but eventually found the role too limiting, writing that social workers were merely "caseworkers patching up the evils and miseries of the industrial system; or propagandists for reform legislation; educators; collectors of facts or figures; or neighborhood and community workers." However, "outside our work, we can join in the radical political movement of socialism; we can get the facts of economic injustice, and talk and write them, helping indict the present economic system."[1]

Jane Addams was born in 1860 in the small town of Cederville, Illinois, the daughter of John Addams and Sarah Addams. John Addams was a prosperous, but not actually rich, businessman. Sarah Addams died when Jane was two years old, her father remarrying when Jane was eight. Upon finishing high school in 1877, Addams wanted to attend Smith College, but acceded to her father's wishes and instead enrolled in nearby Rockford Female Seminary. She graduated first in her class in 1881 and was granted a bachelor's degree a year later when the school became a degree granting college. That same year Addams began studies at the Woman's Medical College in Philadelphia but following her father's death and her recurring health problems she became depressed and returned to her Illinois home after six months. After a period of six years in which she lacked direction, her health significantly improved and she set about her second visit to Europe, accompanied by her college classmate and lifelong friend Ellen Gates Starr. While her first tour had been to experience the social and cultural resources of Europe, this second tour was aimed at learning about the many social and religious movements that were occurring on the continent. The tour ended with an extended visit to Toynbee Hall, a social agency founded by Samuel Barnett and other idealistic young social reformers who built a large residence in a London slum with the intention to live there among the poor and to learn about them and to assist them in any way needed. Inspired by their visit, Addams and Starr resolved to establish a settlement house in Chicago modeled on Toynbee Hall. Upon their return to Chicago they located an old mansion that was in an area that had become a run-down immigrant neighborhood, were able to lease it at an attractive rate, and opened it as Hull House, which was to become the most famous settlement house in America. At the beginning Addams and Starr had no definite plans for the settlement's program, intending to listen to their neighbors and develop programs as needs were revealed. Eventually Hull House provided a kindergarten; boys', girls', workingmen's, and women's clubs; literacy programs; discussion groups of all kinds; health clinics; an art studio; numerous social and cultural exhibits; as well as other programs responding to neighborhood needs. The settlement was staffed mainly by young, college educated men and women who, in return for free room and board at Hull House, exchanged their expertise to help with one or more of the programs. The settlement eventually comprised thirteen buildings and had a staff of sixty-five. Realizing that the problems of the Hull House neighborhood extended to other areas, Addams became involved in politics and social reform. She was a champion for the cause of women's suffrage, was a leader in the development of the Progressive Party's presidential election platform in 1912, and was on the founding executive committee for the National Association for the Advancement of Colored People. She was heavily involved in the labor movement through participation in the building trades strike of 1900, the national anthracite (coal mining) strike of 1902, the Chicago Stockyards strike of 1904, and the textile strike of 1910. As America's participation in World War I became an issue, Addams, like Baldwin, became a committed pacifist, chairing the Woman's Peace Party in 1915 and attending the International Conference of Women at The Hague that same year. Also like Baldwin, Addams's stand as a pacifist was costly for her, resulting in accusations of being a communist or socialist and the revocation of her membership by the Daughters of the American Revolution. Although her reputation in America was never fully restored following her peace activities, her international reputation continued to grow, culminating with her being awarded the Nobel Peace Prize in 1931.

Ida Wells (later Wells-Barnett) was born into slavery in 1862 in Holly Springs, Mississippi. Her father was a skilled carpenter and after emancipation was able to provide stable support for his family. Wells-Barnett began studies at the Shaw School (later becoming Rust College), a school founded by northern Methodist missionaries representing the Freedman's Aid Society of the Methodist Episcopal Church. Her formal education ended in 1876 when her parents died in a yellow fever epidemic that hit the community. Lengthening her skirt to disguise her age Wells claimed she was eighteen and was able to secure a teaching position to support herself. She left her teaching position in Holly Springs to accept a better-paying one in Memphis, and it was here that she became a journalist almost by accident. While on a train she was forcibly removed from the coach in which she was sitting and relocated in a coach reserved for blacks. Humiliated, she filed a suit against the railroad and won the case with a $500 settlement. The decision was soon overturned by the state supreme court. Following this she wrote an account of the incident for a Memphis black church weekly, the *Living Word*, and the article launched her on a career in journalism, resulting in numerous requests from papers all over the country for articles on the plight of blacks and the indignities they were subjected to. Enjoying her work as a journalist and having saved some money, Wells resigned her teaching position and became the editor and co-owner of the Memphis *Free Speech*, a weekly newspaper that quickly gained a wide readership among area blacks. In 1892 Wells-Barnett wrote and published a feature article that clearly established that the horrific lynching of three black men had not been the result of a rape, as claimed by the mob responsible for the lynching, but rather anger from white business competitors of the men's grocery store that was hurting their business in a black neighborhood. Following the publication of her exposé, a white mob destroyed her office and printing press and threatened to lynch her. As Memphis was clearly no longer safe for her, Wells fled, eventually ending up in Chicago, a city that was to remain her home for the rest of her life. It was in Chicago that she married the prominent lawyer and newspaper publisher Ferdinand Barnett, changing her name to Wells-Barnett. In Chicago she continued her anti-lynching campaign, publishing numerous newspaper and magazine articles and frequently speaking on the topic and also becoming involved in social work. She developed a friendship with Jane Addams under whose guidance she established her own settlement house, the Negro Fellowship League. The settlement focused on self-help, research, and social reform, and offered the Black community concrete services in the form of an employment bureau, low-cost lodging, a library, and recreational facilities. Wells-Barnett also worked closely with Jane Addams on many other projects, including increasing the membership of the National Association of Colored Women's Clubs, protesting against a *Chicago Tribune* article in favor of segregated schools, and helping create the National Association for the Advancement of Colored People. In 1910 she became the first woman and the first black person to be appointed as an adult probation officer. Wells-Barnett died in Chicago in 1931, and in 1940 was designated by the city as one of the most outstanding women in its history.

Upton Sinclair was born in 1878 in Baltimore to a mother who was a home-maker and a father who was prone to alcoholism and had chosen the unfortunate career of a liquor salesman. An exceptional student with a gift for writing, Sinclair entered the City College of New York before his fourteenth birthday. He graduated in 1897 at the age of nineteen and entered law school at Columbia University. He never finished his law degree at Columbia, although he enjoyed the school saying his only criticism was that it did not have a class in socialism. By the time Sinclair left Columbia he had published four novels that were met with positive reviews but were not commercially successful. After Columbia he began his lifelong career as a free-lance writer, sometimes being well-off and sometimes nearly impoverished, depending on what assignments he was able to attract. Having grown up in an economically marginal household, and pursuing a career that often left him economically marginal himself, Sinclair developed an animosity toward big business and identified as a socialist. Sinclair was a novelist but found he was drawn to the work of journalists who would soon be called muckrakers (currently identified by the more dignified term investigative reporters). He was especially influenced by those who exposed corruption in government and big business, such as Lincoln Steffens, who wrote of *The Shame of the Cities*; Ida Tarbell who revealed John D. Rockefeller's ruthless business practices in her two-volume *History of Standard Oil*; and Frank Norris, who revealed the Southern Pacific Railroad's stranglehold on California farmers in *The Octopus*. When he was asked by a midwestern weekly, the *Appeal to Reason*, to write a series of articles about factory working conditions, he jumped at the chance. Sinclair and his editor chose the Chicago meatpacking industry as the setting for his study. Because he was a novelist, Sinclair chose to employ the techniques of the muckraking journalists he admired to collect his data, but to present it in the form of fiction. Dressed as a workingman he entered and observed the work on the factory floors of the three largest meatpackers, Armour, Swift, and Morris, that dominated Packingtown, as the Chicago stockyards were called. In the novel, first serialized in *The Appeal*, and later released as *The Jungle*, Sinclair's characters experience a hellish life resulting from exploitative labor management of the big packers, including real estate fraud, poverty, child labor, freezing winter weather, frostbite, on-the-job injury (one character, after working twelve hours in subzero temperature, slices off his own fingers without realizing he has done this), unemployment, death, blood poisoning, breathing disorders, alcoholism, extortion, crime, jail, political corruption, homelessness, and prostitution. As a minor theme of the novel Sinclair also describes the horrifying sanitary conditions in the plants, including men working while standing in pools of blood and entrails, spoiled meat being added to sausages, flies and rats everywhere, and blended meat products, called "deviled chicken" or "potted ham" that actually contained no trace of chicken or pig. In the novel, the main character, Jurgis Rudkos, joins the Socialist Party and the novel suggests that socialism could solve the problems of modern industry and result in a more just social and industrial order. This is the message that Sinclair wanted to communicate through the novel, and Jack London's review suggested that the book "will open countless ears that have been deaf to socialism."[2] It was a disappointment to Sinclair that the message regarding socialism was all but ignored by the reading public (including President Theodore Roosevelt) but the scant 20 pages describing sanitation caused a sensation. Based on this part of the book, President Roosevelt ordered an investigation of the entire food industry and found that conditions were actually worse than described by Sinclair. The resulting public outcry ended with the passage of the Pure Food and Drug Act of 1906 that prominently featured a meat inspection provision. Following the passage of the act, Sinclair sardonically observed, "I aimed at the public's heart, and by accident I hit it in the stomach."

The people just described, only four of a possible hundreds and hundreds of similar examples, were all members of a group who came of age in the late nineteenth and early twentieth centuries who were referred to as progressives, and the years at which they were at the zenith of their careers, roughly 1895 to 1920, is generally referred to as the progressive era. Although these people differed in terms of gender, ethnicity, race, religion, social class background, and geographic location, they shared many convictions. They believed that the massive changes the country was experiencing—population growth, immigration, urbanization, industrialization—had produced serious social problems ranging from city slums, to extremes of wealth and poverty, to corporate abuses. They believed that new ideas and methods were necessary to correct these problems. In particular, they rejected the two guiding ideologies of the nineteenth century, laissez-faire economics and individualism, in favor of broader concepts of social responsibility, and they believed that social order could be achieved through science, organization, and efficiency. Finally, most progressives believed that government itself, as the organized agent of public responsibility, should actively and aggressively address social and economic problems. Obviously, not all Americans were progressives, and many resisted their plans. The decade following the progressive era, popularly known as the roaring twenties, was a time that America turned away from progressivism, and its opponents seemed victorious. However, as we shall see, even the conservative 1920s played a significant role in the reform of American society. The interaction among reformers and the conflict with their opponents made the years between 1895 and 1930 a period of remarkable

2. Ann Bausum, *Muckrakers* (Washington, DC, National Geographic Press, 2007), 55.

ferment and excitement. The progressive's achievements and their failures profoundly shaped the American future, particularly the emergence and development of an American welfare state.

SOCIO-ECONOMIC DEVELOPMENTS AND THE EMERGENCE OF PROGRESSIVISM

The origins of progressivism can be found in the crises of the new urban-industrial order that was emerging in the late nineteenth century. The severe depression and consequent mass suffering of the 1890s, the violent strikes and deployment of what can only be called industrial armies, the political challenges of populism and an obviously ineffective government shattered the complacency with which many middle-class Americans had viewed their nation and made them aware of social and economic inequities that rural and working-class citizens had long recognized. By the turn of the century a returning prosperity had eased the threat of major social violence (a big fear in the 1890s), but the social and technological changes that also were unsettling people continued at an ever accelerating rate.

What were these changes? One was dramatic shifts in the population including its size, composition, and location. The number of people in the United States nearly doubled in the years between 1890 and 1930, growing from 63 million in 1890 to almost 123 million in 1930. Over 20 million of these additional people were immigrants, 14.5 million arriving before 1915, with many coming from southern and eastern Europe, bringing with them social customs and political ideas perceived as at best weird (eating fragrant foods cooked with a lot of garlic and olive oil) and at worst dangerous (advocating socialism and labor organization), by native-born citizens whose origins were mostly western European. The number of racial minorities grew during these years, increasing from 9.2 million to about 12.5 million, but as a percentage of the population this group declined from 12.1 percent to 10.2 percent, a result of the fact that the huge group of immigrants was almost entirely white. As a result of a combination of the growth of industry in the cities with advances in agricultural technology that enabled fewer farmers to feed more people, the majority of the population shifted from rural to urban. In 1890 there were only 11 cities with populations greater than 250,000; by 1930 the number was 37. The 1890 census classified 35 percent of the population as living in urban areas, a percentage that had increased to 56 percent by the 1930 census.[3]

Another area of change that greatly unsettled the progressive generation was a large increase in wealth, including how this wealth was produced and how it was distributed. The consolidation of businesses continued, with the number of businesses capitalized at more than $10 million increasing from a dozen in 1897 to over 300 in 1903, 50 of which were capitalized at more than $50 million, and 17 at more than $100 million. Included in the consolidation of business was the formation of giant trusts including Standard Oil, Consolidated Tobacco, American Smelting, and U.S. Steel, the

---

3. U.S. Bureau of the Census, "Series A 43–56, Number of Places in Urban and Rural Territory, by Size of Place: 1790–1970," *Historical Statistics of the United States, Colonial Times to 1970, Bicentennial Edition, Part 2* (Washington, DC: U.S. Government Printing Office, 1975), 11.

world's first billion dollar corporation.[4] The consolidation of business, accompanied by new inventions and innovative managerial skills and techniques, resulted in a 273 percent increase in the output of manufacturing between 1899 and 1929. The gross national product (GNP) increased from $17 billion in 1900 to $104 billion in 1929. Per capita GNP rose by 73 percent over this same time period. These huge businesses resulted in a small group of extremely wealthy families, popularly referred to as the "upper ten," a term that implied that they were the wealthiest 10 percent of the population, but in reality they were the upper one or at most 2 percent. These were the wealthy capitalists, manufacturers, merchants, landowners, and executives, who owned the majority of the nation's resources and expected to make its key decisions. Their ranks included the nations' roughly four thousand millionaires who, given the value of money at the time, were truly a fabulously rich group. Their most visible and most powerful members were the two hundred or so families worth at least $20 million. Concentrated in the northeast and especially New York State, theirs were the famous names of American capitalism—Vanderbilt, Whitney, Carnegie, Harriman, and Morgan. Probably the richest of them all was John D. Rockefeller, who, forced by anti-trust legislation to break up and sell much of Standard Oil, had a personal fortune that by 1913 amounted to a billion dollars.

A major cause of the public concern with the emergence of a class of extremely wealthy people was that on the other end of industry was the working class who were abused, exploited, and often lived in poverty. Working conditions were difficult and often dangerous. Most workers labored nine or ten hours per day, and many, notably steel and textile workers, usually put in twelve-hour shifts. Wages were minimal; one study calculated that 60 percent of all male workers earned less than a living wage. In Chicago's Packingtown, site of Upton Sinclair's novel, a typical worker could earn only 38 percent of the amount of income needed to support a family of four in 1910.[5] Family survival, then, required women and children to work, often in the lowest paid, most exploited positions. Southern cotton mills employed children as young as seven; coal mines paid twelve-year-old slate pickers 39 cents for a ten-hour day. Poor ventilation, dangerous fumes, open machinery, and an absence of safety programs threatened workers health and sometimes even their lives. In an eerie prediction of current reports and news stories, a 1915 report by the Commission on Industrial Relations identified the critical question of the age to be, "Have workers received a fair share of the enormous increase in wealth which has taken place in the country during the period, as a result largely of their labor?" The conclusion of the Commission: "The answer is emphatically—No!"[6]

SOCIAL WORK AND PROGRESSIVISM

It is probably not too much of a stretch of the imagination to say that progressivism was social work and social work was progressivism. Nearly every activity of progressives led to the development of

4. Alfred D. Chandler, *The Visible Hand: The Managerial Revolution in American Business* (Cambridge, MA: Harvard University Press, 2002).

5. Michael McGerr, *A Fierce Discontent: The Rise and Fall of the Progressive Movement in America, 1870–1920* (New York: Free Press, 2003), 16.

6. U.S. Commission on Industrial Relations, *Final Report* (Washington, DC: U.S. Government Printing Office, 1915), 8.

some kind of social work and every social work development supported some aspect of progressivism. Explanations of how this relationship worked vary, depending on the historical interpretation of the progressive era employed. Early historians saw progressivism as a democratic movement of ordinary Americans, determined to repossess the power accrued by ruthless corporations, corrupt politicians, and misapplied wealth. They saw progressivism as consisting of two parts. One part was an uprising of the plain people against the interests; the other part was a quest for social justice. These were viewed as quite different but related impulses. The popular movement was concerned with anti-trust legislation and corruption, with the goal of keeping the field clear for individual enterprise. The social justice movement was viewed as being more humanitarian and philanthropic, being mainly concerned with poverty and its consequences. This interpretation of progressivism considers it to generally be a continuation of the western and southern farmer's revolt.[7] According to this traditional view of progressivism, the emergence of social work is explained as part of the social justice movement, the settlement houses and the crusade against child labor being its best known features. This explanation, however, leaves large segments of social work unaccounted for. It offers no explanation of psychiatric social work and other aspects of the new profession that demonstrated only marginal concern for social justice issues. In fact, these specialties were often the antithesis of social reform, advocating the adjustment of the individual to a "recognized social reality," rather than attempting to modify the reality.

The first major challenge to the traditional interpretation of progressivism was Hofstadter's status decline theory, most fully developed in his 1955 book *The Age of Reform*. Hofstadter was less focused on the real social and economic problems addressed by the progressives than in the psychological motives that spurred them to action. His main argument is that progressives were members of the traditional nineteenth century American leadership class—clergy, lawyers, business owners in small towns, and professors. They became reformers, he argued, because they had lost status to the newly wealthy, powerful business elite, which had been created by the technological and economic developments of the late nineteenth century, and they were desperately attempting to regain that lost status. According to this interpretation, social workers were members of the traditional elite attempting to modify society in ways that would help them regain lost status. Perhaps this explains why certain persons entered social work, but it does not explain the emergence of the whole profession. What evidence there is indicates that the majority of persons entering social work had little status to protect. For example, Kusmer, in his study of the Chicago Charity Organization Society, concluded that it is unlikely that any of the individuals he studied considered themselves to be victims of a status revolution. Of ten Chicago Charity Organization Society workers whose careers Kusmer traced, "all came from obscure backgrounds; most of them were young; and all were identified with a rising profession and were upwardly mobile."[8]

7. John D. Hicks, *The Populist Revolt: A History of the Farmer's Alliance and the People's Party* (Minneapolis: University of Minnesota Press, 1931), 404–423; George E. Mowry, *Theodore Roosevelt and the Progressive Movement* (Madison: University of Wisconsin Press, 1947), 3–35.

8. Kenneth L. Kusmer, "The Functions of Organized Charity in the Progressive Era: Chicago as a Case Study," *The Journal of American History* 60 (December 1973): 661.

The generation of historians following Hofstadter reinterpreted progressivism as a conservative movement, and their theories help explain those social workers who were upwardly mobile and interested in increasing the status of their profession.[9] Wiebe views progressivism as an expression of the class interests of the "new middle class" of expert professionals and managers, a group in which he includes social workers. This new middle class was interested in reforms that would increase rationality and order and facilitate business and government planning. "A chamber of commerce, mobilized and formidable, desired a cleaner, safer, more beautiful, and more economically operated city. Only the professional administrator, the doctor, the social worker, the economist, could show the way."[10] The progressives, according to this interpretation, believed that professionalism and scientific government would bring opportunity, progress, order, and community. This view of progressivism is very useful in explaining the place of social work in progressivism. According to this view the social worker was an urban technocrat; a young man or woman with a good education, an exaggerated belief in statistics and efficiency, and seeking upward mobility by creating a new profession. However, this theory does not account for the social workers in the settlements who had little or no interest in professionalization or in social work as a vehicle for upward mobility.

The fact that no one theory explains the emergence of social work and social welfare reforms during the progressive movement comes as no surprise to more recent historians who reject the idea that progressivism was a movement at all because it had no unifying organization, central leadership, or consensus on objectives.[11] Instead, it represented the coalescing of different and sometimes even contradictory movements that sought changes in the nation's social, economic, and political life. It can be argued that social work evolved from two of these movements, rational humanistic progressivism and radical humanistic progressivism. The members of both of these groups were concerned with the plight of the individual in the rapidly changing industrial society. However, they approached the problem from opposite ends of the "person-in-environment" equation. The radical group "talked of economic justice, human opportunities and rehabilitated democracy." The rational group used "the language of the budget, boosterism, and social control" within the context of professionalism to describe plans for social programs.[12] The radical group wished to change society, the rational group wanted to change the individual.

Rational humanistic progressivism was represented in social work by the various casework specialties that developed during the progressive era out of the Charity Organization Society Movement. This type of social work had much in common with scientific management, the conservation movement, and the development of professional public school administration. The group being referred to as radical humanistic progressives was represented in social work by the settlements and the various movements growing out of the settlements. This segment of social work had much in common with the labor and the women's movements and, according to Lasch,

9. Gabriel Kolko, *The Triumph of Conservatism: A reinterpretation of American History, 1900–1916* (New York: The Free Press, 1963); Robert H. Wiebe, *The Search for Order, 1877–1920* (New York: Hill and Wang, 1967).

10. Robert Wiebe, *The Search for Order,* 174.

11. Faith Jaycox, *The Progressive Era* (New York: Facts on File, 2005), ix–x.

12. Robert Wiebe, *The Search for Order, 176.*

in some cases may have been nearer to socialism than to progressivism.[13] These two types of social work took markedly different approaches to the solution of social problems. The basic difference being that the Charity Organization Societies emphasized the individual causes of poverty and the settlements stressed the social and economic causes. The charity organizations professed a form of *noblesse oblige*, that the upper classes had a moral responsibility to uplift the needy. The settlements felt that the dependence of classes on each other was reciprocal. Due to these differences, the philosophy of the charity organization movement led to philanthropy directed at individuals and the philosophy of the settlement movement led to reform directed at large groups. These two segments of social work were overlapping. Many charity organization workers lived in settlements and participated in settlement reform activities, and most settlement houses were unable to avoid some form of charity work. School social work, a specialty primarily aligned with casework as developed by the charity organization societies, was begun by settlement houses. Conversely, many reform movements were begun and/or advocated for by charity organizations, for example the anti-tuberculosis campaign initiated by Edward T. Devine of the New York Charity Organization Society. However, the major difference between the two remained—the settlements viewed social progress as coming through social reform and only engaged in charity work when it was unavoidable. The charity organizations saw individual treatment as the main function of social work and only engaged in reform activities when an environmental condition began to impede their work with individuals.

Even though social workers in different practice settings approached reform from different perspectives, it is clear that they were at the very heart of the many reform efforts of the era and that the sum of these efforts was to create the foundations of an American welfare state. Major areas of reform that contributed to this foundation include labor issues, concern for children, government financial assistance for the poor, and crime and criminal justice as a social as well as a legal issue. There were also some progressive issues that social workers were involved in that can be described as deviant themes because, from a historical perspective, it is now clear that they were more repressive than progressive. Among these issues are anti-immigration efforts, Americanization programs, the eugenics movement, and a curious lack of interest in the issue of race.

PROGRESSIVISM AND THE SEEDS OF AN AMERICAN WELFARE STATE

As we have seen, in early America care of the needy was accepted as a public responsibility. However, in the nineteenth century the twin doctrines of individualism and laissez-faire created a strong belief that social welfare should be, to the greatest extent possible, the responsibility of private charity and that government, especially at the federal level, should not be involved. An attempt to reverse this trend was made mid-century by Dorthea Dix, who lobbied Congress to allocate ten million acres of federal land to be used for the support of state mental hospitals. After

---

13. Christopher Lasch, *The New Radicalism in America, 1889–1963: The Intellectual as a Social Type* (New York: Vintage Books, 1965), xiv–iv.

several tries Ms. Dix was successful in having a bill to accomplish this passed by both the House and the Senate in 1854. The bill was vetoed by President Pierce, who argued in his veto message that "It cannot be questioned that if Congress has power to make provision for the indigent insane . . . it has the same powers to provide for the indigent who are not insane, and thus to transfer to the Federal Government the charge of all the poor in all the States." He gave the legal basis for his veto as "I cannot find any authority in the Constitution for making the Federal Government the great almoner of public charity throughout the United States."[14] It is interesting and a little puzzling that social welfare advocates did nothing for the remainder of the nineteenth century to further attempt to involve the federal government in social welfare, particularly as the basis for Pierce's veto was rejected only a few years later with the passage of the Morrill Act that allocated 30,000 acres of land to each state for each member of Congress for the development and support of agricultural and mechanical colleges. This bill was passed by both houses of Congress in 1859 and was vetoed by President Buchanan, using essentially the same arguments as the Pierce veto. The Morrill Act's supporters reintroduced it in the next Congress, where it was once again passed, and was signed into law by President Lincoln in 1862. The US Department of Agriculture was created in this same year and was granted cabinet status in 1889. A system of federally supported agricultural research stations was established in 1887.[15] Together these developments have come to be referred to as the establishment of an agricultural welfare state, the constitutionality of which was never questioned after the original Buchanan veto.[16]

By the late nineteenth century care of the needy had become more of a private matter than a public one. Government social welfare activities had been reduced to providing public institutions for the destitute elderly and the permanently disabled, aid to orphanages, and the provision of indoor relief, that is, poorhouses. The provision of financial or material assistance to people while they remained in their own homes (outdoor relief) had been substantially curtailed and in many areas actually abolished. Most states had established boards of public welfare, but the function of these boards was mainly to supervise the various institutions into which destitute people were placed. As the twentieth century dawned the new generation of progressive reformers was recognizing that the complex of problems associated with rapid industrialization, immigration, a largely unregulated market economy, and urbanization, had created problems of economic deprivation and insecurity that, given the enormity of the task, the private welfare system was not capable of handling. They began to recognize a need for more public involvement in social welfare. Also, as part of the progressives questioning of the doctrine of individualism, progressive reformers argued that since poverty was a social rather than an individual problem, one that was built in to modern industrial society, increased public intervention was not only necessary but was just.

14. John Woolley and Gerhard Peters, "Franklin Pierce XIV President of the United States,1853–1857: Veto Message May 3, 1854." Online at www.presidency.ucsb.edu.

15. Stephen Skowronek, *Building a New American State: The Expansion of National Administrative Capacities, 1877–1920* (Cambridge: Cambridge University Press, 1982).

16. Adam D. Sheingate, *The Rise of the Agricultural Welfare State: Institutions and Interest Group Power in the United States, France, and Japan* (Princeton, NJ: Princeton University Press, 2001).

INCREASING THE SECURITY OF WORKERS

As the national economy evolved from rural and agricultural to urban and industrial, millions of workers headed for the cities in search of higher wages and a better lifestyle, but in the process left behind the traditional security of agricultural life. When faced with hard times, urban industrial workers no longer enjoyed continued access to shelter and food as they had on the farm. Urbanization, and to an even greater extent immigration, also disrupted vital family support networks. In rural communities the extended family had long served as a critical source of support during hard times. When a family member was sick or otherwise incapacitated for a lengthy period of time, others lent a hand to support his or her dependents. Rural neighbors frequently filled in as well. Having left the extended family and farm the typical industrial worker was left entirely dependent on his wages, which meant that a sudden decline or cessation of income could instantly impoverish him and his family.

The risks of cessation of income due to accident or death on the job greatly increased as workers moved from the farm to the city. In Minnesota, for example, in 1910 only 3.5 percent of fatal job-related accidents, and 0.5 percent of non-fatal accidents, were to agricultural workers. In comparison, industrial jobs, particularly those related to railroads, in mines, and in energy-intensive manufacturing carried a far greater risk. In Minnesota in 1910, railroads accounted for 26 percent of fatal accidents (20 percent of non-fatal) and mining accounted for 24 percent of fatal and 43 percent of non-fatal accidents. Although, due to the lack of good public health data in the early twentieth century, it is harder to document the extent of occupational-related disease than accident, it was strongly suspected at the time that industrial workers faced an increased risk of illness compared to agricultural workers. This was thought to be due not only to the prevalence of toxins such as lead and phosphorous in industrial processes, but also to more general unhealthful conditions, such as poor ventilation, which were typical in America's factories, railroads, and mines.[17] In addition to death or injury the industrial worker faced other threats to his income and security, primarily serious illness such at tuberculosis, a decline in the demand for labor, or if he grew too old or feeble to work. Any of these conditions would lead to an interruption in pay with the result that the worker was likely to fall on charity.

Many reformers began to think that some form of insurance might be an attractive alternative to charity to increase the security of industrial workers. The concept of insurance had begun in the fourteenth century by English merchants seeking a means of protecting themselves against loss of cargo at sea. Merchants would enter into agreements with one another that if the cargo of one was lost, all would share in covering that loss, but if the cargo arrived safely and a profit was made, all would share in the profit. By the eighteenth century companies had been developed for the sole purpose of underwriting insurance on a large scale basis, a system safer and more convenient than negotiating each contract among a different set of individuals. The idea of maritime loss insurance was quickly followed by the concept of life insurance. Life insurance was designed for people whose incomes relied on professional or managerial skills—lawyers, architects, and so

---

17. David A. Moss, *When All Else Fails—Government as the Ultimate Risk Manager* (Cambridge, MA: Harvard University Press, 2002), 155–156.

forth—rather than on the ownership of land. By paying a small annual premium a person could create an instant estate that would come to fruition in the case of untimely death. Life insurance was aimed at the professional and business middle class, providing both a protection for property and family, and because it gained cash value over time, it was an attractive investment in the days before the savings bank and stock market appeared to absorb the economic surplus of people with extra income. It enabled the middle class to deal with the economic insecurities of modern urban life in a rational manner. Life insurance provision grew rapidly in the nineteenth century, along with the expansion of trade, industry, and a middle class whose economic security depended on individual skills rather than on ownership of a landed estate.

Also during the nineteenth century another form of insurance developed to rationalize risks to a social class lower than the professional and business people who were buying life insurance. These were the artisan-shopkeepers such as butchers, bakers, goldsmiths, gunsmiths, men who made or did things in their own shops, and the growing group of skilled industrial workers employed in mills, iron works, mines, shipyards, and the like. These workers organized into guilds, friendly societies, and trade societies. These groups had a large social dimension, providing fellowship, a sense of belonging, and recreational activities for their members, but mutual aid was also an important function. These groups generally provided members with a death benefit, the members assessing themselves for a small gift for the family of a deceased member. Some included benefits in cash or the services of a physician in times where a member was seriously ill or recovering from an injury. Some groups would assess the membership to maintain an out-of-work fund to assist members who were temporarily unemployed. A smaller number of groups maintained a residence for elderly members who could no longer work and take care of themselves. While less formal and actuarially based than life insurance, these trade groups attempted, like life insurance, to replace the security that workers had lost by moving from a rural-agricultural to an urban industrial life style.

Another form of insurance, this one aimed at an even lower social class group, unskilled industrial workers, called industrial insurance, began to spread during the late nineteenth century. First developed in Britain in 1850, industrial insurance was introduced in the United States in 1875 by the Prudential Insurance Company. Workers were offered private policies that, for premiums of between five and twenty-five cents a week, provided death benefits in the neighborhood of one-hundred dollars. This benefit was quite small but workers who purchased it took comfort in the knowledge that in case of an untimely death their funeral expenses would be covered and their families would have a small financial cushion. Between 1896 and 1910 the number of private industrial insurance policies sold increased from a little over 8,000 to more than twenty-two million, and the value of coverage increased from $400,000 to $3 billion. Although private industrial insurance sold well enough to make it a viable business for companies such as the Prudential, it was purchased by only a small percentage of industrial workers and was thus not an adequate solution to the problem of financial insecurity in this class. There were two main reasons that more workers did not purchase private protection. One reason is that the cost of premiums was remarkably expensive compared to the benefits paid by the policies. In 1904, for example, insurance companies collected $110 million in premiums but only paid out $31 million in benefits. The companies asserted that the reason for this was the high cost of premium collection that was of necessity done weekly on a door-to-door basis, but critics did not accept this explanation and concluded that the policies exploited unsophisticated purchasers. The second reason that voluntary private industrial insurance was not purchased by more workers is that psychologically most people were not prudent or farsighted enough to rationally plan for all future contingencies.[18] Reformers did not accept the explanations of the insurance industry about the high cost of policies and argued that private insurance would never be adequate as a means of providing comprehensive protection for industrial workers. Labor expert Henry Seager wrote that "experience everywhere has shown that voluntary insurance will not reach the classes which need it most."[19]

With the need for some kind of protection of workers from the insecurity endemic to modern industrial employment, and the demonstrated inability of private insurance to provide this protection, reformers looked across the Atlantic for solutions. European governments had begun, one after the other, to provide public insurance for workers in the latter nineteenth century. Germany was the leader, adopting compulsory health insurance, workplace accident (worker's compensation), and old age and disability insurance between 1883 and 1889. Britain passed worker's compensation in 1897, old age pensions in 1908, and health and unemployment insurance in 1911. Almost every country in Europe had put in place some form of compulsory workers' insurance by the turn of the century. In the United States the federal Department of Labor began to seriously study and promote European models of worker protection releasing three major studies, *Compulsory Insurance in Germany* in 1893, *Workingmen's Insurance* in 1898, and *Workman's Insurance and Compensation* in 1911. This idea of adopting a European approach to worker protection was taken up by the National Conference of Charities and Corrections where a committee on workingmen's insurance was formed in 1901. In 1906 this committee was expanded into a new organization, mainly composed of professors of labor economics, calling itself the American Association for Labor Legislation (AALL). The AALL released its first report at the NCCC's 1906 annual conference advocating that "Workingmen's insurance should be fostered by state legislation."[20] In 1912 the National Conference of Charities and Correction released the Social Standards for Industry that included workmen's insurance as part of its minimum standards to reduce poverty and conserve human resources. These standards, prepared by a committee that included settlement house workers Alice Hamilton and Florence Kelley, became a plank in the Progressive Party's presidential election platform in that year.[21]

Protection of workers and their families from injury or death on the job was the first form of industrial insurance established in the United States. Estimates during the early years of the twentieth century were that around 15,000 workers were killed in on-the-job accidents annually. Many times this number was seriously injured. Workers and their families had, of course, the right to sue their employers for damages, but the law was heavily weighted against them. It was nearly impossible for a worker to win a suit unless he could demonstrate that the employer was entirely at fault. The defenses available to an employer defendant in the nineteenth century were contributory negligence, the fellow servant rule, and assumption of risk. Contributory negligence meant

18. David A. Moss, *When All Else Fails*, 158; James Leiby, *A History of Social Work and Social Welfare in the United States* (Columbia University Press, 1978), 197.

19. Henry R. Seager, "Plan for Health Insurance Act," *American Labor Legislation Review*, 6, no. 1 (1916): 21.

20. National Conference of Charities and Correction, *Proceedings*, 1906, 456.

21. Paul H. Stuart, "Linking Clients and Policy: Social Work's Distinctive Contribution," *Social Work*, 44 (1999): 335–347.

that if the worker had in any way been negligent himself, even in a small way, the employer was absolved of any responsibility for the resulting injury. The fellow servant rule meant that if another employee, rather than the employer, had caused the accident, then the employer was not responsible. Assumption of risk meant that if the employee was aware of the dangers involved in a job, and had accepted the job, then he took on the risk himself and the employer could not be held liable should these risks result in injury or death.

Even though the legal system was heavily biased in their favor, the potential cost of worker accidents began to concern employers by the turn of the century. Labor organizations had been lobbying for safety acts that would spell out employer responsibility and, backed up by government inspection and enforcement, make them liable in the case of accidental death or injury. A number of states passed laws around the turn of the century that began paring back employer defenses against liability. Lawyers, who would come to be called "ambulance chasers," appeared who actively sought out injured workers as clients, would provide representation on a contingency fee basis, and who became skilled in picking juries who would be more sympathetic to injured workers than to wealthy employers. Although successful employee lawsuits and recovery for damages remained the exception rather than the rule, the possibility of large judgments against them began to weigh heavily on the minds of business people. Crystal Eastman, a young lawyer who studied industrial accidents as a researcher working in the famed Pittsburgh Survey, observed in 1910: "The always threatening possibility of having to pay damages as the result of an accident puts [the employer] to the expense of maintaining a special claims department and hiring expert attorneys, although he rarely pays a verdict."[22] Employers began to view industrial accident compensation as a cost of production, one that could be rationalized and managed just like other risks such as fire and flood. Industrial accidents were viewed as not accidents at all, but a normal result of modern industry. Workman's compensation programs made it easier for businesses to guard against losses resulting from industrial injuries and, because these losses were now defined as part of the price of production, they could pass the costs along to the consumer. Thus the business community became not an opponent but a supporter of workers compensation legislation, the conservative National Association of Manufacturers endorsing workmen's compensation in 1911.

Workmen's compensation was a popular idea and as such spread rapidly after to turn of the twentieth century. The first compensation law was passed in Maryland in 1902, but was declared unconstitutional in 1904. Congress passed a law in 1908 to protect federal government employees. Between 1910 and 1913, 22 states enacted some form of workmen's compensation legislation. By 1917 the number increased to 39 and to 43 by 1920. These laws varied from state to state, but the central feature of all was automatic payment to injured workers according to a uniform scale of benefits. Based on the popularity of worker's compensation legislation, its support from both capital and labor, and the speed and ease with which enabling legislation had been obtained, labor advocacy groups such as the AALL were optimistic that other forms of worker security legislation previewed in Europe, such as health, unemployment, and pension benefits, would quickly be adopted in the United States. The road ahead, however, was to prove much more rocky than anticipated.

---

22. Crystal Eastman, *Work Accidents and the Law* (New York: Charities Publication Committee, 1910), 192.

With the campaign for worker's compensation well underway and its success seemingly assured, advocates of workers protection turned their focus to the cause of worker health care and disease prevention. Health insurance had been established in Germany in 1883 and in England in 1911. In a 1915 conference on the subject of health insurance, the AALL declared that this was "the next step in social progress."[23] A committee was formed of leaders of the AALL, along with representatives of organizations of social workers, doctors, manufacturers, labor unions, and women's clubs. The model bill developed would require health insurance for all industrial workers and others earning less than $100 per month. Forty percent of the cost of the insurance would be paid by employers, 40 percent by the covered worker, and 20 percent by the state. Coverage would include any illness, injury, or death that was not insured through workers' compensation, and included non-job related incidents. Insured workers would receive up to two-thirds of wages, medical and surgical care for all family members, and funeral costs in the event of death.

Contrary to the optimism of the early advocates of health insurance, the concept ran into immediate and forceful opposition. The opponents to compulsory health insurance turned out to be remarkably diverse, including manufacturers, druggists, and Christian Scientists. The two major opposition groups were the insurance industry and the medical profession. The insurance industry opposed the model bill because it would interfere in the commercial carriers market for private workers' health coverage and also threaten one of the industry's most profitable lines of business, industrial life insurance. Most workers who purchased industrial life insurance did so for the funeral benefit provision, which would be made superfluous as the proposed bill provided coverage for this expense. The opposition of the medical profession was, according to Leiby, "a little puzzling, because the program had advantages for them: they could serve patients without worrying about ability to pay." However, what concerned physicians was the insertion of a third party between the physician and patient, a party that would fix the relationship, set the fee, and approve the type and amount of services a doctor could provide.[24] The bill was defeated in every state in which it was proposed, including rejection four times in New York State and the defeat by a three to one margin of a constitutional amendment proposed to allow health insurance in California. By 1920, after the final defeat in New York, the AALL and its allies abandoned the campaign for compulsory health insurance for workers.

The risk to urban industrial workers posed by accident and injury had been addressed by enactment of workers' compensation laws. The second area of risk, expenses and loss of income due to medical problems, was addressed, although not successfully as we have seen, by proposals for comprehensive health insurance. This left the final area of risk that workers faced as they moved from rural agricultural employment to urban industrial jobs, the possible loss of income due to being laid off, through no fault of their own, as a result of economic downturns related to the industry that employed them. This problem was addressed through proposals for unemployment insurance. The first unemployment insurance program was enacted in England in 1911. Under this plan, each payday the employer, the worker, and the government would

---

23. Isaac M. Rubinow, *The Quest for Social Security* (New York: Holt, 1934), 207.

24. David A. Moss, *When All Else Fails*, 173–176; James Leiby, *A History of Social Work and Social Welfare in the United States* (Columbia University Press, 1978), 207.

each contribute a premium that would go into a fund from which the worker could draw a fixed benefit for up to 15 weeks of unemployment. The AALL liked the English plan and in 1915 introduced an "American plan" for unemployment compensation. This plan was very similar to the English version with the addition that, as an inducement for prevention, employers and employees who demonstrated better than average employment records were entitled to special refunds. The refund would be paid annually to employers and as a lump sum at retirement to workers. A bill closely based on the AALL plan was introduced into the Massachusetts House of Representatives at the beginning of 1916 but it never got very far. Interest in unemployment insurance had been spurred by a short, but sharp, economic downturn from 1913 to 1915. By the time the unemployment bill was introduced in Massachusetts, the economy had improved and support faded. Bills were introduced in a number of other states between 1916 and 1931, but none were passed. Part of the reason for the failure of this effort was a decision by AALL leaders that health insurance was a higher legislative priority. It was not until the Great Depression hit and unemployment rates reached as high as 40 percent that unemployment insurance reached the top of the reformers agenda.

FOCUSING ON THE NEEDS OF CHILDREN

The major disruptive changes that occurred in the late nineteenth century and led to progressive reforms in the early twentieth century are generally identified as urbanization, industrialization, and immigration. In addition to these changes there also occurred in nineteenth century America a marked change in attitude toward children, which evolved into a conception of children as beings who had unique needs and the right to have those needs fulfilled to a reasonable extent. Viviana Zelizer documents in her book *Pricing the Priceless Child* how during the nineteenth century the concept of the "useful" child who made a valuable contribution to the family economy gradually evolved into the "useless" child of the twentieth century, a child who was economically worthless, in fact very costly, to the family but considered to be emotionally priceless. The reasons for this transformation were many, including the decline in useful tasks that could be performed by children in a maturing industrial economy, the decline in the birth and death rates, and the rise of the compassionate family.[25] The changing view of children, combined with the view of enlightened jurists that parental rights result from the carrying out of parents' duties to their children, created an atmosphere in which children became a focus of progressive interest. As Wiebe notes, "If humanitarian progressivism had a central theme, it was the child. He united the campaigns for health, education and a richer city environment, and he dominated much of the interest in labor legislation."[26]

25. Viviana A. Zelizer, *Pricing the Priceless Child: The Changing Social Value of Children* (Princeton, NJ: Princeton University Press, 1994).
26. Robert Wiebe, *The Search for Order*, 169.

Child Labor

Based on this new conception of childhood, progressives became greatly concerned about child labor. Prior to the late nineteenth century few were concerned about this. The labor of children was considered an economic help for families and was also considered morally valuable, preventing sins like idleness and teaching the virtues of work and responsibility. However, jobs appropriate for children, mainly on family farms, were steadily declining, and children were in ever increasing numbers being put to work in industrial jobs and under conditions that many felt were not appropriate. The percentage of the labor force who were children increased from 14 in 1870 to over 18 in 1900.[27] This worked out to nearly 2 million child employees in the labor force. Contemporary observers, and historians today, believed that many children were not counted and that the official figures were extremely conservative. Reformers argued that child labor should be curtailed because industrial working conditions had become much too dangerous for children; that children working interfered with schooling and thus perpetuated poverty; that children were being exploited, sickened, and maimed by the unrestrained greed of industrialists; and, finally, child labor robbed children of the happy and healthy childhoods that the emerging conception of childhood argued that they were entitled to.

Several industries were of special concern. One was coal mining, where young boys worked in dark and dangerous mines, often for 12 or more hours at a shift. Some worked above ground as breakers, a job that involved sitting for hours at a time over swiftly moving, dusty belts of coal to pick out debris, mainly pieces of slate or shale. Another industry was glassmaking, where boys worked at various tasks in furnace rooms, exposed to long hours of intense heat, often in excess of 100 degrees, and glaring light, combined with the dangers of fumes, dust, and broken glass. Many children worked the night shift. A third industry was textiles, especially cotton mills in the South. In 1900, one in four cotton mill workers were under 15, and children as young as 6 or 7 were often employed. Most children employed in cotton mills worked as spinners, tending long rows of rapidly spinning bobbins to repair breaks in the thread or to change a full bobbin for an empty one. In canneries on the Atlantic and Gulf coasts children as young as 6 shucked oysters, picked shrimp, and processed fruits and vegetables, sometimes 7 days a week, 16 hours a day. Finally, there was concern with urban areas where children roamed the streets, peddling newspapers, working as delivery boys and girls, and as night messengers, a job that was suspected, and later confirmed, as usually a front for prostitution.

Many people concluded that limits needed to be placed on child labor and that it was a problem appropriate for government intervention. Hull House founder Jane Addams stated that it was "inevitable that efforts to secure a child labor law should be our first venture into the field of state legislation."[28] A leader who emerged to jump start the fight against child labor was Florence Kelley. Kelley was a prominent intellectual, daughter of a Pennsylvania congressman, lawyer, translator of Friedrich Engles, and a divorcee with three children. She was one of the most brilliant of the

27. Walter I. Trattner, Crusade for the Children: A History of the National Child Labor Committee and Child Labor Reform in America (Chicago: Quadrangle Books, 1970), 24.
28. Jane Addams, *Twenty Years at Hull House* (New York: Macmillan, 1910).

group that gathered at Hull House under the tutelage of Jane Addams.[29] In 1889 she presented an incisive critique of child labor statistics at a meeting of state labor bureaus. In 1891 the Illinois Bureau of Labor asked her to investigate the sweating system (exploitative home piecework manufacture), part of the results published in *Hull House Maps and Papers*. Partially as a result of this paper she was appointed Factory Inspector for the state of Illinois, a job created by a new factory act. As a factory inspector, Kelley became perhaps the leading national expert on the actual conditions of workers in industry. She became particularly interested in the plight of children in industry. What she found as factory inspector were conditions for child employees even more horrifying than generally believed. As historian James Leiby stated, "What infuriated her was not just the foolish rationalizations of employers and the connivance of parents (including the citizens around Alton, Illinois, who took in foster children from almshouses in surrounding counties to work under harrowing conditions in the glass works), but the general ignorant complacency, the unwillingness of district attorneys to enforce the law and of boards of education to compel attendance at school, and the fatuity of the courts that insisted on a wildly irrelevant "freedom of contract."[30] In 1897 a new governor fired Kelley, and after a few short-term jobs, including that of librarian, Kelley was appointed in 1899 as General Secretary of the National Consumers League. The main idea of the League was to band concerned consumers together to boycott products manufactured by companies that did not meet labor standards set by the League. The League would award a "seal of approval" to companies that met standards and members would only purchase products carrying this seal (this approach was to be used again later in the twentieth century with the slogans "look for the union label" and the "Good Housekeeping Seal of Approval"). By 1905 Kelley had helped found 64 local leagues in 20 states, all looking to her for their reform agenda, on which the major item was child labor. In the meantime she was appointed chair of child labor committees for the National Women's Suffrage Association, the National Congress of Mothers, and the General Federation of Women's Clubs. In 1902 she moved to New York City, living at Henry Street Settlement, where, in collaboration with prominent social worker Lillian Wald, she formed the New York Child Labor Committee. The NYCLC was made up of social workers, reformers, philanthropists, and businessmen and was headed by Robert Hunter of University Settlement. The NYCLC built ties with other civic and religious reform groups and within a year had inspired five child labor bills.

At the 1903 meeting of the National Conference of Charities and Corrections Kelley met with Felix Adler, founder of the Ethical Culture Society, and with Edgar Gardner Murphy, an Alabama Episcopal priest who had founded the Alabama Child Labor Committee and successfully lobbied for the strictest child labor law in the nation. A plan was developed for a nationwide agency to coordinate a unified child labor campaign. Invitations were issued to social welfare leaders throughout the country to a meeting in New York City in April 1904 to plan a new organization. Subsequently, on April 15, 1904 at Carnegie Hall, the National Child Labor Committee (NCLC) convened its first general meeting. Samuel McCune Lindsey of the New York School of Philanthropy was appointed as the first secretary of the new organization. The NCLC investigated

---

29. James Leiby, A History of Social Work and Social Welfare in the United States (New York: Columbia University Press, 1978), 148.

30. James Leiby, *A History of Social Work and Social Welfare in the United States,* 148.

working conditions in several states, drafted a model child labor law in 1904, testified before national, state, and local conferences and legislative committees, and campaigned for compulsory school attendance. The model law called for a minimum age of 16 in mining, 14 in manufacturing, workdays limited to eight hours, no work after 7:00 p.m., and documented proof of age. In 1908, in a master stroke of public relations, the NCLC hired Lewis Hines, a teacher and amateur photographer of New York's poor, as the official NCLC photographer. For the next twenty years Hines produced a photographic record of working conditions in factories, mines, canneries, fields, and on the streets. As historian Walter Trattner observed, Hines photos of "the humane and inhumane elements in industry—the pathetic faces of the working children and the conditions under which they toiled—aroused public sentiment against child labor in a way that no printed page or public lecture could."[31] Hine's photos were widely disseminated by the NCLC to great effect.

One of the early and significant goals of the NCLC was to get the federal government involved in social welfare with, of course, child labor regulation being a major focus. In 1903 Lillian Wald, referring to the agricultural welfare state argued, "If the government can have a department to look after the Nation's farm crops, why can't it have a bureau to look after the Nation's child crop."[32] In her 1905 book *Some Ethical Gains through Legislation*, Florence Kelley further developed the idea of the establishment of a national agency dedicated to the welfare of children. In 1906 the NCLC drafted legislation to establish such a federal agency that was introduced in Congress that same year. The bill met with strong resistance, mostly by southerners who identified it with agitation to prohibit child labor, raised questions about whether such an agency was constitutional, whether the proposed work could not be better done by existing bureaus, and whether it was not really an attack on the rights of parents. The bill died without ever coming to a vote. Turning to President Roosevelt, reformers suggested that he sponsor a national meeting on the welfare of children. Roosevelt found the suggestion interesting and invited 216 social welfare leaders to meet at the White House on January 25 and 26, 1909 to discuss programs for the welfare of children in the United States. The conference met, the first ever White House conference on any subject, and became an every ten year event. The conference concluded that, among other things, a federal Children's Bureau be established and charged with the responsibility of conducting research and collecting data on all aspects of childhood. Roosevelt called on Congress to establish such a bureau, which it did in 1912. President Taft, Roosevelt's successor in the office, appointed Julia Lathrop, a Hull House resident and a member of the Illinois Board of Charities, as first head of the Children's Bureau. To the disappointment of the activists who were central to the movement to create the Children's Bureau, it did not take on child labor as one of its priorities, even though the agency was administratively located in the Department of Labor, and part of its responsibility was to report on "dangerous occupations, accidents and diseases of children [and] employment legislation affecting children."[33] Lathrop, a savvy politician, believed that the issue of child labor was too controversial for a new and tiny federal agency, whose legitimacy was yet to be established, and

---

31. Walter I. Trattner, *Crusade for the Children*, 106.

32. Dorothy E. Bradbury, *Five Decades of Action for Children: A History of the Children's Bureau* (Washington, DC: Children's Bureau, 1962), 1.

33. U.S. 37 stat. 79, the act establishing the Children's Bureau, approved April 7, 1912.

instead chose infant mortality as the bureau's initial focus, an issue no one could argue with, and this remained the focus of the Bureau for two decades.

Although child labor activists developed an early interest in involving the federal government in the issue, the majority of their work was on the state level. In 1900, 28 states had some kind of child labor legislation on the books, but the provisions were minimal. Most of the laws applied only to children employed in manufacturing or mining, and did little more than raise the legal age for employment in factories to 10 and in mines to 12, and this provision was largely meaningless because there was no requirement for age documentation. Some laws limited the work day for children to 10 hours and only eight states protected children from working after 10 p.m. For the next twenty years the NCLC, in conjunction with local reformers, waged a state-by-state battle to improve these laws. In the north, the first target was Pennsylvania where coal mines, glass factories, and other manufacturers employed as many children as all the southern states combined. In 1905 a bill was passed by the Pennsylvania state legislature that required school attendance and proof of age before employment. It was declared unconstitutional by state courts. A modified version was passed in 1909, but glass factories, among the most notorious child labor exploiters, were exempted. In the South the campaign began with an Alabama law passed in 1903 and a Georgia law in 1906, laws that strengthened protections only a little. By 1912 nine states had met NCLC minimum standards set in 1904: minimum age of 14 to work in manufacturing and 16 in mining; work day limited to 8 hours; no night work for those under 16; and a requirement that employers document the age of all employees. By 1914, as a result of the continued campaign by the NCLC, the National Consumers League, the General Federation of Women's Clubs, and others, almost all states had laws covering hours and conditions of child labor in factories, mills, and workshops, and setting minimum age for leaving school.

Although the child labor movement had had some notable success, activists felt that there was still much to be desired. Child labor in home sweatshops, agriculture, canneries, and street trades other than night messenger services remained for the most part completely unregulated at the beginning of the second decade of the new century. By 1913, activists had concluded that federal legislation was necessary to effectively regulate child labor and, perhaps buoyed by the establishment of the Children's Bureau, that federal involvement was possible. The NCLC appointed a committee to write a model law and to circulate it to sympathetic legislators. The legal basis of the model bill was the constitutional power of the federal government to regulate interstate commerce. The bill would prohibit interstate commerce of goods produced by companies that did not meet the minimum standards formulated by the NCLC in 1904. A bill closely following the model bill was introduced in the 63rd Congress, where it passed the House by a large margin in February 1915 but was not acted upon by the Senate and so died at the end of the session. The bill was reintroduced in the 64th Congress in December of 1915 co-sponsored by Representative Edward Keating of Colorado and Senator Robert Owen of Oklahoma. In January 1916 the Keating-Owen bill passed the House by a margin of 343 to 46. The bill was supported by President Wilson, who made it a plank in his reelection platform, saying "We favor the speedy enactment of an effective child labor law." The Republican Party adopted a similar plank.[34] The bill passed the Senate on

---

34. Kirk H. Porter and Donald Bruce Johnson, eds., *National Party Platforms, 1840–1964* (Urbana, IL: University of Illinois Press, 1966), 199, 207.

August 3 by a margin of 52 to 12, with 32 abstentions. The bill was in effect for only about a year before being challenged in North Carolina by a father of two children who would lose their textile mill jobs if the bill were to stay in effect. The judge declared that the law was unconstitutional based on his belief that Congress did not have the right to regulate local labor conditions and that the law denied parents their legal right to their children's earnings. On June 3, 1918 the Supreme Court, by a 5 to 4 margin, upheld the North Carolina ruling, the majority concluding that the law overstepped the legitimate use of the interstate commerce clause.

Even though the Keating-Owens bill was overturned, public support for child labor legislation had become very strong. In 1918, when the United States entered the First World War, the war policies board added the standards specified in the act to all federal war contracts. After the supreme court decision the NCLC immediately began work on constitutionally acceptable alternatives. Based on NCLC work, Senator Atlee Pomeroy introduced a bill that would add a 10 percent tax on the profits of companies that violated the standards specified in the Keating-Owen Act. With little debate the bill passed both houses and was signed into law by President Wilson on February 24, 1919. The Pomeroy Act was declared unconstitutional by an 8 to 1 Supreme Court decision in 1922. However, by this time most states had strengthened their child labor laws and passed compulsory school attendance laws to meet the standards of the overturned federal legislation, and so no further federal laws were pursued. By 1930 less than 5 percent of children between ages 10 and 15 were employed, down from over 18 percent in 1900.

Juvenile Justice

Although nearly 20 percent of children aged ten to fifteen were working at the beginning of the twentieth century, this still left 80 percent who were not. An increasing proportion of these children were living in cities where, with time on their hands and often lax parental supervision because their parents were occupied with earning a living, some engaged in various forms of anti-social behavior and consequently came in contact with the criminal justice system. Prior to the progressive era there were some efforts to treat juvenile offenders differently than adults, mainly the development of a handful of correctional institutions that allowed for the incarceration of children separate from adults: the New York City House of Refuge in 1821; the Philadelphia House of Reformation in 1838; and the Boston House of Reformation in 1836. These were private facilities. In 1847, a public state reform school for boys opened in Westboro, Massachusetts, and one for girls opened in Lancaster in 1845. However, it was not until the end of the nineteenth century that an overall attempt was made to rationalize these reforms into a coherent system of criminal justice for juveniles.[35] Before this time juveniles were processed essentially as adults: they were placed on court dockets with adults; they were detained while awaiting trial in adult jails, and if found guilty they received the same harsh punishments as adults. This resulted in two concerns in the minds of progressives at the end of the nineteenth century. One had to do with the well-being

---

35. Anthony Platt, *The Child Savers: The Invention of Delinquency*, 2nd ed. (Chicago: The University of Chicago Press, 1977), xviii.

of the youth. Based on new theories of psychology and child development the attitude was taking root that crime among children should be considered a problem for humane treatment and reform, rather than for punishment and retribution. The other concern had to do with the safety of society. Because the only options open to judges and juries were to either impose a harsh adult penalty on a child, or to find the child not-guilty even though guilt may have been indicated, many were opting for the latter and letting the child go without any consequences to his or her behavior. Thus, the feeling developed that some children were becoming habitual criminals because they were learning that crime had, for them, no consequences. The result of these concerns was the establishment of the juvenile court.

The juvenile court was first developed in Chicago as a result of efforts of the Chicago Women's Club. In the late 1800s, the club adopted as a project the general improvement of jail conditions in Cook County. While engaged in this effort, the members of the club were shocked to find that children were locked up with adults, and they soon came to the conclusion that there was no way to really improve conditions for these children as long as they were in the adult criminal justice system. In 1895, the members of the club drafted a bill providing for a completely separate court to handle the cases of juveniles. When they submitted the bill to their legal advisor, he questioned its constitutionality, believing that the bill was too broad and that it lacked procedural safeguards. Consequently, the club dropped the bill. It was picked up two years later by the Illinois Conference of Charities, where it gained the support of the Chicago Bar Association and was passed by the legislature. The bill created a juvenile court with jurisdiction for all legal matters pertaining to children under the age of sixteen. It provided for a special judge, a separate courtroom, and the maintenance of separate records. Perhaps the most important aspect was that it called for court hearings to be informal rather than formal.

Although the idea of a juvenile court was first developed in Illinois, its greatest advocate and most successful popularizer was Judge Benjamin Lindsey in Denver. Lindsey was a criminal court judge who was concerned about the same issues that led to the reforms in Chicago. Lacking a law in Colorado, Lindsey simply set about handling juvenile cases that came before him in a different manner than adult cases. In Judge Lindsey's court, juvenile and adult cases were separated, and in the cases involving a juvenile, the well-being of the youth took precedence over legal formalities. Hearings were informal: the judge removed his black robe; the imposing judge's bench was abandoned and cases were heard in less formal settings, often the judge's chambers; adversarial questioning was replaced with fatherly discussions. "Snitching" (confessing to the act) and "ditching" (changing one's behavior) were viewed as essential ingredients to reform. Most important, the judge's disposition of the case was primarily premised on the well-being of the child and not on guilt or innocence. Lindsey's success with Denver's delinquent and dependent children led to the passage of "An Act Concerning Delinquent Children" in 1903, which adopted Lindsey's framework and method for all Colorado courts. Following the passage of this act, in 1904 Lindsey wrote *The Problem of Children and How the State of Colorado Cares for Them*, and a number of articles in both professional journals and lay magazines to drum up support for the movement. The popularity of the juvenile court movement, and of Lindsey himself, is illustrated by the fact that in 1914 a poll by *American Magazine* rated Judge Lindsey in eighth place as "the greatest living American."

The juvenile court was based on the concepts of *parens patria* and *delinquency. Parens patria* is a legal doctrine that states that in cases where people, such as those with mental disorders, are judged to not be responsible for their actions, the courts are given wide discretion to act in their behalf, as a wise parent would. As children under sixteen were now defined as not being fully responsible for their actions, *parens patria* was deemed applicable to the courts dealings with them. The emphasis was to be put on rehabilitation rather than punishment. *Delinquency* was a new sociological concept that had as its object the decriminalizing of antisocial behavior in youth. The basic approach was succinctly stated in an address given to the American Bar Association in 1909 by Julian W. Mack, a judge in the juvenile court in Chicago: "Why isn't it just and proper to treat these juvenile offenders as we deal with the neglected children, as a wise and merciful father handles his own child whose errors are not discovered by the authorities? Why isn't it the duty of the State instead of asking merely whether a boy or a girl has committed the specific offense, to find out what he is, physically, mentally, morally, and then, if it learns that he is treading the path that leads to criminality, to take him in charge, not so much to punish as to reform, not to degrade but to uplift, not to crush but to develop, not to make him a criminal but a worthy citizen."[36]

The concept of *parens patria* and that of delinquency, leading to the creation of the juvenile court met wide public acceptance and support, and the idea caught on quickly. Children were not to be defined as criminals and moral deviants; rather, they were to be thought of as misguided youngsters who needed firm but kindly parenting to get them back on the right track. Ten years after Illinois created the first juvenile court, such courts had been established in twenty-two states and the District of Columbia; within twenty years, only three states, Connecticut, Maine, and Wyoming, lacked separate juvenile courts.

The Return of Public Assistance

As previously discussed, organized charity campaigned tirelessly during the last quarter of the nineteenth century for the elimination of any public financial support outside of the poorhouse. The argument was that only private, scientific charity organizations could help the poor without doing more harm than good. Government, according to these arguments, was incapable of learning the lessons of scientific philanthropy, because it was subject to corruption and political interference, it would fail to attract competent trained administrators because jobs would be filled through political patronage, and it would not provide adequate supervision to recipients. A major danger of government outdoor relief was that it could easily become defined as a right with the inevitable result of pauperizing the recipient, creating a "pathological parasitism." It was a mistake to give applicants cash rather than in-kind benefits such as food and coal, because this would create "temptations to spend money recklessly or foolishly." Finally, organized charity argued that outdoor relief was an attack on the family, encouraging desertion, and destroying the great principle of family solidarity, that which called upon the strong members to support the weak.[37] Also, public relief programs utilized rigid formulas for calculating the amount of relief a family was to

36. Julian Mack, "The Juvenile Court as a Legal Institution," in Hasting H. Hart, ed., *Preventive Treatment of Neglected Children* (New York: Russell Sage Foundation, 1910), 296–297.

37. Mark H. Leff, "Consensus for Reform: The Mothers' Pension Movement in the Progressive Era," *Social Service Review*, 47 (Sept. 1973): 403–404.

receive, violating the cherished scientific charity principle of individuation, that is, using relief as a tool for recipient growth and change, which required that the amount of relief be determined by case goals. As Mary Richmond replied, when queried by a public official about what the adequate amount of assistance was for a family: "Adequate relief is such sum or sums, large or small, as will give, when combined with adequate planning and oversight, the desired result; namely, permanent social betterment in the individual case."[38]

The campaign to end outdoor relief was for the most part successful beginning with New York City suspending all financial assistance in 1874. When a charter was adopted for the consolidated Greater New York City in 1898 it specifically banned the distribution of outdoor relief. Brooklyn abandoned outdoor relief in 1878, followed by Philadelphia in 1879. Chicago, Providence, and Cleveland all followed. By 1900 Baltimore, St. Louis, Washington, San Francisco, Kansas City, New Orleans, Louisville, Denver, Atlanta, Memphis, and Charleston all joined the parade. Boston was the only eastern city to hold out against the movement to abolish outdoor relief.[39]

A major concern about the banning of outdoor relief emerged at the end of the nineteenth century and was tied to a declining faith in orphanages. Popular, as well as expert, opinion was moving in the direction of viewing orphanages as unnatural places for children to grow up, places that rather than molding solid citizens, provided "a kind of life that ruins with its dull routine hundreds of thousands of children."[40] Sentiment was increasing that children's institutions were factories for "human machines," in which the "good innocent child" was made to live with "undesirable children," and in which some children died or were mentally debilitated for a lack of the "most sacred thing in human life—a mother's love." "Only in the home, and from his own mother," it was asserted, could a child "receive the love and personal care necessary to his complete development."[41] Because of the banning of outdoor relief many poor parents were being forced to place their children in institutional care as the only alternative to their living on the street and starving. The highest rate of placement appears to have come in 1910, when it was estimated that 126,000, or more than three children per 1000 child population, were living in orphanages. This was only a part of the family disruption going on at that time, for over 17,000 additional destitute children were placed in foster homes as an alternative to the orphanage.[42] People began to wonder why if the government was giving grants to orphanages, and boarding payments to foster homes, why not just give that money to the children's mothers and enable them to stay at home. One of many observers, Judge Julian Mack of Chicago, for example, asked: "If we take a child away from the

38. Mary E. Richmond to E. Francis O'Neill of the Boston Finance Commission, 5 February 1923, quoted in Sarah Henry Lederman, *From Poverty to Philanthropy: The Life and Work of Mary Richmond* (Ph.D. Dissertation, Columbia University, 1994), 240.

39. Raymond Mohl, "The Abolition of Public Outdoor Relief, 1870–1900: A Critique of the Piven and Cloward Thesis," in Walter I. Trattner, ed., *Social Welfare or Social Control? Some Historical Reflections on Regulating the Poor* (Knoxville, TN: The University of Tennessee Press, 1983), 41.

40. August 1903 editorial in the *New York Journal*, quoted in Matthew A. Crenson, *Building the Invisible Orphanage: A Prehistory of the American Welfare System* (Cambridge, MA: Harvard University Press, 1998), 246.

41. Mark H. Leff, "Consensus for Reform," 410.

42. Muriel W. Pumphrey and Ralph E. Pumphrey, "The Widows' Pension Movement, 1900–1930," in Walter I. Trattner, ed., *Social Welfare or Social Control*, 54.

mother we willingly pay an asylum to care for him; the public pays for his support. Why should not the public funds be paid to the mother herself and keep the family together?"[43]

The event that opened the floodgates to laws enabling states to provide financial assistance to mothers in their own homes was the 1909 White House Conference on Children and Youth. The conference helped to crystalize a growing consensus among child welfare experts that children should be kept in their own homes whenever possible, rather than being placed in the orphanages that Catholics supported, or the foster homes that Protestant child welfare advocates tended to favor. In his opening address President Roosevelt discussed the plight of the widow unable to support her children, saying: "Surely in such a case the goal toward which we should strive is to help that mother, so that she can keep her own home and keep the children in it; that is the best thing possible to be done for that child." At the conclusion of the conference one of the main resolutions stated that "Home life is the highest and finest product of civilization. It is the great molding force of mind and character. Children should not be deprived of it except for urgent and compelling reasons." When misfortune intervened, the document continued, assistance should be given to maintain the family for the children's sake. "The home should not be broken up for reasons of poverty, but only for considerations of inefficiency or immorality." In a nod toward the feelings of organized charity, the resolution expressed the belief that private administration of assistance would be better left to private agencies saying: "This aid should be given by such methods and from such sources as may be determined by the general relief policy of each community, preferably in the form of private charity, rather than public relief."[44]

Mothers' pension advocates instantly grabbed onto the White House Conference resolution that children should not be separated from their parents for reasons of poverty alone. They pretty much ignored, however, the resolution's stated preference for provision of needed assistance by private charity. Although organized charity had been successful in their efforts to ban outdoor relief and gain for themselves the exclusive mission of helping the dependent poor, sentiment against their approach had appeared very early in the process. The prevailing sentiment that organized charity was harsh in its approach to the poor was expressed in a popular saying that the motto of the charity organizations, rather than "not alms, but a friend," should actually be "neither alms nor a friend" and as expressed in poet John Boyle O'Reilly's poem *Bohemia,* which included the line, "The organized charity scrimped and iced in the name of a cautious statistical Christ." Private charity had also lost the confidence of the public in its ability to keep families together when pilot programs to do this failed. The premier program was one launched by the New York Charity Organization Society (COS) in 1898 where the Society was allowed to handle the cases of families considered "worthy" who were applying to place their children in orphanages. The idea was for the COS to demonstrate that a combination of casework services and private financial assistance could prevent the placement, and preserve the homes, of a significant number of children (in effect a foreshadowing of family preservation programs that were to become central to child welfare policy nearly a century later). In two years of effort, the COS had only assisted

43. Quoted in Walter I. Trattner, *From Poor Law to Welfare State*, 6th ed. (New York: The Free Press, 1999), 223.

44. "Letter to the President of the United States Embodying the Conclusions of the Conference on the Care of Dependent Children," reprinted in Robert Bremner, ed., *Children and Youth in America*, Vol. 2, Part 1 (Cambridge, MA: Harvard University Press, 1971), 365.

350 families, with a total of 800 children, while in the same time period nearly 5,000 children were placed in institutional care.[45]

Immediately following the White House Conference, mothers' pension advocates went to work lobbying for states and municipalities to enact legislation, completely ignoring the recommendation about the preference for private charity. To say their efforts were successful would be an understatement. Leff, referring to the opinions of contemporary commentators, notes that the "wildfire spread of widow's pensions exceeded that of any other social or humanitarian idea of the era." Missouri passed the first law in 1911, although it only applied to Kansas City. Illinois passed the first statewide law the same year. By 1913, eighteen additional states had passed similar laws. These laws all provided payments to women, generally widows but some of the laws covered divorced or deserted mothers as long as it could be demonstrated that the woman was not at fault. The grants were meant to cover at least part of the cost of raising children in their own homes, so that they would not have to be placed in foster homes or orphanages. Administration of the mother's pensions in most cases was the responsibility of the juvenile court. States generally established a maximum allowable monthly pension, which ranged from $9 to $15 per month for the first child and $4 to $10 a month for additional children. To be eligible to receive a pension a mother had to demonstrate that she was "a proper person, physically, mentally, and morally fit to bring up her children."[46]

Major professional social work organizations, notably the National Conference of Charities and Corrections, the National Association of Societies for Organizing Charity, and the Russell Sage Foundation mounted fierce resistance to the mothers' pension movement. The resistance was spearheaded by Mary Richmond, at the time head of the Charity Organization Department of the Russell Sage Foundation. The resistance was based on two factors. The first was a genuine belief that mothers' pensions were, philosophically and programmatically, a bad idea. Richmond argued that money was not the main problem faced by widows. She stated, "No group of cases seems to us to need such continuous oversight as . . . pensioned widows with children; 'no volunteer visitor, no pensions,' would be a good rule, we believe."[47] She also believed that public administration, and politics, would preclude the professional administration of relief, using as an example the story of politically fueled, ever rising expenditures for Civil War pensions, asserting that the same thing would happen again if the country instituted the principle of public pensions for mothers. The second argument that organized charity made in opposition to mothers' pensions was related to the pragmatic protection of the charity societies' professional "turf" and financial base. The whole raison d'etre of the charity organizations was the efficient and professional administration of charity. Establishing public pension programs guided by bureaucratic rules rather than professional discretion "strikes at the very vitals of private philanthropy," stated a contemporary analyst.[48] The greatest concern of organized charity about the adoption of mothers' pensions, however, was fiscal. The support of widowed mothers had always been their most effective fundraising

---

45. Muriel W. Pumphrey and Ralph E. Pumphrey, "The Widows' Pension Movement," 55–56.

46. Mark H. Leff, "Consensus for Reform," 400–401.

47. Quoted in Sarah Henry Lederman, *From Poverty to Philanthropy*, 219.

48. Theda Skocpol, *Protecting Soldiers and Mothers: The Political Origins of Social Policy in the United States* (Cambridge, MA: Harvard University Press, 1992), 426.

plea and, if the government began using tax dollars to support widowed mothers, this source of revenue for private agencies was liable to dry up.

By 1913 eighteen states had passed mothers' pension laws, but Richmond and her allies were confident that they would be able to win the battle. Indiana, Minnesota, Massachusetts, and Pennsylvania all had strong organized charity contingents that had succeeded in blocking legislation. Richmond believed that her arguments had been listened to with the result "that all the administrators of the new laws have been put upon the defensive and . . . in a few instances; the laws themselves have been modified." Richmond's greatest victory had been in blocking legislation in New York, the center of organized charity power and influence. In response to this victory in May of 1913 the New York State legislature appropriated $15,000 to establish a commission for studying mothers' pensions, composed mainly of opponents of organized charity. The report of the commission, as anticipated by Richmond, was a scathing attack on organized charity, and concluded that government assistance was the only solution to the problem of impoverished widows with children. Following the publication of the commission's report in 1914 New York passed a mothers' pension law and Richmond conceded defeat and moved on to other interests. By 1919 twenty-two more states had passed such legislation, with seven more and the District of Columbia getting on board by 1931.

From the spirit and the bitterness of the debate between advocates of mothers' pensions and organized charities, it would be natural to conclude that the universal passage of public assistance laws would represent the end of the influence of organized charity in financial assistance programs. This, however, was not the case. When the laws were passed and implemented, public officials found that administering the programs was not as easy as they had anticipated. Ironically, after spending years trashing organized charity and all of its methods and philosophy, these officials turned to the private agencies for help running the programs. The assertion by pension program advocates that their concept of "supervision" of recipients would be far less intrusive and meddlesome than the casework approach of organized charity turned out not to be true. Scientific charity standards quickly became mothers' pension guidelines. Leff observes that as "social caseworkers obtained an ever tightening grip on the programs, it is clear that these investigators were anything but unmeddlesome good friends . . . many mothers' pension agencies vigorously injected themselves into the lives of their 'pensioners.' Use of tobacco and lack of church attendance were evidence of being an 'unfit mother.' " The private charity organizations had lost the battle against public assistance, but then quickly captured the programs, creating in essence the same programs that had been run by scientific charity agencies, with the only difference being that they were now paid for out of public funds.

In addition to the fact that they quickly adopted many of the negative aspects of private charity programs, there were other problems with mothers' pensions. Most of the problems were related to a very low level of financial support allocated by state legislatures, resulting in skimpy grants and incomplete coverage. In 1911 the early Chicago program provided grants averaging only $6.33 per child per month (approximately $156 in 2015 money). Coverage was much greater and more adequate in northern industrial states than in southern states; 1930 per capita expenditures were 82 cents in New York compared to only 3 cents in Louisiana. The Children's Bureau estimated in 1931 that mothers' pension programs were providing aid to less than one-third of eligible families. There was also the problem that the programs served very few minority families. African American families, who constituted about 12 percent of the total number of families, received only 3 percent of total pensions, with a number of counties and some southern states barring them totally from the program. In only two northern states was there recognition of need among black families on a scale at all comparable with that for whites.[49]

In spite of its shortcomings, the development of mothers' pensions represented a quantum leap forward in American social policy. Although many eligible families were not served, a huge number were. By 1931 the number of children remaining in their own homes supported partially by public funds exceeded the total number in institutional and foster care combined. Spending growth for mothers' pensions was faster than almost any other government program. In 1931 the appropriation for mothers' pensions exceeded $33 million, distributed among more than 90,000 families with over 250,000 dependent children. Philosophically mothers' pensions represented the first argument that welfare assistance could be granted as a right and not as a charity dole; that a request for assistance did not constitute evidence of inefficiency or moral turpitude. Advocates argued that mothers, by caring for their children, made a contribution to society similar to a civil servant: "He is paid for his work; she for hers. And she should be paid by those for whom she does it—the citizens of the state, not the subscribers to the charities."[50] The most important contribution of the mothers' pension movement was the rejection of the nineteenth century belief that assistance to the poor was the proper role of the private sector, substituting the at least preliminary recognition that poverty was a problem too large for private charities and was in fact a public problem requiring governmental remedies.

THE PROGRESSIVE ERA IS FOLLOWED BY
THE CONSERVATIVE 1920s

It is, of course, not possible to identify an exact date for the end of a historical era like progressivism, but historians are in agreement that the end was coterminous with the end of World War I, some choosing the year 1918 when hostilities ceased, and some picking 1920 when the Treaty of Versailles was signed officially bringing the war to a close. There is disagreement about the cause of the post WWI rejection of progressivism. Hofstadter attributes it to a reaction to America's involvement in the war. He asserts that America's entry into the war was based on progressive terms, values, and ideals. The war, according to President Wilson, was not being fought for any selfish reasons but rather for ideals such as defense of international law and freedom of the seas. "What is significant," according to Hofstadter, "is that the war was justified before the American public in the Progressive rhetoric and on Progressive terms." Once the war was over and the excitement had died down, the American people began to realize the price they had paid for an essentially idealistic venture. They began to feel that they had been conned by the promoters of the war. "The war purged the pent up guilts, shattered the ethos of responsibility that had permeated

---

49. United States Children's Bureau, *Mothers' Aid, 1931*, in Robert Bremner, ed., *Children and Youth in America*, Vol. 2, Part 1, 396.

50. Mark H. Leff, "Consensus for Reform," 411.

the rhetoric of more than a decade. It convinced the people that they had paid the price for such comforts of modern life as they could claim, that they had finally answered to the full progressive demand for sacrifice and self-control and altruism . . . The pressure for civic participation was followed by widespread apathy, the sense of responsibility by neglect, the call for sacrifice by hedonism."[51] Davis, on the other hand, rejects the notion that the war killed progressivism. He argues that following the defeat of Theodore Roosevelt and the Progressive Party in the 1912 election the movement began to die and was then temporarily resurrected by the war. During the war reform continued to make progress, but after the war ended the previously begun decline was completed.[52] An additional factor was that many leading progressives, including Jane Addams and Roger Baldwin, were pacifists and leaders in the unpopular anti-war movement. When the war ended this left the popular impression that progressives were not patriotic Americans and should therefore not be listened to.

Whatever the reasons for the decline of the progressive era, it is clear that it led to what Jane Addams described as "a period of political and social sag."[53] The 1920s was led by the administrations of three successive conservative Republican presidents, Warren G. Harding, Calvin Coolidge, and Herbert Hoover. Hoover, it should be noted, was a Republican, but was not a conservative in the same sense as Harding and Coolidge, having supported Theodore Roosevelt in the 1912 election, and was widely considered a progressive in the 1920s.[54] All of these men pursued policies that harkened back to the individualism and laissez-faire of the nineteenth century. Different from nineteenth century conservatism, however, was the era's focus on individual freedom, the pursuit of pleasure, and consumerism. The Republicans in the 1920s rolled back many of the economic accomplishments of the progressive era by cutting the income tax, ignoring organized labor and the poor, and allowing big business to dominate federal regulatory agencies. The view of the Republicans was that American capitalism was on the brink of defeating poverty and did not need the assistance of government programs to do so. Herbert Hoover, on the very eve of the Great Depression, famously stated, "In America today, we are nearer a final triumph over poverty than is any other land. We have not reached the goal but . . . we shall soon, with the help of God, be in sight of the day when poverty shall be banished from this nation."[55]

Some reform activities continued in the declining years of progressivism and during the 1920s, but progress was slow and successes were few. Although progressive causes were, as we have seen, mostly liberal, there was always a strong interest in social control in the name of social improvement. These social control aspects lasted into the 1920s and scored some success, notably prohibition and eugenics. Prohibition, enacted by the 18th Amendment to the Constitution, was a result of the temperance movement that had been a cause that built support during the entire progressive years. It was passed in 1917, ratified by the states in 1919, and took effect in 1920. Members of the temperance movement, a number that included many social workers, had argued

---

51. Richard Hofstadter, *The Age of Reform: From Bryan to F.D.R.* (New York: Alfred A. Knopf, 1955), 273.

52. Allen F. Davis, "Welfare Reform and World War I," *American Quarterly*, 19 (Fall, 1967): 516–533.

53. Jane Addams, *The Second Twenty Years at Hull House* (New York: The MacMillan Company, 1930), 192.

54. Joan Hoff Wilson, *Herbert Hoover, Forgotten Progressive* (Boston: Little, Brown, 1975).

55. http://www.brainyquote.com/quotes/authors/h/herbert_hoover.html. Accessed 05/04/2016.

that there was a strong relationship between consumption of alcohol and poverty, sickness, crime, vice, political corruption, and the general demoralization of the working class. The prohibition amendment is generally considered to have been a failure, its main permanent effects being the growth of organized crime and of a large federal law enforcement bureaucracy. However, some historians argue that it was in some ways a success, for example, having reduced the post prohibition per capita annual consumption of alcohol by more than one-half compared to the pre-prohibition level.[56] Prohibition lasted only thirteen years, being repealed with the 21st Amendment to the Constitution that took effect in 1933. The eugenics movement that advocated for the isolation, permanent custodial care, and, most ominously, the forced sterilization of people defined as genetically defective, mainly the mentally retarded, reached its peak in the 1920s. In 1927 in the case of *Buck v. Bell*, challenging the legality of sterilizing a young mother who had been assessed to have a mental age of nine, Oliver Wendell Holmes, Jr. delivered the Supreme Court's decision upholding the Virginia sterilization law, writing, "We have seen more than once that the public welfare may call upon the best citizens for their lives. It would be strange if it could not call upon those who already sap the strength of the state for these lesser sacrifices."[57]

The Nineteenth Amendment to the Constitution, granting women the right to vote, was ratified and became law on August 20, 1920. A result of this amendment, of course, was that women instantly became a major constituency of all elected representatives. Given that women were generally more liberal and more concerned with the rights and welfare of those with little power, especially children, it was anticipated that the Nineteenth Amendment would guarantee the continuation of at least some of the progressive reform agenda. At first it appeared that this would be true, but disappointment followed as reforms were unable to overcome the conservative complacency of the era. A first effort was in the area of infant and maternal health. Studies by the US Children's Bureau had found disturbingly high rates of infant and maternal mortality that they related to a lack of medical facilities and hence inadequate prenatal care, and these studies resulted in the passage of the Promotion of the Welfare and Hygiene of Maternity and Infancy Bill, more commonly referred to as the Sheppard-Towner Act. This act eventually resulted in the establishment of nearly 3000 child and maternal health centers, most in underserved rural areas, strengthened state health departments, and fostered the development of county health units that led to the better administration of local services. The act proved to be a great success, with the nation's infant and maternal mortality rate dropping significantly as a result of its provisions. In 1929 Congress failed to appropriate funds to continue this act due to a combination of persistent political and ideological opposition by conservative politicians, opposition by newly elected President Herbert Hoover, and stiff opposition by the mostly male medical profession that resented control of infant and maternal health by female dominated public health clinics. A second effort was a continuation of the battle against child labor. After the Keating-Owens Act was declared unconstitutional, reformers turned their attention to amending the Constitution. In 1924 Ohio Congressman Israel Moore Fisher proposed a child labor amendment that would give the power to Congress to

56. Jack S. Blocker, "Did Prohibition Really Work? Alcohol Prohibition as a Public Health Innovation," *American Journal of Public Health*, 96 (Feb. 2006): 233–243.

57. Stephen Jay Gould, *The Mismeasure of Man* (New York: W. W. Norton & Company, 1981), 335–336.

"limit, regulate, and prohibit the labor of persons under eighteen years of age." The amendment was passed by both houses of Congress later that same year. However, when it got to the states for ratification it ran into trouble. By 1931 only six states had ratified the amendment; thirty-two states voted against it. By 1932 the amendment was generally regarded as lost. A third reform effort was the work of feminists, led by the National Woman's Party, campaigning for an Equal Rights Amendment. This effort never really gained traction because there was fear among many women that the amendment would nullify progressive laws that had been passed protecting working women. In 1927, reflecting back on efforts of women to advocate for progressive reform during the 1920s, Margaret Dreier Robins, the president of the Women's Trade Union League, called the era "hideous in the public life of our people and in the noisy flaunting of cheap hopes and cheaper materialism."

As fits the conservative, business-dominated era that was the 1920s, the most significant social welfare developments were in the voluntary sector and resulted from increasing business influence on private social agencies. The theme of all these developments was making private social welfare more efficient, rational, well-administered, and, in a phrase, more business-like and, not incidentally, more under the control of the business community. The most important developments were a massive increase in both number and size of philanthropic foundations as a source of social welfare funding; establishment of councils of social agencies to rationalize and coordinate the programs of various agencies; and the development of federated funding as a means of both rationalizing agency fund raising and increasing the donor base to include middle class givers.

As an extension of the Gospel of Wealth that had developed in the late nineteenth century, a philosophy that asserted that rich people were only stewards of their wealth and had an obligation to use it for the benefit of humanity, many of the industrialists who had become rich, as they came to the end of their lives in the 1920s, set up charitable foundations with a portion (or sometimes all) of their estates. There were only a handful of foundations at the turn of the century, 102 in 1920, and by 1931 there were over 350.[58] Most of these foundations, as is still true of foundations today, favored education and health as recipients of their largesse. There were a few, however, notably the Russell Sage Foundation (RSF) and the Commonwealth Fund, that were primarily interested in supporting charity and social work. Since 1909 the RSF had been host and financial supporter of a Charity Organization Department, headed by Mary Richmond, that was dedicated to furthering scientific charity. In addition, the RSF provided money for the establishment of research departments at four early schools of social work, those in New York, Boston, Philadelphia, and St. Louis. In the 1920s the Russell Sage Foundation continued to give away large amounts of money, but as Romanofsky observed, the pattern of their grants "lend support to the notion that the excitement and vitality of the earlier social justice Progressive movement had been dampened by the war and the cynicism it had aroused."[59] Its most important activity in the 1920s was supporting the development of a comprehensive regional plan for the State of New York.

58. Presidents Research Council on Social Trends, *Recent Social Trends in the United States* (New York: McGraw-Hill, 1933), 1202.

59. Peter Romanofsky, ed., *Social Service Organizations*, Vol. 2 (Westport, CT: Greenwood Press, 1978), 651.

The Commonwealth Fund (CF) was established at the end of 1918 by a group of five wealthy philanthropists. The fund supported a few war relief efforts in its early years, but in the 1920s found its focus in the areas of child welfare and the new and exciting area of orthopsychiatry, a specialty in which psychiatric social casework was a key player. In 1922 the CF established the Joint Committee on Methods of Preventing Juvenile Delinquency to act as a coordinating body for the foundation's juvenile delinquency prevention project. This project conceptualized delinquency as a symptom of social and psychological maladjustment and advocated for an individual treatment approach to the problem. Working with the National Committee for Mental Hygiene, the CF supported a series of demonstration clinics in major cities and the famous Institute for Child Guidance in New York City. The CF's program to prevent juvenile delinquency ended in 1927 after influencing the establishment of other child guidance clinics, awakening the social work field to orthopsychiatry, and aiding in the movement of the profession away from social reform toward a more conservative individual treatment model of practice.

Business leaders who were involved with community welfare had a couple of related concerns going into the 1920s. One was that social welfare organizations in the progressive era had sometimes engaged in activities that appeared, at best, to be poorly planned and coordinated, and, at worst, crack brained and influenced by radical social reform thinking. Another was that prosperous business people were being constantly bombarded with requests for help from individuals, groups, and organizations, and the requests for help went on year round and the business person had little in the way of reliable information about which requests were worthy of consideration and which should be rebuffed. These problems were addressed by the development of federated funding (originally called the Community Chest, later the United Way) and of Councils of Community Agencies. Federated funding answered the problem of multiple solicitations by developing a single fund raising campaign in each community with the money being allocated by a single group of social work professionals and lay people who had access (through the efforts of the Council of Community Agencies) to all the necessary data for intelligent allocation. Federated funding had the effect of putting nearly the whole budget of social services under the control of a small group of social workers and influential laypersons who were thus able to impose their goals for social services on every community agency. The result of this was that social services began to reflect the values of the business community from whom most donations, as well as board members, came.

Federated funding began in America in 1887 with the creation of the Associated Charities of Denver. While the citizens of Denver were happy with this effort, the idea did not catch on elsewhere and did not expand until World War I when a number of "war chests" appeared. During the conflict these war chests were organized in great numbers to meet the emergency need for social services caused by the war. Thousands of people never before considered able to participate in philanthropy gave small quantities of money as individuals, and this money in the aggregate produced a level of support never before available to social services.[60] After the war, the same social climate characterized by belief in efficiency, rationality, and expertise, that had given rise to professionalization of both social work and business management, was very receptive to the idea of centralized

---

60. Walter Trattner, *From Poor Law to Welfare State* (New York: The Free Press, 1971), 221.

fund raising. In spite of resistance by some social workers, particularly those in the social settlements, the movement grew so rapidly that by the mid-1920s over 200 cities had adopted the community chest idea.

The drive for financial federation and efficient coordination of services marked the strengthening of the alliance between businessmen and social workers. Financial federation captured the imagination of businessmen by promising efficient coordination and organization of the community welfare machinery, immunity from multiple solicitations, economical collection and distribution of funds, and the development of a broad base of support which would relieve the pressure on a small circle of large givers. The corporation, increasingly regarded as a source of gifts, appreciated the convenience of the community chest. However, federated funding also brought business conservatism into social service funding and provision. In a study of the response of the social settlements to the depression, Trolander found that manufacturers associations advised their members to make contributions to community chests "contingent on the promise that no part of the contribution should be used to promote the passage of, or carry on propaganda for, any 'social-service labor program.'" She concludes that the net result of federated funding was that settlements in cities with strong community chests did not respond to the depression with the social reform programs such as those that had characterized them during the progressive years.[61]

As an adjunct to the community chest, cities established councils of community services to serve as professional social service planning bodies with their major responsibility being to allocate and oversee the spending of the money raised in the federated campaign. As well as struggling to coordinate and rationalize the community welfare machinery, the councils also were given the task of interpretation as a necessary function of fund raising. Thus, the community council became the public relations arm of professional social work, seeking to convince the average citizen that support of welfare was a fundamental civic obligation and also convince the businessman that support of professional social services was profitable in the long run. This function of the council was described in a letter written by Ellwood Street, Director of the St. Louis Community Council, to Dr. Haven Emerson, Medical Editor for the *Survey*, asking for data on the dollar value to business of social services because "I am preparing a speech to be given before business groups on charity as an investment which produces prosperity for the community."[62]

CONCLUSION

In the early twentieth century, progressive reformers responded to the tensions of industrial and urban development by moving to change society and government. Programs and laws were enacted to protect women, children, the impoverished and injured workers. Perhaps the greatest significance of the progressive era for the social welfare of the nation was the rejection of the earlier

---

61. Judith Ann Trolander, *Settlement Houses and the Great Depression* (Detroit: Wayne State University, 1971), 221.

62. Ellwood Street to Haven Emerson, M.D., March 27, 1926; Elwood Street File, Survey Associates Papers, Social Welfare History Archives, University of Minnesota Libraries, St. Paul, MN.

social emphasis on individualism and laissez-faire, and the organization of activities to promote social change and an interventionist state. The trauma of the first world war, or perhaps just a natural weariness with the guilt and demands for sacrifice that came with social reform, brought the progressive era to an end and ushered in the conservative "roaring twenties," an era that saw some return to individualism and laissez-faire, and left the nation's social welfare system poorly positioned to respond to the economic crisis that hit at the end of the decade. However, another set of developments that was in many ways positive, but that also augured poorly for the coming economic crisis, was the continuing and accelerating professionalization of social work, a subject we turn to in the next chapter.

CHAPTER 7

THE BIRTH OF A PROFESSION: 1898–1930

J uly 12, 1884 the Investigation Bureau at the District Office of the New York Charity Organization Society (COS) sent the following form letter, with the blanks filled in, to John Crane of the New York Soldiers and Sailors Protective Association:[1]

Dear Mr. Crane:

Mrs. Jas. W. (Maria) Bates applied to us for assistance and states that in the past she has been helped by your association but is no longer receiving assistance from you.

Will you kindly give us such information as you have concerning the abilities, character, and habits of this applicant?

If you so request, the source of the information which you give will not be made known to anyone.

Hoping for an immediate answer, I am,

Very respectfully,

(Miss) E. J. Scott

Registrar

On July 16 Mr. Crane replied, saying in part: "Your favor of the 15th inst. regarding the family of Mrs. Bates, widow is at hand. We don't wonder at her being a widow as we cannot understand how any man married to her could live very long." He then went on to describe assistance his association had given Mrs. Bates over a period of five months including a hundred pounds of coal, grocery orders for $1.00 on one occasion and $1.62 on another, and $12 to pay rent on her two room apartment. This assistance was given on the basis of her deceased husband having been an army veteran. Mr. Crane explained that his association ceased helping Mrs. Bates because her

---

1. Case files R2—R20, Box 239, Community Service Society Archives, Columbia University Libraries, Rare Book & Manuscript Library, Archival Collections.

attitude and behavior toward them was hostile and abusive and he could see no progress on her part toward self-sufficiency.

At the time Mrs. Bates first applied to the COS for assistance she was a thirty-eight-year-old widow with four sons: Harry, fourteen; Thomas; twelve; William, four; and John, two. She and her sons lived in two rooms in a dilapidated building in the Bronx. She earned a small sum of money by doing knitting in her home, but the income from this was not sufficient to meet the needs of her family. In 1884 a thirty-eight-year-old woman was well into middle age and this, combined with the sexist cast of American society, meant that her opportunities for wage employment were very poor. It appears that Mrs. Bates, in a situation similar to present day welfare mothers, was unable to subsist entirely on either money she earned from work, or from assistance she received from charity.[2] Apparently she managed to subsist for the thirty-year span between her husband's death in 1884 and her own death in 1914 at age sixty-eight by a combination of her small earnings from knitting and a nearly constant process of making the rounds between charities, churches, businesses, and individuals in pursuit of assistance.

Following their investigation of Mrs. Bates in 1884, the COS gave her a $1.00 order for groceries and closed the case, the investigator writing in the Closing Synopsis that "Woman does not desire work but financial assistance." There was apparently no further contact with Mrs. Bates until 1900, from which time until her death in 1914 the case record consists of a long and steady string of inquiries from churches, social agencies, individuals, and businesses inquiring of the COS for information about Mrs. Bates to assist in decisions about whether or not she should be helped. The COS response to every inquiry was prompt and firm, always stating that Mrs. Bates was not a good candidate for relief and that she should not be helped. This recommendation was always based on the COS assessment that Mrs. Bates was "unreasonable . . . quarrelsome, abusive, and drinking." The main problems with Mrs. Bates however, according to the COS agents, was that she was a predatory beggar and that she refused to accept the advice of the COS that she should voluntarily enter an institution (i.e., the poorhouse). Mrs. Bates' response to this recommendation was that she "steadfastly refused to consider it. At times she has threatened bodily violence to visitors from this society." She is quoted at several places in her case record as referring to the COS and its representatives as "Blackguards." A typical response of the COS to inquiries regarding Mrs. Bates was to the G. Hupfel Brewing Company from whom she had solicited assistance in 1912. The Secretary of the Investigation Bureau replied to the Company Chairman that they should not assist Mrs. Bates, concluding, "We thank you for reporting this case to us and will make other efforts to see this old woman and try to have her placed in some institution so she will not be imposing on the public."

There is little doubt that Mrs. Bates was a very difficult and unpleasant woman. However, even given this, it is remarkable just how adversarial and unhelpful the attitude and behavior of the COS was toward her. The cynics' criticism of the COS movement that their motto, rather than "Not alms, but a friend" should actually have been "Neither alms nor a friend" was certainly played out in this case. Michael Katz noted the same dynamics in his review of another COS case in early

---

2. Kathryn Edin, "Surviving the Welfare System: How AFDC Recipients Make Ends Meet in Chicago," *Social Problems* 38 (November 1991): 462–474; Kathryn Edin and Laura Lein, "Work, Welfare, and Single Mothers' Economic Survival Strategies," *American Sociological Review* 62 (April 1997): 253–266.

twentieth century New York City. He observed, "The case records are remarkable for the lack of sympathy in language or tone. Not a drop of sentiment squeezes through the dry narration and frequent condemnation. There is no indication of any empathy between the Visitors and Delia [the client], no appreciation of why she might rather not move to the Bronx [where cheaper housing was available], no clue that her illness, the death of her husband, or her poverty touched visitors enough to override her impudent and assertive manner."[3] These attitudes are precisely replicated in the Bates case. There is not a hint that the agents or visitors had any empathy for her situation or any recognition of the fact that a middle aged widow with four children, no family other than a blind sister who was more a burden than a resource, few skills, and little education, was going to have a very rough time supporting herself in New York City and would probably require some form of long-term help. There also was no indication of any sympathy for Mrs. Bates' apparently forcefully asserted desire to remain independent and not give up her freedom and commit herself to a poorhouse for the rest of her life.

There were some things that could have been done to help Mrs. Bates, even with the limited range of social work knowledge and skill available to a visitor in the early twentieth century, but these appear to never have entered the minds of the COS workers. What could they have done? First, they could have made a realistic assessment of her situation and worked to find some form of long-term assistance for her. This could have been done in conjunction with helping her maximize her income from her knitting. Second, Mrs. Bates is referenced at several points in the case file as saying that her son William (who continued to live with her as an adult) had served in the army in the Philippines and was ill as a result of his service (malaria is a good possibility). She stated that he was due a disability pension from the army but had never received it. It would seem an obvious course for the COS agents to check with the appropriate government office to see if this was true and, if so, to take whatever steps were necessary to see that the family begin receiving this benefit. There is no indication in the case file that they ever so much as thought of doing this. Finally, several of the COS visitors who made entries in the Bates file observed that she was sometimes injured by assaults by her son William when he was drinking. While recognition of domestic violence as a serious social problem was many years away, and techniques for dealing with it had not even been thought of, it would seem that the record would contain at least some expression of concern for the plight of Mrs. Bates and for her safety. It does not.

The overall impression that one gets from reading the Bates file is that of irritation and, even more pronounced, boredom. The COS staff just didn't seem to find Mrs. Bates and her problems very interesting. They were, after all, for the most part the same problems they had been dealing with day after day since the agency was founded in 1877. This boredom was not evident in another case that received services at about the same time as Mrs. Bates—the case of Maraton James Pilgrim.[4] This was the type of case that was increasingly attracting the attention of COSs.

3. Michael B. Katz, "The History of an Impudent Poor Woman in New York City from 1918 to 1923," in Peter Mandler, ed., *The Uses of Charity: The Poor on Relief in the Nineteenth-Century Metropolis* (Philadelphia: University of Pennsylvania Press, 1990), 238–239.

4. Case file R2027, Box 242, Community Service Society Archives, Columbia University Libraries, Rare Book & Manuscript Library, Archival Collections.

In this type of case economic need was only a secondary problem, caused or exacerbated by a primary problem of family or individual adjustment.

Maraton James Pilgrim was a teenager from Mobile Alabama, the son of an upper middle class family. His father was the owner of a wholesale liquor distribution company and his mother was an active member of Mobile society. Maraton was brought to the attention of the New York COS by Mr. Lanorgan, a worker at the Wayfarers' Lodge, a facility that would today be called a homeless shelter, but at the time would have been called a flophouse. Mr. Lanorgan reported to the COS that Maraton had run away from home, arrived in New York City looking for adventure and thinking it would be easy to get along, but had found the going difficult. Upon arriving in the city he had attended services at the Baptist Tabernacle thinking that this connection would be a good resource, but found "the northern people are not as cordial as those in the south." Mr. Lanorgan stated that Maraton would now "appreciate home if he could get back there." He asked assistance from the COS in deciding a course of action in this case.

The New York COS accepted the Pilgrim case with no question about its appropriateness for their services. They immediately wrote to the COS in Mobile, Alabama describing the case, giving detailed contact information, and asking that a worker in Mobile visit Maraton's parents and talk to them about their son. The Mobile agency did this and reported their findings to their New York colleagues:

> Until about 16 months ago he was as exemplary a youth as you could find in Mobile, and he and mother are members and have a pew in one of the foremost churches, but bad companions (sons of reputable and wealthy families, some of them) have almost ruined Maraton. From being an obedient, tractable boy, he has become quite incorrigible and parents are unable to control him. A very bad wealthy boy persuaded him to run away from school, and now for the fourth time he has run away from home, and these adventures of his have proved quite expensive to family and have wrought havoc with mother's already poor health and created such unpleasantness in their once happy home.

For the next five months the worker in Mobile stayed in contact with Mr. and Mrs. Pilgrim, and the New York worker was in frequent contact with Mr. Lanorgon, who was keeping tabs on the day-to-day welfare of Maraton, and the two COS branches corresponded back and forth to develop and implement plans for the young man.

The COS workers suggested a plan to Maraton's parents, which they agreed with, one that would become popular later in the century under the name "tough love." They suggested that the parents not send money to help Maraton out, but rather let him learn how difficult getting by in the world can be, with the goal of his beginning to appreciate the advantages his family can provide him. Mr. Pilgrim was very enthusiastic about this suggestion, saying, "He is thoroughly capable of earning his own living and I am disposed to let him do so." The COS workers recommended that the Pilgrims stay in contact with their son, but send him no money and, when they felt he could return home, require that he figure out how to get there on his own. As part of the plan, perhaps the part that contributed to his mother's accepting it, the COS arranged for Mr. Lanorgon to continue to supervise Maraton's progress and serve as a resource to be sure that no serious harm befell him.

Mr. Lanorgan was quickly able to help Maraton secure a job as a waiter at Moody's Mission (another homeless shelter) for $4 per week. He reported to the COS that the job would not only provide Maraton financial support but that he "should get the full benefit of the lessons he is learning by seeing what a dissipated life brings to the men who are constantly appearing at Moody's Mission." He kept in close contact with the young man and reported that although Maraton was lonely for home, he was doing well. At one point Maraton came to visit him and "looks very much improved with a new suit of clothes." At another time Maraton brought another young man with him who he thought world benefit from a stay at the Wayfarers' Lodge and contact with Mr. Lonorgan. Within three months Maraton had received a raise to $5 per week.

After five months the Pilgrims expressed a willingness to have their son return home. Mr. Lanorgan was able to help Maraton barter for steamship passage from New York to Mobile in return for working as a waiter on the ship during the voyage. After Maraton arrived home his mother wrote to the New York COS:

> I appreciate very much the kind interest taken in my only son. He has been at home since about December 1. Has a good position and is doing well. He works all day, is at home nights, and is very much changed for the better, seeming to have had enough of dissipation. I think his hard and trying experiences in New York were just the lesson he needed to make him appreciate his comfortable home. Send warmest thanks and sincere appreciation.

The COS worker shared the letter with Mr. Lanorgan, who "is delighted with the result of Maraton's return home."

The cases of Maria Bates and Maraton Pilgrim illustrate some of the rapid changes in social work that happened during the first thirty years of the twentieth century. Social work entered the century as a low-level, basically clerical and investigatory trade concerned mainly with protecting the public from unscrupulous charity chiselers, and seeking maximum efficiency in charitable administration. Within three decades it had begun to take on all the trappings of a full-fledged profession, including advanced education and certification, research, theory, and almost an obsession with developing and demonstrating professional practice skills. As part of this process social workers began to deemphasize the charity administration aspect of their work and to form alliances with psychology and psychiatry in becoming experts in individual and family counseling. At the same time, social workers were involved with a number of social reform efforts that set the stage for the formation of America's incomplete welfare state later in the century, but these activities were coming to be defined as outside of the professions mandate. The story of social work during the first three decades of the twentieth century is widely considered to be a sociological case study of the birth of a profession.

SOCIAL WORK'S QUEST TO BE A PROFESSION, 1898–1915

One of the defining characteristics of the progressive era was the idea that more efficient, effective, and scientific means must be developed to manage what was perceived as becoming a chaotic society. The historian Morton Keller has identified this as the heart of progressivism: "However varied were the goals of policymakers, they had a shared sense that the good society was efficient, organized, cohesive. Historians tend to sort out early twentieth-century public thought and action on either side of the fault line of right and left. But it is important to recognize how much overlap there was in social ideologies during the early 1900s. The sense that a new society, turbulent, full of different sorts of people, problems, and ideas, had come into being was as widespread as the awareness that big business, consumerism, and new technology were creating a new economy. Regardless of their place on the ideological spectrum, thinkers and doers sought to cope with this overriding social reality . . . They shared as well a belief in progress, and even in the best way to achieve it: through a better organized, more uniform, more efficient social order."[5]

One of the foremost ideas of progressives was that a key to this more efficient social order was to develop professions, each with the assignment of managing a social issue. Prior to the twentieth century there had been only four occupations that were given the honor of being called professions: medicine, law, the professoriate, and the clergy. Within a few decades of the twentieth century the term "profession" had broadened to refer to any occupation requiring lengthy training, based on science and technology, earning high pay and status and, most important, that had succeeded in getting an exclusive mandate for the management of a pressing social problem. Everyone, it seemed, wanted to be a professional. The literature of the time was full of articles with titles such as "A New Profession," "The Social Secretary: A New Profession," "The Need of Training Schools for a New Profession."[6] In this era, business management, public administration, educational administration, urban planning, public health, as well as many other fields, self-consciously organized into professions. For social work, however, the prospect of being recognized as a profession took on even greater import than it did for these other fields.

Social work by the turn of the twentieth century was very interested, some have said obsessed, with being recognized as a profession for a couple of reasons. One reason is that social work, unlike other professionalizing occupations, had begun as a voluntary activity. One of the core principles of the Association for the Prevention of Pauperism, the Association for Improving the Condition of the Poor, and the COS, was that a personal relationship with a helper was critical for the poor to overcome their problems. An equally important principle was that this helper should be a volunteer providing this service out of the goodness of his or her own heart, out of a sense of charity. An examination of the budgets of the Association for Improving the Condition of the Poor reveals that as time went by, a decreasing proportion of services were provided by volunteers and an increasing proportion by paid staff. It is an indication of the importance of the idea of volunteerism that in his annual reports the general secretary, Robert Hartley, appears to intentionally hide the amount of the agencies budget being spent on paid agents. This personal helping role was exactly the function that social workers were attempting to professionalize. Because this activity had traditionally been performed by volunteers for free, people tended to devalue it and question

5. Morton Keller, *Regulating a New Society: Public Policy and Social Change in America, 1900–1933* (Cambridge, MA: Harvard University Press, 1994), 4.

6. Rita Childe Door, "A New Profession," *Current Literature* 34 (March 1903), 293–294; William Tolman, "The Social Secretary: A New Profession," *Outlook* 77 (July 1904): 594–598; Anna L. Dawes, "The Need of Training Schools for a New Profession," *Lend-A-Hand* 11 (1893): 90–97.

whether or not it was something that people should be paid for, and were especially dubious that people doing this should be paid well. In order to counteract this belief that anyone with a good heart and a willing spirit could provide services to people with problems, proto-social workers felt it extremely important to demonstrate that what they did required a high level of technical skill, scientific knowledge, and professional status.

The second reason for the intense interest of people working in philanthropy to develop what they were doing into a social work profession was the changing role of women in society. The decline of home industries, combined with labor saving machines that reduced the work load of homemakers created a dilemma for women. As Walter Lippman commented, "The mere withdrawal of industries from the home has drawn millions of [working class] woman out of the home and left millions [of middle class women] idle within it."[7] At the same time an increasing number of women were graduating from high school (a relatively high level of education at the time) and college, and many of these women were not interested in traditional domestic female roles. They wanted to independently earn a living and to do this by applying their education and abilities. Most occupations, especially the most desirable ones, were closed to women. It was nearly impossible for a woman, no matter how bright and talented, to become a doctor, lawyer, minister, or business executive. By the late 1800s the vast majority of volunteers at COSs and other social agencies were women, and as these positions began to be replaced by paid agents, most of these agents were also women. As Leiby has noted "Before 1890 women had been mostly patrons or volunteers in charitable enterprise, and for a long time they liked to compare the volunteer, who gave willingly of herself, with the more perfunctory effort and vested interest of the paid agent. But as female paid agents increased in number and authority, beginning as clerks, perhaps, then becoming district agents or executives, the prospect of a new professional identity caught the imagination."[8] Women like Jane Addams, who came from privileged backgrounds and had no necessity to work and make their own way in the world, spoke of the need of a career in terms of self-fulfillment, writing of cultivated and educated young women that "their uselessness hangs about them heavily."[9] For other women, such as Mary Richmond who grew up an orphan in Baltimore, raised by two working class aunts, the desire to increase the occupational status of social work was far more practical. These women had no one to rely on for their daily bread other than themselves and they wanted to earn a living, preferably a good one.

Black Americans were greatly interested in promoting a social work profession for many of the same reasons that applied to women. In the early years of the twentieth century the only professions open to blacks were "teaching and preaching." A few blacks gained entry to traditional professions, but this carried few opportunities and sometimes grave risks.[10] Two types of social work positions became available to blacks early in the century. The first was jobs as social workers

---

7. Quoted in John Ehrenreich, *The Altruistic Imagination: A History of Social Work and Social Policy in the United States* (Ithaca, NY: Cornell University Press, 1985), 35.

8. James Leiby, *History of Social Welfare and Social Work in the United States* (New York: Columbia University Press, 1977), 119.

9. Jane Addams, "The Subjective Necessity of Settlements," in Jane Addams, *Twenty Years at Hull House* (New York: Macmillan, 1916), 94.

10. See, for example, Kevin Boyle, *Arc of Justice: A Saga of Race, Civil Rights, and Murder in the Jazz Age* (New York: Henry Holt, 2004).

and administrators at newly emerging all black social service organizations such as settlement houses (although, according to Davis, there were only ten as of 1910 but a number of white settlements established branches in black neighborhoods), black hospitals, community programs sponsored by black churches, and in the "colored" branches of national organizations such as YMCSs, YWCAs, and Boy and Girl Scouts.[11] The other source of jobs was in main line, primarily white, organizations that created positions for a "colored social worker" to provide services to the agencies' black clientele, organizations such as COSs (many changing their names to the more modern sounding Associated Charities), and State Boards of Charities and Public Welfare. Most likely these jobs were not as desirable as those available to white social workers but there is evidence that the profession was aware of the problem of job discrimination and that at least some white social work executives identified this as problem. For example, Robert Dexter, General Secretary of Associated Charities in Atlanta Georgia, wrote in *The Survey* in 1921, "Differences in salaries, in office equipment, promotions, or appropriations for departments, and indifferences to overwork or poor work are common forms in which this prejudice [against black social workers] manifests itself. The genuine social worker will constantly be on the alert to detect beginnings of prejudice and will fight them with all his might."[12]

Beginning at the end of the nineteenth century, and rapidly increasing due to the growth of jobs in war industries during the second decade of the new century, was what Henri has dubbed "the Great Migration" of blacks from the rural South to the urban North.[13] It is estimated that over 400,000 black Americans made this journey between 1900 and 1920.[14] This group, similar to other groups of immigrants flooding large northern cities, had severe problems that called for the provision of skilled help and created new job opportunities to provide this help. According to E. Franklin Frazier: "Since the mass migration of Negroes to northern cities, there has emerged a relatively large and influential group of leaders who are primarily concerned with the social welfare of Negroes. In fact, the field of social welfare has provided one of the chief fields of employment for the educated Negro."[15] Social work promised a new and exciting career opportunity for educated black people. It promised to open up to them a professional career that was every bit as respectable as education or the ministry and that would enable them to make a decent living, enjoy professional status in their community, and satisfy their desire to be of service to their race. Black leaders in the early years of the twentieth century had tremendous hopes for the power of social work, viewing it as a kind of panacea. Even more than their white colleagues they were committed to a scientific approach. The black leader E. K. Jones wrote in 1928 that social work would "raise the level of intelligence of black people" and "give them a stronger economic foundation," help them gain "a better appreciation of social values," "develop competent and dependable leadership," bring

11. Allen F. Davis, *Spearheads for Reform: The Social Settlements and the Progressive Movement, 1890–1914* (New York: Oxford University Press, 1967), 95.

12. Robert C. Dexter, "The Negro in Social Work," *The Survey* 46 (June 25, 1921): 439–440.

13. Florette Henri, *Black Migration: Movement North, 1900–1920* (Garden City, New York: Doubleday, 1987).

14. Tony Platt and Susan Chandler, "Constant Struggle: E. Franklin Frazier and Black Social Work in the 1920s," *Social Work* (July–August 1988), 293.

15. E. Franklin Frazier, *The Negro in the United States*, rev. ed. (New York: The Macmillan Company, 1957), 550–552.

"closer cooperation" between black and white people, and "remove from the Negro masses the feeling of . . . inferiority."[16]

In 1911 George Haynes, a professor at Fisk University, and Ruth Standish Baldwin, a wealthy New England philanthropist, founded the National Urban League. The organization had two major goals: "to remove barriers to racial equality and to achieve economic empowerment for the country's Negro citizens." Haynes viewed professional social work as the best way to pursue these goals and so set the increase in the number of black social workers as a major strategy of the Urban League. Writing in 1911 he said, "The conditions among Negroes in cities can best be improved by those of their own group whose latent capacity has had superior training directed toward social service."[17] In 1930 the Urban League proudly reported that partially due to its efforts there were 1,500 blacks employed in professional social work positions.

It is probably a safe bet that black social workers in the first three decades of the twentieth century were every bit as effective as their white counterparts when working with clients in one-on-one casework relationships to help resolve problems. However, the black community expected much more of its social workers in terms of elevating the race and demonstrating to white society the error of many of its beliefs regarding their race. The effectiveness of black social workers in achieving this mission is unclear. On the one hand, these early black social workers can be viewed as cultural heroes who, in a shockingly racist and oppressive environment, were able to claw their way into positions of middle class respectability and to serve as models of the possibility of a better future for all their brothers and sisters. Another perspective, however, views these early social workers as sell-outs in the Uncle Tom tradition. Martin and Martin, for example, in their excellent book *Social Work and the Black Experience,* state the thesis that "pioneering black social workers were presented with a great opportunity . . . but they opted to take on the middle-class or bourgeois outlook of the dominant society and to challenge, even to wage war against, black folk culture rather than to learn from it."[18] This "middle class or bourgeois outlook" may explain some of the problem that the Minneapolis Family Welfare Association's "colored worker" Ella Kirby had when making home visits. She initially found her clients, and collateral contacts, to be reticent and "seemed so suspicious of the visitor's mission that they would give no information." She later learned that the problem was that her demeanor, speech, and mannerisms were so foreign to her clients that they thought she was white. She reflected in her case notes that "If they had known that [I] had been colored" they would have related to her in a different manner.[19] Whatever the truth may be about the role and function of black social workers during the first three decades of the twentieth century, one thing is certainly clear—the development of the social work profession and the early manifestation of the civil rights movement were closely and inextricably linked.

16. E. K. Jones, "Social Work Among Negroes," *Annals of the American Academy of Political and Social Science,* 140 (November 1928): 287–293. Quoted in Elmer P. Martin and Joanne Mitchell Martin, *Social Work and the Black Experience* (Washington, DC: NASW Press, 1995), 7–8.

17. George E. Haynes, "Co-operation with Colleges in Securing and Training Negro Social Workers for Urban Centers," *Official Proceedings of the Annual Meeting: 1911, National Conference on Social Welfare* (Chicago, IL: Hildeman, 1911), 384.

18. Elmer P. Martin and Joanne Mitchell Martin, *Social Work and the Black Experience* (Washington, DC: NASW Press, 1995), 3–4.

19. Mark Peel, *Miss Cutler & the Case of the Resurrected Horse: Social Work and the Story of Poverty in America, Australia, and Britain* (Chicago: The University of Chicago Press, 2012), 188.

EDUCATION AS THE KEY TO PROFESSIONALISM

Because professions are based on expert knowledge applied to pressing social problems, the core of any profession is its educational credentials. At the end of the nineteenth century there were no educational programs specifically to teach people to be social workers, although a few preliminary efforts had been made. COSs had developed fairly extensive in-service training programs and a number of worker's discussion and study clubs had been formed. As to formal higher education, social work type classes had been developed at several universities, the most famous being Francis Peabody's Philosophy 11 at Harvard, described in the catalog as "The Ethics of Social Reform. The questions of Charity, Divorce, the Indians, Labor, Prisons, Temperance, etc., as problems of practical ethics—Lectures, essays, and practical observations."[20] Students, legend has it, referred to the course as "Peabo's drainage, drunkenness, and divorce."

The earliest calls for the development of formal educational programs for people working in charity came in 1893 in papers by Nathaniel Rosenau and Anna Dawes. Neither Rosenau or Dawes were interested in training direct service workers, but rather were concerned with the need for agency administrators to be trained experts. Rosenau questioned the criteria used to hire agency executives and criticized the tendency to select the "superannuated clergyman, unsuccessful merchant, or political favorite" to serve as manager of a charitable agency or institution. He argued that it was necessary that persons "take charge of this work who are especially trained, who have a calling for the work, and who mean to devote themselves to it. Dawes, a community leader in Springfield Massachusetts, was concerned with the difficulty of attracting able administrators to smaller cities. She complained that "it is today impossible to get a suitable superintendent of charities for a city of fifteen or twenty thousand inhabitants (or even a larger city) because no one knows anything about how to carry on the work." She concluded that "I am convinced that it is not so much lack of willing individuals as entire lack of opportunity for training that is the real trouble . . . What is needed, it seems to me, is some course of study where an intelligent young person can add to an ordinary education . . . what is now the alphabet of charitable science—some knowledge of its underlying ideas, its tried and trusted methods, and some acquaintance with the various devices employed for the upbuilding of the needy, so that no philanthropic undertaking, from a model tenement-house to a kindergarten to a sand heap, will be altogether strange to his mind." Dawes saw a need for philanthropic education, but she in no way saw this as a vehicle for promoting a new, well paid, profession. Quite the contrary, she saw the poor pay offered by charitable societies as just an unchangeable fact of life, and said the training programs she proposed should be aimed at "able and efficient young men and women who . . . are satisfied, at least temporarily, [to work] for only such remuneration as will furnish them a not too abundant livelihood."[21]

---

20. Frank Bruno, *Trends in Social Work as reflected in the Proceedings of the National Conference of Social Work 1874–1946* (New York: Columbia University Press, 1948), 133.

21. Nathaniel S. Rosenau, "Farewell Address," Charity Organization Society of Buffalo, *Sixteenth Annual Report* (Oct. 27, 1893): 26, 30. Cited in Roy Lubove, *The Professional Altruist: The Emergence of Social Work as a Career, 1880–1930* (Cambridge, MA: Harvard University Press, 1965), 19; Anna L. Dawes, "The Need of Training Schools for a New Profession," paper presented at the International Conference of Charities and Correction, Chicago Illinois, 1893, reprinted in *Sociology in Institutions of Learning*, ed. Amos G. Warner (Baltimore MD: Johns Hopkins Press, 1894), 14–20.

The papers by Dawes and Rosneau provided early recognition of the problems the lack of formal training programs posed for those running charitable organizations. However, their proposals never really lead anywhere. This was not the case with the paper by the prominent COS leader Mary Richmond, presented at the 1897 National Conference of Charities and Correction, titled "The Need of a Training School in Applied Philanthropy." Richmond's paper is remarkable in that in a few pages she laid out the basic principles and structure of social work professional education, principles and structure that remain the basis of social work education today. Unlike previous proposals, Richmond was not concerned with only training agency administrators, but was focused on line workers. She also rejected Dawe's idea that the program should train people "who from a missionary impulse put better education and larger capacity at the service of the public." Richmond believed that people devoting themselves to careers in charity work "have a right to demand something of us in return. Surely, they have a right to demand from the profession of applied philanthropy (we really have not even a name for it) that which they have a right to demand from any other profession—further opportunities for education and development, and, incidentally, the opportunity to earn a living."[22]

Richmond began her proposal for a professional school by recognizing a problem that she was to wrestle with for the remainder of her career—the fact that applied philanthropy was woefully deficient in knowledge and skills, what she referred to as a "professional standard." She identified as a key issue the chicken and egg question of whether a professional standard must be present before developing a school, or if a school is an essential factor in developing a standard. She came down hard on the side that a school needed to be developed first and, utilizing an analogy that would frequently be used in social work in future years, proposed medicine as a model. She said that "we so often turn to the physicians: they are what we merely hope to be . . . is it not probable that the profession of medicine owes a large part of its inheritance of knowledge and principles to its schools . . .?" She then went on to propose the basic elements of a professional program. She first identified what later came to be called the generalist-specialist debate—whether schools should concentrate on general principles and methods applicable in any field of practice, or if they should train specialists in COS work, probation, child saving, and so forth. Her solution to this question, one that remains in place today, was to propose a two year program, with the first year concentrating on generalist principles and skills and students specializing during the second year. She then went on to discuss that philanthropic education should be firmly grounded in academics, and that an affiliation with a university would be a good thing, but that the emphasis should be on practical knowledge. To achieve this she felt the that the school should have "vital connection . . . with the public and private charities of the city," so students "could observe the actual work of charity, and take part in it under the daily supervision of their instructors." Field education has remained the center of social work education to the extent that in 2008 the Council on Social Work Education formally designated field instruction as the "signature pedagogy" of social work. Finally, Richmond identified imparting values, as well as knowledge, as a critical component of social work education, saying "[More] important than any training in detail is the higher ideals

22. Mary Richmond, "The Need of a Training School in Applied Philanthropy," *Proceedings of the National Conference of Charities and Correction, Twenty-Fourth Annual Session Held in Toronto, Ontario, July 7–14, 1897* (Boston, MA: George H. Ellis, 1898), 182.

of charitable service. "Ideals are catching," someone has said. How important, then, to send our young people, our future workers, where ideals can be "caught"!"[23]

It is clear that Richmond was not just throwing out ideas when she presented her paper; she had a definite plan. She indicated that the school should be in a large city, by which she clearly meant New York. She described the type of person who should lead the school, and after her description recognized that "there are [only] a few such men" but that she had one in mind. Finally she spoke of how the school would be financed. Her plan was to find a wealthy donor to endow the project. She did not think this would be a problem using as an example a wealthy man who was giving a great deal of money to a psychologist who was developing complex machinery hoping to discover the color of emotions. She opined, "Now, if such fanciful science as that can find a patron, why should our school go a-begging?"[24] Little time was wasted in implementing Richmond's vision. In the following summer of 1898 a six week Summer School in Applied Philanthropy was launched in New York City, led by Philip Ayers, the Assistant Director of the New York COS. Shoemaker describes the first summer of the school as follows:

> Ayres assembled a group of 27 pioneering students from as far away as Colorado and Minnesota. They were put through their paces with a blistering 6-day-a-week schedule of lectures, classroom discussions, visits to institutions, social research, and practical training. A typical day's schedule was as follows: "June 29: Institutional and placing-out methods in the care of children, an address by Mr. Homer Folks. Provision for babies and for mothers and babies, an address by Miss M.V. Clark. Visit to the home for the friendless and the foundling asylum." That was just the mornings work. In the span of 6 weeks, students visited over 40 institutions; in the days following the visit to the foundling asylum, for example, students visited the College Settlement on Rivington Street, Blackwell's Island, a county poor house, the University Settlement, and so on. They heard 39 lectures by prominent figures in social work, social science, and the reform communities of New York and the nation. For practical experience, students worked in the district offices of the COS. The summer school ended with students' presentations of original research projects, "suitable for publication," the school hoped, on topics ranging from recent immigration, to tenement house and sweatshop conditions, to day nurseries and foster care."[25]

Following this beginning summer course the school quickly grew to fulfill Richmond's total vision. Summer programs were run until 1904 when, financed by a grant from COS board member John S. Kennedy, the school, now named the New York School of Philanthropy, was expanded to a one-year program. Also in 1904 Dr. Edward T. Devine (possibly the man Richmond was referring to in her 1897 paper) became the school's first full-time director. In 1911, John S. Kennedy died, leaving the school one million dollars in his will. The income from this endowment put the school on a permanent footing and enabled it to expand the program to two years, fully implementing Richmond's original plan. Although the school was primarily affiliated with the New York COS, the Kennedy bequest specified that it was to have some connection with Columbia University.

---

23. Mary Richmond, "The Need of a Training School," 181–184.
24. Mary Richmond, "The Need of a Training School," 184–185.
25. Linda M. Shoemaker, "Early Conflicts in Social Work Education," *Social Service Review*, (1998), 183.

This connection was operationalized by the policy that the President of Columbia was to be an ex-officio member of the School's advisory committee. As time went by, the affiliation with the COS became weaker and that with Columbia stronger, until 1940 when the School became a graduate school at Columbia, awarding a Master of Science degree. In 1950 the School formally separated all connections with the COS, now part of a larger organization called the New York Community Service Society.[26]

Following the establishment of the New York School of Philanthropy, education for charity steadily spread to other major cities. In 1904 the Boston School for Social Workers was opened, headed by the COS leader Jeffrey Brackett, with a charity organization focus and program quite similar to the New York School. From the start the Boston School had much closer university ties than was the case in New York, with students able to earn degrees from Harvard or Simmons with part of their curriculum provided by the School for Social Workers. In 1907 a program was started in St. Louis affiliated with Washington University and in 1908 in Philadelphia affiliated with the University of Pennsylvania. These programs differed slightly from those in New York and Boston in that they had a focus on child welfare. In Chicago, the Reverend Graham Taylor, head of the Chicago Commons Settlement House began a lecture series that became an Institute of Social Science and Arts in 1904, with courses offered through the University of Chicago's Extension Division. Two years later the school lost its connection with the University of Chicago, but in 1908, with funding from the newly formed Russell Sage Foundation (RSF), it reemerged as the free standing Chicago School of Civics and Philanthropy.[27]

Black leaders who were advocating for professional social work as a new opportunity for educated blacks were very aware of the necessity of high quality professional education. In fact, one of the original goals of the Urban League was to create opportunities for blacks to gain access to social work education. In 1911 the League's founder George Haynes wrote that the organization had been founded with three main purposes, the third being "to secure and train Negro social workers."[28] He identified two means for achieving this goal. The first was to incorporate social work education into the curricula of existing black colleges. The second was to develop means to send promising graduates of black colleges north to attend the newly established schools of professional social work.

To pursue his first strategy, Haynes began by developing a social work program at Fisk University in Nashville, Tennessee, where he was a professor of sociology. Social work students at Fisk began with a liberal arts foundation, proceeded to a core social science curriculum that included courses in sociology, economics, labor problems, social problems, and statistics and social investigation. Students then moved on to courses in social services, social work methods, and, capping off their education, a field placement in a social service agency. Guest lecturers with expertise in areas such as delinquency and probation, black women and children in cities, and principles of relief gave presentations and attempted to provide a historical perspective regarding

26. Ronald A. Feldman and Sheila B. Kammerman, eds., *The Columbia University School of Social Work: A Centennial Celebration* (New York: Columbia University Press, 2001).

27. Leslie Leighninger, *Creating a New Profession: The Beginnings of Social Work Education in the United States* (Alexandria, VA: Council on Social Work Education, 2000), 16–18.

28. George Haynes, "Co-operation with Colleges in Securing and Training Negro Social Workers for Urban Centers," 386.

the conditions of black people. Within a few years the Fisk social work curriculum was replicated in other black colleges such as Lincoln in Pennsylvania, Wilberforce in Ohio, and Talladega in Alabama.[29]

For his second strategy Haynes budgeted Urban League funds to support two fellowships per year for graduates of black southern universities to attend professional schools of social work in the North. Blacks were admitted as regular students from the very beginning in the schools in New York, Boston, Chicago, and Pennsylvania. Urban League fellows also attended a social work program at the Carnegie School of Technology in Pittsburgh, although what this school was is unclear as it appears to have not lasted long and, other than as a destination for Urban League fellows, it left no record in social work education. In St. Louis, perhaps because the School of Social Economy was affiliated with a private university or perhaps because St. Louis was at the time very much a southern city, blacks were not admitted as regular students. The School, however, reported to the RSF in 1912 that "The School has undertaken extension work among the colored people in St. Louis—a much needed development. Last year there were 32 enrollments in the course provided. A similar course will again be offered this year."[30]

Although the approach of the National Urban League to providing social work education for blacks was successful in many ways, it was not without its critics. Although the undergraduate programs in black colleges appear to have been as good as similar programs in white schools, the fact of the matter was that the profession of social work was actively discouraging this type of program and strongly advocating for specialized schools of social work with the goal of becoming an all graduate trained profession. In addition, black academic leaders such as E. Franklin Frazier argued that black colleges with their limited financial resources, inexperienced teachers, and limited opportunities for field placements were poorly equipped to offer professional social work education. Instead, Frazier argued, they should provide their students with a quality liberal arts education and then send their best graduates to professional schools. The problem with this was that very few graduates of southern black colleges were able to marshal the financial resources to leave home and attend a school in the North.

Social workers in the South fully accepted the mainstream professions position that training at a professional school of social work was necessary for a person to be fully qualified to do social work. Black social workers, and executives of agencies that employed black social workers, were thus very interested in developing a pool of trained black social workers in the South. The program of the Urban League to send qualified students north to study at the existing professional schools had succeeded in providing leaders for black social work in the South, but was far too small a program to have any effect on the need for trained workers at the direct service level. As very few graduates of black colleges had the resources to travel north to pursue professional training, it soon became obvious to social work leaders in the South, both black and white, that a black school of social work should be established south of the Mason-Dixon line and east of the Mississippi river. This issue reached critical mass at the 1920 meeting of the National Conference of Social

29. Robenia Baker Gary and Lawrence E. Gary, "The History of Social Work Education for Black People 1900–1930," *The Journal of Sociology and Social Welfare* 21 (March 2015): 73.

30. St. Louis School of Social Economy Board of Directors to John Glenn, January 10, 1912, Houston Papers, Washington University Archives, St. Louis, MO.

Welfare held that year in New Orleans. A presentation was made at this meeting by Jesse Thomas, National Urban League Field Secretary for the Southern Territory, in which he highlighted the need for professional training of black social workers in the South. Following his talk, Thomas was approached by a delegation of thirteen executive secretaries of Family Welfare Associations in the South who asked him to conduct a survey to ascertain which city would be the most appropriate for the type of school he had proposed, and that the National Urban League take leadership in opening a school in that city. They gave Thomas a commitment that if such a school was opened that their agencies would provide fellowships for qualified black students to attend. Thomas quickly completed the requested survey and the result was that Atlanta was, by far, the best location. An organizational meeting was held in Atlanta on May 12, 1920 at which Dr. John Hope, President of Morehouse College, offered classroom space in Sale Hall, and the services of Gary Moore, Professor of Sociology at Morehouse and graduate of the New York School of Social Work as an Urban League Fellow, as the school's director. The committee accepted Dr. Hope's offer and the school opened for fall semester 1920. Moore remained director of the school for two years and then left to pursue a Ph.D. at Columbia University where, tragically, he died in 1923.

Following Moore as director was E. Franklin Frazier, another Urban League Fellowship graduate of the New York School. Frazier who also had a master's degree in sociology from Clarke University, had just returned to the United States after completing a fellowship year at the University of Copenhagen where he had studied Danish agricultural cooperatives and described how these could serve as a model for rural black agricultural development in America. Frazier was a fiery, confrontational, some said radical, personality, who believed that black social workers should forget about developing competence in psychologically based casework as taught at most schools, and instead work on methods of developing cooperative enterprises and black self-help organizations. He also publically advocated for blacks, in response to the increase in lynchings, to arm themselves and engage in self-defense rather than follow the "deceit and fawning" of "so called Negro leaders" who were counseling non-violence and patience. He stirred up a hornet's nest of controversy in Atlanta when he published an article in a prominent academic journal describing white attitudes and behavior toward blacks as a form of psychopathology which he labeled "the Negro complex," writing that "the behavior motivated by race prejudice shows precisely the same characteristics as that ascribed to insanity."[31] Although he proved to be a brilliant scholar and an able administrator, in 1927 the School's board became so alarmed by Frazier's militancy that they asked him to resign. Frazier left Atlanta for the University of Chicago, where he earned a Ph.D. in sociology. For the remainder of his career he was a professor and prolific scholar at Howard University. He was the first black president of the American Sociological Association.

The curriculum of the Atlanta School of Social Work was both traditional and innovative. It was traditional in that it followed the curriculum of the already existing schools of social work. The curriculum was dominated by the standard courses on social casework, human behavior, fieldwork in social agencies, community organization, and social research. As health was a major concern of agencies working in the black community the curriculum included coursework on medical-social problems. The school's curriculum was also innovative in that it included an emphasis on

31. Edward Franklin Frazier, "The Pathology of Race Prejudice," *Forum* 77, no. 6 (June 1927): 856.

the black experience in America and the relation of that experience to the helping process, a focus that would later be referred to as Afro-centric social work. This aspect of the curriculum was developed by the School's third director Forrester B. Washington who would remain in this position from 1927 until 1954. Like Moore and Frazier before him, Washington was a graduate of the New York School of Social Work as an Urban League fellow. Washington was a bit smoother and more accommodating than Frazier, but he was still what was at the time referred to as a "race man," and as such a strong advocate for a unique black approach to social work. His perspective was summarized by his statement, that "The existence of black people in a predominately unsympathetic and hostile world is sufficient for specialized training for social work in the black community; for this position the writer makes no apologies."[32] Under Washington's leadership the Atlanta School developed a series of courses focusing on the experience of black people in America. Prominent among these courses were The Techniques of Community Organization Among Black People; Industrial Problems of Black People; The Conduct of Social Surveys in the Black Community; Housing Problems of Black People; and Recreational Problems of Black People. Although the curriculum of the Atlanta School was in many ways innovative, it was traditional enough to gain the School accreditation by the newly formed American Association of Schools of Social Work as one of the first group of schools accredited in 1928.

SOCIAL CASEWORK EXPANDS
TO OTHER SETTINGS

Prior to the early 1900s what was beginning to be called social casework had been mostly limited to COSs. However, as more and more people began to recognize the importance of the social environment on different aspects of people's lives, social work began to spread into new areas. Lubove has said, "employment in several institutions whose effectiveness had been limited by a failure to consider the social environment on clients or patients was a decisive episode in the development of social work as a profession . . . The knotty problems of adjustment which social workers confronted in these institutions sparked a search for expertise which differentiated them from other members of the staff and justified claims to professional status."[33]

CHILD PROTECTION

As discussed in the previous chapter, child placement had begun to identify with and be influenced by scientific charity prior to the turn of the century, largely through the work of Charles Birtwell and the Boston Children's Aid Society (BCAS). However, child protective services continued to

---

32. Forrester B. Washington, "The Need for Education of Negro Social Workers," *Journal of Negro Education* 4 (Jan. 1935): 84.

33. Roy Lubove, *The Professional Altruist*, 22

consider itself a law enforcement activity, largely immune from the influence of more progressive agencies such as BCAS and the COSs. This began to change after the turn of the century with Boston once again taking the lead. The Massachusetts Society for the Prevention of Cruelty to Children was founded in 1880 modeled on the New York Society and, like the New York Society was primarily a law enforcement agency. In 1906 this approach came to an end, apparently with some stiff resistance from agency staff. The president of the Society's board, progressive reformer and Massachusetts State Representative Grafton Cushings, reported the following to the board of directors and members of the society:

> The traditional policy of the Massachusetts Society for the Prevention of Cruelty to Children is the prosecution of offenders against children and the taking of children from immoral or unhealthy surroundings, and placing them in homes or institutions . . . There is no attempt to discover the cause of the condition which makes action by the Society necessary, and therefore, no endeavor to prevent a recurrence of these conditions. In other words, there is no "social" work done. It is all legal or police work. A Society for the Prevention of Cruelty to Children thus becomes an arm of the law, a department of the district attorney's office, or an adjunct to the police force, and fills a quasi-public position.

Cushing believed that the society needed to develop:

> . . . along somewhat new lines . . . the times are full of changes, and charitable methods are changing rapidly . . . we cannot feel satisfied until we feel sure that every effort has been made, either by our own officers or through the action of some other organization, not only to see to it that the children who have been taken from parents through our intervention are permanently well cared for, but that the conditions which made our interference necessary are improved.

Cushing then made a statement that has been repeated (although due credit is generally not given to Cushing) in various forms and venues by child welfare social workers with such frequency during the past century that it has become something of a mantra:

> It seems often futile to take from a man and a woman one set of children, and in a few years' time be called on again to take from them another set of children which they have been allowed to bring into the same surroundings of squalor and crime.

The final point Cushings made referred to the aloofness of child protection agencies. He stated that the Massachusetts society would cease this attitude by "entering more closely into relations with other charitable organizations, rather than by standing apart on a different plain, we can best serve our generation."[34]

The general agent of the Massachusetts society, Charles K. Morton, with the backing of the secretary of the influential New York society, vigorously opposed the change of direction that

---

34. Massachusetts Society for the Prevention of Cruelty to Children, *Twenty-Sixth Annual Report, December 31, 1906* (Boston, MA: Griffith-Stillings Press, 1907), 4–6.

Cushings and the board proposed. Cushings summarized the situation by saying, "The difference of opinion as to methods between Mr. Morton and the Directors is radical." Because of the differences, Morton's contract was not renewed. The board hired a new general agent, C. Carl Carstens, who was a social worker with the progressive New York COS. Carstens had a Ph.D. and was an associate of Mary Richmond and Edward Devine, undoubtedly the two leading figures in the development of scientific charity and what was soon to be called social work.[35]

Carstens proved to be a tireless advocate for applying a social work approach to child protection work. Under his leadership, the Massachusetts society quickly developed a program of remedial and preventive casework and environmental reform. Carstens defined a threefold task for the agency:

> It must rescue children from degrading conditions, it must avail itself of every reasonable opportunity to try to reconstruct such families as are moving on to inevitable shipwreck, and, while it is working with each individual instance, it must try to seek out the causes which bring about these bad conditions, so that it may do its part to prevent them.[36]

Carstens was a national figure and had national plans and ambitions. No sooner did he establish the new approach to children's services in Boston, an approach that came to be known as *child protection*, as opposed to the former approach of *child rescue*, than he began to advocate for other anticruelty societies to also adopt it. In doing this he faced heavy opposition, mainly from the established child rescue societies. Elbridge Gerry, the founder of the New York Society for the Prevention of Cruelty to Children, complained about Carstens's activities, saying "There is nothing today which scientific charity does not seek to appropriate to itself; and when it cannot absorb collateral work, it endeavors to obtain possession of the subject of that work and utilize it for its own ends." William Stillman, president of the American Humane Association from 1904 to 1924, complained that "New social reforms are dividing, or seeking to divide, our humane patrimony."[37]

When Carstens and his supporters, a group Stillman referred to as "cranks and bores," failed in a 1912 vote to gain control of the American Humane Society, Carstens disaffiliated the Massachusetts society from the national organization. In 1915, Carstens and other like-minded executives founded the Bureau for the Exchange of Information among Child-Helping Agencies, which in 1921 became the Child Welfare League of America (CWLA). From 1921 until his death in 1939, Carstens served as executive director of CWLA. From that platform, he presided over the spread of a social work approach to child welfare, eventually convincing his rival, the American Humane Association that this was the best approach.[38]

---

35. Massachusetts Society for the Prevention of Cruelty to Children, *Twenty-Seventh Annual Report, December 31, 1907* (Boston, MA: Griffith-Stillings Press, 1908), 17.

36. Massachusetts Society for the Prevention of Cruelty to Children, *Twenty-Seventh Annual Report*, 17

37. Philip G. Anderson, "The Origin, Emergence, and Professional Recognition of Child Protection," *Social Service Review*, 63 (1989): 225.

38. Philip G. Anderson, "The Origin, Emergence, and Professional Recognition of Child Protection," 222–244.

HOSPITALS

Dr. Richard Cabot was the scion of a prominent and wealthy Boston family at the turn of the twentieth century. Cabot was a physician on the faculty of Harvard Medical School and on the staff of the Massachusetts General Hospital. In addition to his medical work, Cabot was involved with numerous charitable agencies and causes in the Boston area. One of these activities was service as a board member of the prominent and progressive BCAS (described earlier). In this role he had become impressed by the casework of the Society's paid staff, who made "careful studies . . . into the character, disposition, antecedents, and record of the child" and then rounded out their investigations by consulting with teachers, physicians, and others who might provide information and insights into the situation and needs of the child and his or her family. The casework method demonstrated by the Children's Aid Society workers, the "focusing of effort on the part of many experts upon the needs of a single child," fascinated Cabot and he began to think that it might be applicable to some of the problems he was concerned about in the delivery of medical care.[39]

Cabot worked in the Outpatient Department of the Massachusetts General Hospital, a setting described as being characterized by barely controlled chaos. Between 800 and 1000 patients came through the Department each day. Most were very poor, many were immigrants who spoke little or no English. Physicians were able to spend only a little time with each patient, focusing only on the presenting symptoms of the patient's condition, and very little on the whole patient. Cabot concluded that once a diagnosis was made by a physician, the treatment recommended in at least 60 percent of cases was completely unrealistic considering the social and economic environment from which the patients came. Cabot would recommend to patients that they stop working, take a vacation, get more sunshine and fresh air, buy dentures, adopt a special diet, and many other treatments and activities which he finally concluded that patients had no way of complying with. Convinced that the treatment he was offering was worthless, and influenced by the practice methods of the Children's Aid Society social workers, Cabot decided that the solution to the treatment problems he was observing in the Outpatient Department was to bring in trained social workers who had the knowledge, skill, and ability to help him deal with the social and economic realities of patients' lives.[40]

In 1905 Cabot hired Garnet Isabel Pelton as the first hospital social worker. Cabot met Pelton in her job as a nurse at Denison House Settlement on Boston's South End. In the first three months 142 patients were referred to Mrs. Pelton by physicians observing things such as "Patient is married—wife and child to support. Too sick to work. No money. Has some kidney condition as yet undetermined." Another wrote, "This man probably has T.B. of one or both kidneys. We cannot tell until 6 weeks have elapsed. He is to come here at least twice a week meanwhile and ought not work." Another doctor referred what he thought might be a mental case, but was not

---

39. Richard C. Cabot, *Social Work: Essays on the Meeting-Ground of Doctor and Social Worker* (Boston: Houghton Mifflin, 1919), xxi–xxii.

40. Claudia Rappaport, "Breathlessness: Richard Cabot's 1908 Conceptualization of Social Work Burnout," Paper presented at the Council on Social Work Education Annual Program Meeting, February 2006, 2.

sure: "This patient tells us stories of abuse at home by his sons. He is depressed and moody. Can you tell us what the conditions are there?" Dr. Cabot himself asked for assistance for a patient with a heart condition: "Working too hard. Does washing. Can she be relieved of some of her work?"[41]

By December of 1905, less than three months after Pelton began work, Cabot reported that she had to refuse to accept cases "because there is no time to attend to them. We are over-run with applications and need more competent help." To address this problem he embarked on a fundraising campaign, which apparently was successful as the size of the Social Work Department had expanded to eight staff by October of 1907. Cabot's most successful hire was Ida Mae Cannon, who joined the Massachusetts General Hospital as a social worker in 1907, shortly following her graduation from the Boston School for Social Workers. Cannon worked for the hospital for forty years, being promoted to Chief of Social Services in 1914. The promotion illustrates the importance that social work quickly assumed at the hospital there being only three chief level positions for the whole organization—chief of medicine, chief of surgery, and chief of social services.

Medical social workers took a special interest in teaching hygiene to young mothers, providing services to children with orthopedic problems, and providing services to pregnant, unwed, young women. However, the most intense interest was the effort to "cure consumption." Tuberculosis accounted for one-third of all deaths of people between the ages of fifteen and fifty-four, inflicting severe emotional and economic strain on patients and families. Once it was revealed to be a communicable disease, a committee of social workers under the sponsorship of Massachusetts General Hospital, investigated the social correlates of tuberculosis such as incidence, symptoms, severity, and possible means of prevention, and then made recommendations which became integral parts of medical treatment. These social workers were among the first professionals to perform a comprehensive analysis of tuberculosis in the United States, building upon the pioneering work of the Tuberculosis Committee of the New York COS.[42]

Medical social workers had to decide early if they were to identify with nursing or social work. Identifying with nursing would have been an obvious step, as many early medical social workers were trained nurses. This also would have solved problems of identification, as nurses already had an established place in the hospital. However, social workers set out to sever any ties they had with nursing for two reasons—they felt that medical social work required different and special skills; and the nurse was clearly subordinate to the physician, and the medical social worker wanted to be the physician's equal. By 1919 hospital social work specializations were available in most schools of social work. Also by this time it was reported that medical social workers were employed by more than 200 hospitals, some social service departments as large as forty or fifty paid workers assisted by a number of volunteers.[43]

41. Roy Lubove, *The Professional Altruist*, 28.

42. Paul Stuart, "Linking Clients and Policy: Social Workers Distinctive Contribution," *Social Work* 44 (1999): 335–347.

43. Francis G. Peabody, *New York Evening Post*, no date, quoted in "Dr. Cabot's Appointment," *The Survey for January 1920*, 482.

MENTAL HEALTH

In the nineteenth century, largely due to work of activists such as Dorothea Dix (see Chapter 5), America built a string of mental hospitals and institutionalization became the treatment of choice for the mentally ill. By 1880 there were 140 public and private mental hospitals caring for nearly 41,000 patients.[44] Care of insane persons was provided by neurologists and the newly profession-alizing specialty of psychiatry (at the time called alienists) and consisted mainly of attempting to keep patients comfortable while hoping for the best although holding out little hope that anything could be done. The prevailing theory of mental illness was that the cause was probably organic and the major research method to uncover the causes was performing autopsies on deceased patients in order to look for brain liaisons. As Rothman has said in regard to prisons, the pride of one generation becomes the shame of another. By the end of the century psychiatrists in rebellion against the mental health establishment began to criticize the institutional approach to treatment and to look for more hopeful ways to explain and treat mental illness.

In 1894 members of the American Neurological Association voted to poll the organization regarding opinions about providing aftercare to mental patients when they returned to their home communities. Over ninety percent of those who responded to the survey were strongly in favor of keeping track of discharged patients and felt that the establishment of privately supported after-care organizations was the best way to do this. In spite of the strong support for the idea of after-care expressed by the association's membership, no concrete action followed. However, interest in aftercare, and in out-patient treatment as an alternative to institutionalization, persisted. Following the turn of the century, a group of young and increasingly influential psychiatrists, notably, Adolf Meyer, Elmer E. Southard, and James J. Putnam, working in conjunction with the emerging men-tal hygiene movement, began to substitute a clinical, empirical, approach to mental illness for the pessimistic institutional isolation and custodial approach of the previous century.

In 1906 Louisa Lee Schuyler conducted a study of aftercare societies in England and presented her findings to the New York State Commission on Lunacy along with a plan for implementation of aftercare services. At the same conference Adolf Meyer presented a paper on aftercare and pre-vention. Following these presentations the conference adopted a resolution requesting that the State Charities Aid Association organize a statewide system of aftecare. In this instance concrete action quickly followed. As reported by French, "in April 1906, the first "after care agent," a gradu-ate of the New York School of Philanthropy, was employed by the State Charities Aid Association. Five years later, acting upon a resolution submitted by the State Charities Aid Association, the first aftercare worker to be paid by state funds was appointed by the State Commission on Lunacy and assigned to Manhattan State Hospital. In the same year an outpatient department was established at Long Island State Hospital, and, in cooperation with Manhattan and Central Islip State Hospitals, a dispensary for nervous and mental diseases, "to be known as the East Side Clinic. . . A social serv-ice worker attends clinics, visits homes of patients, and cooperates with the Board of Education." By May 1914 there were field workers employed in eleven state hospitals. Fourteen dispensaries were maintained by state hospitals and, in New York City alone, there were twenty clinics for

---

44. Gerald N. Grob, *Mental Illness and American Society, 1875–1940* (Princeton, NJ: Princeton University Press, 1983), 4.

mental and nervous disorders."[45] In New York the aftercare program grew at a slow but steady rate. In 1909 117 cases received aftercare services receiving a total of 617 visits. By 1917 it was reported that social workers made 5,731 visits to the homes of patients, found employment for 135, and arranged housing for 51. The program in Massachusetts lagged only slightly behind New York, with Elmer Southard (a colleague of Richard Cabot) establishing a social service department at Boston Psychopathic Hospital (BPH) in 1913. Southard hired Mary Jarrett, a graduate of the Boston School for Social Workers, as Chief of Social Service. Shortly after Southard established social service at BPH the legislature asked the State Board of Charities to study the desirability of establishing social service departments in every state hospital. The recommendation of the Board was positive with the result that in 1914 aftercare was made the responsibility of every state hospital outpatient department. Other states quickly followed the lead of New York and Massachusetts but many aftercare programs were severely hampered by insufficient funds.[46]

Staff employed in mental health settings quickly joined their colleagues in COSs and in medical hospitals in seeking to professionalize their function. Mary Jarrett was a leader in this effort, in 1916 introducing the name "psychiatric social work" to describe the specialization and establishing a six-month internship program at Boston Psychopathic Hospital for social workers wishing to work in mental health. In 1918, in response to increased demand for psychiatric social workers created by America's entry into World War I, the Smith College School for Psychiatric Social Work was established under the auspices of the National Committee for Mental Hygiene and with the participation of the Red Cross. The curriculum included lectures on psychology, sociology, and social psychiatry as well as field work in the form of bi-weekly clinics at the Northampton State Hospital. In 1920 the program was expanded to two full years of study. Schools of social work in New York, Chicago, and Philadelphia also incorporated courses in psychiatric social work in their curricula in response to war demand. In 1920, under the leadership of Mary Jarrett, a Psychiatric Social Workers Club was formed that in 1922 became the Psychiatric Social Work section of the American Association of Hospital Social Workers. In 1926 the section separated from the hospital group and became an independent organization, the American Association of Psychiatric Social Workers.

SCHOOLS

Like hospitals, mental hospitals, and child welfare agencies, schools at the turn of the twentieth century were feeling that they had lost contact with the child's social environment and reformers began to advocate for social work as a way of establishing this contact. Although school social work was an individual treatment specialty it received its original impetus from settlements and civic organizations, rather than from charity organizations. In 1906 four settlement houses cooperated in sponsoring two school social workers (at the time called visiting teachers) for three school districts. By 1913 Boards of Education in many areas of the country began to confer official status on

---

45. Lois Meredith French, *Psychiatric Social Work* (New York: The Commonwealth Fund, 1940), 35.

46. Gerald N. Grob, *Mental Illness and American Society*, 248–249.

visiting teachers, i.e. they became official, permanent, employees of the school districts. In 1921 school social work received an additional boost when the Commonwealth Fund decided to sponsor it as part of its five year program for the prevention of juvenile delinquency.

The progressive educator and the school social worker viewed the child as the key to the problem of urban social control. The ethnic and class divisions of urban society troubled the progressive generation no less than the nineteenth century COS leader. In fact, the search for solutions to these problems was to a great extent what progressivism was all about. For the progressive generation the public school assumed special significance as an instrument of acculturation and social control. The school social workers contact with the child in his own environment was the "logical place to detect symptoms of future inefficiency, whether they be departures from the mental, social, or physical standards."[47]

THE SEARCH FOR FOCUS AND METHOD

By the second decade of the twentieth century the usefulness of social work as a way to address the environmental aspects of a number of areas of social functioning was well on the way to public acceptance. Social work was established and growing as an institutionalized function within child protection, medical care, mental health, and public schools, as well as a few less well established areas such as probation and parole, and even business was experimenting with using social workers to help with employee relations.[48] It was also gradually dawning on COS workers that specialization had made them experts on family adjustment, and, as environment superseded moral defects as an explanation of dependency, they perceived their task to be the discovery of internal and external pressures that interfered with normal family life. Poverty came to be viewed as a symptom of a breakdown of cohesion or of an unsatisfactory relation to other social institutions. The friendly visiting of the COSs began to morph into family casework with the encouragement of the RSF. In 1911 the RSF Charity Organization Department headed by Mary Richmond supported the formation of the American Association of Societies for Organizing Charity with Francis H. McLean as its general secretary. By 1919 Richmond and McLean had accepted that the task of providing financial assistance to the poor was rapidly moving from private to public agencies they changed the name of the organization to the American Association for Organizing Family Social Work. Throughout the 1920s the association led the movement to transform COSs into family social work agencies that specialized in counseling rather than material assistance. In 1930 the name of the organization was changed to the Family Welfare Association of America, and in 1946 the name was once again changed to the Family Service Association of America. As family casework was not thrust into a host institution (school, hospital, etc.) it didn't have the same stimulus to define its professional functions and knowledge base as did the other specialties. However,

---

47. Lydia H. Hodge, "Why a Visiting Teacher?" National Educational Education Association, *Addresses and Proceedings, 1917*, 225.

48. Philip R. Popple, "Social Work Practice in Business and Industry, 1875–1930," *Social Service Review*, 55 (1981): 257–269.

social work leaders were acutely aware that separate, small, specializations, would have little success in improving their status and power within American society (the American Association of Psychiatric Social Workers, for example, had only 96 members in 1926). It was critical for social workers to establish themselves as one unified profession.

THE COMMITTEE ON THE PROFESSIONAL BASIS OF SOCIAL WORK

In 1914 a group of social work leaders who were all active in the National Conference of Charities and Correction (NCCC) met and established within the Conference a Committee on the Professional Basis of Social Work. The group was chaired by Porter R. Lee, a former COS executive and currently the Director of the New York School of Social Work. Other members included Edward T. Devine, a leading social work scholar and faculty member at the New York School, Jeffrey Brackett, former child welfare executive and Director of the Boston School for Social Workers, George Mangold, an economist and child welfare scholar and Director of the Missouri School of Social Economy, Edith Abbott, Associate Director of the Chicago School of Civics and Philanthropy, and Zilpha Drew Smith, Associate Director of the Boston School for Social Workers. The Committee found that among the active members of the NCCC was Abraham Flexner, at the time an Associate of the Bureau of Social Hygiene of New York City (social hygiene was the term used when referring to what would now be called sexual health), but who had previously been employed by the Carnegie Foundation to carry out a study of medical education.[49] The report Flexner wrote on the medical profession resulted in a rapid and nearly complete restructuring of medical education in the United States and a major reform of medical practice. Medicine rose from what it had been prior to Flexner's report, a rather lowly and ineffective profession, to the position it still holds in American society as the zenith of professional effectiveness and status. Having accomplished this for medicine, the Committee hoped he could help increase the power and status of the newly emerging social work profession. The Committee approached Flexner and asked if he would conduct a study of the professional basis of social work and report his results at the 1915 National Conference of Charities and Corrections and he agreed.

Flexner finished his report, titled "Is Social Work a Profession" several weeks prior to the conference and circulated drafts to members of the Committee on the Professional Basis of Social Work so they would have time to prepare responses to be presented at the session on Education for Social Work. He began the report by clearly defining the concept "profession," something that had not previously been done in a satisfactory manner. Flexner listed six criteria separating professions from lesser occupations: they involve essentially intellectual operations with large individual responsibility; they derive their raw material from science and learning; this material they work up to a practical and definite end; they possess an educationally communicable technique; they tend to self- organization; they are becoming increasingly altruistic

---

49. Abraham Flexner, *Medical Education in the United States and Canada: A Report to the Carnegie Foundation for the Advancement of Teaching* (Boston, MA: D. B. Updike, The Merrymount Press, 1910).

in motivation." Flexner concluded that social work was strong in some of the criteria of professionalism. He believed that "the operations of social work are assuredly of intellectual quality," that "no question can be raised as to the source from which the social worker derives his material—it comes obviously from science and learning . . . ; nor is there any doubt on the score of the rapid evolution of professional self-consciousness . . . Finally, in the one respect in which most professions still fall short, social work is fairly on the same level as education, for the rewards of the social worker are in his own conscience and in heaven."[50] In several important criteria, however, Flexner found social work lacking. The main source of social work's deficiency, he believed, was the broadness of its boundaries. Professions, he argued, had to have definite and specific ends. "The high degree of specialized competency required for action and conditioned on limitation of area cannot possibly go with the width and scope characteristic of social work." Flexner thought that this lack of specificity seriously affected the possibility of professional training: "the occupations of social workers are so numerous and diverse that no compact, purposefully organized educational discipline is feasible."[51]

Flexner's conclusion was negative. He did not think that at the stage of development social work had reached in 1915 it could legitimately be considered a profession. However, he voiced an optimistic, although cautionary, note at the end of his paper: "At the moment therefore,. . . it may be that social work will gain if it becomes uncomfortably conscious that it is not a profession in the sense in which medicine and engineering are professions; that if medicine and engineering have cause to proceed with critical care, social work has even more."[52]

Following Flexner's presentation, members of the Committee on the Professional Basis of Social Work presented papers outlining their ideas as to how social work could meet the challenges he identified. Jeffrey Brackett, Edward Devine, and Porter R. Lee all presented papers outlining the steps they felt social work must take in order to achieve full professional status. The significant fact about all of these papers is the degree to which they emphasized the individual treatment aspect of social work and, while recognizing social work's involvement with macro social issues such as poverty and social justice, relegated these to a position of secondary importance conducted as extra-professional activities. The reports also were unanimous in their arguments that a critical issue for social work was the necessity of developing educationally communicable techniques. These two areas, central to Flexner's criticism, were seen as closely related—in order to develop educationally communicable techniques it would be necessary to narrow the boundaries of social work. The prevailing belief among these professional leaders was that focusing on individual treatment (which was coming to be called social casework) would sufficiently narrow the focus of the profession to enable the development of expert practice techniques.

The papers presented in response to Flexner were in general agreement on what the problem and solution to social work's professional position was, but varied somewhat on the degree to which they emphasized individual treatment as the core professional function to the exclusion of macro activities such as administration and social reform. The most treatment oriented was

50. Abraham Flexner, "Is Social Work a Profession?" *Proceedings, National Conference of Charities and Corrections, 1915* (Chicago: Hildmann Printing Co., 1915), 581.

51. Abraham Flexner, "Is Social Work a Profession?" 588.

52. Abraham Flexner, "Is Social Work a Profession?" 590.

Brackett who argued that: "In [a school of social work] the chief lessons to learn are indeed in the wide field of group and individual psychology . . . interpreted through actual situations in groups or individuals lives." He felt that one of the school's chief goals was to get students "to appreciate the value of technique in 'casework' in any part of the field, with its necessary relations to measures for improving general conditions and advancing useful knowledge."[53]

The response by Edward Devine placed a bit less emphasis on the centrality of an individual treatment approach to social work and less enthusiasm about relegating macro issues to the professions periphery. This is understandable given Devine's broad background in reform movements. However, Devine still considered the development of individual treatment technique to be the number one priority of a school of social work: "A course, therefore, which deals with individuals and families and their complicated disabilities is fundamental in the curriculum of a professional school for social workers. . . Social movements . . . may, I think, be studied with profit; but the school might send out students who had not studied these particular matters and still expect them confidently not to disgrace the school. But any student who does not understand [individual problems and how to deal with them] would be equally a disgrace to a school, regardless of his type of work."[54]

Porter R. Lee presented a paper reporting the deliberations of the whole committee. This dealt mainly with defining what were the boundaries and responsibilities of the profession of social work. The main thrust of the report was that social work needed to develop professional expertise based on scientific knowledge: "When we speak of social work as a profession we are making large claims for ourselves. . . Professional standing implies expertness. . . expertness implies responsibility and power gained by hard work which other persons, including other kinds of experts, do not have . . . No organized activity . . . can claim professional standing until it rests upon scientific knowledge, and has developed definite methods of using knowledge to reach its goal." The committee defined the responsibility of social work for the solution of social as well as individual problems in a way that kept the boundaries of the profession narrow and relegated social reform and other macro practice activities to secondary status. Lee reported that the primary professional responsibility of social work was individual treatment and its responsibility for social problems was limited to research into these problems as they affect individual functioning. The committee believed that social work's "function requires a technical skill . . . the tests of this technical skill we believe to be two: the diagnosis and treatment of disabilities so far as they are influenced by the social routine of the disabled person or family, and the determination of the general effect upon human welfare of different phases of the economy and social life."[55] Having now clearly identified and articulated the professional basis of social work, the only task left, and it was a big one, was developing techniques with which to carry out the functions identified.

53. Jeffrey Brackett, "The Curriculum of the Professional School of Social Work," *Proceedings, National Conference of Charities and Correction, 1915* (Chicago: Hildmann Printing Co., 1915), 611–612.

54. Edward T. Devine, "Education for Social Work," Proceedings, National Conference of Charities and Correction, 1915 (Chicago: Hildmann Printing Co., 1915), 609.

55. Porter R. Lee, "Committee Report: The Professional Basis of Social Work," Proceedings, National Conference of Charities and Correction, 1915 (Chicago: Hildmann Printing Co., 1915), 599–600.

THE DEVELOPMENT OF PRACTICE TECHNIQUE

Although the paper the Committee on the Professional Basis of Social Work asked Abraham Flexner to write served to focus the attention of professional leaders on the need for social workers to develop a technique to guide their practice, this problem had been on the forefront of Mary Richmond's mind for a quarter of a century. In 1890 while she was still a relatively inexperienced COS leader in Baltimore she delivered her first important public speech before the annual meeting of that group in which she began to explicate the skills needed to be an effective charity worker. At this early point in her career she was a little naïve stating that only two things were necessary for successful work among the poor—"one is much good will, and the other is a little tact."[56] She spent much of the rest of her career, until her death in 1928, expanding on her vision of social work (or at least social casework) skills and techniques.

The method that Richmond developed to study social work practice technique was that of case analysis. She began this as a formal process in 1893 when she organized the first of a series of educational conferences in Baltimore for which she asked participants to bring case histories with them that could be subjected to systematic analysis in the search for general principles that could improve their work. In 1899 she used the data she had gathered through these case histories to write her first full-length book about social work practice *Friendly Visiting Among the Poor*. In this book Richmond lays out many principles that still form the basis of social work practice technique. Among these are individualization, now referred to as differential diagnosis and treatment, which calls for assistance to be given that will best fit the particular need of the particular client. She also predicts the modern problem solving process with her conception of a helping process based on facts and purposeful action. The concept of therapeutic relationship is foreshadowed when she writes that "Friendly visiting means intimate and continuous knowledge of and sympathy with a poor family's joys, sorrows, opinions, feelings, and entire outlook on life . . . The friendly visitor should get well acquainted with all the members of the family without trying to force their confidence. A fault of beginners is that they are unwilling to wait for the natural development of trust and friendliness." She identifies the social work role of brokerage, advising that the friendly visitor "must confer with sources of relief that are or can be interested." The idea of use of self is identified by Richmond when she discusses "the power of taking our own interests with us when we visit. In our contact with poor people we do not always give ourselves as generously as we might. Intent upon finding out about them, we forget that they might be interested to hear about us." And last, she identifies the technique that she would focus on developing for the following sixteen years—assessment—saying "In getting acquainted, the visitor has the definite object of trying to improve the condition of the family. This is impossible unless he has a fairly accurate knowledge of the main facts of family history. . . One advantage of visiting under the guidance of a charity organization society is that a thorough investigation has been made of the family circumstances before the visitor is sent." She presents a detailed outline of a complete assessment with a final caveat: "Its

---

56. Mary Richmond, "The Friendly Visitor," paper presented at the 1890 Annual Meeting of the Baltimore Charity Organization Society, reprinted in Joanna C. Colcord (ed.), *The Long View: Papers and Addresses by Mary E. Richmond* (New York: Russell Sage Foundation, 1930), 39–42.

seemingly inquisitorial features are justified by the fact that it is not made with any purpose of finding people out, but with the sole purpose of finding out how to help them."[57]

Richmond's leadership in the pursuit of knowledge for the new profession was recognized in 1905 when she was appointed editor of the Field Department of the leading social work journal of the time *Charities and the Commons.* In this position she issued a national call to share cases which provided more data for her work on developing a social work method. In 1909 the extremely well endowed RSF was established with Richmond among its first full-time employees as Director of the Charity Organization Department. With this new job Richmond was free to devote full time to collecting and analyzing cases and developing social work practice theory and technique.

Among the first tasks that Richmond undertook upon taking the new job at Russell Sage was researching and writing a substantial, scholarly, treatise on social work practice technique. She began this project in 1910 and devoted six years to it, publishing the results under the title *Social Diagnosis* in 1916 (with a 1917 copyright) just in time to be received by the profession reacting to the Flexner report as the explication of the educationally communicable technique that they were seeking. In this book Richmond analyzed the common elements of social casework regardless of agency or institutional setting, what we would now call generalist social work practice. The question with which she began her book was, "When a human being, whatever his economic status, develops some marked form of social difficulty and social need, what do we have to know about him and about his difficulty (or more often his difficulties) before we can arrive at a way of meeting his need?" To answer this question the social worker must engage in social diagnosis which Richmond defined "as the attempt to make as exact a definition as possible of the situation and personality of a human being in some social need—of his situation and personality, that is, in relation to the other human beings upon whom he in any way depends or who depend upon him, and in relation also to the social institutions of his community."[58]

Social Diagnosis was a formal, scholarly, but backward looking, explication of social work practice knowledge as it had been developed during the late nineteenth and early twentieth centuries. The expertise that social work had developed was a methodology of investigation and the results of the investigation were usually turned over to some other professional for action. The charity worker studied the character and circumstances of relief applicants and then reported the results to a committee who made decisions about the type, amount, and duration of aid to be granted. The visiting teacher studied the family and neighborhood environment of the child experiencing school problems and then turned the results over to the teacher or principal for use in their educational planning for the child. The medical social worker visited the patient in his or her own home and reported back to the physician with information critical for the patients care and, conversely, communicated information from the physician to the patient's family regarding their role in patient care. Likewise, the psychiatric social worker conducted a study of the mental patients home environment and reported information relevant to the treatment plan to the attending psychiatrist. The physician Abraham Myerson, described the role of medical and psychiatric social workers "as the sensory and motor apparatus of the physician, while at the same time she builds

---

57. Mary E. Richmond, *Friendly Visiting Among the Poor: A Handbook for Charity Workers* (New York: The Macmillan Company, 1899), 179–195.

58. Mary Richmond, *Social Diagnosis* (New York: Russell Sage Foundation, 1917), 26, 357.

up an independent social science which, in the long run, helps govern the knowledge and conduct of the physician."[59] It was this attribute of the social worker's role that Flexner identified as one of the reasons he did not consider social work to have achieved full professional status, writing "The social worker takes hold of a case, that of a disintegrating family, a wrecked individual, or an unsocialized industry. Having localized his problem, having decided on its particular nature, is he not usually driven to invoke the specialized agency, professional or other, best equipped to handle it? . . . he is, as social worker, not so much an expert himself as the mediator whose concern is to summon the expert."[60]

The concern focused by Flexner's comments was that social work had expertise in investigation, or diagnosis or assessment if you will, but once this was done had little idea of what to do to solve the problems identified. Social work practice had been based on the assumption that if adequate knowledge could be attained about the individual, then the logical course of action would be obvious. Thus the weight of professional activity was on the collection of facts in order to establish a cause-cure relationship. By the time of the publication of *Social Diagnosis* social workers, including Richmond herself, were beginning to question this assumption. In 1920 Richmond quotes an unnamed judge who said to her "After the investigation has been made and recorded, the treatment seems to drop to a lower level almost as suddenly as though it went over the edge of a cliff." Richmond commented that "This is an exaggeration, of course; but is it not high time that we began to fix our attention with concentrated determination upon what ought to be the [next] period of our development; namely, upon the period of sympathetic and adaptable treatment."[61] It seems that most social work leaders anticipated that Richmond would follow up *Social Diagnosis* with a similarly scholarly and brilliantly conceptualized text on the question of treatment technique. This never was to be. Richmond published the well regarded reflection on social work practice titled *What is Social Casework* in 1922, with the famous definition of casework as "those processes which develop personality through adjustments consciously effected, individual by individual, between men and their social environment." However, after this, with her health declining, she turned her attention to the social policy questions surrounding marriage laws, advocating for states to raise the minimum age for marriage, never returning to the problem of social work treatment technique.

The ink was barely dry on *Social Diagnosis* before Richmond's colleagues began to criticize it. The criticism was respectful, for Richmond was a revered and respected figure in the profession, but was criticism none-the-less. The critics, led by leaders in the tiny but prestigious specialty of psychiatric social work, based their criticism on the fact that Richmond largely ignored the newly emerging, and exciting, field of psychiatry, and specifically did not use insights gained from Freud's theory and techniques of psychoanalysis. Robinson, in her 1930 book *A Changing Psychology of Social Casework*, summarized the criticism: "it is the sociological rather than the psychological basis which organizes and gives unity to her presentation in *Social Diagnosis* . . . There is

---

59. Abraham Myerson, "The Psychiatric Social Worker," *Journal of Abnormal Psychology* (1917), 225.

60. Abraham Flexner, "Is Social Work a Profession?" 585, 588.

61. Mary E. Richmond, "Some Next Steps in Social Treatment," paper given at the 1920 National Conference of Social Work, reprinted in Joanna C. Colcord and Ruth Z. S. Mann (eds.), *The Long View; Papers and Addresses by Mary E. Richmond* (New York: Russell Sage Foundation, 1930), 485.

no reference in Miss Richmond's book to Freud or to William A. White's *Mechanisms of Character Formation* which appeared in 1916."

By a sociological approach Richmond's critics were referring to the fact that *Social Diagnosis* described processes by which accurate *objective* information could be obtained and analyzed regarding a client's situation and then making case plans based on this information. Thus, information (or evidence, to use Richmond's term) would be collected about a client's family, job, neighborhood, financial situation, health and so forth. Robinson describes the sociological approach as: "When the problem was simply perceived in its social and mass aspects rather than its psychological and individual aspects, it was easier to know what to do and how to do it. The earliest case records are of simple effective action. Families "cooperate" or "fail to cooperate," in which latter instance the case is closed. A complete plan of treatment could be mapped out in advance for different types of problems."[62] The treatment plan for a client who was unemployed would be to help him find a job; for the ill client, find medical care; for the child with school problems, help the parents learn to assist the child's studying or help find a tutor; and so forth. Critics complained that this rational model did not explain the irrationality that they saw in their practice. They would help an unemployed man get a job and within a few weeks he would have sabotaged it and again be unemployed; they would help a woman obtain quality medical care and she would not follow the physician's instructions; they would help a family construct a workable budget only to see them blow an entire week's wages on a Sunday outing.

Specialists in the newly emerging field of psychiatric social work began, shortly following the end of World War I, to aggressively argue that case workers should make use of psychiatric knowledge in their practice. They argued that what was important was not the objective facts of a client's situation, as in the sociological approach, but rather how the client perceived and reacted to these facts. Mary Jarrett argued that the "special function of social casework is the adjustment of individuals with social difficulties. It is the art of bringing an individual who is in a condition of social disorder into the best possible relation with all parts of his environment." The most important aspect of social disorder was the mental functioning of the client. Jarrett analyzed all of the cases that Mary Richmond had used as examples in *Social Diagnosis* and concluded that fifty percent presented a clearly psychiatric problem, and another fifteen percent strongly suggested a psychopathic condition.[63] A new conception of scientific casework developed, rooted in Freud and the mysteries of the psyche, personality, and emotions. As Lubove has observed: "The psychiatric social worker emerged as the queen of caseworkers, for if her point of view was relevant to all casework, then no group was better qualified by training and experience to speak for the profession."[64]

If social workers thought, and they appear to have, that utilizing psychiatric knowledge would lead to expert treatment techniques, they were to be disappointed. The optimistic expectation of answers from psychiatry was expressed by Mary B. Sayles when she wrote, "It is not difficult to identify some of the methods and processes here described as well-established elements in the skill of many a good social worker . . . Psychiatry, however, stands in an entirely different relation

---

62. Virginia Robinson, *A Changing Psychology of Social Casework* (Chapel Hill, NC: University of North Carolina Press, 1930), 108.

63. Mary C. Jarrett, "The Psychiatric Thread Running Through All Social Case Work," *Proceedings, National Conference of Social Work* (Chicago: Hildmann Printing Co., 1920), 587–593.

64. Roy Lubove, *The Professional Altruist*, 86.

to social casework. Through the interpretation of the processes of mental life revealed by a close study of all the aspects of personality as well as environment, this branch of science is bringing a new and fundamental contribution to the technique of understanding and adjusting individual lives."[65] In spite of the faith that social workers such as Sayles had in psychiatry to provide answers to treatment questions, psychiatrists themselves were not so confident. Dr. Lawson G. Lowrey, for example, wrote in 1930, "I think most of us would agree that whereas there are many people in this country who can write a most satisfying and elevating textbook on the causes of behavior disorders, there isn't any person, so far as I know, who is really qualified to write a textbook on treatment." Social worker Porter R. Lee agreed with Lowrey, writing, "When we come right down to the real essentials of treatment, we know almost nothing." Charlotte Towle, in a somewhat ironic statement, both praised the sociological approach of *Social Diagnosis* and blamed it for the slow development of treatment techniques based on psychiatric knowledge: "Social diagnosis has attained an adequacy which has not yet been realized in treatment. The technique involved in this phase of our work is perhaps being stressed at the expense of treatment."[66]

By 1930, thanks to Richmond's two books *Social Diagnosis* and *What Is Social Case Work*, and through faith in the possibility that psychiatric knowledge would eventually contribute effective treatment techniques, social workers felt they were well on the way to addressing and correcting one of the professional deficiencies addressed by Flexner, namely that social work did not have a educationally communicable technique. This left only the second major deficiency addressed by Flexner, the broadness of social work's boundaries. Of this Flexner had written, "professions need to be limited and definite in scope, in order that practitioners may themselves act; but the high degree of specialized competency required for action and conditioned on limitation of area cannot possibly go with the width and scope characteristic of social work."[67] Social work leaders in the 1920s were also focused on remedying this perceived deficiency.

DEFINING THE PROFESSION'S BOUNDARIES

During the 1920s a group of social work executives and board members met annually under the name The Milford Conference to grapple with the question of what were the boundaries of the profession. In 1929 they released a report based on their deliberations titled *Social Case Work: Generic & Specific*. This report reflected the determination of social work leaders to establish a group identity based on a generic skill. The conclusion of the report stated the "emergence of a strong conviction unanimously held by the members . . . that a functional conception which has come to be spoken of as 'generic social case work' was much more substantial in content and much more significant in its implications for all forms of social case work than were any of the

65. Mary B. Sayles, "Introduction," in Mary B. Sayles, ed., *Three Problem Children: Narratives from the Case Records of a Child Guidance Clinic* (New York: Joint Committee on Methods of Preventing Delinquency, 1924), 10.

66. Albert T. Poffenberger, "Trends in Therapy: Specific Psychological Therapies," *American Journal of Orthopsychiatry* 9 (Oct. 1939), 755–760.

67. Abraham Flexner, "Is Social Work a Profession?" 586.

specific emphases of the different case work fields." By this conception, caseworkers differed not in purpose or in methodology but only in administrative setting. Each setting required a measure of specialized knowledge and technique, but the "distinguishing concern" of all caseworkers was the "capacity of the individual to organize his own normal social activities in a given environment."[68]

The significance of the Milford Report is not just that it defined social case work as a generic skill that did not vary across practice settings, but that the conference met under the assumption that social work *was* social casework, directed at individual adjustment, and that macro activities such as social reform were outside the borders of the profession. This is an assumption that was not shared by all social workers and they let their feelings be known. Abraham Epstein, writing in 1928, spoke of social work's "loss of zeal." Of the type of social worker described in the Milford Report Epstein lamented: "His prescriptions are no longer compounds of social panaceas and far-visioned dreams, but of all the new discoveries of psychology, psychiatry and the 'science' of case work. The questions of a living wage, abolition of the slums, women and child labor, the lack of economic opportunity, the insecurity of life, and so forth no longer attract him."[69] Richard C. Cabot, founder of medical social work was another leader concerned with the direction reflected by the Milford Report. In 1927, referring to the previous ten years of the Massachusetts Conference of Social Work, Cabot complained: "164 speakers out of 165 have dealt not with our ends, but with the means to our ends such as institutional care, psychiatric examinations, habit clinics, mental hygiene, financial federations, family budgets, and so forth. Only one speaker dealt with the objects for which all this apparatus and technique are marshaled."[70]

In response to criticisms such as these, Milford Conference participant Porter R. Lee, set down a rationale for the individual treatment approach to social work that was quickly accepted as the authoritative statement on social work's professional boundaries. Lee agreed with those who argued that social work had a dual focus, treatment on one hand and social reform on the other, and that this duality was natural and inevitable, and that the two aspects were complementary. However, Lee argued that rather than being completely parallel in development the two aspects of social work were evolutionary, with reform (which he referred to as "cause") playing the most important role in the early years of the profession and then being gradually replaced by treatment (which he referred to as "function"). Lee argued that a "cause," once successful, naturally tended to "transfer its interest and its responsibility to an administrative unit" which justified its existence by the test of efficiency, not zeal, by its "demonstrated possibilities of achievement" rather than by the "faith and purpose of its adherents." The emphasis of the "function" was upon "organization, technique, standards, and efficiency." Fervor inspired the "cause" while intelligence directed the "function." Lee felt that once the "cause" had been won it was necessary that it be institutionalized as a "function" in order that the gains be made permanent. This he saw as the primary task of professional social work."[71] Lee was, in effect, differentiating between social welfare and social work. Social welfare was seen as the institution in society charged with managing the problem of dependency through social reform, program development, and social legislation. Once the social

68. American Association of Social Workers, *Social Case Work: Generic and Specific: A Report of the Milford Conference*, Studies in the Practice of Social Work No. 2 (New York: American Association of Social Workers, 1929), 3, 16.

69. Abraham Epstein, "The Soullessness of Present-day Social Work," *Current History*, 27 (1928): 391.

70. Richard C. Cabot, ed., *The Goal of Social Work* (Boston: Houghton Mifflin, 1927), 392.

71. Porter R. Lee, *Social Work as Cause and Function, and Other Papers* (New York: New York School of Social Work, 1937), 4–9.

welfare institution had created policies and programs to deal with social problems social work was called in as the professional technology to staff and administer them.

CONCLUSION

Social work underwent a remarkable transformation between 1900 and 1930. One of the major changes was the gradual lessening of concern within the new profession for social reform. This change in orientation was dramatic. In 1906 Edward T. Devine, in his Presidential address to the National Conference of Charities and Corrections had painted a broad responsibility for social work:

> It is embodied in a determination to seek out and to strike effectively at those organized forces of evil, at those particular causes of dependence and intolerable living conditions which are beyond the control of the individuals whom they injure and whom they too often destroy. Other tasks for other ages. This be the glory of ours, that the social causes of dependency shall be destroyed.[72]

The radical alteration of this view can be seen in the 1930 Presidential Address to the same organization (now called the National Conference of Social Work) by Miriam Van Waters:

> Social work has realized that a program cannot make men moral, religious or happy . . . The true springs of action are in the internal nature of man. Hence, the uselessness of programs, particularly those dependent upon State action or force.[73]

The definition of social reform as tangential to professional social work was probably not a mistake by the professions leaders. It is not possible for one profession to take responsibility for an entire social institution. Even medicine found it necessary to cede control of public health to other specialists in order to focus on the core area of individual patient care. What was a mistake was the rejection of the sociological approach to direct practice that had been so painstakingly and effectively developed by Mary Richmond, E. Franklin Frazier, and others over a period of many years of study and experience. The professions leaders uncritically accepted Flexner's opinion that the type of social work described by Richmond was not fully professional. They looked for an alternative and found it in the seductive new fields of psychology and psychiatry even though these fields gave little indication of offering concrete techniques that could be applied to social work practice. As the historian Roy Lubove noted in his masterful study of the professionalizing of social work:

> Apparently Flexner did not consider the possibility that liaison and resource mobilization in a complex urban society [Richmond's sociological approach] was a professional function requiring

---

72. Edward T. Devine, "Presidential Address," *Proceedings, National Conference of Charities and Corrections* (Chicago: Hildmann Printing Co., 1906).

73. Miriam Van Waters, "Presidential Address," Proceedings, National Conference of Charities and Corrections (Chicago: Hildmann Printing Co., 1930), 19.

considerable skill and specialized training. Drawing his models from the traditional professions like medicine, law, and the ministry, he did not recognize that the ability to mobilize the many specialized services of a community on behalf of a single individual or to serve as liaison among social groups and institutions was a pivotal task in modern society and no less "professional" than any other. . . Like Flexner, social workers failed to realize that the opening of lines of communication between individuals, classes, and institutions, and community resource mobilization, could be defended as legitimate "professional" responsibilities.[74]

74. Roy Lubove, *The Professional Altruist*, 106–107.

CHAPTER 8

CRISES: THE GREAT DEPRESSION AND WORLD WAR II

Harry Hopkins's boyhood was so stereotypical ideal mid-American that it almost seems to follow the script of an old Andy Hardy movie. Hopkins was born in Sioux City Iowa on August 17, 1890 to David Aldana Hopkins, known as Al, and to Anna Pickett Hopkins, the fifth of six children, one of whom died in infancy. Al was a hail fellow well-met, who was good natured, outgoing, friendly, loved sports—especially bowling—and was not beyond placing the occasional wager on an event, once winning $500 betting on a bowling tournament. In contrast, Anna was a prim, somewhat dour, devoutly religious Methodist churchwoman, not entirely approving of her husband's character. But, for whatever reasons, the marriage seemed to work and provided Harry and his siblings with a stable home life, although Harry once remarked that he had grown up surrounded by "conservative narrow mindedness." The family moved around a bit during Hopkins's early years, mostly to small Midwestern towns with one stint in Chicago, the only large city they ever lived in. In 1901 the Hopkins family left Chicago and moved to Grinnell, Iowa, a college town chosen by Anna out of a desire to return to a small town and for the educational and cultural opportunities available there because of Grinnell College. After moving to Grinnell Al provided the family with a modest, but adequate, living by running a small store and working as a harness maker. Harry was a popular student in the local schools; earned money with a paper route; was a member of the Stars, a local boys club; had a steady girlfriend; and played football, baseball, tennis, and basketball, which he played well enough to be considered a good prospect for the Grinnell College team. During summers he worked at a local brickyard and as a hired hand for a nearby farmer.[1]

1. William W. Bremer, "Hopkins, Harry Lloyd," in Walter I. Trattner, ed., *Biographical Dictionary of Social Welfare in America* (New York: Greenwood Press, 1986), 399–402.

In 1908, following his mother's plan, Harry went two blocks down the street and enrolled in Grinnell College. Although located in the middle of rural Iowa, Grinnell College was a well-respected, academically rigorous center of progressive social reform thinking. In the 1890s it became a center of Social Gospel Christianity under the leadership of President George A. Gates and Professor of Applied Christianity George D. Herron. At the beginning Harry struggled academically, probably due to poor preparation for higher education, and was dead last in his class at the end of his freshman year. He quickly overcame any educational deficiencies he brought with him to Grinnell, and by his junior year had reversed his ranking and was near the top of his class. At Grinnell Harry continued to be a popular, socially active student as a member of the social committee of his freshman class; secretary of the sophomore class; president of the senior class; treasurer of the campus YMCA chapter; member of the college annual staff; associate editor, assistant sports editor, and business manager of the campus newspaper; musical director and vice president of the men's literary society; and vice chairman of the College Council (the student government association). During his college years, Harry came under the influence of professors who were leading progressive thinkers, including Professor of Political Science Jesse Macy, Professor of Philosophy John D. Stoops, college President John H. T. Main, and Professor of Sociology Garret P. Wyckoff. These men impressed upon Harry that concern for the human condition was at the center of Christianity, that Darwin's scientific method was the new key to truth, and that religion would become truly Christian, and social sciences truly scientific only when they applied themselves to the "problems of social life."[2]

The member of his family that Harry was closest to was his oldest sister Adah, who graduated from Grinnell in 1905 and moved to New York to become a social worker. With the encouragement of Adah, who at the time was working as registrar of the New York School of Philanthropy, Harry accepted a job in New York arranged by his philosophy professor Louis D. Hartson, as director of junior boys programs at Northover Camp in New Jersey, a camp for inner city boys run by the New York settlement Christadora House. When the summer ended Harry accepted an offer to work as a district visitor for Christadora House investigating requests for aid. As a district visitor Harry got a quick introduction to the lives of the big city poor, visiting the homes of applicants for aid and interviewing them in detail about their living situations. He also confronted aspects of the lives of the poor that he did not understand, such as when the teenagers in a boys group he was supervising stood in silence to honor four convicted murderers on the day of their execution. The boys' behavior shocked him, but also led to a desire to understand it.[3]

From the very beginning of his social work career Hopkins demonstrated the ability to impress and gain the sponsorship of influential men. The first was John A. Kingsbury, a national figure in social welfare, policy advisor to Theodore Roosevelt, and general agent for the New York Association for Improving the Condition of the Poor (AICP). Meeting Hopkins through his work at Christadora House, Kingsbury made him his friend and protégé, hiring him in 1913 as an AICP visitor in the waterfront district, an area considered to be too dangerous for a female worker. His career at the AICP advanced rapidly, becoming Supervisor of Relief for the lower east side in fall

---

2. George McJimsey, *Harry Hopkins: Ally of the Poor and Defender of Democracy* (Cambridge, MA: Harvard University Press, 1967), 8–11.

3. George McJimsey, *Harry Hopkins*, 18.

of 1914, and Supervisor of the AICP tuberculosis clinic in early 1915. While at the AICP Hopkins conducted a study to find out why relief applications were rapidly increasing. The results of the study were to shape his attitudes toward welfare and unemployment for the remainder of his career, and were to have significant impact on later New Deal programs. Hopkins results found that, contrary to popular belief, fewer than six percent of relief applicants were homeless vagrants, the vast majority being men who simply could not find work. He concluded that structural and economic conditions, not personal shortcomings was at the root of poverty, and that the social response should be programs to create meaningful jobs for the unemployed, not the demeaning make-work activities such as raking leaves or chopping wood that were often required of relief recipients. He also recommended the establishment of employment exchanges that, unlike the common practices of the AICP and Charity Organization Society relief, should be free from any association with the stigma of charity and should concentrate on assuring the applicant that they have "no interest whatever in [his] private affairs . . . outside of determining his fitness for the position which he is applying for."[4]

In the fall of 1915, following the passage of the mother's pension act in the state, New York City Mayor Mitchel appointed a Board of Child Welfare to manage the program in the city and, on Kingsbury's recommendation Hopkins was appointed the board's executive secretary. This job gave Hopkins the chance to develop large scale organizational skills. He recruited and supervised the office staff, handled correspondence with government and private agency officials, attended state and local conferences, and lobbied and oversaw the movement of bills through the state legislature. He maintained close ties to visitors employed by the board and used information they gained during their investigations to develop policy recommendations to the board. He made it a point to assure that aid was granted on a professional, not a patronage, basis, that the amount was determined by need and not by political influence or connections. In spite of the good work he did, Hopkins tenure with the Child Welfare Board was short, a victim of exactly the type of political influences he fought so hard to keep out of the program. In 1916, Mayor Mitchel lost his bid for reelection to a Tammany Hall candidate, Hopkins ally Kingsbury was forced from the board, and several other board member who Hopkins respected resigned. In December of that year in an act of solidarity Hopkins resigned his position as executive secretary.

Hopkins, unemployed following his resignation from the Child Welfare Board, heard through his professional grapevine that the American Red Cross was looking for people to help develop and manage programs to provide services to the families of soldiers. He was hired by the organization thinking that the job would just be a temporary thing that would support him while he looked for something permanent. Contrary to this expectation, the Red Cross job lasted for five years, involved a number of assignments, and catapulted him into the upper echelons of social work administration. In quick succession Hopkins was assigned to manage disaster relief in the Gulf division; Associate Manager of the Gulf division retaining responsibility for disaster relief but also with responsibility of managing all field staff; manager of the newly enlarged southeastern division; and finally, after a new round of consolidation, manager of the whole southern district. At the Red Cross Hopkins also increased his involvement in professional social work, bringing social

4. Quoted in George McJimsey, *Harry Hopkins*, 21.

work standards to services provided by the organization, implementing an extensive in-service training program for the staff and, outside of the Red Cross, was, in 1922, a founding member of the American Association of Social Workers, an organization that eventually grew into the current major professional organization, the National Association of Social Workers. As McJimsey has noted, "All of this he accomplished in a way that showed his particular genius for administration. He had clearly mastered the professional social worker's skills of organizing and processing, and he had enriched them with the intuition and personality traits of the successful executive. More than anything else, he showed a strong sense of purpose."[5]

Because his home life had become very unsettled due to the amount of traveling required by his Red Cross duties, by 1922 Hopkins was again looking for a new job.[6] He once again turned to his friend and mentor John Kingsbury who was busy organizing a large public health project to be sponsored by the New York AICP. Kingsbury hired Hopkins to direct his project, but when it ran into political difficulties involving mainly a turf battle with the city health department, Hopkins, having little patience for the fight, left to become general director of the New York Tuberculosis and Health Association. In 1924 the Tuberculosis and Health Association inaugurated the Bellevue Yorkville Health Demonstration Project. The strategy of the project was to coordinate previously independent health agencies, even redesigning agency organizational structures to conform to those of the demonstration project. Hopkins career in public health lasted until his resignation in 1932 when he accepted Governor Roosevelt's invitation to become Director of the New York Temporary Relief Administration. The public health jobs had taught him critical administrative skills in coordinating independent services by providing advice and information, and the value of demonstration projects, at the time a new and innovative idea. As he said in an address to the National Conference of Social Work: "Why should there not be organized social welfare demonstrations the purpose of which would be not only to analyze the social work of a community, but to set up adequate experimental machinery to try out on a scientific basis the theories expounded for years by social workers."[7]

When the stock market crashed in 1929, ushering in the worst economic depression in terms of depth and length in American history, Harry Hopkins training and experience as both a social work practitioner and administrator positioned him as uniquely qualified to play a significant role in the nation's response to the crisis. His experience as a direct practitioner at Christadora House and as a district visitor for the AICP had enabled him to know the poor and to discount stereotypes both among the general public and many of his social work colleagues that poverty was mainly due to moral shortcomings or adjustment difficulties. Hopkins had learned that poverty was mainly due to unemployment, under employment, or exploitation, and had much more to do with structural flaws in the economic and social structure than to any personal shortcomings of the poor. His experience as an administrator with the AICP had taught him basic management skills.

5. George McJimsey, *Harry Hopkins*, 24.

6. Hopkins and his first wife Ethel, after having three children, divorced in 1928. Perhaps due to his feelings of guilt about not paying more attention to his family, Hopkins agreed to a ruinous financial settlement of one half of his salary for child support. This settlement, combined with Hopkins taste for a first-class life style, resulted in his having lifelong financial problems in spite of earning a large salary.

7. Harry L. Hopkins, "The Place of Social Work in Public Health," *Proceedings of the National Conference of Social Work* (Chicago: University of Chicago Press, 1926), 222–227.

At the Red Cross he had gained skill in program and organizational design and coordination and crisis management. At the Child Welfare Board he had learned about the political realities of running a public social welfare program. His public health work impressed upon him the value of the demonstration project which experimented with administrative techniques and tested results with statistical objectivity. By developing precise and commonly accepted standards, demonstration projects created models for other social agencies to apply. When the economy crashed Hopkins was an obvious person to help respond to the crisis, but with the White House in Republican control, it was several years before his talents were called upon.

THE CRASH OF 1929

Republican Warren G. Harding, with Calvin Coolidge as vice president, became president after handily winning the 1920 election with the promise of a "return to normalcy" following the trauma of war, revolution, race riots, labor unrest, and political hostility between President Wilson and Congress. Although the Harding administration had some bright spots, such as his signing the Sheppard-Towner Maternity act and his public criticism of the system of racial segregation in the South, most historians judge that it marked a new record for non-achievement and corruption. Harding and all members of his administration believed that whatever helped business helped the government and the entire nation, one time calling for "less government in business and more business in government." Harding died in office in 1923 and was succeeded by Vice President Coolidge who won the office on his own in the 1924 election. Since he shared his predecessor's economic views, famously declaring that "the business of America is business," there was no change in policy except for a new emphasis on honesty. With Andrew Mellon, one of the wealthiest men in America, as Secretary of the Treasury in the Harding, Coolidge, and Hoover administrations, a radical pro-business and pro-wealthy policy was aggressively pursued. A tax law was passed in 1926 that reduced both the federal surtax and estate tax rate from 40 percent to 20 percent and eliminated the gift tax, a huge boon to the wealthy at the expense of everyone else. Credit was expanded adding fuel to the economy. The money flowing into the financial network encouraged banks to buy government bonds and to loan money to investors to buy stocks, bonds and real estate. The banks also began to encourage consumer credit buying. Although these easy credit policies resulted in a growing burden of indebtedness and many uncollectible loans, they generated enormous prosperity. Corporate income in the U.S. grew 28 percent in five years, from $8.3 billion in 1923 to $10.6 billion in 1928. The great majority of Americans, farmers and minorities being notable exceptions, shared this prosperity. The gross national product grew from $128 billion in 1921 to $204 billion in 1929.

The economic prosperity was accompanied by a long and steady surge in the stock market. The total market value of stocks rose from $27 billion in 1925 to $67 billion in the summer of 1929. From June to August 1929 the market increased by 25 percent. The general attitude of the American people became that money was there for the taking, and anyone who did not invest all they could spare or borrow was a fool. Then, catching nearly everyone off guard, the market experienced several shocks in the fall of 1929, leading some investors to lessen their exposure to stocks, but because bankers were acting to stabilize the market, no massive sell-off occurred. Stability seemed to have been restored until October 29, 1929, called "Black Tuesday" when, for whatever reasons of psychology apply, investors panicked and dumped stocks at any price. Gains for the whole previous year were lost in one day. Confidence in the economy disappeared and the slide continued, until it hit bottom in 1932. Between 1929 and 1932 U.S. Steel stock fell from $262 a share to $22, Montgomery Ward dropped from $138 to $4. It is not known whether or not Harry Hopkins personally lost money in the crash, but most likely he did not. Although he earned a handsome salary, three to four times that of the average American, he was well known for spending all of it on high living, including first class train travel, five star hotels, stylish clothes, a beautiful home in a fashionable suburb of New York City, and a summer cottage at Woodstock. Because of this life style he had financial problems his whole adult life and it is doubtful that he had any extra funds available for stock market speculation. However, living in New York City, and having numerous friends and associates who were business volunteers on boards and committees, he had a perfect vantage point from which to watch the crisis unfold.

The stock market crash led immediately to a slide in the whole economy. Between 1929 and 1932 the index of industrial output fell from a high of 119 to only 68, a drop of nearly 43 percent; steel mills were at 12 percent capacity and auto factories at 20 percent. Banks became insolvent, with 1,345 failing in 1930 alone. Unemployment skyrocketed with thousands of employees being laid off each week during the depressions first three years. At its peak at the end of 1932 the unemployment rate was 25 percent, more than 13 million individuals. For those fortunate enough to still have jobs, wages fell sharply; personal income in 1932 was half of what it had been in 1929. The depression began to feed on itself in a vicious circle: shrinking wages and employment cut into purchasing power, causing business to slash production and lay off workers, thereby further reducing purchasing power.

The Wall Street crash was mainly caused by speculative fever that ran rampant throughout the country in the 1920s, and the lack of rigorous and effective government control of banks and the financial industry in general. However, the crash of 1929 marked the beginning of the depression, but did not cause it. The depression stemmed from basic weaknesses in the economy. Most damaging was the unequal distribution of wealth and income that had resulted from the radical pro-business and pro-upper class policy of the national administrations. In 1929 the richest 0.1 percent of the population had as much total income as the bottom 42 percent. Although the government did not yet keep official poverty statistics, current estimates were that more than one-half the nation was living at or below the subsistence level. The result was that there were not enough people with purchasing power to maintain the economy. If people do not have enough money to buy the products industry is producing, industry will not be able to sell those products. Other factors contributing to the economic collapse can be found in the basic structure of American business—many industries dominated by oligopolies that repressed competition; weaknesses in specific industries, notably agriculture, coal mining, textiles, and banking; international economic problems that were exacerbated by the Harding and Coolidge administrations restrictive trade policies; and government policies that encouraged speculation and shied away from business regulation. In short, the same government policies that shaped the booming 1920s economy also pointed to economic disaster.

HERBERT HOOVER BECOMES PRESIDENT
AND RESPONDS TO THE DEPRESSION

During his first term President Coolidge choose not to run for reelection, even though he probably could have easily won a second term. In his stead the Republican Party choose Herbert Hoover, a man who had never been elected to any office, but was a well-known and much respected public figure. Following graduation from Stanford University in 1896 Hoover pursued a spectacular career in large scale international mining that made him a millionaire, and brought him international fame for managing the evacuation of American citizens from Europe at the onset on World War I. During the war, Hoover administered food relief to Belgium and, following the armistice, to war refugees throughout Europe. He served as Secretary of Commerce under President Harding, and then used his role in organizing the response to the catastrophic Mississippi River flood of 1927 as a prelude for his campaign for the presidency in 1928. Hoover's campaign was the first to use modern professionally produced media as a tool, releasing a short film, titled *Master of Emergencies,* shown in theaters along with first run movies. Hoover's Democratic Party opponent was the popular governor of New York Alfred E. Smith. Harry Hopkins, who had by this time given up any socialist leanings he had as a youth, was now a solid member of the Democratic Party and he supported Smith in the election. Smith was a Catholic in a time when this was a much bigger deal than now, and his religion became an issue, costing him many votes among Protestants. Public contentment with prosperity also served Hoover. The public felt that things had been going well for eight years under two Republican administrations and saw little reason for change. Hoover won an overwhelming victory in the election, carrying forty states.

Hoover billed himself as "master of emergencies," but as the old saying goes, he hadn't seen anything yet. Less than a year into his administration the market crashed ushering in the longest and deepest depression in American history. Although Hoover had obviously not caused the depression, having been in office less than nine months when it commenced, it was his responsibility to lead the response to the crisis, which he did, with the result that the situation only got worse during the remaining three years of his presidency. Because of the poor results of his administration's attempts to turn the economy around he is popularly remembered as inept, foolish, and a total, laughable failure. This assessment is not really fair because from all evidence Hoover was a well-qualified, competent, and compassionate person. In 1921, as Secretary of Commerce, he had convened a conference on unemployment to deal with the problem of a short post-war depression, and he was abreast of advanced thought on this subject as well as on general economic theory. That he was a man of principle, intelligence, and integrity was conceded even by his critics. He was also somewhat of a genius at the art of administration and organization, a characteristic it has been pointed out that he shared with Harry Hopkins.[8] Hoover's failure to respond effectively to the depression had to do with two characteristics not related to his preparation or competence: his guiding theory of economics (one he shared with the majority of educated Americans, it must be said), and his social philosophy regarding the proper role of government in relation to helping out the victims of the poor economy.

---

8. Elizabeth S. Clemans, "Organizing Powers in Eventful Times," *Social Science History,* 39, no. 1 (Spring 2016): xx–xx.

At the time Hoover was responding to the depression there was no such field as macroeconomics—the study of the determination of the level of income, employment, and their fluctuations, and theories about how the economy can be managed through monetary policy (management of the money supply) and fiscal policy (use of government revenue and spending, taxes, and debt). Economists had devoted most of their attention to understanding what is now called microeconomics—the study of relative prices, allocation of resources, and distribution of income. The closest thing to a theory of macroeconomics was the belief among enlightened thinkers such as Hoover in the business cycle. This belief was that the economy constantly progressed through a series of natural economic cycles. The economy would improve and the markets rise, until there was a certain amount of waste, inefficiency, and over-value built in, at which time it would decline until these had been eliminated. Depending on how much the economy had grown beyond its natural level a decline could be a small adjustment, a recession, or a full-blown depression. The important point here is that the belief was that this was a natural process and there was nothing that anyone could do to prevent it, and that any attempts to interfere with the process would only make it worse and recovery to take longer. Thus, according to this way of thinking, the proper response to an economic downturn was for the government to do nothing. The strongest advocate of this position in the Hoover administration was Secretary of the Treasury Andrew Mellon who advised the president that the federal government should stand aside while inflated values were liquidated and the economic situation readjusted itself to normal. His advice was simple and brutal: "Liquidate labor, liquidate stocks, liquidate the farmers, liquidate real estate."[9]

Hoover was not quite as radically committed to the doctrine of non-intervention as Mellon, but he was very timid in the amount of government action he approved. His initial effort to tinker with the economy was to recommend that the federal reserve reduce the discount rate (interest that the central bank charges to member banks on loans that they in turn pass on to borrowers) in order to ensure that investment capital, previously provided by the stock market, would be available for normal business needs. The main thrust of Hoover's economic program was to convene a series of personal meetings with business and labor leaders and obtain from them pledges to not lay off workers and to retain existing wage levels in order to protect consumption. He also obtained pledges from business leaders to promote by voluntary action the expansion of the construction and maintenance work of the country. The vast majority of business leaders who agreed to the president's requests soon repudiated these pledges, slashed wages and laid off workers. Of this situation Hoover said "You know, the only trouble with capitalism is capitalists; they're too damn greedy."[10] As the economic situation deteriorated, and voluntary cooperation by businesses proved ineffective, Hoover became a little more interventionist. He successfully lobbied Congress to reduce income taxes to increase consumer's buying power, and he increased the public works project budget, to provide economic stimulation. He created the Federal Farm Board to lend money to cooperatives and to buy agricultural products to stabilize crop prices. His most successful effort came near the end of his term, the Reconstruction Finance Corporation, which lent federal funds to banks, insurance companies, and railroads so that the resultant profits could "trickle

9. Herbert Hoover, *The Memoirs of Herbert Hoover* (New York: Macmillan, 1952), 30.

10. Quoted in Joan Hoff Wilson, *Herbert Hoover: Forgotten Progressive* (Boston: Little Brown, 1975), xx.

down" to ordinary Americans. These efforts had relatively little effect on the economic situation, which continued to get worse.

While Hoover pursued ineffective policies attempting to restore the economy, the problem of relief grew worse. This was Hoover's second major shortcoming in dealing with the depression—that he strongly held to the outdated view that the needs of victims of economic downturn in a modern, highly interconnected economy could be adequately dealt with primarily by private charity, whose main source of income was voluntary contributions, and secondarily by local governments whose income was generally limited to property taxes. He absolutely believed that the federal government should have nothing to do with providing direct assistance to needy individuals. He believed that federal charity would delay the natural forces of recovery, would result in a decrease in private giving to agencies, would be inflexible and thus not responsive to local needs, and was probably unconstitutional because it would violate local responsibility and states' rights. His main objection was philosophical and he summarized this with the statement "You cannot extend the mastery of government over the daily lives of the people without at the same time making it the master of their souls and thoughts."[11] He was not unaware or insensitive to the plight of those unemployed and impoverished by the depression, saying shortly before the winter of 1930 "As a nation we must prevent hunger and cold to those of our people who are in honest difficulties."[12] He did not, however, authorize any direct assistance as a way of helping these people; instead he appointed two committees—the Cabinet Committee on Unemployment and the President's Emergency Committee for Employment. The committees primarily served as information resources and cheerleaders for local communities organizing to help the unemployed, turning out endless letters of encouragement, advice, and collecting information, pamphlets, and books that could in turn be distributed to local groups.

Hoover's unemployment committees did not collect any original empirical data on the true relief situation in the country or, as far as can be told, even made much of an effort to look for data collected by others. Both committees primarily relied on telephone calls to governors and other state officials who, for the most part assured them that the situation was well in hand. On the basis of information given to him by the unemployment committees Hoover based his repeated claims that unemployment and distress were being adequately met by private agencies and local government. They were not. Because of this laxity by the federal government, no national level data is existent regarding the relief situation, so data from individual cities is the best that is available, and it does not tell a pretty story. Romasco has described the situation in New York City, the largest and richest city, with the largest and most advanced private social welfare system in the nation. By the summer of 1930 the leaders of the major social agencies in the city were becoming increasingly worried about the unemployment and relief situation. Following the president's urging, and with advice and encouragement from his unemployment committees, they formed the Emergency Employment Committee and launched a campaign to increase their inadequate budgets. Harry Hopkins, at the time heading the Tuberculosis and Health Association, teaching

11. Quoted in Walter I. Trattner, *From Poor Law to Welfare State: A History of Social Welfare in America,* 6th ed. (New York: The Free Press, 1994), 277.

12. Quoted in Allen Nevins, Henry Steele Commager, with Jeffrey Morris, *A Pocket History of the United States,* 9th ed., (New York: Pocket Books, 1992), 416.

part time for his friend Porter R. Lee at the New York School of Social Work, and helping his former AICP colleague Bill Mathews operate an Emergency Work Bureau, was asked to join the committee and help plan the campaign. The campaign, in terms of revenue generated was quite successful, especially considering that the donor base was itself suffering from the poor economy. The original goal of the campaign was $2,000,000, which was quickly increased to $6,000,000, and by the December 17 end of the campaign a total of $8,269,000 had been collected. Other groups cooperating with the Emergency Committee, mainly a committee formed by Mayor James Walker, and a teacher's organization, the School Relief Fund, totaled $4,569,948. However, with 300,000 unemployed in 1930, increasing to 800,000 in 1931, in addition to the usual number of people needing assistance for reasons not directly related to the economic meltdown, even this large amount raised, and distributed by the most efficient and effective private social agencies in the country, proved to be woefully inadequate. As Romasco concludes his analysis of the situation "By the beginning of the third depression winter, even New York, the largest and wealthiest city in the country, with unmatched resources upon which to draw and an above-average relief organization, had failed miserably in coping with unemployment."[13] The situation in other large cities, as well as small towns and rural areas, was even worse than in New York.

STATE ACTION: FRANKLIN ROOSEVELT AND HARRY HOPKINS IN NEW YORK

In 1928 Al Smith, governor or New York, became the democratic candidate for president, thus opening the way for Franklin Roosevelt to run for governor on the democratic ticket. Roosevelt, a popular politician, easily won the election and, along with President Hoover, entered office just in time to be faced with one of the worst economic situations the country had ever faced. In many ways Roosevelt was not that different than Hoover, being in principle fairly conservative, favoring a laissez faire economic philosophy, believing that minimum government was best, in local responsibility whenever possible, and in balanced budgets. There were, however, a couple of major differences between Roosevelt and Hoover in terms of style and practice that resulted in their taking very different approaches to dealing with the depression. One was that unlike Hoover's reliance on his various commissions' collection of anecdotal data regarding the effect of the economic situation on citizens, which led him to believe that the situation was being adequately dealt with, Roosevelt looked for hard data. Early in the depression he requested that the New York State Joint Committee on Unemployment Relief of the, and the New York State Charities Aid Association, conduct studies to obtain hard data on how citizens of New York were faring. The data collected told him that many private charitable organizations had closed their doors because they had run out of money, and the remaining private and local government agencies were reaching fewer than one-third of those eligible for unemployment relief, and this one-third were not receiving assistance in amounts adequate to even meet their basic needs. The second major difference between

13. Albert U. Romasco, *The Poverty of Abundance: Hoover, the Nation, the Depression* (London: Oxford University Press, 1965), 155.

Roosevelt and Hoover was that Roosevelt believed that when abstract ideological belief, such as laissez-fair or minimum government, was weighed against the reality of human suffering, the proper response was to address the suffering and place the ideology aside. The third difference was that Roosevelt developed a strong justification for the rights of unemployed workers to receive governmental assistance. This belief was that inasmuch as governmental relief funds came from taxation, which was paid by the entire community, and most of those needing aid had paid taxes during their days of self-support, they were not receiving something for nothing because they were merely receiving money back that they had previously paid into the system. Thus, receiving relief was no different from sending children to public school or calling the fire department.

By 1931 as the depression continued to deepen and suffering increase, Roosevelt understood from looking at New York data that private agencies and local governments were absolutely unable to respond to the crisis to any meaningful extent, and that the federal government was going to continue to do nothing but act as a cheerleader claiming that the situation was well in hand. By August 1931 Roosevelt was convinced that bold action on the state level was necessary and he called a special session of the state legislature to consider the emergency. He asked the legislature to allocate funds to aid the unemployed who were destitute, he told them, due to conditions over which they had no control. He said "Modern society acting through its government owes the definite obligation to prevent the starvation or dire waste of any of its fellow men and women who try to maintain themselves but cannot [aid to the unemployed] must be extended by government, not as a matter of charity, but as a matter of social duty."[14] Responding to Roosevelt's request the legislature passed the Temporary Emergency Relief Act (TERA), called the Wicks Act, and set up the Temporary Emergency Relief Administration to implement its provisions. Roosevelt signed the bill on September 23, 1931 with an initial appropriation of $20 million to fund it from November 1, 1931 to June 1, 1932. In 1932 another $5 million was added to extend the emergency period until November 15, 1932, at which time a bond issue would be placed on the ballot asking voters to approve an additional $30 million to continue benefits through 1933. Voters approved this by a four to one margin.

Roosevelt appointed a three member board to administer the TERA. Chair of the board was Jesse Isadore Strauss, president of Macy's Department Store (who in 1932 offered Hopkins a job as a Macy's executive at a salary of $25 thousand per year, more than double his salary), John Sullivan, president of the New York Federation of Labor, and Philip J. Wickser, a prominent Buffalo attorney. The board offered the job of executive director to William Hodson, Head of the New York City Welfare Council and one of the most prominent social workers and poverty experts in the country. Hodson was interested in the job but when he approached his board asking for a leave of absence they turned him down. Hodson knew Hopkins from professional social work activities and recommended him for the job. Hopkins, seeing the job as a huge opportunity both in terms of his career and also the potential the position offered to make a significant impact on the state's unemployment crisis, asked the Tuberculosis and Health Association board for a leave of absence and this was granted. On October 8, 1931 Hopkins became the executive director of the Temporary Emergency Relief Administration.

14. Quoted in Joan M. Crouse, *The Homeless Transient in the Great Depression: New York State, 1929–1941* (Albany, NY: The State University of New York Press, 1986), 54.

Hopkins did not remain as executive director of TERA for long. Barely five months after Hopkins's appointment, the Chairman of the Board, Isdadore Strauss resigned. Impressed with his work in the five months he had served, Roosevelt appointed Hopkins to replace Strauss as chair, thus putting him in charge of both relief policy and administration. The first thing Hopkins did in his new position was to join the campaign for the $30 million dollar bond issue to allow the program to continue. As we have seen, the campaign was overwhelmingly successful, but Hopkins was not entirely reassured by the success, predicting that the $30 million would not be nearly enough, estimating that at least $150 million would be necessary to adequately meet needs until the following June. He pointed out that at the time the bond issue passed there were a half million New York citizens who were eligible for aid under the program but who were not receiving it because of lack of funds.

Hopkins was a whirlwind of activity during his time with the TERA. He made funds available to local communities for both work and home relief. Work relief was administered locally by Emergency Work Bureaus that hired the unemployed for jobs in public works projects. Hopkins exerted every effort to ensure that the projects the state funded were not make work such as the old Charity Organization Society wood yards or raking leaves or shoveling snow, but were meaningful contributions to the community such as building schools, maintaining parks, or repairing roads. The state covered the wages of the men employed by the Emergency Work Bureaus and the local community provided matching funds by in-kind contributions of the materials necessary for the projects. For home relief, meaning traditional charity for people who were for one reason or another unable to work, administration was assigned to local welfare departments and the state picked up 40 percent of expenditures. The TERA was the central administration for both work relief and home relief programs and employed regional directors and field supervisors to investigate complaints, audit accounts, and organize relief procedures. To encourage professionalism Hopkins required that each local agency "employ at least one trained and experienced investigator on its staff." In less than a year well over one-half of the welfare districts were employing trained social workers.[15] In the first seven months of Hopkins work at TERA, over 312,000 families were assisted at a cost of $17,484,546 in state funds; with local matching funds the total spent for unemployment relief alone was over $35 million.

Roosevelt, as governor of New York, was, of course, primarily concerned with the situation in that state, but realizing that the problem was national in scope and that the federal government was not going to take responsibility for dealing with the mass suffering, he began, early in his term, to meet with governors of other states to encourage them to join his efforts to help the unemployed and the traditional poor. In 1932 the Illinois governor appointed the Illinois Emergency Relief Commission and the legislature allocated $18,750,000 to fund it. Very modest appropriations were made in 1931 by Oklahoma, New Hampshire, and California. Ohio passed a law that empowered local communities to issue bonds to fund unemployment relief, based on the questionable assumption that the bonds could be marketed. In 1932 New Jersey appropriated $9,616,033 and Pennsylvania $22 million for unemployment, but in Pennsylvania the courts ruled that the allocation was in violation of the state constitution. Here was the problem of dealing with a national

15. Emma Octavia Lundberg, "The New York State Temporary Emergency Relief Administration," *Social Service Review*, 6 (1932): 545–566.

problem on a state-by-state basis: the vast majority of states faced constitutional problems in selling bonds or raising taxes to support poor relief and it was estimated that it would take at least two years to amend the constitutions so they could do this. The practical consequence of tax and constitutional difficulties was that most states were able to do nothing to relieve the exhausted cities, counties, and voluntary agencies. By 1932 only eight states were providing assistance for the unemployed, and in none of these, not even New York, could it be said that the problem was being adequately taken care of.

In 1932, under intense pressure from all sides, Hoover finally took some action to deal with the plight of the unemployed in the country, although it was too little and too late. After private social welfare agencies, professional social work organizations, the governors of all industrial states, and a parade of prominent citizens had taken up the call for a federal relief effort, the president finally approved a relief bill. The law allowed the Reconstruction Finance Corporation, created earlier to make federal loans to businesses, to lend up to $300 million to states for unemployment relief. Hopkins filed an application for New York to receive federal aid and received $13 million during the last days of the Hoover administration and the state received another $6.5 million after Roosevelt took office as president.

By 1932 the country was in desperate straits. Newspapers were full of stories of families reduced to eating dandelion greens picked from public parks or roadsides in order to stay alive, and of formerly proud and self-sufficient men committing suicide because they could no longer support their families. Threats of revolution were heard and were taken seriously as the nation watched other countries, notably Germany and Italy, fall to fascism as the citizens gave up freedom for economic security. Communists, socialists, and other radicals organized formal protests. Communists organized the jobless into "unemployment councils" that staged hunger marches, demonstrated for relief, and blocked evictions. Socialists built similar organizations, including the Baltimore's People's Unemployment League, which had twelve thousand members. There were also rural protests. Communists organized some of them, as in Alabama where the Croppers' and Farm Workers' Union mobilized black agricultural laborers in 1931 to demand better treatment. In the Midwest, the Farmer's Holiday Association, organized among family farmers in 1932, stopped the shipment of produce to urban markets hoping to drive up prices.

Hoover had become the most unpopular president in history, perceived as both ineffectual and callous to the suffering of the nation. When speaking in public he was often jeered by the audience as a president had never been jeered before. Leuchtenburg describes him during the waning days of his presidency as "a pathetic figure, a weary, beaten man."[16] The event that put the cherry on Hoover's sundae as far as voters were concerned was his handling of the Bonus Army protest in Washington. Veterans of World War I had been promised bonuses to be paid in 1945 with the intention of helping them in their retirement years as an extra thank-you for their service to the country. In 1932 many of these veterans were unemployed and destitute and they proposed that the bonuses be paid immediately, a not unreasonable request. This proposal was ignored by the Hoover administration. The Bonus Army was formally organized in Portland Oregon, led Walter W. Waters, an unemployed cannery worker who had served as a sergeant in the war. Waters called

16. William E. Leuchtenburg, *Franklin Roosevelt and the New Deal* (New York: Harper & Row, 1963), 16.

for veterans to gather in Washington D.C. to press their request for the bonus with the president. The veterans came from all over the country, hopping trains for transportation and living on handouts from sympathizers along the way. By June some 20,000 were camped in a shanty town, by this time popularly called a "Hooverville," on the flats of the Anacostia River in Washington. Hoover refused to meet with representatives of the "army," but they convinced Representative Wright Patman to introduce a bill in the House authorizing immediate payment of the bonus. The bill passed the House on June 15, but the Senate turned it down two days later. In the over two months that the veterans were in Washington, not a single member of the administration met with them. Most of the veterans became discouraged and went home, but about 2,000 stayed at the encampment. At the end of July, responding to unfounded reports that the protestors were being led by communists and were planning violence, Secretary of the Army Patrick J. Hurley sent federal troops to evict the protestors from their ramshackle village, attacking them with tear gas and clubs, and setting fire to their shacks. The remnants of the Bonus Army fled into Maryland and the protest ended. The assault provoked widespread condemnation in the press and in popular discourse. "What a pitiful spectacle is that of the great American Government, mightiest in the world, chasing unarmed men, women and children with army tanks," said the *Washington News.* The protesters were not communists or radicals of any kind, but simply anxious and discouraged Americans, and if there were any criminals among them, noted one critic, there were fewer than in President Hoover's cabinet. The incident confirmed the public's perception of Hoover as harsh and insensitive.[17]

Even though Hoover had become tremendously unpopular, the Republicans nominated him to run for a second term in 1932. The Democrats nominated Franklin Roosevelt who won in a landslide. Roosevelt won every state south and west of Pennsylvania. It was the worst defeat of a Republican candidate in history except for 1912 when the party split and in essence ran two candidates who split the vote. Between November 1932 when Roosevelt was elected, and March 1933 when he officially took office, the situation of the country deteriorated even more, as unemployment increased, farm prices decreased, and production and consumer spending continued to decline. In February of 1933 panic struck the banking system. Nearly six thousand banks had failed and desperate Americans rushed to withdraw their funds from the remaining banks, putting them at risk of failing as well. With the federal government under Hoover immobilized, state governments shut the banks to prevent their failure. By March Hoover stated that "We are at the end of our string." That same month Roosevelt came to Washington to take command, bringing Harry Hopkins with him to attempt to do for the whole nation what he had done for the state of New York.

ROOSEVELT AND THE NEW DEAL

In his presidential campaign Roosevelt had promised the American people a "new deal" and they had given him an overwhelming mandate to deliver it. When he entered office on March 4, 1933,

---

17. William E. Leuchtenburg, *Herbert Hoover* (New York City: Henry Holt, 2009), 136.

with the nation at the very bottom of the economic crisis, Roosevelt had to address it on three policy and program fronts—recovery, relief, and reform. Recovery was concerned with getting the country back on its feet economically: increasing production and consumption, reversing the economic decline and returning to economic growth, reducing unemployment to something like the three to four percent that economists believe indicates a healthy economy, and addressing other indicators that are now identified as macroeconomics.[18] Relief meant taking steps to address the mass suffering that was being experienced by the millions of unemployed and their families. Reform meant identifying what had gone wrong with economic policies and structures that had caused the crash, and developing means to counteract these in the future so such a severe crash does not happen again. As we have seen, Hoover followed a long precedent of presidential inactivity in depression times, basically waiting unobtrusively for recovery. It cannot be said that he did nothing for he took a few timid steps such as encouraging the Federal Reserve to reduce the discount rate, establishing the Reconstruction Finance Corporation and belatedly authorizing it to lend money to states for direct relief to citizens, but his actions were hardly assertive and had little, if any, effect. In his vision for the New Deal Roosevelt, by contrast, promised bold action, saying in a speech shortly before accepting the 1932 Democratic party nomination: "The country needs, and unless I mistake its temper, the country demands bold, persistent experimentation . . . It is common sense to take a method and try it. If it fails, try another. But above all, try something."[19]

Upon entering office Roosevelt assumed leadership of a nation with a collapsing financial system, crippling unemployment, and malfunctioning agricultural and industrial sectors. He promised "action and action now" telling the people in one of his famous radio fireside chats that "the only thing we have to fear is fear itself—nameless, unreasoning, unidentified terror, which paralyzes needed efforts to convert retreat into advance." He immediately called Congress into session and pushed a bold agenda. In what came to be called the Hundred Days of the New Deal, the Democratic dominated Congress passed fifteen major laws, some designed by Roosevelt himself and some by a diverse group of advisors including academic experts informally referred to as Roosevelt's brain trust, politicians, and social workers. The most immediate crisis that Roosevelt faced was that of the banking system. Thousands of banks had failed during the Hoover administration and the level of gold reserves had fallen below legal limits. By 1933 the nation was experiencing a "run" on its banks, dramatically depicted in the famous Jimmy Stuart movie "It's a Wonderful Life," that was putting the remaining banks at risk of failure. On March 5, thirty-six hours after taking the oath of office, the new president declared a bank holiday, ordering all banks to cease operations. Seven hours later Congress passed the Emergency Banking Act that extended government assistance to sound banks and guidelines for reorganizing weak ones. The act required banks to obtain permission to reopen, based on a formal inspection of the banks management and resources. On March 13 banks in federal reserve cities were eligible to reopen. By March 15 banks controlling 90 percent of banking resources had resumed operations and public confidence in the new administration, inspired by another fireside chat, was reflected by the fact that deposits immediately

18. Chris Farrell, "Why Not Target a 3% Unemployment Rate?" *Bloomberg Business Week*, May 2, 2013. http://www.bloomberg.com/news/articles/2013. Retrieved May 2, 2016.

19. Franklin D. Roosevelt, *Works of Franklin D. Roosevelt*, Address at Oglethorpe University, May 22, 1932. Retrieved from New Deal Network, http://www.newdeal.feri.org/speeches/1932.html. Accessed June 21, 2016.

exceeded withdrawals. Although 4000 banks would never reopen, the worst of the crisis appeared to be over. The Emergency Banking Act was an emergency measure and was replaced on June 16, 1933 by the Banking Act of 1933 which, among other things, set up the Federal Deposit Insurance Corporation that guaranteed the return of money in savings accounts up to $2,500.[20] Further reform of the financial industry was accomplished by the passage of the Glass-Steagall Act that separated investment from commercial banking to protect depositors from losses due to speculative activities by the bank and by the creation of the Securities and Exchange Commission to regulate the stock market.

Having addressed the crisis in the financial sector of the economy Roosevelt turned his attention to the production sector where farms were failing and businesses were going bankrupt. In May of 1933 the New Deal addressed problems in the rural economy by establishing the Agricultural Adjustment Administration created to combat the depression in agriculture caused by crop surpluses and resultant low prices. The method employed by the AAA was to pay subsidies to farmers who agreed to restrict production. That the government was paying farmers not to grow food when people across the nation were going hungry caused a fierce backlash. Secretary of Agriculture Henry Wallace defended the government's production control practice as being analogous to corporations pursuing policies that maximized profits. He argued that "Agriculture cannot survive in a capitalistic society as a philanthropic enterprise."[21] In addition to the criticism that the AAA was denying food to a hungry land, it was also criticized for benefiting large, commercial, farmers and harming small family farms. In response to the provisions of the act, large growers were evicting tenant farmers whose land they wanted to lay fallow so as to collect subsidies, which they in turn invested in farm mechanization which further put small farmers out of business. In 1936 the Supreme Court ruled the AAA unconstitutional, but the act established a practice of farm subsidies that is still in existence.

The continuing slide in prices, wages, and employment in industry was also addressed during the hundred days with the passage of the National Industrial Recovery Act, which created the National Recovery Administration. The act suspended anti-trust laws, authorized industrial and trade associations to draft codes setting production quotas, price policies, wages and working conditions, and other business practices. The codes that were developed were heavily weighted toward the interests of big business, but some attention was paid to the interests of labor. Section 7a of the law guaranteed workers the right to organize and bargain collectively. John L. Lewis of the United Mine Workers Union called this an Emancipation Proclamation for labor. Support for the NIRA quickly declined when it became clear that big business was using it to advance their own goals and to discriminate against small businesses, consumers, and labor. Businesses regularly ignored Section 7a and the NRA did little to enforce it. Roosevelt tried to reorganize the NRA to make it more responsive to the needs of small business and labor, but it remained unpopular and was declared unconstitutional by the Supreme Court in 1935. The NIRA did, however, prepare

20. Helen M. Burns, *The American Banking Community and the New Deal Banking Reform* (Westport, CT: Greenwood Press, 1974; Charles Sterling Popple, *Development of Two Bank Groups in the Central Northwest: A Study in Bank Policy and Organization* (Cambridge, MA: Harvard University Press, 1944), 253–259.

21. Arthur M. Schlesinger, Jr., *The Age of Roosevelt—The Coming of the New Deal: 1933–1935* (Boston: Houghton Mifflin, 1958), 63.

the way for stronger pro-labor legislation, notably the Wagner National Labor Relations Act that set up the National Labor Relations Board. This guaranteed workers' right to organize unions and forbade employers to adopt unfair labor practices, such as firing union activists or forming company unions.

Although Roosevelt was not focused on the problem of unemployment during the early stages of the New Deal, the problem was indirectly addressed in the NIRA through the establishment and funding, in the amount of $3.3 billion, of the Public Works Administration (PWA). The purpose of the PWA was to jump start the economy through the quick release of money into the economy by establishing a rapidly adopted public construction program. The PWA did not itself do any construction, rather it provided grants to states and cities, based on carefully reviewed proposals, with the expectation that 70 percent of the cost would be funded by the smaller governmental unit. This massive amount of money spent on construction projects would, of course, provide jobs for the unemployed, but this was secondary to the goal of stimulating the industrial economy. The PWA was placed under the direction of Harold Ickes, Secretary of the Interior, a poor choice because, having a personality 180 degrees from that of Harry Hopkins, he was cautious and suspicious by nature. Leuchtenburg describes him as "vain, quarrelsome, suspicious of mankind, a man who saw little but a void of wickedness beyond the arc of his own righteousness."[22] As a result of Icke's cautious administration, and of Roosevelt's tendency to raid the PWA budget to fund programs for the increasingly favored Hopkins, the PWA had little short-term effect on the country's economic problems. In the long term, however, Icke's careful selection of only projects that would have large payoffs for the nation resulted in a long list of things from which we still benefit. A partial list of PWA accomplishments includes the Tri-borough bridge, the Lincoln Tunnel, the La Guardia Airport, and a new psychiatric ward at Bellevue Hospital in New York City, the Skyline Drive in Virginia, the Overseas Highway in the Florida Keys, the San Francisco—Oakland Bay Bridge, electrification of the Pennsylvania Railroad, the port of Brownsville Texas, and a magnificent library at the University of New Mexico. In addition, during its years of operation the PWA built 70 percent of the country's new schools, 65 percent of its courthouses, and 35 percent of hospitals and public health facilities, as well as the aircraft carriers Yorktown and Enterprise, the heavy cruiser Vincennes, as well as numerous smaller ships; the Army Air Corps received grants for more than a hundred planes and over fifty military airports.

Toward the end of the hundred days, having launched bold programs aimed at recovery and reform, Roosevelt turned his attention directly to the issue of relief. Harry Hopkins was ready. He and his social work colleague William Hodson of the New York Welfare Council and the Russell Sage Foundation had begun work on a plan as soon as Roosevelt was elected, and had preceded the president elect to Washington to advocate for it. The plan called for a huge appropriation, between $600 million and $1 billion, given as grants rather than loans to the states, with the states providing a match. Hopkins wanted a bill passed before Hoover left office, but Congress took no action. When Roosevelt took office, Hopkins, a respected and trusted associate of the president but not yet a member of his inner circle, was unable to schedule a meeting for he and Hodson to push their plan. As an alternate route to the president they turned to fellow New York social worker Francis

22. Leuchtenburg, *Franklin Roosevelt and the New Deal*, 70–71.

Perkins, who had been appointed as Secretary of Labor. They met with Perkins at the Washington Women's club, a venue so bustling with activity that under a stairwell was the only place they could find to sit and talk. Hopkins and Hodson gave her their grim forecast that unless something was done quickly by the federal government to address unemployment the country would not survive. They argued that the president would need to set up an emergency agency to grant funds to the states for unemployment relief. Perkins left the meeting convinced of the soundness of their arguments and promised to push their plan with the president. Exactly what Perkins said to Roosevelt is not known, but her efforts were successful and in April 1933 the president asked Congress to approve the establishment of a new department to be named the Federal Emergency Relief Administration (FERA) with an initial budget of $500 million. The $500 million was divided into two parts, the first to be paid to the states as a matching grant with one federal dollar for three state dollars, the second to be granted directly to the states with no strings attached. Congress complied with the president's plan and in May he asked Hopkins to Washington to head the new agency.

Roosevelt offered Hopkins the job as head of the new FERA on Friday May 19 and Hopkins eagerly accepted. The next day Hopkins name was sent to the Senate who approved his appointment without comment. Hopkins met with the president on the morning of May 22. Immediately following the meeting Hopkins walked over to his office in the rather run-down Walker-Johnson Building, claimed a standard government issue blond pine bureaucrats desk as his own and began to spend money. In his first two hours on the job Hopkins spent over $5 million, sending grants to states that had filed applications for assistance from the Hoover administration. The next morning, over a picture of Hopkins, the *Washington Post* headline read "Money Flies."[23] He then began firing off telegrams to the governors of states that had not filed applications, telling them about available grants and saying that they could obtain one by simply sending him a telegram and following it up later with a formal application. While Harry Hopkins and his staff at the FERA were responsible for determining the size and composition of grants to the states, responsibility for administering the funds remained with the states and localities. Hopkins immediately established the policy that FERA funds were to be administered by government agencies, nullifying the practice of public money being funneled through private agencies, and requiring that every state establish a state public welfare department. Although the main emphasis of federal relief was on emergency work programs, the aid covered all forms of unemployment and dependency, including straight cash grants to people in their own homes, and a surplus commodity program to provide food relief. In spite of Hopkins strong preference for work relief programs an excessively large proportion of FERA money went for direct relief grants.

As the winter of 1933/1934 approached it was becoming clear that a new crisis was approaching. The NIRA was falling far short of stimulating the economy to the extent needed to create an adequate number of jobs (Hopkins estimated that six million would be needed). The number of direct relief recipients was not declining and the costs were increasing as recipients stayed on the rolls longer and the size of their grants increased. Finally, Secretary Ickes pinch-penny administration of the Public Works Administration had limited expenditures to a trickle, creating few jobs. In order to avert the coming crisis, Hopkins and his chief assistant, Alabama social worker

23. "Money Flies," *Washington Post* (May 23, 1933), 1.

Aubrey Williams, prepared a proposal for the president, arguing for a vast work program to fund projects directed, managed, and paid for by the federal government. Hopkins was not optimistic about his chances of getting Roosevelt to endorse the plan because of increasing pressure from conservatives to balance the budget, and opposition from organized labor who strongly opposed governmental "make work jobs" that would compete with union workers. The president surprised Hopkins, approving the program, called the Civil Works Administration (CWA) to be under the FERA and Hopkins' direction, and funded at $750 million, $350 to come from the FERA budget, and $400 million from Ickes Public Works Administration.

The CWA was intended by Roosevelt to be a very temporary program, to get the nation through the winter, and so was approved to run only from November 8, 1933 until the end of March 1934. Once again Hopkins demonstrated his exceptional ability to move things along (and not incidentally to spend money) fast. In less than two weeks from the beginning of the program 800,000 unemployed people had been placed in CWA jobs, after two more weeks the number was two million and, at its high point in mid-January 1934 4.25 million were employed in jobs funded by the program. Hopkins tried to convince Roosevelt to extend the CWA and make it a permanent part of the New Deal. Roosevelt rejected this proposal insisting that the CWA end on schedule. Although he recognized that the program had been a great success, and had been central to the country getting through the winter, he felt that extending it would send the message that his recovery program had failed and that the depression was permanent. The president felt that his recovery programs were succeeding and that there would be an economic upturn in the spring making the CWA jobs unnecessary.

Later in 1934 events conspired to change Roosevelt's mind about a large government jobs program. The first event was the unexpected overwhelming endorsement of the New Deal received from the American people in the off-year elections in November of 1934. It is generally expected that the party in power will experience losses in an off-year election. Democrats were optimistic about the 1934 election, predicting that they would lose only thirty-seven seats in the house, a loss small enough that they could claim it as a victory. When the results came in people were stunned to find that the Democrats had actually gained thirteen seats in the House and nine in the Senate. The new House would be composed of 322 Democrats, 103 Republicans, and ten representatives from minor parties. The Senate's roster was sixty-nine Democrats and 31 Republicans, the largest majority ever held by one party. William Allen White opined that Roosevelt "has been all but crowned by the people."[24] The second factor contributing to Roosevelt's renewed support of work relief was his increasing concern with the number of people receiving direct home relief, i.e. welfare. Roosevelt had come to agree with Hopkins that direct relief given in the traditional way, involving means tests and social work supervision, ultimately degraded and pauperized the recipient. Welfare, he declared, was "a narcotic, a subtle destroyer of the human spirit ... I am not willing that the vitality of our people be further sapped by the giving of cash, of market baskets, of a few hours of weekly work cutting grass, raking leaves, or picking up papers." He proposed that help for the employable unemployed should take the form of jobs, not welfare, saying that "We must make

24. William E. Leuchtenburg, *Franklin Roosevelt and the New Deal*, 116–117.

it a national principle that we will not tolerate a large army of unemployed . . . I do not want to think that it is the destiny of any American to remain permanently on the relief rolls."[25]

Hopkins, excited about the president's strengthening support for a jobs program, and jubilant about the results of the mid-term election, crowed to his senior staff, "Boys—this is our hour. We've got to get everything we want—a works program, social security, wages and hours, everything now or never. Get your minds to work on developing a complete ticket to provide security for all the folks of this country up and down and across the board."[26] Within a few days Hopkins and his staff had produced a plan, tentatively titled a Plan to End Poverty, which he presented to Roosevelt at his Warm Springs, Georgia retreat over Thanksgiving weekend. Roosevelt returned to Washington and proposed to Congress the Emergency Relief Appropriations Act, largely following Hopkins recommendations, and Congress passed the act in April, 1935. The act was funded at almost $5 billion dollars, the largest single appropriation in history up to that time, to fund emergency public employment. The act created the Works Progress Administration (WPA), which Roosevelt immediately appointed Hopkins to head, with the charge of setting up work relief programs to assist the unemployed and to give a boost to the economy. The WPA was in operation from 1935 to 1943, at which time the war economy had created an employee shortage rather than a job shortage so a federal work program was no longer justified. During these eight years the WPA created jobs for nine million people and spent nearly $12 billion dollars. The majority of the spending was on construction projects that used large amounts of manual labor. However, the WPA also expanded the definition of work relief and launched projects to support students and white collar workers. Students were supported through the National Youth Administration, under the direction of Hopkins protégé Aubrey Williams, which gave part time jobs to high school and college students, enabling them to continue their educations while learning additional job skills and doing productive work. White collar workers were given support through the Federal Arts Project, the Federal Writers Project, and the Federal Music Project. These projects created a fair amount of political heat for the WPA as the press was fond of making fun of some of the activities supported and implying that they were a waste of money. The still used term "boondoggle" was coined to describe WPA arts, writers, and music grants. Refreshingly, unlike many administrators, Hopkins was never willing to wilt before these criticisms, by apologizing, saying the project was a mistake, or referring the allegation to a committee for investigation. For example, he was once asked at a press conference to justify a WPA funded project investigating ancient safety pins. Hopkins response was, "Why should I? There is nothing the matter with that. They are damn good projects—excellent projects. That goes for all the projects up there. . . I have no apologies to make. As a matter of fact, we have not done enough. . . Every one of those [projects] is under the direction of competent research people. You can make fun of anything; that is easy to do."[27]

25. William E. Leuchtenburg, *Franklin Roosevelt and the New Deal*, 124; George McJimsey, *Harry Hopkins*, 76.

26. Quoted in Robert E. Sherwood, *Roosevelt and Hopkins, An Intimate History* (New York City: Harper, 1950), 64–65.

27. Harry Hopkins press conference, April 4, 1935. Quoted in Henry H. Adams, *Harry Hopkins: A Biography* (New York: G. P. Putnam's Sons, 1977), 62.

THE SOCIAL SECURITY ACT

After his mandate in the 1934 election, Roosevelt wanted to consolidate the New Deal and he launched new social and economic reforms that some have called the Second New Deal. Among this new group of reforms was the Wagner National Labor Relations Act that guaranteed labor's right to organize; the Banking Act of 1935 that increased the authority of the Federal Reserve Board over the nation's currency and credit system and limited the power of the private bankers whose irresponsible behavior had contributed to the depression; the Public Utility Holding Company Act that expanded federal authority over public utilities that had previously exploited consumers and frustrated government regulators; the Revenue Act of 1935 that established graduated income taxes and increased corporate and estate taxes; and establishment of the Resettlement Administration that focused on land reform and helped poor farmers. A major second new deal goal of Roosevelt was to reform the hodge-podge of federal emergency relief programs into one unified, permanent program of social security to rationalize the nation's relief practices. He particularly wanted the permanent program to separate employment related issues, such as unemployment insurance and retirement, which he was comfortable with being federal level programs, from other types of relief that had fallen under the poor law such as assistance to broken families and the disabled, which he felt was properly the responsibility of the states and localities.

Roosevelt was receiving the most pressure for a permanent federal program from people concerned with the plight of the elderly in the depression. The population of elderly citizens was rapidly rising, having increased as a proportion of the population at a rate double of other demographic groups. Older citizens suffered from unemployment at a rate much higher than younger groups, and once unemployed their chances of ever regaining their jobs was very low. State pension programs were rare, less than 5 percent of the population being covered, and private pensions were even rarer. The tradition of elderly parents being cared for in the homes of their adult children was also breaking down as depression burdened children were having trouble just supporting their own families often making adding an elderly parent to the household an impossibility. This increasing concern with the plight of the elderly was manifested in several crackpot, but not easily dismissed, program proposals that were garnering significant popular support. One such program was the End Poverty in California (EPIC) program envisioned and publicized by popular writer Upton Sinclair who, while actually socialist in his leanings, used his program to get himself nominated as the Democratic candidate for the California governorship in 1934. The EPIC program proposal garnered wide popular support with tens of thousands joining End Poverty Leagues and supporting Sinclair's bid for governor, although he eventually lost his bid for the office. The EPIC program called for generous pensions for retired workers to be financed out of a state income tax with levels as high as 30 percent, a revised and much increased inheritance tax, and government confiscation of unused factories and farm land. Another popular proposal was that of Dr. Francis E. Townsend. Townsend believed that the depression could be solved by giving pensions of $200 per month to everyone over age 60 with the condition that they could not be working and that they would have to spend the money within a month. The pensioners would be removed from the labor force, freeing up jobs for younger workers, and their spending would increase demand for goods and services, thus stimulating the economy. By January of 1935 Townsend clubs had been organized across the nation and Townsend was publishing a newspaper with a readership of over 200,000. Another proposal, and this one with even more political power behind it was the Share Our Wealth program of Senator Huey Long of Louisiana. Long's program called for, in essence, the confiscation of all personal fortunes exceeding $3 million. The government would then provide each family in the nation with an annual income of $2000 (the average family income at the time was less than $1500), and a $5000 grant to buy a house, a radio, and a car. The plan also included old-age pensions, public works, a shorter work week, and other measures that were highly appealing. By 1935 it was claimed by Long's staff that there were 27,000 Share Our Wealth Clubs with membership exceeding 7 million, probably an exaggeration but surely a cause for concern in the Roosevelt administration.

Roosevelt was concerned with these radical reform proposals, especially as he observed other western democracies turning to radical solutions, mainly fascism, in response to depression suffering. In 1934 he sent Hopkins to Germany to meet with Adolph Hitler and to Italy to meet with Benito Mussolini, with the stated purpose being to discuss their social welfare systems and see if America could learn anything from them, but also to get another perspective on the ominous political situation in central Europe. Hopkins met with Mussolini but was unable to meet with Hitler due to political events that were rapidly unrolling in Germany. Roosevelt believed that a system of security was essential for the nation's social and economic stability, and to ensure that the political upheaval in Europe did not visit the United States. In a radio fireside chat he stated "Democracy has disappeared in several other great nations not because the people of these nations disliked democracy but because they had grown tired of unemployment and insecurity, of seeing their children hungry while they sat helpless in the face of government confusion and government weakness through lack of leadership in government. Finally in desperation they chose to sacrifice liberty in the hope of getting something to eat. We, in America, know that our democratic institutions can be preserved and made to work. But in order to preserve them we need to act together to meet the needs of the nation boldly, and to prove that the practical operation of democratic government is equal to the task of protecting the security of the people."[28]

In the spring of 1934 Roosevelt appointed a Committee on Economic Security (CES) to develop recommendations for a permanent plan of social security. The president's charge to the committee was "I am looking for a sound means which I can recommend to provide at once security against several of the great disturbing factors in life – especially those which relate to unemployment and old age." He was looking for a program to provide "some safe-guard against misfortunes which cannot be wholly eliminated in this man-made world of ours."[29] The committee was chaired by Secretary of Labor Francis Perkins, and the members were Secretary of the Treasury Henry Morganthau, Secretary of Agriculture Henry Wallace, Attorney General Homer Cummings, and, the only non-cabinet level member, FERA Director Harry Hopkins. University of Wisconsin economics professor and authority on social insurance Edwin Witte was hired as the projects executive director and was given a budget of $145,000 and authorized to hire a staff of

28. The American Presidency Project, Franklin D. Roosevelt, XXXII President of the United States: 1933–1945, 50, *Fireside Chat,* April 14, 1938. http://www.presidency.uscb.edu. Accessed July 21, 2016.

29. CES Report, "Letter of Transmittal, Washington, DC, January 15, 1935." *Social Security Reports and Studies,* https://www.ssa.gov. Accessed July 21, 2016.

twenty-one experts. Among these experts was Witte's student Wilber Cohen who was to remain with the Social Security Administration for thirty-five years, eventually becoming the Secretary of the Department of Health, Education and Welfare. In late June, Hopkins arranged quarters for the committee's technical staff in the Walker-Johnson Building and for clerical support from FERA staff.

The technical staff of the CES began their work in earnest at the end of June starting with a meeting with the president where he provided additional guidance. He told the staff, according to Witte's recollection, that all forms of social insurance must be self-supporting, without subsidies from general tax sources. However, he said he understood that assistance from general tax revenues would have to be given to people without means (i.e. the unemployable poor).[30] Based on the president's guidance, input from the expert staff, and their own predilections, the CES came to pretty easy agreement about the general form for a policy to deal with retirement and to take care of the unemployable poor. Unemployment insurance however proved to be a more difficult matter with the CES being split between advocates for three different options. Harry Hopkins argued for a system that would make the WPA a permanent federal program. People who became unemployed through no fault of their own would be given cash relief for a period of time that was brief but sufficient for them to find new employment if employment was available. If they did not find new employment by the end of the allotted benefit period they would be given a federally supported job through WPA or some similar agency. The job would pay more than welfare benefits, but less than the prevailing wage thereby motivating them to continue to pursue private market employment. A second group advocated for short-term cash benefits, not followed by any guaranteed job, which were funded and administered nationally, with uniform rules and benefit structure so everyone would get exactly the same benefit regardless of where they were living. The main argument for this plan was that it would insure uniform standards in a country where workers frequently moved from state to state and where state governments were often badly mismanaged. The third group advocated for what was called the Wisconsin plan, after the residence of its designers Paul Rauschenbush and his wife Elizabeth Brandeis (daughter of the Supreme Court Justice). This plan called for the federal government to require employers to pay for unemployment insurance, which would be collected by the central government, but 90 percent of the money would be returned to the states to be distributed to the unemployed under clear federal guidelines, but with states having discretion about a number of aspects of the program. The main argument in support of this national-state system was that it would permit experimentation on a problem where many questions still had not been answered.

The CES submitted their report to Roosevelt in early January 1935 and he forwarded it to Congress on January 17, requesting that they take quick action and pass a social security bill. In his letter of transmittal he was quite clear that he felt he was sending them a conservative program and that this was by design. He wrote, "It is overwhelmingly important to avoid any danger of permanently discrediting the sound and necessary policy of federal legislation for economic security by attempting to apply it on too ambitious a scale before actual experience has provided guidance for the permanently safe direction of such efforts. The place of such a fundamental in our future

30. CES Report, "Introduction," *Social Security Reports and Studies,* https://www.ssa.gov. Accessed July 23, 2016.

civilization is too precious to be jeopardized now by extravagant action."[31] Based on Roosevelt's letter and the CES report a social security bill was introduced in the Senate by Robert F. Wagner of New York and in the House by David Lewis of Maryland. Predictably, the bill was attacked by conservatives who argued that a program of guaranteed social security went against time tested American traditions of self-help, self-denial, and individual responsibility. The opposition to the bill was more spirited, however, from liberals who thought the benefits proposed were too meager. Representative John McGroarty of California proposed amending the bill along the lines of the Townsend plan to give all retirees a monthly pension of $200. This proposal failed, but impressed Congress with the need for some kind of legislation to satisfy the popular demands for some type of old-age assistance. After voting down the McGroarty proposal, and some that were even more radical, the House passed the Social Security Act in April by a vote of 371-33. In June the Senate passed the bill by a margin of 77 to 6 and the president signed it into law on August 15, 1935.

The Social Security Act closely followed the proposal of the Committee on Economic Security, which had closely followed the guidance of the president. Under the act destitution was addressed along three lines. The first line addressed the problem of unemployment during a person's working years, and retirement when the person became too old to work. This part of the plan was defined as entirely a federal responsibility. The retirement program, called Old Age Insurance (OAI) was the centerpiece of the act. To fund OAI a trust fund was set up that was to be funded by a payroll tax split between employees and employers. The program was to be actuarially sound, that is, the trust fund was to be large enough that payments of benefits would be equal to or less than income from payroll tax revenues. For this reason benefits from OAI were not scheduled to begin until 1942 when the fund would have grown to a level sufficient to support claims against it. The second part of the federal responsibility was unemployment insurance. The advocates for the Wisconsin plan in the CES won the debate here. The plan required employers to contribute a percentage of their payroll for unemployment insurance premiums to the federal government who would administer the fund, but stipulated that 90 percent would be returned to the states to set up their own unemployment insurance plans in accordance with standards approved by a federal Social Security Board, which was to be set up to administer the entire law. The second line of defense against destitution concerned the group of people the CES referred to as "genuine unemployables—or near unemployables." This group comprised the old poor law categories of the deserving poor—the elderly poor (who for one reason or another were not covered under OAI), dependent children, and the blind. Following Roosevelt's strongly and frequently stated desire to get the federal government out of "the business of relief" the CES deferred responsibility for this group to the states and the social workers in their employ, writing: "With the Federal Government carrying so much burden for pure unemployment, the State and local governments . . . should resume responsibility for relief. The families that have always been partially or wholly dependent on others for support can best be assisted through the tried procedures of social casework, with its individualized treatment."[32] While the act delegated primary responsibility for the care of this group of dependents to the states and localities, it did not completely absolve the central government of responsibility. The

31. CES Report, Letter of Transmittal, https://www.ssa.gov. Accessed July 23, 2016.
32. *Report of the Committee on Economic Security*, p. 25, https://www.ssa.gov. Accessed July 24, 2016.

act provided for federal matching funds to assist in the support of these groups. The federal government would assume 50 percent of the cost of aid to the elderly through the OAA, and 30 percent of Aid to Dependent Children and of Aid to the Blind . The third line of the Social Security Act essentially restored the provisions of the highly effective and popular Sheppard-Towner Maternal and Child Health Act that had reduced maternal and child deaths during the 1920s, but had been abandoned by the Hoover administration in 1928. The Supreme Court had not been kind to many of Roosevelt's new deal programs, for instance overturning both the Agricultural Adjustment Act and the National industrial Recovery Act. The president had learned, however, and he crafted the Social Security Act in a manner that resulted in it being upheld by the court in two separate decisions, *Steward Machine Co. v. Davis* and *Helvering v. Davis*.

The Social Security Act of 1935 can be criticized on a number of fronts as an astonishingly conservative response to the needs of a modern industrial society that had just been dramatically shown how vulnerable its citizens were to problems in the economy. In no other western state's welfare program was the burden of paying for a retirement system taken out of the current earnings of the workers themselves. Other nations paid for these benefits out of general tax revenues. Not only did the payment of premiums cause financial problems for individual workers but, by taking billions of dollars out of the economy, it slowed economic growth by decreasing spending. Roosevelt was aware of this criticism but responded unapologetically explaining "I guess you're right on the economics, but those taxes were never a problem of economics. They are politics all the way through. We put those payroll contributions there so as to give the contributors a legal, moral, and political right to collect their pensions and their unemployment benefits. With those taxes in there, no damn politician can ever scrap my social security program."[33] The political savvy demonstrated by Roosevelt in this plan is demonstrated by the fact that social security has ever since been commonly referred to as "the third rail of politics," meaning that if you touch it your political career is dead. Another criticism of the act is that it did not cover all workers, excluding many who were most in need of coverage such as farm laborers and domestics. The fact that these were groups that included a large proportion of minority workers has not been lost on the act's critics. The act's relegating the care of the dependent poor—the elderly, children, and the blind—to the states, who had traditionally been neglectful of these groups, was another aspect of the act seen as a shortcoming. Another, related, problem was the act's outright ignoring of another group of the needy, namely working age adults with no children who were indigent for health or mental health or some other reason, relegating their care to budget strapped counties and private charities. Finally, sickness, which in normal economic times is the leading cause of joblessness and destitution, was ignored. The CES strongly felt that a health insurance provision should be included, but after encountering major opposition from health provider groups, mainly the American Medical Association, they stated in their final report: "We are not prepared at this time to make recommendations for a system of health insurance."

A major theory of the policy making process is incrementalism, which argues that, in general, only the smallest change of existing policy is possible. One of the leading proponents of this theory, Charles Lindblom, argues that policymakers "see policy making as a never-ending process in

33. Arthur Schlesinger, Jr., *The Coming of the New Deal* (Boston: Houghton Mifflin, 1959), 308–309.

which continual nibbling substitutes for a good bite."[34] The Social Security Act, with all its flaws and shortcomings was one of the rare events in policy history where more than incremental change, a "good bite" to use Lindblom's phrase, occurred. The act reversed historic assumptions about the nature of social responsibility: it established the proposition that the individual has clear-cut social rights; it replaced the American idea that welfare was a Christian responsibility with the idea that it was a responsibility of government; it finally and forcefully repudiated the Pierce veto by assigning some, although not all, responsibility for social welfare to the federal government; it implied that destitution was no longer always a matter of individual weakness; and it finally established a permanent framework upon which to begin the construction of a modern welfare state. As historian David Kennedy concluded:

> No other New Deal measure proved more lastingly consequential or more emblematic of the very meaning of the New Deal. Nor did any other better reveal the tangled skein of human needs, economic calculation, idealistic visions, political pressures, partisan maneuverings, actuarial projections, and constitutional constraints out of which Roosevelt was obliged to weave his reform program. Tortuously threading each of those filaments through the needle of the legislative process, Roosevelt began with the Social Security Act to knit the fabric of the modern welfare state. It would in the end be a peculiar garment, one that could have been fashioned only in America and perhaps only in the circumstances of the Depression era.[35]

THE DECLINE OF THE NEW DEAL

Hopkins had for years been nationally known and respected as a social worker and public welfare administrator, but he was unknown to most Americans at the time he joined the New Deal. Likewise, he was respected and valued by Roosevelt who primarily viewed him as a trusted employee who was effective at getting things done. By the end of Roosevelt's first term this had all changed. Hopkins' Works Progress Administration had become the best known and most effective of the New Deal programs, and Hopkins himself had become one of Roosevelt's most prominent spokesmen. Roosevelt had hundreds, perhaps thousands, of acquaintances, but very few people he considered to be friends. By 1936 Hopkins and Roosevelt's relationship had become one of personal friendship.

Roosevelt handily won election to a second term as president in the 1936 election, but following the flurry of reform measures enacted during his first term, his strong mandate was seriously weakened. In addition to the predictable weakening of a president's support during his second term, there were several factors that contributed to Roosevelt's problems. One was the president's proposal to restructure (critics said "pack") the Supreme Court by allowing him to name a new justice for each justice aged past seventy. This was viewed by almost everyone, not only Roosevelt's

---

34. Charles E. Lindblom, *The Policy Making Process,* 2nd ed., (Englewood Cliffs, NJ: Prentice-Hall, 1980), 4–5.

35. David M. Kennedy, *Freedom from Fear: The American People in Depression and War, 1929–1945* (New York: Oxford University Press, 2005), 258.

critics, as a threat to the traditional checks and balances system central to American democracy and created a backlash the intensity of which stunned the president. People were also becoming fearful that Roosevelt was polarizing the nation with rhetoric that referred to "economic royalists" and contrasted them to "one-third of a nation, ill-housed, ill-clad, ill-nourished."[36] Statements such as this by the president contributed to polarizing American politics along the lines of rich versus poor and reform versus reaction. Less recognized, but highly significant, was that the tenuous coalition Roosevelt had managed to create within the Democratic Party began to fray in response to the president's increasingly strong identification with liberal, labor, and urban factions within the party. The old north/south and urban/rural splits began to reappear. As Patterson concluded from a careful study of Roosevelt's relations with Congress, it was "the urban nature of the [New Deal] measures themselves that Congressional conservatives found most disturbing." Even without the Supreme Court debacle, Patterson argues, "sizable conservative opposition to measures of this sort [Social Security Act and labor legislation] would have developed."[37] By the beginning of Roosevelt's second term an alliance had developed between Republicans and conservative Democrats that, while not powerful enough to enact laws undoing New Deal programs, was powerful enough to impede any new legislative initiatives from the White House or liberal Congressional colleagues. The result was a legislature in 1937 that did very little legislating.

As has been previously noted, Roosevelt's basic disposition was fairly conservative and, while he was willing to engage in deficit spending to ease the human suffering caused by the nation's economic crisis, he was uncomfortable with the practice, thinking that a balanced budget was essential to a healthy economy. In 1936 and 1937 the economy was in a strong upswing fueled by a large increase in the combined total spending of federal, state, and local governments. This deficit spending caused the president to become increasingly worried about the danger of an inflationary boom leading to an economic collapse. He also wanted to woo the support of congressional conservatives who demanded governmental economy and a balanced budget. In 1937 Roosevelt acceded to these pressures and applied strong brakes to the rising economy. Among the measures applied was a stiff increase in the requirement of the amount of cash banks must hold in reserve, forcing them to convert loans and investments into cash; the Federal Reserve Banks sold government bonds to reduce the money supply; federal spending for public works projects, the WPA, and cash home relief was cut back. The president promised a balanced budget. In response to the government austerity measures, businessmen curtailed spending, investment was cut back, and orders declined. The result was that between spring of 1937 and spring of 1938 the economy plunged into a severe recession within the depression. Industrial production fell by 33 percent during this period and by its low point was one-third below its mid-1929 level. Gross National Product declined 5 percent between 1937 and 1938. The unemployment rate leaped to over 19 percent. On October 29, 1938, known as "Black Tuesday" the stock market broke completely

36. Franklin D. Roosevelt, Inaugural Address, January 20, 1937, *Public Papers and Addresses of Franklin D. Roosevelt*, Vol. 2, 1937 (Ann Arbor, MI: University of Michigan Library, 2005), http://quod.lib.umich.edu/p/ppotus/492538. Accessed August 1, 2016.

37. James T. Patterson, *Congressional Conservatism and the New Deal: The Growth of the Conservative Coalition in Congress, 1933–1939* (Lexington: University of Kentucky Press, 1967), 160–162.

as 17 million shares were dumped, making this the worst day for the market since 1929. Critics dubbed this the Roosevelt recession.

The Roosevelt recession brought to a head a debate that had been simmering in both the national administration and in the discipline of economics since the beginning of the depression. Conservative politicians, supported by many economists, believed that prosperity produced by governmental actions such as the large influx of money into the economy by the WPA was artificial and self-defeating, leaving government with a huge debt to pay off that would ultimately damage the economy. They were in support of the traditional goal of a balanced budget and a pro-business policy to encourage private investment. But a growing number of economists, and of politicians who listened to them, were becoming convinced by the arguments put forth by the British macro-economist John Maynard Keynes in his widely read 1936 book *The General Theory of Employment, Interest, and Money*. One of the main arguments of Keynes is that the proper response of government to a recession is to reverse the decline of aggregate money demands for output, and this should be done with expansionary monetary and fiscal policies. Keynes refuted the conservative belief that a mounting federal budget deficit in the midst of a recession, reflecting increased government payments of unemployment benefits, jobs programs, and decreased revenues resulting automatically from decreases in national income, should be responded to by tax increases or expenditure cuts to reduce or eradicate the deficit. Keynes's essential argument was that governments should spend their way out of recessions and depressions, and a budget deficit was a tool, not a problem.

Hopkins, by the time of the 1937–1938 recession had become Roosevelt's closest advisor on all matters, not just social welfare policy. He was not a formal student of economics, but it would not be incorrect to describe Hopkins as an intuitive Keynesian. Since his earliest years with Roosevelt Hopkins had been an advocate for an expansionist budget. Recording his notes on a meeting he had with Roosevelt in 1934 to help write a speech he recalled "I pressed as hard as I could for an economy of abundance in America rather than one of scarcity which had characterized the New Deal up to the present."[38] The title of Hopkins' only book, *Spending to Save—The Complete Story of Relief*, published in 1936 is a double entendre, referring to public relief as both saving the families of unemployed workers at the same time it saves the nation by providing economic stimulation. Since the beginning of the recession Hopkins and his chief assistant Aubrey Williams, assisted by Leon Henderson, the chief economist of the WPA had been collecting data and working on a proposal to try to convince Roosevelt of the error of listening to his conservative critics. When the market experienced a second major drop on March 25, 1938 Hopkins was ready and he and Williams descended upon Roosevelt with a fully developed proposal. The plan called for a program of heavy public works projects, combining loans and grants, increased spending for highways, flood control, expansion of the National Youth Administration, the Civilian Conservation Corps, and the Works Progress Administration and a host of other projects all calculated to stimulate the economy and rekindle the recovery. Roosevelt held a series of meetings with his cabinet and advisors and incorporated most of Hopkins' plan into a formal legislative proposal. On April 14 Roosevelt described his plan to the public in another fireside chat. He then

38. Quoted in Henry H. Adams, *Harry Hopkins: A Biography* (New York: G. P. Putnams' Sons, 1977), 70.

submitted the plan, the total package amounting to nearly $5 billion to Congress who passed it with very little modification.

Historians generally recognize 1938 as the end of the New Deal. New Deal initiatives had done a tremendous amount of good in reducing the suffering caused by the economic catastrophe, but they had failed to completely restore prosperity. Roosevelt was successful in moving forward only a few rather minor social welfare programs in his second term, mainly the National Housing Act that created the United States Housing Authority, and the Social Security Act Amendments of 1939 that began the incremental process of improving the law by increasing payment amounts, adding survivor's benefits, and expanding the number of workers covered. The infusion of money from Hopkins 1938 plan revived the faltering economy, but was nowhere near the amount of spending that would be necessary to end the depression. Only the vast expenditures necessitated by the coming of World War II would bring full recovery.

MINORITY GROUPS IN THE NEW DEAL

It has been frequently noted that the United States has a dual welfare system. One part of that system is aimed at the problems encountered by white males who have strong connections with the labor market. This part of the system is relatively generous in terms of benefits, and does not stigmatize its recipients. Benefits obtained under this system are given names that indicate no connection with welfare, names such as "insurance" and "pension." The other part of the system is extremely stingy in benefit amounts and is highly stigmatizing. This part of the system is always identified as welfare. Its recipients tend to be women and minorities. This dual welfare system has roots that predate the depression, but they were institutionalized by the New Deal. In spite of the fact that the system set up by the New Deal was in many ways a great leap forward in United States social welfare policy, and, realistically, it probably achieved all that was possible politically, the Roosevelt years gave minority groups little cause for celebration.

African Americans did benefit it small ways from New Deal programs, mainly due to protests they staged against discriminatory policies in work and benefit programs, and the active support by first lady Eleanor Roosevelt of civil rights for blacks. Harry Hopkins and Secretary of the Interior Harold Ickes promoted non-discrimination in federal job programs, advocated for blacks being granted relief jobs in proportion to their share of the population, and Ickes banned segregation and discrimination in Department of the Interior jobs, causing the secretaries of other federal agencies to follow suit. Black illiteracy dropped during the 1930s because of federal education projects, and the number of black college students and graduates more than doubled, in part because the National Youth Administration provided aid to students enrolled in black colleges. However, Roosevelt never pushed for civil rights issues because he feared antagonizing Southern Democrats in Congress whose support he needed. The Civil Conservation Corps was segregated, and the National Recovery Administration programs so often specified lower wages and benefits that the black press began to refer to the NRA Blue Eagle as "a predatory bird," and wrote that NRA really stood for "Negro Run Around" or "Negroes Ruined Again."

The situation of Native Americans was also somewhat improved by the New Deal. More than eighty thousand Indians worked in the Civil Conservation Corps where they were trained in agriculture, forestry, and animal husbandry, along with basic academic subjects. The projects they worked on, along with a smaller number employed in PWA and WPA projects, built schools, hospitals, roads, and irrigation systems on reservations. Probably more important than these direct benefits received by Indians, was that in 1933 Roosevelt appointed the first truly progressive Commissioner of Indian Affairs, John Collier. Collier reversed the traditionally racist federal Indian policy by prohibiting interference in Indian religious or cultural affairs, directing the Bureau of Indian Affairs to employ more Indians, and forbid the practice by Indian schools of suppressing native languages and traditions. Collier also lobbied through Congress the Indian Reorganization Act, sometimes called the Indians' New Deal. The act guaranteed religious freedom, reestablished tribal self-government, and halted the sale of tribal lands. For his efforts, Collier was attacked by conservatives as an atheist and a communist.

Hispanic Americans fared worse than other groups under the New Deal. Those who were not citizens were completely ignored by all programs. Hispanics who did participate in federal work programs often received lower wages than did Anglos. Most importantly, as most Hispanics in the U.S. were employed as agricultural workers, they were excluded from benefits of the Social Security Act and from rights and protections of the Wagner National Labor Relations Act.

ONE CRISIS ENDS AND ANOTHER BEGINS: WORLD WAR II

When Roosevelt was in his second term as president, the Twenty-Second Amendment to the Constitution was not in existence, so there was nothing to prevent him from seeking a third term. However, traditionally presidents had not served more than two terms and Roosevelt was concerned that his personal estate could not withstand much more of the neglect his being in office caused, so he was not planning to seek a third term in 1940. Roosevelt was, of course, greatly concerned that his legacy, particularly the New Deal, be protected from his conservative detractors both within and outside of the Democratic Party. He needed to select the best successor, and the evidence indicates that he picked Hopkins. One of Hopkins major drawbacks in terms of a presidential candidacy was his close association with social work and relief. This was problematic for two reasons. One reason was that this would create kneejerk opposition among the not insignificant number of people who hated the whole idea of public welfare. The other was that it opened Hopkins up to criticism as lacking broad enough experience to handle all the requirements of a president. In order to counter these potential criticisms Roosevelt, at the end of 1937, appointed Hopkins to the Cabinet as Secretary of Commerce. This, it was felt, would give him two years before the Democratic Convention to demonstrate a broader base of expertise and to curry favor with the business community.[39]

---

39. Serle F. Charles, *Minister of Relief: Harry Hopkins and the Depression* (Syracuse New York: Syracuse University Press, 1963), 206–219.

Roosevelt's anointing Hopkins to be his presidential successor effectively ended his role as the nation's chief social worker and as the president's advisor on social welfare issues. Hopkins relationship with Roosevelt became ever closer, and his advisory role expanded to include virtually all areas of concern to the president. It was widely recognized that he was the chief of Roosevelt's "inner cabinet." His presidential ambitions, however, did not go very far for two reasons. The first is that after 1938 the world diplomatic situation deteriorated at a rapid rate and Roosevelt, and his many supporters, concluded that a war was likely and he should remain at the head of the nation to meet the crisis. Hopkins, ever the Roosevelt loyalist, was fine with this and even agreed to floor manage Roosevelt's nomination at the 1940 convention. He skillfully did this, avoiding criticism about the president seeking a third term by making it appear that the nomination was the result of a spontaneous draft by the delegates.[40] The second reason was Hopkins declining health. In 1935 he was diagnosed with a duodenal ulcer for which he was successfully treated with instructions to improve his diet (which he did) and to slow down the pace of his life (which he did not do). In 1937 Hopkins experienced trouble eating and, after a strong push by the president, went to the Mayo Clinic in Rochester Minnesota at the end of the year. The doctors diagnosed stomach cancer and recommended immediate surgery. On December 20 the surgery was performed with two-thirds of Hopkins stomach removed. Against all odds, the surgery was successful and Hopkins returned to work. In late 1939 his symptoms once again appeared and he returned to the Mayo Clinic. The doctors there concluded that his cancer had not reappeared, but that he had developed some kind of condition that was preventing his body from absorbing nutrients. He was starving to death. Following a heroic course of treatment involving blood transfusions, intravenous feeding, and vitamin and iron injections his health improved enough to permit him to go home in September, 1939. However, feeling that his health was preventing him from maximum efficiency Hopkins resigned from governmental service in August of 1940.

Roosevelt was not willing to let Hopkins go so easily. Following Hopkins resignation as Secretary of Commerce, Roosevelt moved Hopkins into the Lincoln bedroom in the White House and created for him the position of Assistant to the president. He lived at the White House for three-and-a-half years, and devoted himself to assisting Roosevelt with wartime policies. He mainly served as Roosevelt's personal emissary to world leaders in war policy negotiations. Among his most significant activities were that he coordinated efforts to meet Great Britain's need for supplies, administered the lend-lease program, served as envoy to the British and Soviet governments, attended the Yalta Conference, and negotiated the format for the Potsdam Conference. He is attributed with writing the speech in which Roosevelt made the famous statement that "the United States must be the great arsenal of democracy." Russian Historian Valeri Lungblind asserts that Hopkins was the individual that "Winston Churchill considered second only to Franklin D. Roosevelt as an architect of the anti-Hitler coalition from 1939 to 1944."[41] The ability that Hopkins demonstrated during wartime discussions with world leaders or their representatives to dissect a complex subject, focus attention on its most important elements, and by force of reason

40. George McJimsey, *Harry Hopkins*, 129.

41. Valeri Lungblind cited in Christopher D. O'Sullivan, *Harry Hopkins, FDR's Envoy to Churchill and Stalin* (New York: Rowman & Littlefield, 2015), 117.

and expression to cause others to see things as he did, resulted in Winston Churchill referring to him as "Lord Root of the Matter."[42]

AFTERWORD

Hopkins was not liked by all, but was universally respected as patriotic, honest, and ethical to a fault. A 1939 editorial page cartoon pictures the WPA headquarters with a plaque being installed reading "To the Everlasting Honor of Harry L. Hopkins, An American Boy From Iowa Who Spent *9 Billions* Of His Country's Money *And Not A Dollar Stuck To His Fingers!*" Following Roosevelt's death and his own resignation from official duties, Hopkins was awarded the Distinguished Service Medal by President Harry S. Truman in September, 1945. Four months later he died in New York City. It is an interesting footnote to history that in 1995–96 the National Security Agency declassified a large number of World War II era messages from the Soviet NKGB (predecessor to the Cold War era KGB), and a number of these messages referred to a Soviet agent code named "19." Based on a process of elimination a number of foreign policy historians concluded that "19" was Harry Hopkins.[43] Hopkins was also under suspicion because during the 1920s and 1930s, like many social workers, he was openly sympathetic to the Russian experiment with communism; during the war he consistently advocated for aid to the Soviets with asking little or nothing in return; and he had occasionally expressed his opinion that Stalin was a strong and competent leader. After further documents came to light, including the notebooks of Soviet KGB agent Alexander Vassiliev, it became clear that "19" was actually Laurence Duggan, a State Department Official who committed suicide in 1948 when it appeared that the FBI was closing in on him and that his activities as a Soviet agent might be uncovered.[43] In the final analysis it appears that Harry Hopkins was exactly what he appeared to be—a good hearted, extremely competent, patriotic American who was central in establishing our welfare system, warts and all, and whose diplomatic efforts were central to victory in World War II. He was the social worker who almost became president.

---

42. Bill McIlvine, "Lord Root of the Matter," *American History* 35, no. 1 (April 2000): 30.

43. Harvey Klehr and John Earl Haynes, "Harry Hopkins and Soviet Espionage," *Intelligence and National Security*, 29, no. 6 (2014): 864–879.

CHAPTER 9

THE DEPRESSION: A CRISIS FOR THE NEW PROFESSION, 1930–1945

W hen John Willems graduated from the University of Wisconsin in June of 1933 it was not the joyous occasion he had pictured when he began as a freshman in September of 1929.[1] As he worked on his degree in economics he had a ring side seat as the economy got progressively worse and worse, culminating in a non-farm unemployment rate of 25 percent at his graduation time. Willems diligently looked for a job in business but, predictably, not only did not have a job by his graduation; he didn't even have any prospects. He realized, however, that he was more fortunate than many of his classmates because his family were the owners of a fairly prosperous dairy farm outside of Green Bay Wisconsin. Although the value of the farm had drastically declined, and the family's once bountiful income had shrunk, the farm was still a viable business and he had the option of returning home and helping his father run it. Having no other prospects, this is what he did.

Over the next year Willems continued to seek a college graduate level job but other than a few interviews was making no progress. That is, until on a spring 1934 Thursday afternoon his father returned from his weekly civic group lunch with a lead. The speaker at lunch was Walter P. Smith, Director of the newly organized City of Green Bay Department of Public Welfare. The charge of the department was to efficiently and humanely tend to the needs of the unemployed poor in Green Bay by administering programs mostly paid for by the Federal Emergency Relief Administration, the Wisconsin Emergency Relief Administration, Brown County, and the City of Green Bay. Mr. Smith announced during his talk that he was seeking to hire four investigators and eight visitors. The investigators would be responsible for taking applications for relief, conducting

---

1. John Willems is a composite portrait of several public welfare investigators discussed in the "Green Bay [Wisconsin] Welfare Department Board Minutes, 1932–1986" and who left case records contained in the "Green Bay Welfare Department Case Files, 1932–1986," Special Collections, Cofrin Library, University of Wisconsin Green Bay. The names of all clients are pseudonyms as per a confidentiality agreement.

family studies to ascertain exactly what the applicant's family situation was, working out detailed family budgets, auditing the family's financial situation to determine exactly what their resources and monthly income was, and then determining if the family was eligible for assistance and, if so, how much and what kind. A visitor would be responsible for taking up a case once the investigator had determined eligibility, developing a relationship with the family, and meeting with the family once every two weeks in the family home or the visitor's office. The purpose of the visitor's work was to monitor changes in the family's financial situation and adjust the benefit level accordingly, help the family develop and implement plans to become financially independent, and to help the family resolve other problems of living they might encounter. These jobs all required that applicants hold a college degree and carried a starting salary of $80 per month with a raise to $85 after six months and to $90 after one year. In 1934 when the national average wage was $1,071, a small but nice apartment could be rented in Green Bay for $15 a month, and a new Model B Ford could be purchased for $490, $80 per month was a modest wage, but was acceptable for a first job.

Willems got up the next morning, put on his one good suit, and drove his father's car to the Welfare Department office in the City Hall Building. He was given an employment application which he filled in and left with the receptionist. Three days later he received a phone call inviting him to come for an interview with Mrs. Helen DuBois, Casework Supervisor. He met with Mrs. DuBois who informed him that she was a professional social worker with a diploma from the New York School of Social Work. She had spent four years in Chicago as a caseworker for Associated Charities and had recently relocated to Green Bay after her husband finished dental school and came home to set up his practice. She explained that she would like to hire trained social workers for all the investigator and visitor positions in the new department but could not because (1) the city council was insisting that the department hire only local people and there were virtually no trained social workers in Green Bay and (2) even if she could go outside of the city to hire, no one with professional training would be willing to work for $80 per month (she did not share this with Willems, but her salary was $150 per month). She explained that she would provide on the job training to the new investigators and visitors and was confident that, in spite of lack of formal training, they would be up to the job. Two days later Mr. Smith called and, on the advice of Mrs. DuBois, offered John Willems a job as a relief investigator.

True to her word, Mrs. DuBois implemented a rigorous training program as soon as Willems began work. She lent him one of the Department's copies of Mary Richmond's influential book *Social Diagnosis* and several essays on interviewing techniques and told him to study these carefully. She then went over a number of forms he would use to guide his investigations. The process would begin when a family applied for relief by filling out a two page, fourteen item, Affidavit and First Application for Emergency Relief. This form, signed under oath, briefly stated the family's composition, debts, and resources. Following receipt of the application Willems would do a family case history beginning with a Family Record Face Sheet on which he would list detailed information about the family beginning with names and birth dates, work history, marital status, information on relatives, church affiliation, and a list of all social agencies the family was involved with. The face sheet would be accompanied by a narrative in which Willems would describe the family's reason for application, any health problems, education level, property owned, debts, resources such as insurance policies, work history, and information on any relatives who could potentially be of help. He would then complete a detailed family budget sheet on which would be listed all of the family's monthly expenses and income. By subtracting the expenses from the income Willems would arrive at the amount of aid the family was eligible to receive. Following the collection of all of this information from the family Willems was then to set about confirming it. To do this he was to use a series of inquiry forms to be sent to the family's land lord, banker, insurance agent, former employers, and even a form on which business people with whom the family dealt affirmed that "I am unable at this time to give him further credit." Mrs. DuBois also explained that although Willems's job title was investigator and, as such, his main job responsibility was establishing and monitoring eligibility for assistance, he would share with the visitors some of the responsibility for establishing relationships with recipients, regularly visiting in their homes, and helping them with any problems preventing them from being as independent as possible.

Willems began work on July 1, 1934 and worked for the Green Bay Department of Public Welfare for the next four years. During this time he carried a case load that averaged seventy-five families, quite a load considering he was required to have contact with each family at least once every two weeks. Most of the cases were pretty routine, mainly dealing with unemployed men who were desperate to get back to work. The major types of assistance that the department could provide these men was grocery orders, rental assistance, medical care, and most importantly, referral and certification to one of the federal jobs programs such as Work Progress Administration (WPA) or the Civilian Conservation Corps (CCC). Very little cash relief was given. A typical case was that of Charles Gillis who was fired from his job of seventeen years as a foreman at a local produce company. It was determined that he had no relatives who could help out, but had a life insurance policy with a cash value of $50 that could support the family for a month. Following this the family was certified to receive groceries, rent assistance, and Mr. Gillis was referred to the WPA for work relief. Over the course of the following two years the department was successful in helping Mr. Gillis get a temporary WPA job, helped him find summer employment during one summer, and provided medical services to help with a vision problem of one of the family's children. On several occasions John Willems went with Mr. Gillis to talk to his former employer and see if he could be taken back with the company. This was finally successful when he was rehired, as a truck driver rather than a foreman, and the case was closed.[2] Another typical, if slightly more humorous, case was that of Dudley Simon, married with no children. Mr. Simon had made a good living between 1930 and 1936 brewing illegal beer in his garage and selling it to local speakeasies. In 1933 prohibition ended, the large commercial brewers in Milwaukee reopened, legal bars and clubs opened, and Mr. Simon lost his market. When John Willems left the department in 1938 Mr. Simon still had not found new employment.[3]

Some of Willems's cases were not routine at all and made him wish that he had received more intense social work training. One such case was that of Richard and Adele Martens. The Martens case was opened in 1936 when Mr. Martens was hospitalized due to severe burns received in a job related accident. The Martens were married in 1916, adopted one child, and then Mrs. Martens gave birth to four more. The marriage was troubled, with allegations that Mr. Martens drank excessively and when drinking was prone to domestic violence. The Martens divorced in 1929 but

2. Green Bay, Wisconsin, Welfare Department Case Files, Case 140, Special Collections, Cofrin Library, University of Wisconsin Green Bay.

3. Green Bay, Wisconsin, Welfare Department Case Files, Case 170.

remarried in 1934 after Mrs. Martens became pregnant, giving birth to another son four months after the remarriage. John Willems spent a good deal of time trying to help Mr. Martens find a job, but when the man became despondent due to his inability to support himself and his family, he spent more and more time just talking to Mr. Martens, "hoping to get his spirit up." In 1936, in a horrific incident, Mr. Martens committed suicide by cutting his own throat with a straight razor in front of his wife. After the suicide, Willems continued to work with the family, continuously recertifying them for assistance. In the summer of 1937 he approved the family to receive a seed assortment and, making good use of his farm boy background, helped Mrs. Martens's older children plant and tend to a vegetable garden. As the oldest child grew up, Willems helped him find work first in a National Youth Administration employment program, then a brief job with a WPA project in Green Bay, and finally in a Civil Conversation Corp program. When Willems left the department in 1938, the oldest boy, having found that he liked the regimentation of the CCC job, was planning on entering the army.[4]

The vast majority of Willems's cases were two-parent families where unemployment of the breadwinner (in all cases the husband) was the major problem. In the Martens case he worked with Mrs. Martens after the death of her husband, but his focus quickly shifted to the oldest son with the goal of helping him become employed so he could support the family. Very few of his cases involved female clients. One case that did involve only a woman was that of Anna Pauwels. Mrs. Pauwels, born in 1872, was married to George Pauwels in 1905. The couple never had any children. In 1936 Mr. Pauwels died, leaving his wife with no resources on which to live. Having never worked outside of the home Mrs. Pauwels found herself in desperate straits and finally, very reluctantly, she applied to the Green Bay Department of Public Welfare for assistance. The case was assigned to John Willems for investigation and he quickly certified Mrs. Pauwels for rent assistance, grocery assistance, and arranged for a very small monthly cash grant from the Green Bay Diocese Apostolate (Mrs. Pauwels was a long and faithful member of a local Catholic congregation). Because she had never worked and was sixty three years old, the chances of Mrs. Pauwels finding a job in the 1936 economy were virtually zero. Willems recognized this and accordingly never recorded employment as a goal. Mrs. Pauwels, however, was not happy with being financially dependent on the city and her church and badly wanted to be self-sufficient and thought that starting her own business would be the way to do this. So, for three years Willems patiently and earnestly helped her in what he must have realized were doomed entrepreneurial efforts. Mrs. Pauwels first attempt was to start a used clothing business. She somehow gathered a large supply of good quality used clothing, cleaned and repaired the garments, and found racks on which they could be attractively displayed. The one thing she did not have, and could not find because she had no money to pay rent, was shop space in which to operate this business, and so, after several months of having to beg friends for space to store her stock while she looked for free shop space, she gave up this effort. The next thing she tried was to open a boarding house. She found space and found ten people willing to pay her for room and board. However, the man she was renting the space from never made renovations he had promised in order to make the space livable, so she had to abandon this plan. Her third effort was to begin a sewing business, specializing in

4. Green Bay, Wisconsin, Welfare Department Case Files, Case 220.

remodeling clothes to reflect the latest styles. She was once again successful in attracting business, but quickly found that she would need supplies (matching thread, buttons, and so forth) that she did not have money for. Her final attempt was the result of a relationship she developed with a local man. Recognizing that Mrs. Pauwels had artistic ability he offered to pay for mail order water color painting lessons thinking that when she completed the course she would be able to find work as a commercial artist. The man made the first payment for the course but when the relationship soured (Willems recorded that the man "wanted more for his $65 than just friendship") he refused to pay for the remainder of the course. By this time Mrs. Pauwels had reached the age of sixty-five and was eligible for what both she and John Willems referred to as a "pension." This was actually an Old Age Assistance grant provided under the new Social Security Act. After several months of advocacy, Willems was successful in getting Mrs. Pauwels approved for this grant and her case was closed. Closing Mrs. Pauwel's case appears to be the last official act of John Willems as an employee of the Green Bay Department of Public Welfare, as his name disappears from department records after this.[5]

A number of historians have studied social work case records in recent years and the picture they paint of the profession in the past, although not entirely unsympathetic, is generally not flattering.[6] Peel, for example, found that the case records of the social workers he studied in Minneapolis "dramatized an explanation of inequality that highlighted the importance of making plans, the dangers of dependency, and the wisdom of middle-class self-sufficiency . . . [the social workers] ignored the fact that most of their clients simply wanted limited and temporary help so they could eventually carry forward their own decisions and aspirations." Reading cases dealing with family violence in Boston, Linda Gordon found that they offered evidence of unfounded assumptions, intrusions, and class biases on the part of the social workers. The social workers studied by these historians generally placed far too much responsibility for problems on the individual experiencing them and far too little on the social and economic environmental components of the problems. For the most part evidence of these negative attitudes and class and ethnic biases are lacking in the case records of John Willems and his untrained colleagues in Green Bay. The staff, as well as the board, of this agency seemed to accept as obvious that the problems their clients were experiencing were a result of the country's economic situation, and acted under the assumption that people would go back to work as soon as work was available. The records contain an occasional, if rare, statement that could be taken as class bias or negative stereotyping such as when a visitor referred to Mrs. S. as "rather a large woman, well dressed; a person of very little refinement and not much education" and reported a neighbor as saying that the S "boys appear to be rough and use bad language." These statements could, of course, be true, but exactly why the visitor felt it necessary to include them in the case record is unclear. In another record the visitor makes quite

5. Green Bay, Wisconsin, Welfare Department Case Files, Case 260.

6. Beverly Stadum, *Poor Women and Their Families: Hard Working Charity Cases, 1900–1930* (Albany, NY: State University of New York Press, 1992); Regina Kunzel, *Fallen Women, Problem Girls: Unmarried Mothers and the Professionalization of Social Work, 1890–1945* (New Haven, CT: Yale University Press, 1993); Karen W. Tice, *Tales of Wayward Girls and Immoral Women: Case Records and the Professionalization of Social Work* (Urbana, IL: University of Illinois Press, 1998); Linda Gordon, *Heroes of Their Own Lives: The Politics of Family Violence: Boston 1890–1960* (Urbana, IL: University of Illinois Press, 1998); Mark Peel, *Miss Cutler and the Case of the Resurrected Horse: Social Work and the Story of Poverty in America, Australia, and Britain* (Chicago, IL: University of Chicago Press, 2012).

an issue out of the fact that the oldest son in the family had gotten his girlfriend pregnant and consequently " Winford is being married next month by compulsion," and that Winford is going to be married to a Baker girl on October 19 "because he has to." The visitor records that she told Winford and the Baker girl that "they had better not expect the city to support them." However, after making these indignant statements, the worker clipped the wedding announcement from the paper and taped it into the case record, and amended her statement about not expecting the city to support them by adding the clause "until after the baby arrives."

The time period covered in this chapter, 1930 to 1945 could be titled "a tale of two social works." Coming into the depression in 1930 social workers had for many years been attempting to construct a profession that would fight poverty through private agencies, studying and coming to understand the individual causes of dependency, and stamp out poverty one case at a time through the development of skilled professional techniques. In order to be able to gain the necessary skills social workers would have to receive advanced technical training in problems of poverty and dependency and develop skills through intense professional supervision. Social work was viewed as something that not just anyone could do and the minimum education and qualifications increased until by the onset of the depression the goal was for all social workers to be trained on the graduate level. With the onset of the depression and the huge and rapid increase in poverty and dependency, anti-poverty programs exploded in terms of number and consequently number of employees. The new programs were almost exclusively public, whereas in the past social workers had mostly worked in private programs. The new jobs created by the public programs expanded so rapidly that even if the profession had claimed them as its own, there is no way that an adequate number of trained social workers could have been produced to fully meet staffing needs.

THE CHANGING POLICY CONTEXT
OF SOCIAL WORK PRACTICE

We have argued elsewhere that social work is a "policy based profession" by which we mean that the very nature and substance of social work practice is determined by the policy environment in which it finds itself.[7] As the policy context changes over time so must the profession. Medicine deals with the human body, which remains stable; the legal profession deals with a body of law that changes over time, but also with legal principles that remain stable. Social work, on the other hand, deals with public and voluntary programs concerned with immediate problems and priorities and reflecting values and beliefs that are constantly shifting. If a major health policy, such as the Affordable Care Act, is implemented, it will influence medical services but not the basic nature of medical practice. A major Supreme Court decision will influence the material a lawyer works with, but the function and practice of law will not change. A major public welfare bill, such as the Social Security Act, can change the basic structure of social work and the function of practice.

---

7. Philip R. Popple and Leslie Leighninger, *The Policy Based Profession: An Introduction to Social Welfare Policy for Social Workers*, 6th ed. (Boston: Pearson, 2015).

The Green Bay Department of Public Welfare and John Willems and the thousands of other social workers hired by such agencies were a result of a fundamental policy shift in the way poverty was handled in the United States and changed the whole theoretical basis of social work practice. In previous chapters we have discussed the development of the Charity Organization Society movement. More than just a coming together of groups of civic minded citizens in communities across the country, the COS movement constituted a national social welfare policy in regards to handling poverty. The COS approach to poverty was based on the belief that people were poor largely due to individual problems and that these problems could be solved, and the whole problem of poverty ameliorated, by the provision of skilled individual social services. The basis for all of these services was the provision of material assistance in a form and amount that was based on what were believed to be scientific principles, individualized to each case in the precise manner that was thought to have the greatest probability of solving the families underlying problems that were leading to its dependency. The COS people believed that prior to their movement, material assistance had been doled out based on moral and arbitrary criteria that in some cases gave people too much assistance, in some gave them too little, and in all cases did little or nothing to solve the problems that caused the family to need assistance in the first place. A major goal of the COS movement was to establish a profession of social work that would have scientific knowledge and technical skills to ensure that every family needing assistance would be given just the right amount for the right period of time, and that this correct grant, along with the skilled advice and direction of the social worker, would eventually lead to the family becoming independent.

This technical skill that would enable social workers to assist each individual case in a correct, non-moralistic, non-judgmental way was the topic of Richmond's ground breaking book *Social Diagnosis*. This book, unlike modern social work practice texts, contains almost nothing related to human behavior, behavior change, and interpersonal skills that enable a social worker to relate to a client in a positive way. Rather, Richmond's book is almost entirely concerned with techniques for collecting social evidence, that is, data on the situation and character of a family applying for relief. It is assumed that once valid and reliable evidence related to families' problems has been collected and analyzed that the correct course of action (the treatment plan) will become apparent. As Lederman has observed:

> . . . Richmond argued, both in the book and afterwards with her critics that treatment was inherent in diagnosis. Consider the following passage. "The processes which lead up to social diagnosis and thence to the shaping of a plan of social treatment may be divided into the collection of evidence and the drawing of inferences therefrom," Richmond implied that once the evidence was collected, the case worker could draw inferences which would then comprise the treatment plan. Chapter V was entirely devoted to "inferences."[8]

Social workers in the years between the founding of the COS movement and the onset of the Great Depression viewed material relief not as an end in itself, and certainly not as a unconditionally

---

8. Sarah Henry Lederman, *From Poverty to Philanthropy: The Life and Work of Mary E. Richmond*, Ph.D. Dissertation, Department of History, Columbia University, 1996.

offered benefit for those in need, but as a tool. The correct relief package was the main tool the social worker had to move a family in the direction of constructive change. Like any tool, relief in the hands of the amateur, the incompetent, or the poorly trained, could do incalculable harm, in most cases turning a temporary problem into a permanent state of dependency. Thus, in Richmond's formulation of casework theory, it was imperative that the social worker have complete discretion about the size, type, and duration of material aid given a family. Two cases of identical composition, need, income, and resources, could receive very different benefit packages if the social worker, based on proper professional collection of social evidence, diagnoses one family as having the spirit of independence, but in need of long term help and the other family as "wanting charity more than work," and so in danger of sinking into permanent dependency if anything more than short term assistance were given along with a stern talking to about the value of work and independence. In 1923 a Boston official asked Richmond what the proper amount of relief was for a family, and Richmond replied that it "is such sum or sums, large or small, as will give, when combined with adequate planning and oversight, the desired result, namely, permanent social betterment in the individual case."[9]

A basic, foundational element, of COS philosophy was opposition to public outdoor relief. The public sector was supposed to provide institutional care (the poorhouse, orphanage, mental hospital, etc.), but the provision of direct assistance to people in their own homes was to be the exclusive responsibility of the private COS type agency. There were a number of aspects of public provision of relief that Richmond and her COS associates objected to. Problems of graft, corruption, patronage, and incompetence were among them. In at least three places (two in *Social Diagnosis* and once in an article in *Charities* Review) Richmond used the case of Albert Gough to illustrate the superiority of the work of the Associated Charities to that of public agencies.[10] Gough was a homeless man who wandered in to an Associated Charities office and requested assistance. It was soon discovered that Gough was an escaped inmate of a local state mental hospital where he had been a resident for sixteen years. The Associated Charities social worker was familiar with family law in the state and knew that family members were legally required to support members disabled by conditions such as mental illness. Thus, the first thing she did was to search for the man's family. Using investigative techniques described by Richmond in her book (among other things, using city directories from 16 years ago when Gough had first appeared at the hospital to find addresses of people with his last name) and making proper inferences from the information gained (eliminating names from neighborhoods the worker knew to be of a racial or ethnic composition making it unlikely that Gough would have lived there) and after many days of work, the social worker located and contacted Gough's family. The lesson to be learned from the Gough case, as stated by Richmond, was

> . . . the point to be made here is that the failure of a state's public institutions to discover this man's family, who had been eager for news of him all these years, is not so much a failure properly to adjust a question of legal support as it is a far graver failure. It is true that the state at the present

9. Quoted in Sarah Henry Lederman, *From Poverty to Philanthropy,* 240.

10. Mary E. Richmond, "Albert Gough, Single: An Annotated Case Record," *Charity Organization Bulletin* 2, no. 6 (1911): 61–71. Mary E. Richmond, *Social Diagnosis* (New York: Russell Sage Foundation, 1917), 196, 267, 268.

per capita cost of maintenance had expended $3,160 for his care, but it had done something more wasteful than this; it had neglected through this whole period to utilize a therapeutic agency of the first importance. The man's family proved to be sterling people, whose affection and sympathy achieved wonders for his mental health even after years of lost opportunity.

During the early years the COS movement made some headway in its campaign to eliminate public outdoor relief, for example successful efforts to get public assistance totally eliminated in New York City and Philadelphia. In spite of the spirited battle that Mary Richmond and her COS colleagues fought against public welfare, it turned out to be inevitable. Private organizations, no matter how great their determination and how good their motives, were simply not capable of managing a massive and growing problem such as poverty in a modern urban industrial environment. By 1915 twenty states had implemented mothers' pension programs and Richmond conceded defeat and gave up organizing active opposition to the expansion of public relief. As the nation moved through the prosperous and optimistic 1920s clear signs of the inability of the private agencies to handle poverty, even with the assistance of the many widow pension programs, were emerging. In a 1926 article in the COS journal *The Family*, Edward Lynde cites figures from 96 Associated Charities agencies that show the agencies spending three times as much for material relief than they had ten years previously.[11] Three years later, just before the onset of the depression, in the same journal, Linton Swift reported that 75 percent of the relief being distributed by family agencies (the new term for the COSs) was coming from public funds. He bemoans the fact that "With these developments we have in many cities gradually lost our former character as an independent private and experimental agency, and have drifted toward the status of a semi-official public agency, responsible to the entire community for the administration of a large central relief fund."[12]

When the depression hit with its full force in the early 1930s its effect on the social work profession was immediate and immense. Initially, true to Swift's prediction, private family agencies became semi-official public agencies. Their structure, staffing, and social work approach remained basically unchanged, but the money they were administering was coming almost entirely from public coffers. This quickly changed, however. In 1933 when the new Roosevelt administration enacted the Federal Emergency Relief Act, with social worker Harry Hopkins at its head, one of the first things he did was issue Regulation Number One. This was the gist of the regulation:

Grants of Federal emergency relief funds are to be administered by public agencies . . .This ruling prohibits the turning over of Federal Emergency Relief funds to a private agency. The unemployed must apply to a public agency for relief, and this relief must be furnished direct to the applicant by a public agent.[13]

11. Edward D. Lynde, "The Significance of Changing Methods in Relief Giving," *The Family,* 8, (July, 1927): 135–144.

12. Linton B. Swift, "The Relief Problem in Family Social Work," *The Family,* 10 (March 1929): 3–11.

13. Federal Emergency Relief Administration, *Rules and Regulations* no. 1, June 23, 1933. Cited in Paul A. Kurzman, *Harry Hopkins and the New Deal* (Fair Lawn, NJ: R. E. Burdick, 1974), 83.

This ruling did two major things with one stroke of the pen: it removed the historic role of relief giving from private social agencies and it mandated that state's set up public welfare departments in their stead.

For the profession of social work, long dominated by the family agencies, this created nothing less than a crisis. The most influential approach to social work practice was that described in Mary Richmond's *Social Diagnosis*. Although late in her career Richmond attempted to paint a broader theoretical focus for casework, writing about "the influence of mind on mind" and the "development of personality" in the "adjustment . . . between men and their social environment," she never offered so much as a hint about how a social workers mind would act upon a client's, or how personality could be developed, or how the relationship between a man and his social environment could be adjusted.[14] For most social workers their practice was predicated on their ability to make decisions about the aid packages a client could receive, and for this Richmond gave good advice. Moving this function to public agencies meant both that private agency workers would not have the tool of relief, which was the whole basis of their practice expertise, and public agency workers would administer relief but, because of the nature of public policy, would have little discretion in regard to the relief package a client received. As family agency social worker Emily Mitchell Wires lamented in a 1936 article:

> Any discussion of the place of the social caseworker in public welfare must meet the objection that case work theory is not applicable to the practice of emergency relief administration. To support this objection, one is reminded of the restrictions, represented by the rules of the public organization, which seem to narrow one's field of effort to such an extent that case work is out of the question (though not actually in violation of these rules). The rigidity of budgetary regulations, for instance, seems to leave no room for individual treatments: we cannot conscientiously grant to one family, no matter what its needs or standards, an allowance any more generous than that to another.[15]

This evolution of relief giving from being a responsibility of private, professional, social work agencies to one of public, bureaucratic organizations, created two large questions for the social work profession. The first was what was to be the role of social work in the new public welfare agencies, and the second was what was to be the basis of social casework practice when the social worker was not responsible for, and had no discretion over, the dispensing of material relief?

THE NEW PUBLIC SOCIAL WORK

When the Federal Emergency Relief Act was passed in 1933 it posed more problems for professionally trained social workers than just the loss of responsibility for decisions regarding material relief and the effect of this on social work practice theory and skill. Most of the fears that social workers had of the consequences of the establishment of public welfare programs turned out, at

14. Mary Richmond, *What Is Social Casework?* (New York: Russell Sage Foundation, 1922), 98–100.
15. Emily Mitchell Wires, "The Application of Case Work Theory to Public Welfare Practice," *The Family* 17 (April 1936).

least initially, to be true. The first effect of the new public programs was an increase in the number of social work jobs far in excess of the ability of the profession to fill. In 1930, according to the US Census, there were 36,000 people holding full time, paid, social work positions. The 1933 *Social Work Yearbook* estimated that about one third of these people were qualified social workers according to the standards of the American Association of Social Workers.[16] By the 1940 census the number of paid, full time, social work positions had increased to 69,677, most in the new public welfare departments, while the number of persons with qualifications recognized by the AASW had only increased to approximately 20,000.[17] Thus, in ten years the gap between the number of qualified social workers and the number of social work jobs had increased from approximately 24,000 to nearly 50,000.

The fear among professional social workers that the development of public welfare departments would lead to staffing by unqualified workers had been present since before the massive increase in staff brought on by the depression. In 1926 the AASW established a Committee on Standards, Personnel, and Service in Public Agencies. After several years work the committee recommended that social work positions in public service should be defined as professional, requiring social work training, and should be part of a civil service system, filled through competitive examination, conducted by professional social workers. When the FERA was passed and states began hiring the large number of new social workers, the recommendations of AASW were ignored. The new public welfare departments did not have any kind of merit system and, other than stating a preference for a college degree, had few requirements for the new cadre of social workers. The patronage system that hired most of the new public welfare workers was in most cases not of the sinister Boss Tweed variety. Rather, most of these people were probably hired in a manner similar to John Willems—he was known about town as a nice young man from a good family, his father was acquainted with the public welfare director as well as with most of the prominent citizens of Green Bay, so why spend a lot of time and effort to hire someone you don't know even if that person has some type of fancy professional credential?

As indicated by Mrs. DuBois in her interview with John Willems, even if she were to try to find a qualified social worker for the job, it is doubtful that she could have. When faced with this new mass of untrained social workers, the response of the profession was to double down and increase the basic requirements for earning recognition as a professional social worker. New requirements for membership in the American Association of Social Workers were implemented effective July 1, 1933. These requirements specified a complex combination of undergraduate education, professional preparation, and supervised work experience, requiring a minimum of seven years preparation in order to be considered a professional social worker. However, looking toward the future the association stated, "As a preferred method, a six-year preparation is allowed to those who graduate from an approved university and then complete a two-year graduate course in a school of social work."[18] The AASW was aware of the problems caused by its increasing membership requirements

16. Walter W. West, "Social Work as a Profession," *Social Work Yearbook: 1933* (New York: Russell Sage Foundation, 1933), 494.

17. Arlien Johnson, "Social Work as a Profession," *Social Work Yearbook: 1941* (New York: Russell Sage Foundation, 1941), 549.

18. Grace F. Marcus, "Social Work as a Profession," in Russell H. Kurtz, ed., *Social Work Yearbook, 1937* (New York: Russell Sage Foundation, 1937), 489.

during a time when the profession was expanding most rapidly by the addition of people who did not meet these requirements. Prior to the 1933 adoption of the increased membership requirements a proposal was made to admit non-professionally trained social workers as associate members. This proposal was voted down by the membership in 1933.[19] This proposal was reintroduced in 1940 and again in 1942, but was again voted down by a membership affirming its belief in selective membership requirements founded on high standards of formal professional education. The membership felt that selective membership requirements were necessary for the realization of the association's purposes and for reliable service to clientele.[20]

But it was quickly recognized that the work of the new public welfare workers involved some complex tasks. These workers spent most of their time doing eligibility reviews and this was a pretty routine bureaucratic task requiring a good mind, an in-depth knowledge of agency rules, and enough arithmetic to figure family budgets. But, as Leiby has noted, "it was never simply that. Rules were often complicated and allowed a degree of discretion. Applicants were likely to be ashamed, defensive, uncooperative or even hostile, pitiable, or offensive. It took a degree of patience, tact, insight, and skillful interviewing to bring out the facts and put them together so they could be understood or accepted. There were always problems besides the financial ones, trouble to shoot." Elizabeth Dexter, a person who came into public welfare work from a psychiatric social work background, was one of many who argued that social work training was necessary to equip workers to handle the bewilderment and embarrassment of the applicant and to investigate the full range of client problems.[21]

The federal agency responsible for coordinating with the states in the implementation and day-to-day operation of the new public welfare laws was the Bureau of Public Assistance, part of the Social Security Board. There were a number of professional social workers in the Bureau who felt that professional social work should change and bend its definition of social work to help creatively meet the staffing needs of the new agencies and the needs of clients for high quality professional services. Jane Hoey, the head of the Bureau, had definite ideas that reflected an orientation toward professional social work. Hoey realized that there were not enough trained social workers to occupy staff public welfare worker positions but, following the lead of Harry Hopkins, head of the Temporary Emergency Relief Administration, she lobbied to have supervisory, training, and administrative positions filled by trained professionals. Josephine Brown, Hoey's chief assistant advocated for the social work profession to reduce the basic credential for membership to a bachelor's degree in social work, and reached out to state agricultural universities proposing that they develop undergraduate programs aimed at staff jobs in the new welfare departments. She felt that professional social work training was not only at too advanced a level for the needs of the new departments, but it was heavily oriented toward urban problems, so undergraduate programs at universities targeted toward the needs of rural areas would precisely fit the bill.

In spite of efforts of people like Hoey and Brown, main stream professional social work refused to give recognition to its new, lesser trained, colleagues. The 1931 annual meeting of the National

19. "The Vote on the Membership Requirements," *The Compass*, 14 (May, 1933): 4.

20. Arlien Johnson, "Social Work as a Profession," *Social Work Yearbook: 1943* (New York: Russell Sage Foundation, 1943), 517.

21. Leslie Leighninger, *Social Work: Search for Identity* (New York: Greenwood Press, 1987), 19.

Conference of Social Work was devoted to discussing the nation's economic crisis and the reaction and position of professional social work to it. The conferees were unanimous in their support for government efforts to assist victims of the depression, recognizing that only the government, not private agencies, had the resources and capacity to meet the crisis. However, much fear was expressed regarding what the new order would mean for professional social work. The nucleus of the fear was that social work values would be drowned in the swelling tide of public assistance, standards of professional work would be abandoned, and that professional status would be lost.[22] Throughout the depression the major organizations did nothing but argue for continued high entry requirements, often advocating for increases. The response of the American Association of Schools of Social Work to Brown's efforts to institute undergraduate social work education at state agricultural colleges was to form the Professional Education Consultation Service. This service would sniff out agricultural colleges that were considering establishing undergraduate social work programs. They would then contact the college president and offer to send consultants free-of-charge. The consultants would look at the college's plan and would explain to the president how professional social work training should only be on the graduate level. They would then offer an alternative proposal for the college to offer a pre-social work major with the goal of providing excellent preparation for the students to go on to graduate professional education to become fully qualified, excellent, social workers.[23]

SOCIAL WORKERS UNIONIZE

Their abandonment by the main stream social work organizations was keenly felt by the excluded public agency workers who faced a number of workplace problems in addition to the fact that they were not adequately prepared for their jobs. Working conditions for the new group of relief workers were not good. Although many were college educated, salaries were poor. Caseloads were high, offices were often dumpy, high work quotas were imposed, staff cuts were common, and workers were sometimes required to take payless vacations. These conditions, accompanied by the rejection of the organized social work profession, prepared the way for the trade union movement to begin in social work. Union leader Jacob Fisher said: "Employee organization appealed to the more progressive relief workers as the only bulwark against low wages, and the lack of job tenure and the primitive working conditions obtaining in the great majority of relief agencies."[24] Shapiro, writing in *The Compass*, the official journal of the AASW, explained the rise of unions as "efforts to prevent reduction of wages and regression in standards through utilizing existing channels failed. The dividing line between the employing group and the workers became sharper and forced the workers into the recognition of the difference between the interests of their employers and their

22. George Springer, "The Challenge of Hard Times," *Survey*, 66 (1931): 380–385.

23. Personal conversation with Professor Sue Spencer, October 21, 1976. Professor Spencer was a 1931 graduate of the University of Chicago School of Social Service Administration, and served as a member of the Professional Consultation Service.

24. Jacob Fisher, "The Rank and File Movement 1930–1936," *Social Work Today*, 3 (Feb. 1936): 7.

own. Along with the rest of the working masses, whether intellectual or industrial, social workers found the American standard of living crumbling around them with all types of retrenchments schemes in full blast."[25]

The groups comprising the rank and file movement in social work had their start not as labor organizations but, rather, as discussion clubs formed by relief workers in several cities. At the beginning these workers were mostly employees of private agencies, but worked for these agencies as a result of contracts with local governments to administer public relief funds, so they were, for all practical purposes, public welfare workers. (The purpose of Hopkins's Regulation Number 1 was to prohibit this practice, but this did not happen until three years later). The first group was the Social Workers Discussion Club of New York, founded in 1930. The stated purpose of the club was to be "an open forum for the analysis of basic social problems and their relation to social work." The club reflected the feelings of younger workers that professional social work was failing to meet the challenge of the depression.[26]

The New York club declared itself a union in 1931, changing its name to The New York Association of Federation Workers. The stated purpose of the group was to promote the interests of employees of agencies supported by the Jewish Federation of New York. Members of the group presented a paper at the Jewish Social Service Conference stating: "It is possible to work out a theory and practice for such an organization in terms of the lag in the status of social work, the existence of organization within the employer group, and the unsatisfactory nature of the protection afforded by the executive group, and the decline of laissez faire in our corporate life."[27] By 1932 there were discussion clubs in Boston, Philadelphia, Chicago, St. Louis, Kansas City, and Los Angeles. These groups began through contact with members of the New York group at the 1932 meeting of the National Conference of Social Work and, as a result, most of the groups closely resembled the New York model. Primary issues were "unemployment, public relief, social insurance, the Negro, war and fascism, mental hygiene and social chaos, the intellectual and the crisis."[28]

Although social work unions began in private agencies, it was in the new and rapidly growing public agencies that they found their real base. The Chicago discussion club was, from the beginning, composed mostly of public employees and was more interested in personnel problems than in the general social issues that were the focus of the other clubs. The Chicago club organized opposition to payless vacations, salary reductions, uncompensated overtime, and generally poor working conditions. In 1933 the Chicago club officially became a union, The Federation of Social Service Employees.[29] Also in 1933 employees of the public Home Relief Bureau of New York founded the Home Relief Bureau Employees Association. This quickly grew to be the largest rank and file group in the country with over 1000 members within a few months of its organization. In the following year employee groups were formed in Cincinnati, Cleveland, Detroit, Minneapolis, Newark, Philadelphia, and Pittsburgh.

25. Lillian Shapiro, "Other Forms of Security," *The Compass* 14 (Dec. 1932): 6.

26. Jacob Fisher, "Trade Unionism in Social Work," *Social Work Yearbook: 1937* (New York: Russell Sage Foundation, 1937), 503.

27. *New York Times*, June 11, 1933, 26:3.

28. Jacob Fisher, "The Rank and File Movement 1930–1936," 5

29. Jacob Fisher, "The Rank and File Movement 1930–1936," 5.

With the rapid spread of unions in social agencies people began to feel that some form of coordination would be desirable. In 1933 representatives of four discussion clubs met at the National Conference of Social Work and set up a national organizing committee that never got off the ground. At the next National Conference meeting held in Kansas City in 1934 representatives from a dozen employee groups met and called for a national convention of employee groups. This meeting, held in Pittsburgh in 1935 and including representatives of thirty groups, resulted in the formation of the National Coordinating Committee of Rank and File Groups in Social Work. The Committee stated its purpose as threefold: (1) to promote cooperation among social work employee groups on economic, social welfare, and professional issues; (2) to support a broad program of social welfare in cooperation with other workers and professional groups, and (3) the maintenance and advancement of professional and vocational standards in the field of social work.[30]

The social work employee groups quickly resolved any ambivalence they may have felt as professionals identifying as union members and began to affiliate with national labor organizations. In 1936 nine employee groups in public agencies joined the American Federation of Labor (AFL). The AFL also chartered unions of private agency workers in New York and Chicago. When later in the year the Congress of Industrial Organizations (CIO) was formed the majority of social work groups saw its objectives as more consistent with theirs than those of the AFL and switched affiliation. Social work union membership grew rapidly after the affiliation with national organizations. It is estimated that approximately 11,500 social workers were union members in 1938, of these 8,500 were in twenty eight public welfare locals of the State, County, and Municipal Workers of America, which was affiliated with the CIO. About 1,000 were in three locals of the State, County, and Municipal Employees of America, affiliated with the AFL. Around 2000 were in seven locals of private agency workers affiliated with the United Office and Professional Workers of America, another CIO group. By the beginning of the Second World War social work unions had been completely absorbed into the national bodies. It is difficult to estimate the number of social workers who were union members because clerical, maintenance, and support staffs of social agencies are all lumped in with social workers. At the high point of membership these groups probably had around 21,500 members with social workers comprising slightly more than half.[31] At the same time the AASW, representing trained social workers mostly employed in private agencies, had a membership of approximately 11,500.[32]

Although union membership was overwhelmingly composed of untrained social workers, there were a number of trained workers who joined unions, including a number who held joint membership in the AASW and in a social work union. The professional social workers who allied themselves with the rank and file movement generally questioned the relevance of professional social work to the problems of the Depression. They felt that major social and political change, not skilled individual treatment, would be necessary to lift the nation out of the economic crisis. They often shared the political philosophy of the union leadership which was decidedly Marxist. The

30. Jacob Fisher, "Trade Unionism in Social Work," 504.

31. Frank C. Bancroft, "Trade Unionism in Social Work," *Social Work Yearbook: 1941* (New York: Russell Sage Foundation, 1941), 559–563.

32. "National Agencies—Private," *Social Work Yearbook:1941* (New York: Russell Sage Foundation, 1941), 642.

first issue of *Social Work Today*, a journal devoted to the interests of the rank and file movement in social work, summarized the feelings of union workers regarding the Depression: "How do social workers fit into the picture? Are they exempt from its implications? Are their interests those of the owning class, or do they belong with the teacher and the engineer in the emerging alliance of professional and industrial workers? . . . Under the cumulative pressure of four years of continuous contact with the victims of our chaotic social order, some have learned to question the traditional dogmas of the profession and to examine critically the shibboleths of "awareness," "bearing witness," "social engineering," and "community integration." They are painfully aware of many things that do not submit to awareness. They wonder who is doing the engineering and whether it is social. They suspect that talk of community integration is a pleasant fiction to hide the ugliness of our class society. They are sick of merely bearing witness."[33]

Although many AASW members supported the social work unions, the relation between the professional group and the unions was generally characterized by animosity. It appears that AASW preferred to mention the unions as little as possible. When mention was made it was usually an objective statement of size, membership composition, and so forth, or occasionally a guest article in *The Compass* written by a person who was a member of both AASW and a union. Occasionally there was a direct attack as when prominent social work leader Virginia Robinson wrote in the AASW journal *The Compass* that union social workers were "scornful of social work and professional workers. *Social Work Today* . . . started off with an attack on everything in social work. It revealed its philosophy as conservative and reactionary; it accused it of capitalist domination. Social action alone was worthwhile and social work as a technical, professional field received scant consideration."[34] Union social workers were also hostile when addressing the topic of the AASW and its definition of social work. In nearly any issue of *Social Work Today* one can find criticism of the AASW. In the 1935 issue a glossary was published that said that AASW (among other things), "Is dominated by high-salaried social work executives who fear to offend contributors. Has displayed little interest in the social work employee not an AASW member. Has done little to raise salaries or improve working conditions." In the first issue of *Social Work Today* a cartoon is published showing two women talking across a desk with the caption "Relief supervisor (to a $20 a week investigator): Now, remember, above all, that your attitude must always be professional!"[35]

While the fundamental difference between AASW and the social work unions was their definition of the qualifications necessary for a person to be considered a social worker there was also a philosophical difference regarding how social work was to be organized and how it fit into the division of labor in society. The unions were based on the principle of staff or craft solidarity. They felt that social workers were labor, as opposed to management, and their interests were one with those of labor. AASW, by contrast, was based on the professional principle of selection for membership by qualification. This professional principle held that social work was complex enough to require a high degree of preparation, like law or medicine, and that entry to the profession should be carefully regulated in order to protect the public.

33. *Social Work Today*, 1 (March–April 1934), 1.
34. Virginia Robinson, "Is Unionization Compatible with Social Work?" *Compass*, 18 (May 1937), 5–9.
35. *Social Work Today*, 1 (March–April 1934), 3.

Unionization in general was a major social issue preceding and during the Depression. The 1920s and 1930s were periods witnessing some very violent labor-management conflict. The relation of social work to the labor issue in general was another major difference between AASW and the unions during the late 1920s and early 1930s. Going into the Depression social work was well on the way to developing a very individualistic bias. Writing in the 1929 *Proceedings of the National Conference of Social Work*, Nell Scott proposed a psychological, casework approach for dealing with unions. She did not consider direct involvement to be a proper social work role, writing, "I still venture to maintain that family case workers are doing a different thing in a different way, that our first obligation is to cultivate an awareness in our own ranks of the struggle and its significances in the individual's personality development as he participates with his fellows. The social worker can be of service with her particular contributions only if she is something of a nonparticipant." Scott felt that a social worker could get involved in the union's struggle but implies that in doing so she is not acting as a social worker, explaining, "She might do it only if she were going into the field of [public relations], if she were participating shoulder to shoulder with him (the union member) in the fight. These are two roles. The social worker can help in either way, but may maintain only one role at a time. She must do the best informed and the clearest thinking, in order that she may not confuse her function as an exponent of the art of developing personality through many experiences, not the least of which is group participation."[36] Social workers who were active in the rank and file movement had a very different view of the proper social work role in relation to the labor movement. The editorial in the first issue of *Social Work Today* explained this view: "There is a growing body which is applying in another spirit the charge to all social workers to know their clients and to help them free themselves. They have heard the voice of labor speak compellingly in its own behalf. They are coming to feel that whatever skill and knowledge they may have can be put to most effective use supporting by publicity and action the organization of labor and its fight for adequate relief and social insurance."[37]

The basic socio-political philosophy and the stand toward social planning based on this philosophy was another area of difference between AASW and the unions. The unions appear on the surface to have been somewhat further to the left on the political spectrum than was the AASW. *The Compass*, the official AASW journal, carried articles of a mostly apolitical nature. The journal concerned itself mainly with professional and practice concerns. A definite political stance was rarely taken. *Social Work Today*, the rank and file journal, was constantly filled with fiery political material. It contained articles praising life in the USSR, condemning fascism in Germany and Spain, ads for May Day tours of the USSR, as well as arguments that the capitalistic system was at the root of American social and economic problems. An interesting example of the politics, and the feelings about social work practice, of the editors of *Social Work Today* is seen in a book review of a novel titled *I Love*, translated from Russian: "Here is a novel of especial interest to social workers, since it concerns itself with the material of social work. There is no introspective soul searching in this story, no probing after unconscious motivations. Sanza [the novel's protagonist] begins life as the typical delinquent, doomed to a succession of prison sentences. But the society he lives

36. Nell Scott, "Social Workers and Labor Unions: Social Work Touches on Organized Industry," *Proceedings of the National Conference of Social Work* (New York: Russell Sage Foundation, 1929), 363–364.

37. *Social Work Today*, 1 (March–April 1934), 1.

in furnishes him with the ideal of a better world that he can help realize, and with guidance and leadership he soon becomes part of the surging force that is building a new life and new hope."[38]

Although on the surface the AASW appeared to be much more conservative than the unions, the difference may have been more illusory than real. First, the AASW may not have been as conservative as the rank and file movement liked to accuse it of being. Reed's paper on the "Efforts of Social Workers Toward Social Reorganization" shows that professional social workers were willing to openly advocate radical social change when they felt it necessary, and that they often did during the Depression years.[39] On the other hand, the union membership may not have been as radical as its leadership. Writing in the July 1936 issue of *The Survey*, Maurice Taylor wrote, "Membership in AFW (Association of Federation Workers) has come, on the part of many, through coercion and an unwillingness to face isolation. There has been a conflict of emotions among certain workers who, while recognizing the desirability of organization for certain ends, and not sure how the methods employed square with their individual professional philosophy."[40]

The different philosophies of the AASW and the unions resulted in interest in different, although sometimes overlapping, issues. For its part the AASW was mainly interested in issues concerning advancement of social work as a profession. For example, in 1929 the AASW pursued four major activities: (1) membership requirements; (2) negotiating an agreement with the US Census Bureau to classify social work as a profession rather than its previous classification as a semi-profession; (3) a committee was organized to study preparation for social work and a series of job analyses sponsored by the Russell Sage Foundation was worked on; and (4) another committee prepared a study of the relationship of social work to several closely related fields. In addition to these activities, chapters in California attempted to get a licensing bill through the state legislature.[41] During the Depression the interests and activities broadened a bit beyond such narrow professional status concerns. The organization began to devote increasing attention to problems of public policy as well as with personnel practices. In 1939 the AASW was divided into three divisions to reflect its broadened major interests. These divisions were Government and Social Work; Employment Practices; and Personnel Standards.

The unions, for their part, were primarily concerned with two types of issues. The first and most important concerns were issues dealing with wages and working conditions. Emphasis was placed on support of the merit system, achieving collective bargaining rights for public employees, and the inclusion of private agency employees under the provisions of the Social Security Act. The second, and less important type of issues concerning social work unions were various social issues. Relief, public works, social security, the labor movement, fascism, war, and the like, were all of interest.

The involvement of the United States in the Second World War brought about changes in the activities of both the AASW and the unions, but the thrust of their activities was still different. The basic protective function of the unions, the fight for recognition, collective bargaining, and

---

38. Edith Waller, book review of *I Love. Social Work Today*, 3 (Jan. 1936), 30.

39. Ellery F. Reed, "Efforts of Social Workers toward Social Reorganization," *Social Forces*, 14 (Oct. 1935), 87–93.

40. Maurice Taylor, "Tactics of Social Work Unions," *The Survey*, 72 (Oct. 1936), 234.

41. Ida White Parker, "Social Work as a Profession," *Social Work Yearbook, 1929* (New York: Russell Sage Foundation, 1929), 437.

the merit system, continued. However, an increasing emphasis was placed on the war effort. For example, activities of the State, County, and Municipal Workers of America (CIO), to which the majority of unionized social workers belonged, were in three main areas—they marshalled thousands of union and non-union government employees for volunteer civilian war services; they cooperated with city governments in setting up emergency social services to be brought into action in the event of invasion; and they worked with the administration around wage stabilization, increase in sub-standard wages, office and staff efficiency, and interpretation to the community of the basic role of social services in total war mobilization.[42]

Like the unions, the AASW changed its programs in response to the war. However, the AASW was less concerned with the total war effort than with the specific effects of the war on social conditions and therefore, social work practice. "The program of the American Association of Social Workers reflects the effort of professional social workers to cope with the important problem of social dislocation at home and abroad." One of the most active groups was the Committee on Organization and Planning of the Social Services in the War and Postwar Period. This committee was concerned with formulating a platform statement of social services, and promulgation and interpretation of the Association's position on public social services, and the assembly of data to support this position.[43]

The rank and file movement rose to be a significant force in social work very quickly, going from obscurity to prominence in a few short years. It began its decline and reached its demise almost as quickly. Beginning in 1929, the movement reached its zenith and began its decline around 1936. The reason for the rapid decline can be attributed to both internal and external factors. The internal factors were the result of union members maturing and gaining social work experience. In the early years of the movement the typical member was a raw, young, brand new social worker quick to accept radical explanations of social problems being the result of an oppressive capitalist social system. He or she was also quick to resent what they saw to be the pretensions of professionally trained and oriented social workers who they felt lorded over them with claims of largely illusory knowledge and skills. By 1936 these union members tended to be seasoned social workers who, having faced situations like John Willems when he failed to prevent the suicide of the depressed Mr. Martens, began to appreciate the need for in-depth knowledge and a high degree of technical skill. *Social Work Today*, which began with mostly articles critical of American society and full of praise for the Soviet Union, by 1936 closely resembled *The Compass* with most articles focusing on casework technique.

Another factor in the decline of the rank and file movement is the gradual disillusionment of members in the face of little evidence of effectiveness on the part of the unions. Relatively early in the movement Taylor had noted, "the threat of strike as used by labor in industry is held inapplicable to social work which operates on a non-profit basis."[44] The movement's journal *Social Work Today*, which played up union achievements as much as possible, reported little of consequence

---

42. Frank C. Bancroft, "Trade Unionism in Social Work," *Social Work Yearbook: 1943* (New York: Russell Sage Foundation, 1943), 523.

43. Joseph P. Anderson, "Social Work as a Profession," *Social Work Yearbook: 1945* (New York: Russell Sage Foundation, 1945), 452.

44. Maurice Taylor, "Tactics of Social Work Unions," 112.

during its nine years of publication. It is true that working conditions in public agencies improved, but this was probably more a result of the relief situation stabilizing and public welfare workers being changed from temporary to permanent employees than of any direct union action.

Equally significant in the decline of the rank and file movement were external factors. As the 1930s progressed some of the working conditions that had fueled resentment among public welfare workers improved. Pay increased a bit, some of the workers were promoted to supervisory and management positions, and in 1939 amendments to the Social Security Act gave the Social Security Board authority to require that states establish merit systems. Another external factor that contributed to the decline of the rank and file movement was the gradual improvement of the economy and the end of the Depression as a result of America's entry into World War II. America's entry into the war rapidly changed the economy from being characterized by a job shortage to one characterized by a labor shortage. When the public welfare departments had begun in 1933 most of the people they employed were there because it was the only job available to them, a situation bound to contribute to dissatisfaction. By the early 1940s any public welfare department employee unhappy with his or her job could easily enter another line of work. Finally, the war itself led to a more patriotic, conservative, nation. During the chaos of the Depression the public's faith in the social and economic system of the nation was shaken. Public sentiment encouraged people to experiment with new ideas, among which were socialism, communism, and unionism. The three were often closely related, and were even more so in the public mind. The success of the New Deal in restructuring American Capitalism, especially as the nation entered the war, coupled with patriotism stirred by the war, changed the temper of the times to one of less tolerance of radical ideas.

The end of the rank and file movement in social work came with virtually no mention of its passing. In May of 1943 *Social Work Today* published volume nine, number six. The editorial page spoke in a very optimistic tone of the future of the journal and announced that it would be published during the summer for the first time. It even contained a preview of the summer issue and solicited suggestions for future issues. Not only did the promised summer issue not appear, the journal was never to appear again. In a similar, if less abrupt, fashion, mention of the rank and file movement gradually faded out of the *Social Work Yearbook*. From 1935 to 1943 there was an article devoted to the movement in each volume. In 1945 the article became "Labor and Social Work" and was mainly concerned with professional social workers practicing in blue collar unions, providing what are now called employee assistance services. Only scant mention was made of social workers as union members. In the 1947 *Yearbook* coverage was down to one column. The 1947 volume was the last to contain any mention of social work unions at all.

THE PROFESSIONAL ELITE

The group we are calling the professional elite are those social workers who had advanced training and membership in the AASW. These are the social workers who had been organizing and advocating for social work to be recognized not only as a full profession, but as a high status one. For these folks the Depression and the taking over of anti-poverty programs by the public sector necessitated some fairly quick decisions about the direction the profession should take. An obvious move for these social workers to take would have been to say "Well, we've been in the business of studying, administering, and reforming anti-poverty programs for over fifty years. We are the experts in this area and everyone recognizes this. We will move our organizational base from the family service (formerly COS) agencies into the new government public welfare departments." As we have already discussed, the profession did not do this. It did, in fact, quite the opposite, refusing to recognize public welfare as a legitimate part of social work practice and denying membership to the legion of new, lesser qualified, public welfare workers. This, of course, left the profession with a major problem—if anti-poverty work was no longer to be central to the profession, what was its center to be? Having decided what professional social work was not—it was not to be the main profession in the emerging public welfare system, and it was not going to offer skilled professional casework services to public welfare recipients—social work leaders continued with their efforts to define what social work is. One of the major questions of concern to professional leaders was derived from the fact that social work was practiced in so many organizational settings. Social workers worked in hospitals, mental hospitals, child welfare agencies, juvenile justice agencies, and numerous other settings. The question was asked whether social work had a generic set of skills that could be applied to any setting, or was it really a number of separate professions, the child welfare worker being significantly different than the psychiatric social worker, for example. In order to address this question a group of seventeen agency executives from six national organizations met for two days each summer from 1923 to 1929 in Milford Pennsylvania at what came to be called the Milford Conference.

The final report of the Milford Conference was published in 1929 under the title *Social Casework: Generic and Specific.* The main conclusion of the report was "the emergence of a strong conviction unanimously held by the members of the Conference that a fundamental conception which had come to be spoken of as "generic social case work" was much more substantial in content and much more significant in its implications for all forms of social case work than were any of the specific emphases of the different case work fields." Although social workers may work in many agencies dealing with many "deviations from accepted standards of normal social life" (the report listed 42 ranging from alcoholism to vagrancy), social case work skill was not in the undoubtedly necessary knowledge about the problem being dealt with, but that "the distinguishing concern of social casework is the capacity of the individual to organize his own normal social activities in a given environment."[45]

Having concluded that social case workers were characterized by one generic set of skills, it now became imperative that those skills be more clearly and closely delineated. As reviewed in the last chapter, the profession was already moving toward a psychology/psychiatry based practice that was oriented toward casework/counseling with people with individual adjustment problems. This direction was set with the Red Cross Home Service during the First World War, described in Mary Jarrett's 1919 "The Psychiatric Thread Running Through All Social Casework," and received full development in Virginia Robinson's 1929 book "*A Changing Psychology of Social Casework.*"

---

45. American Association of Social Workers, "Social Case Work: Generic and Specific: An Outline, A Report of the Milford Conference," *Studies in the Practice of Social Work* no. 2 (New York: American Association of Social Workers, 1929): 3, 16.

As a result of choosing to emphasize a generic individual casework definition of the profession and to deemphasize social change and economic justice issues, the major professional knowledge development activity during the Depression years was a curious little intellectual battle between two psycho-therapeutic approaches to casework known as the functional school and the diagnostic school.

THE FUNCTIONAL/DIAGNOSTIC DEBATE

When social work entered its "psychological phase" in the late 1920s most schools and agencies followed the lead of the New York School (Columbia University) uncritically accepting the theories and methods of Sigmund Freud. This approach came to be called the diagnostic school of social casework. A smaller group of social workers centered at the University of Pennsylvania and led by Jessie Taft and Virginia Robinson, developed what was called the functional school of casework, based on the theories of Freud's renegade disciple Otto Rank. Although both of these schools of practice were psycho-therapeutic, both were rooted in Freudian psychology, and both viewed the role of the caseworker as that of a therapist, there were several significant differences in their respective approaches to social casework, differences that assumed much greater significance at the time than they do when viewed from a historical perspective.

The first difference between the schools was in their understanding of human nature. The Freudian diagnostic school took a basically negative view of the nature of humanity, viewing people as driven by unconscious forces (the id) with the result that people were perceived as having an essentially selfish nature. The result of this conception was that the diagnostic practitioner worked from a psychology of illness, with the worker responsible for diagnosing and treating a pathological condition and the center of change residing in the worker. The functional school believed in a psychology of growth occurring within the context of relationship, with the center of change in the client, not in the worker. The relationship between the worker and client was the factor that released the client's own power for choice and growth. While the diagnostic school used the terms "treating" or "treatment" the functional school used the term "helping."

The second difference between the schools, an outgrowth of the first, is the concept of time and diagnosis in the case work process. The diagnostic school was a long term therapeutic model based on an in-depth investigation of the clients' life history. The functional school believed in short-term treatment, focusing on the here and now. A central technique of functional treatment was that of "partializing," focusing only on the immediate issues of concern to the client. The diagnostic school, by contrast, believed in the importance of examining and treating the total personality of the client, even if the client had come only for help with a limited and specific problem. The functional school rejected the necessity of a formal diagnosis of the client's problem and the setting of specific treatment goals, believing that these would emerge in the course of the worker/client relationship. The diagnostic school insisted on the importance of differential diagnosis and on setting short and long-term treatment goals.

A third, and critical, difference between the two schools was their view of the place of the social agency in the casework process. Because the diagnostic school was based on a belief in illness as the basic problem plaguing any client, and discovery of the root causes of the problem as the basis for a cure, it was inconsequential whether the worker was seeing the client in a hospital, child welfare, mental health, or any other specific setting. The role of the worker, and the goal of the treatment, was to diagnose the client's fundamental problem and, based on the assumptions of the medical model, once the dynamics of the problem were uncovered the cure would naturally occur. Whether the problem manifested itself in a behavioral problem, parent child difficulties, marital tension, or whatever, the problem, process, and cure would be the same so the agency within which the process occurred was not important. The functional school, on the other hand, believed that the social agency setting of the client/worker encounter was of paramount importance. The functional school saw the experience of the client in his or her relationship with the social worker within the specific agency setting and how the client used the agency's functions as the key to personal change and problem solution. These workers saw the purpose of the agency as representing partial or social work's overall purpose and as giving focus, direction, and content to the worker's practice. Casework method was viewed as not a form of social treatment of individuals but a method for administering some specific social service with such psychological understanding of, and skill in, the helping process that the agency's service had the best chance of being used for the individual's and society's welfare. Dunlap nicely summarizes this important principle of the functional casework approach: "The agency gives focus, direction, and content to the worker's practice. By so doing the agency protects both the worker and the client. Casework is not a form of psychosocial treatment, but a method for administering a specific social service."[46]

Another difference between the two schools, one that was the result of their differing conceptions of the purpose of treatment, was that of time. Because the diagnostic school viewed the role of the social worker to be getting at the root (usually childhood) causes of a client's problems, treating the total personality of the client, and viewed the client as ill and needing to be cured, the case work process was open ended and could, usually did, take place over a long period of time. The functional school, believing that the role of the social worker was to help the client make the best use of specific services offered by a social agency in order to solve a specific problem, focused on the here and now and on offering short term services. The functional school believed in partializing, that is focusing only on the immediate issues presented by the client.

A final important difference between the two schools was their conception of client psychology. The diagnostic school was based on the classic Freudian conceptualization of human psychological functioning resulting from the id, ego, and superego, which had each developed over the course of a person's lifetime. Change could only result from uncovering all the events that had impacted this largely subconscious development and this change had to be guided by the case worker. The functional school, while accepting the idea of classic Freudian personality development, rejected the idea that the client's total personality had to be unraveled to solve a problem and based treatment on the concept of "will". According to this approach, clients possessed a conscious will and were characterized by the potential for self-determination. They could use their will and their power of self-determination to change even if they (and their social worker) never fully understood the root causes of their problem. The role of the social worker was only to help

46.   Katherine M. Dunlap, "Functional Theory and Social Work Practice," in Francis J. Turner, ed., *Social Work Treatment*, 4th ed. (New York: The Free Press, 1996), 319–340.

the client use his or her will to solve their own problems, not to provide the solution for them. As Taft noted in 1932, "The anxious parent, the angry school teacher, the despairing wife or husband, must bear their own burdens, solve their own problems. I can help them only in and for themselves, if they are able to use me. I cannot perform magic on the bad child, the inattentive pupil, the faithless partner, because they want him made over in their own terms ... the [social worker] must accept [his or her] final limitation and the right of the other,—perhaps his necessity, — to refuse help or to take help in his own terms, not as therapist, friends or society might choose. My knowledge and my skill avail nothing unless they are accepted and used by the other."[47]

Given the truly large and significant issues that social workers were wrestling with in the 1930s—should social work focus on individual treatment or social change; should social work be practiced in the public or the private sector; must all social workers have graduate level training; should social work seek a complex technical skill or should they merely be friends and neighbors—it seems odd that so much time and energy would be devoted to the functional/diagnostic debate, an issue that can, in historical perspective, be clearly seen as a tempest in a teapot. But at the time it was seen as a huge issue, one that Dunlap has described as "the great schism." She explains: "Each group defended its stance with evangelistic fervor, for each believed it had found the way to end psychic pain and mental illness. The polemic was public and painful ... "[48] Ehrenreich describes the debate as "extraordinarily bitter, even vitriolic." Graduates of the two functional graduate schools, Pennsylvania and North Carolina, could not get jobs in agencies run by diagnostic case workers, and vice versa. Helen Harris Perlman recalls: "going to a conference in Atlantic City—I think it was 1938—where a group of us went into a restaurant and a very bright waiter met us at the door and asked: "What side of the room do you want to sit on, the diagnostic or the functional?"[49]

So the question is, why did this disagreement about a relatively petty difference between two case work approaches assume such outsize proportion? The reason, according to historian John Ehrenreich, is that the real issue behind this schism was not about two different approaches to social work practice but was really a much larger issue about what was the nature and basis for the social work profession itself. The diagnostic school was based on Flexner's belief that a profession had to have complete autonomy, that is, the practitioners had to have a skill that was not dependent on an office in an organization as the basis for its authority. The caseworker's authority was based on superior knowledge and skill, not on a position within an organization. Thus the diagnostic school's belief that the practice of the social worker was the same whether occurring in a child welfare agency, a hospital, or a private practice therapy setting. The functionalists belief that social work practice occurred within an agency context and largely consisted of helping a client identify and make use of the appropriate agency services to address his or her problem, was viewed by the diagnostic school as relegating social work to a semi-professional status at best. Adherents of the functionalist approach, for their part, believed that it was the diagnostic school that provided a

47. Jessie Taft, "The Time Element in Mental Hygiene Therapy as Applied to Social Case Work," *Proceedings of the National Conference of Social Work* (New York: Russell Sage Foundation, 1932), 369.

48. Katherine Dunlap, "Functional Theory and Social Work Practice," 324.

49. John H. Ehrenreich, *The Altruistic Imagination: A History of Social Work and Social Policy in the United States* (Ithaca, New York: Cornell University Press, 1985), 125–126.

weak basis for professionalism. Functionalist leader Jessie Taft, for example, argued that the diagnostic school's embracing of psychoanalysis as the foundation of social work "rules out the administering of actual services as the core of casework with its own authentic skill and goal and forces the worker to an unwarranted assumption of psychoanalytic diagnostic authority. . . It leaves case work with nothing it can do in its own right, so that its only hope is to obtain the services of a psychiatrist or a highly specialized psychiatric social worker to direct the many case workers who lack special training and first-hand experience of psychoanalysis."[50]

Although a functional school of casework continued to exist, by the mid-1940s it was clear that it had lost the battle for intellectual dominance of social work and that the profession was clearly led by the diagnostic school. Ehrenreich observes, " Social work succeeded in ignoring Taft and Robinson's challenge to the underlying basis of social work professionalism and their effort to bring social work into a new relation with the newly developed welfare state . . . It is ironic . . . that social work, so desperately anxious to this day about its "knowledge base," [was] so quick to dismiss what must count as its most intellectually rigorous and culturally important contribution to the theory and practice of helping emotionally troubled people."[51]

THE BROADENING BEGINS

By the 1930s the traditional, elite, model of the social work profession, a model based more on sociological theory and political aspirations than on reality, was firmly dominant in the field. Social work, as defined by the AASW and by schools of social work, was narrowed to casework following a medical model. This definition was fine but it excluded more than half of people working at full time paid jobs that the general public, and the workers themselves, considered to be social work. Among those excluded from the elite's definition were people working in settlement houses, YMCAs, and community centers. These agencies provided services mainly in the form of group activities to a clientele who were considered to be functioning normally, that is, lacking any psychopathology. The social workers in these agencies considered themselves to have skills in group leadership rather than therapy and counseling. These social workers were often trained at the graduate level, held membership in the AASW, and considered themselves to be fully qualified professional social workers. Another group of highly trained, professionally qualified social workers who did not fit the narrow casework definition of a professional were those who were involved in the fund raising, planning, implementing, coordinating, and assessing the programs that the caseworkers and group workers practiced in. Some of these people worked in the administration of large social agencies and many worked in federated funding programs, now called the United Way, but earlier in the twentieth century called Red Feather or Community Chest. This group of social workers was beginning to identify itself as community organization. And finally, of course, there was the vast army of social workers with less than graduate training who were employed by the emerging public welfare system.

50. John H. Ehrenreich, *The Altruistic Imagination,* 129–136.
51. John H. Ehrenreich, *The Altruistic Imagination,* 137–138.

Recognition of Group Work

Caseworkers were initially skeptical about how professional the activities of group workers were, saying that leading hobby clubs, self-help classes, and political action groups were fine activities, but hardly rose to the level of professional technique. Group workers, for their part, were convinced that something positive happened when people participated in a well-run group but they had a hard time identifying what it was and how it happened. When Mary P. Follett described the formation of opinion and organization for action as it occurred in small groups as the kernel of democratic process, group workers eagerly seized upon it. At long last they saw the basis for analysis of process in what they had previously been doing in an opportunistic way. At about the same time the progressive education movement was pointing out the values of free association and the leadership rather than authoritarian role of the good teacher. This was easily translated to apply to the approach of a good social group worker.[52]

Group workers looked to education rather than psychiatry for the philosophical and theoretical basis for their practice. It was the writing of John Dewey, rather than Sigmund Freud, that group workers read and discussed. In fact, during the 1920s there was a good deal of discussion of whether group work belonged more to the profession of education than to social work. However, by the 1930s group workers were unified in their desire to be identified as professional social workers. In 1934 fifty group workers gathered at the annual meeting of the National Conference of Social Work and formed the National Association for the Study of Group Work. From that year forward group work was given official recognition, and a place on the agenda, at every meeting of the National Conference.

In 1935 Wilber Newstetter, a leader in the effort to have group work recognized by the National Conference and by the profession of social work, presented a paper at the annual meeting titled "What Is Social Group Work?" Newstetter defined group work as an educational process that had two foci. The first was the development and social adjustment of an individual through voluntary group association and the second was the use of this association as a means of furthering other socially desirable ends. For example, a group might be formed at a community center with the practical purpose of setting up a youth baseball league in the community. Over time the group would achieve this practical end, but in the process of doing so the group members would grow as human beings and as citizens of a democracy. Newstetter said that the technique, or process, of group leadership "is determined by (1) the objectives of the worker; (2) the adjustive efforts within the group itself; (3) the worker's observation and interpretation of the adjustive efforts within the group; (4) the skill of the worker in the selection and application of technique."[53] As time went on group workers became seduced by the lure of psychotherapy that had trapped case workers and began to more and more define group work as a psychological technique and as a therapeutic adjunct to casework.

Group work was quickly accepted as a full member of the profession of social work with relatively little controversy. There were several reasons for this rapid acceptance. The first is that social

52. Mary P. Follett, *The New State* (New York: Longmans, Green and Co., 1918), 24–33.

53. Wilber I. Newstetter, "What Is Social Group Work," *Proceedings: National Conference of Social Work, 1935* (New York: Russell Sage Foundation, 1935), 191–199.

settlements, community centers, and similar agencies, had a long and well-respected place in the development of social work and the main function of these agencies was to host groups of many types. The second reason is that advocates, and leaders, of group work had long had an affiliation with respected schools of social work. Newstetter, for example, was a faculty member at the prestigious Western Reserve School of Applied Social Sciences. Finally, and perhaps most important, was that caseworkers quickly recognized the potential of groups for the psychological treatment of clients who did not respond to one-on-one counseling. As the Pumphreys have noted "Within the child guidance movement, it soon became apparent to caseworkers that in many children obstreperous or withdrawn behavior was only a symptom of their failure to relate to their peers and work cooperatively with others. Referral to interest groups usually was unsuccessful, as also frequently was casework. Efforts were then made to develop relationship ability by specially designed group experience. From beginnings such as Slavson's group therapy, based on psychiatric knowledge, [group work] became a recognized type of social work."[54]

Recognition of Community Organization

It should be recalled that the original primary purpose of the Charity Organization Society movement was not the establishment of social casework, but the organization of community agencies to rationally plan, fund, and administer social services. Casework, and the whole social work profession, grew out of COS plans that indicated that recipients of charity were also in need of skilled individual services. This led, as we have seen, the profession of social work, and the COS agencies themselves, into a radical over emphasis on the importance of individual treatment. However, even with this emphasis on case work, the COS agencies never lost their interest in identifying community needs, planning for programs to address these needs, and seeking funding to support these programs. It was the COS movement that created and led the anti-tuberculosis movement that eventually resulted in the establishment of public health departments and the profession of public health; the tenement house reform movement that led to strengthened housing laws and eventually to the establishment of municipal public housing authorities; and many other community organization activities on the local level.

As the programs of social agencies grew and became more complex social workers began to seek ways to bring order out of what often seemed like chaos. Two issues were prominent in this effort. One was that agency administrators and boards felt a need for some way to work out operational problems caused by gaps and overlaps in their services. The second issue was that financial contributors to agencies were concerned that they were receiving an increasing number of requests for donations, and were finding the number of requests bothersome and were also concerned that they lacked the time or expertise to separate worthy from unworthy requests. Shortly following the beginning of the twentieth century community and social work leaders in a number of communities began to meet to discuss these concerns. These meetings had two major outcomes. The

---

54. Ralph E. Pumphrey and Muriel W. Pumphrey, eds., *The Heritage of American Social Work: Readings in Its Philosophical and Institutional Development* (New York: Columbia University Press, 1961), 162.

first was the establishment in most major cities of a Council of Social Agencies (sometimes called the Community Council), an agency staffed by professionally trained and experienced social workers who were responsible for assessing community needs, identifying the agencies addressing these needs, identifying gaps and overlaps in services to meet the needs, advocating for the establishment of new agencies, or new programs within existing agencies to address these needs and, finally, devising ways to fund the services. The problem of funding was addressed by a movement known as federated funding. This movement, now primarily led by the United Way, grew out of the World War I war chest movement. The strategy then, as now, was to greatly expand the donor base by soliciting from a large number of small givers, usually solicited at their workplace, in addition to the smaller number of large donors. The federated funding agency, in cooperation with the Council of Community Services, would then take all the money and, based on research and the formal establishment of community social service goals, would evaluate agencies in terms of their efficiency, effectiveness, and relevance to the established goals, and would distribute and oversee the spending of the social service funds. The slogan of these early Red Feather or Community Chest agencies was "put all your ask its in one basket."[55]

When the profession turned so sharply toward a definition of itself as being based on skilled individual case work services, people who worked in community organization (most of whom had actually been trained and began their careers as case workers) began to feel, like the group workers, that they had been left out and to organize and advocate for official recognition of their specialty. In 1933 the National Conference of Social Work officially recognized a Community Organization Section that met at each subsequent annual meeting to discuss common concerns. The major result of these discussions was the issuance, in 1939, of a report authored by Robert Lane, referred to as The Lane Report but officially titled "The Field of Community Organization." This report identified community organization as a field of social work practice comparable to case work and group work. Lane identified community work as both a process and a field of social work but as a rule not offering direct help to specific clientele. The objectives of community organization practice were identified as first, fact finding for planning and action; second, initiating, developing, and modifying social work services and programs; third, setting standards; and finally, fourth, promoting coordination between organizations, groups, and individuals.

SOCIAL WORK 1945

At the end of the Second World War, social workers were unanimous in defining social work as comprising three methods—case work, group work, and community organization. Schools of social work generally required students to select one of these fields as their area of specialization. Group work was moving further away from its educational and task group roots and becoming defined more and more as group therapy. The vast majority, around 85 percent, of students selected the case work specialization. Although, as Ehrenreich has noted, social work and a number of

55. Roy Lubove, *The Professional Altruist: The Emergence of Social Work as a Career, 1880–1930* (Cambridge, MA: Harvard University Press, 1965), 180, 182, 197–199.

other mental health disciplines quietly absorbed many of the theories, attitudes, and techniques of the functional approach to casework "it remains true in a deeper sense that the latter [the functional school] lost the debate within social work." In 1945 there were 42 accredited schools of social work and only two, the University of Pennsylvania and the University of North Carolina, were teaching the functional approach. This embracing of the diagnostic approach left social work with a problem that was to plague it for years, as noted by Trattner "what distinguished psychiatric casework from psychotherapy, except for the social workers' inferior education and training? Were psychiatric social workers mere handmaidens to psychiatrists?"[56]

The main challenge to the traditional social work profession, that of the undergraduate trained workers in the new public welfare departments, had largely been put to rest by 1945. The rank and file movement had died, proposals for admitting BA level workers to AASW as associate members had been defeated on several occasions, and attempts to get the American Association of Schools of Social Work to accredit undergraduate programs yielded little success. There was, however, a good deal of cooperation between the new public welfare departments and the social work profession. The Social Security Act specified that every public welfare department have at least one professionally trained social worker for every 20 case workers. As illustrated by the case example that opened this chapter, local welfare offices such at that in Green Bay, turned to *Social Diagnosis* and to the procedures of family social work agencies to develop their policies, procedures, manuals, and even their forms looked exactly like those developed in professional social work agencies. Early in 1934 the Federal Emergency Relief Administration allocated $420,000 to send staff to accredited social work schools for professional training (although only for part of a year, not for a degree) and 1137 caseworkers benefitted from this training. However, the profession steadfastly held to its position that only graduate trained social workers would be recognized as members of the profession.

56. Walter Trattner, *From Poor Law to Welfare State: A History of Social Welfare in America,* 6th ed. (New York: The Free Press, 1994), 268.

CHAPTER 10

AMERICA'S WELFARE STATE EXPERIMENT: 1945-1974

In the hit Broadway musical *West Side Story* that played to sold out crowds in the late 1950s and 1960s, and that became an Academy Award winning movie in 1961, members of a teenage gang sing the following verse parodying their social worker:

> *Officer Krupke, you've done it again.*
> *This boy don't need a job, he needs a year in the pen.*
> *It ain't just a question of misunderstood;*
> *Deep down inside him, he's no good!*[1]

West Side Story, which was a retelling of *Romeo and Juliet,* moved to twentieth century New York, revolved around two Manhattan gangs, the Sharks and the Jets. Like most good art, *West Side Story* was fictional, but the fiction was firmly rooted in reality. Gangs were at the time becoming a great concern in low income neighborhoods. In reality there were no gangs named the Sharks and Jets in Manhattan, but there were the Sportsman and the Dragons. These two large gangs controlled the area around the Cahan Houses project, a large high rise apartment complex at the foot of the Williamsburg Bridge. The Sportsman controlled the territory to the north of the projects and the Dragons the area to the south. These gangs were not as dangerous as gangs have become in the twenty-first century, now being essentially criminal business enterprises dealing in drugs, prostitution, and so forth, but they were violent none-the-less, fighting being one of their major pass times. As the journalist Robert Rice noted in an 1965 article in *The New Yorker*, by fighting "I don't mean

1. "Gee Officer Krupke," *West Side Story,* Music by Leonard Bernstein, lyrics by Stephen Sondheim, copyright 1956, 1957 Amberson Holdings LLC and Stephen Sondheim. Copyright renewed. Leonard Bernstein Music Publishing Company LLC, Publisher.

wrestling on the sidewalk or fisticuffs in the park but murderous fighting with bricks and broken bottles and bicycle chains and knives and, if possible, guns."[2]

A group of eight boys—Thomas Burke, Ismael Flores, Pedro Flores, Antonio Vidal, Carlos Cintron, Cesar Santiago, Harry Young, and Alfonso Jimeniz—all lived in Cahan Houses and attended P.S. 5 elementary school. They became fast friends and together hung out at the Grand Street Settlement House where they, and six or eight others who rotated in and out of the group, constituted one of the many youth clubs sponsored by the agency, naming themselves the Continentals. As the Continentals they participated in a number of the settlement's activities, but their main focus was basketball, an activity they were good enough at to one year win the middle school championship. Middle junior high school was an age when boys in the Lower East Side had to make a decision whether or not to join a gang. Joining had the benefit of providing protection for the member, but also required that the member buy into the aggressive, violent, life style of the gang. The Sportsman were mostly black and the Dragons were Puerto Rican. The Continentals, being Puerto Rican, were recruited by the Dragons. The Continentals were not averse to fighting for self-defense, and they were not opposed to a little criminal activity or general mischief, but they did not have the stomach for the very violent, hyper aggressive behavior of the Dragons. So, the solution the boys hit upon was to adopt the street name the Cahanmen and identify themselves as an independent street gang. For whatever reason the Dragons recognized the legitimacy of the Cahanmen as a gang and for the most part left them alone. The only real enemy of the Cahanmen was another small independent gang named (no kidding) the Bopping Ballerinos. The Ballerinos would conceal themselves on rooftops or behind fences at 3:00 when the Cahanmen got out of school and bombard them with rocks and bottles. Nights could be even more deadly, Tony Vidal reporting that "Everybody had a secret way to get home."

The Continentals, nee Cahanmen, had never been model youth, being continually in trouble with their parents, the school authorities, and on occasion, the police, but until junior high they were relatively functional young people. At age eleven or twelve they began to go quickly downhill, cutting school, drinking wine, and later alternating the wine drinking with smoking marijuana. By the time the boys were fifteen heroin had become a scourge in the city with an estimated 50,000 addicts by the early 1960s, and the boys added this to their list of vices. By age sixteen all of the boys had dropped out of school, essentially becoming full-time heroin addicts. Given their low level of education, generally anti-social attitude, and drug and alcohol habits, getting and keeping a job was not in the cards. The boys supported themselves and their drug habits by a combination of stealing (sometimes from their own families), hustling, and scheming. The difference between hustling and scheming is that scheming was verbal behavior (i.e., you talk your Mom into giving you twenty dollars because you convince her you need a new coat) and hustling is active behavior (you pawn the coat your mother gave you for three dollars).

The boys continued to hang out at the Grand Street Settlement House, although after age sixteen this mostly consisted of nodding off while high sitting on the front steps. In the early 1960s the settlement was doing very well, launching a number of new programs funded mostly by the federal Mobilization for Youth (MFY) program. The MFY programs run by the settlement were aimed at

2. This quote, as well as general information related to this case history, is from Robert Rice, "Junk," The New Yorker, May 27, 1965, 50–61 and 124–142.

reducing juvenile delinquency and addressed just about every social problem in the lower east side except narcotics addiction. The reason the agency had not yet addressed the drug issue is that, by their own admission, they did not understand it, they did not realize just how extensive it had become, and they viewed it as an individual behavior problem and they were more interested in addressing structural problems such as unemployment and community disorganization. The thinking of the Grand Street social workers was that heroin was "a disease about which little is known, and that little is of little help." However, by 1963 the agency was coming to realize that its programs were all being negatively affected by the area's drug abuse problem. Two examples were the World of Work employment program that included forty-five addicts among its participants, and not one was able to complete the program, and two coffee shops run by the agency that were intended to be wholesome hang-out places for neighborhood youth that had quickly devolved into locations for addicts to nod in.

By the fall of 1963 the leadership of the Grand Street Settlement had decided that they would have to address the problem of drug use among their young people. Being a settlement house they had relatively little interest in programs providing individual psychotherapy or counseling as an approach. Numerous individual drug treatment programs were already being run, to little obvious effect, by area family service and mental health agencies. The bread and butter of settlements has always been group programs and so the agency naturally took a group approach to this new target for their services. The Grand Street social workers came to be heavily influenced by the work of criminologist Donald R. Cressey who had applied the differential association theory of Edwin Sutherland to correctional work with criminals. According to Cressey this theory has "provided an alternative principle on which to base the diagnosis and treatment of criminals, namely, that the behavior, attitudes, beliefs, and values which a person exhibits are not only the *products* of group contacts but also the *properties* of groups. If the behavior of an individual is an intrinsic part of groups to which he belongs, attempts to change the behavior must be directed at groups. . . persons become criminals principally because they have been relatively isolated from groups whose behavior patterns (including attitudes, motives, and rationalizations) are anticriminal or because . . . something has brought them into relatively frequent association with the behavior patterns of criminal groups."[3]

Based on the theories of Cressey and Sutherland, and a set of six practice principles that social psychologist Dorwin Cartwright[4] had developed from these theories, the Grand Street social workers wrote a funding proposal and submitted it to Mobilization for Youth. The proposal, titled "Draft Proposal for an Experimental Group and Work Treatment for Young Addicts" proposed to find an existing group of about twenty young addicts and assign a full-time social worker to work with them. Under the leadership of the social worker the young men would make a group resolution to give up drug use. Once they had all signed on to this resolution they would, as a group, enter a hospital for detoxification. Once the members were clean they would leave the city for some kind of recreational program in the country that would last several weeks. Following this period the group would return to the city, but not to their old neighborhood and would live and

3. Donald R. Cressey, "Changing Criminals: The Application of the Theory of Differential Association," *American Journal of Sociology*, 61 (September 1955): 116–120.

4. Dorwin Cartwright, "Achieving Change in People: Some Applications of Group Dynamics Theory," *Human Relations*, 4 (1951): 381–392.

receive job training together. The hope was that the group members would first lose their chemical addiction to heroin and then, under the leadership of the social worker, would develop strong group norms that were opposed to drug use.

The Grand Street social workers identified the Continentals as a group that might be interested in such a program. After four years of more or less constant drug use the boys were showing signs of fatigue. In fact, several of the members had attempted to kick the drug habit on their own but, with the exception of Pedro, did not succeed. As journalist Robert Rice observed when reporting on the group, "It is hard to exaggerate the panic felt by a habitual user of heroin when he wakes in the morning with a churning stomach, an itching nose, watery eyes, sore joints, and not enough money for his next dose. All the Continentals woke up that way more mornings than not for nearly four years." In addition, all of the group members were having problems with their girlfriends who were tired of going to movies, parties, and so forth with partners who only sat there and nodded off, generally not even remembering the activity the next day. Social worker Roger Crawford, who was described as a burly Philadelphian who was charming almost to the point of being seductive, was assigned to the group with the goal of getting them to agree to participate in the experimental group drug rehabilitation program. Crawford explained the proposal to the group carefully, a little at a time, over a period of several weeks, with the result that they agreed to its terms with scarcely an objection. Because there were only eight Continentals available to join the project Crawford and two additional social workers assigned to the project, Angel Camacho and Patrick Kelley, worked with the group to identify eight additional addicts that would be acceptable group members. These eight were recruited, making the treatment group sixteen, a number acceptable to the funding agency.

The hope was for the project to begin in April of 1964, but difficulties finding a hospital willing to take the group and also with finding a location to host the second stage, the "camp experience" stage, delayed the program's beginning until summer. Before the program even began two of the group members were arrested and jailed and one of the late addition boys was murdered, leaving a group of thirteen to check into Manhattan General Hospital on June 29 to begin the detoxification stage of the project. On the second day in the hospital one of the non-Continentals signed himself out, a few days later a second left, and ten days later a third. All of the Continentals and three of the additional participants stuck it out for the full three weeks of treatment.

Following completion of the hospital detoxification program the eleven remaining participants were transported to a camp in the Catskills, about 100 miles from New York City. The camp was a conventional summer camp, its owner had decided to not open that summer due to health issues, but he was happy to rent it to Grand Street for a program that he did not have to run. For the first three weeks of this stage of the project the boys engaged in typical summer camp activities—swimming, boating, fishing, crafts, and so forth—however, they soon became bored with this and so the social workers arranged for part time jobs for them clearing brush for the power company. After six weeks the social workers felt that group cohesiveness had been maximized and that a firm anti-drug culture had developed that would be sufficient to keep the boys clean. It was therefore decided that it was time to return the group to the city and begin the third stage of the process, reintegration into mainstream life.

The group returned to the city on September 1, 1964 and took up residence in housing provided by a church on the edge of the Grand Street neighborhood. This was too close to their old environment for the liking of the social workers, but was the best situation that could be found. Everyone realized that this was the beginning of the most difficult phase of the project and, unfortunately, it was during this stage that the project broke down. Tommy was the first to fall, returning to drug use only a week after returning to the city. He was, in violation of one of the basic principles of the project, given a second chance and allowed to return to the housing. He repaid this kindness by leaving again for a drug binge, this time taking Cesar with him. Cesar then convinced Alfonso to join them and it was soon revealed that Harry had been using since his first day back in the city. At this point the social workers relocated the remaining five participants to a hotel far from their home neighborhood. Of these five, three, Ishmael, Tony, and Chino began job training programs but found them too stressful and returned to their old addict street lives. Only Frankie and Leroy remained in the project after the end of October. Frankie was clean but not sober, having begun to drink heavily. He was still on probation, and because drinking was a violation of the terms of his probation, he was returned to jail. Leroy was the single participant for whom the project could be considered a success. By December he had found a good office job, was planning on returning to college, and appeared to be heading for a full recovery. The project was terminated in January 1965 with the Continentals' status being summarized by the project evaluator as, "Group cohesiveness, except as expressed against the staff, was gone; education was a dead issue; work, after the need for Christmas money was gone, was neglected . . . No further progress was envisaged in this situation."

We begin this chapter with a description of this program not because the program itself was particularly significant—it was after all only one of hundreds of drug treatment programs that have had limited success at best—but rather because it encapsulates the spirit of the 1945 to 1974 era regarding social issues in the United States. This was a heady, incredibly optimistic time in social work and social welfare, as well as in the nation in general, in which a problem approach was followed that consisted of several related aspects. First a problem was "discovered," often with much fanfare, publicity, and outrage. In the case of the Grand Street project the problem was drug abuse. Also discovered, as we shall discuss later, were juvenile delinquency, poverty, child abuse, foster home failure, and "snake pit" mental hospitals. Next, governmental and private organizations would commit large sums of money dedicated to finding solutions to the problems identified. Then social science experts would be called upon to provide explanations of the problems and professionals, notably social workers, would be hired to implement programs informed by the social scientists to address the problems. Finally, the programs would be assessed, by objective social scientists evaluating results, by journalists looking for a good story, and by politicians seeking an issue for political gain, with, in nearly all cases, the conclusion being that the program had cost too much, promised too much, accomplished too little and may even, in hindsight, seemed silly. A 52 page article in the premier literary magazine *The New Yorker*, reporting on the program described earlier was titled "Junk." This title was a double entendre referring to heroin, at the time colloquially referred to as junk, and also to the program, which the author considered to be junk, i.e. worthless and useless.

1945–1974: AN ERA
OF GRAND EXPECTATIONS

The 1947 movie *The Best Years of Our Lives* won seven academy awards. The movie follows the readjustment to civilian life of a group of military veterans and, besides being a well-acted and directed movie, its immense popularity was due to the fact that the anxieties of the characters reflected the anxieties of the nation as a whole. "Hard times are coming" one of the characters predicts reflecting the wide spread fear that the depression was just waiting in the wings to reappear once the huge government defense expenditures for the war were cut back. There was a good basis for these fears: 12.1 million military personnel had been released from the services without jobs to come home to. The Pentagon had cancelled $15 billion of defense contracts within two days of the Japanese surrender. Some economists were predicting 8 million unemployed by 1946, an unemployment rate of more than 13 percent of the labor force. But the pessimists were wrong. Four years of war with full employment and little in the way of consumer goods available to spend income on had resulted in a tremendous backlog of consumer demand. The nation's immense productive capacity built up supplying war materials was quickly converted to producing cars, washing machines, radios, clothing, and all other types of consumer products. Rather than the economy sinking into another depression, America experienced a quarter century of the fastest economic growth in history, a rate of 2.5 percent per year. Economist Ha-Joo Chang has labeled the years from 1945 to 1973 the golden age of capitalism.[5]

Part of the reason that America was able to sustain a quarter century of economic stability and growth was that people had formed an uneasy consensus behind government regulation and stimulation of the economy. The United States, as well as most other western democracies, rejected classical economic theory (the market keeps all producers alert and efficient, so government should leave it alone) and began to employ in its stead counter-cyclical macroeconomic policies, known as Keynesian economics, preventing wild swings in the market by expanding government spending and money supply from the central bank during economic downturns when unemployment is increasing and reducing them during upturns when inflation becomes a concern. Roosevelt's New Deal policies, which had been attacked and thwarted by conservatives since their implementation in 1937, became widely accepted and safe from repeal. In 1944 Congress passed the GI Bill of Rights that provided higher education benefits for millions of veterans and home buying assistance. One result was a building boom that went on for years and stimulated the entire economy. The Employment Act of 1946 and the Taft-Hartley Act of 1947 represented liberal and conservative approaches to managing the economy, but more important illustrated that both the left and the right were willing to have the federal government involved in this management.

The facts that America had won a war on two sides of the world, and then entered a period of nearly unbelievable prosperity, created a national euphoria, a belief that not only could America lead the world, but could solve old problems at home. Historian James Patterson refers to the attitude in America between 1945 and 1974 as "grand expectations." This refers to the American people's ever greater expectations following the end of World War II that they could create a better

5. Ha Joon Chang, *Economics: A User's Guide* (London: Pelican Books, 2014), 79–80.

world abroad and a happier society at home. Faith in the wealth of the United States and in the capacity of the federal government to promote progress also aroused an unprecedented rights consciousness. Patterson explains: "I call this grand quest for opportunity at home a rights revolution. It affected all manner of Americans, including people who were disadvantaged—minorities, the poor, women, and many others—and who demanded greater access to the ever-richer society that was glittering around them. The quest resulted in significant and lasting improvement in the economic and legal standing of millions of people. No comparable period of United States history witnessed so much economic and civic progress. In this golden age it often seemed that there were no limits to what the United States could do both at home and abroad."[6]

The center piece of this rights revolution was, of course, the civil rights movement by Black Americans, whereby they moved from legally mandated and enforced second class status to fully equal and entitled citizens. The wartime experience of fighting for freedom abroad while not being free at home sensitized a generation of African Americans to the injustice of their situation at home. One Black soldier encapsulated this feeling when he wrote, "Just carve on my tombstone, here lies a black man killed fighting a yellow man for the protection of a white man." Another wrote a "Draftee's Prayer":

Dear Lord, today
I go to war:
To fight, to die,
Tell me what for?
Dear Lord, I'll fight,
I do not fear,
Germans or Japs;
My fears are here,
America![7]

These veterans, along with their kin who had migrated from the rural south to the urban north in record numbers to work in war industries, exited the war with a resolve to close the gap between America's ideal of equality and its performance.

Early efforts by Blacks to improve their situations resulted in a wave of racist violence across the south; Black veterans seeking to vote were special targets. However, many white Americans felt uneasy about the contradiction between a crusade for freedom abroad and racial discrimination at home. At the end of the war Swedish social scientist Gunnar Myrdal published the results of a six year study of race relations in the United States commissioned by the Carnegie Foundation. The 1000 page report, titled *An American Dilemma*, looked at the gap between what he identified as the "American Creed," a sincere and deeply felt commitment to freedom and equal opportunity, and the social reality of the way African Americans were treated. In spite of the vast distance between the theory and the reality of life for minorities in America, Myrdal was optimistic about the

---

6. James T. Patterson, *Grand Expectations: The United States, 1945–1974* (New York: Oxford University Press, 1996), vii–viii.

7. William Leuchtenburg, ed., *The Unfinished Century: America Since 1900* (New York: Little, Brown & Co., 1973), 454.

future: "Not since Reconstruction has there been more reason to anticipate fundamental changes in American race relations, changes which will involve a development toward the American ideals . . . America relative to all the other branches of Western civilization, is moralistic and 'moral conscious.' . . . The main trend in its history is the gradual realization of the American Creed . . . In this sense the Negro problem is not only America's greatest failure but also America's incomparably great opportunity for the future."[8]

With the combination of a Black population who were determined to overcome their subservient role in society and a white population that was at the very least ambivalent about segregation in America, progress came quickly although not without a great deal of conflict. Following the war's end, President Truman and the Supreme Court engaged in a series of actions that presaged a new attitude toward equality and justice. In 1946 Truman appointed a federal level Committee on Civil Rights, ordered the Justice Department to support the NAACP in civil rights lawsuits, and ordered federal housing agencies to eliminate racially restrictive policies in public housing programs. In 1948 in the case of *Shelley v. Kramer* the Supreme Court declared deed restriction based on race to be illegal. In 1948 Truman ordered that there be "equality of treatment and opportunity" in the armed forces. In 1954 the Supreme Court ruled racial segregation in public schools to be inherently unequal and therefore unconstitutional. In a style that became popular in the 1950s the court relied on social science theory and research as the basis for their decision. Thurgood Marshall, the NAACP attorney representing the plaintiffs and later himself a Supreme Court Justice, argued that sociological evidence proved that segregation harmed black children. Psychologist Kenneth Clark testified about his research where black children, when asked to pick between a white and a black doll, most frequently chose the white doll because they said it was "prettier" and the black doll looked "bad." From this research he concluded that segregation had harmed the children's self-image. This series of executive and court actions combined with acts of civic protest by African Americans and their white supporters, notably the 1955 Montgomery bus boycott, a series of sit-ins that began at a Greensboro North Carolina Woolworth's lunch counter, and a number of freedom rides in the Deep South in the early 1960s eventually led to the passage of the 1964 Civil Rights Act and the 1965 Voting Rights Act.

From the very brief summary of civil rights in the era 1945 to 1974, it would be easy to conclude that America moved from being a racist to an anti-racist society during these years. While it is undoubtedly true that attitudes by the white majority toward blacks and other minorities were mitigated during these years, it is also true that a strong undercurrent of racism survived. It is this undercurrent that makes the civil rights progress during this era very significant for the history of social welfare. Prior to 1945 most programs that make up the formal institution of social welfare in this country were aimed at the needs of, and overwhelmingly served, the white population. Government programs such as Social Security, Old Age Assistance, Aid to Dependent Children, public housing, surplus commodities (food assistance), children's programs, school services, and numerous others, were clearly aimed at the white population. Blacks were, at the very least, discouraged from applying. Private charities such as United Fund Agencies, community centers, free clinics, and so forth were also mainly

8. Gunner Myrdal, *An American Dilemma,* (New York: McGraw-Hill, 1964), lxi, lxx, 1021 (Reprint of 1944 original).

serving the white population. Programs and services to blacks tended to be run on a mutual aid basis with black institutions such as churches, black colleges, and black medical schools offering help to their neighbors. In most areas (certainly south of the Mason-Dixon line) Blacks knew not to bother to apply for mainstream programs because they realized that they would be turned down. As long as social welfare programs largely served a white clientele, especially the sick, elderly, handicapped, and widowed mothers (the "deserving poor") they were relatively non-controversial. Voters and politicians viewed them as serving "people like us" who were just down on their luck. With the success of the civil rights movement agencies were banned from discrimination based on race, and minorities felt empowered to demand their rights, not only to vote but to receive all the benefits to which they were legally entitled. As a result, during this era social welfare programs began to be viewed as targeted to minority group members, and in addition to members who were not the "deserving poor," for example an unwed mother, substance abuser, or a member of the chronically unemployed. This resulted in a loss of popular support for social welfare programs and steadily increasing opposition to them even in an era when they grew at a tremendous rate.

In this era America had "grand expectations" of our ability to solve social problems. The nation began the era identifying and learning about a number of issues, launched bold initiatives to attempt to solve the problems, and by the end of the era had become disillusioned with the results of our efforts. One of the approaches that was experimented with was the provision of expert social work services, directed at the victims of the various social problems, as a way to solve the problems. Areas with heavy social work involvement were poverty/public welfare, child protection, and mental health. By the end of the era there was a mutual disengagement between social work and poverty/public welfare as policy makers figured out that a case-by-case "retail" approach was not an effective anti-poverty strategy, and social workers figured out that those within the profession who had long argued that public welfare was not a venue hospitable to professional social work practice were correct after all. However, by the end of the era social work had become central to the mental health system with its new and growing focus on community care, and had become clearly recognized as the central profession in the rapidly growing child welfare system.

1945–1958: THE CONFIDENT YEARS

The era from the end of World War II until the late 1950s have sometimes been referred to as the confident years because this was a time of almost smug self-satisfaction among Americans that their nation was the greatest in history and was up to any challenge internationally or at home. However, this period could just as well be called the worried years. The biggest worry was, of course, the very real threat of nuclear holocaust. But there were also a number of fears related to American social welfare. Major areas of popular concern were the health of the nation, both physical and mental; the teenager as a newly recognized social group, and particularly with juvenile delinquency; and, most worrisome, the fact that poverty was still evident, in fact appeared to be growing, seemingly immune to the nation's almost unbelievable affluence.

Health and Mental Health

One of the byproducts of any war is that a great deal of data is gathered regarding the physical and mental health of the young men of the nation as a result of the screening process for the military draft. We are always shocked to find that the "flower of our youth" is not nearly as fit and hearty as we thought. This was especially true of the Second World War where fifteen million young men underwent physical and mental screening. To qualify for the draft a conscript had to stand at least five feet tall and weigh 105 pounds; possess twelve or more of his natural thirty-two teeth; not have flat feet, venereal disease, or hernias. Even with these low standards more than forty of every hundred men were rejected. Nearly two million of these were rejected for psychiatric reasons. In addition, by the end of the war half a million men from the army ground forces alone were discharged for psychiatric reasons.

Although the nation was very concerned about health care issues in the years immediately following the end of World War II, little progress was made on the issue for two related reasons. The first was highly organized opposition to governmental involvement in health care led by the medical profession orchestrated by the American Medical Association. Paul Starr has documented in his classic book *The Social Transformation of American Medicine*, how physicians were unique in that their profession was able to escape control by both the bureaucracy (government) and the corporation (business). They thus had the luxury of practicing as fully autonomous professionals and were hyper-vigilant in protecting this privilege. In order to protect this autonomy physicians opposed any government health program in an almost knee-jerk fashion. The second impediment to progress in governmental support of health care was the extreme anti-communism and anti-socialism of the era. National health insurance programs had originated, and experienced the most growth, in countries that Americans considered to be socialistic in leaning and thus were perceived as dangerous (the first step on a slippery slope, so to speak) by most citizens. These two reasons for opposition to national health insurance are closely related, as the fear of communism/socialism was exploited by the AMA to support its largely self-serving position.

The original plans for the Social Security Act had included a national health insurance scheme but this was dropped out of fear that it might bring down the whole effort. Beginning in 1939 the annual reports of the Social Security Board included lengthy discussions of health issues. In 1942 the Board expressed support for a unified and comprehensive social insurance system that would include a health plan. In 1943 the Board drafted a bill for national health insurance that was introduced by Senators Wagner and Murray and by Representative Dingell. As its drafters and sponsors expected, the Wagner-Murray-Dingell bill signaled the beginning of a political debate that would come to climax in the postwar years. Facing opposition by the AMA, the Insurance Economics Society of America, the Pharmaceutical Manufacturers Association of America, and other groups, the bill never made it out of committee. After the war the bill was resurrected as part of President Truman's Fair Deal program, but by 1950 it became apparent that the bill was dead and advocacy for it ended.

With no "public option" available to deal with the perceived health crisis in America, the country began to pursue private plans. One major event was that during the war, when wages were frozen to prevent employers from competing for each other's scarce workers by bidding up salaries, the War Labor Board ruled in 1943 that certain work benefits, including health insurance coverage, should be excluded from wage and price controls. Thus, employers began to use generous health benefits to attract workers. In the rapidly expanding economy following the war, where large corporations faced little competition and had profits large enough so unions could successfully negotiate for greater fringe benefits, the provision of health insurance as a job perk continued to rapidly increase. By the mid-1950s it was estimated that two-thirds of American workers were covered by employer sponsored health insurance plans.

There was one major government incursion into health care in the years immediately following the war, but in keeping with the spirit of the times, this involved governmental support of the private health care system. This was the passage of the Hospital Survey and Construction Act (the Hill-Burton Act). This act allocated federal grants and loans to build and improve the nation's hospitals. Basically the act provided better "workshops" for physicians to pursue the private practice of medicine. The act allocated $75 million per year to accomplish its objectives. Although the Hill-Burton Act was mainly a benefit to middle class citizens with health insurance, and to physicians, it did include some benefits for other groups. One was that the act prohibited hospitals receiving funds under the act from discriminating on the basis of race, color, national origin, or creed, although until 1963 the provision of "separate but equal" facilities was permitted. The act also required facilities that received funding to provide a "reasonable volume" of care each year for those residents in the facility's area who needed care but could not afford to pay.

The problem of the mental health of the nation revealed by the disturbing findings of draft screening and military psychiatric problems was addressed in the postwar years by two federal initiatives. The first was aimed specifically at returning veterans and took the form of a reinvigorated Veterans Administration under whose aegis a nationwide program of mental health services to veterans was established, including a wide distribution of mental hospitals and community clinics, many located near medical schools. In addition to providing a high quality of in-patient care, the facilities extended outpatient services, demonstrating the value and practicality of mental health services at the community level. Also, as part of its total service to all veterans, the V.A. committed its facilities to training programs in psychiatry, clinical psychology, and what was then known as psychiatric social work. The second federal initiative in the area of mental health was the passage in 1946 of the National Mental Health Act that established what was to become the National Institute of Mental Health, designed to primarily develop preventive approaches. The National Mental Health Act provided for an extensive mental health program by enabling the states and private institutions to obtain federal grants for research, professional training, and community mental health programs. Basically, the National Mental Health Act authorized a broad national program to combat mental illness under the aegis of the federal government.

Prior to World War II, mental health was dominated by a perspective that fused Freudian psychology with clinical medicine to produce a model of mental illness described by Rochefort as "the individually mentally ill person was a deviant whose abnormality required treatment; emotional breakdown akin to a disease having symptoms and other properties of organic illness; treatment for the disease should take place on a basis of one-to-one contact between the psychiatrist and his patient; and psychoanalysis should be considered a specialty on a par with other branches of medicine."[9] This model was seriously challenged in the 1950s by research and demonstration projects largely supported by the NIMH and the Veteran's Administration. This challenge came from several directions. First was the realization that the number of mentally ill people that had been revealed by World War II draft screening could not possibly be cared for using the one-on-one medical model. Second, the development of tranquilizing drugs, mainly reserpine and chlorpromazine, made hospitalization unnecessary for a large number of patients. Next, a number of exposes revealing the horrific conditions in state mental hospitals were released in the popular press (for example, the *Life Magazine* article "Bedlam USA" and the *Reader's Digest* article "The Shame of Our Mental Hospitals), and in the academic social science literature (for example, *The Mental Hospital* by Stanton and Schwartz, and *Asylums* by Goffman).

In response to the increasing concern about mental health care the American Medical Association and the American Psychiatric Association began in the early 1950s to organize for a "Flexner like" study of the mental health system in the United States. The result of these efforts was the passage, in 1955, of the Mental Health Study Act, that established and funded a Joint Commission on Mental Illness and Health. In September of that year the Joint Commission established four goals to guide its work: (1) to study mental illness and health and the various "medical, psychological, social, economic, cultural and other factors that relate to etiology"; (2) to discover, develop, and apply appropriate methods for the diagnosis, treatment, care, and rehabilitation of the mentally ill and mentally retarded; (3) to evaluate and improve the recruitment of personnel; and (4) to conduct a national survey and to develop a comprehensive program. The final report of the Commission, titled *Action for Mental Health* was not completed until 1960 and not released until 1961 when the Commission felt there would be a more receptive political climate. The major recommendations of the report were for an expanded NIMH research program focusing on basic rather than applied research; for a major expansion of mental health manpower including social workers; that a goal should be established to have a ratio of one outpatient mental health clinic for each 50,000 citizens; that state mental hospitals should be much smaller and that their role should be to provide short term intensive treatment rather than long term custodial care; and, finally, that spending on mental health services should greatly increase, doubling in five years and tripling in ten. As Rochefort summarizes the gist of the report, "the Joint Commission drew up the blueprint for a substantially revised public mental health system, one that would begin to substitute the principle of community care for custodialism and that would depend, at least in the beginning, on a large infusion of federal monies."[10]

Juvenile Crime

During the early years of the twentieth century adolescence was for the first time recognized as a separate and significant stage of growth and development. Psychologist G. Stanley Hall was the

9. David A. Rochefort, *From Poorhouses to Homelessness: Policy Analysis and Mental Health Care*, 2nd ed. (Westport, CT: Auburn House, 1997), 42.

10. David A. Rochefort, *From Poorhouses to Homelessness*, 55.

first, in 1905, to publish a formal study of this period of growth and development.[11] Identification of adolescence was generally thought to be related to the rapid increase in the number of young people in secondary school, a development that kept them out of the full-time work force and thus created a period between childhood playtime and adult employment. However, it was not until the Second World War that the teenager was created and recognized as a significant social type. The war brought major and rapid changes in the lifestyles of American families. For many families the temporary or permanent loss of the father to combat and the mother's working away from home in a war industry job led to transformations in parenting. As a result, older children had to take on greater responsibilities inside and outside the home, for example seeing themselves off to school, preparing their own meals, and maintaining the household without the constant presence and support of parents. Thousands of adolescents became what we now term latchkey children. For the young person this greater responsibility had the benefit of greater freedom. Out of the autonomy of the latchkey lifestyle a new type of child emerged. The war years saw the advent of what became known as the teenager, a distinct childhood classification with its own culture and personality.

Disturbing to a great number of Americans was that one defining characteristic of the new teenage personality and culture was the rejection of authority that at times verged on lawlessness. As the 1940s turned into the 1950s the topic of juvenile delinquency became a major concern in American society. Newspapers and magazines published story after story chronicling youth crime. The problem even became a Hollywood interest with sixty films dealing with delinquency released in the 1950s decade. This concern was not unfounded as statistics at the time supported the perception that juvenile crime was increasing. The FBI reported a rapidly increasing number of arrests of teenagers throughout the 1950s. The agency's semiannual *Uniform Crime Reports* provided documentation of juvenile crime increases throughout the decade. In 1959 the FBI analyzed the historical trend and reported that the number of juvenile crimes had increased by 220 percent from 1941 to 1957. In response to queries that this increase might just reflect the growth in the number of young people in the population the Bureau had an answer ready: "By directly comparing percentages of the rise in delinquency and the growth in the young population, we find that juvenile arrests' have increased two and one-half times as fast."[12]

Given the conservative tenor of the late 1940s and the 1950s one would expect that this concern with juvenile crime would be met with a tough law and order reaction, and there was some activity in this direction. In 1946 Attorney General Tom Clark called a National Conference on the Prevention and Control of Juvenile Delinquency to investigate the problem and to make recommendations as to how to respond. The conference provided little in the way of increased understanding of the problem but did succeed in increasing the public's perception and fear, partially as a result of a radio broadcast by Clark entitled "America's Town Meeting of the Air" in which he cited examples of vicious juvenile crime and figures that indicated a growing trend in such

---

11. G. Stanley Hall, *Adolescence: Its Psychology and Its Relations to Physiology, Anthropology, Sociology, Sex, Crime, Religion and Education* (New York: Macmillan, 1905).

12. U.S. Department of Justice, *Uniform Crime Reports for the United States, 1959* (Washington, DC: U.S. Government Printing Office, 1960), 17.

crimes.[13] However, at least as far as federal policy was concerned, the get tough approach found little traction. Instead the government opted for a prevention and rehabilitation approach. Barnosky poses a question and an answer explaining this response: "What kept the government's response centered on policies of prevention and rehabilitation? The answer lies in a set of institutions that framed the issue and biased it in favor of progressive solutions. These institutions—the Children's Bureau, the National Institute of Mental Health (NIMH), and the Senate Judiciary Committee to Investigate Juvenile Delinquency—provided friendly venues for progressive ideas and prevented others from being considered. They also linked experts sympathetic to progressive ideas to policymakers. Consequently, they were able to limit the debate to policies they favored."[14]

The experts that the federal agencies were linking to policy makers were liberal sociologists and social workers who were seeking explanations of delinquency in the new and rapidly changing social environment of the 1950s. Pre-war theories, notably those of Clifford Shaw and Henry McKay, and of William Foote Whyte had explained delinquency in a structural fashion, relating it to immigration and to disorganized communities. Shaw and McKay argued that delinquency was concentrated in low income inner city areas, heavily populated by recent immigrant families, characterized by social disorganization in these groups whose culture had been shattered by the "new cultural and racial situation of the city." In his influential text *Delinquency Areas* Shaw concluded that delinquency was one of many symptoms of disorganization in urban life, "associated, area by area, with rates of truancy, adult crime, infant mortality, tuberculosis, and mental disorder."[15] Whyte, in his influential study, *Street Corner Society: The Structure of a Slum*, argued a variation of Shaw's theory, that the immigrant neighborhood he studied did not so much lack organization, but that there was a "failure of its own social organization to mesh with the structure of the society around it."[16]

The structural explanations of poverty proposed by Shaw, McKay, Whyte, and others continued to have influence well into the 1950s.[17] The youth crime of the 1950s, however, was different than that explained by structural theories. In addition to its increase, and its increasingly violent character, delinquency as we entered the second half of the century, was clearly not restricted to immigrant communities. To account for these changes social scientists began to look at delinquency as a subculture within the larger culture, one with its own norms and values that favored crime over law abiding behavior. One of the more influential examples of this theory was developed by Harvard anthropologist Walter Miller. Miller argued that people in lower class communities were frustrated by middle class norms of success and the values associated with these, and as a result of this frustration developed, and passed along to their children their own set of norms and values related to success. He identified six values that have a high priority for young males in impoverished neighborhoods: trouble, toughness, smartness, excitement, fate, and autonomy.

13. James Gilbert, *A Cycle of Outrage: America's Reaction to the Juvenile Delinquent in the 1950s* (New York: Oxford University Press, 1986), 37.

14. Jason Barnosky, "The Violent Years: Responses to Juvenile Crime in the 1950s," *Polity*, 38 (July 2006): 315.

15. Clifford R. Shaw with Frederick M. Zorbaugh, Henry D. McKay, and Leonard S. Cottrell, *Delinquency Areas* (Chicago: University of Chicago Press, 1929).

16. William Foote Whyte, *Street Corner Society: The Social Structure of an Italian Slum in Chicago* (Chicago: University of Chicago Press, 1943).

17. See, for example, Solomon Korbrin, "The Chicago Area Project: A 25-Year Assessment," *Annals of the American Academy of Political and Social Science*, 322 (March 1959).

Miller believed that the internalization of lower-class values combined with a need to demonstrate their "manhood" can cause some young males to defy authority and participate in fighting and other activities that tend to be interpreted by middle-class people as signifiers of juvenile delinquency.

A second major theory, one that was to have a great impact on the approach policy makers took to the problem of juvenile crime in the decade that was to follow, was referred to as opportunity theory and was the product of social worker Richard Cloward and sociologist Lloyd Ohlin. Cloward and Ohlin's opportunity theory was different from prior cultural theories in that it argued that juvenile delinquents were not responding to sub-cultural values that were different from those of the larger society, but rather they were responding to main stream values such as achievement and success. Where the problem lay, according to Cloward and Ohlin, was that in the communities in which the youth live legitimate means of successfully meeting these values were blocked. The combination of internalized values of success and achievement with the lack of opportunity for successful pursuit of these values created intense frustration and resentment among the youth. This frustration led to one or a combination of responses by the juveniles. The first was engagement in criminal activities that represented an attempt to fulfill a legitimate value (material success) through illegitimate means (robbery, pushing drugs, pimping/prostitution, and so forth). The second reaction was violence that was a reaction to the frustration created by blocked opportunity. The third reaction was retreatism, i.e. a withdrawal from participation in the larger society that is frustrating the young person. In the vignette that opened this chapter the Sportsmen and Dragon gangs were an example of a violent response, the Cahanmen exemplified retreatism. All three gangs responded to their perceived lack of opportunity by resorting to criminality. Cloward and Ohlin's opportunity theory was to become a centerpiece of the aggressive liberal social programs of the sixties.

The intense popular and academic interest in juvenile delinquency in the 1950s led to President Kennedy, in spring of 1961 shortly after taking office, to create the President's Committee on Juvenile Delinquency and Youth Crime. In the same year the Juvenile Delinquency and Youth Offenses Control Act, a measure that, among other things, helped fund and operate a number of local projects for the prevention and treatment of delinquency in inner-city neighborhoods, was passed. This act funded a number of local projects to test various responses to the youth crime problem, notably the Mobilization for Youth project, jointly funded by the federal government and the Ford Foundation that formally tested theories of delinquency, but most had disappointing results and did not spread beyond their local demonstration areas. What the new interest in delinquency did do, however, was to serve as a platform for a new approach to poverty, one that emphasized structural conditions, mainly blocked opportunity, rather than individual pathology or immorality, as an explanation for the problem and a theoretical basis for combatting it.

Poverty and Public Welfare

When the Aid to Dependent Children (ADC) program was passed as part of the 1936 Social Security Act it stirred up relatively little controversy. The program, which was later changed to Aid to Families of Dependent Children (AFDC), was targeted to support the children of single mothers, mostly widows and divorcees, who were experiencing financial hard times. The main reason that this program did not receive more opposition was the belief that it was mainly a response to the hard times of the depression and that when the depression abated the ADC program would shrink in size and perhaps even disappear. This did not occur. As the country experienced the unprecedented prosperity of the 1940s and 1950s ADC not only did not shrink, but it grew at an alarming rate. The program had 546,000 recipients in 1940; 1,222,000 in 1950; and 2,233,000 in 1960.[18] As the program increased in size it ate up proportionally larger shares of state budgets. In the aggregate, states' revenues increased 138 percent between 1945 and 1955 while their ADC expenditures rose by 270 percent.[19] The anomaly of the country experiencing record economic growth, low unemployment levels, but with a rapidly growing problem of welfare dependency, resulted in great concern from citizens and their elected representatives.

In 1952, concerned about growing opposition to AFDC and related programs, the *Social Service Review*, the leading academic social work/social welfare journal in the country published a survey of magazine and newspaper articles between 1949 and 1952 on the subject of public welfare. What they found was that these articles "reveal a growing distrust on the part of the public as to whether the current operation of the public assistance program is serving the common welfare in a way that will strengthen both the individual recipients and the total nation." Examples given of journalistic criticisms included an article from Lyon County Kansas that reported that in one month in 1951 the county had expended an amount on public welfare that exceeded the total expenditure of the entire year of 1929; a *New York Times* article reported that a grand jury in Delaware County Pennsylvania accused the Pennsylvania Department of Public Assistance with "subsidizing immorality" by making grants to mothers of illegitimate children; an article in the *Saturday Evening Post* criticized the Oklahoma Department of Public Welfare saying "The case histories disclose countless examples of indolence and sloth, show clearly how the taxpayer supports men and women who not only don't work but who are breeding a society of illegitimates besides." After reviewing the newspapers and magazines the author concluded that dissatisfaction with public welfare programs could be separated into five categories: "(1) The cost of public assistance throughout the country is rising. (2) The public assistance program is encouraging increased illegitimacy and makes it easier for fathers to desert their families. (3) [As the *Saturday Evening Post*] vividly states "Relief chiselers are stealing us blind." (4) Secrecy of names of recipients and of the amount of payments is a violation of the taxpayers' right to know how their money is being spent. (5) Federal control of the program is less efficient than if authorities for administration were delegated to the states."[20]

The controversy that surrounded ADC beginning in the 1950s is not really surprising as it appears that the designers of the program did not really understand what they were passing and

18. U.S. House Ways and Means Committee, *1998 Greenbook: Background Material and Data on the Programs within the Jurisdiction of the Committee on Ways and Means*, Table 7-2 (Washington, D.C.: U.S. Government Printing Office, 1999).

19. Sarah A. Soule and Yvonne Zylan, "Runaway Train? The Diffusion of State-Level Reform in ADC/AFDC Eligibility Requirements, 1940–1967," *American Journal of Sociology*, 103, (March. 1998): 736.

20. Hilda C. M Arndt, "An Appraisal of What the Critics Are Saying about Public Assistance," *Social Service Review* 26 (December 1952): 464–475.

certainly did not predict what the program would eventually become. Scholars often romanticize New Deal programs and characterize the designers as humanists and liberals with a far-reaching vision of a just society and a realistic plan for achieving it. However, the evidence indicates that the designers of the ADC program supported it only because they believed that the program was temporary and would wither away as the economy improved and social insurance came into effect. Further, the designers of ADC never imagined that the program would support the children of unwed mothers. Franklin Roosevelt characterized welfare as "a narcotic, a subtle destroyer of the human spirit" and argued that federal job creation was far preferable to welfare.[21] Edith Abbott, a social worker and prominent social reformer, advocated for ADC with the assurance that it would support only "nice" families. Social worker and Secretary of Labor Frances Perkins supported the program under the misunderstanding that the term *dependent mother* referred only to women who were widows, married to disabled workers, or divorced due to no fault of their own. It never occurred to her that unwed mothers would be included in the definition of *dependent*. Historian Linda Gordon states:

> The authors of the New Deal welfare programs, often thought of as spiritual allies of contempo-
> rary liberals, would severely disapprove of what the New Deal programs have subsequently become
> with liberal encouragement: a source of more-or-less permanent support for single mothers who, in
> many instances are not white and "not nice."[22]

The most popular explanation as to why poverty and welfare dependency continued amidst the prosperity of the 1950s was given by the Harvard economist John Kenneth Galbraith in his best-selling book *The Affluent Society*. The main purpose of Galbraith's book was to explain the new American economy, one that Galbraith described as remarkable because, for the first time in history, the non-poor members greatly outnumbered the poor. However, Galbraith observes that "We must remember that we still have a great many poor people [but] poverty survives in economic discourse partly as a buttress to the conventional economic wisdom. Still . . . it can no longer be presented as a universal or massive affliction. It is more nearly an afterthought." Galbraith argued that the poverty that remained in the United States was of two types. One type he named *case poverty* and can be found in any community, rural or urban, regardless of how prosperous the times. Case poverty is related to some defect of the individuals so afflicted, "mental deficiency, bad health, inability to adapt to the discipline of modern economic life, excessive procreation, alcohol, insufficient education, or perhaps a combination of several of these handicaps—have kept these individuals from participating in the general well-being." The other type of poverty Galbraith

21. Sar Levitan and Frank Gallo, "Jobs for JOBS: Toward a Work-Based Welfare System," *Occasional Papers* 1993–1 (Washington, DC: Urban Institute, March 1993).

22. Terry Mizrahi, "The New 'Right' Agenda Decimates Social Programs, Devalues Social Work and Devastates Clients and Communities," HCSSW Update (School of Social Work, Hunter College of the City University of New York, Spring 1996), 1. Sar Levitan and Frank Gallo, "Jobs for JOBS: Toward a Work-Based Welfare System," *Occasional Papers* 1993–1; G. D. Reilly, "Madame Secretary," in K. Louchheim, ed., *The Making of the New Deal: The Insiders Speak* (Cambridge, MA: Harvard University Press, 1997); Linda Gordon, *Pitied but Not Entitled: Single Mothers and the History of Welfare, 1890–1935* (New York: Free Press, 1994), 299.

referred to as *insular poverty*—"that which manifests itself as an 'island' of poverty." In this geographic island of poverty nearly everyone is poor and so poverty cannot be explained by individual inadequacy. Galbraith did not attempt to give an in-depth explanation of the reasons that these islands of poverty exist amongst the affluence of the rest of the country, he only observes that they do in fact exist. Although Galbraith argues that insular poverty cannot be explained by individual inadequacy, he does place much of the blame on individuals because they choose to "spend their lives at or near the place of their birth. This homing instinct causes them to bar the solution, always open as an individual remedy in a country without barriers to emigration, to escape the island of poverty in which they were born." Galbraith concludes that poverty in the United States cannot be cured by continued general economic growth because growth "cannot improve the position of those who, by virtue of self or environment, cannot participate or are not reached."[23]

The popular attitude regarding poverty and welfare exemplified by the news articles summarized in the *Social Service Review* article, and the lower key and more sophisticated explanation given in Galbraith's book led to two policy approaches to the problem in the 1950s. The harsh popular attitude was embraced by many politicians who recognized a vote-getting issue when they saw one. The result was a series of punitive and poorly thought out attempts at welfare reform, generally with the aim of limiting the number of people who could qualify for welfare benefits. These policies included "suitable home" and "man in the house" rules, and residency requirements. The suitable home and man in the house rules stated that aid would not be given to children who were living in immoral environments, generally defined as home situations in which it appeared that the mother was having a sexual relationship with a man to whom she was not married. Some states enacted policies whereby social workers, when establishing eligibility for aid, were required to look in closets and under furniture to see if there was evidence of a non-related male living in the home. Applicant mothers were sometimes required to sign affidavits like the following:

I _____ do hereby promise and agree that until such time as the following agreement is rescinded, I will not have any male callers coming to my home nor meeting me elsewhere under improper conditions. I also agree to raise my children to the best of my ability and will not knowingly contribute or be a contributing factor to their being shamed by my conduct. I understand that should I violate this agreement, the children will be taken from me.

Louisiana was so enthusiastic about this means of cutting welfare rolls that in 1960 it cut 6,281 families, with 23,489 children, from its welfare rolls based on suitable home rules. Public outcry in response to this move led to federal intervention with the result that benefits were reinstated to about half of the affected families.[24] These rules were struck down in all states in the 1968 Supreme Court decision in the case of *King v. Smith*. Residency requirements were policies that denied benefits to any person who had not resided in a locale for a certain period of time, sometimes as long as five years. By the mid-1950s these requirements were in effect in all but three states. The

23. John Kenneth Galbraith, *The Affluent Society* (Boston, MA: Houghton Mifflin Company, 1958), 322–327.
24. James T. Patterson, *America's Struggle against Poverty in the Twentieth Century* (Cambridge, MA: Harvard University Press, 2000), 85–86.

New York Times reported in 1956 a story from Ohio where a mother and her eight children, who had not eaten in two days, were "Under a court ruling . . . put on a train with instructions to return to Livingston, Ala., because the children are not eligible for relief under Ohio law." At the court session a welfare department official told the judge that "if these people are allowed to remain here, Your Honor, word will get back to the South and we will be flooded with similar families."[25] Residency requirements were struck down by the Supreme Court in the 1969 *Shapiro v. Thompson* decision.

Although restrictive, punitive, policies attempting to restrict eligibility to welfare benefits were the most frequent and popular attempts to stem the growth of the welfare population in the 1950s, liberal social welfare advocacy groups such as the American Public Welfare Association (APWA) and the National Association of Social Workers (NASW) were beginning to get the attention of policy makers. These organizations lobbied Congress advocating an explanation of welfare dependency, predicting Galbraith's idea of case poverty that most people were on welfare due to some individual shortcoming. The solution to the problem of the growth of the welfare rolls, they argued, was to provide social services to help recipients resolve their problems and thereby become independent. One result of the lobbying efforts of these groups was that the 1956 amendments to the Social Security Act included a revision and expansion of the statement of purpose for public assistance programs. The revised statement made explicit that in addition to enabling the States to give financial aid to needy persons the purpose is to encourage the States to provide services to help recipients toward independent living, to strengthen family life, and to help keep children in their own homes. To help operationalize these new purposes of public assistance, the 1956 amendments included money being allocated for social work training for public assistance workers and for federal support of social services as part of state public welfare programs. In order to strengthen social work education for public welfare practice the act authorized $5 million per year for a period of five years "to be used by States to make grants to institutions of higher learning for training personnel for the public assistance programs and for establishing fellowships or traineeships and special short-term courses of study."[26]

1958–1968: BOLD EXPERIMENTS

The 1950s, those halcyon years of *Leave It to Beaver* and *Ozzie and Harriet*, are now looked back upon as an era of smug self-satisfaction where little progress was made in any area other than middle class Americans enriching themselves, often at the expense of others. Historian Eric Goldman, writing in *Harper's Magazine* in 1960, opined, "We've grown unbelievably prosperous and we meander along in a heavy, humorless, sanctimonious stultifying atmosphere, singularly lacking in the self-mockery that is self-criticism. Probably the climate of the late 1950s was the dullest and dreariest

25. "Cleveland Sends 9 Negroes South," *New York Times*, June 9, 1956, 17.

26. Charles I. Schottland, "Social Security Amendments of 1956: A Summary and Legislative History," *Social Security Bulletin* (September 1956): 3–15.

in all our history." Fred Siegel, reviewing the results of opinion polls in the late 1950s and in 1960 found that they reported that the American people were "relaxed, unadventurous, comfortably satisfied with their way of life and blandly optimistic about the future." In the area of social welfare, however, the years from the end of World War II until 1958 were, to use the term that historian Clark Chambers used to describe the 1920s, a "seedtime for reform." It was an era that saw little really major advancement in programs to benefit the needy and to reduce inequality, but where knowledge was gathered, and momentum built up, which lead to major attempts to reduce poverty and increase equality. Significant areas of reform that began with commissions and research in the 1950s that were to blossom into bold policy initiatives in the 1960s were juvenile delinquency and community disorganization, public assistance, child welfare, and community mental health.

Poverty and Public Assistance

By the end of the 1950s, the country was feeling restless and ready for change. John F. Kennedy was campaigning for the presidency on the assertion that the country was stagnating, and he promised to get it "moving again" toward "new frontiers." Shortly after his election, the 1960 census was completed and it revealed that the country clearly needed to get moving again. The census data revealed that the New Deal and the Second World War had not eliminated poverty as was popularly believed. In addition, the data indicated that poverty was not restricted to people living in certain deprived areas or to members of certain groups, as Galbraith had asserted, but that it was common and widespread. Following the release of the census data a number of scholarly books were published that demonstrated the true nature and extent of poverty in America. These books, generally turgid and dull as academic tracts are prone to be, sailed under the radar, so to speak, until the journalist and public intellectual Dwight MacDonald published a lively review in the *New Yorker* in 1963 titled "Our Invisible Poor." The book he found the most interesting, and most compelling, was *The Other America: Poverty in the United States*, by left-wing journalist Michael Harrington. Harrington had compiled an impressive body of statistics, and on the basis of these concluded that fifty million Americans, about one-fourth of the population, were living in poverty. Harrington addressed the question of why, if there are so many poor people in the United States, the problem was not obvious to everyone. His explanation was that "The other America, the America of poverty, is hidden today in a way it never was before. Its millions are socially invisible to the rest of us." The reason that the poor were invisible, according to Harrington, is that they lived off the beaten track, areas to which most people rarely if ever went; that due to mass production they are dressed in a manner that does not clearly identify them as poor; that many are old so tend to stay inside out of the view of others; and, finally, the poor are politically invisible-—"It is one of the cruelest ironies of social life in advanced countries that the dispossessed at the bottom of society are unable to speak for themselves." After the review by MacDonald, the sale of Harrington's book went through the roof and it was read by many influential policy makers, including President Kennedy, and the poverty problem moved from the backwaters of public policy to the very center of the national agenda. In light of this "rediscovery of poverty," the federal government attempted to attack the problem from three different approaches under three different presidents during the 1960s.

The approach of the Kennedy administration was embodied in Public Law 87-543, known as the Social Service Amendments, signed into law on July 25, 1962. This law grew out of the recommendations of the Ad Hoc Committee on Public Welfare appointed by Health, Education, and Welfare Secretary Abraham Ribicoff in May 1961 and out of a report by George Wyman at about the same time. Wyman was an administrator with experience in a wide variety of social welfare agencies that included local, state, and federal agencies. The ad hoc committee was composed of twenty-five public and voluntary social welfare leaders, mostly social workers. Three members of the committee were deans of schools of social work and a fourth dean served as a consultant. The recommendations in the report of the Ad Hoc and Wyman committees were heavily influenced by social workers and other social service and social science experts who contended that providing intensive social services would rehabilitate and bring financial independence to the poor. The act provided increased federal support at a 75 percent match to the states to enable them to provide social services to recipients of public assistance. In reality, the act represented a very old approach, harkening back to the Charity Organization Society, of providing individual services to help people lift themselves out of poverty, with little attention directed toward altering the social conditions that caused the poverty.

The Social Service Amendments rapidly increased the number of social workers in public welfare settings. Recommendation number 12 of the Ad Hoc Committee stated, "To make possible the rehabilitative services so strongly advocated [by the committee], the goal should be established that one third of all persons engaged in social work capacities in public welfare should hold master's degrees in social work. " Money was allocated for welfare departments to send employees to graduate school in social work, and for these schools to incorporate additional public welfare content into their curricula.

The reports of the Wyman and the Ad Hoc Committee were heavily influenced by cultural theories, notably those of anthropologist Oscar Lewis who had formulated, and promulgated in five books, the culture of poverty theory. Lewis explained poverty as a "subculture with its own structure and rationale, as a way of life which is passed down from generation to generation along family lines." He proposed that poverty was not only something negative—want and deprivation—but that it also included positive aspects, some rewards without which the poor could not carry on. The culture of poverty develops, according to Lewis, as a reaction by the poor to their marginal position in society; and it "represents an effort to cope with feeling of hopelessness and despair which develop from the realization of the improbability of achieving success."[27] When social workers advocated providing professional services to welfare recipients, they did so in the belief that these services would address this culture and its feelings of helplessness and despair and thereby improve recipient's lives. They assumed that the services would be judged on this basis. Unfortunately, the basis on which Congress supported these services was that they would help people become self-supporting, thereby reducing the welfare rolls, and it was on this basis that the services were judged. After the passage of the amendments, the welfare rolls rose at a faster rate than ever, making social workers and allied social scientists suspect in policymakers' eyes and causing the policymakers to look for a new approach to the "welfare problem."

27. Oscar Lewis, *Five Families: Mexican Case Studies in the Culture of Poverty* (New York: Basic Books, 1959).

The new approach came in 1964 when, in his State of the Union message, President Johnson called on Congress to enact a thirteen-point program that would declare "unconditional war on poverty." This "war" was launched in July of 1964 with the passage of the Economic Opportunity Act. Whereas the social service approach of the Kennedy administration had been based on the culture of poverty theory, the Economic Opportunity Act was more influenced by Cloward and Ohlin's opportunity theory, originally directed toward juvenile delinquency, but now more broadly interpreted to explain poverty in general. In response to opportunity theory's assertion that the main problems of poor people were mainly structural conditions that blocked legitimate opportunities for success, the OEO took a number of steps to remediate these structural conditions. Toward this end the act created the Office of Economic Opportunity, Volunteers in Service to America (VISTA), the Job Corps, Upward Bound, the Neighborhood Youth Corps, and the Community Action Program (CAP).

There were several additional reasons behind President Johnson's War on Poverty. One was pressure from the civil rights movement for an attack on hunger and poverty. An example of the intensity of this pressure was a march for "jobs and freedom" that brought two hundred thousand people to Washington, D.C., and culminated in a historic speech by Martin Luther King, Jr. The major reason, however, was probably the growing awareness of the extent of poverty in the United States and the continued growth of the welfare rolls despite the Social Service Amendments. A significant new development in the War on Poverty programs was that they made a concerted effort to include input from the poor themselves in the design and administration of the programs; this was done under the Economic Opportunity Act's provision for "maximum feasible participation" of the poor, which encouraged participation of low-income people on boards and staffs of community programs, and deemphasized services by professionals such as social workers.

If anything, the War on Poverty programs were even less successful than the Social Service Amendments. Congress and taxpayers stuck to reducing welfare rolls as the primary criterion for success, and far from shrinking, the rolls increased at a record rate, with more than one million persons being added between 1963 and 1966. In addition, the War on Poverty drew severe criticism for other reasons. Mayors were upset because the federal government was funding programs in their towns over which they had no control; members of Congress were upset about lawsuits brought against government agencies by government-funded legal services; and citizens were upset by the aggressiveness and hostility of the poor, who had found a voice through the "maximum feasible participation" concept. As a result of these criticisms, the Economic Opportunity Act of 1966 sharply curtailed the Community Action Program.

Two War on Poverty programs that perhaps have had little effect on reducing welfare rolls but have had an immense impact on improving the lives of the poor were the 1964 Food Stamp Act and the 1965 Medicare and Medicaid amendments to the Social Security Act. The Food Stamp Act replaced the commodities program that had provided nutritional assistance for the poor by making surplus agricultural produce available to them for no cost. Although better than nothing, the commodities program provided no choice; the type of food available largely depended on the commodities for which there was a surplus. The Food Stamp Program (now the Supplemental Nutrition Assistance Program, called SNAP) provides vouchers (now a debit card) that can be used just like cash for the purchase of food and thus permit recipients the same range of choice that anyone else has in his or her weekly shopping. The Medicare program expanded federal support for health care for the elderly, and the Medicaid program did the same for children and mothers receiving support under the AFDC program.

Toward the end of President Johnson's term in office, the mood of the country began to drift to the right. In 1966, on the same day the new Economic Opportunity Act was signed into law, the Republicans gained fifty-one seats in Congress, mostly replacing liberal democrats. In 1968, with the election of President Richard Nixon, the Republicans added the White House to their list of victories. With the conservative mood of the country, sentiment grew for limiting "soft" services, such as social work assistance and community action, and for emphasizing "hard" services, such as day care and work training and support programs. The Social Security Amendments of 1967 reflected this mood, setting up the Work Incentive Program (WIN), which required all AFDC recipients with no children under age six to register for work or for job training and to accept employment or training as soon as it was available and offered. The purpose of this policy was to attempt once again to force welfare recipients to "stop being lazy and to get to work." True to the experience of all such programs in the past, the number of welfare recipients who expressed a desire for the jobs or training promised by the WIN program far exceeded the ability of state job services to supply work or training. Another part of the amendments instituted a formula whereby a welfare recipient's grant was reduced by only a percentage of earned income when that person became employed. Also funded was day care for welfare recipients who were employed or in training.

Child Welfare

In addition to poverty, another area that burst unto the social welfare policy scene in the late 1950s and 1960s is that of child maltreatment. Attention to this problem resulted from the activities of two professions and highlighted two separate yet related aspects of the problem. First, and most dramatic, was the belated recognition by the medical profession of abuse as a child health problem. Second, social work researchers identified a huge number of children drifting in foster care, with little hope of reunification with their families yet with no alternative plan.

The basic structure of the child protective services system was put in place with the passage and implementation of Title V (later Title IV) of the Social Security Act that authorized the Children's Bureau to fund and assist states in providing child welfare services for dependent and neglected children. Although child protective services after this date were officially a responsibility of government, the services were spotty and poorly funded. Prior to the late 1950s three states had no protective services at all. In the states that did have services, an American Humane Association survey found that "much of what was reported as child protective services was in reality nonspecific child welfare services or nonspecific family assistance services in the context of a financial assistance setting." In addition, the survey found that child protection services provided by private agencies had undergone a long term decline.[28] Two events in the late 1950s and early 1960s were to cause child welfare to explode on the national agenda, one being the discovery by social workers of great problems in the foster care system and the other was the recognition of child abuse as a social problem by physicians.

FOSTER CARE

During the first half of the twentieth century, procedures for home study, child placement, and supervision were developed by social workers. As these procedures were developed, Title V of the Social Security Act was passed in 1935 to provide public funding of foster homes. As an anti-institutional bias developed during the twentieth century, the number of children in orphanages declined and the number in foster care increased until foster care became the clear method of choice for placement of dependent and neglected children. Foster care became a standard item in the child welfare social workers toolkit. It was a resource that existed with little examination until the late 1950s, when a study by social workers Henry Maas and Richard Engler opened the floodgates of criticism. Maas and Engler wanted to know what was actually happening in the foster care system and to find out they sent researchers into nine communities thought to be representative of the country as a whole. The researchers looked at a number of aspects of foster care in each of the communities including length of time in care, number of foster placements per child, contact with families of origin, case plans for foster children, and number of contacts of the children's families with agency social workers. As there was no central data reporting mechanism for foster care, the Maas and Engler study provided the first valid look into the overall picture of foster care in the United States. The facts they uncovered were disturbing. First, they found that the assumption that foster care was a temporary respite for children and families was untrue. The average length of placement was three years, many children were destined to grow up in foster care, and less than one-quarter of foster care children were likely to permanently return home. Equally disturbing was the finding that the parents of foster children indicated, in most cases, that they either had no relationship or a negative relationship with the child placement agencies, or in only one-third of the cases did a parent ever visit a child in care. In an afterword to the study, Child Welfare League of America Executive Director Joseph Reid referred to foster children as "orphans of the living."[29]

MEDICINE RECOGNIZES CHILD ABUSE

In the late 1940s and early 1950s, radiologists began to recognize injuries that we now know were related to abuse and neglect—injuries that doctors had previously tended to view as accidental. In 1960, a social worker at Children's Hospital in Pittsburgh published an article that attributed

28. Vincent DeFrancis, *Protecting the Abused Child*. Hearing before the Subcommittee on Children and Youth, 93rd Congress, on the Child Abuse Prevention and Treatment Act (S1191), 323–331.

29. Henry Maas and Richard Engler, *Children in Need of Parents* (New York: Columbia University Press, 1959).

the resistance of physicians to diagnosing intentional injury to children to both repugnance of the problem and a difficulty in assuming an objective attitude with abusive parents.[30]

C. Henry Kempe, the physician instrumental in overcoming this resistance recalls, "When I saw child abuse between 1956 and 1958 in Denver, our house staff was unwilling to make this diagnosis [child abuse]. Initially I felt intellectual dismay at diagnoses such as 'obscure bruising,' 'osteogenesis imperfecta tarda,' 'spontaneous subdural hematoma.' " In 1960, Kempe used his prerogative as program committee chair of the American Academy of Pediatrics to plan a plenary session on child abuse. The rest of the committee agreed, provided he could come up with a catchy title for the session. The title Kempe coined was "The Battered Child Syndrome." Shortly after the meeting, Kempe, with the assistance of a psychiatrist and a radiologist, published an article with the same title in the journal of the American Medical Association.[31]

As Williams has noted "The speed of public and professional response, enhanced by media coverage, was incredible."[32] In 1962, the US Children's Bureau held a conference to draft model child welfare legislation. That same year, the amendments to the Social Security Act required all states to develop a plan to provide child protective services in every political subdivision. In 1963, eighteen bills were introduced in Congress dealing with child abuse, and eleven of them passed. By 1967, all states had passed laws requiring professionals to report child abuse. Increased public awareness of the problem of child maltreatment, combined with the reporting laws, resulted in a massive increase in the number of referrals and thus the sizes of caseloads of child welfare agencies. In 1967, there were only 9,563 child abuse reports nationally; by 1980 reports had increased to over one million. That number has continued to increase such that by the end of the century the number peaked at more than three million.[33]

Community Mental Health

The report of the Joint Commission on Mental Illness that had been in the works since 1955, titled *Action for Mental Health"* released in 1961, found a receptive audience in the Kennedy administration. President Kennedy's family had itself been affected by mental illness in the case of the President's sister Rose who had been institutionalized. The administration developed a legislative package to address the issue of mental illness which Kennedy outlined in a special message to Congress on February 5, 1963. The president proposed both that Congress strengthen existing programs and that it fund several new ones. For existing programs he asked for grants to augment

30. Elizabeth Elmer, "Abused Young Children Seen in Hospitals," *Social Work*, 5 (1960): 98–102.

31. C. Henry Kempe, "Child Abuse: The Pediatrician's Role in Advocacy and Preventive Pediatrics," *American Journal of Diseases in Children*, 132 (1978): 255–260.

32. G. J. Williams, Introduction to Part 2: "Protection of Children Against Abuse and Neglect: Historical Background." In G. J. Williams and J. Money eds., *Traumatic Abuse and Neglect of Children at Home* (Baltimore, MD: Johns Hopkins University Press, 1980), 63–83.

33. U.S. Department of Health and Human Services, Administration for Children and Families, Children's Bureau, *Child Maltreatment 2014*. Available from http://www.acf.hhs.gov/programs/cb/research-data-technology/statistice-research/child-maltreatment

the training of professional personnel, to expand existing research, and to upgrade the quality of institutional care until new programs and facilities could be built. For new programs and facilities, Kennedy proposed federal matching grants to the states for construction of Comprehensive Community Mental Health Centers. Kennedy described the purpose of his proposed "comprehensive community mental health system" to be the provision of emergency psychiatric facilities, outpatient and inpatient services, foster home care, and related services in every community in the country. His goal was to reduce the number of patients under custodial care in state mental hospitals by 50 percent within two decades. Kennedy's proposed legislation received remarkable bipartisan support and enthusiastic endorsement from the professional mental health community. The only part that engendered controversy was the proposal to provide federal funding for mental health center staffing that was opposed by the American Medical Association who saw in it the seeds of "socialized medicine" and of national health insurance. By early fall of 1963 the House and the Senate agreed on and passed a version of the act that excluded the staffing provision, and allocated $150 million total funding for the new mental health centers program. The president signed the legislation on October 31, 1963. In 1965 the act was amended to authorize the federal funding for the employment of professional and technical personnel that has been cut from the 1963 bill. Funding for staffing was set at $73.5 million for 1966 to 1968. In 1967 the act was once again amended, extending the staffing and construction grants for an additional three years and authorizing funding for the continued support of three hundred currently funded centers, as well as for establishing three hundred more. In 1968 the Alcoholic and Narcotic Addiction Rehabilitation Amendments provided funds for the building and staffing of specialized facilities for the treatment of drug addiction and alcoholism. Although, as we will later see, the Community Mental Health Act fell short of many of the promises of its designers, the statement made in 1964 by Robert Felix, then Director of the National Institute of Mental Health, is undoubtedly true: "This statute has touched off one of the most dynamic revolutions in the history of the mental health movement."

1967–1974: THE DREAM FADES

America's flirtation with becoming a European style welfare state, begun in the Kennedy administration in 1961 and promoted with enthusiasm by Lyndon Johnson, came to an end in 1968 with the election of Richard Nixon to the White House, accompanied by a Republican gain of 51 seats in Congress, most replacing liberal Democrats. Nixon appealed to what he labeled the silent majority and was contemptuous of social scientists and reform-minded professionals such as journalists and social workers, a group his combative vice president, Spiro Agnew, labeled the "nattering nabobs of negativism." Several factors contributed to the nation's quick rejection of the welfare state experiment. One, illustrated by the Republican's electoral success in 1968, was a general swing to the right among the general population who were fed up with vocal and aggressive protest movements, urban riots mainly attributed to the poor and minorities, and increasingly intense anti-Vietnam war protests. Much of the blame for these unpleasant events was laid at the feet of political liberals, professional social reformers including social workers, and their poor constituents. Publically expressed attitudes toward the poor and the welfare programs that assisted them returned to former levels of negativity. As summarized by Patterson, "A survey in 1967 revealed that 42 percent of Americans thought poverty resulted from 'lack of effort'; only 19 percent blamed 'circumstances beyond control.' A poll two years later found that 58 percent of respondents thought that poverty was caused by a 'lack of thrift and proper money management by poor people.' 55 percent said that it was the result of 'lack of effort by the poor.' A total of 84 percent agreed with the statement: 'There are too many people receiving welfare who ought to be working,' and 71 percent said 'Many people getting welfare are not honest about their need.' Only 34 percent agreed with the statement, 'Generally speaking, we are spending too *little* money on welfare in this country.' " An article in *Time Magazine* reported that the increase in social programs had "stretched some cities to the verge of bankruptcy." The *Time* article concluded by saying that "The failure of the United States welfare system is in large measure a defeat for liberalism"[34]

The increasingly negative perception of social reforms was reinforced by data coming in that indicated that the programs were falling far short of the results promised by their designers. The biggest concern was with the AFDC program that in spite of utilizing more than 33,000 social service workers to help clients become self-supporting was growing at an ever increasing rate. The number of recipients of AFDC benefits grew from slightly more than 3 million people in 1960 to over 5 million in 1967 to nearly 11 million by 1974. In addition to the cash benefits received by this group, generous in-kind benefits, mainly food stamps, public housing, and Medicaid, had been added that amounted to annual expenditures of over $9 billion per year. As the economy slowed in the early 1970s the perception of AFDC as a failed program and a money pit increased. Congress expressed its concern about the AFDC program by once again amending the Social Security Act in 1967. These amendments distinguished between "soft" services, such as social casework, and "hard" services such as employment training and day care, and emphasized the later. A centerpiece of the act was the Work Incentive Program (originally labeled WIP but quickly changed to WIN) that required recipients to accept jobs or job training or have their benefits cut off. To implement this change from a social service to an employment focus for the AFDC program, the Welfare Administration section of the Department of Health, Education, and Welfare was reorganized. The Welfare Administration Bureau was replaced with the Social and Rehabilitation Service, headed by Mary Switzer, a specialist in vocational rehabilitation. The Bureau of Family Services, the stronghold of social work in HEW, was divided into two divisions, the Assistance Payments Administration that was strictly concerned with administering the financial grants to recipients and the Community Services Administration that supervised social work services. This split operationalized a new philosophy in HEW that made social services strictly voluntary on the part of welfare recipients. Recipients were no longer required to accept social work services to help deal with the problems leading to their welfare dependency, but they _were_ strictly required to accept job placement and job training services.

The AFDC program was not the only one to deliver disappointing results when evaluated. Programs to combat crime and delinquency such as the much touted Mobilization for Youth were quickly found to be ineffective. Researcher Robert Martindale, for example, concluded that "with a few isolated exceptions, the rehabilitative efforts that have been reported so far have had no

34. James T. Patterson, *America's Struggle Against Poverty*, 167.

appreciable effect on rehabilitation."[35] Early reviews of the new community approach to mental health services were also expressing disappointment with results of the approach. Evaluations concluded that fewer than half the proposed community mental health centers had actually been opened and that those that had were understaffed, underfunded, and were failing to take responsibility for the care of former, present, and potential state hospital patients. As to the implementation of a new approach to mental health care, studies tended to confirm the conclusion of the Ralph Nader Study Group: "community mental health centers tend to involve only a renaming of conventional psychiatry, a collection of traditional clinical services that are in most cases not responsive to the needs of large segments of the community, and which often leave community people indifferent, sometimes antagonistic."[36]

When Richard Nixon defeated Hubert Humphrey by a slim margin and became president in 1969 he was aware of the shortcomings of the nation's social programs and made no bones about his dislike for public welfare, social work, and especially the War on Poverty. Nixon was a great disciple of traditional American values, especially those of hard work and limited federal government power. He was fond of comparing welfare recipients to his mother who, during hard economic times, had taken a job emptying bedpans in a health care facility in order to help support her family and to prevent its having to ask for help. When he was reelected in 1972, this time by a huge margin, he made his disdain for social work and social welfare even more explicit.

One of Nixon's first, and most significant, reforms was to launch a program he called the "New Federalism." The intent of this initiative was to "reverse the flow of power and resources from the states and communities to Washington and start power and resources flowing back . . . to the people all across America."[37] His intent was to get the federal government out of the business of designing, implementing and supervising social programs with its staff of primarily Democrat social activists. Instead he would take the money that was allocated for these programs and give it to the states and cities. They could then look within themselves for solutions to their problems instead of looking to Washington, they could discuss their own priorities and debate solutions, and they could work with their local publics and constituencies. "Revenue sharing" was the key to the "New Federalism" that would Nixon hoped; reverse the long trend toward a huge federal establishment. Nixon got much of what he wanted in the State and Local Financial Assistance Act of 1972, and with the authority provided by this act he moved to vigorously cut back on many social programs of the sixties. He did not get everything he wanted, however, as Congress in an effort to protect federal social spending passed Title XX of the Social Security Act in 1974, signed by Gerald Ford in 1975 after Nixon left office, that allocated money to states according to a prescribed formula for use in programs to enhance individuals ability to be self-supporting, and to improve family care or self-care, community based care, and institutional care. Title XX represented a continued commitment by the federal government, to the tune of $2.5 billion annually, to provide a

35. Robert Martinson, "What Works?" *The Public Interest* 35 (Spring 1974): 22–54.

36. B. S. Brown, "A Look at the Overlook," *Mental Hygiene* 56, (April, 1972); 6; Franklin D. Chu and Sharland Trotter, *The Madness Establishment,* Ralph Nader's Study Group Report on the National Institute of Mental Health (New York: Grossman, 1974).

37. Quoted in Walter I. Trattner, *From Poor Law to Welfare State: A History of Social Welfare in America,* 6th ed. (New York: Free Press, 1996), 338.

variety of social services to people who were near or under the poverty line. The bill, however, also reflected a growing conservative concern about runaway costs for social services by changing what had been an uncapped mandate into a program capped at the $250 billion appropriated.[38]

When Nixon took office in 1969 he recognized that the heart of the "welfare problem" was clearly the AFDC program. The program had problems along three dimensions. The first was that of adequacy. Even with the patchwork of in-kind programs that had been added, the amount of AFDC benefits was clearly not enough to support the families on the program. The second problem was equity. High benefit states, such as New York, provided grants that were three or four times as much as those of low benefit states such as Mississippi. The third problem was that the program lacked incentives to motivate people to become self-supporting and as a result trapped many recipients in a cycle of permanent dependency. Of course, these were all components of the bigger problem that was that the program continued to grow in numbers and cost and nothing seemed able to stem this tide. Giving credence to the old saying that politics makes strange bedfellows, Nixon turned to liberal social scientist (and later Democratic Senator) Daniel Patrick Moynihan, for advice regarding welfare reform. Moynihan devised what they called the Family Assistance Plan, a guaranteed annual income strategy where every family in the country would get a minimum annual income. This was a liberal's approach to welfare, but was made palatable to Nixon by setting the income level very low, and coupling benefits to an elaborate system of penalties and incentives designed to force recipients to work. The plan, according to Trattner, was "motivated, in part at least, by a desire to destroy the network of bureaucrats and social workers . . . established by the [Economic Opportunity Act] and other programs of the decade, and in part by a fear that the Democrats, who controlled the Congress, would pre-empt the issue and propose a more liberal program."[39]

The Family Assistance Plan proposed that the entire welfare system be federalized, with grants administered directly by the Social Security Administration. The amount of grants would be the same for every state. Unemployed families would receive $1600 per year (the poverty line in 1969 for a family of four was $3790) and the head of household would be required to register for work placement and/or enter a job training program. The working poor would be allowed to keep a portion of the grant, under a complex formula, until their total income reached $4000, at which time benefits would zero out. Another part of Nixon's welfare reform proposal, one that received much less publicity, was to also federalize what were known as the "adult categories" of financial assistance—Aid to the Blind, Aid to the Permanently and Totally Disabled, and Old Age Assistance. After a spirited debate, the Family Assistance Plan passed the House in 1970, lost in the Senate, was reintroduced with more liberal benefits in 1971, and once again made it through the House but was killed by the Senate. The part federalizing the adult categories did, however, pass, establishing the Supplemental Security Income program, moving benefits for the "deserving poor" from state to federal administration.

Counter to logic, under Nixon, a staunchly anti-welfare and social program conservative, programs for the poor and troubled not only continued to grow under his administration, but grew at record rates. He signed into law the Rehabilitation Act of 1973 that protected physically disabled

38. Martha Derthick, *Uncontrollable Spending for Social Services Grants* (Washington, DC: Brookings Institution, 1975).
39. Walter I. Trattner, *From Poor Law to Welfare State,* 338.

persons from discrimination; legislation establishing the Earned Income Tax Credit (E.I.T.C), a negative income tax administered by the Internal Revenue Service that provided low income families with dependent children a refundable tax credit equal to 10 percent of their earned income; the Comprehensive Employment and Training Act (CETA), which established hundreds of thousands of public service jobs in both public and private organizations; Title XX of the Social Security Act that allocated $2.5 billion annually to the states to be used by them with broad discretion for programs to meet the needs of their low income citizens. Nixon also supported expansion of the Food Stamp Program, increases in social security (OASDI) benefits and indexing benefit levels to inflation through automatic cost to living (COLA) adjustments to be made each year inflation rose by 3 percent or more. Increases in social welfare spending during the Nixon years, adjusted for inflation, were nearly twice that of the Kennedy and Johnson administrations combined. Most commentators agree with policy analyst Sar Levitan that "the greatest extensions of the modern welfare system were enacted under the conservative Presidency of Richard Nixon . . . dwarfing in size and scope the initiatives Lyndon Johnson's Great Society."[40]

Child Welfare Takes Center Stage

Reforms of the Nixon administration were in almost all cases bad for the social work profession. Although social work had not yet been completely driven from the public assistance/anti-poverty arena the handwriting for this exclusion was on the wall. However, the professional turf social work was losing in public assistance it was making up for by gains in public child welfare. As discussed earlier, public child welfare services authorized by the Social Security Act in 1935 had deteriorated to the point of being almost non-existent by the 1950s. In 1956, the Children's Bureau reported that in the whole country only 5,628 staff was employed by public child welfare agencies. With the publicity directed toward child abuse resulting from its "discovery" by the medical profession, by 1962 35 states and the District of Columbia passed legislation giving local public social service agencies responsibility and authority for child welfare services. The federal response to the problem of child maltreatment was mainly to sponsor a series of conferences on child abuse reporting laws and to develop model legislation. By 1967 every state and the District of Columbia had enacted some form of child abuse and neglect reporting law to permit individuals to report suspected cases while being protected from legal repercussions, and requiring professionals working with children to report suspected cases. The passage of reporting laws combined with the media attention devoted to child maltreatment resulted in a massive growth in the number of child abuse and neglect referrals. In 1967 nationally there were only 9,563 child maltreatment reports; by 1974 the number had increased to almost 300,000. In 1971 Senator Walter Mondale became chairman of the newly created Subcommittee on Children and Youth and in 1973 began hearings on the issue of child abuse and neglect. The hearings confirmed the arguments made by both the American Humane Association and by the Children's Bureau that efforts by both the public and private sectors to

40. Sar Levitan and Clifford Johnson, *Beyond the Safety Net: Reviving the Promise of Opportunity in America* (Cambridge, MA: Ballinger, 1984), 2.

combat child abuse and neglect were seriously deficient. The result of these hearings was the Child Abuse Prevention and Treatment Act (P.L. 93-247) passed by overwhelming majorities in both the House and the Senate and signed into law by President Nixon on January 31, 1974. The act

- Provided funds to states to set up child abuse and neglect prevention and treatment programs
- Authorized research into child abuse prevention and treatment
- Created the National Center on Child Abuse and Neglect
- Created the National Clearinghouse on Child Abuse and Neglect Information
- Established state grants for hiring and training personnel and to support innovative programs aimed at preventing and treating child maltreatment

As a result of these developments the number of social workers employed in child welfare capacities increased from slightly more than 5,000 in 1955 to more than 30,000 in 1974.

CONCLUSION

The years 1945 to 1974 witnessed a massive increase in the size and expense of the social welfare system in the United States. During these years a pattern was followed where a problem would be recognized and publicized, scholars and journalists would analyze and attempt to explain the problem and speculate about possible solutions, pressure would build for the government, often aided by private foundations, to act against the problem, and finally, supported by the booming economy programs would be launched. Health, mental health, crime and delinquency, aging, poverty, and child welfare all went through this process. Public spending on social welfare programs during these years grew from $9 billion, which was 4.4 percent of gross national product and 8.4 percent of total government outlays, to $289 billion, which was 19.1 percent of GDP and more than half of total government spending.[41]

As social welfare moved from the margins to the center of American concerns people began to ask how welfare fit with American values and lifestyles and, more specifically, if we had become, or should become, a welfare state like many in Western Europe. In an effort to address this question the International Conference of Social Work asked the Russell Sage Foundation to sponsor a study of the place of social welfare in American society. The foundation agreed that this was an important question and contracted with sociologists Harold Wilensky and Charles Lebeaux (who was on the faculty of a school of social work) to conduct a study and prepare a report on this subject. In 1958 they published their report titled *Industrial Society and Social Welfare: The Impact of Industrialization on the Supply and Organization of Social Services in the United States.* This book, revised in 1965, was required reading for students in schools of social work for more than a decade.

---

41. U.S. Census Bureau, *Statistical Abstract of the United States: 1999,* Table No. 1422, Social Welfare Expenditures Under Public Programs and National Health Care Expenditures: 1929 to 1997. Available at https://www.census.gov/library/publications/1999/compendia/statab/119ed.html.

Wilensky and Lebeaux's analysis revolved around two ideas central for understanding social welfare in the United States. The first was an analysis of American society as being what they labeled a "culture of capitalism." They argued that the culture of capitalism was based on a radical individualism that attributed all credit for success and all blame for failure on the rational, self-interested, acquisitive individual. He or she gets all the credit as well as all the blame. Those who achieve are, by definition, virtuous; those who do not are at least incompetent and perhaps even lazy and immoral. Their second major idea was the identification of two different conceptualizations of social welfare in industrial societies, which they labeled *institutional* and *residual*.

The institutional conception, according to Wilensky and Lebeaux is dominant in most western European democracies and "implies no stigma, no emergency, no 'abnormalacy' [on the part of those receiving services]: Social welfare becomes accepted as a proper, legitimate function of modern industrial society in helping individuals achieve self-fulfillment. The complexity of modern life is recognized. The inability of the individual to provide for himself, or to meet all his needs in family and work settings, is considered a 'normal' condition; and the helping agencies achieve 'regular' institutional status."[42] In other words, the institutional conception recognizes that life in modern society is so complex that nearly everyone will need help achieving and maintaining health and self-sufficiency, and that the level of this help needs to be greater than the forms the basic institutions, mainly family and market, can provide. Families cannot provide 100 percent of the care needed by their children; the economy cannot provide 100 percent employment for the entire population at all times; and families and churches cannot care for all the elderly now that people are living many years past retirement and an ever increasing proportion of the population is elderly. Social welfare is viewed as a first-line, permanent social institution.

The other view of social welfare in industrial societies is labeled by Wilensky and Lebeaux as the residual conception. This view is "based on the premise that there are two 'natural' channels through which an individual's needs are properly met: the family and the market economy. These are the preferred structures of supply. However, sometimes these institutions do not function adequately: family life is disrupted, depressions occur. Or sometimes the individual cannot make use of the normal channels because of old age or illness. In such cases, according to this idea, a third mechanism of need fulfillment is brought into play—the social welfare structure. This is conceived as a residual agency, attending primarily to emergency functions, and is expected to withdraw when the regular social structure—the family and the economic system—is again working properly. Because of its residual, temporary, substitute characteristic, social welfare thus conceived often carries the stigma of 'dole' or 'charity.' " In this conception, social welfare is not an institution but an emergency backup system. If the other institutions of society could be made to perform properly—the family to take responsibility for its elderly members, the church to care for the less fortunate, and the economy to provide enough jobs for everyone—social welfare programs would not be necessary.

During the years 1945 to 1974 America flirted with the idea of becoming a welfare state. Not only did the size and expenditures of social welfare programs grow at a dizzying pace, but it appeared that our attitudes or, to use Wilensky and Lebeaux's term, our conception of social

---

42. Harold L. Wilensky and Charles N. Lebeaux, *Industrial Society and Social Welfare* (New York: Russell Sage Foundation, 1958), 140.

welfare seemed to be changing. We began to view welfare as a right, recipients as people who were victims of impersonal social forces rather than personal failures, to talk of empowering the poor, and to chide ourselves to stop "blaming the victim." Academics and policy experts began to argue that America was not only becoming a welfare state, but an institutional welfare state. Wilensky and Lebeaux, in a 1965 revision of their book opined, "As the residual conception becomes weaker, as we believe it will, and the institutional conception increasingly dominant, it seems likely that distinctions between welfare and other types of social institutions will become more and more blurred. Under continuing industrialization all institutions will be oriented toward and evaluated in terms of social welfare aims. The 'welfare state' will become the 'welfare society,' and both will be more reality than epithet."[43]

Wilensky and Lebeaux, along with most social welfare scholars, were wrong in their belief that America was becoming an institutional welfare state. When Richard Nixon became president in 1969 the rhetoric about social welfare took a sharp turn to the right and became critical to the point of being harsh. But, as we have seen, the growth of social welfare programs did not slow but in fact increased. What had changed was not the nation's commitment to help the poor and afflicted, but the attitude upon which that help was given. American's rejected the idea that welfare was a right of the recipient, but not the idea that helping was an obligation of the rest of us. They rejected the idea that people should be able to violate social norms (such as having children outside of marriage) and then expect help without any consequences. And, probably most important, they rejected the idea that welfare was a substitute for work and people could chose to be long term recipients of aid without making substantial efforts to become self-supporting. America had become a welfare state, but it was clearly a residual welfare state.

43. Harold Wilensky and Charles Lebeaux, *Industrial Society and Social Welfare,* 2nd ed. (New York: The Free Press, 1965), 147.

CHAPTER 11

SOCIAL WORK PRACTICE, 1945–1974

Anna Deck received a bachelor's degree in anthropology from Oberlin College in 1958 and an MSW from New York University in 1960.[1] She was unusual in that she choose to double major at NYU following the curriculum for both casework and group work, thus gaining her professional qualifications in two of the three professional practice methods. Immediately following graduation she went to work for a Jewish Community Centers Association where she mainly applied her group work skills in leading all sorts of developmental and recreational groups for the agency's mainly middle class and relatively pathology- free clientele. Although this was a pretty good job and Anna felt she was making good use of her skills, she found it a little boring. So when she was told about a job as a social worker in a new inner city project named Mobilization for Youth (MFY), working in one of its neighborhood service centers, she immediately applied. She was invited for an interview and spoke with the agency's assistant chief, who explained to her that she would be working mostly with minority group members who were very poor, each with multiple problems that involved crime, drug abuse, single parenthood, abuse, exploitation, and just about any problem you could think of. He offered his opinion that each day would be different, stress would sometimes be high, and that her social work education, even with her two-method concentration, would probably not have adequately equipped her for the challenges she would face. When she was offered the job she accepted without hesitation.

Early in her tenure as a MFY social worker Anna was buzzed by the receptionist, who told her that there was a neighborhood resident in the waiting area who would like to see her. Seeing a drop-in was not at all unusual because the agency realized that appointments were not in the style of residents of their neighborhood, so they saw people in a first come, first served basis. Anna escorted the client, who she was introduced to as Cassandra Smith, to her office and asked how she could be of help. Mrs. Smith was a black woman somewhere in her early twenties, tall, thin of a type that people sometimes called wiry, clear eyed, well spoken, and apparently very intelligent. Her

---

1. Anna Deck is a pseudonym. The case is based on Francis P. Purcell and Harry Specht, "The House on Sixth Street," *Social Work* 10, no. 4, (Oct. 1965): 69–76.

physical appearance did not, however, match her personal presence. She appeared dirty, unkempt, with wrinkled clothes and matted hair. The reason for her rough physical appearance became clear when she explained her problem to the social worker. Mrs. Smith and eleven other families were residents of an apartment building on Sixth Street and there had been no gas, electricity, heat, or hot water to the apartments for more than four weeks. She and her four children were entirely supported by a welfare grant and this meager resource was exhausted, so she came to the MFY center in desperation because she could not run her household any longer without utilities.

Later that same day Anna visited the Sixth Street building with Mrs. Smith and a community worker. Community workers were program staff members who were neighborhood residents, generally with little formal education, whose job was to relate to their neighbors in ways that outsiders could not and to encourage them to organize and take independent social action. The community worker in this case was of Puerto Rican descent, spoke Spanish, and his easy manner and knowledge of the neighborhood enabled him and Anna to become involved quickly with Mrs. Smith and her neighbors. Their visit confirmed what Mrs. Smith had said about the condition of the building. Upon entering the building through a broken front door Anna was nearly overpowered by the stench of garbage and decay, had to swat flies and roaches out of the way, and her foot was run over by a rat the size of a small dog. Following the building visit Anna did a little research and found that the Rent and Rehabilitation Administration (the New York City agency that paid the low income tenants rent) had reduced the payment to the landlord to one dollar per month for each apartment because the landlord had failed to respond to orders to repair the building. The landlord had not made any utility payments for several months and so services to the building had been discontinued. With dirt and disorganization increasing daily, the mothers were tired and demoralized. They were afraid to sleep at night because the building was infested with rats. There was a constant threat of fire because the tenants had to use candles for light. There were also seventeen vacant apartments in the building that had been invaded by homeless men and drug addicts.

Anna's first task was to decide on a point of intervention to help Mrs. Smith and her neighbors with their problems and then select the methods to be used. One of the basic beliefs of MFY was that "Too often, the client system presenting the problem becomes the major target for intervention, and the intervention method is limited to the one most suitable for that client system." A traditional social work approach at the time would have been to define Mrs. Smith as the client and to work with her using casework methods to resolve her problem as defined by her and the social worker. Following this approach the social worker would help her find a new place to live, organize her life so she was less likely to face this problem again, and work with her to strengthen aspects of her personality that contributed to her problems. Mobilization for Youth, however, was a leader in questioning this approach to social work practice and was experimenting with replacing it with an approach that viewed a client as embedded in a social system that was in many ways interrelated, and that to truly help the client it is necessary to change multiple aspects of the system. Consequently, the agency was as interested in facilitating social change as it was in individual change. Aspects of the system that were involved in this case were defined as Mrs. Smith, her neighbors, the land lord, the public utility companies, the Rent and Rehabilitation Administration, the welfare department, the police, and various other city agencies responsible for health and welfare.

Anna worked on this case for four months. During this time she made use of all social work methods (casework and group work that she had been trained in, and community organization that she had to learn along the way), as well as assistance from the community worker, a lawyer, a city planner, and various civil rights organizations. Anna functioned as a social work generalist providing casework services to individuals and families when they had specialized needs or during especially trying times such as when they were relocated. Group work, administration, and community organization were handled by another agency social worker who had specialized in community organization. Anna also provided immediate and concrete assistance to individuals and families such as small financial grants, medical care, homemaking services, child care, and transportation.

With as much participation as possible from the building residents, Anna and her team formulated and implemented a plan to address the specific problems of the Sixth Street building residents as well as to improve the situation of all low-income housing residents in the MFY neighborhood. Included in the plan was legal action against the landlord and the various agencies who were denying the tenants services to which they were legally entitled. Mrs. Smith proved to be a natural and competent leader and, with support and encouragement from MFY staff, she and the other residents became articulate and effective in negotiating with the various agencies. They were successful in having the city codes administration condemn the building so their problem would not be replicated with a new group of tenants. With the building condemned the welfare department was legally obligated to find alternative housing for the families.

Following the condemnation of the building the welfare department offered to move all of the residents into shelters or hotels, but this offer was rejected by the mothers because shelters would mean splitting up families and the hotels were really flop houses that were inhabited mostly by prostitutes or drug addicts. Following much discussion the mothers decided that they would publicly embarrass the officials responsible for the problem, hoping that this would goad them into action. The strategy for doing this was to first send a telegram to city, state, and federal officials accusing the city and state agencies of racism because the residents of the building were all either black or Puerto Rican. The second step was to move out of the apartment building and take up residence in the basement of a local church. Once these steps had been taken the group contacted the media and provided material for several stories about the racism charges and that the mothers were living in a church basement because of the failure of public agencies to do their jobs. These stories were successful in embarrassing the welfare department and the Rent and Rehabilitation Administration and motivated them to increase their efforts to find suitable housing for the families.

After four months the building had been condemned and boarded up and all of the families had been relocated to alternative housing. The agency administrators and social workers who had worked on the case assessed its outcome and concluded that it was both disappointing and hopeful. On the disappointing side was the outcome that the tenant's court cases had been dismissed on technicalities. The tenants had all been provided alternative housing but some of it was out of the neighborhood and most was almost as bad as the Sixth Street apartments. The agency also suspected that they may have played into the hands of the landlord who, now that the building was condemned and empty, was eligible to apply for Urban Development funds to rehabilitate it into middle income housing. On the hopeful side was the assessment that the case had strengthened the capacity of neighborhood residents to work together as a community. Two agency administrators concluded: "The organization that began to develop in the neighborhood has continued to grow, but it is a painstaking job. The fact that the poor have the strength to continue to struggle for better living conditions is something to wonder at and admire."

The case of "The House on Sixth Street," which was published in the NASW journal *Social Work* in 1965, is an example of the rapid changes that were occurring in social work practice in the 1960s and 1970s. A view of client problems as rooted in complex social systems began to replace the narrow psychodynamic approach that had for many years dominated the field. Recognizing client problems as having system dimensions led to the corollary recognition that social workers must engage in social action as well as individual treatment to effectively address issues. Finally, it was recognized that the traditional methods of casework, group work, and community organization were so inextricably interwoven in practice that this traditional division was no longer valid, and practice theory began to move toward a conception of integrated methods and eventually generalist practice.

DOMINANCE OF THE PROFESSIONAL ELITE: 1945–1960

Prior to the Great Depression the elite segment of the social work profession had worked tirelessly to gain recognition of social work as a major profession, one on par with medicine, law and the clergy. A central tenet of these efforts was that fully qualified social workers should be graduates of professional schools, preferably on the graduate level. This was codified in 1937 when the American Association of Social Workers (AASW) passed the resolution that "all professional education for social work was to be offered as graduate study after October 1, 1939."[2] These schools were accredited by the AASW, established in 1919, the body recognized by the federal Committee on Accrediting, as the official social work accreditation body.

As we have seen, in the 1930s in conjunction with the implementation of the huge public welfare programs resulting from the Social Security Act, the number of social work jobs rapidly increased, most requiring less than a master's degree, and it was quickly recognized that some type of training programs should be established to meet the technical needs of these new positions. The existing schools of social work were clearly not able to meet this need because, in addition to limiting their training to the graduate level, they were heavily concentrated in the northeastern region of the country, were few in number, produced a limited supply of graduates, and were heavily focused on the needs of private agencies in urban centers. In response to this problem state universities and agricultural colleges began to develop undergraduate social work programs, mainly within existing sociology departments, aimed at the needs of public agencies and rural areas. One proposal from a sociology department chair at a state agricultural college said that the remedy to the problem of social work education for public service in rural areas was "to tackle the problem from the grassroots and try to build up at least one school in each state that can train farm-reared people" and design the social work curriculum "from the farm viewpoint rather than the standpoint of highly

2. Ernest V. Hollis and Alice L. Taylor, *Social Work Education in the United States—The Report of a Study Made for the National Council on Social Work Education* (New York: Columbia University Press, 1951), 29.

developed urban techniques."[3] These programs sought direction and help from AASSW, but the response they received was generally less than helpful. During the years 1936 to 1941 more effort was expended by the AASSW Executive Committee to develop ways to discourage the establishment of new programs than to help the existing ones. As Sophenisba Breckinridge, a member of the AASSW Executive Board, explained the associations attitude toward undergraduate social work education it "might be described as believing thoroughly in birth control . . . It is . . . easier to keep an institution out than to get it out, and we must be assured of graduate quality [in social work education]"[4]

In response to the need for trained social workers in rural states, and to the unhelpfulness of the AASSW, W. R. Bizzell, President of the University of Oklahoma, sent a memo to forty state universities proposing the development of a new accrediting organization for schools with undergraduate social work programs and one-year social work graduate degrees. Bizzell listed seven reasons for establishing a new accrediting body, which quickly came to be referred to as the "seven deadly sins" of the AASSW. Among these were that the AASSW standards were not practical in any but the largest schools; the Association reflected the goals and structure of privately endowed schools of social work; it ignored the needs of rural populations; state universities should have the responsibility of training students for publically funded social service positions; and that the AASSW was "an autocratic organization dominated by the thinking of two or three schools."[5]

In response to the Bizzell memo the AASSW proposed a special membership category for one-year graduate programs (such as that at the University of Oklahoma) but refused to make any accommodation for undergraduate programs. Their concern was that accepting the legitimacy of undergraduate professional training might confirm the public view of social work as a job that could be done by any reasonably well-educated individual. Undergraduate programs continued to grow and, faced with the rejection by AASSW, in1942 banded together to form the National Association of Schools of Social Administration (NASSA). The 34 schools that joined as charter members were for the most part social work programs in state universities and land grant colleges. All were "identified with the tradition that tax-supported institutions have a responsibility for meeting the needs of the states for professional and quasi-professional personnel."[6]

The existence of two separate accrediting bodies for programs providing training for what the public perceived as the same profession was of concern to agencies, funding bodies, universities, and, most significantly, the Joint Committee on Accrediting, the body that accredited the individual accrediting agencies. As a result of pressure by these groups two committees were formed and issued reports dealing with the situation. The first committee was set up by the US Children's Bureau and the Joint Committee on Accrediting in 1944. The committee held only one meeting, attended by representatives of AASSW and NASSA. The NASSA, predictably, pushed for formal

3. Letter from W. Kumlien to S. Breckinridge, 7/27/35, quoted in Leslie Leighninger, "Graduate and Undergraduate Social Work Education: Roots of Conflict," *Journal of Education for Social Work*, 20, (Fall 1984): 69.

4. Breckinridge to Wayne McMillen, 1/7/36, quoted in Leslie Leighninger, "Graduate and Undergraduate Social Work Education," *Journal of Education for Social Work*,20 (Fall 1984): 70.

5. Leslie Leighninger, "Graduate and Undergraduate Social Work Education," 70

6. Ernest V. Hollis and Alice L. Taylor, *Social Work Education in the United States,* (New York: Columbia University Press, 1951), 37.

recognition of undergraduate education in social work, while AASSW stuck to its position that a two year master's program was the only legitimate form of professional social work education. No solution or compromise was reached. The second committee, the Joint Committee on Education for Social Work, was sponsored by the Russell Sage Foundation, met for nearly a year and took its task of negotiation and cooperation seriously. This committee agreed upon a set of eight recommendations, including that the AASSW and the NASSW merge into one organization that would be responsible for accrediting all levels of social work educational programs. The NASSA board accepted all eight recommendations while the AASSW board accepted only three rather minor ones: that a national study be conducted; that a National Council on Social Work Education be formed; and that another study committee be formed. As a result of the formation, in 1946, of the National Council on Social Work Education, there were now three official social work education organizations. These committees had failed to reach any compromise about the shape and form of social work education largely because, as noted by Leighninger, they "differed greatly in their attitudes toward professionalism and their degree of commitment to public welfare. AASSW was chiefly concerned with matters internal to a profession—the need to develop autonomy, raise practice and academic standards, and strengthen the profession's educational base. NASSA was concerned largely with external matters—the needs of the public social services, and the pressures exerted by institutions of higher education."[7]

Frustrated by the inability of the AASSW and the NASSA to resolve the social work accreditation issue, in November 1947 the Joint Committee on Accrediting announced that if the two organizations did not resolve their differences the Committee would declare a moratorium on *all* accrediting of social work education. Faced with this threat, a joint committee of the two organizations obtained funding from the Carnegie Foundation for a study, to be led by an outside educational expert, to examine "the provision and distribution of educational facilities in relation to present . . . demand for social service personnel."[8] Earnest Hollis, Chief of College Administration for the US Department of Education, was hired as the outside expert to lead the study of social work education. Alice Taylor, a well-known social worker and a Training Consultant in the US Bureau of Public Assistance, was hired to assist Hollis. Their study, *Social Work Education in the United States*, was published in 1951. The report was disappointing to hardliners in both the NASSA and the AASSW. Many members of the NASSA were disappointed with the report because it did not support the idea that undergraduate programs could provide entry level training for social work practice. Hollis and Taylor instead supported the expansion of undergraduate social work education, but viewed it as pre-professional, preparing students for graduate professional study in social work analogous to pre-med or pre-law studies. Many AASSW members were disappointed with the report because it did advocate for undergraduate social work education, albeit defined as preprofessional, and they felt that undergraduate social work programs were not necessarily superior to general study in the social sciences.

Although few were completely satisfied with the Hollis-Taylor report most saw its main recommendation that social work professional education be limited to the graduate level, but that

---

7. Leslie Leighninger, "Graduate and Undergraduate Social Work Education," 73.

8. Memo, Sue Spencer to members, National Council on Education for Social Work, n.d., cited in Leslie Leighninger, "Graduate and Undergraduate Social Work Education in the United States," 74.

undergraduate programs be expanded to provide pre-professional education, as a reasonable compromise. The hard reality was that the Joint Committee on Accrediting was insisting that social work unify its accrediting function and NASSA did not have the resources to continue as an independent body. Following the release of the report and its consideration by all involved, another committee was formed that represented both educational associations as well as public welfare agencies. This committee rapidly developed an action plan with the result that in 1952 a new accrediting organization was formed, the Council on Social Work Education (CSWE). The new organization replaced both previous groups, which were immediately disbanded. Although the new organization represented a compromise between the more extreme positions of its predecessors, there clearly was an imbalance between American Association of Schools of Social Work (AASSW) and NASSA concerns and interests. On the new organizations board undergraduate programs were given ten seats and the graduate programs were given twenty. Most importantly, under the new structure undergraduate programs were not eligible for any kind of accreditation and baccalaureate prepared people were not recognized as professional social workers.

Although the establishment of the CSWE represented a victory for the traditional social work elite by defining the master's degree as the only route to becoming a professional social worker, it flew in the face of job market reality. At about the same time as the establishment of the new organization the US Bureau of Labor Statistics released data on occupants of jobs within its definition of social work. Only 16 percent of these jobs were occupied by people meeting the CSWE definition of a professionally trained social worker.[9] Because of this reality, which did not change much over time, the graduate/undergraduate debate continued and was not finally resolved until 1974.

A NEW ERA OF CHANGE FOR SOCIAL WORK PRACTICE

With MSWs firmly in control of the profession, social workers in the 1950s continued to strive toward the goal of becoming a psychotherapeutic, individual treatment specialty. Two significant trends in the 1950s facilitated this process. One was the gradual shifting of professional attention from the poor toward the needs and problems of the middle class. This was largely due to the continuing social work rejection of public welfare as an appropriate setting for professional practice with the accompanying belief that because public agencies were dealing with the problems of the poor, social work agencies had less responsibility to do so. Social workers Richard Cloward and Irwin Epstein reviewed historical literature and agency documents and traced an evolution of the relationship of social work and the poor. They found that until the Great Depression private (read "professional") social agencies defined their mission as providing both material assistance and social casework services to the poor. When the great federal programs were established in the 1930s a new division of labor was established with the public agencies being responsible for material assistance and the private agencies providing social casework services. Cloward and Epstein

---

9. U.S. Department of Labor, Bureau of Labor Statistics, "Social Workers in 1950," cited in Harold Wilensky and Charles Lebeaux, *Industrial Society and Social Welfare* (New York: Russell Sage Foundation, 1956), 292.

found that over time the private agencies began to more and more refer poor clients back to pub-lic agencies for services, reserving their resources for middle income clients experiencing non-economic relationship or adjustment problems. They conclude "The private agency, we suggest, did not respond to the development of public programs by defining a new role with respect to its traditional clientele, the poor, instead, it moved toward a new clientele, economically more fortu-nate than the old. At the same time, a new conception of the private agency began to emerge."[10] This conception was as a psychodynamic counseling agency providing services to a clientele with both the value system to make use of insight based therapy and, to the extent possible, the financial resources to pay for it.

The second trend, obviously related to the first, was that casework began to closely resemble psychotherapy as provided by several other professions, notably psychiatry and clinical psychol-ogy. In 1962 Fernando Torgerson published a careful literature review in which he attempted to develop a definition that would differentiate and define casework as different from psychotherapy. He failed to find any difference in the theory and practice of psychotherapy and casework, but finally concluded that the difference was in the goals of the two professions. He argued that psy-chotherapy aims at the resolution of inner psychological conflicts, at structural personality change, and at emotional maturation, in the final analysis expecting the client to give up old, destructive, patterns of behavior. Casework, by comparison, aims at helping an individual come to a decision with regard to a social problem so that he or she can move toward a solution with conviction and with strength to live with the consequences of that decision.[11]

Social work leaders were aware that the person in environment equation that was the profes-sion's *sine qua non* was tilting decidedly toward the person side, however their expressions of con-cern were tepid at best. In 1953 the great casework theoretician and teacher Helen Harris Perlman urged her colleagues to "put the social back in social work" but later confessed that she thought it was a lost cause. Also in 1953 AASW President Benjamin Youngdahl asked at an address to the organization's delegate assembly if their "function as social workers was limited to the treatment of social pathologies, or do we also have a positive or preventive function to perform?" He concluded that of course social workers had this second function to perform, but the best proposal he could make was that they develop skills in "statesmanship," which he defined as "all those activities which would have for their primary purpose the prevention of illness, maladjustment, and need, and which would relate individual need to the culture and existing social institutions in such a positive way as to bring improvement and a lessening of individual ills." In 1958 Herbert Bisno asked "How Social Will Social Work Be," and concluded that social work was heading toward 1) a continuing de-emphasis on controversial social action; 2) a related lessening of attempts to influence social policy and the acceptance of the role of technician-implementer; and 3) a change in the ideology

---

10. Richard A. Cloward and Erwin Epstein, "Private Social Welfare's Disengagement from the Poor: The Case of Family Adjustment Agencies," in Mayer Zald, editor, *Social Welfare Institutions: A Sociological Reader* (New York: John Wiley and Sons, 1965), 626.

11. Fernando G. Torgerson, "Differentiating and Defining Casework and Psychotherapy," *Social Work*, 7 (April, 1962): 39–47. See also Helen Harris Perlman, "The Basic Structure of the Casework Process," *Social Service Review* 27 (September, 1953): 308–315; Cora Kasius, ed., *Social Casework in the Fifties* (New York: Family Service Association of America, 1962); Gordon Hamilton, "A Theory of Personality: Freud's Contribution to Social Work," in Howard J. Parad, ed., *Ego Psychology and Dynamic Casework* (New York: Family Service Association of America, 1958), 11–37.

of social work that will lessen the gap between its system of ideas and that of the dominant groups in society. Ernest Greenwood, social work's preeminent expert on the sociology of the professions noted the trend toward de-emphasis on social action and attributed this to the pursuit of professional status, saying this was the price of achieving the public acceptance accorded a profession. He stated "Extrapolation from the sociologist's model of the professions suggests a reality basis for these fears. It suggests that the attainment of professional prestige, authority, and monopoly by social workers will undoubtedly carry disturbing implications for the social action and social reform components of social work philosophy. The anticipated developments will compel social workers to rethink and redefine the societal role of their profession."[12]

Although social workers themselves were timid in their assessments of the implications of the pursuit of professional status at the expense of interest in poverty and social change, there were those outside the profession who were not timid at all. In 1957 Marion K. Sanders, a journalist whose "beat" was social issues, including social work, published a stinging critique of social work's professional pretensions in the influential and intellectually weighty magazine *Harpers*, accusing social work of being "a profession chasing its tail." She assessed social work as being preoccupied with the pursuit of professional status and as a result of this as having lost track of the purpose of the profession. She accused the profession of being obsessed with jargon, tending to obscure issues with overly complex analyses, having abandoned public welfare, and becoming preoccupied with individual counseling and even attempting to retreat to private practice. She concluded that social workers should "... accept the overwhelming demand for their services as proof enough that the profession is esteemed enough and stop chasing the tail of status. Thus invigorated, they might lift their eyes from the trees of individual behavior to the woods full of social problems, moving in large numbers from the backwaters of private philanthropy to the mainstream of public welfare. . . And while they are so engaged they may find it wise, for a time at least, to leave the talking and conferring to others. Especially the talking."[13]

Just as the massive social unrest of the 1930s caught social work unprepared, narrowly focusing on an individual treatment model in a world that was suddenly questioning the status quo and interested in changing social structures, the social discontent of the 1960s found social work once again focusing on a narrow approach designed to adjust individuals to a recognized reality, even though that reality may be unjust. The wave of social criticism and demand for social change and social action that engulfed the nation following Kennedy's election in 1961, broke over social work with sudden and enthusiastic demands that the profession reverse the 1950s trend toward individual, psychotherapeutic practice and that it embrace the new national ethos of relevance and change. Professional leaders, however, did not forget the concerns that social action could be hazardous to the profession. Early in the movement Hyman Weiner advised his social work colleagues that they certainly should be involved in social action, but that they would need to do this as members of professional organizations or as private citizens. He believed that there was

12. Helen Harris Perlman, "Social Work Method: A Review of the Past Decade," *Social Work* 10 (October 1965): 178; Benjamin Youngdahl, "Social Work at a Crossroads," *Social Work Journal* 34, no. 3 (July 1953): 11;Herbert Bisno, "How Social Will Social Work Be?" *Social Work* 1 (April 1956); 12–18; Ernest Greenwood, "Attributes of a Profession," *Social Work* 2 (July 1957): 55.

13. Marion K. Saunders, "Social Work: A Profession Chasing Its Tail," *Harpers*, March 1957, 56–62.

little possibility for social workers to integrate a social change role within their daily jobs. In a similar vein Lydia Rapoport observed that social workers have to maintain a dual identification and loyalty, on the one hand to their employing agency and on the other to the profession, with the primary tie being with the agency. She argued that the time for social workers to engage in social action was at hand, but that it would be effective only if they were represented by sound and powerful professional organizations and by schools of social work that were less responsive to agency dictates. She observed that the liberal political climate represented a rare opportunity and that "It is up to the social work profession to take advantage of this positive objective situation and translate words into action."[14]

Social workers took seriously the observation that if change was to come to the profession it would need to be led by the schools and professional organizations. Schools responded to the new social atmosphere by rapidly expanding in both number and enrollment and by curriculum revisions. By 1970 there were seventy accredited schools of social work in the United States, with an additional ten working toward accreditation. These schools enrolled over 13,000 students, more than double the enrollment in 1965. There was a dramatic shift in the concentration choice of students, casework students declining from a high of 80 percent in the late 1950s to only 36 percent in 1970, community organization students increasing from less than 1 percent to more than 10 percent, with group work remaining at a steady 10 percent (the remaining percentage of students choose administration, policy, generic, or combined concentrations).[15] This new bumper crop of students was also much more demanding than their predecessors, insisting on greater student involvement in the educational process and more attention by the faculty to the need for social action and social change. A wave of student protests swept the schools involving walk outs, sit-ins, student strikes, and numerous other aggressive protest strategies. Bell weather results of these protests were that students at Berkeley were invited to be non-voting members of the school's Executive Committee and voting members of all other non-personnel related faculty committees; students at NYU were invited to attend all faculty committees; at Michigan students transformed the Student Council to a Student Union and successfully demanded curriculum revisions to include courses on legal aid, psychology of change, and the sociology of social movements. On March 17 and 18, 1967 a conference was held at Washington University (St. Louis) to organize a Congress of Students of Social Work with the stated purpose being to "take a more radical and objective position about issues on the social work scene as well as our own schools." The Congress sought to include trained and untrained social workers as well as recipients of services. One observer of the student movement in schools of social work noted with some sense of irony that ". . . today's students will be tomorrows administrators, and thus in turn the ultimate target for newer reformers."

Professional organizations were rocked with demands for change even more dramatically than were the schools. Virtually every annual meeting of professional social work and social welfare professional organizations in the last half of the 1960s was disrupted by a combination of walkouts,

14. Hyman J. Weiner, "Towards Techniques for Social Change," *Social Work* 6 (April 1961): 26–35; Lydia Rapoport, "In Defense of Social Work," *Social Service Review* 34 (March 1960): 71.

15. Arnulf M. Pins, "Changes in Social Work Education and Their Implications for Practice, *Social Work*, 16 (April 1971): 5–15.

picketing, and attendees shouting down presenters. Particularly hard hit was the hundred year old National Conference of Social Welfare, which was at the time still the nation's preeminent social welfare organization. Groups staging protests and making demands at each meeting between 1968 and 1973 included the National Welfare Rights Organization, the National Association of Black Social Workers, the National Federation of Student Social Workers, Trabajabores Sociales de la Raza, the Association of Puerto Rican Social Service Workers, the National Congress of American Indians, the Asian American Social Workers, the Social Welfare Workers Movement, as well as other groups representing gay social workers, prisoners, and various labor organizations. NCSW President John Kidneigh summarized the 1969 Annual Conference in New York saying "It is an understatement to say that the week was a week of action. Forceful take-overs of General Sessions, demonstrations, picketing, marches on Sears, seizure of the registration area, unauthorized money-raising accompanied by cajoling demands, and bushels of hastily prepared leaflets and propaganda materials, were some of the features that provided a week of tension, devotion, excitement, anger, pity, and intense concern." The protests revolved around two issues. The first was whether NCSW would demonstrate inclusiveness in its own organization. The most successful example of this was a demand by the National Association of Black Social Workers to be allowed to select representatives on the Executive Committee and on all planning committees of the Conference. The second issue was that the Conference take a stand on social issues and become the "national voice of social welfare." Demands in this area included that people "who speak, write, research and evaluate the black community be black people" and that white social workers ". . . involve themselves with solving the problem of white racism—America's number one mental health problem." Groups also called on the Conference to repudiate the existing welfare system.[16]

NEW APPROACHES TO PRACTICE

Although leaders such as Weiner and Rapoport had argued forcefully that social action/social change activities could and should not be integrated into social work practice methods, most social workers felt that practice theory needed to change to incorporate a greater concern for the social environment. Beginning in the early 1960s intense effort was directed toward doing exactly this. These efforts focused on developing and refining macro methods, conceptualizing casework (soon to be called direct practice) as being as concerned with social change/social justice as with helping people adjust to a recognized reality, integrating systems thinking into social work methods, and finally, toward the end of the era, blurring the lines between the traditional methods of casework, group work, and community organization and conceptualizing them as one integrated method.

16. Wayne Vasey, "The San Francisco Story," in *Social Welfare Forum, 1968* (New York: NCSW, 1968), 156–163; John C. Kidneigh, "The New York Conference Story," in *Social Welfare Forum, 1969* (New York: NCSW, 1969), 178–187; Howard E. Pruntz, "Chicago Scene II: Report from a Participant," in *Social Welfare Forum, 1970* (New York: NCSW, 1970), 156–160; Howard E. Pruntz, "The New York Story—A Participant's Viewpoint," in *Social Welfare Forum, 1969* (New York: NCSW, 1969); Margaret E. Berry, "Confrontation at the National Conference on Social Welfare," *Social Service Review* 63, (Dec. 1989): 630–656.

THE DEVELOPMENT OF MACRO METHODS

As was discussed earlier, community organization was accepted as a social work technique in the 1930s and was given equal status in social work education with that of casework and group work, even though the number of students selecting this method was extremely small. In 1962 community organization was re-conceptualized in a statement developed by the Committee on Community Organization of the National Association of Social Workers. This statement defined a dual purpose for community practice—the strengthening of community capability for problem solving and the achievement of specific goals. Like other social workers, the community worker was seen as using a problem solving process, but the community organization process was rooted in the techniques of study, structuring, and conciliation. Community workers were responsible for organizational work with communities, as well as community development and planning. An important change from previous conceptualizations of community practice was that this statement broadened the clientele of community workers from the community leaders who had previously been the focus, to include indigenous citizens who might also be the recipients of social services.

In addition to the traditional macro role of community organization, social workers began to argue for the development of skills in politics and social policy. Wade, for example, observed that key social welfare decisions were now being made in the public and not the private sector. If, he argued, social workers are to make a contribution to these decisions they must develop effective ways to bring their expertise about social conditions and problems to the attention of politicians who will, in the final analysis, make the decisions about how to deal with these conditions. Social workers must develop direct and indirect methods of political action with the same energy and devotion that they have given to the shaping of techniques and methods of direct practice in the past. He concluded "Only in this way can our profession have a significant impact on community life. If we ignore politics, it will continue to ignore us, and the chances are that our profession will thus lose its great potential as an instrument of a democratic society."[17] In a similar vein, philosopher Charles Frankel argued that social workers needed to seriously address themselves to the study of our social and political organization and to develop a "serious, deliberate, and controversial concern with social policy." Of social workers Frankel said "He is doing his job efficiently and he is also encasing himself in his job. He is tinkering with the broken products that are brought to the repair shop, but he is not asking himself why so many of these broken products are being brought in."[18]

Social work leaders and scholars were generally sympathetic to the development of social action methods but voiced concern that this could be a fad, and that methods needed to be carefully developed and "the criteria used for determining activity ought not to be based on popularity of the activity, the degree of satisfaction which the participants might gain, or the amount of publicity generated." Thursz argued that the criterion for selection of methods should be the degree to

17. Alan D. Wade, "Social Work and Political Action," *Social Work* 8, (Oct. 1963): 3–10.
18. Charles Frankel, "Obstacles to Action for Human Welfare," in *Social Welfare Forum, 1961* (New York: NCSW, 1961), 272–282.

which they bring the group closer to its goals. The assessment of a social action strategy should be based on goal achievement. In order to do this, practitioners of social action social work should, like those applying other methods, develop parameters. They need to collect and analyze data. They need to develop methods of diagnosis of situations from which various options for intervention can be developed, and periodically reviewed and modified. In other words, advocates for social action need to do the same type of work as other social workers to develop effective methods and to evaluate these in a hard-nosed fashion. He concluded "Professional social action is not based on whim or even urgent concern—no matter how justified. The concern must be translated into a well-developed plan of action, with contingency options and built-in phases for reaching short-term objectives."[19]

Even though they had not yet developed methods to compare with those of casework and group work, within only a few years macro social workers found that they had moved from the fringes to the very center of the social work profession. In schools of social work students in the community organizations specialization had grown from less than 1 percent of students in 1958 to more than 10 percent in 1970. Graduates were finding jobs in the large, federally financed, social action programs such as Mobilization for Youth, Model Cities, War on Poverty, and the Community Action Program. Schorr commented in 1966 that "For one reason or another, the dazzle that once hovered over casework--especially psychiatric social work—now lights up social policy. Those who were interested in social policy ten years ago could have held their conventions in a telephone booth (if they had a dime); today they deliver the major addresses at our national conferences." However Schorr, himself a prominent leader in the area of social policy, was concerned that social work not develop an interest in policy at a cost to direct practice. He mused "To promote policy by heaping scorn upon practice is like arguing that all building contactors should be architects. It is precisely in day-to-day practice that we should find what is wrong with yesterday's policy. Practice and policy are—or ought to be—symbiotic . . . basically we all serve a practice profession—most of us by practicing and some of us not. We shall do a better job if we see it as one job."[20]

DEVELOPMENTS IN DIRECT PRACTICE METHODS

In the 1960s all of the counseling professions, including social casework, began to broaden their repertoire of theories and techniques. Prominent among new approaches to individual treatment were role theory, reality therapy, transactional analysis, and various techniques based on behavioral theory.[21] Social work, however, had a more difficult challenge than the other counseling professions for two reasons. The main problem for social work was that the profession had

19. Daniel Thursz, "Social Action," in Robert Morris, ed., *Encyclopedia of Social Work*, 16th ed. (New York: NASW Press), 1191.

20. Alvin Schorr, "Editor's Page," *Social Work* 11 (July 1966): 2.

21. Eric Berne, *Transactional Analysis in Psychotherapy: A Systematic Individual and Social Psychiatry* (New York: Grove Press, 1961); William Glasser, *Reality Therapy* (New York: Harper and Row, 1965); Edwin J. Thomas, ed., *The Socio-Behavioral Approach and Applications to Social Work* (New York: Council on Social Work Education, 1967).

always defined the person-in-environment perspective as what differentiates it from other helping professions, so social work had to deal with the fact that these new approaches focused heavily on the individual side of the equation and thus presented exactly the same problem for theory development as the older psychodynamic approaches. The second problem facing those who were attempting to revise social work practice theory was that the traditional division of practice into the three methods of casework, group work, and community organization was being challenged as an artificial division and one that should be revised.

Caseworkers were as anxious as anyone else to demonstrate that they were relevant and could be vehicles for social change and not simply "running dogs of capitalism" serving the economic and social elite by pacifying the poor and oppressed. They were, after all, living in the sixties just like everyone else. So, incorporating concern with the social environment became a priority among those revising casework theories. One popular proposal was to develop a conception and practice of radical casework. The radical caseworker was not a prisoner of the collective status quo when working with individuals, but rather willing to overtly and covertly resist pressures for conformity. The radical caseworker is willing to challenge the standards and values of society when they can be shown to be irrelevant or to have hurtful consequences, that valid and relevant standards are not implemented, or that the standards people live by are faulty. One way that a social worker could practice radical casework was to act as an insurgent within the social service bureaucracy in which he or she is employed, seeking to change its policies and purposes in line with the values cherished by social work. Caseworkers were advised to act as rebels within a bureaucracy, humanizing its established policies and procedures.[22] Rein summarized the core idea of radical casework (which, in hindsight, no longer looks at all radical) as "A radical casework approach would mean not merely obtaining for clients social services to which they are entitled or helping them adjust to their environment, but also trying to deal with the relevant people and institutions in the clients' environment that are contributing to their difficulties . . . a radical casework approach would mean not merely obtaining for the clients the services to which they are entitled or helping them adapt to the expectations of their environment, but it would also encourage the individuals to alter their external circumstances as well as seeking directly to change the framework of expectation and the level of provision that are contributing to these difficulties."[23] As scholars moved to incorporate some "radical" casework ideas two essential roles for the social worker were identified and incorporated into main stream practice theory—social brokerage and advocacy. Brokerage was defined as "standing between the client, or the customer, and the bureaucracy that is supposed to deliver the service," and advocacy was moving beyond brokerage to "whereby the social worker or other helper stands next to the client and fights with him in partnership."[24]

Discussions of radical casework and the addition of new roles to social work practice models were really just tinkering with the way social workers had always practiced. But there was a hunger

22. Henry Miller, "Value Dilemmas in Social Casework," *Social Work* 13 (January 1968): 26–33; Scott Briar, "The Casework Predicament," *Social Work* 13 (January 1968): 2–12; Irving Piliavin, "Restructuring the Provision of Social Services," *Social Work* 18 (January 1968): 34–41.

23. Martin Rein, "Social Work in Search of a Radical Profession," *Social Work* 20 (April 1970): 28.

24. Bertram M. Beck, "A (New) Social Work Model," *Social Service Review* 40, no. 3 (Sept. 1966): 270–274; Mary J. McCormick, "Social Advocacy: A New Dimension in Social Work," *Social Casework* 51 (Jan. 1970): 3–11.

in the field to do something more substantial, to develop a new paradigm to use a word from the philosophy of science that was getting the attention of social workers. A major development in this direction was the attempt to apply general systems theory to social work practice. Gordon Hearn, a leading advocate for the development of formal theory to guide social work knowledge building, had been looking at systems theory since the late 1950s. Under his leadership a full day workshop to present and discuss a systems approach to social work practice was held at the 1968 CSWE Annual Program Meeting in Minneapolis. Major papers from this session were published the next year in a monograph sponsored by the Council.[25] The most widely read, most frequently cited, and most influential application of systems concepts to social work was published in a 1969 article in *Social Casework* by Sister Mary Paul Janchill. Janchill directly addressed the loss of a focus on clients' social environment that accompanied the adoption of Freudian psychoanalytic theory. Psychoanalytic theory, she observed, ". . . led to a shift in values. There was a growing conviction among caseworkers that the salient features of need were to be understood in the personality of the client: the forces *within his psyche* that served to establish a given relationship between him and his environment . . . recasting the very definition of task for the caseworker by shifting the focus from *problem* to *person* and from the socioeconomic frame of reference to the psychosocial." (italics in original). At the same time that psychoanalytic (and other psychodynamic approaches) were focusing attention on the person side of the person-in-environment equation, social science theory was developing (largely outside of social work theory) that focused the attention nearly exclusively on social environmental contributions to social problems. Janchill argued that a bridge was needed between the individualistic psychodynamic theories and the environmentally oriented social science theories. She observed that the development of ego psychology and role theory was attempting to serve as this bridge, but that they were not proving to be sufficient. She argued that general systems theory would provide this bridge by providing conceptual tools that activate an understanding of the relational determinates of behavior in the person-in-situation (environment) configuration. She explained that "systems theory is not a body of knowledge; it is a way of thinking and of analysis that accommodates knowledge from many sciences."[26]

Janchill described the basic concepts of systems theory and how they could be applied to casework theory. Reading this description one cannot avoid thinking about Sanders criticism of social work for the overuse of jargon. The jargon of systems theory can only be described as mind numbing. First, systems must be identified as open or closed. Closed systems are mainly machines; people exist in open systems. She then describes a set of highly abstract concepts that she argues can be used to analyze and understand open social systems. These concepts are input; throughput; output, systems as cycles of events; negative entropy; information input, negative feedback, and the coding process; steady state and dynamic homeostasis; differentiation; and equifinality. Janchill's descriptions of the applications of these concepts to social work are abstract almost to the point of being meaningless. For example, the concept of input " . . . permits an assessment of an individual's resources in terms of his inner psychic equipment as well as all the outer sources that

25. Gordon Hearn, ed., *The General Systems Approach: Contributions Toward An Holistic Conception of Social Work* (New York: Council on Social Work Education, 1969).

26. Sister Mary Paul Janchill, "Systems Concepts in Casework Theory and Practice," *Social Casework* 50 (Feb. 1969): 74–82.

make contact with the affective life." As an example of the concept of throughput she says " . . . the mother-child relationship cannot be understood in isolation; the mother must be seen in hyphenated relation to the father, the grandparents, and all her other role partners in all her statuses if one is to achieve an understanding of the characteristics of her relationship with her child." For output she uses the example of depression which systems theory enables interpretation ". . . by means of its latent functional consequences: the control it gives the patient in environmental systems, such as the family and employment." The level of abstraction becomes ever greater as she explains the other concepts ending with equifinality which she proposes as ". . . a subject for renewed cathective interest by caseworkers that should lead to creative experimentation in methods by which human growth and happiness may be influenced and achieved."[27]

As Robert Leighninger noted in an analysis of the potential usefulness of general systems theory for social work ". . . [the practitioner] must deal daily with the lives of real people, not imaginative constructs. After a yeasty session with intoxicating ideas, theorists can always sit in the back seat and sing; but the practitioner is the one who has to get behind the wheel and drive safely home." [28] Although Janchill's presentation of general systems theory as a framework to guide social work practice was too general and too abstract to be of a great deal of use, her popularization of the perspective and of systems concepts was rapidly embraced by practice theorists and developed into a form that was useful for social work practitioners. Gelfand, writing four years after Janchill, observed that the most important contribution of systems theory to social work practice was the focus it generated in environmental concerns and in pointing out that a major question for social work practice is "To what part of the client's system should the practitioner address himself?" He concludes that "If only for its powers to sensitize the milieu, the teaching of the system concept will continue to be given a prominent role in the diagnostic education of the social practitioner."[29]

In the 1950s and 1960s ego psychology had begun to supplant the Freudian psychodynamic perspective as the basis for casework theory. However, with ego psychology the problem remained of social work being excessively focused on the individual side of the person-in-environment construct and the resulting dualistic conceptualization of social work as addressing the person through casework, and the environment through community organization and political action. In the early 1970s social work practice theorists, notably Carol Germain and Alex Gitterman used ecological theory from biology to combine systems theory with ego psychology to develop what they called the life model of social work practice. The life model, focusing on the transactions between person and environment, conceptualized problems in living faced by individuals, families, and groups, into three categories: (1) problems and needs associated with tasks involved in life transitions; (2.) problems and needs associated with tasks in using and influencing elements of the environment; and (3) problems and needs associated with interpersonal obstacles which impede the work of a family or a group as it deals with transitional and/or environmental tasks. Gitterman and Germaine argued that this ". . . conceptualization of people's needs into three interrelated areas of problems-in-living transcends former methodological distinctions among casework, family

27. Sister Mary Paul Janchill, "Systems Concepts in Casework Theory and Practice," 78–81.

28. Robert D. Leighninger, "Systems Theory," *Journal of Sociology and Social Welfare,*" 5 (Dec. 1978): 446–480.

29. Bernard Gelfand, "Emerging Trends in Social Treatment," *Social Casework* 53 (June 1972): 160.

therapy, and group work, and provides a life model for intervention."[30] Germain and Gitterman got the idea of applying ecological constructs to social work from the work of William E. Gordon whose writings suggested that the concern of social work was in neither the person or the environment side of the equation, but that the distinctive domain of social work lies at the interface of the person and environment, the area that has traditionally been referred to as social functioning.[31] In this view the purpose of social work is the realization of human potential. "Its knowledge is related to the coping capacities of people and the qualities of the impinging environment. Its professional interventions are directed either to strengthening and enhancing the coping capacities of people or to meliorating the environment, or to both."[32] Germain viewed ecological theory as a derivative of general systems theory, but useful for social work because it was at a lower level of abstraction and is, therefore, closer to human phenomena.[33]

THE DEVELOPMENT OF INTEGRATED METHODS

As social work expanded into areas of social policy and social action, and as the knowledge base rapidly grew, social workers became concerned that the traditional conceptualizations of social work practice were no longer adequate. In 1965 the National Association of Social Workers asked Harriett Bartlett to chair a committee to study the way social work practice was thought about in the profession and to prepare a report analyzing social work practice. The result was the 1970 monograph *The Common Base of Social Work Practice*. In the monograph Bartlett reflected the growing concern in the profession that the classic three method conceptualization of social work practice as casework, group work, and community organization was becoming problematic. Boiled down to its basics the argument was that caseworkers work with groups, group workers with individuals, and community workers with individuals and groups, as well as that all social workers work with organizations and segments of the community. It was seen as obvious, therefore, that every social worker needed knowledge and skill related to all levels of practice—individuals, groups, organizations, and communities. Bartlett forcefully argued that ". . . the common elements in social work need to be identified and established as the base for all social work practice . . . all social workers

30. Alex Gitterman and Carel B. Germain, "Social Work Practice: A Life Model," *Social Service Review,* 50 (Dec. 1976): 601–610.

31. William E. Gordon, "Basic Constructs for an Integrative and Generative Conception of Social Work," in Gordon A. Hearn, ed., *The General Systems Approach: Contributions Toward an Holistic Conception of Social Work* (New York: Council on Social Work Education, 1969), 5–11. It is interesting to note that Gordon, one of the leading social work scholars of the 1950s and 1960s, had no social work training himself. He was educated as a forest ecologist but when he received his Ph.D. in the midst of the Great Depression he was unable to find work in his field. Based on his scientific training he obtained employment with the Minnesota Department of Public Welfare as a statistician. Working for a social agency, alongside of social workers, he fell in love with his accidental profession and went on to devote his life to furthering social work research and theory. It was late in his career when he realized the connection between his training as an ecologist and his interest in social work practice.

32. Carol B. Germain, "An Ecological Perspective in Casework Practice," *Social Casework* 54 (June 1973): 326.

33. Carel B. Germain, "General-Systems Theory and Ego Psychology: An Ecological Perspective," *Social Service Review,"* 78 (Dec. 1978): 535–550.

need to be able to view the full interventive repertoire of the profession and to understand how the various interventive actions are combined and used in practice . . . [this] means that all social workers will be aware of the full range of interventive measures encompassed by their profession, not as skills to be learned but as ways of offering help, influencing situations, and bringing about social change, and will take them into account in their own planning and actions."[34]

Bartlett's work was immediately, although not completely uncritically, embraced by the social work profession.[35] Two books quickly followed the publication of Bartlett's monograph, with each, in a slightly different form, answering the call for a model of practice that integrates knowledge across both levels and fields of practice. The first of these was *Social Work Practice: Model and Method* by Allen Pincus and Anne Minahan published in 1973.[36] They implicitly used a systems framework for organizing their treatment of social work practice but, thankfully, avoided the overly arcane and complex treatments that this framework had received in some other applications to social work. Four systems are identified as providing the context of all practice—the change agent system, the client system, the target system, and the action system. After identifying and discussing these systems, within the value base of social work, Pincus and Minahan present a detailed description and explanation of "a common core of concepts, skills, tasks and activities which are essential to the practice of social work." The bulk of the book is devoted to describing the practice skill areas that they see as cutting across all levels and fields of social work practice. These areas are described by Pincus and Minahan as assessing problems, collecting data, making initial contacts, negotiating contracts, forming action systems, maintaining and coordinating action systems, exercising influence, and terminating the change effort. These skills are presented as cutting across all levels of social work practice and also all fields of practice with the intention of accomplishing one or more of the functions of social work practice that are described as:

1. Help people enhance and more effectively utilize their own problem-solving capacities.
2. Establish initial linkages between people and resource systems.
3. Facilitate interaction and modify and build new relationships between people and societal resource systems.
4. Facilitate interaction and modify and build relationships between people within resource systems.
5. Contribute to the development and modification of social policy.
6. Dispense material resources.
7. Serve as agents of social control.

The second book to develop and secure a conceptualization of integrated methods as the basis for social work practice was *Social Work Practice: A Unitary Approach* by Howard Goldstein, also

34. Harriet M. Bartlett, *The Common Base of Social Work Practice* (New York: National Association of Social Workers, 1970), 17, 80.

35. Mary E. Burns, Review of *The Common Base of Social Work Practice* by Harriet Bartlett, *Social Service Review* 43 (Dec., 1971): 503–505.

36. Allen Pincus and Anne Minahan, *Social Work Practice: Model and Method* (Itasca, IL: F. E. Peacock, 1973).

published in 1973.[37] Goldstein begins with pretty much the same observation made by Bartlett and then by Pincus and Minahan: "The profession of social work finds itself in a dilemma. Its years of maturation have been marked by first a one, then a two, and finally, a three method conception of practice which has tended to segment its knowledge and its clientele into categories labeled Individual, group, and community. Now, a plea for recognition of the fact that social work does have a common knowledge base is heard with increasing frequency." He then goes on to argue that the problem with conceptualizing social work practice is not one of too little knowledge but rather of too much knowledge and ". . . how this knowledge can be systematized and ordered so as to afford the profession a coherent foundation for practice. . . With due regard for the immensity of the task, it is the intent of this book to contribute to the need for ordering and systematizing pertinent knowledge and to affirm the reality of a common or unitary base for professional practice." To accomplish the task he set out for himself Goldstein explicitly uses social systems theory as the major organizing framework for social work goals and objectives and learning theory as the means to conceptualize social work practice. After devoting more than half the book to describing the organization and framework of social work practice Goldstein develops a process model of practice to describe how a social worker using a unitary approach actually does the work. He describes the process model as comprising three interrelated dimensions—target, strategy, and phases. The target refers to the social unit receiving professional services defined as individual, family, group, organization, or community. This would look like the method conception of social work practice that Goldstein has explicitly rejected except that "this distinction does not imply that these are discrete units; practice with any one unit requires awareness of how that unit is part of, includes, or is in relation to all others." By strategy Goldstein means a social work method divided into three major role activities—study and evaluation, intention and intervention, and appraisal. The final dimension of the model is phases of practice which Goldstein divides into induction, core, and ending.

Compared to previous social work practice "standard" texts, those by Pincus and Minahan, and by Goldstein were only a blip on the radar. Richmond's *Social Diagnosis* served as the standard practice I text from its publication in 1917 until almost 1940. It was then replaced by Gordon Hamilton's *Theory and Practice of Social Casework* published in 1940 and revised in 1951. Hamilton's book was then eclipsed by Helen Harris Perlman's *Social Casework—A Problem Solving Process* that reigned supreme from its publication in 1957 until the early 1970s. The Goldstein and the Pincus and Minahan books were both published in 1973 and quickly came to dominate the social work practice textbook market. However, their dominance did not last long. Neither book was ever revised into a second edition and by the late 1970s they had largely been replaced by newer introductory practice books, all unquestioningly accepting integrated methods as *de rigueur*. However, they are hugely significant in that these were the books that took Bartlett's idea of a common base for social work practice, explicated and translated it into a fairly consistent practice theory, and got the notion of integrated methods as basic to social work practice widely accepted in the field. By the time the books by Pincus and Minahan and Goldstein faded from dominance the classes in

37. Howard Goldstein, *Social Work Practice: A Unitary Approach* (Columbia, SC: University of South Carolina Press, 1973).

schools of social work with titles of social casework, social group work, and community organization had nearly disappeared.

The developers of integrated methods argued that this conceptualization was different than generalist social work practice which, as will be discussed in the following section, provided the theoretical justification for recognition of BSWs as entry level social work practitioners. Pincus and Minahan were quite explicit about this saying "Our [integrated methods] model in not intended to provide a base for a generalist practitioner, as opposed to the specialist. It can set the foundation for either one, depending on how the practitioner builds on it and incorporates his special knowledge and interests regarding particular social problems, client groups, resource systems, theoretical orientations, and social science knowledge."[38] However, looking at the work of integrated methods and that on generalist practice, it is hard to see any major, substantive, differences.

SOCIAL WORK PRACTICE IN PUBLIC WELFARE, THE RECOGNITION OF UNDERGRADUATE LEVEL SOCIAL WORKERS, AND THE DEVELOPMENT OF GENERALIST PRACTICE

In spite of the massive growth of public welfare programs that were overwhelmingly staffed with non-MSW trained social workers, the organized social work profession continued throughout the 1950s and most of the 1960s to reject proposals to recognize undergraduate trained social workers as professional colleagues. Although proposals were regularly made to the AASW and to its replacement, the National Association of Social Workers, to develop at least some form of associate membership for these workers, the constituency continued to vote these proposals down. In a similar fashion, the CSWE steadfastly refused to develop any formal accreditation relationship with undergraduate social work programs, insisting that these programs could only function as pre-professional programs providing preparation for graduates to attend graduate school, and certainly these programs should not include any content on actual social work practice.

Public welfare departments did not accept the rebuffs and continued to place their faith in professional social work as the main hope for providing quality and effective services for financial assistance, and child protective service, recipients. In the 1930s when the Federal Emergency Relief Administration was formed one of the early policies was that every state welfare department was to employ at least one trained social worker, in a supervisory position, for every twenty field staff members. When the American Public Welfare Association was formed in the early 1930s as a representative association of public welfare officials and social work leaders, it promoted an expansion of services in public assistance and the development of professional standards in public welfare work. The association equated training for this work with education in a professional school of social work. State public welfare departments frequently brought in trained social workers to

---

38. Pincus and Minahan, *Social Work Practice: Model and Method,* xii.

provide in-service education for their field staff and, as their budgets allowed, send staff to workshops and training sessions at schools of social work. Some departments were even able to grant a few staff one year of educational leave to attend a school of social work.

Professional social work continued to give lip service to the need for trained workers to provide services to public welfare recipients. About this they were in agreement with the public agencies. Where they differed, however, was that public agencies, with strong support from state agricultural colleges, advocated for establishing training programs on the undergraduate level for workers in public assistance jobs, and jobs in rural areas. The profession strongly believed that social workers in public welfare, just like in any other agency, needed to be fully trained, meaning to have earned an MSW degree. This was not really a possibility for several reasons. One was that there were not enough schools of social work and not enough graduates to come anywhere near the number that would be needed to staff public assistance casework positions. In 1971, for example, there were only 75 schools of social work producing 5000 graduates per year and this output was not even enough to fill the needs of urban private agencies, not to mention the needs of public welfare organizations. State welfare administrators also opposed increased standards for public welfare caseworkers because, particularly those in rural offices, had difficulty filling positions with people with any college degree, much less a master's degree. Finally, state legislatures showed little interest in spending the significantly greater amount of money it would cost to hire graduate trained social workers.

The attitude of government policymakers toward professional social workers began to change in the 1950s. The reason for this change in attitude was concern about the anomaly (see chapter 10) of increasing numbers of public welfare recipients in a growing economy. When the ADC program had been passed as part of the 1934 Social Security Act most people believed that it was necessary because the economy was not providing enough jobs for everyone. It was assumed that when the economy fully recovered the program would wither away, or at least exist in a greatly reduced fashion. In the 1950s with the economy roaring and ADC numbers, and cost, increasing everyone was puzzled and concerned. The explanation that was generally accepted was that of economist John Kenneth Galbraith that the growth was due to what he termed "case poverty." What he meant by this is that people who have to rely on public assistance in a booming economy have to do so because there is something wrong with them. Galbraith did not spend much time discussing what these individual (case) problems might be but most people agreed that they were some combination of mental illness, low education and skills, and the whole host of deficits that fell under the new label of culture of poverty. These were all things that social workers were believed to have a great deal of knowledge about and skills to remediate.

The US Congress began to address the issue of public welfare staffing with the 1956 Social Security Act amendments in which $5 million per year, renewable for five years, was allocated for social work training of public assistance staff. This money was allocated on the basis of states splitting costs with the federal government on a 50/50 basis. Because of the high cost of the match no state took advantage of the program. When Kennedy was elected in 1960, bringing with him to Washington a more activist and social science oriented administration, more meaningful steps were taken. In 1961 the newly appointed secretary of the Department of Health, Education and Welfare, Abraham Ribicoff, addressed social workers at the annual meeting of the National Conference of Social Welfare. He told his audience that public welfare was in trouble, and that a new approach was needed, one "whose keystone concepts are prevention and rehabilitation." He appealed to the social work profession to put the "social back into social work" and to help public welfare clients "to become responsible citizens serving their own and the public interest." In May of 1961 Secretary Ribicoff appointed an Ad Hoc Committee on Public Welfare and President Kennedy appointed George Wyman to make a report formulating "recommendations and suggestions for administrative and program actions relating to procedures and operations in the Children's Bureau and the Bureau of Public Assistance." Ribicoff's committee comprised twenty-five social welfare leaders, mainly social workers and including deans of three schools of social work, and Wyman consulted with largely the same group.

Based largely on the recommendations contained in the reports of the Ribicoff and Wyman committees, Congress passed Public Law 87-543 in spring of 1962, a bill that was generally referred to as the social service amendments. The influence of professional social work can be clearly seen in President Kennedy's message supporting the bill in which he said:

> It is essential that State and local welfare agencies be staffed with enough qualified personnel to insure constructive and adequate attention to the problems of needy individuals—to take the time to help them find and hold a job—to prevent public dependency, and to strive, where that is not possible, for rehabilitation—and to ascertain promptly whether any individual is receiving aid for which he does not qualify, so that aid can be promptly withdrawn... Unfortunately, there is an acute shortage of trained personnel in all our welfare programs. The lack of experienced social workers for programs dealing with children and their families is especially critical... I recommend, therefore, that Federal assistance to the States for training additional welfare personnel be increased; and that in addition, the Secretary of Health, Education, and Welfare be authorized to make special arrangements for the training of family welfare personnel to work with those children whose parents have deserted, whose parents are unmarried, or who have other serious problems.[39]

The 1962 amendments placed the responsibility for solution of the "welfare mess" squarely in the lap of the social work profession, taking as a matter of faith the idea that social work had the skills necessary to solve the problem and that the only challenge was finding enough trained social workers to do the job. In order to rectify this problem the bill allocated a large amount of money to fund social work education for public welfare employees. Three and a half million dollars was allocated for fiscal year 1962–63 and $5 million for each succeeding fiscal year. This amount was to be used as a match for state funds with the federal government paying 75 percent and the states paying 25 percent. The major purpose of these funds was to pay for state public welfare caseworkers to attend schools of social work as full-time students to earn MSW degrees. Employees who took advantage of this opportunity were expected to return to work for the state agency for a set amount of time, generally two years for each year of graduate school. In addition to funds for employee stipends the Secretary of the Department of Health, Education and Welfare was allocated $1 million for 1962–1963 and $2 million each year thereafter for grants or contracts with universities to strengthen their capacity to provide in-service training for public welfare personnel. The 1962

---

39. Message from President John F. Kennedy: Public Welfare, February 1, 1962, House Document Number 325.

amendments were followed up by more amendments in 1967 that continued the employee grad-uate school stipend program and increased funding to expand and strengthen the capacity of schools of social work to provide training for public welfare agency personnel. Section 707 of the 1967 amendments allocated $3 million for grants to school of social work for the 1967–68 fiscal year and $5 million for each of the succeeding fiscal years.[40]

In their vigorous and successful lobbying for federal support of social work and social work education as the solution to the welfare problem in the United States, the profession was making a bold claim. It is clear that Congress defined the welfare problem not as helping recipients resolve individual problems thus making their lives better, but as stopping or reversing the growth of the size and cost of the AFDC program. Congress was endorsing and supporting social work services as a method of reducing welfare costs. The House Committee on Ways and Means, for example, linked the goals and means of the 1962 amendments in these words: "Experience has shown that adequately trained personnel can be one of the largest factors in reducing ultimately the cost of public assistance programs."[41] Although the vast majority of the profession was wildly enthusiastic about the future of social work in public welfare, there were a few who issued words of caution. In a 1964 editorial in the NASW journal *Social Work*, Howard J. Parad identified two risks posed to the social work profession by the legislation authorizing social services in public welfare departments. The first risk was that the social work job classifications in these agencies were insufficient to hire professionally trained social workers. He argued that these agencies need to extricate themselves from "the logically absurd position of paying poverty wages to those who are asked to wage the war against poverty." His more serious concern was that social work may have set itself up for failure. He wrote ". . . we must also be mindful of the fact that unrealistic expectations have been aroused in some quarters concerning the tax-saving possibilities of casework services in public assistance. If, as we are often told, 90 percent of assistance recipients are, for one or another compelling reason, unemployable in today's job market, can such services move people 'from relief rolls to payrolls'? Are we perhaps postponing for ourselves a boomerang of criticism that might jeopardize the con-tribution of casework in enhancing the well-being and social functioning of many people, even though they may not be restored to gainful employment?" Social work research leaders Aaron Rosen and Ronda Connaway clearly identified the risk of the social service amendments to social work stating that the profession identified its goal as increasing the capacity of people to utilize varied available resources, whether they are economic, educational, aesthetic, social, or personal in nature, and defined activities toward these ends as justified in themselves. The public welfare amendments, however, defined social services only as means for reducing economic dependency. They explain, "Viewed in this light, the public mandate given to social work activities directed at increasing the capacity of individuals to utilize social resources is conditioned by, and contin-gent on, an empirical, factual demonstration of the correspondence and efficacy of such activities

40. Wilber J. Cohen and Robert M. Ball, "Public Welfare Amendments of 1962 and Proposals for Health Insurance for the Aged," *Social Security Bulletin* 26 (Oct. 1962): 3–22; Wilber J. Cohen and Robert M. Ball, "Social Security Amendments of 1967: Summary and Legislative History," *Social Security Bulletin* 31 (Feb. 1968): 23–42; Michael J. Austin, Jude Mary Antonyappan, and Leslie Leighninger, "Federal Support for Social Work Education: Section 707 of the 1967 Social Security Act Amendments," *Social Service Review* 70 (March 1996): 83–97.

41. U.S. House of Representatives, Committee on Ways and Means, "Report Accompanying H.R. 10606" (March 10, 1962), 3.

(methods) in relation to the *public* purpose of reducing economic need. To the extent that social work is not successful in demonstrating such a relationship (regardless of other benefits that may accrue to individuals), it will be in great danger of forfeiting the public mandate and trust demonstrated in the 1962 amendments."[42]

The concerns expressed by Parad and by Rosen and Connaway proved to be right on the money. During the 1960s when social services were expanded under the theory that they would reduce welfare rolls, the AFDC caseload nearly tripled, going from 3,005,000 recipients in 1960 to 8,466,000 in 1970. This increase was generally considered by people outside of social work as evidence that the social service approach to the welfare problem had proven to be a failure. Congress responded by deemphasizing, and reducing funding, for "soft services" such as social casework and by increasing emphasis and funding for "hard services" such as employment training, vocational rehabilitation, child care, transportation, and the like. The election of Richard Nixon in 1968 and his landslide reelection in 1972 represented the end of the federal government's experiment with social work services as a solution to poverty. Shortly before the 1972 reelection Nixon's top aide John Ehrlichman was quoted in the *Wall Street Journal* saying that under the Nixon administration's second term social workers would "just have to go out and find honest labor somewhere else," and referred to the profession as "parasites sucking the fiscal blood."[43] The Nixon administration made good on its threat in 1973 when funds for support of training in social work, rehabilitation, and aging were reduced from $44.7 million to zero.

The historian James Leiby concluded, "The main finding of the 1960s . . . was that efforts to reform or rehabilitate [welfare recipients] did not work . . . "[44] Blaming of the social work profession for the failure of the social service strategy to the welfare problem, however, has generally been unfair for several reasons. For one thing the notion that a few thousand professional social workers could make a significant impact on the dependency problems of a caseload of literally millions is on the face of it absurd. Although the number of social worker positions was steadily increased, growing from 22,000 in in 1963 to 33,000 in 1967, the program size increased apace keeping the average caseload size at about sixty intensive cases per worker. A survey of AFDC recipients in 1967 concluded that "social service is little more than a relatively infrequent, pleasant chat. It is rarely threatening but also not too meaningful in the sense of either helping poor people get things they want or of changing their lives."[45] With sixty cases, workers were not really able to provide intensive services to any of their clients. The second reason is that Congress became disillusioned with the approach in a few short years, before anyone could reasonably expect results to begin showing up in macroeconomic numbers. It was almost as though policymakers were saying, "Okay, the poverty problem has always been with us—let's see if social workers can solve it in five or six years." Then there is the problem that of all the public welfare employees who were

---

42. Aaron Rosen and Ronda S. Connaway, "Public Welfare, Social Work, and Social Work Education," *Social Work* 14 (April, 1969): 87–94.

43. *Wall Street Journal*, October 19, 1972, 20.

44. James Leiby, *A History of Social Welfare and Social Work in the United States* (New York: Columbia University Press, 1978), 332.

45. Joel F. Handler and Ellen Jane Hollingsworth, "The Administration of Social Services and the Structure of Dependency: The Views of AFDC Recipients," *Social Service Review*, 43 (Dec. 1969): 406–420.

sent to school with stipends to earn MSW degrees, very few returned to positions in the AFDC program. In almost all cases, states assigned the newly minted MSWs to child protective services positions or to higher level jobs in administration or training. Even in child welfare divisions, few MSWs were assigned to direct service positions, mostly because these positions paid way too little for a person with a graduate degree. Rumors flew around most state public welfare departments that a clinical social work consultant position was going to be created for MSW level workers that would be at a high pay grade and would be assigned especially difficult cases, basically a clinical social work position in the public bureaucracy, but none of these rumors turned out to be true. Finally, those social workers who had been arguing for years that a public welfare bureaucracy was not a setting conducive to professional social work practice turned out to not be entirely wrong. Caseworkers presenting at American Public Welfare Association conferences complained about the number of forms required for each case, the increased amount of dictation required by depart- ment policy, the "social study" guidelines that, if completely followed, would result in a document for every case that exceeded ten pages in length, and the prescribed list from which goals for each case must be selected, a list that kept changing requiring repeating the process several times for each case. The result, according to Dwight Weisner, a senior caseworker, was that "accountability, interview reporting, and recording, all have one thing in common, they take time—*time* away from the client. . . We feel that the increased time spent at our desks as a result of implement- ing these [policies] has in this respect ironically limited our effectiveness."[46] The American Public Welfare Association reported in 1963 that the turnover among public welfare caseworkers was 26 percent per year and attributed much of the blame for this high rate to the bureaucratic hassles associated with doing this job.[47]

Although many of the reasons for the failure of the social service approach to public welfare were outside of the control of the social work profession, it must be said that the profession did not do all it could to help the approach succeed. Going into the 1960s the profession's self-image was that of a private agency based, mental health focused discipline. Although social work accepted the money and the jobs that came with the social service amendments it never really changed this image to embrace public welfare practice. The curriculums of schools of social work changed little to accommodate a focus on direct services in public welfare settings. A few schools added admin- istration tracks designed to send public welfare workers back to their agencies as supervisors or administrators, but little attention was devoted to methods of direct practice to help welfare recipi- ents become self-supporting. Also, the culture of graduate schools of social work was such that public welfare stipend students were very clearly given the message that their preferred career path should be to return to the public welfare agency for the minimum time necessary to repay their sti- pend commitment and then, as soon as possible, take a job in a private mental health agency where they could begin to practice *real* professional social work. As a result, very few stipend recipients were still working in public welfare three years after receiving their graduate degrees.[48]

46. Dwight O. Weiser, "The Caseworkers Speak Up: The Caseworker and the 1962 Amendments," *Public Welfare* 23 (January, 1965): 7–11.

47. Clyde W. Linville, Jr. "Staffing Problems Under The New Service Amendments," *Public Welfare* 21 (October, 1963): 203.

48. These observations, admittedly anecdotal, are based on the author's experience as a public welfare stipend recipient.

The massive expansion of entry level social work positions resulting from the 1956, 1962, and 1967 amendments blew the long smoldering issue of recognition of baccalaureate level workers into full flame. Advocates for the expansion of the definition of the profession to include BSW level workers based their argument on several factors. The first was that schools of social work were nearly all located in large urban centers disproportionately in the northeastern part of the country. These schools poorly served rural, southern, and western regions. Undergraduate programs located in state agricultural and teachers colleges could extend professional social work to these areas. Another argument was that states could not afford to pay MSW level salaries to the large and increasing pool of public welfare workers. Rather than upgrading these positions to the MSW level virtually all states defined the positions as requiring a bachelor's degree in any field. Advocates for BSW recognition made the logical argument that, while an MSW might be desirable this was not possible, so a BSW degree was far superior to no professional social work training at all. And finally it was argued, and supported by hard data, that the demand for trained social workers far outstripped the capacity of graduate schools to provide a sufficient supply. In spite of the fact that these arguments were valid and seemingly convincing, the profession as represented by NASW and CSWE continued to resist the expansion of professional boundaries. In 1964 and again in 1967 the NASW membership convincingly voted down proposals to change minimum membership requirements to a bachelor's degree and either two years of graduate school, or two years' experience in a social welfare organization.[49]

NASW and CSWE, as well as other organizations such as the Department of Health, Education, and Welfare and the Southern Regional Education Board, were aware and acutely concerned about the staffing (at that time called "manpower") crisis in social work. In the 1960s a number of studies were funded by various federal agencies and private foundations to analyze the staffing problems in social agencies. All of these studies documented the need for an increase in the number of trained social workers and identified ways that baccalaureate level workers could help fill the need.[50] By far the most influential of these studies was that of the Department of Health, Education and Welfare Task Force on Social Work Education and Manpower, appointed in 1963 and releasing its report in 1965. The task force was chaired by Milton Wittman, the chief of the social work section for training and manpower resources of the National Institute of Mental Health, and directed by Dorothy Bird Daly, later to become dean of the Catholic University National School of Social Service. Among other findings and projections, the report concluded that only 25 percent of social work jobs were filled by trained social workers and projected that by 1970 there would be 100,000 more social work jobs than trained personnel available to fill them. In keeping with the conclusions of other studies of the era the report emphasized "the critical need for the advancement of undergraduate education in social welfare both for direct entry of graduates into practice and as preparation for graduate education."[51] This report went further than the other studies and

49. David M. Austin, "Broadening the Membership Base: Where Next?" *Social Work* 13 (January, 1968): 113–116.

50. Edward E. Schwartz, ed., *Manpower in Social Welfare* (New York, NASW Press, 1966); Bernice Madison, *Undergraduate Education for Social Welfare* (San Francisco: Rosenberg Foundation, 1960); Robert Barker and Thomas Brigg (eds.), *Manpower Research on the Utilization of Baccalaureate Social Workers: Implications for Education* (Washington, D.C.: United States Government Printing Office, 1972); Robert Teare and Harold MacPheeters, *Manpower Utilization in Social Welfare* (Atlanta: Southern Regional Educational Board, 1971).

51. U.S. Task Force on Social Work Education and Manpower, *Closing the Gap in Social Work Manpower* (Washington, DC: U.S. Department of Health, Education, and Welfare, November 1965), 80–81.

looked at the job functions of graduate and undergraduate trained social service personnel and concluded that the tasks performed by the two levels were not clearly differentiated. The authors argued that undergraduate trained social workers often faced unrealistic expectations about what they were capable of doing, while graduate trained social workers often were not able to use their specialized skills. Among other recommendations the task force report advocated for establishing two classifications of social work, one at the graduate and the other at the undergraduate level of preparation, and encouraged professional organizations (NASW and CSWE) to broaden their base of membership eligibility to include both levels of social worker and for state governments to establish two level licensing requirements.

As is not an uncommon occurrence, the factor that finally lead to the resolve of the undergraduate/graduate debate in social work was money. As previously discussed, the 1967 amendments to the Social Security Act included a large amount of money for the support and expansion of social work education. This provision of the act was heavily informed by the HEW study with the result that it specified that fifty percent of the funds be allocated to the support of BSW programs. At the same time the Southern Regional Educational Board also began to allocate funds to support the development of undergraduate social work education in the southern states. As a result new BSW programs quickly emerged and older programs expanded until, within a few years, there were 170 BSW programs enrolling more than 25,000 full time degree students, and granting more than 7,000 BSW degrees. By way of comparison, at the same time graduate programs enrolled 16,869 students and granted 9,080 MSW degrees. In the face of the massive growth of BSW programs, and the seemingly irrefutable logic of arguments for recognition of undergraduate trained social workers, a national referendum was again taken of NASW members, who this time approved the motion that membership be granted to "Any person who holds the baccalaureate degree, having completed an undergraduate program in social work that meets the criteria established by the Council on Social Work Education." Following this referendum, the CSWE began work on the criteria for review of undergraduate programs and applied to the US Department of Education for approval to accredit BSW programs. This approval was granted in 1973 and in 1974 CSWE began the accreditation process. Within one year 200 programs were reviewed with 135 being granted accreditation for varying lengths of time, with five years being the maximum. An additional seven programs were placed in candidacy but were not granted full accreditation.

The recognition of the BSW as the beginning level professional practice degree forced the social work profession to reorganize curriculum content. Prior to this recognition the undergraduate degree was defined as providing a pre-professional foundation for graduate study, where all the necessary content and skills would be provided. This now needed to be rethought. The solution, quickly adopted, was that proposed by Werner Boehm in a 1959 CSWE publication that presciently looked at future curriculum options. In this pamphlet Boehm proposed that social work practice could be divided between generalist skills and specialist skills. Boehm proposed that generalist skills could be taught at the undergraduate level and the graduate level would build on this foundation and teach specialist skills:

> . . . the social work general practitioner . . . provides liaison and basic counseling in relation to specific, concrete services such as foster home placement, homemaker, day care, aftercare arrangements, and referral service to specialized community programs. The general practitioner is first-line

case service provider; he coordinates the services, provides accountability, and furnishes case advocacy as appropriate. His is what has been called the social brokerage function . . . The social work
specialist . . . provides counseling, focusing on interpersonal problems, psychotherapeutic case services, consultation to other community services in health, education and the like, and as expert is
available in relation to other human service utilities. Among his functions could be included policy
advocacy which would call for review and revision of agency policies which are found to be dysfunc-
tional in relation to outcome.[52]

The social work curriculum was re-organized with the undergraduate degree and the first year
of the two year graduate program both covering foundation and generalist practice content. The
BSW curriculum and the first year MSW curriculum were conceptualized as covering exactly the
same material. The second year of the MSW curriculum was defined as the specialization year.
This lead to the development of advanced standing programs that permitted students who had
earned a BSW with a good grade point average to earn the MSW in one year.

CONCLUSION: REFORM AND REACTION

Between 1945 and 1974 the nature and structure of the social work profession and of social work
practice was radically altered. From an exclusively graduate trained, private agency based, profession with a heavy emphasis on psychiatrically focused practice, the profession evolved to one in
which macro practice, public welfare, generalist practice utilizing integrated methods, and social
policy and reform were its organizing principles. Although seldom mentioned, and really barely
noticed, the old debate between the diagnostic and the functional schools had quietly evolved
from the 1950s where the diagnostic school was the clearly dominant influence to the 1970s
where functional concepts, (client self-determination, freedom of choice, agency policy focus, the
use of time as a treatment element, and an emphasis on relationship) had come to dominate social
work practice theory and technique. After the vigor, and sometimes even rancor, with which the
functional/diagnostic battle had been waged it is ironic, and a bit sad, that the eventual dominance
of functional ideas in social work practice was never really recognized.

It seems that every period of reform is followed by one of reaction. This was true of the 1960s
era reforms in social work theory and practice with the reaction from the profession coming from
several different directions. One reaction came from social work agency administrators who were
unhappy with the quality of graduates coming out of the reformed social work curriculums. An
example of this reaction to the changed focus of social work and social work education came in
the form of a position statement adopted by the Family Service Association of America Board
of Directors on May 22, 1972. The statement was developed by an Ad Hoc Committee of executive and supervisory staff members for a number of family service agencies, chaired by Sidney
Berkowitz, Executive Director of Jewish Family and Community Services of Chicago. The

---

52. Werner Boehm, *Objectives of the Social Work Curriculum of the Future* (New York: Council on Social Work Education, 1959): 16–17.

statement accuses schools of social work, reflecting changes in the social work professional culture, as deemphasizing practice with individuals and small groups, with the result that students "do not develop a commitment to, nor even an awareness of the need for, working with individuals and families. They do not emerge with an adequate theoretical base for practice in usable form... They discover that education has not prepared them for the positions they seek." This situation was attributed to the emphasis by social work educators on social work activity with and for larger groups, community, and policy and their "denigration of individual needs." The source of the problem, the task force concludes, is that social agencies no longer had significant involvement in setting the goals of the total curriculum or in changes in educational programs. The report concludes "Our recommendation, therefore, is that some means be found for redressing this situation and bringing the agencies and schools together, at the top administrative level as well as through field instruction, for the purpose of developing mutually acceptable goals."[53]

A second source of reaction came from the elite segment of the profession formerly known as psychiatric social workers but by the late 1960s called clinical social workers. By the early 1970s these social workers began to identify their interests as different from the rest of the profession and began to establish their own professional organizations. By 1972 there were 14 state level societies for clinical social work, affiliated with the National Federation of Societies for Clinical Social Work and the number was growing. There were two basic motivations behind the formation of these societies. The first was concern with protecting funding for social workers practicing psychotherapy. Some states had passed legislation that defined psychotherapy as a medical specialty thereby preventing social workers from receiving reimbursement for counseling and therapy services. The societies for clinical social work quickly organized and began intense lobbying for licensing of social workers to practice and be reimbursed for psychotherapeutic services. The societies (with, it must be noted, the support of other professional organizations such as NASW) had great success in this effort with social work gaining licensure in all fifty states, Puerto Rico, and the District of Columbia. In addition, most Canadian provinces also began to license social workers. The second motivation for the founding of these societies was a general dissatisfaction of clinical social workers with the direction the profession had taken. Statements by representatives of clinical societies indicated a "deep concern that NASW has ignored the [clinical] practice area," that "NASW no longer represents the professional social worker," and that societies for clinical social work were "... clearly in response to the National Association of Social Workers' (NASW) lowering of membership standards to include BSWs and its move in the direction of endorsing a multilevel licensing standard which includes BSWs and paraprofessionals."[54]

Many, if not most, members of clinical social work societies continued to strongly identify with the social work profession and often maintained concurrent membership in NASW and a clinical society. However, there were those whose dissatisfaction was so great that they advocated for defining clinical social work as an entity separate from the larger profession. These practitioners felt

53. Position Statement of Family Service Agencies Regarding Graduate Schools of Social Work, *Smith College Studies in Social Work*, 43 (February 1973): 108–110.

54. Mary E. Pharis, "Societies for Clinical Social Work," *Social Work* 18 (May 1973): 99–103; Mary E. Pharis and Barbara E. Williams, "Further Developments in Societies for Clinical Social Work: A Ten-Year Follow-Up Study," *Clinical Social Work Journal*, 12 (March, 1984): 164–178.

a ". . . profound dissatisfaction with the trend against clinical training in many graduate schools of social work, the endorsement by the CSWE of the undergraduate degree as the entry-level degree, and with what is viewed as NASW's disinterest in the clinician and its acceptance of members with bachelor's degrees." [55] The trend toward defining clinical social work as outside of the larger social work profession was given support from those in other clinical professions who argued for the formation of a "fifth profession" specializing in individual and group therapy that would comprise those currently in clinical social work, psychiatry, clinical psychology, and psychoanalysis.[56]

This reaction against the broadening of social work's boundaries, although continuing to the present day, had little effect on the overall direction of the profession. The movement was quickly successful in getting legal recognition of social work as a mental health service profession with title protection and eligibility for insurance reimbursement, and all the other benefits of licensing. Also, a couple of schools of clinical social work were founded, notably in Chicago and California, but these offer clinical doctorates that require an accredited MSW as a basic entrance requirement and so can be viewed as an effort to enhance, not replace, main stream social work education. In addition, the traditional professional organizations such as NASW have become more sensitive to the desires of clinical practitioners. However, by 1974 social work had clearly and irrevocably changed its self-image away from that of being an elite, all-graduate trained profession focused on clinical practice, into that of a more generalist, multi-level and multi-method, discipline, heavily involved with public policy, and with a social justice and macro-social focus.

55. Mary E. Pharis. "Societies for Clinical Social Work," 103.

56. William E. Henry, John H. Sims, and S. Lee Spray, *The Fifth Profession* (San Francisco: Jossey-Bass, 1971).

CHAPTER 12

ENDING WELFARE AS WE KNOW IT

I n the 1960s and 1970s there was a standard lecture given in every school of social work's foundation social policy course describing the current structure and future direction of the social welfare system in the United States. The lecture began by describing the institutional and residual conceptions of social welfare as developed by Charles Wilensky and Charles Lebeaux (see chapter 10).[1] Basically, the institutional conception viewed social welfare as a front line social institution providing benefits and services that were needed by everyone in order to function in a complex, modern, social environment. Services under this conception are viewed as a normal need and no stigma is attached to their receipt. The residual conception, by contrast, views the major social institutions, mainly the family, church, and economy, as being able to provide for all the needs of members of society as long as these institutions are functioning well. Under this conception social welfare benefits and services are necessary only when the individual is experiencing some problem preventing the major social institutions from carrying out all their tasks. Thus the receipt of social welfare benefits and services in considered abnormal and is stigmatized. Following the presentation of Wilensky and Lebeaux's conceptions of social welfare the presentation would move to the English policy scholar T. H. Marshall and his theory of citizenship. According to Marshall, western industrial democracies followed a pattern in the expansion of the rights granted to people merely by virtue of their being citizens of the society.[2] These rights are of three types: civil, political, and social. The civil aspects of citizenship arose with the emergence of the bourgeoisie in the eighteenth century and involve a set of individual rights—liberty, freedom of speech, right to travel without interference, equality before the law, and the right to own property. Political rights, the access to the decision making process through participation in the choice of leaders by universal suffrage, emerged in the nineteenth century as a result of demands of the working class. Marshall argues that in the twentieth century social rights began to appear, defined

1. Harold L. Wilensky and Charles N. Lebeaux, *Industrial Society and Social Welfare,* enlarged paperback ed. (New York: Russell Sage Foundation, 1958), 34–35.

2. T. H. Marshall, *Class, Citizenship, and Social Development: Essays by T. H. Marshall* (New York: Anchor Books, 1965).

as a right to a certain share of the nation's wealth regardless of ability or willingness to participate in the creation of that wealth. In programmatic terms social rights involve the provision of welfare, security, and education as a matter of rights and these programs become major components in the definition of citizenship in the twentieth century.

Following the presentation of these two major theories of welfare and the welfare state the welfare system in the United States would be discussed. First, the various major benefit programs in the country would be listed and categorized as either residual (AFDC, nutrition, housing, and so forth) or institutional (Old Age Survivors and Disability Insurance, Medicare). The professor would then turn to a discussion of similar programs in Western Europe and the Scandinavian countries, emphasizing the point that many more of the programs in these places fit into the institutional conception of social welfare than in the United States. Statistics on government spending on US social welfare programs would be compared to that of other western industrialized nations, emphasizing that the United States spent significantly less than its peers. The analysis would conclude that the United States was a laggard welfare state. After the presentation of the theories, programs, and data the sunny conclusion would be presented that the United States was traveling the same road as its European peers, that the establishment of a liberal welfare state based on citizenship as described by Marshall was inevitable, and the United States might be a laggard, but by the end of the careers of the students sitting in the class full welfare state status would be achieved.

As the optimistic 1960s (which sociologically ended in 1974) came to an end, and developments in social welfare in the United States appeared to be deviating from the path that had been predicted, and a new generation of scholars began to develop new theories of the welfare state in Europe as well as the United States. They categorically rejected the notion that there is only one type of welfare state and instead theorized that there are numerous models and they differ according to the society in which they are located. Probably the most influential of these scholars is the Swedish political scientist Gosta Esping-Anderson, who described "three worlds of welfare capitalism." He categorizes the United States as a liberal or individualist/market model of a welfare state. In this type of welfare state citizens are primarily considered to be market actors. There is a reluctance to replace market relations with social rights, and citizens are encouraged to seek their welfare in the market, for example, through subsidies for private welfare benefits (such as 501c retirement plans). Basic security schemes tend to be means tested and benefit levels modest. Social worker Charles Atherton contrasts European regimes, which he labels redistributive welfare states because one of their major functions is shifting income from the non-poor to the poor, with the United States which he labels a programmatic welfare state that "devotes a portion of its gross national product, through taxation, to the solution of certain social problems without changing the basic nature of the economy." Social worker Neil Gilbert argues that the United States. has moved from becoming a European style welfare state to an "enabling state," that is, a system of social welfare with a primary focus on "public support for private responsibility" meaning promoting work rather than protecting labor, privatization rather than public provision, and selectivity rather than universal entitlement.[3]

3. Gosta Esping-Anderson, *Three Worlds of Welfare Capitalism* (Princeton, NJ: Princeton University Press, 1990); Charles R. Atherton, "The Welfare State: Still on Solid Ground," *Social Service Review* 63 (June 1989); Neil Gilbert and Barbara Gilbert, *The Enabling State: Modern Welfare Capitalism in America* (New York: Oxford University Press, 1989).

These theorists are only a few of many who have reevaluated the concept of the welfare state in the late twentieth century. Robert Goodwin and Deborah Mitchell in 2002 edited a three volume set containing seventy articles on the subject.[4] However they may differ in focus or detail, most scholars agree that the United States may briefly have been on the path to becoming a European style welfare state, but it has evolved into something else. Characteristics of the American welfare state, as it has evolved since the 1970s, are as follows: First, it has very little interest in redistribution of income. Second, it is focused on work. The economic institution, i.e., the job market, is viewed as the normal way for a person to be supported. Financial assistance is seen as residual and as only a temporary measure until the dependent person connects, or reconnects with the market. Third, benefits to working people, or to people who are not working for reasons that are apparent (children, elderly, the disabled), are reasonably adequate, those to people who are not working for reasons that are not clear and apparent (i.e., single parents, substance abusers, people with personality disorders), are minimal to the point of being inadequate. Finally, concern with the social and economic roots of poverty and related social problems has been replaced with a focus on individual behavior and responsibility by the poor and afflicted, major concerns being crime and broken families.

This evolution of the American welfare state since the mid-1970s has been accompanied with some major revisions in service delivery philosophy and design. These changes have been a direct result of the conservative swing in American society that began with the Nixon administration when, early in his first term he announced "the New Federalism" in domestic affairs centering on a new vision of how power should be shared between the federal government and the states. "After a third of a century of power flowing from the people and the states to Washington, it is time for a New Federalism in which power, funds, and responsibility will flow from Washington to the states and to the people," he said. [5] Nixon announced an intention to reform the welfare system, including the way revenue was shared between the federal government and the states, but, perhaps due to a focus on the Vietnam War and the Watergate scandal that eventually ended his tenure as president, he made little progress with his reform initiatives. When Ronald Reagan was elected in 1984 he adopted Nixon's New Federalism proposal as his own and quickly moved to turn over to the states many of the federal government's domestic programs. By doing this he believed that it would "end cumbersome administration" and make the programs "more responsive to both the people they are meant to help and the people who pay for them."[6] His main method of doing this was to replace categorical funding with block grant funding. Categorical funding, which previous to the Reagan Administration, had been the major way that the federal government helped the states provide social services, is the most restrictive means of federal funding. Categorical grants can be used only for specifically aided programs and are usually limited to narrowly defined activities. Most categorical social welfare grants required states to match the federal contribution at a

4. Robert B. Goodwin and Deborah Mitchell, *The Foundations of the Welfare State,* 3 vols. (Northampton, MA: Edward Elgar Publishing, 2000).

5. Quoted in Bruce Katz, "Nixon's New Federalism 45 Years Later," *Brookings: The Avenue, Rethinking Metropolitan America,* August 11, 2014, retrieved from www.brookings.edu/blogs/the-avenue/posts/2014/08/11

6. President Ronald Reagan, *State of the Union Address* (Washington, DC: U.S. Government Printing Office, January 26, 1982).

25 percent level, although a few services, notably administration, staff development, and social work education, required only a 10 percent match. Categorical programs were in most cases entitlements, meaning that the funding was uncapped and the states were required to provide benefits and services to everyone who qualified, regardless of the cost. Block grants are not entitlements, which mean that states provide benefits and services to people who qualify only up to the point that the funding ceiling is reached, after this point qualified applicants are placed on a waiting list and only get the benefit when their name reaches the top of the list. Block grants are less restrictive on the states. They must be used only for a specifically aided set of programs but are not limited to narrowly defined activities. The federal government gives each state a designated amount of money, and a set of broad general goals that the state is to use the money to pursue, but the specific means the state uses to do this are not specified.

The Reagan administration operationalized its plans for converting social service funding to a block grant program via the 1981 amendments to Title XX of the Social Security Act that created the Social Services Block Grant (SSBG). Funding for the SSBG was originally capped at $2.9 billion, this being reduced to $2.4 billion for fiscal 1982, and the funding level has been capped at $1.7 billion every year since 2001. On the surface this looks like the federal funding for social services has decreased, but it actually hasn't because policy now allows states to transfer up to 10 percent of the money they are allocated by the federal government for the TANF block grant to the SSBG, increasing its total funding level to $2.9 billion in 2011. States may use their SSBG funds to pursue five basic goals:

- Achieving or maintaining economic self-support to prevent, reduce, or eliminate dependency
- Achieving or maintaining self-sufficiency, including reduction or prevention of dependency
- Preventing or remedying neglect, abuse, or exploitation of children and adults unable to protect their own interests, or preserving, rehabilitating, or reuniting families
- Preventing or reducing inappropriate institutional care by providing for community-based care, home-based care, or other forms of less intensive care
- Securing referral or admission for institutional care when other forms of care are not appropriate or providing services to individuals in institutions

States have broad discretion in spending SSBG funds in pursuit of these broad goals. Examples of social services, as specified in law, that relate to the SSBG's broad goals are child care, protective services for children and adults in foster care, services related to the management and maintenance of the home, adult day care, transportation, family planning, training and related services, employment services, referral and counseling services, meal preparation and delivery, health support services, and services to meet the special needs of children, the aged, the mentally retarded, the blind, the emotionally disturbed, the physically handicapped, and alcoholics and drug addicts.[7]

Another major policy thrust that has intensified since the 1970s is the privatization of social services. Privatization, also called outsourcing or contracting out, refers to the government

7. Karen E. Lynch, *Social Services Block Grant: Background and Funding* (Washington, DC: Congressional Research Service, August 28, 2012), 2.

transferring activities to private providers rather than providing the service itself. The official government definition of privatization is "the transfer of government services, assets, and/or enterprises to private sector owners and suppliers, when [they] have the capability of providing better services at lower costs."[8] This is, of course, not new. The government has always contracted with private business to develop and manufacture weapons for national defense, contracted with private firms to build bridges and highways, as well as many other activities. It is also not new in the social service area where government has contracted with private non-profit, and private for-profit organizations to provide benefits such as child care, nursing home care, as well as other services. However, the administration of large programs delivering services and benefits to clients has previously been restricted to governmental agencies. The beginning of this restriction was in the 1930s when Harry Hopkins, the social worker working as an advisor to President Roosevelt helping to develop regulations for the implementation of the Social Security Act, developed a policy that government benefits could only be administered by governmental agencies.

In the 1970s and 1980s, with the enthusiastic support of the conservative administrations of Reagan and Bush, contracting out various aspects of social service provision accelerated. Common programs for privatization were child support enforcement and the automating of various aspects of benefit delivery. Examples include the defense contractor BDM International that contracted with New Mexico to automate their welfare system in 1988; Lockheed-Martin that set up child support collection systems in several states; and Curtis & Associates and the job-brokerage firm America Works that implemented workfare programs in Buffalo, San Francisco, as well as other large cities before 1990. The zenith of welfare privatization was achieved in 1996 when the Personal Responsibility and Work Opportunity Act became law and included the provision that a state may administer its welfare program "through contracts with charitable, religious, or private organizations," thus repudiating Hopkins dictum that government benefit programs could only be administered by government agencies. States can now contract with private firms to run the state's whole welfare system. Under the old system, only government agencies could determine who was eligible for assistance and how much they could receive, but this requirement vanished with the new law. The states are still the only ones empowered to set eligibility levels, but it is up to the private contractors to determine which individuals fit the criteria. Large companies that have moved into the welfare service delivery market include Ross Perot's Electronic Data Systems, defense contract giant Lockheed-Martin (who for a period of time ran Florida's entire welfare system), IBM, Anderson Consulting, and IBM. Smaller businesses specifically established to manage government programs include America Works, Curtis and Associates, and Maximus Incorporated. Although these companies are small compared to the giants listed previously, such as IBM, they are hardly small in any absolute sense—Maximus, for example, is a $700 million business.

Since 1974 social welfare benefits and programs have continued to expand in the United States, but no one any longer sees this growth as evidence of our moving toward a liberal, citizenship rights based welfare state. Development has been entirely within the framework of an American individualistic/market model of a welfare state, guided by the new federalism philosophy and

8. Executive Office of the President, Office of Management and the Budget, *Management of the United States Government, Fiscal Year 1990* (Washington, DC: U.S. Government Printing Office, 1989), quoted in Diana DiNitto and David Johnson, *Social Welfare—Politics and Public Policy,* 8th ed. (Boston: Pearson, 1989), 87.

operationalized through the dual trends of block grants and privatization. Within this new framework there have been major developments in public financial assistance, child welfare, mental health, health care, and family service. The role and place of the social work profession within this welfare state model has also undergone a remarkable transformation, exiting entirely from the financial assistance arena, but gaining significant ground in mental health and in child welfare.

FINANCIAL ASSISTANCE TO THE VERY POOR AND THE WORKING POOR

When Dwight McDonald wrote his 1963 essay review of Michael Harrington's 1958 book *The Other America* he emphasized the point that the poor in America were invisible. The book and essay came at a time when America was experiencing a wave of sympathy and concern for the poor and was launching the wide variety of anti-poverty experiments discussed in Chapter 11. By 1975 liberal supporters of anti-poverty efforts were wishing that the poor had not become quite so visible. Several developments had begun to seriously erode the sympathy that the average citizen had been feeling for the poor, especially the welfare poor. One development was the result of community action programs implemented during the 1960s that gave the poor a voice, and the rest of the country discovered that the poor not only were not grateful for the assistance they were receiving, they were angry. The major vehicle for this anger was the National Welfare Rights Organization (NWRO), founded in 1966 by civil rights activist Dr. George Wiley. Wiley orchestrated events such as a 155 mile march by welfare recipients and their supporters from Cleveland Ohio to the state capitol in Columbus, followed by rallies in twenty other cities. At these rallies, and at hearings arranged by the NWRO, angry statements were made by welfare recipients that were widely reported in the press. For example, in 1970 testimony before a committee chaired by Senator Eugene McCarthy, in response to questions about work requirements for recipients, NWRO representative Mrs. Ethel Crump declared, "We only want the kind of jobs that will pay $10,000 or $20,000" (the average American worker at the time earned $6,186), "we aren't going to do anybody's laundry except for ourselves!" At the same hearing Vice Chairman of the New York City NWRO Chapter, Mrs. Beulah Sanders, asserted that "You can't force me to work! You better give me something better than I'm getting on welfare. I ain't taking it . . . . I heard that Senator Long said as long as he can't get his laundry done he's going to put welfare recipients to work . . . Those days are gone forever! . . . We ain't going to clean it!"[9] The average American, as well as their elected representatives, took offense at such statements and support for liberal welfare programs began to erode.

The anger of the poor and their activist supporters was given teeth by another War on Poverty development, the Legal Services Corporation. The NWRO organized and demonstrated but legal services, and other legal advocacy groups, sued and established something that had not been previously recognized, the concept of welfare rights. *King v. Smith* (1968) ruled that substitute father

9. Vincent J. Burke and Vee Burke, *Nixon's Good Deed: Welfare Reform* (New York: Columbia University Press, 1974), 161–162.

rules (stating that having a sexual relationship with a man made a woman ineligible for welfare benefits) did not conform to the Social Security Act resulting in the elimination of these "suitable home" regulations. *Shapiro v. Thompson* (1969) struck down residency requirements establishing that people did not have to reside in a state for a certain period of time before becoming eligible for welfare assistance. *Goldberg v. Kelly* (1970) ruled that benefits could not be taken away without due process. As a result of these lawsuits, activities of groups such as the NWRO that publicized welfare programs and encouraged people to apply for benefits, and a few other factors, the welfare rolls more than quadrupled between 1960 and 1975, causing great concern about the cost of welfare programs and fear that the rolls would continue to grow until they ate up most of federal and state budgets. The skyrocketing welfare rolls continued the erosion of support for liberal welfare programs.

Another cause for concern about welfare programs, specifically AFDC, was the rather dramatic shift that had occurred in American values regarding women and work. When the AFDC program had been designed it was based on a strong value that a mother's primary responsibility was to stay home and care for her children. Based on this, motherhood was defined as a legitimate reason for a woman to not work, even if this meant that she was supported by public aid. By the end of the 1960s values had changed to the point that being self-supporting was considered to be more important than being a stay-at-home mom; i.e. motherhood was no longer seen as a justification for not working. When the AFDC program started, less than one married woman in ten worked outside of the home. By the mid-1970s, more than half of American mothers worked. As Senator Daniel Patrick Moynihan testified before his Senate colleagues, "A program that was designed to pay mothers to stay home with their children cannot succeed when we observe most mothers going out to work."[10] Or as one angry citizen told the Senate Finance Committee during hearings on the 1967 amendments to the Social Security Act: "What gives the welfare mother the right to sit home while others work?"[11]

The final factor leading to a reaction against the welfare poor was the economy. The twenty-five years of almost unbroken prosperity and economic growth following the Second World War came to an end in the 1970s. For a number of complex reasons, growth in the US economy slowed to a crawl and inflation increased to double digits. The problem was severe enough that a new word was developed to describe a slow economy accompanied by high inflation—stagflation. A recession began in the late 1970s and became sharp between 1980 and 1982, resulting in an unemployment rate of ten percent. Concern with the economy, concern with the meteoric rise in the welfare rolls, resentment toward the poor resulting from the concept of welfare rights, all combined to fuel a shift in popular concern from ending poverty to a concern with controlling welfare.

In the 1950s and 1960s popular opinion and social legislation was guided by the work of liberal social scientists and journalists such as Michael Harrington, Francis Fox Piven, and Richard

---

10. Daniel Patrick Moynihan, "Beyond Welfare," Statement before the Senate Subcommittee on Social Security and Family Policy, January 23, 1987. Quoted in Michael Novak et. al., *The New Consensus on Family and Welfare: A Community of Self-Reliance*. Report of the Working Seminar on Family and American Welfare Policy (Washington, DC: American Enterprise Institute for Public Policy Research, 1987).

11. Quoted in Vincent Burke and Vee Burke, "Nixon's Good Deed," 164.

Cloward. As popular resentment toward the welfare poor increased a new group of conservative academics and journalists emerged who changed the focus from concern with the social environmental causes of poverty to concern that it was characteristics of the poor themselves that was causing their poverty. It is perhaps ironic that the basis for the new conservative attack on welfare was partially inspired by the work of liberals such as Daniel Patrick Moynihan whose report, "The Negro Family: The Case for National Action," and journalist Bill Moyers CBS special, "Crisis in the Black Family." Both decried the startling increase in single motherhood among Blacks and strongly implied that the phenomenon was partially the result of welfare policy. Moyers documentary featured interviews with a young man named Timothy McSeed who could be described as the poster child for anti-welfare stereotypes. McSeed readily, and somewhat proudly, admitted to fathering at least six children and supporting none of them. When asked by Moyers if he was concerned about his failure to support his children he responded that he was not because, "Welfare gives them a stipend for the month. What I can't do the government does." The mother of two of McSeed's children tells Moyers, "I don't like welfare because it makes me lazy."[12]

Up until the late 1970s "think tanks" such at the Urban Institute, the Brookings Institution and the Russell Sage Foundation had almost always had a decidedly liberal bias and produced studies and position papers generally supportive of reforms that would expand benefits to the poor and oppressed. By the early 1980s this had changed with the emergence of several well-funded and influential organizations that supported conservative scholars to produce works that were critical of the poor and argued that well intentioned social programs had miserably failed and needed to be reformed in a conservative direction. The first salvo in the intellectual assault on welfare and poverty was fired by scholar George Gilder, co-founder of the conservative Discovery Institute and director of its Center on Wealth, Poverty and Morality, and most fully explained in his popular 1980 book *Wealth and Poverty*. Based on his fame resulting from this book, Gilder was invited to give testimony to the Senate Committee on Finance, Subcommittee on Public Assistance, which he did, titling his testimony *How to Think About Welfare Reform for the 1980s*. The gist of Gilder's argument is that generous welfare programs destroy families by making the father superfluous, that generous benefits "destroy the key role and authority of the father. He can no longer feel manly in his own home . . . his response to this reality is that very combination of resignation and rage, escapism and violence, short horizons and promiscuous sexual activity that characterizes everywhere the lives of the poor." Gilder goes on to make the rather startling argument that poverty in the United States is not the result of economic factors, but rather of government policy that has deprived poor families of strong fathers. Gilder concludes with the recommendation that welfare policy should offer only emergency aid and at the lowest possible level, a level well below that which can be obtained through work (an update of the English Poor Law principle of less eligibility). This policy will "offer some promise of relieving poverty without creating a welfare culture that perpetuates it . . . from the viewpoint of the poor, successful reform must make welfare worse, not better. The welfare problem is that it is already much too good."[13]

12. Daniel Patrick Moynihan, *The Negro Family: The Case for National Action* (Washington, DC: U.S. Department of Labor, 1965); Bill Moyers, "The Vanishing Family: Crisis in Black America," CBS, Jan. 25, 1986.

13. George Gilder, *Wealth and Poverty* (New York: Bantam Books, 1980); George Gilder, *How to Think about Welfare Reform for the 1980s: Hearings before the Subcommittee on Public Assistance*, 96th Cong., 2d sess., 1980.

By far the work most influential in changing the direction of welfare policy in the United States from a structural approach to an approach based on individual behavior was *Losing Ground*, a best seller written by political scientist Charles Murray with support from the conservative American Enterprise Institute. As can be inferred from the title, Murray's main thesis was that liberal welfare policies implemented during the 1960s had actually done more harm than good. Murray was mainly speaking of the Aid to Families with Dependent Children (AFDC) program, but also included other programs like food stamps, subsidized housing, Medicaid, workers' compensation, and unemployment insurance. Murray argued that these programs functioned to divert people from normal incentives to work, marry, and form stable lives. Murray argued his points using what he called a "thought experiment," the imaginary case of a young unmarried Philadelphia couple he called Phyllis and Harold. Phyllis becomes pregnant and Murray describes how they would deal with this development in 1960, before the advent of all the Great Society welfare programs, and in 1970 when benefits from these programs are available (it is assumed that Phyllis wants to have and keep the baby). Murray concludes that in 1960, with few benefits available, Harold and Phyllis would have married because there would be no other way to support and raise the child (Murray also assumes that Harold was a nice guy and would not have simply abandoned Phyllis or, like Timothy McSeed in the Bill Moyers interview, have responded to his girlfriend's pregnancy with the statement "Mama baby, Daddy maybe"). As a result of this forced choice the couple would marry, Harold would become employed, and they would be on the first step of the American ladder to success. In 1970 Murray pictures a very different outcome. Because benefits available from social programs would have a value in excess of Harold's earning capacity, the couple would choose not to marry. High benefits with few requirements made it far more attractive for the young couple to rely on the welfare state than to look for work and earn their own income. Harold would hang around for a while, but with his role as a father made largely superfluous by the government, he would eventually drift away and Phyllis and the baby would become long term welfare recipients. As Patterson notes, Murray's depiction of the poor was much different than the traditional conservative one: "His view of these people reflected an ironic departure from the nineteenth century visions of the downtrodden in the slums. The conservatives had often depicted slum dwellers as intemperate, shiftless, and immoral. To Murray these people were crassly rational calculators of their own self-interest: the benefits of welfare, Murray thought, induced them to quit work and live off the public trough." This thinking led Murray to a startling conclusion: don't just reform welfare; abolish it. By eliminating welfare programs "I am hypothesizing, with the advantage of powerful collateral evidence, that the lives of large numbers of poor people would be radically changed for the better." DeParle summarizes the effect of Murray's book: "Pre-Murray, welfare's main critics had attacked on equity grounds: it was costly, wasteful, unfair to taxpayers. Post-Murray, the criticisms became much more profound: welfare was the evil from which all other evils flowed, from crime to family breakdown. To cut was to care."[14]

14. Charles Murray, *Losing Ground: American Social Policy 1950–1980* (New York: Basic Books, 1984); James T. Patterson, *America's Struggle against Poverty in the Twentieth Century* (Cambridge, MA: Harvard University Press, 2000); Jason DeParle, *American Dream: Three Women, Ten Kids, and a Nation's Drive to End Welfare* (New York: Penguin Books, 2004).

Although conservatives were taking the lead in the new American attitude toward welfare and the poor, liberals also jumped on the bandwagon. In a popular 1982 book journalist Ken Auletta popularized the term "the underclass" to describe part of the poverty population who had basically checked out of American society and did not follow many of its accepted patterns of behavior such as work and law abidance.[15] As one frightened liberal exclaimed after reading Auletta's book, "An American version of a *lumpenproletariat* (the so-called underclass), without work and without hope, existing at the margins of society, could bring down the great cities, sap resources and strength from the entire society and, lacking the usual means to survive, prey upon those who possess them."[16] Journalist Nicolas Lehman researched the tie between welfare and the sharecropper background of many recipients, bringing in a racial link that Murray and Gilder had ignored. Sociologist William Julius Wilson published *The Truly Disadvantaged,* which established the reigning explanation for that segment of the welfare population referred to as the underclass. Where Murray identified welfare itself as the problem, Wilson described a complex interplay between industrial decline, desegregation, and self-defeating cultural forces. Wilson put little emphasis on welfare, but he did argue that ghetto life had entered a tragic new state, and defended the word *underclass* from those on the left who felt it too harsh, and encouraged liberals to speak more bluntly about behavioral aspects of poverty.[17] Liberal journalist Mickey Kaus in an essay in the left leaning *New Republic* attacked standard programs that emphasized voluntary education and training for the poor and had produced poor results. He argued that rather than offering training the government should offer guaranteed jobs saying, "Our goal, in contrast, is to break the culture of poverty through work requirements."[18] DeParle observes, "Murray and Kaus hailed from opposite poles—one called for a radical constriction of government, the other for several million government jobs. But they proceeded from a common assumption, that welfare was destroying American life."[19]

So, by the 1970s America's major social concern had shifted from "what can we do about poverty?" to "what can we do about welfare?" A consensus had emerged from both the right and the left that welfare (especially AFDC) was damaging to the poor and a threat to the social and fiscal welfare of the rest of the population. The sentiment of policymakers, reflecting that of the general population, was growing that welfare recipients should be required to work, or to at least be in some kind of work preparation. Welfare policies emphasizing work always carried provisions rewarding work behaviors on the part of recipients (the carrot) and penalizing failure to exhibit these behaviors (the stick). As welfare policy evolved from the 1962 Social Service Amendments to the 1996 Personal Responsibility and Work Opportunity Reconciliation Act, which totally replaced the AFDC program, the reward provisions diminished and the penalty provisions increased. The change in expectations that welfare mothers should work rather than stay home was first hinted at in the otherwise liberal, service oriented 1962 Social Security Act amendments.

15. Ken Auletta, *The Underclass* (New York: Random House, 1982).

16. Quoted in James Patterson, *America's Struggle Against Poverty,* 209.

17. William Julius Wilson, *The Truly Disadvantaged: The Inner City, the Underclass, and Public Policy* (Chicago: University of Chicago Press, 1987).

18. Mickey Kaus, "The Work Ethic State," *The New Republic,* July 7, 1986, 128–140.

19. Jason DeParle, *American Dream,* 98.

These amendments included provisions encouraging work by allowing recipients to deduct work expenses from earned income before these earnings were deducted from benefits. The amendments also made clear that the terms "prevention and rehabilitation," the watchwords of the act, meant getting recipients out to work and off the rolls, although the methods prescribed were counseling and services rather than penalties for not participating.

The first serious attempt to establish firm work expectations as conditions of welfare receipt was the Work Incentive Program (WIN) established as part of the 1967 Social Security Act amendments. The WIN program was the first to explicitly employ a carrot and stick approach to motivate welfare recipients to enter the job market. The WIN program required states to refer a portion of their AFDC recipients with school age children to work programs and, as an incentive to take jobs, allowed program participants to keep the first $30 of their wages and one-third of anything beyond that without decreasing their welfare benefits (a provision that was referred to as the "thirty and a third rule"). As Patterson has pointed out, the WIN program with its stress on "workfare" (combining work and welfare) had little more effect in the 1960s and 1970s than it had for the Charity Organization Societies in the late nineteenth century. Although the 1967 amendments included provisions for subsidized day care for participants, the number of slots available was tiny compared to the need. In practice welfare agencies interpreted work requirements as pertaining to only fathers in states where two parent families were eligible for AFDC, school dropouts over sixteen, and the few mothers of school age children who had access to free day care. WIN program statistics in 1972 broke down as follows: 2.8 million AFDC recipients were eligible for the program; 700,000 of these were deemed "appropriate for referral" by local welfare department officials; 400,000 of these were enrolled in WIN by mid-1972. Approximately one quarter of these completed training, and only 52,000, less than 2 percent of the original pool, actually found jobs, making on average only slightly more than the minimum wage.[20] Analyses of the WIN program identified lack of appropriate jobs for participants as the major problem. To attempt to deal with this problem the Comprehensive Employment and Training Act (CETA) was passed in 1973 that provided block grants to states to subsidize jobs for low income people. CETA was replaced in 1982 by the Job Training Partnership Act (JPTA) that was more narrowly focused on placing AFDC and food stamp recipients in jobs or job training. Neither CETA nor JTPA was significantly more effective than WIN, and were opposed and subjected to budget cuts by conservatives who supported work requirements for welfare recipients but were opposed to the federal government being involved in what they viewed as artificial job creation.

Among the sea of failures of welfare reform and anti-poverty programs, one stands out as a success, the Earned Income Tax Credit (EITC), originally passed in 1975. The EITC set the stage for later welfare reforms. The program could be referred to as America' stealth welfare program because, due to its being attached to wage employment, and administered by the Internal Revenue Service, the fact that it is a welfare program is generally ignored. The EITC is designed to supplement the income of the working poor, defined as persons who are employed for at least half the year with poverty level-level incomes. In 1978, the EITC was made a permanent part of the Internal Revenue Code, and it has been expanded and made more generous through periodic

---

20. James T. Patterson, *America's Struggle against Poverty in the Twentieth Century,* 170.

revisions in 1986 and 1990. Under the EITC, if a person qualifies for the credit, he or she can get a tax return that is significantly more than the taxes that were withheld. There are three benefit schedules: one for taxpayers with no children, one for taxpayers with one child, and one for taxpayers with multiple children. People on each of these schedules receive benefits according to what are called *phases*. As of 2014 unmarried people with no children receive a benefit equal to 7.65 percent of earned income up to an income of $5,974, at which point (referred to as the *phase–in point*) they receive a maximum benefit of $457. The benefit then stays at a constant $457 until income reaches $6,740 (the *plateau point*) at which point the benefit begins to decrease until it becomes zero at an income of $23,440 (the *phase-out point*). For unmarried people with one child, the benefit is 34 percent, the phase-in point is $8,080 with a benefit of $2,747, the plateau point ends at $14,810, and the benefit ends at the phase-out point $40,463. For unmarried people with two children, the benefit is 40 percent, the phase-in point is $11,340 with a benefit of $4,536, the plateau ends at $14,810, and the benefit ends at the phase-out point of $40,295. For people using the married filing jointly status, the phase-out thresholds are increased by $2,000. All dollar amounts are now indexed to inflation. In 2009, through funds provided by the American Recovery and Reinvestment Act, the EITC program was expanded to provide families with three or more children with a larger benefit of up to $5,657. The EITC program has gradually and without fanfare become by far the largest antipoverty program in the United States. Almost 25 million families received more than $48 billion in refunds through the EITC in 2007, with an average benefit of $1,974 per family. By comparison, in 2006, the Temporary Assistance to Needy Families program provided benefits to slightly fewer than two million families at a total federal cost of slightly more than $17 billion.

In what can be considered to be almost a footnote to social welfare history, in 1977, in the midst of the national conservative reaction against welfare and the poor, President Carter proposed a program that was basically a liberal expansion of Nixon's failed Family Assistance Act. Carter's Program for Better Jobs and Income (PBJI) proposed replacing the entire welfare system with a two track system, one for people who were able to work and one for those who were not able. Those who could work were to receive wage supplements in addition to EITC, help in finding employment in the regular wage economy, or one of 1.4 million public jobs to be created paying slightly more than the minimum wage. For the second group, SSI, AFDC, General Assistance, and food stamps were to be combined into one program with one eligibility standard. All poor people (except those who refused to work) were to be given a floor income of $4,200 for a family of four (the poverty line for this family was $6,020), and were to have only one-half of earned income subtracted from benefits. That marginal tax meant that families of four earning up to $8,400 a year would receive some federal assistance (median household income in 1977 was $13,570). Carter's PBJI ran into the same opposition as Nixon's FAP. Conservative doubted the ability of the federal government to efficiently create and administer a job creation program, and liberals felt the income floor was much too low. Another problem is that Carter insisted that the program be designed with no increase in overall federal welfare spending. In the end, Carter did not vigorously push for the program's passage and it died by 1979 in an unenthusiastic Congress.

The 1980 election changed the balance of power in Washington with the Republican Party winning the presidency, a majority in the Senate, and picking up 31 seats in the house. With the "mandate" provided by the election the Reagan administration set out to accomplish a revolution in social and economic policy, seeking to reduce the welfare state to its bare bones. When Reagan was reelected in 1984 by an even greater majority of the vote, he announced his intention to "reform welfare." In response to Reagan's announced intent, a number of public policy groups, including the National Governor's Association, chaired by Arkansas Governor Bill Clinton, conducted studies of ways to reform the system. The reports of the policy elites agreed on three points: first, the breakdown of the family and inadequate inner city educational systems were generating a permanently dependent underclass; second, that a reformed welfare system should be based on the concept of reciprocal responsibilities between government and welfare recipients; and third, that states should be given greater discretion over certain aspects of welfare policy. Unfortunately for the Republican desire to reform welfare in a direction guided by Charles Murray's *Losing Ground*, the elections for the Senate and House did not reflect the Republican landslide of the presidential election. In 1984 the Republicans controlled the Senate by a small margin, but the Democrats controlled the House. In 1986 the Democrats regained control of the Senate and in 1988 their majority in both houses became even greater.

In 1988 liberal Democratic Senator Daniel Patrick Moynihan introduced a major welfare reform bill, the Family Support Act. The act was passed after intense debate and included major revisions that were demanded by conservative Republicans. In keeping with the focus on work for welfare recipients the new law expanded federal mandates requiring states to move their welfare recipients into jobs or job training programs and simultaneously gave states more discretion in designing programs to accomplish this. The major feature of the law was the Job Opportunities and Basic Skills Training Program (called JOBS) that required states to provide welfare recipients with assessment, training, education, work experience, and job search assistance. As Goldberg and Collins note, "the Family Support Act represented a dramatic shift in welfare policy from income support to a focus on moving welfare clients toward self-sufficiency."[21] The act's guiding principle was that work should always pay, that is that any work behavior engaged in by a welfare recipient should result in a net gain in income. In order to accomplish this the bill required states to allow recipients who left the rolls due to earned income to retain their Medicaid and child care benefits for one year after leaving the welfare rolls, as well as improving on the "thirty and a third" rule by raising certain earnings disregards. All recipients were required to participate in the JOBS program with the exception of mothers of children under three, or under six if the state could not provide subsidized child care. In regard to fathers, the act required all states to adopt the AFDC-UP program (an expansion of AFDC that made two parent families eligible for benefits), and outlined stronger measures aimed at forcing absent fathers to make child support payments. The program required that at least one parent in a two parent household be engaged in work or work training for at least sixteen hours per week. States were required to have at least 20 percent of welfare recipients in jobs or in job training.

The Family Support Act was supposed to stabilize welfare policy and put an end to the steady drum beat for welfare reform that had been present for two decades. This was not to be as welfare rolls continued to rise and it soon became obvious that the Family Support Act and JOBS program were no more successful in fixing the problems in the welfare system than previous reforms had

---

21. Gertrude Schaffner Goldberg and Sheila D. Collins, *Washington's New Poor Law: Welfare "Reform" and the Roads Not Taken, 1935 to the Present* (New York: The Apex Press, 2001), 174.

been. Reasons for its failure were many. First was the failure of Congress to appropriate nearly enough money to enable AFDC recipients to receive the education and training promised by the act. Second, even for recipients fortunate enough to obtain job training through the program there were not nearly enough jobs in the late eighties/early nineties economy to provide them with employment, much less employment that provided for a significantly better level of living than that provided by welfare. Then there was the problem that the AFDC program was so poorly administered by the states that recipients who did find work in most cases did not report it to welfare officials because it would result in a decrease in their grants. As Patterson notes, "The majority of adults on AFDC failed to report savings, earnings, or other sources of income, much of which would have been deducted, in accordance with AFDC rules, from their welfare checks."[22] The main problem with the FSA and its JOBS program was that it failed to address the major concern with the American welfare system which was that the size of the program and the cost continued to increase at an ever greater rate. Between 1988 when the FSA was passed, and 1994 when Newt Gingerich included welfare reform as one of the planks in his Contract with America, the number of families receiving AFDC increased from 3.748 million to 5.046 million. It should be noted that the cost of the AFDC program did not rise as fast as the number of recipients because Congress, following Gilders recommendations, had let the actual value of grants decline as inflation continued. In constant dollars the average AFDC monthly grant declined from $676 in 1970 to $336 in 1995.

In his 1992 campaign for the presidency Bill Clinton made welfare reform one on the major planks. He promised that, if elected, he would "scrap the current welfare system and make welfare a second chance, not a way of life." As catchy as this phrase was, it was one that Clinton's young speech writer Bruce Reed came up with that really caught fire. Clinton, using Reed's words, promised that "In a Clinton administration we're going to put an end to welfare as we know it." However, during the first two years of Clinton's presidency he showed relatively little interest in reforming welfare. It was not until the Republicans captured both houses of Congress in the 1994 mid-term elections that welfare reform returned to center stage. The new Speaker of the House Newt Gingerich opened the 1994 104th Congress by announcing what he called the "Contract with America," a set of ten ideologically driven planks, with proposed implementing legislation, that, if passed in their entirety, would have resulted in the most radical restructuring of American government since the New Deal. A major target of the "Contract" was the welfare system that was to be reduced in size and turned over to the states in the form of block grants. Gingerich's welfare reform proposal was heavily based on the thinking of Charles Murray as described in his best-selling book *Losing Ground*. While previous Republican proposals for reform had attacked poor people for abusing welfare programs, Gingerich attacked the programs for abusing the poor. He didn't complain, as Reagan had, of high-living "welfare queens" but instead reminded the public that poor children were suffering and welfare was to blame. While Reagan had spoken of welfare recipients whose "tax-free cash income alone is over a hundred fifty thousand dollars," Gingerich talked of "twelve-year-olds having babies" and "seventeen-year-olds dying of AIDS." The rhetoric

22. James Patterson, *America's Struggle Against Poverty in the Twentieth Century*, 225.

did more than soften the message. It created logic for deeper cuts in welfare benefits: it's cruel to be kind; the less we spend the more we care.

After the Democratic losses in the 1994 midterm elections Clinton's advisors concluded that he had to make good on his pledge to "end welfare as we know it." Clinton's new political strategist Dick Morris, urged him to "fast forward on the Gingerich agenda" and sign a welfare bill, even if he had to hold his nose while doing so. He needed, according to Morris, to get welfare off the table. A widely read article by Mickey Kaus in the influential and liberal *New Republic* called Clinton's failure to end welfare "the fundamental strategic mistake of the Clinton presidency."[23] The Republicans, led by Gingerich, were working feverishly to pass a welfare reform bill that they believed that Clinton, backed into a corner, would have to sign. It took three tries before they accomplished their goal. The first attempt was passed on March 24, 1995, and was included as part of a larger budget reconciliation bill that sought to reduce the budget deficit, almost entirely by cutting programs benefitting the poor. President Clinton vetoed the bill stating as part of his reason that it made too many extreme cuts, especially in Medicare and that it would impoverish more than a million children. In January 1996 the Republican led Congress made another try at welfare reform, this time passing it as a separate piece of legislation. Clinton vetoed this one saying, "it does too little to move people from welfare to work." In late July 1996 both the House and the Senate passed a third version of welfare reform. By the next month the House-Senate conference committee had finished marking up the bill and on August 22, 1996 President Clinton signed it into law.

> The Major Provisions of H.R. 3734, the Personal Responsibility and Work Opportunity Reconciliation Act of 1996 are:
> - The Aid to Families with Dependent Children (AFDC) program was ended and replaced by the Temporary Assistance to Needy Families (TANF) program.
> - Under TANF states receive a block grant in an amount calculated to be the highest of (1) the average payment they received in fiscal years 1992 through 1994; (2) the amount they received in fiscal year 1994; or (3) the amount they received in fiscal year 1995. This provision put a cap on the amount that states could receive to subsidize their welfare program, in contrast to AFDC that had been an uncapped entitlement program that gave states the right to reimbursement for 75 percent of the cost of AFDC grants up to an unlimited amount. States have much more freedom regarding how to spend TANF money than they had under AFDC, but when it is spent they have no right to additional funds from the federal government. A contingency fund was set up to help states that exceed their block grant amounts, but this is available only under specific and limited conditions (i.e., an exceptional increase in unemployment).
> - Adults receiving cash benefits are required to work or participate in a state designed program after two years or their payments will be ended. This work requirement is defined as one individual in a household working at least thirty hours per week.

---

23. Mickey Kaus, "They Blew It," *The New Republic*, Dec. 5, 1994.

- States were required to have at least 50 percent of their total single parent welfare caseloads in jobs by 2002. States failing to meet this requirement were subject to a reduction of their block grant by 5 percent or more in the following year. States are allowed various exemptions and disregards in this calculation with the result that, as of 2015, although no state had actually reached the goal of having 50 percent of recipients in jobs, no sanctions were levied.
- States are allowed to sanction, through a reduction or termination of cash benefits, people who fail to fulfill the work requirement.
- Payments to recipients using federal funds must end after a maximum of five years for all spells (times receiving assistance) combined, thereby requiring that families become self-supporting at that point.
- Persons immigrating to the United States after the passage of H.R. 3734 will be ineligible for most means tested programs, including TANF, the Supplemental Nutritional Assistance Program (food stamps), and Medicaid, for their first five years of residence.
- Illegal aliens will be barred from all means tested programs.

The central philosophy, and in many states the program name, of TANF is a concept known as "work first." For conservatives this represented a return to, and victory of, traditional American values of work and self-reliance. For social workers and their liberal supporters it was a statement of despair and resignation over the fact that programs aimed at uplifting and rehabilitating welfare recipients had failed (if the criteria for success was getting people off the welfare rolls). The social service approach of the 1960s that attempted to help welfare recipients solve personal problems that were theoretically preventing them from working had certainly failed to increase labor force participation. Most work oriented rehabilitation programs, such as WIN and JOBS had also demonstrated limited success. The appeal of the "work first" approach resulted from a number of experimental evaluations of two types of work program approaches conducted in the 1980s and 1990s. These approaches are known as Human Capital Development (HCD) and Labor Force Attachment (LFA). The WIN, CETA, and JOBS programs were all based on the HCD approach that is based on the belief that for the poor to escape welfare they first need to improve their education and skills, that is, increase their human capital. The LFA programs emphasized low cost, short-term services, emphasizing job search skills and labor market experience. This strategy posits that the nonworking poor can best build work habits and skills, advance their positions in the labor market, and eventually escape welfare dependency by gaining work experience at any job regardless of how unstable or low paying it is. The event that convinced policymakers that the Labor Force Attachment, or work first, approach should be the centerpiece of the TANF program was a study conducted in California in 1993 by the Manpower Development Research Corporation. This study evaluated the results of a California welfare-to-work program called GAIN. The study compared the programs of six counties, five of which employed traditional Human Capital Development approaches that provided education and training for welfare recipients with the goal of making them competitive for more and better paying jobs. The sixth county, Riverside, was a Labor Force Attachment approach that stressed basic job search classes and encouraged participants to take the first job they could find. "Get a job, any job" was the guiding motto of the Riverside program. When all the data was analyzed after two years, the Riverside program had increased its participant's earnings by more than 50 percent, a result about three times greater than that of the five other programs.[24]

So, TANF was implemented in 1996 as a hard-nosed, no nonsense, work-first philosophy. To boil it down to its basics, TANF requires that recipients begin an intense job search as soon as they enter the program; requires that they take any job that is available; sanctions (kicks out of the program) recipients for any infraction of the rules, often something as minor as missing a required meeting; and limits a person's eligibility for aid to two years for any one spell and five years for all spells combined. TANF discourages entering the program by offering applicants a one-time cash grant, supposedly enough to solve their immediate problem (typically about $1000) in return for giving up their eligibility to apply for additional benefits. Some states require a month-long job search before applicants can collect benefits. Some route recipients through rounds of job-search and motivation classes so tedious they discourage many from even completing the application process. As DeParle has noted, "If the welfare law has worked . . . it has largely worked as a deterrent, creating enough hassles that those with other options make other plans."[25]

President Clinton expressed reluctance to sign the PRWORA, and the expectation that welfare reform would continue, saying, "You can put wings on a pig, but that still does not make it an eagle." He continued, "This is not the end of welfare reform; this is the beginning. We have to fill in the blanks."[26] Senator Moynihan, however, did not share Clinton's optimism that the law would be reformed and improved, saying that the votes simply would not be there to significantly modify the law. The law has now been in place for more than twenty years and it appears that Senator Moynihan was correct; there have as yet been no major modifications to soften this law and there are not any on the policy radar screen. Why has this welfare reform law been perceived as so successful when all previous laws were seen as failures? The answer is simple: under all previous welfare reforms the size of the welfare rolls increased, usually at an ever faster pace. Under TANF the size of the rolls has significantly declined. During 1995, the last full year of the AFDC program, the caseload size was 13,660,192 recipients and 4,870,903 families. By 2015, under the TANF program these numbers had declined to 3,102,936 recipients in 1,346,931 families, a truly remarkable drop. Given that cost and caseload size has always been the major criteria that policymakers apply when evaluating welfare programs, it is not hard to see why TANF is generally considered to be a successful welfare reform.

However, as the TANF program has matured, and clearly demonstrated effectiveness as measured by the criteria of cost and caseload size, calls for expanded evaluation measures are being heard. Critics are wondering if, in addition to caseload reductions, policymakers should also be looking at the degree to which TANF provides a safety net for people facing hard times; the success of TANF in lifting children out of deep poverty; and how successful the program is in increasing sustained labor force participation. An example of such demands is the October 2012 Congressional Research Service Report to Congress on TANF that concludes, "Policymakers also face questions about whether the sole focus of assessment of TANF's success ought to be

24. Stephen Freedman, Jean Tansey Knab, Lisa A. Bennetian, and David Navarro. *The Los Angeles Jobs-First GAIN Evaluation: Final Report on a Work First Program in a Major Urban Center* (Oakland, CA: MDRC, 2000).

25. Jason DeParle, "Dream Deferred," *Washington Monthly*, September 2004.

26. "Clinton Signs Controversial Welfare Bill," *Dallas Morning News* (23 August, 1996), sec. A, 32.

welfare-to-work. TANF has evolved into a program where cash assistance represents less than 30 percent of its funds. Policymakers thus face questions of whether consideration might be given to developing measures and assessment on how well TANF does in meeting other goals related to improving the circumstances of families with children."[27] The results of studies that have looked at these other evaluation criteria have not been encouraging. Findings have shown that of all the people who leave the TANF rolls, only about 60 percent leave because they have a job; the other 40 percent leave because they have been sanctioned.[28] Of those former recipients who do find jobs, their wages are very low, the jobs are unstable, and few provide any benefits.[29] Services to support TANF recipients in finding and keeping jobs have also been analyzed and found to be inadequate. As one example, that of transportation, where an evaluation by Lens concludes "none of [current transportation reform] attempts really address the root of the problem, and transportation problems persist. To get welfare recipients to work, no less than a radical restructuring of public transportation systems may ultimately be needed."[30]

CONCLUSION

Although there are very strong arguments that the TANF program has not improved the lives of the poor in any overall manner, and in fact may have actually increased the suffering of the poor, these arguments are pretty much beside the point. TANF represents a shift in American social welfare thinking, a shift that says that work is the most important American value and that people should be self-supporting at almost any cost. The TANF program, unlike all its financial assistance predecessors, has succeeded in reducing the welfare rolls and so most people, including a majority of policymakers, are satisfied with it and major reforms in the foreseeable future are unlikely.

27. Shannon Bopp and Gene Falk, *Temporary Assistance to Needy Families (TANF): Welfare-to-Work Revisited,* Congressional Research Service Report to Congress, October 2, 2012.

28. Jeounghee Kim and Myungkook Joo, "Work-Related Activities of Single Mothers Before and After Welfare Reform," *Monthly Labor Review* (December 2009): 3–17.

29. Pamela Loprest, "How Are Families Who Left Welfare Doing over Time? A Comparison of Two Cohorts of Welfare Leavers," *Economic Policy Review* (Federal Reserve Bank of New York) 7 (September, 2001): 9–11; Robert G. Wood, Quinn Moore, and Anu Rangarajan, "Two Steps Forward, One Step Back: The Uneven Economic Progress of TANF Recipients," *Social Service Review* (March 2008): 10.

30. Vicki Lens, "TANF: What Went Wrong and What to Do Next," *Social Work* 47 (July 2002): 280–285.

CHAPTER 13

SOCIAL WORK IN THE CONSERVATIVE 21ST CENTURY WELFARE STATE

S ocial work educators were shocked in 2007 to find themselves the target of an attack by the National Association of Scholars (NAS), an ultra-conservative group that is mostly concerned with what it sees as the problem of "political correctness" on American college campuses. The attack was laid out in a 27-page report titled "The Scandal of Social Work Education" and was quickly supported by the political commentator George Will in a *Washington Post* column titled "Code of Coercion." The report asserts that social work education has an unredeemable liberal bias that reflects the National Association of Social Workers (NASW) Code of Ethics and is further enshrined in Council on Social Work Education (CSWE) accreditation standards. Particularly troubling to the authors of the report and to Mr. Will is the emphasis on social justice that "today generally equates with the advocacy of more egalitarian access to income through state-sponsored redistribution. The phrase is also frequently used to justify new entitlement rights for individuals and whole categories of people, i.e. legally enforceable claims of individuals against the state itself." The NAS report asks, "How far has the trend toward advocacy in social work education gone?" The answer it comes up with is this: "On the basis of numerous anecdotes and fragments of evidence it began to appear increasingly likely that even within the ideologically colored environment of the contemporary university, social work education constituted an especially advanced case of politicalization, in which dogma, tendentiousness, and coerced intellectual conformity were becoming integral to the definition of the field." Will concludes his editorial with the statement that "there might as well be signs on the doors of many schools of social work proclaiming 'conservatives need not apply.' "[1]

---

1. National Association of Scholars, *The Scandal of Social Work Education* (Princeton, NJ: NAS, 2007); George Will, "Code of Coercion," *The Washington Post*, October 14, 2007.

Events such as the NAS attack and the supporting national editorial by George Will, combined with the unexpected election of Donald Trump to the presidency in 2016 and the accompanying Republican majority in both the House and the Senate, as well as the majority of governorships, has brought home to social workers that they are now existing in a conservative society dominated by business and not social work values. The "culture of capitalism" so clearly explicated in 1958 by Wilensky and Lebeaux has, rather than softening as predicted, instead come roaring back with a vengeance.[2] This strengthening of conservative values, which is generally argued to have begun in the late 1970s, with the accompanying development of the programmatic welfare state discussed in the previous chapter, has led to some significant changes in the social work profession and in social work practice. Unlike previous eras where the evolution of social work practice largely involved development of new knowledge and methods (i.e., integrated methods, cognitive behavioral therapy), recent developments have been dominated by changes in the organizational arrangements under which social services are delivered.

SOCIAL WORK DISENGAGES
FROM FINANCIAL ASSISTANCE

The origin of professional social work was the administration of charity. The Charity Organization Societies, which were the direct predecessors of public welfare, were 100 percent professional social work organizations. In fact, as we have previously discussed, it was the COSs under the leadership of Mary Richmond that invented professional social work, including professional education, methods, journals, and the first textbooks. When the inevitable shift from private charity to public welfare began in the first few decades of the twentieth century with the growth of widow's pension laws and was completed with the passage of the Social Security Act in 1935, most of social work leadership were happy to turn the responsibility for the administration and delivery of welfare over to public bureaucracies. Social work leaders had begun to see their expertise and social function as the delivery of skilled individual and family counseling services that were viewed as more professional activities and more worthy of graduate trained workers. However, as we have seen, the new public welfare agencies were not so quick to let social work off the hook. They had been given a serious and complex social problem to manage and viewed social work as the only group in society who had any knowledge and skill relevant to the task. One of the first acts of Harry Hopkins as Director of the Federal Emergency Relief Administration (predecessor to the Social Security Administration) was to formulate a policy that required each agency to employ one professionally trained social worker for every twenty direct service staff. Jane Hoey, a social worker who served as Director of Public Assistance in the Social Security Administration from its inception until the 1950s was a staunch advocate of professional staffing of public welfare agencies. The result of professional social work being unwilling to firmly commit to public welfare while the

---

2. Harold Wilensky and Charles Lebeaux, *Industrial Society and Social Welfare* (New York: The Russell Sage Foundation, 1958), 33–48.

public welfare apparatus continued to turn to the profession for help created an ambivalent relationship that persisted for much of the twentieth century.

The disengagement of social work from public assistance began in the late 1960s following the disappointing results of the massive federal investment in social services mandated by the 1962 social service amendments. As we have seen, policymakers disillusioned by the social service strategy for welfare roll reduction, referred to as soft services, began to emphasize hard services such as job training, job placement, and concrete supportive services such as day care and transportation. This shift was operationalized by the reorganization of the Department of Health, Education, and Welfare's Bureau of Family Services into two new divisions. One was the Assistance Payments Administration, which was charged with supervising state arrangements for relief payments, focusing on making them simple and minimizing discretion by eligibility determination staff. The other was the Community Services Administration, which supervised social work services, which were now defined as strictly voluntary on the part of the recipient. The result was what was known as separation of services: one welfare department staff member was responsible for administering a recipient's grant, and another, a social worker, was available to provide services, but only at the recipients request, no longer as a requirement for receipt of aid.

The 1996 Personal Responsibility and Work Opportunity Reconciliation Act (PRWORA), the act that replaced AFDC with TANF, allocates a large amount of money for social services under the Social Services Block Grant (SSBG). This is a capped grant to states meaning that they are allocated a specific sum of money and cannot exceed that amount regardless of the level of need. This is in contrast to AFDC that was an entitlement, meaning that the federal government was required to fund states to provide services to everyone who met eligibility requirements regardless of the cost. States may use their SSBG money in any way they see fit in order to achieve the stated goals of TANF. Typical ways states spend their SSBG money is on services related to the management and maintenance of the home, training and related services, employment services, family planning, referral and counseling services, and services to meet the special needs of children, the aged, the mentally retarded, the blind, the emotionally disturbed, the physically handicapped, and alcoholics and drug addicts.[3] What is significant for our purposes here is that nowhere in the PRWORA or in the SSBG legislation is social work so much as mentioned as a social service provider.

Agencies administering TANF still employ a large number of people, usually called Financial and Employment Planner/Case Mangers (FEPs), to provide direct social services to TANF recipients. New York Times reporter Jason DeParle chronicles one FEP in Milwaukee named Michael Steinborn.[4] The description of Steinborn's background, how he got his job, his job functions, and day-to-day activities is very reminiscent of those of John Willems's job in 1934 with the Green Bay Department of Public Welfare described in chapter 9, or of Dwight Weisner in 1962 with the Fond du Lac Department of Public Welfare mentioned in chapter 11. Just like Willems and Weisner, Steinborn is responsible for some fifty-five cases at a time. He is responsible for developing an individualized employment plan for each case and for providing the services necessary to implement

3. Karen E. Lynch, "Social Services Block Grant: Background and Funding," Congressional Research Service Report for Congress, August 28, 2012, 2.

4. Jason DeParle, "Dream Deferred: The Most Inspired Employee in America's Most Lauded Welfare Agency Can Barely Do His Job," *Washington Monthly* (September 2004_: 18–30.

the plan. As DeParle describes the job, the FEP is "part sheriff and part shrink" and is supposed to monitor progress and to get to the bottom of things. The original proposal for the TANF program in Wisconsin asserted that "More of the success of Wisconsin Works will ride on the talents . . . [of the] financial planners [FEPs] than on any other collective feature of the new design."[5] There is one big difference between the jobs of Willems and Weisner, who worked for Wisconsin county governments that were implementing federal programs, and Steinborn, who works for a profit-making corporation listed on the New York Stock Exchange (Maximus) that contracts with the state of Wisconsin to administer part of its federal TANF block grant. This difference is that Willems and Weisner considered themselves, and were considered by their employing agencies, to be social workers. They were given social work supervision and training, some of their peers were sent to schools of social work for one year of graduate training in the case of Willems and for two-year MSWs in the case of Weisner, and were expected to study and learn social work practice techniques. Their agencies had as a goal to eventually be fully staffed with professionally qualified social workers. This is not the case with Mike Steinborn and the Milwaukee TANF agency (called Wisconsin Works, generally shortened to W2). Not only does his job as a Financial and Employment Planner/Case Manager not require a social work degree, it doesn't require a degree at all. Steinborn attended Marquette University for several years but left without a degree and then bounced around for several years, mostly working in construction, before landing the job as a FEP with Wisconsin Works. The stated requirement for a FEP with the W2 program is "Minimum of an associate's degree or two years related experience and/or training; or equivalent combination of education and experience is preferred." The salary offered for a beginning FEP is sufficient to attract a newly minted BSW, currently about $39,000 per year with a full benefit package and ample opportunity for advancement, but the agency makes no effort to recruit trained social workers. There is nothing, of course, to prevent BSW level social workers from taking jobs as FEPs, but the evidence is that few, if any, do. An analysis of the LinkedIn pages of 36 FEPS found that few had college degrees and those who did generally had degrees in liberal arts, or in the case of two human services majors, basically a non-accredited, non-professional social work degree. Also analyzed was a random sample of accredited BSW programs that found no content at all specifically related to the roll, function, or skills needed by a TANF FEP worker.[6]

The social work profession has always been ambivalent about working in public assistance programs, thinking it a setting not conducive to high-quality practice. A typical opinion is that of Chaiklin and Frank that "Inadequate resources, high staff turnover, and other demoralizing conditions make the attempt to deliver service in public welfare an exercise in achieving the impossible dream."[7] With this as a typical attitude it is not surprising that the profession watched passively as social work was cut out of public assistance legislation. There have been a few statements from the profession indicating a tepid interest in reengaging with public assistance, for example the National Association of Social Workers policy recommendation on the proposed 2015 reauthorization of TANF, which, under the heading "Enhance the capacity of the welfare system infrastructure,"

5. Jason DeParle, "Dream Deferred," 23.

6. Philip Popple, "TANF Social Services: Where Are the Social Workers?" unpublished manuscript, February, 2015.

7. Harris Chaiklin and Carol Frank, "Separation, Service Delivery and Family Functioning," *Public Welfare* 31 (Winter 1973): 2.

reads in its entirety: "The additional tasks for service provision being placed on frontline workers, such as social workers, calls for a significant investment in training to enhance their capacity to responsibly serve vulnerable families."[8] It is interesting that the NASW statement blithely ignores the fact that there are no frontline social workers in the welfare system infrastructure. There has also been the occasional article in a professional journal lamenting the exit of social work from public assistance and offering some very good analyses of how the profession could reestablish a helpful relationship with the TANF program.[9] However, unless policymakers begin to recognize the shortcomings of the TANF program, mainly that it has reduced the welfare rolls but not the suffering of the poor, social work reengagement with public assistance is unlikely.[10]

FAMILY AND CHILDREN'S SERVICES

In the progressive era[11] when public assistance programs began to replace the charity function of Charity Organization Societies, their national association, the American Association of Societies for Organizing Charity went through a process of redefining its mission and that of the member agencies. In 1918, as part of this process, Francis McLean, General Secretary of the Association, surveyed member agencies and asked, "Should the family or the community be the particular unit of charity organizations?" The membership of 170 agencies was unequivocal in its response. They believed that their fundamental purpose was casework with disorganized families whether or not the families were destitute. In order to reflect the new focus of the organization, it changed its name in 1919 to the American Association for Organizing Family Social Work, eventually becoming the Family Service Association of America. For more than the following half century this group represented the elite of the social work profession, publishing *Social Casework*, the top practice journal; taking the lead in establishing the Academy of Certified Social Workers (ACSW), a voluntary certification that preceded formal licensing; publishing an annual volume of cases to be used for family therapist education and training; assuming leadership roles in the National Association of Social Workers and the Council on Social Work Education; funding stipends for students in schools of social work interested in working for a FSSA agency; and tirelessly advocating for social work to be an all graduate trained profession focusing on skilled counseling and therapy with individuals and families.

Until well past mid-century family and children's services agencies received the majority of their funding from Community Chests, which later became the United Way. A 1954 Family Service Association of America memorandum stated that member agencies relied on the community

8. National Association of Social Workers, "Temporary Assistance for Needy Families (TANF) Reauthorization: NASW Recommendations," 2015.

9. Gregory Washington, Michael Sullivan, and Edwina Thomas Washington, "TANF Policy: Past, Present, and Future Directions," *Journal of Health and Social Policy*, 21 (2006): 13.

10. University of Wisconsin-Madison, Institute for Research on Poverty, "TANF turns 20," *Fast Focus: Research/Policy Brief*, No. 26-2017 (March, 2017).

11. Unless otherwise noted, information for this section is from Patricia Winsten, *A Century of Service: 1911–2011— Alliance for Children and Families*, http://alliance.org/centennial/book. Accessed Feb. 21, 2017.

chest for nearly 90 percent of their total income, some receiving over 95 percent of revenue from this single source. These member agencies tended to be small, almost completely staffed by MSW social workers, and offered traditional psychodynamic oriented child and marriage therapy. Their national organization, the FSAA, was basically a trade organization: the make-up of its board was one-third member agency executives and two-thirds people nominated by member agencies.[12]

Beginning in the 1960s and accelerating in the 1970s and 1980s, the comfortable cocoon of family and children's services agencies, that of relying on the United Way for near total support and having the freedom to specify and define their own role, began to crumble. It gradually became clear that United Way funding would be an ever diminishing proportion of agency revenue. As United Way funding declined, agencies began to rely more and more on government contracts. In recognition of the increasing importance of government policy for member agencies' well-being, the FSAA established a Washington, DC–based Office for Governmental Affairs. As the agencies faced an ever tightening and more competitive funding environment there was a recognition that financial resources must be obtained outside of the United Way and government contracts. Agencies were recognizing that they had to develop a business plan.[13]

By the end of the 1970s United Way support assumed only a small proportion of agency funding, the bulk now coming from contracts with multiple levels of government and an increasing amount from fees and insurance reimbursement. The FSAA and other national leaders cautioned member agencies that small agencies risked extinction. It was becoming clear that agencies needed to consolidate to achieve economies of scale and to maximize impact. In response to these recommendations across the country local United Way organizations were assessing community needs and in many instances recommending mergers between organizations to increase efficiency and provide more comprehensive services.

As funding and organizational structure became central concerns of the Family Service Association of America it began to evolve from an organization dominated by social workers with service to member agencies as its major task, to one with a business/corporate focus with finance and policy advocacy as its major priorities. The vehicle for this change was the Task Force on Organizational Renewal established in 1982. One recommendation of the task force was that the board change from being dominated by agency executives to one with lay representatives with no vested interest who would bring a business focus and a national perspective (and, not incidentally, the capacity to make large contributions themselves). Member agencies were asked to recommend corporate leaders in their communities to the national FSAA board.

One motivation for moving toward a business oriented board was that the organization had begun to experiment with offering for-profit services. i.e. becoming a business itself. In 1979 the organization entered into a contract with Xerox Corporation to develop and manage its employee assistance plan. To manage and expand its for-profit services the FSAA created the National Service to Industry division. Early for-profit programs focused on mental health, but as the list of corporate clients grew, a Dependent Care Program was added that helped with elder and child care

---

12. John E. Hansen, "Family Service Association of America: Part 1," Social Welfare History Project, Virginia Commonwealth University, http://socialwelfare.library.vcu.edu/organizations/family-service-association-of-america-part-i/

13. Lester M. Solomon, "The Marketization of Welfare: Changing Nonprofit and For-Profit Roles in the American Welfare State," *Social Service Review,* 67 (Mar., 1993): 16–39.

needs and a Crisis Management Program to help with mass casualty incidents, workplace catastrophes, and community disasters. In 1992 a contract was signed with General Motors Corporation to manage its drug and alcohol program. By the time the GM contract was signed, for-profit activities of the FSAA were producing revenues in excess of $6 million per year and were growing at a rate of 37 percent.

The former Family Services Association of America has continued to rapidly grow and change in response to an ever changing social service marketplace. With the increasing growth and importance of its for-profit activities the FSAA, was concerned that its tax status as a 501(c)3 (non-profit) organization was in jeopardy. To address this concern, in 1992 the organization restructured with a parent holding company called Families International that comprised a non-profit corporation called Family Service America (FSA) and a for-profit corporation called Family Enterprises Incorporated (FEI). In 1998, once again with an eye toward economies of scale in a tight funding environment, the not-for-profit division of Families International, Family Services America, merged with the National Association of Homes and Services for Children, and the name of this division was changed to the Alliance for Families and Children. In 2006 United Neighborhood Centers of America, the direct descendent of the National Federation of Settlement Houses founded by Jane Addams in 1911, entered into an affiliation agreement with the Alliance for Families and Children thus becoming a sister organization.

Along with the changes in organizational structure and funding, the family service national organization was also going through a process of reassessing the focus and goals of its member agencies. Family Service America was concerned that as family agencies had evolved there had been a pullback from community involvement "into the office and behind the desk". The social upheaval of the 1960s, combined with the goals of programs funded by the government that, among other things, promoted care in the least restrictive environment, caused agencies to reexamine their focus. The evolution was slow, but by the 1990s new approaches to behavioral health care began to concentrate on community centered institutions. This concern gained focus through the 1995–1997 Family Service America strategic plan titled "Prospects and Strategies for Community Centered Family Service." The plan, heavily influenced by Robert Putman's book *Bowling Alone*, emphasized the loneliness and isolation of families in modern society. It concluded that to strengthen families, agencies must tackle the problems affecting communities. The report did not recommend that agencies abandon their traditional counseling/therapy function aimed at problems such as divorce, substance abuse, domestic violence, and so forth but rather that agency administrators seek a balanced portfolio of resources and services brought to families, saying "individual services and community organizing can work together to improve families' chances."[14]

In order to operationalize a focus on community focused services Family Services America began, in the 1990s, to seek grants for pilot projects that, if successful, could be spread to member agencies. Two of note are the Families and Schools Together (FAST) program and the Ways to Work program. Families and Schools Together was developed and piloted at Family Services Madison in Wisconsin. The eight week program works with parents of elementary school children who are assessed as being at risk of school failure. Evaluations of the program indicated that its

---

14. Michael Sviridoff and William Ryan, "Community-Centered Family Service," *Families in Society*, 78 (Mar., 1997): 128–139.

level of success merited expansion so nationwide expansion was funded by a group of foundations. By 1996, FAST had spread to 350 schools in 25 states and two Canadian provinces. By 1997 the program was funded at a level of more than $20 million. The Ways to Work program was piloted in Minnesota, initially providing small loans to low-income families who could not obtain loans elsewhere and were thus prey to predatory lenders. The program has attracted millions of dollars in private grant funding and also from the federal Departments of Transportations and Labor. The program currently has offices across the country, all housed within member agencies of the Alliance for Families and Children. Many of these programs have expanded beyond only offering loans to providing general family financial counseling provided by Certified Financial Counselors.

By the end of the twentieth century family and children's services agencies had been fundamentally reformed. From elite social work agencies that could be said to have been the heart of the profession, they had evolved into general community social service agencies that employ, but are not dominated by, social workers. Some, such as Family and Children's Services of Dallas Texas merged and re-merged with other community mental health agencies to finally become The Family Partnership, an agency that still primarily provides clinical therapy to families and children but now defines itself as a mental health agency rather than a social work agency. The agency still employs clinical social workers as therapists but they serve alongside of Licensed Professional Counselors, Licensed Marriage and Family Counselors, and both clinical and counseling psychologists. Most former family and children's services agencies, however, have merged with other community agencies and still offer some traditional clinical services, but also offer a number of other community service programs. Family and Children's Services of Kalamazoo Michigan merged with other community agencies and now offers clinical services as well as foster care and adoption under a contract with the State of Michigan. It is unusual in that it has retained the Family and Children's Services name. Family and Children's Services of Minneapolis, arguably once one of the most prestigious social agencies in the nation that, among other things, was highly influential in the establishment of schools of social work at both the University of Minnesota and at Washington University in St. Louis, has merged with other agencies and is now known as The Family Partnership. Under this new name the agency offers a mix of counseling, educational, advocacy, and financial literacy programs. Family and Children's Services of Jacksonville Florida, a relatively young agency founded in 1956, now called Family Foundations, offers some traditional family counseling, but focuses more on its 1,000 in 1,000 (Moving 1,000 people out of poverty every 1,000 days) anti-poverty program, and its family financial counseling program. Sadly, a number of family and children's services agencies, notably the storied Family Services of Philadelphia, once headed by Mary Richmond and largely responsible for the establishment of the University of Pennsylvania School of Social Work (now the School of Social Policy and Practice), have succumbed to financial pressures and simply shut their doors.

CRIMINAL JUSTICE

Ever since the Walnut Street Jail was opened in Philadelphia in 1790, signifying the beginning of the idea that it was possible to not simply punish, but to also rehabilitate criminal offenders, there has been an ongoing tension in the criminal justice institution. On one side of the debate is the pro-punishment school of thought (now known as the *Justice model*) that believes that the function of the criminal justice system is simply to impose a penalty on a wrongdoer and to do whatever is possible to right any wrong that has been done. On the other side of this debate is the rehabilitation school of thought that views lawbreakers not as bad people in need of punishment but rather as people who are demonstrating a serious adjustment problem and are in need of help. Since its early beginning in the late nineteenth century, when social work was known as charities and corrections, the profession has been a leading advocate for the rehabilitation approach. Under the leadership of social workers probation and parole was developed, juveniles were removed from the adult correctional system and dealt with as young people needing help rather than as criminals deserving punishment, and correctional counseling programs were instituted within prison walls.[15] In the 1960s the community focused Mobilization for Youth program, created and led by Columbia University School of Social Work professor Richard Cloward, was a major effort at a community focused rehabilitation and prevention approach to juvenile delinquency.

Until the late twentieth century social workers were heavily involved in the formal correctional system. One of the 13 volumes in the 1959 CSWE curriculum study was devoted to the curriculum for teaching correctional social work. By the mid-1960s probation departments had been established in all fifty states and 2,300 counties and approximately fifty percent of probation and parole officers were trained social workers. A national study at this time by the National Council on Crime and Delinquency, headed by social worker Milton Rector, recommended that all new probation officers and supervisors be required to have an MSW degree and two years of casework experience.[16]

In the late 1970s and accelerating into the twenty-first century the criminal justice system took a sharp turn away from rehabilitation and adopted a radical punishment approach. A major reason for this shift was a public reaction to high and increasing crime rates. While crime rates, especially those of violent crimes, were increasing, the public perception was that they were increasing at rates far greater than was actually the case. A result was that there was a clamor for a get tough on crime approach, responded to by policymakers with a number of laws such as mandatory minimum sentences for violent crimes and drug related offenses, "three strikes and you're out" laws mandating that people convicted of a third offense, even if the offenses were minor, be given a mandatory life sentence; federally mandated guidelines that limited the ability of judges to consider mitigating circumstances before imposing a prison sentence; and "truth in sentencing" policies that made it more difficult for inmates to gain early release for good behavior (including participation in prison rehabilitation programs). A second reason for the decrease of interest in rehabilitation and increased emphasis on punishment was a series of studies of rehabilitation programs that generally concluded the programs had little effect. The results of these studies were summarized in an article by Robert Martinson in the influential policy magazine *The Public Interest* in which he concluded that "with a few isolated exceptions, the rehabilitative efforts that have been

15. Albert Roberts and D. Springer, Social Work in Juvenile and Criminal Justice Settings, 3rd ed. (Springfield, IL: Charles C. Thomas, 2007).

16. Albert Roberts, "Emergence of the Juvenile Court and Probation Services," in Albert Roberts, ed., *Juvenile Justice Policies, Programs, and Services*, 2nd ed. (Springfield, IL: Nelson Hall, 1998).

reported so far have had no appreciable effect on rehabilitation." Criminologist Robert Walker wrote, "as instruments of rehabilitation, American prisons are an obscene joke."[17]

The result of the turn away from the rehabilitation approach has been a staggering increase in the number of people in prison or under some form of correctional supervision in the United States. From 1980 to 2015 the prison population in the US increased from 319,598 to over 1.5 million; the population in local jails increased from 182,228 to over 700,000; the population under community correctional supervision (parole and probation) increased from 1,118,097 to 3.8 million. These numbers make the United States the world leader in incarceration, locking up 670 people per 100,000 population, compared to Russia which locks up 439, Rwanda with a rate of 434, and India that incarcerates only 30 people per 100,000. The racial disparities in the correctional population explosion have also been stunning. Although blacks comprise only 13.2 percent of the population, they account for 35.4 percent of the prison population; Hispanics who make up 17 percent of the population represent 21.6 percent of prisoners; and non-Hispanic whites at 62.6 percent of the population occupy only 33.8 percent of prison beds. Although exact statistics are hard to come by, most agree that the poor and the mentally ill are greatly overrepresented in the correctional population. It has been documented that over half of all prisoners were living in poverty the year before their arrest and have little chance of rising out of poverty when released.[18]

The turn away from an interest in rehabilitation to a hard focus on incarceration and related issues such as maintaining order in prisons, has led to a major change in the role of social work in the correctional system. This change was encapsulated in 1984 in a statement by Norman Carleson, Director of the federal Bureau of Prisons: "We have to divorce ourselves from the notion that we can change human behavior, that we have the power to change inmates. We don't." Treger and Allen note that "As the concept of rehabilitation faded, do did social work in the justice system." Jobs such as probation and parole officer, juvenile probation office, and correctional counselor were redefined as quasi-police roles as opposed to social work roles. Criminal justice system employers redefined entry qualifications away from social work credentials and more frequently specified a degree in criminal justice as the preferred credential. As a result, very few social workers currently work in the formal criminal justice system.

The mutual disengagement of social work and the formal correctional system does not mean that social work has abandoned the problem of crime in society and of ways that social workers can engage with the problem. Social workers interested in crime, now called forensic social workers, occupy a number of new and innovative roles. Social workers currently work in victim assistance, victim-offender mediation and restitution, domestic violence, innocence projects, crisis intervention with crime victims, survivor assistance, post release counseling and support, as well as other roles. In addition social workers are increasingly acting in judicial support roles as expert witnesses (usually hired as independent consultants, not employees of the criminal justice system)

17. Robert Martinson, "What Works?—Questions and Answers about Prison Reform," *The Public Interest* 35 (Spring 1974): 22–54; Robert Walker, *Sense and Nonsense About Crime, Drugs, and Communities* (Independence KY: Cengage Learning, 2011), 218.

18. Danielle Kaeble, Lauren Glaze, *Correctional Populations in the United States, 2015*, http://www.bjs.gov/content/pubs/cpus14.pdf. Accessed April 10, 2017.

providing pre-sentencing studies and reports, mitigating factor testimony in capital murder cases, and home studies for independent adoptions.[19]

Social work professional organizations, horrified by the massive and disproportionate increase in the number of people under correctional supervision in the United States and committed to social work's historic social justice mission, have joined other organizations such as the Prison Moratorium Project and Just Leadership USA, in a movement, referred to as decarceration, to reverse this trend. A major project titled the Smart Decarceration Initiative was begun in 2014. The initiative is housed in the Center for Social Development at Washington University's George Warren Brown School of Social Work, and was accepted as a grand challenge by the American Academy of Social Work and Social Welfare. The concept paper for the initiative states the objective thus: "Effective decarceration will be occurring when (1) the incarcerated population in US jails and prisons is substantially decreased; (2) existing racial and economic disparities in the criminal justice system are redressed; and (3) public safety and public health are maximized."[20] The initiative held its first national conference, titled From Mass Incarceration to Effective and Sustainable Decarceration, in St. Louis in September of 1915, and will be releasing a book based on the conference sessions titled *Smart Decarceration: Achieving Criminal Justice Transformation in the 21st Century.* While it is too early to predict the outcome of the decarceration movement there are some hopeful signs. One is that support for the movement is coming from conservatives as well as liberals. Liberals support the movement because they are horrified at the injustice of the mass-incarceration movement. Conservatives support the movement because, after demanding get-tough criminal justice policies, including more and harsher prison sentences, they are now horrified by how much it is costing, an amount estimated by the Pew Center to be more than $52 billion annually. Another hopeful sign is that the prison population has, after more than forty years of increases, begun to decline, falling from a high of 1.6 million in 2006 to a little less than 1.5 million in 2015.[21] This is a small decrease, but may be the beginning of a new trend that may also lead to a renewed interest in rehabilitation.

MENTAL HEALTH

The deinstitutionalization movement of the 1960s and early 1970s left tens of thousands of seriously and persistently mentally ill people, many former mental hospital patients, on the streets or living with families not equipped to care for them. The massive system of community mental health centers and funding for these, was not provided at nearly the level needed to meet the

19. Albert R. Roberts, David W. Springer, and Patricia Brownell, "The Emergence and Current Developments in Forensic Social Work," in Albert R. Roberts and David W. Springer, eds., *Social Work in Juvenile and Criminal Justice Settings,* 3rd ed. (Springfield, IL: Charles C. Thomas, 2007), 5–24.

20. Carrie Pettus-Davis and Matthew W. Epperson, *From Mass Incarceration to Smart Decarceration: American Academy of Social Work and Social Welfare Grand Challenges Initiative Concept Paper* (St. Louis: Washington University in St. Louis, 2014).

21. Pat Nolan, "Conservative and Liberals Join Together for Criminal Justice Reforms," *Huffington Post,* April 16, 2015, http://www.huffingronpost.com/pat-nolan/conservative-andliberals_b-7057184.html.

problem. To make matters worse, no network of supportive services was developed. In addition to these seriously mentally ill people the mental health system was facing increasing pressure for services from people with problems that had formerly been considered problems in living (marital discord, unruly children, persistent sadness, and so forth), or defined as moral issues (drug and alcohol abuse), who were now arguing that these were pathological conditions needing professional treatment.

The failure of the community mental health system to live up to the promises of its designers was addressed by the Presidential Commission on Mental Health established by President Carter in February 1977 with First Lady Rosalynn Carter as the honorary chairperson. The commission released its report in 1978 and strongly argued for greater investment in mental health services, noting that although the mental health problem was one of the largest the country was facing in terms of the number of people involved and the level of their suffering, only 12 percent of health expenditures were devoted to it. It emphasized the need to develop more community based services and to make them flexible so as to serve the needs of varying social and racial groups. Based on the report of President Carter's commission the Mental Health Systems Act was passed in 1980 authorizing increased federal funding to improve the community mental health system with an emphasis on serving people with severe and long term mental illnesses, children and adolescents with serious mental health issues, and other groups that were defined as unserved or underserved. One month after the passage of this bill the Reagan administration took office and chose not to implement it, instead rolling mental health funding into the Omnibus Budget Reconciliation Act and, under the New Federalism, returned responsibility for mental health services to the states in the form of block grants, cutting the overall federal budget for these programs by 25 percent.

In addition to the lack of adequate funding for community services there were several reasons that the mental health system was not able to effectively handle the demand for community based (outpatient) mental health services in the final decade of the twentieth century. One major problem was a shortage of professional personnel. Until the late twentieth century the primary provider of mental health services was psychiatrists aided by an inadequate number of social workers and a large number of custodial personnel all under the direct supervision of psychiatrists. It is difficult to get an accurate fix on the number of board certified psychiatrists in practice, but the best, admittedly rough, estimate is that the number has remained fairly constant at about 45,000. With a total national population of over three hundred twenty million, and estimates that around 12 percent are in need of mental health care, the inadequacy of this number is apparent. The second problem was a lack of a funding mechanism to pay for mental health services for individuals. The cost of mental health treatment is beyond the means of most people and entering the last quarter of the twentieth century there were few government programs that individuals could call upon for help in paying for counseling and therapy. In addition, for those fortunate enough to have private health insurance, most plans either did not provide for mental health services or, at best, provided very limited benefits. Third party payers, both government and private insurers, argued that they could not cover mental health problems because there was no accurate way to diagnose these problems and, once diagnosed, the prevailing psychodynamic (Freudian) treatment methods were open ended so treatment could potentially go on for years and no one would really know when the problem was solved.

The problem of the inability to make precise and accurate diagnoses of mental health problems was addressed by the development of the Diagnostic and Statistical Manual (DSM). Psychiatrists, later assisted by psychologists and social workers, began working on this tool shortly after the Second World War and the passage of the National Mental Health Act. The first version was published in 1952 and, although it was only a rough glossary of descriptions of diagnostic categories, it was the first official manual of mental disorders to focus on clinical use. The DSM was revised in 1968 as the DSM II, but like its predecessor was fairly vague and general in its definitions of disorders and was of limited use as a tool for providing reliable clinical diagnosis and was not specific enough to meet the needs of insurance providers. To address this problem the American Psychiatric Association began work on a major revision that was completed and published in 1980 as the DSM III. This revision was a major improvement as it introduced a number of innovations, including explicit diagnostic criteria, a multi-axial diagnostic assessment system, and an approach that attempted to be neutral with respect to causes of mental disorders (i.e. did not favor one psychological theory over another). The DSM III provided a system that was explicit enough to enable private insurers and government policymakers to provide specific benefits attached to specific disorders (i.e. a specific type of substance abuse disorder calls for 21 days of in-patient treatment; a certain behavioral or relationship problem requires 12 outpatient therapy sessions, and so forth). The DSM III was revised in 1987 as the DSM IIIR, replaced by the DSM IV in 1994, and by the DSM V in 2013.

Once a reliable and standardized method had been developed for diagnosing and classifying mental health problems the issue of length of treatment remained. Prior to the latter part of the twentieth century the dominant approach to therapy was a psychodynamic one that was based on the belief that in order to cure a mental problem it is necessary to find the cause of the problem, often residing years previously in the patients childhood, and that the problem could only be uncovered through extensive and lengthy talk therapy, often lasting years. A popular example of this belief was a 1978 Sally Fields movie (which was based on an actual case history, but there is some reason to believe that the story was fraudulent) in which the main character Sybil exhibited multiple personalities. After years of therapy from a gifted psychiatrist, the cause is finally uncovered—as a small child Sybil was forced to kiss her dead grandmother goodbye at her funeral, an event so traumatic that it caused her personality to fracture. Once the cause is uncovered Sybil's recovery is spontaneous. There were two main problems with this approach to mental health treatment. First, there was very little evidence that it actually worked and, second, it was far too expensive to base a mental health system upon. This problem was addressed in the 1970s and 1980s with the development of a number of treatment techniques collectively referred to as short term treatment. Brief therapy approaches are less concerned with how a problem arose than they are with current factors supporting it and preventing change. Among the more popular short term techniques are cognitive behavioral therapy developed by psychologists, focusing on exploring relationships among a person's thoughts, feelings, and behaviors; and solution focused therapy, developed by social workers, which is goal oriented, targeting the desired outcome of therapy as a solution rather than focusing on the symptoms or issues that brought the person to therapy.

Brief therapy techniques, combined with ever more effective psycho-pharmaceuticals, reduced the time necessary for mental health treatment to a level where government programs and private insurance could cover the cost of treatment. Although, as mentioned earlier, under the

Reagan administration's New Federalism, the federal government greatly reduced its involvement with the mental health of the nation, it is ironic that the Reagan administration, by expanding Medicare and Medicaid eligibility to include mental health problems, made the federal government the country's largest mental health services payer. As the century moved toward its end, private insurers also were subjected to increasing pressure to pay for mental health problems in the same manner that they covered physical health conditions (an issue referred to as parity). This led to the development of the Managed Behavioral Health Care industry and to research programs studying its effectiveness. This research suggested that utilization could be managed, cost controlled and quality maintained through managed care. The rise of managed care, utilizing DSM diagnostic techniques and short term treatment, made parity in private insurance coverage affordable and hence possible. States and the Federal Employees Health Benefits program responded by establishing parity coverage for mental health services. Private insurers were required to provide parity for mental health care first through the Mental Health Parity Act of 1996, which required parity with respect to aggregate lifetime and annual dollar limits for mental health benefits. This act was expanded by the Mental Health Parity and Addictions Equity Act of 2008, which required that financial requirements and treatment limitations applicable to mental health or substance use disorder benefits are no more restrictive than those applied to other medical or surgical benefits.

As the Managed Behavioral Mental Health system expanded, so did the need for trained mental health professionals. Psychiatrists, previously the dominant mental health professionals, were too few in number and too expensive to meet the exploding need for care. Also, psychiatry lost interest in providing talk therapy, preferring to concentrate on new developments in neuroscience and psycho-pharmaceuticals. This left a huge opportunity for other mental health professions to expand. Although psychology has generally been thought of as a mental health treatment profession, for most of its history it has had little interest in direct practice, preferring to define itself as a research science with the goal of explaining, not treating, human behavior. As opportunities for financial reimbursement expanded late in the century, psychology Ph.D. programs added clinical practice tracks and, when these failed to provide a sufficient number of practicing psychologists, and also continued to place too much emphasis on science and research to please the practice community, schools of professional psychology developed, offering the Psy.D. degree specifically aimed at training clinicians. Social workers, by contrast, have been intensely interested in providing psychotherapy ever since Virginia Robinson wrote *A Changing Psychology of Social Casework* in the late 1920s. In order qualify for psychotherapy reimbursement, social workers have been seeking professional licensing for many years. The first social work licensing law was passed in Puerto Rico in 1934, California licensed social workers in 1945. As receiving third party payment as independent practitioners moved from a possibility, to a probability, to a done deal with the advent of Managed Behavioral Health Care, the pace of licensing accelerated. Seven more states passed licensing laws in the 1960s, 14 more in the 1970s, and 27 in the 1980s. By 1992 all 50 states, the District of Columbia, Puerto Rico, and the Virgin Islands all regulated social work practice.

By the end of the twentieth century the mental health professional work force had changed both in numbers and in composition. Between the mid-1970s and 2000 the number of psychiatrists doubled, the number of psychologists tripled, and the number of social workers in mental health quadrupled. By the century's end more than 70,000 social workers were practicing in the mental health arena. It is widely reported in both the social work and mental health policy literature that social work is now the largest provider of mental health treatment in the country. This is not true, however. With practically no notice, Licensed Professional Counseling, a discipline that has grown out of university departments of school and rehabilitation counseling, has grown to surpass all other mental health providers with more than 108,000 counselors licensed by states or by the National Board for Certified Counselors. Salary differentials between mental health professions have also been reduced. The relative salary of psychiatrists has declined, while that of psychologists and social workers has increased. In 1969 psychologists earned nearly 50 percent more than social workers, but by 1999 the gap had been reduced to less than ten percent.

CHILD WELFARE

As we have seen in the 1960s numbers, mainly the massive increase in the AFDC caseload drove financial assistance policy and fueled calls for reform. In the 1970s in a parallel process numbers fueled calls for policy reform in child welfare. In the case of child welfare policy, the numbers were the massive increase in the number of cases caused by the media frenzy following the discovery of the battered child syndrome in the early 1960s. As Williams has noted, "The speed of public and professional response was incredible."[22] In 1962, the US Children's Bureau held a conference to draft model child welfare legislation. That same year, the Social Security Act was amended to require all states to develop a plan to provide child protective services in every political subdivision. In 1963, 18 bills were introduced in Congress dealing with child abuse and neglect, and 11 of them passed. By 1967, all states had passed laws requiring professionals to report child abuse. Increased public awareness of the problem of child maltreatment, combined with the reporting laws, resulted in a massive increase in the number of referrals and thus the sizes of caseloads of child welfare agencies. In 1967 there were only 9,562 child abuse reports nationally; by 1980, reports had increased to over 1 million. The number has continued to increase until it was over 3 million by the mid-1990s and has vacillated around this number for every year since.[23] Accompanying the increase in child maltreatment referrals was a corresponding increase in the number of children in out-of-home care. The number of children in foster care increased from 163,000 in 1961 to more than half-a-million in 1977. This increase in the number of children in foster care was perceived as a crisis for the obvious reason that at a cost of thousands of dollars per year per child the situation constituted a threat to federal and state budgets. Child protective services were a legal entitlement and the cost could not be controlled by using block grants, caps, and waiting lists. The government was obligated to provide services to all who needed them, regardless of the cost.

A first response to the rapidly emerging problem of child maltreatment was a section in Title XX of the Social Security Act, passed in 1972, which made protective services mandatory in all states and provided federal funding to pay for these services. Once funding was in place

---

22. Gertrude J. Williams, "Cruelty and Kindness to Children," in Gertrude J. Williams and John Money, eds., *Traumatic Abuse and Neglect of Children at Home* (Baltimore, MD: Johns Hopkins University Press, 1980), 76.

23. U.S. Department on Health and Human Services, Administration on Children and Families, Children's Bureau. *Child Maltreatment 2014* (2016). Available from http://www.acf.hhs.gov/programs/cb/research-data-technology/statistics-research/child-maltreatment

for services, however, it quickly became apparent that no one had much useful information on just how to design action programs. This realization led to the passage in 1974 of the Child Abuse Prevention and Treatment Act (CAPTA). This act had two major components. First, it established within the Department of Health and Human Services the National Center for Child Abuse and Neglect, a research and data clearinghouse designed to help remedy the huge gaps in knowledge that were becoming apparent as attempts were made to remedy child protection problems. The second component was a model statute for state child protection programs, which was eventually adopted in all 50 states. The model statute specified the following provisions:

(1) A standard definition of child abuse and neglect
(2) Standard methods of reporting and investigating child abuse and neglect
(3) Guarantee of immunity for those reporting suspected injuries to children and neglect
(4) Development of prevention and public education efforts to reduce the incidence of child abuse and neglect[24]

CAPTA provided only a limited amount of funding to support these activities by the states (initially only $2.2 million), but in spite of this, all 50 states were in compliance with the provisions of the bill by 1980.

Even with the passage and implementation of the Title XX provisions and of CAPTA it could not really be said that there was a national system of foster care or child welfare in the 1970s. The provisions specified the systems that states were required to set up, but were silent on how they should deal with the problem of child maltreatment once the systems were in place and the cases started rolling in. A 1978 report the Children's Defense Fund concluded, "There is no overall explicit federal policy toward children out of their home" but there was " an implicit policy reflected in federal funding priorities [that] acts as a disincentive to the development of strong programs ensuring children their own or adoptive families."[25] Studies supported or collected by the new National Center for Child Abuse and Neglect, as well as influential journalistic and legalistic treatises on foster care, such as Goldstein, Freud, and Solnit's influential *Beyond the Best Interests of the Child,* identified several major issues regarding foster care.[26] The first was that foster care was in many, if not most, cases not a temporary but rather a long term situation. The second was what has come to be called "foster care drift." This referred to the finding that many children in foster care were not in one stable long term foster home but were placed in a series of homes. The final issue was that agencies placing children in foster care rarely had any kind of long term plan for the children other than for them to remain in care until such time as they could be returned home (often never).

24. Leah Costin, Howard Karger, and David Stoez, *The Politics of Child Abuse in America* (New York: Oxford University Press, 1976), 119.

25. Jane Knitzer, Mary Lee Allen, and Brenda McGowan, *Children Without Homes: An Examination of Public Responsibility to Children in Out-of-Home Care* (Washington, DC: Children's Defense Fund, 1978), 8.

26. J. Goldstein, Anna Freud, and Alfred Solnit. *Beyond the Best Interests of the Child* (New York: The Free Press, 1973).

This concern about children "adrift" in the foster care system led to the development of a guiding principle of child protective services and to a focus for federal child welfare policy; the concept of permanency planning. According to child welfare experts Anthony Maluccio and Edith Fein:

> "As a formal movement, permanency planning emerged in the 1970s as an antidote to long-standing abuses in the child welfare system, especially the inappropriate removal of children from their homes and the recurring drift of children in foster care. Its philosophical and programmatic emphasis was on the primacy of the family as the preferred environment for child rearing. Permanency planning was then extensively promoted through the landmark, federally funded 'Oregon Project,' which demonstrated that children who had been adrift in long-term care could be returned to their biological families or placed in adoption through intensive agency services emphasizing aggressive planning and casework techniques."[27]

A series of federally funded demonstration projects in the 1970s experimented with different methods of implementing permanency planning. These projects plus research sponsored by the National Center for Child Abuse and Neglect increased knowledge regarding problems in the foster care system, as well as solutions to these problems. This increased knowledge led to the passage of Public Law 96-272, the Adoption Assistance and Child Welfare Act of 1980, a law that, according to Sribnick, "provided for the first time a national policy for children who had been removed from their parents or who were in danger of being removed from their homes due to maltreatment or neglect."[28] This act directs federal fiscal incentives toward permanency planning objectives—namely, the development of preventive and reunification services and adoption subsidies. In order for states to be eligible for increased federal funds, they must implement a service program designed either to reunite children with their families or to provide a permanent substitute home. Before removing children from their homes state agencies are required to document that they have made "reasonable efforts" to avoid placing the child in substitute care. If, following the provision of services demanded by the reasonable efforts provision, placement is deemed unavoidable, they are required to take steps, such as the establishment of foster placement review committees and procedures for regular case review, to ensure that children are placed appropriately, and that they are returned home or else are moved on to permanent families in a timely fashion. The act also creates fiscal incentives for states to seek adoptive homes for hard-to-place children, including children who are disabled, older, or members of minority groups.

When the permanency planning approach was implemented under the Adoption Assistance and Child Welfare Act it appeared, for a while, that the problem of foster care was under control. The number of children in care declined from 520,000 in 1977 to 275,000 in 1984. However, after 1984 a number of factors in the social environment kicked in and caused this trend to reverse. Among these factors were the crack cocaine epidemic, economic problems leading to increased poverty and unemployment, AIDS, and a sharp rise in births to single mothers, particularly teenagers. This increase led social workers and policymakers to look for ways to build upon and

---

27. Anthony N. Maluccio and Edith Fein, "Family Preservation in Perspective," *Family Preservation Journal* 6 (2001): 1.

28. Ethan G. Sribnick, "The Origins of Modern Child Welfare: Liberalism, Interest Groups, and the Transformation of Public Policy in the 1970s," *The Journal of Policy History* 23 (April, 2011): 152.

improve the permanency planning approach. The method that they hit upon was referred to as family preservation services. This approach is based on the belief that in many cases where out-of-home placement appears to be imminent, it is possible to prevent placement by the provision of intense services delivered in the child's home over a brief, time-limited period. Family preservation services begin when a child is referred to a state protective services agency as being in danger of serious harm. A social worker investigates the complaint and, if the complaint is confirmed, decides if the family is a good candidate for family preservation services. For the family to be considered an appropriate case for family preservation services, the child must be at risk of placement, but the social worker must be convinced that the child can remain safely in his or her own home if intensive services are provided. Depending on which of several models of family preservation services is being applied, the family is given services for periods ranging from four to six weeks in the most intensive models to three to six months in the less intensive models. The social workers providing services have small caseloads and work with each family for many hours per week, sometimes twenty or more. After provision of the brief, intensive services, the agency withdraws to a supervisory role and leaves the family to function—presumably with a greatly improved level of child care and problem-solving capacity.

In 1993 family preservation became an explicit part of federal child welfare policy with the passage of P.L. 103-66, the Family Preservation and Support Program, which was part of the Omnibus Budget Reconciliation Act. The provisions of this act had a federal cost of $1 billion over five years to provide states with funds for services to avoid foster care placement for children and to preserve and strengthen families. As the act included a 25 percent matching requirement from the states, the amount to be spent on family preservation services over five years was actually $1.25 billion. A basic principle of social policy is that every solution contains within it the seeds of a new problem. In the case of family preservation policy criticisms quickly developed that by emphasizing child removal as a decision of last resort, social workers were exposing children to unacceptable levels of risk. Formal evaluations of family preservation programs, such as that of the Illinois Families First program conducted by the University of Chicago's Chapin Hall Center for Children, combined with powerful anecdotal accounts of child deaths prompted calls to reevaluate the approach.[29] For example, family violence expert (and dean of the University of Pennsylvania's School of Social Policy and Practice) Richard Gelles calls for a return to a child protection, rather than a family preservation approach to child welfare, writing in 1996:

> "Children must come first in the words and deeds of the agencies that are entrusted with protecting them. It is time to move beyond the lip service paid to children and to develop a social structure, from top to bottom, that guarantees their safety, both by supporting families so that abuse will not occur in the first place and by absolutely guaranteeing the future safety and developmental integrity of children who have been abused and neglected."[30]

29. Duncan Lindsey, *The Welfare of Children,* 2nd ed. (New York: Oxford University Press, 2004), 52–56.

30. Richard Gelles, *The Book of David: How Preserving Families Can Cost Children's Lives* (New York: Basic Books, 1996), 171–172.

As a result of these criticisms, Congress reformed the Family Preservation and Support Program in 1997, this time calling it the Adoption and Safe Families Act. This revision added some child protection features to the earlier act, the most important being: specifying a number of situations in which reasonable efforts to preserve the family (for example the murder of a sibling) are not required; shortened deadlines for initiating termination of parental rights hearings; increased requirements for background checks of foster and adoptive parent applicants; shortening the timeline for permanency from 18 to 12 months; and several items designed to make adoption an easier and more desirable solution to family dysfunction. Although many critics view the Adoption and Safe Families Act as primarily a reaction against the emphasis on family preservation in the earlier act, this is only partially true. Under the new title *Promising Safe and Stable Families*, the act continues the federal family preservation and support services program. It actually authorized an increase in expenditures earmarked for family preservation of $20 million per year in 1999, increasing to a maximum of $305 million in 2001, increasing to $505 million in the 2004 budget. While the act continues support for a family preservation approach to child welfare, Congress added several provisions emphasizing that "the child's health and safety shall be of paramount concern."[31]

The Child Abuse Prevention and Treatment Act was again reauthorized in 2003 as P.L.108-36, the Keeping Families and Children Safe Act. The reauthorization was for a period of two years, at which time it was maintained under continuing resolutions until 2010 when it was reauthorized until 2015. The act was funded for $39.9 million for 2010 and at $1.030 billion for 2011 through 2015. Changes made to the law under the Keeping Families and Children Safe Act were minor. The act included a number of administrative provisions designed to improve program operation and data collection, to improve systems for supporting and training individuals working in child welfare, and to strengthen coordination among the various agencies that respond to child maltreatment and to dating and domestic violence. The major provision related to social work practice in the reauthorization is the encouragement of a "differential response" approach to child protective services. This provision, heavily lobbied for by the American Humane Association, the Child Welfare League of America, and the Children's Defense Fund, allows agencies to respond to maltreatment reports in different ways based on factors such as the type and severity of the alleged maltreatment, the number and sources of previous reports, and the willingness of the family to cooperate with the agency.

The combination of P.L. 96-272, with its requirement that agencies demonstrate "reasonable efforts" to prevent foster home placement of children, and P.L. 103-66 and 108-36, each providing massive federal financial incentives to provide family preservation services, made family preservation the policy of choice in child welfare for the twenty-first century. Although a backlash developed, embodied in the passage in 1997 of the Adoption and Safe Families Act, family preservation continues to be the policy of choice for dealing with the problem of child maltreatment. Virtually every state had developed and implemented some form of family preservation by the end of the twentieth century, and so far in the twentieth-first there has been no serious challenge to family preservation as the policy of choice.

---

31. Public Law 105-89-Nov. 19, 1997; Sec. 101 "Clarification Of The Reasonable Efforts Requirement." Available at https://www.congress.gov/105/plaws/publ89/PLAW-105publ89.pdf.

The American Indian Child Welfare Act

At the same time that America was struggling with the general crisis in child welfare caused by the recognition of child maltreatment and the corresponding increase in referrals and foster home placements, a smaller crisis was developing in the American Indian community. This crisis was a direct result of social changes affecting the supply of adoptable infants. In the 1960s and 1970s birth control technology improved, abortion became legal, and social norms underwent a startling and rapid change that made single motherhood socially acceptable. The result of these changes was that the supply of what were referred to as "blue-ribbon babies" (healthy white infants born to primarily middle-class white unwed mothers) declined to practically nothing. The response of social agencies and couples wishing to form a family through adoption was to begin to define groups of children who had previously been classified as hard-to-place, or even unadoptable, as adoptable. Older and handicapped children came to be considered good candidates for adoption. In addition, the previous practice of attempting to match a child as completely as possible with adoptive parents (i.e., it was considered desirable, although not essential, that a child with red hair be place with a couple where one spouse had red hair) was ruled out as an important adoption principle. As this principle was ruled out, transracial and transcultural adoption came to be defined as not only acceptable but desirable. As Jacobs notes, "Thus out of necessity, due to changing middle-class, white gender dynamics, the adoption of Indian children by non-Indian families became more acceptable in this period."[32]

In the 1960s social agencies identified the American Indian community as a rich potential source of adoptable infants to replenish the supply diminished by the factors just identified. Two projects were developed by prestigious professional organizations that sought to increase the adoption of Indian children by non-Indian parents. One was the Indian Adoption Project jointly sponsored by the Child Welfare League of American and the federal Bureau of Indian Affairs. This project was later incorporated into a new project, the Adoption Resource Exchange of North America (ARENA) a more widely focused project dedicated to placing "hard-to-place" or "special needs" children, that continued to place Indian children with non-Indian adoptive families. The result of these efforts was a rapid increase in the number of Indian children placed permanently with non-Indian families and the steady circulation of anecdotal accounts of violation of biological parents rights and disregard of Indian culture and practices (notably the importance of the extended family in the rearing of Indian children) in child removal and placement decisions. In1968, responding to an inordinate number of complaints from tribal members regarding the behavior of child welfare officials, the Devils Lake Sioux Tribe of North Dakota requested that the Association on American Indian Affairs (AAIA) conduct an investigation of the situation. The AAIA investigation found that of 1,100 Devils Lake Sioux living on the reservation, 275, or 25 percent, had been separated from their families. Suspecting that the practice affected other Indian communities, the AAIA analyzed national data from state and private social service agencies. They found that in most states with large American Indian populations, 25 to 35 percent of

---

32. Margaret D. Jacobs, "Remembering the 'Forgotten Child': The American Indian Child Welfare Crisis in the 1960s and 1970s," *American Indian Quarterly*, 37, no. 1/2 (Winter/Spring, 2013): 136–159.

Indian children had been separated from their families and placed in foster or adoptive homes or institutions, a rate far greater than that for non-Indian children. Indian families and their advocates charged that the reason for these disproportionate statistics was at least partially due to social workers using ethnocentric and middle-class criteria to unnecessarily remove Indian children from their families. In response to this problem Indian activists and their allies sought to bring Indian child welfare under the control of Indian nations.

In 1976 the AAIA presented its findings to the Senate Select Committee on Indian Affairs, who responded that they found the situation "shocking [and that it] cries out for sweeping reform at all levels of government." The Committee further found that state, local, and federal officials had abused their child removal powers to "strike at the heart of Indian communities by literally stealing Indian children."[33] The result of the hearings was the passage, in 1978, of the Indian Child Welfare Act. The first thing the act did was to create a uniform system for standardizing statistics and procedures regarding placement of Indian children because these varied so greatly across the country that keeping tabs on the situation was nearly impossible. The main thrust of the act was to "ensure Indian families will be accorded a full and fair hearing when child placement is at issue, establish a priority for Indian adoptive and foster families to care for Indian children . . . and generally promote the stability and security of Indian family life."[34] The act sought to shift the balance of power in child placement decision making to tribal communities so that they could regulate their own child welfare issues by keeping the children in the tribe and protecting the Indian children as Indians. Under this act, all child welfare court proceedings involving Indian children must be heard in tribal courts if possible, and tribes have the right to intervene in state court proceedings. The Indian Child Welfare Act also established the Indian Child Welfare Grant program that allocates approximately $11 million annually to support a broad array of child welfare services.

Child Welfare Staffing and Professional Social Work

In the late 20th century, unlike public assistance practice where social work completely lost its seat at the table, or mental health where social work gained in both numbers and authority but failed to achieve professional dominance, social work established its status as the main profession in child protective services. As noted by Whitaker, by the late 20th century more MSWs were employed by child welfare agencies than any other area of social work practice and it had become clear "that child welfare 'belonged' to social work and—unlike any other discipline—that the social work profession embraced child welfare by preparing its graduates for child welfare practice and envisioning the practice area broadly."[35] Be this as it may, the staffing of public child welfare agencies continues to be plagued by serious problems. Most are related, directly or indirectly, to the massive growth in staffing needs of these agencies caused by the previously noted explosion in the

---

33. Senate Select Committee on Indian Affairs, *Indian Child Welfare Act of 1977: Hearings before the United States Select Committee on Indian Affairs*, 95th Cong., 1st sess. (Washington, DC: US Government Printing Office, 1977), 538.

34. Senate Select Committee on Indian Affairs, *Hearings before the United States Select Committee*, 539.

35. Tracy R. Whitaker, "Professional Social Workers in the Child Welfare Workforce: Findings from NASW," *Journal of Family Strengths*, 12 (Issue 1, 2012): Article 8. Available at http://digitalcommons.library.tmc.edu/jfs/vol12/iss1/8

number of abuse and neglect referrals and the accompanying increase in the number of children in out-of-home care. Precise and current statistics describing child welfare agency staffing are not easily available; however those that are estimate that the number of professional positions in child welfare increased from 14,000 in 1967 to 30,000 in 1974, to more than 74,000 in 2000, and that the number has continued to increase at an ever greater rate.[36]

The result of the massive increase in the number of child welfare positions was initially responded to by many states in the 1980s and 1990s by downgrading the qualifications for entry level positions to less than a bachelor's degree. The reasons for this downgrading are fairly simple and had little to do with the perceived desirability of a social work degree for such jobs. States downgraded jobs in response to budget problems (it's more expensive to hire someone with a degree, and even more expensive to hire a specialized professional degree holder), and difficulties that state merit systems have in filling positions, particularly in rural areas (it's hard to find a degree holder, much less a BSW or MSW, to staff the child welfare office in Lidgerwood North Dakota or Borger Texas). Child welfare scholars defined this situation as a crisis and referred to it as the "de-professionalization of child welfare."[37] Although people continue to express concern about this de-professionalization of child welfare, the statistics that are available indicate that progress is being made. A 1988 study found that only 28 percent of child welfare workers had professional social work training. A 2008 study found this number to have increased to nearly 40 percent. A report from the American Public Human Services Association found that "A bachelor's degree was the predominant minimum academic degree required, but states require social work licensing at varying rates for each category of worker: 29 percent for CPS workers; 53 percent for in-home protective service workers; 42 percent for foster care and adoption workers; and 33 percent for multiple programs."[38]

A large part of the reason for the increase in the number of social work prepared workers in child welfare agencies has been support from the federal government. At about the same time that the government was withdrawing its support for professional training for public assistance workers, the 1980 Child Welfare and Adoption Assistance Act was passed that included support for a child welfare training program. The program provides funding to schools and departments of social work to support students preparing for child welfare careers. The federal government pays for 75 percent of the cost of the program and allows schools to provide their 25 percent through in-kind matching including faculty salaries, overhead expenses, and curriculum development costs. States were slow to begin to use the Title IV-E program until the mid-1990s when participation increased rapidly. In 1990 Title IV-E provided only about $44 million to states for child welfare education, by 1995 this had increased to $142 million, and to $286 million in 2002. A 2013 study

36. Philip R. Popple and Leslie Leighninger, *The Policy Based Profession: An Introduction to Social Welfare Policy Analysis for Social Workers,* 6th ed. (Boston: Pearson, 2015), 220.

37. Alberta Ellett, "Policy Analysis of De-professionalization of Child Welfare," Unpublished paper, Louisiana State University School of Social Work, 1996.

38. Alice Lieberman, H. Hornby, and M. Russell. "Analyzing the Educational Backgrounds and Work Experiences of Child Welfare Personnel: A National Study," *Social Work* 33: 485–489; Richard Barth, E. C. Lloyd, S. L. Christ, M. V. Chapman, and Nancy Dickinson, "Child Welfare Worker Characteristics and Job Satisfaction: A National Study," *Social Work* 53 (June 2008): 199–209; American Public Human Services Association, *Report from the 2004 Child Welfare Workforce Survey,* February, 2005.

of Title IV-E training found that at least 1,853 students received funding from the program during the 2011–2012 academic year.[39]

Although progress is being made in the qualifications of child welfare personnel, there are still a number of serious concerns regarding staffing. The concerns fall into three main groups. The first is that in spite of efforts described, agencies find an insufficient number of qualified candidates in the recruitment pool. Second, child welfare agencies are often unable to compete with other segments of the economy in terms of salary, benefits, and working conditions. According to the Bureau of Labor Statistics in 2002 the average salary of a child protective service worker was $10,570 less than that of a public school teacher and $17,257 less than that of a registered nurse. The workload of CPS workers is also excessive; the Child Welfare League of America estimates that staff should be increased by 50 percent to be adequate to the demands of the job. Third, as a consequence of these conditions, agencies are unable to retain staff. Child welfare worker positions turn over at a rate of 22.1 percent per year and at any one time 8.5 percent of positions are vacant. Out of frustration over the inability of state agencies to solve these staffing problems on their own, a number of children's rights organizations have filed class action suits that have, among other things, included provisions specifically targeted to improving the child welfare workforce. Cases have been successfully pursued in Kansas, Connecticut, Washington, DC, Pennsylvania, New Mexico, New York, Kentucky, Massachusetts, and other states. The judgments in these cases typically order state governments to upgrade the child welfare system to make it able to meet the requirements of P.L. 96-272 and P.L. 103-66. Orders generally require the states to greatly increase the number of social workers in the child welfare system, hire more professionally trained (both BSW and MSW level) social workers and supervisors, improve in-house staff training, decrease caseloads in some instances by as much as two-thirds, increase training of foster parents, provide special therapeutic foster homes for seriously disturbed children, and develop permanent placement plans for children within six months of their entry into the system.[40]

CONCLUSION

During the previous century, the questions of defining the social welfare institution in the United States, generally posed as to whether or not the country is a welfare state and the place of social work within this institution, were regularly and enthusiastically debated by social work practitioners and academics. Schools of social work each had at least a couple of courses with titles such as "the social welfare institution" and "social work as a profession" in which these issues were debated and discussed. Professional journals regularly devoted special issues to the topic of

39. National Association of Social Workers, *Fact Sheet: Title IV-E Training Program* (Alexandria, VA: NASW, 2003); Joan Levy Zlotnik and Jessica A Pryce, "Status of the Use of Title IV-E Funding in BSW and MSW Programs," *Journal of Public Child Welfare*, 7, no. 4 (2013): 430–446.

40. Child Welfare League of America, "Research Roundup—Child Welfare Workforce," September 2002; American Public Human Services Association, *Report from the 2004 Child Welfare Workforce Survey,* (Washington, DC: APHSA, February 2005); Julie Farber and Sara Munson, "Strengthening the Child Welfare Workforce: Lessons from Litigation," *Journal of Public Child Welfare* 4 (June 2010): 132–157.

conceptualizing social work and conferences regularly addressed this theme. Social work scholars frequently and vigorously debated the question of what should be the nature and focus of social work research, mainly should the discipline focus on basic research or should it concentrate on translational research, that is, taking findings and theories from basic social sciences and translating them into forms useful for social work policy and practice. As we have moved into the twenty-first century this fertile self-examination seems to have ended. This is unfortunate because there are critical professional issues crying out for debate.

Social workers continue to define themselves as experts functioning at the intersection of the individual with his or her social environment. As such, they continue to find a place in many programs of the social welfare institution—health, aging, schools, and community development, to name just a few. They have had a dominant position, however, in only three social institutions—public welfare, mental health, and child welfare—and thus these have been the focus of this book. There are critical issues facing social work in each of these that should be engaged and discussed by the profession and, it would not be too much of an overstatement to say, the professions long term prosperity and even survival depend on. In public welfare, the institution that led to the creation of social work, the profession no longer has any involvement at all. Research evaluating the TANF program is unanimous in the conclusion that, while the policy has been successful in drastically reducing the number of recipients, those that remain are worse off than ever. Social work has knowledge and skills that could be of great help in improving this program and bettering the lives of its clients. Social workers could also be a positive influence for humanizing policies of the TANF program thereby improving the lives of our poorest fellow citizens. Also, in a more self-serving sense, as the number of graduates of schools of social work continues to increase and competition for jobs becomes more rigorous, the profession should not be ignoring the huge job market potential in the TANF program. The profession needs to reengage with TANF and once again become service providers and reenergize our historic role as advocates for our poorest citizens.

In the area of mental health, social work has succeeded in achieving its paramount professional dream of becoming licensed as independent service providers empowered to practice without external supervision and to bill individuals, government, and insurance providers for services rendered. However, having achieved licensure in mental health, social work has totally failed to protect itself from what the sociologist William Goode refers to as charlatans and encroachers, mainly in the form of the development of the licensed professional counselor profession (LPC).[41] Mainly due to its training being more tightly focused (LPC students are not required to take courses in macro human behavior, social policy, advocacy, or other non-clinical topics required for the BSW and MSW degree); shorter (LPC masters degrees generally require 36 semester hours as compared to the 60 hour MSW requirement); and more accessible (the Council for Accreditation of Counseling and Related Educational Programs lists 756 accredited programs with 104 additional programs in candidacy, compared to 264 MSW programs accredited by the Council on Social Work Education), LPCs have quickly become the largest mental health profession. Social work scholars and professional organizations have made little note of this threat to our professional turf. They need to do so. Social work, with its emphasis on the social environmental element in human

41. William J. Goode, "Encroachment, Charlatanism, and the Emerging Profession: Psychology, Sociology, and Medicine," *American Sociological Review* 25 (Dec. 1960): 902–914.

problems in living, provides a unique and critical perspective on mental health treatment, one that is in danger of being drowned out by the sheer number of LPCs.

Finally, child welfare remains as the only institution in which social work is the dominant profession. The job of child welfare social workers is very difficult, perhaps this is the reason that no other profession has shown any interest in challenging social work's dominance in this field, but, due to strong advocacy by the profession and its allies, the job is getting better. Staffing levels of public child welfare agencies has improved in terms of both numbers and professional qualifications, caseload sizes have been drastically reduced, sometimes to fewer than twenty cases per worker, and pressure is developing for salary levels that adequately compensate workers for the complexity, difficulty, and stress of this job. The social work profession needs to recognize that child welfare is a large, perhaps the largest, part of its future and continue to emphasize this field in both its political activities and its educational programs.

INDEX